Lecture Notes
in Business Information Processing   **291**

More information about this series at http://www.springer.com/series/7911

Slimane Hammoudi · Leszek A. Maciaszek
Michele M. Missikoff · Olivier Camp
José Cordeiro (Eds.)

Enterprise Information Systems

18th International Conference, ICEIS 2016
Rome, Italy, April 25–28, 2016
Revised Selected Papers

 Springer

Editors
Slimane Hammoudi
MODESTE/ESEO
Angers
France

Olivier Camp
MODESTE/ESEO
Angers
France

Leszek A. Maciaszek
Wroclaw University of Economics
Wroclaw
Poland

José Cordeiro
EST
Instituto Politécnico de Setúbal (IPS)
Setúbal
Portugal

Michele M. Missikoff
ISTC-CNR
Institute of Sciences and Technologies
 of Cognition
Rome
Italy

ISSN 1865-1348   ISSN 1865-1356   (electronic)
Lecture Notes in Business Information Processing
ISBN 978-3-319-62385-6   ISBN 978-3-319-62386-3   (eBook)
DOI 10.1007/978-3-319-62386-3

Library of Congress Control Number: 2017945276

Printed on acid-free paper

This Springer imprint is published by Springer Nature
The registered company is Springer International Publishing AG
The registered company address is: Gewerbestrasse 11, 6330 Cham, Switzerland

Preface

The present book includes extended and revised versions of a set of selected papers from the 18th International Conference on Enterprise Information Systems (ICEIS 2016), held in Rome, Italy, during April 25–28.

ICEIS 2016 received 257 paper submissions from 42 countries, of which 9% are included in this book. The papers were selected by the event chairs and their selection is based on a number of criteria that include the classifications and comments provided by the Program Committee members, the session chairs' assessment, and also the program chairs' global view of all papers included in the technical program. The authors of selected papers were then invited to submit a revised and extended version of their papers having at least 30% innovative material.

The purpose of ICEIS is to bring together researchers, engineers, and practitioners interested in the advances and business applications of information systems. Six simultaneous tracks were held, covering different aspects of enterprise information systems applications, including enterprise database technology, systems integration, artificial intelligence, decision support systems, information systems analysis and specification, internet computing, electronic commerce, human factors and enterprise architecture.

The papers selected to be included in this book contribute to the understanding of relevant trends of current research on enterprise information systems, including issues with regard to enterprise engineering, heterogeneous systems, security, software engineering, systems integration, business process management, human factors and affective computing, ubiquitous computing, social computing, knowledge management, and artificial intelligence.

We would like to thank all the authors for their contributions and also the reviewers who helped ensure the quality of this publication.

February 2017

Leszek Maciaszek
Michele M. Missikoff
Slimane Hammoudi
José Cordeiro
Olivier Camp

Organization

Conference Co-chairs

Olivier Camp   MODESTE/ESEO, France
José Cordeiro   Polytechnic Institute of Setúbal/INSTICC, Portugal

Program Co-chairs

Slimane Hammoudi   ESEO, MODESTE, France
Leszek Maciaszek   Wroclaw University of Economics, Poland
     and Macquarie University, Sydney, Australia
Michele M. Missikoff   Institute of Sciences and Technologies of Cognition,
     ISTC-CNR, Italy

Program Committee

Miguel Angel Martinez Aguilar   University of Murcia, Spain

Adeel Ahmad   Laboratoire d'Informatique Signal et Image de la Côte d'Opale, France

Patrick Albers   ESEO, École Supérieure d'Électronique de l'Ouest, France

Mohammad Al-Shamri   Ibb University, Yemen
Rainer Alt   University of Leipzig, Germany
Andreas S. Andreou   Cyprus University of Technology, Cyprus
Oscar Avila   Universidad de los Andes, Colombia
Tamara Babaian   Bentley University, USA
Cecilia Baranauskas   State University of Campinas, Unicamp, Brazil
Ken Barker   University of Calgary, Canada
Jean-Paul Barthes   Université de Technologie de Compiègne, France
Lamia Hadrich Belguith   ANLP Research Group, MIRACL, University of Sfax, Tunisia

Orlando Belo   University of Minho, Portugal
Domenico Beneventano   Università di Modena e Reggio Emilia, Italy
Jorge Bernardino   Polytechnic Institute of Coimbra, ISEC, Portugal
Frederique Biennier   INSA Lyon, France
Sandro Bimonte   IRSTEA, France
Marko Bohanec   Jožef Stefan Institute, Slovenia
Jean-Louis Boulanger   CERTIFER, France
Daniel Antonio Callegari   PUCRS Pontificia Universidade Catolica do Rio Grande do Sul, Brazil
Luis M. Camarinha-Matos   New University of Lisbon, Portugal

Roy Campbell	University of Illinois at Urbana-Champaign, USA
Manuel Isidoro Capel-Tuñón	University of Granada, Spain
Glauco Carneiro	Salvador University (UNIFACS), Brazil
Angélica Caro	University of Bio-Bio, Chile
Nunzio Casalino	LUISS Guido Carli University, Italy
Marco A. Casanova	PUC-Rio, Brazil
Luca Cernuzzi	Universidad Católica Nuestra Señora de la Asunción, Paraguay
Shiping Chen	CSIRO, Australia
Max Chevalier	Institut de Recherche en Informatique de Toulouse UMR 5505, France
Nan-Hsing Chiu	Chien Hsin University of Science and Technology, Taiwan
Witold Chmielarz	Warsaw University, Poland
Daniela Barreiro Claro	Universidade Federal da Bahia (UFBA), Brazil
Pedro Henrique Gouvêa Coelho	State University of Rio de Janeiro, Brazil
Francesco Colace	Università degli Studi di Salerno, Italy
Cesar Collazos	Universidad del Cauca, Colombia
Antonio Corral	University of Almeria, Spain
Mariela Cortés	State University of Ceará, Brazil
Sharon Cox	Birmingham City University, UK
Broderick Crawford	Pontificia Universidad Catolica de Valparaiso, Chile
Vincenzo Deufemia	Università di Salerno, Italy
Dulce Domingos	University of Lisbon, Portugal
César Domínguez	Universidad de La Rioja, Spain
Sophie Ebersold	Université Toulouse II-Le Mirail, France
Hans-Dieter Ehrich	Technische Universität Braunschweig, Germany
Fabrício Enembreck	Pontifical Catholic University of Paraná, Brazil
Sean Eom	Southeast Missouri State University, USA
João Faria	University of Porto, Portugal
Antonio Fariña	University of A Coruña, Spain
Edilson Ferneda	Catholic University of Brasília, Brazil
Maria João Silva Costa Ferreira	Universidade Portucalense, Portugal
Paulo Ferreira	INESC-ID/IST, Portugal
Jiri (George) Feuerlicht	Prague University of Economics, Czech Republic
António Figueiredo	University of Coimbra, Portugal
Rita Francese	Università degli Studi di Salerno, Italy
Ana Fred	Instituto de Telecomunicações/IST, Portugal
Lixin Fu	University of North Carolina, Greensboro, USA
Johannes Gettinger	University of Hohenheim, Germany
George Giaglis	Athens University of Economics and Business, Greece
Daniela Giordano	University of Catania, Italy
Feliz Gouveia	University Fernando Pessoa/Cerem, Portugal

Virginie Govaere	INRS, France
Janis Grabis	Riga Technical University, Latvia
Maria Carmen Penadés Gramaje	Universitat Politècnica de València, Spain
Sven Groppe	University of Lübeck, Germany
Wieslawa Gryncewicz	Wroclaw University of Economics, Poland
Rune Gustavsson	Blekinge Institute of Technology, Sweden
Hatim Hafiddi	INPT, Morocco
Karin Harbusch	Universität Koblenz-Landau, Germany
Wladyslaw Homenda	Warsaw University of Technology, Poland
Wei-Chiang Hong	Oriental Institute of Technology, Taiwan
Miguel J. Hornos	University of Granada, Spain
Kai-I Huang	Tunghai University, Taiwan
Miroslav Hudec	University of Economics in Bratislava, Slovak Republic
San-Yih Hwang	National Sun Yat-sen University, Taiwan
Abdessamad Imine	Laboratoire Lorrain de Recherche en Informatique et Ses Applications, France
Arturo Jaime	Universidad de La Rioja, Spain
Kai Jakobs	RWTH Aachen University, Germany
Paul Johannesson	Royal Institute of Technology, Sweden
Nikitas Karanikolas	Technological Educational Institute of Athens (TEI-A), Greece
Dimitrios Katsaros	University of Thessaly, Greece
Andrea Kienle	University of Applied Sciences, Dortmund, Germany
Marite Kirikova	Riga Technical University, Latvia
Alexander Knapp	Universität Augsburg, Germany
Natallia Kokash	Leiden University, The Netherlands
Fotis Kokkoras	TEI of Thessaly, Greece
Christophe Kolski	University of Valenciennes, France
John Krogstie	NTNU, Norway
Rob Kusters	Eindhoven University of Technology and Open University of The Netherlands, The Netherlands
Wim Laurier	Université Saint-Louis, Belgium
Ramon Lawrence	University of British Columbia Okanagan, Canada
Jintae Lee	Leeds School of Business at University of Colorado, Boulder, USA
Alain Leger	France Telecom Orange Labs, France
Joerg Leukel	University of Hohenheim, Germany
Lei Li	Hefei University of Technology, China
Da-Yin Liao	Straight & Up Intelligent Innovations Group Co., USA
Luis Jiménez Linares	University of de Castilla-La Mancha, Spain
Panagiotis Linos	Butler University, USA
Stephane Loiseau	LERIA, University of Angers, France
João Correia Lopes	INESC TEC, Universidade do Porto, Portugal

Maria Filomena Cerqueira de Castro Lopes	Universidade Portucalense Infante D. Henrique, Portugal
Wendy Lucas	Bentley University, USA
André Ludwig	University of Leipzig, Germany
Mark Lycett	Royal Holloway, University of London, UK
Jose Antonio Macedo	Federal University of Ceara, Brazil
Leszek Maciaszek	Wroclaw University of Economics, Poland and Macquarie University, Sydney, Australia
Cristiano Maciel	Universidade Federal de Mato Grosso, Brazil
Rita Suzana Pitangueira Maciel	Federal University of Bahia, Brazil
Riccardo Martoglia	University of Modena and Reggio Emilia, Italy
Katsuhisa Maruyama	Ritsumeikan University, Japan
David Martins de Matos	L2F/INESC-ID Lisboa/Instituto Superior Técnico, Portugal
Wolfgang Mayer	University of South Australia, Australia
Brad Mehlenbacher	North Carolina State University, USA
Jerzy Michnik	University of Economics in Katowice, Poland
Marek Milosz	Lublin University of Technology, Poland
Michele M. Missikoff	Institute of Sciences and Technologies of Cognition, ISTC-CNR, Italy
Pascal Molli	LINA, University of Nantes, France
Lars Mönch	FernUniversität in Hagen, Germany
Francisco Montero	University of Castilla-la Mancha, Spain
Carlos León de Mora	University of Seville, Spain
João Luís Cardoso de Moraes	Federal University of São Carlos, Brazil
Fernando Moreira	Universidade Portucalense, Portugal
Pietro Murano	Oslo and Akershus University College of Applied Sciences, Norway
Tomoharu Nakashima	Osaka Prefecture University, Japan
Alvaro Navas	Universidad Politécnica de Madrid, Spain
Rabia Nessah	IESEG School of Management, France
Vincent Ng	The Hong Kong Polytechnic University, Hong Kong, SAR China
Ovidiu Noran	Griffith University, Australia
Edson OliveiraJr	Universidade Estadual de Maringá, Brazil
Andrés Muñoz Ortega	Catholic University of Murcia (UCAM), Spain
Claus Pahl	Dublin City University, Ireland
Philippe Palanque	Institut de Recherche en Informatique de Toulouse, France
Tadeusz Pankowski	Poznan University of Technology, Poland
Hugo Parada	UPM, Spain
Eric Pardede	La Trobe University, Australia
Viviana Patti	University of Turin, Italy
Luis Ferreira Pires	University of Twente, The Netherlands

Pierluigi Plebani	Politecnico di Milano, Italy
Geert Poels	Ghent University, Belgium
Luigi Pontieri	National Research Council (CNR), Italy
Filipe Portela	Centro ALGORITMI, University of Minho, Portugal
Robin Qiu	Pennsylvania State University, USA
Ricardo J. Rabelo	Federal University of Santa Catarina, Brazil
Daniele Radicioni	University of Turin, Italy
T. Ramayah	Universiti Sains Malaysia, Malaysia
Pedro Ramos	Instituto Superior das Ciências do Trabalho e da Empresa, Portugal
Francisco Regateiro	Instituto Superior Técnico, Portugal
Ulrich Reimer	University of Applied Sciences St. Gallen, Switzerland
Nuno de Magalhães Ribeiro	Universidade Fernando Pessoa, Portugal
Michele Risi	University of Salerno, Italy
Sérgio Assis Rodrigues	COPPE/UFRJ – Federal University of Rio de Janeiro, Brazil
Alfonso Rodriguez	University of Bio-Bio, Chile
Daniel Rodriguez	University of Alcalá, Spain
Oscar Mario Rodriguez-Elias	Institute of Technology of Hermosillo, Mexico
Luciana Alvim Santos Romani	Embrapa Agricultural Informatics, Brazil
Jose Raul Romero	University of Cordoba, Spain
David G. Rosado	University of Castilla-la Mancha, Spain
Michael Rosemann	Queensland University of Technology, Australia
Gustavo Rossi	Lifia, Argentina
Artur Rot	Wroclaw University of Economics, Poland
Francisco Ruiz	Universidad de Castilla-La Mancha, Spain
Indrajit Saha	National Institute of Technical Teachers' Training and Research, India
Belen Vela Sanchez	Rey Juan Carlos University, Spain
Luis Enrique Sánchez	Universidad de Castilla-la Mancha, Spain
Manuel Filipe Santos	Centro ALGORITMI, University of Minho, Portugal
Sissel Guttormsen Schär	University of Bern, Switzerland
Isabel Seruca	Universidade Portucalense, Portugal
Ahm Shamsuzzoha	Sultan Qaboos University, Oman
Jianhua Shao	Cardiff University, UK
Markus Siepermann	TU Dortmund, Germany
Alberto Rodrigues Silva	Instituto Superior Técnico, Portugal
Sean Siqueira	Federal University of the State of Rio de Janeiro (UNIRIO), Brazil
Spiros Sirmakessis	Technological Educational Institution of Messolongi, Greece
Hala Skaf-Molli	Nantes University, France
Michel Soares	Federal University of Sergipe, Brazil
Ricardo Soto	Pontificia Universidad Catolica de Valparaiso, Chile

Chantal Soule-Dupuy	Université Toulouse 1, France
Patricia Souza	UFMT, Brazil
Hatem Ben Sta	Université de Tunis a El Manar, Tunisia
Clare Stanier	Staffordshire University, UK
Chris Stary	Johannes Kepler University of Linz, Austria
Vijayan Sugumaran	Oakland University, USA
Hiroki Suguri	Miyagi University, Japan
Lily Sun	University of Reading, UK
Jerzy Surma	Warsaw School of Economics, Poland
Ryszard Tadeusiewicz	AGH University of Science and Technology, Poland
Tania Tait	Maringá State University, Brazil
Mohan Tanniru	Oakland University, USA
Sotirios Terzis	University of Strathclyde, UK
Claudine Toffolon	Université du Maine, France
José Tribolet	INESC-ID/Instituto Superior Técnico, Portugal
Theodoros Tzouramanis	University of the Aegean, Greece
Domenico Ursino	Università degli Studi Mediterranea Reggio Calabria, Italy
Vadim Vagin	Moscow Power Engineering Institute (National Research University), Russian Federation
José Ângelo Braga de Vasconcelos	Universidade Atlântica, Portugal
Michael Vassilakopoulos	University of Thessaly, Greece
Maria Esther Vidal	Universidad Simon Bolivar, Venezuela
Stephanie Vie	University of Central Florida, USA
Gualtiero Volpe	Università degli Studi di Genova, Italy
Bing Wang	University of Hull, UK
Dariusz Wawrzyniak	Wroclaw University of Economics, Poland
Hans Weghorn	BW Cooperative State University Stuttgart, Germany
Hans Weigand	Tilburg University, The Netherlands
Robert Wrembel	Poznan University of Technology, Poland
Stanislaw Wrycza	University of Gdansk, Poland
Mudasser Wyne	National University, USA
Hongji Yang	Bath Spa University, UK
Stefano Za	CeRSI - LUISS Guido Carli University, Italy
Eugenio Zimeo	University of Sannio, Italy

Additional Reviewers

Boris Almonacid	Pontificia Universidad Católica de Valparaíso, Chile
Marcio Bera	State University of Maringá, Brazil
Solvita Berzisa	Riga Technical University, Latvia
Magdalena Cantabella	Universidad Católica San Antonio de Murcia, Spain
Claudia Cappelli	UNIRIO, Universidade Federal do Estado do Rio de Janeiro, Brazil
Luisa Carpente	University of A Coruña, Spain

Fernando William Cruz	Universidade de Brasilia, Brazil
Delia Irazù Hernandez Farias	UPV/UNITO, Spain
Fausto Fasano	University of Molise, Italy
Cristian Galleguillos	Pontificia Universidad Católica de Valparaíso, Chile
Javier David Fernández García	Vienna University of Economics and Business, Austria
Ricardo Geraldi	State University of Maringá, Brazil
Rafael Glauber	Federal University of Bahia, Brazil
Magalí González	Universidad Católica Nuestra Señora de la Asunción, Paraguay
Djilali Idoughi	University A. Mira of Bejaia, Algeria
Christos Kalyvas	University of the Aegean, Greece
Janis Kampars	Riga Technical University, Latvia
Shixong Liu	University of Reading, UK
Leandros Maglaras	De Montfort University, UK
Anderson Marcolino	University of São Paulo, Brazil
Eirini Molla	University of the Aegean, Greece
Dario Di Nucci	University of Salerno, Italy
Fabio Palomba	University of Salerno, Italy
Roberto Pereira	University of Campinas (UNICAMP), Brazil
Victor Reyes	Pontifica Universidad Catolica de Valparaiso, Chile
Jorge Saldivar	Catholic University Nuestra Señora de la Asunción, Paraguay

Invited Speakers

Claudia Loebbecke	University of Cologne, Germany
Sergio Gusmeroli	Engineering Ingegneria Informatica SPA, Italy
Wil Van Der Aalst	Technische Universiteit Eindhoven, The Netherlands
Jan Vom Brocke	University of Liechtenstein, Liechtenstein

Contents

Enterprise Architecture

Invited Paper

Responsible Data Science: Using Event Data in a "People Friendly" Manner

Wil M.P. van der Aalst[✉]

Department of Mathematics and Computer Science,
Eindhoven University of Technology,
PO Box 513, 5600 MB Eindhoven, The Netherlands
`w.m.p.v.d.aalst@tue.nl`
`http://www.vdaalst.com/`

Abstract. The omnipresence of event data and powerful process mining techniques make it possible to quickly learn process models describing what people and organizations really do. Recent breakthroughs in process mining resulted in powerful techniques to discover the real processes, to detect deviations from normative process models, and to analyze bottlenecks and waste. Process mining and other data science techniques can be used to improve processes within any organization. However, there are also great concerns about the use of data for such purposes. Increasingly, customers, patients, and other stakeholders worry about "irresponsible" forms of data science. Automated data decisions may be unfair or non-transparent. Confidential data may be shared unintentionally or abused by third parties. Each step in the "data science pipeline" (from raw data to decisions) may create inaccuracies, e.g., if the data used to learn a model reflects existing social biases, the algorithm is likely to incorporate these biases. These concerns could lead to resistance against the large-scale use of data and make it impossible to reap the benefits of process mining and other data science approaches. This paper discusses *Responsible Process Mining* (RPM) as a new challenge in the broader field of *Responsible Data Science* (RDS). Rather than avoiding the use of (event) data altogether, we strongly believe that techniques, infrastructures and approaches can be made *responsible by design*. Not addressing the challenges related to RPM/RDS may lead to a society where (event) data are misused or analysis results are deeply mistrusted.

Keywords: Data science · Process mining · Big data · Fairness · Accuracy · Confidentiality · Transparency

1 Introduction

Big data is changing the way we do business, socialize, conduct research, and govern society. Data are collected on anything, at any time, and in any place [5]. Organizations are investing heavily in Big data technologies and data science has emerged as a new scientific discipline providing techniques, methods,

© Springer International Publishing AG 2017
S. Hammoudi et al. (Eds.): ICEIS 2016, LNBIP 291, pp. 3–28, 2017.
DOI: 10.1007/978-3-319-62386-3_1

and tools to gain value and insights from new and existing data sets. Data abundance combined with powerful data science techniques has the potential to dramatically improve our lives by enabling new services and products, while improving their efficiency and quality. Big Data is often considered as the "new oil" and data science aims to transform this into new forms of "energy": insights, diagnostics, predictions, and automated decisions. However, the process of transforming "new oil" (data) into "new energy" (analytics) may negatively impact citizens, patients, customers, and employees. Systematic discrimination based on data, invasions of privacy, non-transparent life-changing decisions, and inaccurate conclusions occur regularly and show that the saying "With great power comes great responsibility" also applies to data science.

Data science techniques may lead to new forms of "pollution". Technological solutions that aim to avoid the negative side effects of using data, can be characterized by the term *"Green Data Science"* (GDS) first coined in [4]. The term refers to the collection of techniques and approaches trying to reap the benefits of data science and Big Data while ensuring fairness, accuracy, confidentiality, and transparency. Citizens, patients, customers, and employees need to be *protected against irresponsible uses of data* (big or small). Therefore, we need to separate the "good" and "bad" of data science. Compare this with environmentally friendly forms of green energy (e.g. solar power) that overcome problems related to traditional forms of energy. Data science may result in unfair decision making, undesired disclosures, inaccuracies, and non-transparency. These irresponsible uses of data can be viewed as "pollution". Abandoning the systematic use of data may help to overcome these problems. However, this would be comparable to abandoning the use of energy altogether. Data science is used to make products and services more reliable, convenient, efficient, and cost effective. Moreover, most new products and services depend on the collection and use of data. *Therefore, we argue that the "prohibition of data (science)" is not a viable solution.* Instead we believe that technological solutions can be used to avoid pollution and protect the environment in which data is collected and used.

In this paper we use the term *"Responsible Data Science"* (RDS) rather than "Green Data Science" (GDS). Our notion of *responsible* is inspired by the emerging field of *responsible innovation* [15,21]. From the overall "responsibility" notion, we distill four main challenges specific to data science:

- **Fairness:** *Data science without prejudice* - How to avoid unfair conclusions even if they are true?
- **Accuracy:** *Data science without guesswork* - How to answer questions with a guaranteed level of accuracy?
- **Confidentiality:** *Data science that ensures confidentiality* - How to answer questions without revealing secrets?
- **Transparency:** *Data science that provides transparency* - How to clarify answers such that they become indisputable?

This paper discusses these so-called "FACT" challenges while emphasizing the need for technological solutions that enable individuals, organizations and society to reap the benefits from the widespread availability of data while ensuring Fairness, Accuracy, Confidentiality, and Transparency (FACT).

The "FACT" challenges are fairly general. Therefore, the second part of this paper focuses on a specific subdiscipline of data science: *process mining* [5]. Process mining can be used to discover what people actually do, check compliance, and uncover bottlenecks. Process mining reveals the behaviors of workers, customers, and other people involved in the processes being analyzed. The unique capabilities of process mining also create a range of "FACT" challenges. For example, analysis may reveal that workers taking care of the most difficult cases are slower than others or cause more deviations. Moreover, the filtering of event data may be used to influence the outcomes in such a way that decision makers are not aware of this. These examples illustrate the negative side-effects that *Responsible Process Mining* (RPM) aims to avoid.

This paper extends the ICEIS 2016/ENASE 2016 keynote paper [4] by introducing the data science discipline and by elaborating on RDS and RPM. The remainder of this paper is organized as follows. Section 2 introduces the field of data science and uses the example of photography to illustrate the impact of digitization in our daily lives. In Sect. 3 we elaborate on the four general "FACT" challenges. Section 4 introduces process mining as a technology to analyze the *behavior* of people and organizations. In this more specific setting, we revisit the four "FACT" challenges and mention possible solution directions (Sect. 5). Finally, Sect. 6 concludes the paper.

2   Data Science

Many definitions have been proposed for data science [11,24]. Here, we use a definition taken from [5]:

> *Data science is an interdisciplinary field aiming to turn data into real value. Data may be structured or unstructured, big or small, static or streaming. Value may be provided in the form of predictions, automated decisions, models learned from data, or any type of data visualization delivering insights. Data science includes data extraction, data preparation, data exploration, data transformation, storage and retrieval, computing infrastructures, various types of mining and learning, presentation of explanations and predictions, and the exploitation of results taking into account ethical, social, legal, and business aspects.*

The definition shows that the data science field is quite broad. Data science has it roots in different fields. Like computer science emerged from mathematics, data science is now emerging from a range of disciplines (see Fig. 1).

Within statistics, one of the key areas in mathematics, there is a long tradition in data analysis. Statistics developed over four centuries starting with the work of John Graunt (1620–1674). Although data science can be seen as a continuation of statistics, the recent progress in data science cannot be attributed to traditional statisticians that tend to focus more on theoretical results rather than real-world analysis problems. The computational aspects, which are critical for larger data sets, are typically ignored by statisticians [5,27]. The focus is on generative modeling rather than prediction and dealing with practical challenges related to data quality and size. It was the data mining community that realized major breakthroughs in the discovery of patterns and relationships (e.g., efficiently learning decision trees and association rules). Data science is also closely related to data processing. Turing award winner Peter Naur (1928–2016) used the term "data science" long before it was in vogue [5]. In 1974, Naur wrote: "A basic principle of *data science*, perhaps the most fundamental that may be formulated, can now be stated: The data representation must be chosen with due regard to the transformation to be achieved and the data processing tools available" [19].

As Fig. 1 shows, the roots of data science extend beyond mathematics and computer science. Other areas include ethics, law, economics, and operations management.

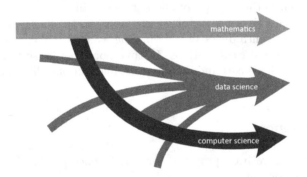

Fig. 1. Just like computer science emerged from mathematics, data science is now emerging from multiple disciplines.

To illustrate the relevance of data science, let us consider the development of photography over time as sketched in Fig. 2. Photography emerged at the beginning of the 19th century. Until 1975 photos were analog and for a long time Kodak was the undisputed market leader. At the peak of its success Kodak developed the first digital camera. It could make 0.01 megapixel black and white pictures and marked both the beginning of the digital photography and the decline of Kodak as a company (see Fig. 2). In 2003, the sales of digital cameras exceeded the sales of traditional cameras for the first time. Today, we make photographs using smartphones and tablets rather than cameras. The remarkable transition from analog to digital photography illustrated by Fig. 2 has had an impact that goes far beyond the photos themselves. The digitization of photography enabled new applications. For example, photos can be shared online (e.g. Flickr, Instagram, Facebook, and Twitter) and changed the way we communicate and socialize (see the uptake of the term "selfie"). Smartphone apps can even be used to detect eye cancer, melanoma, and other diseases by analyzing photos. Photos capture "events" showing what is really happening. This is enabling new forms of data analysis.

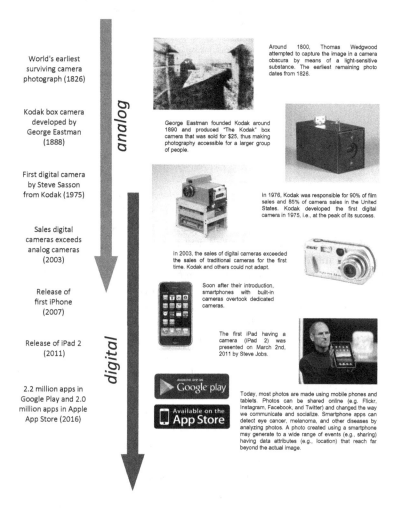

Fig. 2. Example of digitization: digital photography changed the way we make and use photos. Moreover, the digitization of photos enabled new forms of analysis.

Similar developments can be witnessed in all economic sectors. Consider for example the music industry. The transition from analog to digital music has quite some similarities with Fig. 2.

Looking at the timeline in Fig. 2, one can easily see why data science is now emerging as a new discipline. The exponential growth of data over the last decades has now reached a "tipping point" dramatically changing the way we do business and socialize. After explaining why and how data science emerged as a new discipline, we now use Fig. 3 to introduce the three main aspects of data science:

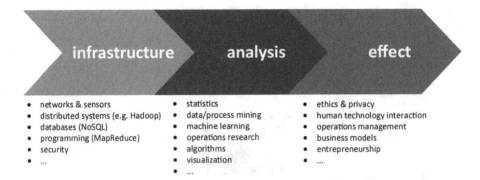

Fig. 3. The data science landscape composed of three main aspects: infrastructure, analysis, and effect.

- **Infrastructure:** *How to collect, store, and process (large amounts of) data?* The infrastructure provides the basis for analysis. Data need to be collected and stored. Systems may need to be distributed to cope with larger amounts of data. Databases may need to be tailored towards the application and special programming models may need to be employed.
- **Analysis:** *How to turn data into insights, answers, ideas, and decisions?* Using the infrastructure different types of approaches can be used to extract value from data. This includes machine learning, data/process mining, statistics, visual analytics, predictive analytics, decision support, etc.
- **Effect:** *How to positively impact reality?* The application of data science may impact individuals, processes, organizations, and society. There may be trade-offs between different goals and stakeholders. For example, privacy concerns may conflict with business targets.

Figure 4 provides yet another view on the data science landscape by sketching the "data science pipeline". Individuals interact with a range of hardware/software systems (information systems, smartphones, websites, wearables, etc.) ❶. Data related to machine and interaction events are collected ❷ and preprocessed for analysis ❸. During preprocessing data may be transformed, cleaned, anonymized, de-identified, etc. Models may be learned from data or made/modified by hand ❹. For compliance checking, models are often normative and made by hand rather than discovered from data. Analysis results based on data (and possibly also models) are presented to analysts, managers, etc. ❺ or used to influence the behavior of information systems and devices ❻. Based on the data, decisions are made or recommendations are provided. Analysis results may also be used to change systems, laws, procedures, guidelines, responsibilities, etc. ❼.

3 Responsible Data Science (RDS)

Figure 4 also lists the four "FACT" challenges mentioned in the introduction. Each of the challenges requires an understanding of the whole data pipeline. Flawed analysis results or bad decisions may be caused by different factors such as a sampling bias, careless preprocessing, inadequate analysis, or an opinionated presentation. We use the term *Responsible Data Science* (RDS) for data science approaches that try to exploit data while avoiding negative side-effects. RDS is synonymous with "Green Data Science" (GDS) [4]. The latter term is based on the metaphor that "data is the new oil" and that we should develop technologies to avoid the "pollution" caused by irresponsible uses of data.

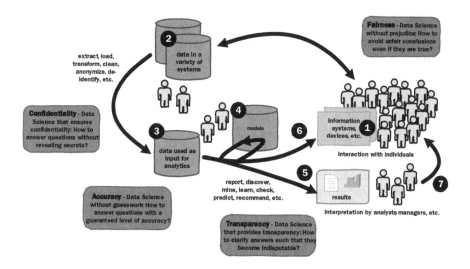

Fig. 4. The "data science pipeline" facing the four "FACT" challenges.

RDS advocates taking the third aspect ("effect") in Fig. 3 as leading when designing or using the first two aspects ("infrastructure" and "analysis"). Whenever possible, infrastructures and analysis techniques should be responsible by design.

The remainder of this section elaborates on the four "FACT" challenges: Fairness, Accuracy, Confidentiality, and Transparency.

3.1 Fairness - Data Science Without Prejudice: How to Avoid Unfair Conclusions Even if They Are True?

Data science techniques need to ensure *fairness*: Automated decisions and insights should not be used to discriminate in ways that are unacceptable from a legal or ethical point of view. Discrimination can be defined as "the harmful treatment of an individual based on their membership of a specific group or category (race, gender, nationality, disability, marital status, or age)". However, most analysis techniques *aim to discriminate* among groups. Banks handing out loans and credit cards try to discriminate between groups that will pay their debts and groups that will run into financial problems. Insurance companies try to discriminate between groups that are likely to claim and groups that are less likely to claim insurance. Hospitals try to discriminate between groups for which a particular treatment is likely to be effective and groups for which this is less likely. Hiring employees, providing scholarships, screening suspects, etc. can all be seen as classification problems: The goal is to explain a response variable (e.g., person will pay back the loan) in terms of predictor variables (e.g., credit history, employment status, age, etc.). Ideally, the learned model explains the response variable as well as possible without discriminating on the basis of sensitive attributes (race, gender, etc.).

To explain *discrimination discovery* and *discrimination prevention*, let us consider the set of all (potential) customers of some insurance company specializing in car insurance. For each customer we have the following variables:

- name,
- birthdate,
- gender (male or female),
- nationality,
- car brand (Alfa, BMW, etc.),
- years of driving experience,
- number of claims in the last year,
- number of claims in the last five years, and
- status (insured, refused, or left).

The status field is used to distinguish current customers (status = insured) from customers that were refused (status = refused) or that left the insurance company during the last year (status = left). Customers that were refused or that left more than a year ago are removed from the data set.

Techniques for *discrimination discovery* aim to identify groups that are discriminated based on *sensitive* variables, i.e., variables that should not matter. For example, we may find that "males have a higher likelihood to be rejected than females" or that "foreigners driving a BMW have a higher likelihood to be rejected than Dutch BMW drivers". Discrimination may be caused by human judgment or by automated decision algorithms using a predictive model. The decision algorithms may discriminate due to a sampling bias, incomplete data, or incorrect labels. If earlier rejections are used to learn new rejections, then prejudices may be reinforced. Similar "self-fulfilling prophecies" can be caused by sampling or missing values.

Even when there is no intent to discriminate, discrimination may still occur. Even when the automated decision algorithm does not use gender and uses only non-sensitive variables, the actual decisions may still be such that (fe)males or foreigners have a much higher probability to be rejected. The decision algorithm may also favor more frequent values for a variable. As a result, minority groups may be treated unfairly.

Discrimination prevention aims to create automated decision algorithms that do not discriminate using sensitive variables. It is not sufficient to remove these sensitive variables: Due to correlations and the handling of outliers, unintentional discrimination may still take place. One can add constraints to the decision algorithm to ensure fairness using a predefined criterion. For example, the constraint "males and females should have approximately the same probability to be rejected" can be added to a decision-tree learning algorithm. Next to adding algorithm-specific constraints used during analysis one can also use preprocessing (modify the input data by resampling or relabeling) or postprocessing (modify models, e.g., relabel mixed leaf nodes in a decision tree). In general there is often a *trade-off between maximizing accuracy and minimizing discrimination* (see Fig. 5). By rejecting fewer males (better fairness), the insurance company may need to pay more claims.

Discrimination prevention often needs to use sensitive variables (gender, age, nationality, etc.) to ensure fairness. This creates a *paradox*, e.g., information on gender needs to be used to avoid discrimination based on gender.

The first paper on discrimination-aware data mining appeared in 2008 [22]. Since then, several papers mostly focusing on fair classification appeared: [8, 14,26]. These examples show that unfairness during analysis can be actively prevented. However, unfairness is not limited to classification and more advanced forms of analytics also need to ensure fairness.

3.2 Confidentiality - Data Science That Ensures Confidentiality: How to Answer Questions Without Revealing Secrets?

The application of data science techniques should not reveal certain types of personal or otherwise sensitive information. Often personal data need to be kept *confidential*. The General Data Protection Regulation (GDPR) (see also Sect. 6) focuses on personal information [10]: *"The principles of data protection should apply to any information concerning an identified or identifiable natural person. Personal data which have undergone pseudonymisation, which could be attributed*

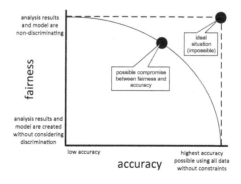

Fig. 5. Tradeoff between fairness and accuracy.

to a natural person by the use of additional information should be considered to be information on an identifiable natural person. To determine whether a natural person is identifiable, account should be taken of all the means reasonably likely to be used, such as singling out, either by the controller or by another person to identify the natural person directly or indirectly. To ascertain whether means are reasonably likely to be used to identify the natural person, account should be taken of all objective factors, such as the costs of and the amount of time required for identification, taking into consideration the available technology at the time of the processing and technological developments. The principles of data protection should therefore not apply to anonymous information, namely information which does not relate to an identified or identifiable natural person or to personal data rendered anonymous in such a manner that the data subject is not or no longer identifiable."

Confidentiality is not limited to personal data. Companies may want to hide sales volumes or production times when presenting results to certain stakeholders. One also needs to bear in mind that few information systems hold information that can be shared or analyzed without limits (e.g., the existence of personal data cannot be avoided). The "data science pipeline" depicted in Fig. 4 shows that there are different types of data having different audiences. Here we focus on: (1) the "raw data" stored in the information system ❷, (2) the data used as input for analysis ❸, and (3) the analysis results interpreted by analysts and managers ❺. Whereas the raw data may refer to individuals, the data used for analysis is often (partly) de-identified, and analysis results may refer to aggregate data only. It is important to note that confidentiality may be endangered along the whole pipeline and includes analysis results.

Consider a data set that contains sensitive information. Records in such a data set may have three types of variables:

- *Direct identifiers*: Variables that uniquely identify a person, house, car, company, or other entity. For example, a social security number identifies a person.
- *Key variables*: Subsets of variables that together can be used to identify some entity. For example, it may be possible to identify a person based on gender, age, and employer. A car may be uniquely identified based on registration date, model, and color. Key variables are also referred to as *implicit identifiers* or *quasi identifiers*.
- *Non-identifying variables*: Variables that cannot be used to identify some entity (direct or indirect).

Confidentiality is impaired by unintended or malicious disclosures. We consider three types of such disclosures:

- *Identity disclosure*: Information about an entity (person, house, etc.) is revealed. This can be done through direct or implicit identifiers. For example, the salaries of employees are disclosed unintentionally or an intruder is able to retrieve patient data.
- *Attribute disclosure*: Information about an entity can be derived indirectly. If there is only one male surgeon in the age group 40–45, then aggregate data for this category reveals information about this person.

– *Partial disclosure*: Information about a group of entities can be inferred. Aggregate information on male surgeons in the age group 40–45 may disclose an unusual number of medical errors. These cannot be linked to a particular surgeon. Nevertheless, one may conclude that surgeons in this group are more likely to make errors.

De-identification of data refers to the process of removing or obscuring variables with the goal to minimize unintended disclosures. In many cases *re-identification* is possible by linking different data sources. For example, the combination of wedding date and birth date may allow for the re-identification of a particular person. *Anonymization* of data refers to de-identification that is irreversible: re-identification is impossible. A range of de-identification methods is available: removing variables, randomization, hashing, shuffling, sub-sampling, aggregation, truncation, generalization, adding noise, etc. Adding some noise to a continuous variable or the coarsening of values may have a limited impact on the quality of analysis results while ensuring confidentiality.

There is a trade-off between minimizing the disclosure of sensitive information and the usefulness of analysis results (see Fig. 6). Removing variables, aggregation, and adding noise can make it hard to produce any meaningful analysis results. Emphasis on confidentiality (like security) may also reduce convenience. Note that *personalization often conflicts with fairness and confidentiality*. Disclosing all data, supports analysis, but jeopardizes confidentiality.

Access rights to the different types of data and analysis results in the "data science pipeline" (Fig. 4) vary per group. For example, very few people will have access to the "raw data" stored in the information system ❷. More people will have access to the data used for analysis and the actual analysis results. Poor cybersecurity may endanger confidentiality. Good policies ensuring proper authentication (Are you who you say you are?) and authorization (What are you allowed to do?) are needed to protect access to the pipeline in Fig. 4. Cybersecurity measures should not complicate access, data preparation, and analysis; otherwise people may start using illegal copies and replicate data. See [18, 20, 23] for approaches to ensure confidentiality.

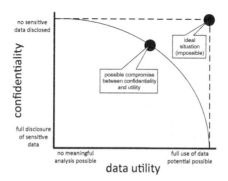

Fig. 6. Tradeoff between confidentiality and utility.

3.3   Accuracy - Data Science Without Guesswork: How to Answer Questions with a Guaranteed Level of Accuracy?

Increasingly decisions are made using a combination of algorithms and data rather than human judgement. Hence, analysis results need to be *accurate* and should not deceive end-users and decision makers. Yet, there are several factors endangering accuracy.

First of all, there is the problem of overfitting the data leading to "bogus conclusions". There are numerous examples of so-called *spurious correlations* illustrating the problem. Some examples (taken from [28]):

- The per capita cheese consumption strongly correlates with the number of people who died by becoming tangled in their bedsheets.
- The number of Japanese passenger cars sold in the US strongly correlates with the number of suicides by crashing of motor vehicle.
- US spending on science, space and technology strongly correlates with suicides by hanging, strangulation and suffocation.
- The total revenue generated by arcades strongly correlates with the number of computer science doctorates awarded in the US.

When using many variables relative to the number of instances, classification may result in complex rules overfitting the data. This is often referred to as the *curse of dimensionality*: As dimensionality increases, the number of combinations grows so fast that the available data become sparse. With a fixed number of instances, the predictive power reduces as the dimensionality increases. Using cross-validation most findings (e.g., classification rules) will get rejected. However, if there are many findings, some may survive cross-validation by sheer luck.

In statistics, Bonferroni's correction is a method (named after the Italian mathematician Carlo Emilio Bonferroni) to compensate for the problem of multiple comparisons. Normally, one rejects the null hypothesis if the likelihood of the observed data under the null hypothesis is low [9]. If we test many hypotheses, we also increase the likelihood of a rare event. Hence, the likelihood of incorrectly rejecting a null hypothesis increases [17]. If the desired significance level for the whole collection of null hypotheses is α, then the Bonferroni correction suggests that one should test each individual hypothesis at a significance level of $\frac{\alpha}{k}$ where k is the number of null hypotheses. For example, if $\alpha = 0.05$ and $k = 20$, then $\frac{\alpha}{k} = 0.0025$ is the required significance level for testing the individual hypotheses.

Next to overfitting the data and testing multiple hypotheses, there is the problem of *uncertainty in the input data* and the problem of *not showing uncertainty in the results*.

Uncertainty in the input data is related to the fourth "V" in the four "V's of Big Data" (Volume, Velocity, Variety, and Veracity). Veracity refers to the trustworthiness of the input data. Sensor data may be uncertain, multiple users may use the same account, tweets may be generated by software rather than people, etc. These uncertainties are often not taken into account during analysis assuming that things "even out" in larger data sets. This does not need to be the case and the reliability of analysis results is affected by unreliable or probabilistic input data.

According to *Bonferroni's principle* we need to avoid treating random observations as if they are real and significant [25]. The following example, inspired by a similar example in [25], illustrates the risk of treating completely random events as patterns.

A *Dutch government agency is searching for terrorists by examining hotel visits* of all of its 18 million citizens (18×10^6). The hypothesis is that terrorists meet multiple times at some hotel to plan an attack. Hence, the agency looks for suspicious "events" $\{p_1, p_2\} \dagger \{d_1, d_2\}$ where persons p_1 and p_2 meet on days d_1 and d_2. How many of such suspicious events will the agency find if the behavior of people is completely random? To estimate this number we need to make some additional assumptions. On average, Dutch people go to a hotel every 100 days and a hotel can accommodate 100 people at the same time. We further assume that there are $\frac{18 \times 10^6}{100 \times 100} = 1800$ Dutch hotels where potential terrorists can meet.

The probability that two persons (p_1 and p_2) visit a hotel on a given day d is $\frac{1}{100} \times \frac{1}{100} = 10^{-4}$. The probability that p_1 and p_2 visit the *same* hotel on day d is $10^{-4} \times \frac{1}{1800} = 5.55 \times 10^{-8}$. The probability that p_1 and p_2 visit the same hotel on two different days d_1 and d_2 is $(5.55 \times 10^{-8})^2 = 3.086 \times 10^{-15}$. Note that different hotels may be used on both days. Hence, the probability of suspicious event $\{p_1, p_2\} \dagger \{d_1, d_2\}$ is 3.086×10^{-15}.

How many candidate events are there? Assume an observation period of 1000 days. Hence, there are $1000 \times (1000 - 1)/2 = 499,500$ combinations of days d_1 and d_2. Note that the order of days does not matter, but the days need to be different. There are $(18 \times 10^6) \times (18 \times 10^6 - 1)/2 = 1.62 \times 10^{14}$ combinations of persons p_1 and p_2. Again the ordering of p_1 and p_2 does not matter, but $p_1 \neq p_2$. Hence, there are $499,500 \times 1.62 \times 10^{14} = 8.09 \times 10^{19}$ candidate events $\{p_1, p_2\} \dagger \{d_1, d_2\}$.

The expected number of suspicious events is equal to the product of the number of candidate events $\{p_1, p_2\} \dagger \{d_1, d_2\}$ and the probability of such events (assuming independence): $8.09 \times 10^{19} \times 3.086 \times 10^{-15} = 249,749$. Hence, there will be around a quarter million observed suspicious events $\{p_1, p_2\} \dagger \{d_1, d_2\}$ in a 1000 day period!

Suppose that there are only a handful of terrorists and related meetings in hotels. *The Dutch government agency will need to investigate around a quarter million suspicious events involving hundreds of thousands innocent citizens.* Using Bonferroni's principle, we know beforehand that this is not wise: there will be too many false positives.

Example 1: Bonferroni's principle explained using an example taken from [5]. To apply the principle, compute the number of observations of some phenomena one is interested in under the assumption that things occur at random. If this number is significantly larger than the real number of instances one expects, then most of the findings will be false positives.

When we say, "we are 95% confident that the true value of parameter x is in our confidence interval $[a, b]$", we mean that 95% of the hypothetically observed confidence intervals will hold the true value of parameter x. Averages, sums, standard deviations, etc. are often based on sample data. Therefore, it is important to provide a confidence interval. For example, given a mean of 35.4 the 95% confidence interval may be $[35.3, 35.6]$, but the 95% confidence interval may also be $[15.3, 55.6]$. In the latter case, we will interpret the mean of 35.4 as a "wild guess" rather than a representative value for true average value. Although we are used to confidence intervals for numerical values, decision makers have problems interpreting the expected accuracy of more complex analysis results like decision trees, association rules, process models, etc. Cross-validation techniques like k-fold checking and confusion matrices give some insights. However, models and decisions are often presented unequivocally thus hiding uncertainties. Explicit vagueness or more explicit confidence diagnostics may help to better interpret analysis results. Parts of models should be kept deliberately "vague" if analysis is not conclusive.

3.4 Transparency - Data Science That Provides Transparency: How to Clarify Answers Such That They Become Indisputable?

Data science techniques are used to make a variety of decisions. Some of these decisions are made automatically based on rules learned from historic data. For example, a mortgage application may be rejected automatically based on a decision tree. Other decisions are based on analysis results (e.g., process models or frequent patterns). For example, when analysis reveals previously unknown bottlenecks, then this may have consequences for the organization of work and changes in staffing (or even layoffs). Automated decision rules (❻ in Fig. 4) need to be as accurate as possible (e.g., to reduce costs and delays). Analysis results (❺ in Fig. 4) also need to be accurate. However, accuracy is not sufficient to ensure acceptance and proper use of data science techniques. Both decisions ❻ and analysis results ❺ also need to be *transparent*.

Figure 7 illustrates the notion of transparency. Consider an application submitted by John evaluated using three data-driven decision systems. The first system is a black box: It is unclear why John's application is rejected. The second system reveals it's decision logic in the form of a decision tree. Applications from females and younger males are always accepted. Only applications from older males get rejected. The third system uses the same decision tree, but also explains the rejection ("because male and above 50"). Clearly, the third system is most transparent. When governments make decisions for citizens it is often mandatory to explain the basis for such decisions.

Deep learning techniques (like many-layered neural networks) use multiple processing layers with complex structures or multiple non-linear transformations. These techniques have been successfully applied to automatic speech recognition, image recognition, and various other complex decision tasks. Deep learning methods are often looked at as a "black box", with performance measured empirically and no formal guarantees or explanations. A many-layered neural network is not

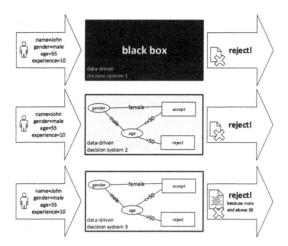

Fig. 7. Different levels of transparency.

as transparent as for example a decision tree. Such a neural network may make good decisions, but it cannot explain a rule or criterion. Therefore, such black box approaches are non-transparent and may be unacceptable in some domains.

Transparency is not restricted to automated decision making and explaining individual decisions, it also involves the intelligibility, clearness, and comprehensibility of analysis results (e.g., a process model, decision tree, regression formula). For example, a model may reveal bottlenecks in a process, possible fraudulent behavior, deviations by a small group of individuals, etc. It needs to be clear for the user of such models (e.g., a manager) how these findings where obtained. The link to the data and the analysis technique used should be clear. For example, filtering the input data (e.g., removing outliers) or adjusting parameters of the algorithm may have a dramatic effect on the model returned.

Storytelling is sometimes referred to as "the last mile in data science". The key question is: How to communicate analysis results with end-users? *Storytelling is about communicating actionable insights to the right person, at the right time, in the right way.* One needs to know the gist of the story one wants to tell to successfully communicate analysis results (rather than presenting the whole model and all data). One can use natural language generation to transform selected analysis results into concise, easy-to-read, individualized reports.

To provide transparency there should be a clear link between data and analysis results/stories. One needs to be able to *drill-down* and inspect the data from the model's perspective. Given a bottleneck one needs to be able to drill down to the instances that are delayed due to the bottleneck. This related to *data provenance*: it should always be possible to reproduce analysis results from the original data.

The four "FACT" challenges depicted in Fig. 4 are clearly interrelated. There may be trade-offs between them. For example, to ensure confidentiality we may add noise and de-identify data thus possibly compromising accuracy and transparency.

4   Process Mining

The goal of *process mining* is to turn event data into insights and actions [5]. Process mining is an integral part of data science, fueled by the availability of data and the desire to improve processes. Process mining can be seen as a means to bridge the gap between data science and process science. Data science approaches tend to be process agonistic whereas process science approaches tend to be model-driven without considering the "evidence" hidden in the data.

4.1   What Is Process Mining?

Figure 8 shows the "process mining pipeline" and can be viewed as a specialization of the Fig. 4. Process mining focuses on the analysis of *event data* and analysis results are often related to *process models*. Process mining is a rapidly growing subdiscipline within both Business Process Management (BPM) [2] and data science [3]. Mainstream Business Intelligence (BI), data mining and machine learning tools are not tailored towards the analysis of event data and the improvement of processes. Fortunately, there are dedicated process mining tools able to transform event data into actionable process-related insights. For example, *ProM* (www.processmining.org) is an

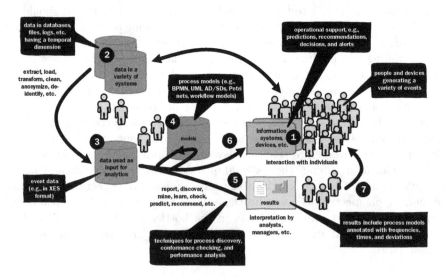

Fig. 8. The "process mining pipeline" relates observed and modeled behavior.

open-source process mining tool supporting process discovery, conformance checking, social network analysis, organizational mining, clustering, decision mining, prediction, and recommendation (see Fig. 9). Moreover, in recent years, several vendors released commercial process mining tools. Examples include: *Celonis Process Mining* by Celonis GmbH (www.celonis.de), *Disco* by Fluxicon (www.fluxicon.com), *Interstage Business Process Manager Analytics* by Fujitsu Ltd. (www.fujitsu.com), *Minit* by Gradient ECM (www.minitlabs.com), *myInvenio* by Cognitive Technology (www.my-invenio.com), *Perceptive Process Mining* by Lexmark (www.lexmark.com), *QPR ProcessAnalyzer* by QPR (www.qpr.com), *Rialto Process* by Exeura (www.exeura.eu), *SNP Business Process Analysis* by SNP Schneider-Neureither & Partner AG (www.snp-bpa.com), and *PPM webMethods Process Performance Manager* by Software AG (www.softwareag.com).

4.2 Creating and Managing Event Data

Process mining is impossible without proper *event logs* [1]. An event log contains event data related to a particular process. Each event in an event log refers to one *process instance*, called *case*. Events related to a case are ordered. Events can have attributes. Examples of typical attribute names are activity, time, costs, and resource. Not all events need to have the same set of attributes. However, typically, events referring to the same activity have the same set of attributes. Figure 9(a) shows the conversion of an CSV file with four columns (case, activity, resource, and timestamp) into an event log.

Most process mining tools support XES (eXtensible Event Stream) [13]. In September 2010, the format was adopted by the IEEE Task Force on Process Mining and became the de facto exchange format for process mining. The IEEE Standards Organization is currently evaluating XES with the aim to turn XES into an official IEEE standard.

To create event logs we need to extract, load, transform, anonymize, and de-identify data from a variety of systems (see ❸ in Fig. 8). Consider for example the hundreds of tables in a typical HIS (Hospital Information System) like Chip-Soft, McKesson and EPIC or in an ERP (Enterprise Resource Planning) system like SAP, Oracle, and Microsoft Dynamics. Non-trivial mappings are needed to extract events and to relate events to cases. Event data needs to be scoped to focus on a particular process. Moreover, the data also needs to be scoped with respect to confidentiality issues.

4.3 Process Discovery

Process discovery is one of the most challenging process mining tasks [1]. Based on an event log, a process model is constructed thus capturing the behavior seen in the log. Dozens of process discovery algorithms are available. Figure 9(c) shows a process model discovered using ProM's *inductive visual miner* [16]. Techniques use Petri nets, WF-nets, C-nets, process trees, or transition systems as a representational bias [5]. These results can always be converted to the desired

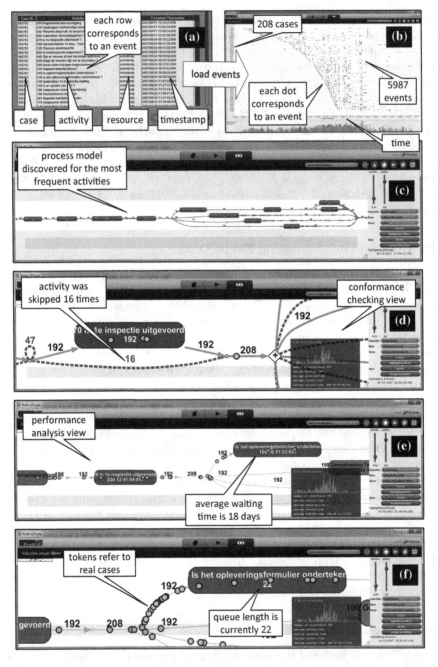

Fig. 9. Six screenshots of ProM while analyzing an event log with 208 cases, 5987 events, and 74 different activities. First, a CSV file is converted into an event log (a). Then, the event data can be explored using a dotted chart (b). A process model is discovered for the 11 most frequent activities (c). The event log can be replayed on the discovered model. This is used to show deviations (d), average waiting times (e), and queue lengths (f).

notation, for example BPMN (Business Process Model and Notation), YAWL, or UML activity diagrams.

4.4 Conformance Checking

Using conformance checking discrepancies between the log and the model can be detected and quantified by replaying the log [6]. For example, Fig. 9(c) shows an activity that was skipped 16 times. Some of the discrepancies found may expose undesirable deviations, i.e., conformance checking signals the need for a better control of the process. Other discrepancies may reveal desirable deviations and can be used for better process support. Input for conformance checking is a process model having executable semantics and an event log.

4.5 Performance Analysis

By replaying event logs on process model, we can compute frequencies and waiting/service times. Using alignments [6] we can relate cases to paths in the model. Since events have timestamps, we can associate the times in-between events along such a path to delays in the process model. If the event log records both start and complete events for activities, we can also monitor activity durations. Figure 9(d) shows an activity that has an average waiting time of 18 days and 16 h. Note that such bottlenecks are discovered without any modeling.

4.6 Operational Support

Figure 9(e) shows the queue length at a particular point in time. This illustrates that process mining can be used in an online setting to provide operational support. Process mining techniques exist to predict the remaining flow time for a case or the outcome of a process. This requires the combination of a discovered process model, historic event data, and information about running cases. There are also techniques to recommend the next step in a process, to check conformance at run-time, and to provide alerts when certain Service Level Agreements (SLAs) are (about to be) violated.

5 Responsible Process Mining (RPM)

This section discusses challenges related to fairness, accuracy, confidentiality, and transparency in the context of process mining. The goal is not to provide solutions, but to illustrate that the more general challenges discussed before trigger concrete research questions in the process mining domain.

5.1 Classification of RPM Challenges

Tables 1 and 2 map the four generic "FACT" challenges introduced in Sect. 3 onto the five key ingredients of process mining briefly introduced in Subsects. 4.2–4.6. Using both dimensions we obtain a classification consisting of $4 \times 5 = 20$ possible problem areas.

It is impossible to discuss all 20 potential problem areas listed in Tables 1 and 2. Therefore, we discuss four selected problem areas in more detail.

5.2 Example: Confidentiality and Creating and Managing Event Data

Let us now explore one of the cells in Table 2. Event data may reveal confidential information as highlighted in Fig. 10. The class model shows the information found in event logs using XES [13], MXML, or some other logging format. Process mining tools exploit such information during analysis. In Fig. 10 three levels are identified: *process model level*, *case/instance level*, and *event level*. The case/instance level consists of *cases* and *activity instances* that connect *processes* and *activities* in the model to *events* in the event log. See [5] for a detailed description of the typical ingredients of an event log. For RPM it is important to note that events and cases often refer to individuals. A case may correspond to a customer, patient, student, or citizen. Events often refer to the person executing the corresponding activity instance (e.g., an employee).

Event data are notoriously difficult to fully anonymize. In larger processes, most cases follow a unique path. In the event log used in Fig. 9, 198 of the 208 cases follow a unique path (focusing only on the order of activities). Hence, knowing the order of a few selected activities may be used to de-anonymize or re-identify cases. The same holds for (precise) timestamps. For the event log in Fig. 9, several cases can be uniquely identified based on the day the registration activity (first activity in process) was executed. If one knows the timestamps of these initial activities with the precision of an hour, then almost all cases can be uniquely identified. This shows that the ordering and timestamp data in event logs may reveal confidential information unintentionally. Therefore, it is interesting to investigate what can be done by adding noise (or other transformations) to event data such that the analysis results do not change too much. For example, we can shift all timestamps such that all cases start in "week 0". Most process discovery techniques will still return the same process model. Moreover, the average flow/waiting/service times are not affected by this. However, if one is investigating queueing or resource behavior, then one cannot consider cases in isolation and shift cases in time.

Moreover, event data can also be stored in aggregated form as is done for streaming process mining where one cannot keep track of all events and all cases due to memory constraints and the need to provide answers in real-time [5,7,29]. Aging data structures, queues, time windows, sampling, hashing, etc. can be used to keep only the information necessary to instantly provide answers to selected questions. Such approaches can also be used to ensure confidentiality, often without a significant loss of accuracy.

Table 1. Relating the four challenges to process mining specific tasks (1/2).

	Creating and managing event data	Process discovery	Conformance checking	Performance analysis	Operational support
Fairness Data Science without prejudice: How to avoid unfair conclusions even if they are true?	The input data may be biased, incomplete or incorrect such that the analysis reconfirms prejudices. By resampling or relabeling the data, undesirable forms of discrimination can be avoided. Note that both cases and resources (used to execute activities) may refer to individuals having sensitive attributes such as race, gender, age, etc.	The discovered model may abstract from paths followed by certain under-represented groups of cases. Discrimination-aware process-discovery algorithms can be used to avoid this. For example, if cases are handled differently based on gender, we may want to ensure that both are equally represented in the model?	Conformance checking can be used to "blame" individuals, groups, or organizations for deviating from some normative model. Discrimination-aware conformance checking (e.g., alignments) needs to separate (1) likelihood, (2) severity and (3) blame. Deviations may need to be interpreted differently for different groups of cases and resources	Straightforward performance measurements may be unfair for certain classes of cases and resources (e.g., not taking into account the context). Discrimination-aware performance analysis detects unfairness and supports process improvements taking into account trade-offs between internal fairness (worker's perspective) and external fairness (citizen/patient/customer's perspective)	Process-related predictions, recommendations and decisions may discriminate (un)intentionally. This problem can be tackled using techniques from discrimination-aware data mining
Accuracy Data Science without guesswork: How to answer questions with a guaranteed level of accuracy?	Event data (e.g., XES files) may have all kinds of quality problems. Attributes may be incorrect, imprecise, or uncertain. For example, timestamps may be too coarse (just the date) or reflect the time of recording rather than the time of the event's occurrence	Process discovery depends on many parameters and characteristics of the event log. Process models should better show the confidence level of the different parts. Moreover, additional information needs to be used better (domain knowledge, uncertainty in event data, etc.)	Often multiple explanations are possible to interpret non-conformance. Just providing one alignment based on a particular cost function may be misleading. How robust are the findings?	In case of fitness problems (process model and event log disagree), performance analysis is based on assumptions and needs to deal with missing values (making results less accurate)	Inaccurate process models may lead to flawed predictions, recommendations and decisions. Moreover, not communicating the (un)certainty of predictions, recommendations and decisions, may negatively impact processes

Table 2. Relating the four challenges to process mining specific tasks (2/2).

	Creating and managing event data	Process discovery	Conformance checking	Performance analysis	Operational support
Confidentiality Data Science that ensures confidentiality: How to answer questions without revealing secrets?	Event data (e.g., XES files) may reveal sensitive information. Anonymization and de-identification can be used to avoid disclosure. Note that timestamps and paths may be unique and a source for re-identification (e.g., all paths are unique)	The discovered model may reveal sensitive information, especially with respect to infrequent paths or small event logs. Drilling-down from the model may need to be blocked when numbers get too small (cf. k-anonymity)	Conformance checking shows diagnostics for deviating cases and resources. Access-control is important and diagnostics need to be aggregated to avoid revealing compliance problems at the level of individuals	Performance analysis shows bottlenecks and other problems. Linking these problems to cases and resources may disclose sensitive information	Process-related predictions, recommendations and decisions may disclose sensitive information, e.g., based on a rejection other properties can be derived
Transparency Data Science that provides transparency: How to clarify answers such that they become indisputable?	Provenance of event data is key. Ideally, process mining insights can be related to the event data they are based on. However, this may conflict with confidentiality concerns	Discovered process models depend on the event data used as input and the parameter settings and choice of discovery algorithm. How to ensure that the process model is interpreted correctly? End-users need to understand the relation between data and model to trust analysis	When modeled and observed behavior disagree there may be multiple explanations. How to ensure that conformance diagnostics are interpreted correctly?	When detecting performance problems, it should be clear how these were detected and what the possible causes are. Animating event logs on models helps to make problems more transparent	Predictions, recommendations and decisions are based on process models. If possible, these models should be transparent. Moreover, explanations should be added to predictions, recommendations and decisions ("We predict that this case be late, because ...")

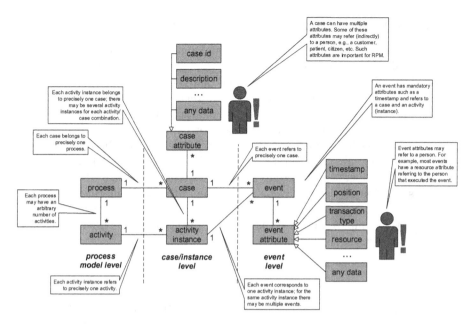

Fig. 10. The typical ingredients of an event log described in terms of a class model highlighting data elements referring to individuals.

5.3 Example: Accuracy and Process Discovery

As mentioned in Table 1 the accuracy of a discovery process model may depend on a variety parameter settings. A small change in the input data (log or settings) may completely change the result. One of the main problems of existing techniques is that they do not indicate any form of confidence level. Often parts of the model can be discovered with great certainty whereas other parts are unclear and the discovery technique is basically guessing. Nevertheless, this uncertainty is seldom shown in the model and may lead to incorrect conclusions. To support RPM, we need to develop process discovery techniques that indicate confidence information in the models returned.

5.4 Example: Transparency and Conformance Checking

Conformance checking [6] can be viewed as a classification problem. What kinds of cases deviate at a particular point? However, if model and log disagree, then there may be multiple explanations for each deviation. For example, there may be multiple log-model "alignments" having the same costs. Moreover, the costs assigned to deviations may be arbitrary. As mentioned in Table 2 it is vital that conformance diagnostics are interpreted correctly. Moreover, the "process mining pipeline" (Fig. 8) needs to be managed carefully to avoid misleading conclusions caused by, for example, data preparation problems.

5.5   Example: Fairness and Performance Analysis

Process mining provides the ability to show and analyze bottlenecks in processes with minimal effort. Bottleneck analysis can also be formulated as a classification problem. Which cases get delayed more than 5 days? Who worked on these delayed cases? Performance problems can be related to characteristics of the case (e.g., a citizen or customer) or the people that worked on it. The process itself may be "unfair" (discriminate workers or cases) or decision makers can make "unfair" conclusions based on a superficial analysis of the data. Table 1 mentions *internal* fairness (worker's perspective) and *external* fairness (citizen/patient/customer's perspective) as two concerns. Note that the employee that takes all difficult cases may be slower than others. Evaluating employees without taking such context into account will lead to unjustified conclusions.

The above examples illustrate that our classification can be used to identify a range of novel research challenges in process mining.

6   Epilogue

This paper introduced the notion of *"Responsible Data Science"* (RDS) from four angles: *fairness, accuracy, confidentiality,* and *transparency.* We advocate the development and use of positive technological solutions rather than relying on stricter regulations like the *General Data Protection Regulation* (GDPR) approved by the EU Parliament in April 2016 [10]. GDPR aims to strengthen and unify data protection for individuals and replaces Directive 95/46/EC [12]. GDPR is far more restrictive than earlier legislation. Sanctions include fines of up to 4% of the annual worldwide turnover.

GDPR and other forms of legislation can be seen as environmental laws protecting society against "pollution" caused by irresponsible data use. However, legislation may also prevent the use of data (science) in applications where incredible improvements are possible. Simply prohibiting the collection and systematic use of data would be turning back the clock. Next to legislation, positive technological solutions are needed to ensure RDS. Green data science needs technological breakthroughs, just like the innovations enabling green energy.

The paper also discussed the four "FACT" challenges in the context of process mining. In today's society, *event data* are collected about anything, at any time, and at any place. Today's process mining tools are able to analyze such data and can handle event logs with billions of events. These amazing capabilities also imply a great responsibility. Fairness, accuracy, confidentiality, and transparency should be key concerns for any process miner. There is a need for a new generation of process mining techniques and tools that are responsible by design. However, sometimes painful trade-offs are inevitable. Figure 5 and Table 1 both show the need for trade-offs between fairness and accuracy. Other trade-offs are needed between confidentiality and transparency (see Fig. 6 and Table 2).

We invite researchers and practitioners to contribute to RDS and RPM. These topics are urgent: without proper tools and approaches the use of data may come to a grinding hold. People like Michael Jordan warned for a

"Big data winter", due to the simple-minded and statistically unsound approaches used today. Irresponsible uses of data (science) may trigger restrictive laws and effectuate resistance of customers and citizens.

Acknowledgements. This work is partly based by discussions in the context of the *Responsible Data Science* (RDS) collaboration involving principal scientists from Eindhoven University of Technology, Leiden University, University of Amsterdam, Radboud University Nijmegen, Tilburg University, VU University, Amsterdam Medical Center, VU Medical Center, Leiden University Medical Center, Delft University of Technology, and CWI.

References

1. van der Aalst, W.M.P.: Process Mining: Discovery, Conformance and Enhancement of Business Processes. Springer, Berlin (2011)
2. van der Aalst, W.M.P., Management, B.P.: A comprehensive survey. ISRN Softw. Eng. 1–37 (2013). doi:10.1155/2013/507984
3. Aalst, W.M.P.: Data scientist: the engineer of the future. In: Mertins, K., Bénaben, F., Poler, R., Bourrières, J.-P. (eds.) Enterprise Interoperability VI. PIC, vol. 7, pp. 13–26. Springer, Cham (2014). doi:10.1007/978-3-319-04948-9_2
4. van der Aalst, W.M.P.: Green data science: using big data in an "environmentally friendly" manner. In: Camp, O., Cordeiro, J. (eds.) Proceedings of the 18th International Conference on Enterprise Information Systems (ICEIS 2016), pp. 9–21. Science and Technology Publications, Portugal (2016)
5. van der Aalst, W.M.P.: Process Mining: Data Science in Action. Springer, Berlin (2016)
6. van der Aalst, W.M.P., Adriansyah, A., van Dongen, B.: Replaying history on process models for conformance checking and performance analysis. WIREs Data Mining Knowl. Discov. 2(2), 182–192 (2012)
7. Burattin, A., Sperduti, A., van der Aalst, W.M.P.: Control-flow discovery from event streams. In: IEEE Congress on Evolutionary Computation (CEC 2014), pp. 2420–2427. IEEE Computer Society (2014)
8. Calders, T., Verwer, S.: Three naive bayes approaches for discrimination-aware classification. Data Min. Knowl. Disc. 21(2), 277–292 (2010)
9. Casella, G., Berger, R.L.: Statistical Inference, 2nd edn. Duxbury Press, Delhi (2002)
10. Council of the European Union. General Data Protection Regulation (GDPR). Regulation (EU) 2016/679 of the European Parliament and of the Council of 27 April 2016 on the protection of natural persons with regard to the processing of personal data and on the free movement of such data, and repealing Directive 95/46/EC, April 2016
11. Donoho, D.: 50 years of Data Science. Technical report, Stanford University, September 2015. Based on a Presentation at the Tukey Centennial Workshop, Princeton, NJ, 18 September 2015
12. European Commission: Directive 95/46/EC of the European Parliament and of the Council on the Protection of Individuals with Wegard to the Processing of Personal Data and on the Free Movement of Such Data. Official Journal of the European Communities, No L 281/31, October 1995

13. IEEE Task Force on Process Mining: XES Standard Definition (2013). www.xes-standard.org
14. Kamiran, F., Calders, T., Pechenizkiy, M.: Discrimination-aware decision-tree learning. In: Proceedings of the IEEE International Conference on Data Mining (ICDM 2010), pp. 869–874 (2010)
15. Koops, B.J., Oosterlaken, I., Romijn, H., Swierstra, T., Van den Hoven, J. (eds.): Responsible Innovation 2: Concepts, Approaches, and Applications. Springer, Berlin (2015)
16. Leemans, S.J.J., Fahland, D., Aalst, W.M.P.: Exploring processes and deviations. In: Fournier, F., Mendling, J. (eds.) BPM 2014. LNBIP, vol. 202, pp. 304–316. Springer, Cham (2015). doi:10.1007/978-3-319-15895-2_26
17. Miller, R.G.: Simultaneous Statistical Inference. Springer, Berlin (1981)
18. Monreale, A., Rinzivillo, S., Pratesi, F., Giannotti, F., Pedreschi, D.: Privacy-by-design in big data analytics and social mining. EPJ Data Sci. **1**(10), 1–26 (2014)
19. Naur, P.: Concise Survey of Computer Methods. Studentlitteratur Lund, Akademisk Forlag, Kobenhaven (1974)
20. Nelson, G.S.: Practical Implications of Sharing Data: A Primer on Data Privacy, Anonymization, and De-Identification. Paper 1884–2015, ThotWave Technologies, Chapel Hill (2015)
21. Owen, R., Bessant, J., Heintz, M. (eds.): Responsible Innovation. Wiley, Hoboken (2013)
22. Pedreshi, D., Ruggieri, S., Turini, F.: Discrimination-aware data mining. In: Proceedings of the 14th ACM SIGKDD International Conference on Knowledge Discovery and Data Mining, pp. 560–568. ACM (2008)
23. President's Council of Advisors on Science and Technology: Big Data and Privacy: A Technological Perspective (Report to the President). Executive Office of the President, US-PCAST, May 2014
24. Press, G.: A very short history of data science. Forbes Technology (2013). http://www.forbes.com/sites/gilpress/2013/05/28/a-very-short-history-of-data-science/
25. Rajaraman, A., Ullman, J.D.: Mining of Massive Datasets. Cambridge University Press, Cambridge (2011)
26. Ruggieri, S., Pedreshi, D., Turini, F.: DCUBE: discrimination discovery in databases. In: Proceedings of the ACM SIGMOD International Conference on Management of Data, pp. 1127–1130. ACM (2010)
27. Tukey, J.W.: The future of data analysis. Ann. Math. Stat. **33**(1), 1–67 (1962)
28. Vigen, T.: Spurious Correlations. Hachette Books, New York (2015)
29. van Zelst, S.J., van Dongen, B.F., van der Aalst, W.M.P.: Know what you stream: generating event streams from CPN models in ProM 6. In: Proceedings of the BPM2015 Demo Session. CEURWorkshop Proceedings, vol. 1418, pp. 85–89 (2015). http://ceur-ws.org/

Databases and Information Systems Integration

Story-Telling and Narrative: Alternative Genres Linking IS Publication and Practice

Antonio Ghezzi[1(✉)] and Eileen Lavezzari[1,2]

[1] Department of Management, Economics and Industrial Engineering,
Politecnico di Milano, Via Lambruschini 4B, 20156 Milan, Italy
{antoniol.ghezzi,eileen.lavezzari}@polimi.it,
eileen.lavezzari@it.bosch.com
[2] Bosch Group Italy - Diesel Systems - Sales and Marketing (VHIT/SMP),
Strada Vicinale delle Sabbione 5, 26010 Offanengo, CR, Italy

Abstract. Genres of communications significantly influence the evolution of a field of research. In the Information Systems (IS) domain, a debate has recently emerged on the chance to implement alternative genres in the representation of IS publication and practice. We hence propose to apply story-telling and narrative as alternative genres to write publications reporting IS research. By presenting a narration exemplifying the implementation of these genres, we argue that the incremental introduction of their principles would be beneficial to IS research, enabling a revisited representation of IS themes that extends the boundaries of canonical genres. In parallel, thanks to the peculiarity of the story narrated, we claim that story-telling and narrative are also powerful instruments supporting IS practice. The mediating role of action research in enhancing the link between story-telling and narrative used as writing genres and practices will also be recognized.

Keywords: Alternative genre · Story-Telling · Narrative · Action research · Information systems publication · Information systems practice

1 Introduction

"The universe is made of stories, not atoms."
Muriel Rukeyser (1913–1980)

The evolution of a field of research like that on Information Systems (IS) inherently relates not only to the content of investigation – in either its theoretical or empirical forms – and to the methodologies applied to conduct the research endeavor; it is also significantly shaped by the writing genre traditionally applied as a vehicle to report its content and findings.

In the last years, an intriguing debate has emerged among Editors and Authors of Academic Journals – commonly recognized as the most suitable outlet for scientific publications – with regards to the genres to be applied when writing academic publications [1, 2]. As the concept of genre represents a meaningful pattern of communication which consists of a sequence of speech acts [3], IS scholars and practitioners are currently discussing the opportunity to apply alternative genres in IS research representation. According to [4], the term "alternative genres" refers to unconventional forms of

S. Hammoudi et al. (Eds.): ICEIS 2016, LNBIP 291, pp. 31–52, 2017.
DOI: 10.1007/978-3-319-62386-3_2

thinking, doing, and communicating scholarship and practice. In particular, it is related to innovation with respect to epistemological perspectives, research methods, semantic framing, literary styles, and media of expression. Furthermore, [2] defines "alternative genres" as a new and larger class of publication genres, which would encompass the narratives and presentational innovations such as theatre, video and other types of presentational genres.

Providing an opportunity to better understand specific issues in an innovative way, alternative genres add value to the existing set of publication genres in IS research, and as such should be of interest for the IS community [2]. Alternative genres should not only be considered as a source of new types of research output, but also as an addition and enrichment of dominant publication genres; put differently, a combination of traditional and alternative techniques can provide deeper and more profound understanding of the analysed phenomena.

By reflecting new forms of analysis that serve as a source of inspiration, innovation and insight generation, alternative genres as such could potentially change the current perception of the world [5]. The creation of alternative genres category could act as a driver for getting creative ideas within the business ecosystem. On the contrary, an establishment of a new formal category carries the risk of disaccreditation of the published papers within the category, and hence should be tackled according to the accreditation procedures [2]. By motivating scientists and researchers to propose more reflexive works, such as literature reviews, narratives and essays, top journals could set the platform for the publications of more enigmatic papers as well as practice-oriented papers, resulting in larger inclusion of alternative genres [1].

Ultimately, the aim of the emerging debate on genres is to sustain the quest for alternative, fresh standpoints that "challenge or reframe our taken-for-granted assumptions, perceptions and practices related to representing IS research" [6].

With the intention to contribute to this on-going debate, our study puts forward the proposal to apply story-telling and narrative as an alternative genre to write publications reporting IS research. Well-grounded in an interpretative philosophical assumption, story-telling and narrative could support the understanding of IS phenomena through the meanings that people assign to them. More precisely, we aim at exploring and exploiting the interpretive power of these alternative genres, "aimed at producing an understanding of the context of the information system, and the process whereby the information system influences and is influenced by the context" [7].

In addition to the role of story-telling and narrative in IS publication, we will argue that this genre is also valuable to link IS publication and practice. The mediating role of action research in enhancing the link between story-telling and narrative used as both writing genres and practice will also be recognized.

The remainder of this Section will present the salient points of the alternative genre proposed.

1.1 Story-Telling and Narrative as Alternative Genres – Definition, Structure and Principles

Considering the significance and pervasiveness of the topic, several definitions for story-telling and narrative have been provided. The Oxford English Dictionary defines a narrative (or story) as "any account of connected events, presented to a reader or listener in a sequence of written or spoken words, or in a sequence of (moving) pictures". According to [8], narrative is the main conventional form of organising human experiences and memories through stories; stories hence inherently have an anecdotal base based on anthropological observation [9]. Consistently with this paramount role assigned to narrative, [10] claims that "a narrative is a communicative relation which is often conflated with straightforward understanding of what a story is. Narrative is a particular form of representation implementing signs and how it is necessarily bound up with sequence, space and time".

Indeed, narratives are not only chronologies or reports of evidence: stories represent poetic elaborations of narrative material, aiming to communicate facts as experience, not facts as information [11].

Focusing on story-telling as a publication genre, [2] defines it as a way to organize a discourse and the resulting narrative. Each story has two meanings: (i) the story itself, i.e. the set of events that we want to report; and (ii) the narrative, i.e. what is being told.

Like all genres, story-telling and narrative should conform to a canonical structure and a set of principles.

As proposed in different studies on narrative structure (e.g., see [8, 9]; Tolstoy, 1899; [12]), the traditional way to organize stories is the "three-act form", where: the first act is used to provide context and introduce the complication – or the "inciting incident" [13]; the second act further develops the complication, builds up the tension and creates a narrative climax; and the third act presents the resolution, drawing the narration's conclusions as well as the "moral of the story" [12], and possibly leaving one or more issues pending for further reflection [8]. Such structure is almost canonical in narrative, and evidences of it are found from ancient representations in Greek theatre to contemporary cinema [14].

[9] Argues that stories have recurring structures, made of one or more cycles of interaction between the protagonist and her or his external and internal context. Narrative is hence built on the following main structural components:

- Context;
- Complication;
- Protagonist (P);
- Cycle/s of P's internal (thoughts and feelings) and external (words and actions) responses, and consequences of P's external responses;
- End of the story, with/without a complete solution.

Beyond their traditional structure, studies have investigated the principles and features of story-telling and narrative. [15] Identify four key elements of the narrative method: (i) experience; (ii) time; (iii) personal knowledge; and (iv) reflection and deliberation. All four elements are interconnected and of vital importance for story-telling. Experience and time are present all around us, and as such influence human behaviour. Considering that without time, no experience can be gained, it can be easily concluded that time is a critical dimension of experience. Through the process of learning, knowledge is obtained, and as such determines a person's image of the wold and of her/himself. Reflection puts the emphasis on the past events in a sense of revision and reproduction, whereas deliberation conveys a sense of preparation for the future. It is clear enough that reflection commonly implies a preparation for the future and that deliberation implies past considerations; hence, narrative requires a balanced treatment of past, present and future. Overall, a storyteller is influenced by his or her personal experience and knowledge, as well as senses of reflection and deliberation, at all points of life; consequently, so are the storyteller's stories.

According to [8], story-telling and narrative are fundamental tools not only for reality representation, but also for "reality construction". The ten features of narratives he sketches constitute a reference framework when shaping or analysing a narrated story, which consists of: (i) narrative diachronicity – a narrative is a unique pattern of events over time, and as such, it is irreducibly durative; (ii) particularity – narrative takes as its reference particular happenings, which however, are their vehicle rather than destination; a story's suggestiveness lies in the emblematic nature of its particulars, which may embody specific meanings; (iii) intentional state entailment – narrative is about characters acting in a setting, and the story's happenings shall be relevant to their intentional states while engaged in the story itself; however, intentional state does not necessarily determine the course of events, as characters' action may depart from their intentions, and narrative can provide the basis for interpreting the reasons (not the causes) behind the characters' actions; (iv) hermeneutic composability – an act of hermeneutic interpretation of the meaning of what is expressed is implied in narration, where neither a rationalist truth nor an empirical demonstrability of the meaning apply; this applies to all parts of the story's whole, which need to be interpretatively composed and constituted by the narrator in the light of the overall narrative; (v) canonicity and breach – narrative shall concern how "an implicit canonical script has been breached, violated, or deviated from" [8] in a manner to tear apart the canonical script's legitimacy; "the breach component in a narrative can be created by linguistic means as well as by the use of a putatively delegitimizing precipitating event in the plot" [8]; (vi) referentiability – a narrative refers to reality, even though it could depart from it and embrace a fictional account of events; (vii) genericness – narrative, as all other genres, is both a "conventional way of representing human plights and a way of telling that predisposes our minds and sensitivities in particular ways [...]. While [genres] may be representation of social ontology, they are also invitations to a particular style of epistemology. As such, they may have quite as powerful an influence in shaping our modes of thought as they have in creating the realities that their plots depict" [8]; (viii) normativeness – as narrative ultimately rests on the breach of conventional expectations, where a breach presupposes a norm, narrative is constitutionally normative; this does not, however, imply a normative approach according to which each trouble in the story should be ultimately resolved; (ix) context sensitivity and negotiability – the context of narrative is assimilated according to the reader's background, though the reader inevitably takes the narrator's intentions into account when approaching his or her story, thus making narrative a viable instrument for cultural negotiation; (x) narrative accrual – narratives can (and should) accrue to create a story of some sort, which may eventually take the form of culture, history, tradition or field-specific knowledge.

Further recommendations and elements of story-telling refer to the need to see the story as a whole [16], which implies that some degree of central control is necessary to ensure that the story makes sense as a unit: to attain this notion successfully, a central entity or narrator should perform a unifying and orchestrating activity [17]. [18] Add that a good narrative involves a balance between what Aristotle referred to as logos – i.e. internal consistency of the message, ethos – i.e. credibility of the writer, and pathos – i.e. emotional appeal. [18] Also highlight that narrative is often used in the context of action research, proposing five principles for assessing the quality of narrative research reports: (i) historical continuity; (ii) reflexivity – the ability to stimulate reflection; (iii) dialectics – the dialectical elaboration of the story; (iv) workability – the production of usable practices; and (v) evocativeness – the emphasis on ethos and pathos.

Eventually, story-telling or anecdote enhancement should also follow the principles of privacy and confidentiality for material gathered, and that of non-judgement – since the purpose of observation is to capture things as they are, not as the narrator would like them to be [9].

After discussing the definitions, structure, principle and feature of the genre, the next section will present an exemplification of story-telling and narrative as an alternative genre to write a publication investigating the IS theme of Enterprise Resource Planning implementation in a small-medium enterprise. The story narrated employs the aforementioned principles and reports a research conducted by the authors in the timeframe December 2011–April 2013.

2 Alternative Genre Application – A "Story" on the Use of Stories and Narrative in the Implementation of an ERP System

"Are we sure this is the only way?"

The Chief Executive Officer looked around the roundtable where his team of executives was sitting together with the marketing and technology representatives of the partnering IT vendor and our team of academic researchers. The faces and expressions he saw did not convince him. Without waiting for a reply, he said: *"I need you to consider and explain to me all the implications related to this project. Enlighten me"*.

We were expecting this question: our role was that of researchers and advisors of the company's management team and possible facilitators of the change to be introduced. We had been working side-by-side with CEO for three months, and we knew that, in his mind, a proper assessment of multifaceted implications made all the difference. The reason for his stance had deep roots in the story of his organization.

Since the early fifties, his company had come a long way. Started as a family business manufacturing glass products, it soon became a national designer and manufacturer of display cases; when it was commissioned a set of installations for an art museum, the company's founders and managers envisioned a clear opportunity for future growth. In the period 1970–2000, the company nurtured both technical and cultural skills in the fields of artistic installation, museum exhibitions and works conservation; such competences allowed it to become a global exhibition designer involved in several projects with renown institutions, such as the British Museum, the Tower of London Museum, the Louvre in Paris, the Museum of Modern Arts and the Metropolitan Museum in New York. In 2012, the company owned an international portfolio of projects and had gained worldwide recognition.

As the company grew globally, however, it was shaped by two diverging thrust: on the one hand, the CEO aimed at maintaining the company's inheritance of small-medium enterprise and its craftsman approach towards each activity and work; on the other, a compelling need for organic development and structuration was perceived by the management. As a result, the organizational evolution was to some extent convoluted and not fully consistent: while some functions (e.g. design and manufacturing) operated with a high degree of structuration and technology support, others (e.g. administration, procurement, project management and marketing) were almost completely unstructured. Furthermore, Information Technology did not evolve alongside the company's manufacturing technologies. The little IT function was largely focusing on maintaining the computers used for running Computer Aided Design and Computer Aided Manufacturing software; data analysis and storing was either based on mere spreadsheets, or more frequently, on paperwork.

In early 2012, when this story takes places, it was time to make a strategic decision about IT. The management team had been consulting a shortlist of IT vendors for three months, and the most promising solution proposed was that of implementing an Enterprise Resource Planning (ERP) system to centralize and support information management and workflow throughout the functions. The Marketing Manager from the vendor was selling the idea that an ERP would have solved all problems the company was facing. "*It will be a 'panacea of all evils'*", he used to tell everyone he met.

However, the CEO had profound doubts about this change, and his worries were somewhat justifiable. The CEO had been in charge of leading the company for more than thirty years, inheriting it from his father, and he was well aware of its organizational inconsistencies: he foresaw the introduction of such a pervasive system would determine radical modifications in several areas, with unpredictable results. He had always played a key role in human resource management, including selection and recruiting, so he expected some of his employees to eventually resist to or impair the IT project. On top of this, he held a Philosophy and Literature background, which gave him an anti-conformist and original perspective on many strategic or organizational issues, including technology: he had contrasting feelings concerning IT, which he liked to philosophically define as "*a robot with huge potential to enhance human's capabilities, but after all, a robot with no will and no creative value in itself other than that of the human utilizing it*".

The meeting with the management, the IT vendors and the academic researchers was meant to make a final decision concerning ERP implementation in the company. However, considering the CEO's eclectic character, a twist was just around the corner.

The vendor's Marketing Manager started addressing the hot question on impacts: "*We are aware an ERP has multidimensional impacts, but don't worry, we have done this before: our solutions are modular, flexible, scalable, interoperable and secure. They support a wide range of activities and processes, and we will take care of the integration with you legacy systems*".

"*Our legacy systems...*". The CEO made a long reflective pause. "*What about our cultural legacy? And our human resources legacy? How do you take those into account?*".

The Marketing Manager seemed puzzled: the one spoken by the CEO was clearly a language he was not familiar with. He almost mumbled when formulating an answer:

"Well... we essentially perform process mapping and requirements identification through standard models, like UML...".

"And what in the world is UML?" the CEO interrupted. *"Please, I am quite an old man, would you mind sparing me this purely technical language? Whenever that language is used, it seems to me it is used on purpose, and the purpose is quite often to make things more obscure than they actually are. I am firmly convinced IT language is an unnecessary mystification created to put off rather than involve".* After this openly provoking statement, the Marketing Manager remained silent for a while, as all the other participants to the meeting did. The CEO had deliberately created a breach in an otherwise ordinary client-supplier meeting: it was then time for him to make his point.

> *"Let me tell you what we will do this time. I want no technical language, no 'UML': I want you to tell me a story. The story of why and how my company would benefit from IS. And when I say you, I mean all of you, all of us: not only our partners, even each and every manager and employee in my company will need to narrate how this information system would affect the way she or he works and live. You are my partners, colleagues and friends, I want to read your stories, hear your voice, in a language we can all understand. That's what we will do".*

The request sounded as bizarre as it was resolute. Some of the company's own managers tried to question it, but the CEO was inflexible. The meeting was closed with the action point to start gathering story-telling and narrations from all people possibly influenced by ERP implementation.

In a private discussion following the meeting with the IT vendors, the CEO revealed his motives to us: *"My father used to tell me you should never reckon without your host. My hosts are my employees: if I want to change something so radical in my organization, I need my decision to be shared. Or I'll be paying the consequences when nobody uses the newly implemented systems, or worse, they feel threatened by it and lose their motivation and creativity. And frankly... I also see this as a great opportunity to pursue some sort of a 'literature crusade' to acculturate my Human Resources at all levels. They will benefit from it, you'll see".* The grin on his face clearly showed he wanted to go all the way.

If the beginning of the story was unconventional, what that followed was even more unexpected.

An inter-firm client-supplier team was constituted, with the aim to collect, interpret, relate and synthesise the narrations from all parties involved, in all their forms. In such an endeavour, significant support came from the Project Manager appointed by the CEO: funnily enough, he was an Architect with little or no knowledge of IS. We soon realized his alienated perspective would have caused some problems in the first phases of the project: when we asked about his new appointment two weeks after he got it, he burst out *"I hated this assignment in the first place [...]. Now I'm starting to under-stand its relevance, but I'm still not sure if I'm the right person for the job...",*

Eventually, we had to admit he actually provided a fresh look at the issue of interest. When discussing with the academic researchers in the middle of the project, his peculiar view of what IS should be and how they should be described emerged. And it was revealing.

He told us: *"My job as an Architect is to design an environment where people live and which people enjoy, not just a tool. As time went by I started seeing IS as the environment I had to design. Indeed, IS is way more than a tool: it is a pervasive way of doing things which changes people's work, and in turn, life. As such, its implementation should be investigated in terms of employees' feelings about it, not only through convoluted programming languages and weird modelling schemes. And the investigation of human's ideas and feeling is surely best achieved through story-telling".*

As a whole, the effect of the CEO's decision to involve both white and blue collars in the narration of their perspective on the IT revolution underway exceeded the brightest expectations. As the word spread, almost each employee felt compelled to tell her or his story about the workplace and how IT could affect it, from her or his peculiar perspective.

As the process of stories gathering was completed, the Project Manager met with the academic researchers to start drawing some conclusions.

"Take a look at what I have here" he said, quite satisfied with the results of his team's work. Out of sixty-two employees, they collected more than ninety narrations – including one from the IT vendor – in different forms: short stories, essays, mottos, and even rhymes.

A manager structured his story as an historical essay on the role of technology in human history, concluding with positive remarks on its adoption by the company:

"Throughout the history of mankind, technology innovations have marked fundamental milestones enabling our evolution. [...]".

Enthusiastic narrations of how IT could positively influence working practices were delivered: and sometimes, they showed biased or inaccurate expectations that required realignment. An example of this came from a Project Manager involved in international projects. What she wrote seemed to relate more to a Decision Support Systems than to an ERP:

"Finally, IT! I was waiting for you! Now I'll be able to get the right information at the right time, analyse them, extract the charts I need and keep full control of my projects' time, cost and quality".

Some ironic statements were also there. The Project Manager was giggling as he handed two sheets to us:

"If we adopt an Information System, maybe Mary [family name omitted] will refrain from losing or mistyping all the notes I hand her. Adam".

Attached to this statement with a paper clip, a witty reply followed:

"To my dearest Adam [family name omitted],
My ability to mistyping your handwritten notes is inversely proportional to your ability to write sense-making notes.
With deliberate irony,
Mary"

On the other hand, not everyone was fully content with the innovation. Several stories or narration showed a critical stance towards the new system. A short story came from an employee in the administration:

"Average Joe works in the archival department, spending most of his time reading, storing, retrieving and relating paper documents. He is quite happy with it. Then, IT comes into play, promising to help Joe in doing his job, while saving, let's say, 50% of his time. Joe is even happier in the first place, but then he starts thinking 'what will I do with the remaining half of my time? Will I be relocated? Or worse, will my managers start to believe they do not really need me?'. Eventually, Average Joe feels IT is basically stealing his job. And then, he is happy no more."

Another personal, first-person narration was delivered by an account manager in procurement, and showed some resentment towards the new company's orientation:

"My job in the supplier selection department is extremely delicate. I am working with people, managing contracts. I have been carrying out my tasks in the best way possible, always. Then that smart guy from the IT vendor comes in, and tells me what I have been doing for years is now obsolete. Now, I am quite an easy-going lady, so I'm trying to grin and bear it. However, I easily foresee that when the new IT stuff is introduced, I will be feeling lost. I won't know where to start from, I will lose motivation and my performance will plummet. How can technology replace human interaction and rationality after all?"

The Project Manager read these two contributions and thoughtfully said *"We are going to need to work on this. We'll have to restate the urging need for innovation, but we must communicate a feeling of security and stability to everyone"*.

It was then the turn for the IT vendor narration. *"They made me sweat in the early phases. Their answer to all our requests was 'No way. We don't work like that'"*, said the Project Management. *"Eventually, they made an effort to understand our unstructured requirements formulated through story-telling; they even came up with their own story"*. Indeed, the supplier delivered a fascinating – though not fully original – statement envisioning and projecting all benefits of IT:

"We have a dream. We are dreaming of a world where information flow freely. We are dreaming of a company where there's no boundary between people and units. We are dreaming of a place where technology unites, and helps people communicating and sharing their experiences [...]. We have this dream. Do you wish to share this dream with us?"

"Martin Luther King would have liked this..." said the Project Manager, and we all laughed at the joke. Amusingly enough, a modification of these very words soon became part of the IT vendor's institutional mission.

When we asked about internal resistance to this alternative project, he commented: *"Few people actually complained, and if they did, they had to do it with an essay or a motto: I recall this one from one manager..."* and he searched the narrations pile, taking out a small card with this quotation written on:

"What I think of this idea of using story-telling? Frankly, my dear, I don't give a damn".

Again, he mildly smiled. *"They were then confronted with other manuscripts showing different perspectives, rather than compelled to follow an order. This should hopefully increase their empathy towards their fellow colleagues, their bosses and the new system"*.

All in all, everyone participated in the process, and to various extent, became part of it.

The CEO considered this a first, significant success which would have enabled his company to move forward. Indeed, it was this strong participation to the 'story-telling project' who made him decide to give the implementation process his 'green light'.

At the kick-off meeting, he held a plenary talk with all employees. All eyes were on him as he stepped on stage, and once again, he approached the audience with a story, in the form of a metaphorical narration.

"When we are babies... – well, I guess we do not recall much of that period, I am now assuming what our parents told us is truthful – our mother is the world. Our eyes are made to look at her and our arms to hang on her. As we grow up, we find out there is much more to discover out there, much more to see; reality literally expands its boundaries in front of us. Reality is there for us to experience, but also there to be crafted and created. And not only reality changes: we change as well. Hence, we constantly change in an ever-changing world: this is, let's admit it, the most frightening of things. Very few of us like to change: it is at least annoying, maybe even frustrating. However, if we reflect on it, it is also the greatest gift of all. As we change, as we grow, we gradually become familiar with new instrument to experience and even shape our world: legs to walk around; hands to write or make gestures; a mouth to speak, and sometimes misspeak; and above all, a mind to learn, to understand, to compare, to induce and deduce. A mind to create.

Today, as individuals, as an organisation, as a family, we choose to change again. We choose to depart from our previous 'weltanschauung' and to extend our boundaries even further; we choose to learn how to use a new tool, which will influence the way we work as well as the way we live.

But, my friends, be not afraid. Perceive technology as an extension of your hands, you mouths, your minds: perceive it as your next step of evolution and growth. It won't change who you are: it will only provide a further means of expressing yourselves. It won't be good or bad in itself: it will reflect how prone you are to learn and experiment. It won't make you a better worker or a better person: but I am convinced the way you approach this process may influence your attitude towards the next big changes in your life.

So, take it from me: be open to change, be eager to experiment and learn, and fundamentally, be ready to live."

When he left the stage after his speech, he finally knew.

He knew he had convinced them, and he knew he had convinced himself.

He was right: the ERP implementation would have required approximately eleven months, fairly below the average of eighteen and a half months reported by analysts in the Panorama Consulting Group's ERP Report he took as a reference. In the first months following implementations, promising efficiency gains would have been reported, with peaks in those functions – administration, procurement and marketing & sales –and processes – budgeting, call for tender proposals formulation, vendor rating, project procurement, requirement planning and resource allocation – where IT was largely unused and data were scattered around many units and owners.

"So far, we already cut the lead time to formulate a business proposal for the call for tenders we want to compete in from two weeks to six days" a manager in charge of budgeting would have commented. *"We are also beginning sorting out some of the issues about planning requirements and having the right resources just when we need them. The system's introduction is not mature yet, so we are just scratching the surface: this means that, hopefully, there's a lot more to come".*

And above all, in line with what the CEO cared about the most, the overall project would have reinforced organizational culture and shared values; it would have created a sense of unity and common direction; it would have improved organizational climate and control tensions; it would also have strengthened the ties with the IT supplier. This all, thanks to the unconventional approach taken from the very beginning.

The Marketing Manager from the IT vendor would have reinforced this opinion in one of his last comments: *"We really had a hard time finding the motivation to undertake the 'story-telling' pilot project, but now we recognize its value. Users got growingly involved in the system as they tried to investigate its influence on their everyday activities; eventually, they became interested about how the system worked, and often, they were positively impressed. Users were part of the project since its early phases, and to my understanding gained through my professional experience, this is key for successful implementation"*.

As he was leaving the auditorium, the CEO walked through the whole team who originally met around a table to shape the company's IT future – the team he originally provoked and shocked with his proposals – shaking hands with everyone. *"It will be a good project"* he whispered to his staff. Then the door closed behind him.

3 Reflection

The implementation of story-telling and narrative as an alternative genre in IS publication brings about several intriguing implications: our main argument in this study is that such implications cross the boundaries of IS publication, to affect IS practice as well. Indeed, our exemplary application in Sect. 2 presents a meta-role for story-telling, both content and vehicle of the narration: we hence propose that story-telling could frame both IS publication and practice, thus constituting a link between these two halves of the same whole. Elaborating on the findings from [4, 18], we also argue that story-telling shows significant synergies with action research methodology applied to IS, and the two could be mutually reinforcing.

3.1 Story-Telling and Narrative in IS Publication

The story we narrated, written according to the main principle presented in Sect. 1.1, shows the potential – and possible drawbacks – of story-telling and narrative when used as writing genres in IS publication. The story fundamentally follows the traditional three-act form, the "inciting incident" [13] being the CEO's unconventional stance and bizarre request on the use of story-telling.

It also conforms to [9] structure, which, however, is revisited in its flow. Our narration is structured as follows:

- Introduction of the Protagonist (CEO);
- Context and CEO internal characterization;
- Complication determined by CEO's external response and contrast with the "Antagonist" (IT Vendor's MM);
- First cycle/s of CEO's internal (thoughts and feelings) and external (words and actions) responses, and consequences of CEO's external responses (involving Managers, Employees, Suppliers and Action Researchers);

- Introduction of a Co-protagonist (PM);
- Second cycle/s of PM's internal (thoughts and feelings) and external (words and actions) responses, and consequences of PM's external responses (involving Managers, Employees, Suppliers and Action Researchers);
- End and "moral of the story".

Opening the narration with a direct intervention from the would-be protagonist is a narrative device to enhance the "*in medias res*" perception in the reader, capture attention and build up the tension; the introduction of an antagonist, a main co-protagonist and several characters with minor roles is essential to provide different angles, while narrative unity and holism is ensured by the main plot's structure; moreover, ending the story with its moral – provided by a surprisingly revealing speech by the protagonist – facilitates the interiorizing of its meaning and stimulates empathy in the reader. Story-telling hence serves as a learning enabler [15], where the context and the meaning are constantly negotiated between the writer and the reader to achieve a common ground [8].

This restructuring demonstrates a high potential of flexibility and adaptability of the genre to the context; it also sheds light on the power of story-telling to manage and convey meaning, personal motives and soft determinants (e.g. protagonists' internal responses; subplots and stories-in-the-story; figures of speech like metaphors, puns, irony, sarcasm) which would have largely been "lost in translation" in traditional scientific writings.

An essential role enabling this genre to fulfil its literary task is that of the narrator: it is recommendable that the narrator overlaps with the writer/researcher [17, 18], playing the part of the "quasi-omniscient narrator", so as to provide insightful or intriguing details on several characters' internal and external responses, while maintaining control of how the story and the narration develop; this may include anticipating or postponing elements, or adding additional perspectives, to attract the reader's attention while facilitating her or his understanding.

Considering [8] features of narrative, they should be taken into full account and partly reinterpreted to ensure narrative is valuably adopted as an alternative genre in IS research. We specifically refer to referentiability, whereas a narration should possess strong ties with the real events that occurred, so as to avoid fictitious extensions of the story – regardless of their fascinating power. Normativeness should also be revisited, as uncanny events should not only be made comprehensible, interpretable and thus bearable, they should also be resolved – at least in part – in the story narrated, to underscore the actual contribution of action research to the issue under scrutiny, and the study's contribution to literature and practice. At least, the story should imply which events or actions led to the failure to find a solution to the inciting incident and/or to emerging open issues, so as to provide a contribution in the form of anti-advices. After all, the story should be "workable" [18].

On the contrary, the principle of genericness is particularly revealing, as it discloses how alternative genres influence not only the way reality is depicted, but also our modes of thought. Innovations in genres, as supported in this study, should hence be celebrated not only as a change in the content of imagination, but also in its *modus operandi*. Intentional state entailment discloses a possible dualism between characters' intentions and external responses, and calls for a narration which accounts for both and provides the basis for an hermeneutic composition and interpretation of the story's meaning.

Context sensitivity and negotiability is also key, as it shows how narrative creates a common ground for confrontation and synthesis of different perspectives: this is valuable for both IS writing – where a number of alternative standpoints may coexist and be negotiated within the whole story – and IS practice, where narrative could serve as an instrument for conflict resolution.

More broadly, the story's writer/research/narrator should look for a constructive cooperation with the IS community, thus aiming to ensure narrative accrual and the development of an incremental and possibly ever-growing contribution from stories published in IS journals. Narrative accrues once shared culturally, and IS academic journals would provide a legitimate, extremely suitable instrument for the creation of incremental knowledge on information systems based on story-telling and narrative: such extension in genres, sponsored in a growing number of IS works (e.g. [1–4]), would represent an enriching deviation which, however, maintains complicity with the canon of traditional scientific writing.

Such complicity could be preserved by proposing the argument that story-telling and narrative genres are an extension and revisiting of the writing approach currently used to report case studies and action research endeavours. Both these options are hence considered below.

Case studies are "empirical inquiries that investigates a contemporary phenomenon within its real-life context, especially when the boundaries between phenomenon and context are not clearly evident" [19]. The aim of case research is understanding complex phenomena and thus building new theory – or extending existing theories – on them [20]. The application of story-telling and narrative principles and features would constitute a beneficial revisiting and extension of case writing traditionally found in many IS publications, with specific reference to studies addressing ERP implementation (e.g., see [21–25]). Following the claim that ERP implementations are complex undertakings [23] which need to be assessed in a multidimensional fashion, we argue that story-telling could support the investigation of otherwise left-aside organizational perspectives. Being ERP implementation a socio-technical challenge [25], studies addressing this issue – as well as the more general theme of IS introduction – should consider social dynamics and human-related motives [7], which, from a publication writing standpoint, are best described through the narration of a story; at the same time, story-telling as an IS practice could stimulate the inherently human feelings of empathy and identification with the narrated characters and events, thus driving change towards the intended outcomes.

Exploiting the genre's advantages, while controlling for its disadvantages, would constitute a normative breach that enables IS publications based on cases to overcome the limitations of canonical scientific writing (i.e. constraints on figures of speech, rhetorical devices and styles available; structural rigidity; limited accountability of internal responses and motives, and limited perception of the intentional state vs. external response dualism; limited empathy and involvement evoked in the reader), thus providing a truly multifaceted account of the "organizational drama" [26] behind IS adoption.

Action research, as a form of qualitative research [27], is described as a setting in which a client is involved in the process of data gathering, which is prevailingly under the charge of a researcher [28]. According to [29], "action research aims to contribute both to the practical concerns of people in an immediate problematic situation and to the goals of social science by joint collaboration within a mutually acceptable ethical framework".

When reporting action research, style of communication matters. A recent study from [4] investigates how the need to report action research's results in IS publications leads to the selection of different styles, revealing the importance of the notion of "style composition". The results of their study also provide indication that styles adopted by IS action researchers vary according to the three different sections of the article – premise, inference and contribution – and have been changing in time.

Action research, as part of the broader qualitative research stream, could also benefit from a thoughtful design of interviews to generate and gather data that provide insight into people's experiential life [30], reshaped through story-telling: different interviewing methods such as appreciative interviews, laddering interviews and photo-diary interviews can provide enriched descriptions beyond the realist genre when incorporated in a narrative or case study.

Elaborating on the findings presented in [18], we argue that narrative and story-telling could constitute a fundamental genre to report action research in IS publication. To support our argument, while enabling a smoother introduction of this alternative genre in the IS journals' publication canon, we propose to extend the template designed in [4] – directed to IS action researchers to support their publication structuring – by explicitly including a "Narration" building block.

The revisited template would hence follow this structure: (i) Introduction; (ii) Background; (ii) Framing; (iv) Methods; (v) *Narration*; (vi) Results; and (vii) Discussion.

In Narration (v), the case or project experience of the action researcher is represented by means of story-telling and narrative. To ensure intra-template balance of the overall structure, the Narration phase could be introduced in Methods (iv), in term of its founding principles and features; its key messages, interpretation and "moral" could be synthesized in Results (vi) and be further explored in Discussion (vii).

This process of incremental inclusion would make story-telling more easily acceptable for mainstream IS journals – where a radical restructuring and revisiting of the traditional scientific writing may have a difficult uptake – thus serving as an "accreditation" procedure, consistently with the issue addressed in [2]; nevertheless, it would preserve the value of stories and add their contribution to the action researchers' overall study, and it would facilitate narrative accrual [8].

When discussing the genre's limitations, story-telling and narrative mostly rely on the reader's interpretative ability, which could in turn be affected by cultural setting and personal characteristics [31]. In line with this, [32] noticed a sort of independence of the story and its interpretation: "a story, once told, no longer belongs solely to the storyteller", and might have an uncontrolled evolution unrelated to the intended purpose the storyteller had in the first place. Narrative meanings may also be difficult to be coded in results; and IS researchers might show some rigidity and unwillingness to adopt story-telling, due to their scientific writing background, and to the fear of a reduction in the purely informative power of their publications. Among those who adopt the alternative genre on the contrary, a risk to run into what we define the "novelist syndrome" could arise: the writer/researcher could wish to add fictitious or instrumental elements to the story to make it more appealing [9], though this would constitute a clear departure from a scientific approach, undermining the publication's contribution.

A summary of the main advantages and disadvantages of story-telling and narrative as alternative genres in IS publication is reported in Table 1.

Table 1. Advantages and disadvantages of story-telling and narrative as alternative genres in IS publication.

Advantages	Disadvantages
• Focus on communication, discussion and interpretation (not just reporting) of key findings, results and messages • Focus on building a consensus and a common culture of shared understanding • Role of "learning enabler" • Provision of a vehicle to messages and meanings related to sub-plots or characters' internal responses, personal motives and soft determinants, which may risk to be "lost in translation" in a traditional report or writing style • Accountability of the "emotional state" vs. "external response" dualism • Passionate, non-aseptic discourse underscoring multiple angles • Stimulation of empathy and involvement in the reader • Provision of a hint at the "organizational drama" behind any IS implementation • Availability of figures of speech such as metaphors, similes, climax, twists and rhetorical styles such as irony and sarcasm • Context sensitivity and negotiation – coexistence and negotiation of different standpoints in the whole story; • Flexibility and adaptability to context • Holism and unity provided by the quasi-omniscient narrator	• Uncontrolled evolution and unintended meanings • Possible independence between the story and its interpretation • Influence of cultural setting and personal characteristics on interpretation of the genre • Difficult coding of narrative results • Rigidity of IS researchers in adopting storytelling, due to scientific writing background • Possible reduction of the purely informative power of the narration • "Novelist syndrome": possible low adherence to reality, due to the addition of fictitious or instrumental elements to the story ("fish tales" swapping experiences and escalating) to inflate its appeal

In the next paragraphs, we will further elaborate on these alternative genres' contribution with reference to IS practice.

3.2   Story-Telling and Narrative in IS Practice

The story told reveals that narrative had a paramount practical role in enabling IS implementation within the company analysed.

The CEO perceived this alternative genre approach as necessary to reduce the negative outcomes of a transition from a largely manual to an automated information management. An alternative perspectives on IS, together with little or no knowledge of IT, gave the CEO and the Project Manager a fresh look at the implementation problem: the outcome was a rather innovative way to tackle it. The CEO's Philosophy and Literature background led him to force managers, employees and even IT vendor representatives to tell their experiences in a literary fashion: employees/users were requested to express their working expectations and feelings related to the new IS, and this made for better interiorizing of change and reduced long-term resistance.

Hence, he had IT modelling languages replaced by story-telling to describe the main features related to ERP implementation, including: requirements identification; IS expected benefits and drawbacks; and organizational impacts, for each employee and user role.

By doing so, the CEO performed an interesting paradigm shift in the classical approach to change management [21]: he created and inflated an initial "communication resistance" aimed to lessen the impact of any future "user resistance". As the story discloses, the process of approaching ERP implementation through writing created early inter and intra-organizational tensions, which, however, in the short term eased participation, involvement and commitment to use the newly introduced system: this determined more time spent in planning and processing unstructured information, but contemporarily, a shorter lead time in implementing the system, and above all, less waste of resources in transition management.

In his quest to revolutionize the traditional approach towards implementation supported by the IT vendor, he even renamed UML (Unified Modelling Language) with the Latin acronym "*Unicus Modus Linguae*" he coined, asserting that human's truly unique language of communication is story-telling rather than conceptual modelling.

These results, of interest for IS practice, were largely determined by the leader's extravagancy and eclecticism: even though formalizing extravagancy is far from being an easy task, another point we wish to make in this study is that an attempt should be made to include the alternative approach based on story-telling and narrative in IS practice, so as to overcome social resistance to technology-induced change, thus increasing the rates of acceptance and success for IS projects.

This is in line with the literature claiming that stories can be used for multiple purposes [32] and have various functions, examples being entertainment, creating trust and openness among colleagues, becoming aware of operating biases and values, and thinking outside the box to generate creative solutions and breakthroughs [33]. Since story-telling is the time-honoured practice of using fictional techniques to engage [34], stories and narratives are an important part of the solution for organizational problems: gradually, leaders are starting to make widespread use of stories for enlisting the commitment that enables change [35].

In [36] it is stated that stories, parables, chronicles, and narratives are powerful means for influencing mind-sets of involved parties. Literature mostly focuses on the effect of stories in building a consensus and a common culture of shared understanding. Stories should invite reader and listener to suspend judgments, understand the message of the story, and consequently decide which level of truthfulness it carries. Furthermore, [36] discusses the usage of tales, letters, poems, songs, and so forth by subordinated groups that existed in history (e.g. black slaves, Mexican Americans, Native Americans) to express their pain and everyday difficulties; those stories were claimed to be their survival and liberation tool. A parallel can be driven between stories of these historical out-groups and contemporary employees: indeed, the creation of informal groups in the business environment is an inevitable incidence, and as such, those groups develop their own intragroup rules and dynamics and hence, are capable of opposing certain corporate decisions or initiatives – as it could have been the case in the company analysed in our study. Therefore, listening to stories helps acquiring ability to see the world through other eyes (e.g. executives and managers can understand concerns or resistance employees are experiencing due to a certain occurrence in the company – as it happened to the Project Manager after he read the short stories written by the employee in Administration and the account manager in Procurement).

As claimed in [37], knowledge in the organization is conveyed through mentoring and story-telling. Managers should be aware of and capable of understanding the cognitive processes behind these types of learning, because ignorance, lack of absorptive capacity, lack of pre-existing relationships, and lack of motivation can become barriers to transfer of knowledge and best practices within the organizations [34].

Discussing the importance of leadership in management of meaning through story-telling, [38] claim that the use of language, rituals, drama, stories, myths, and symbolic constructions can play an important role in the leader's efforts to establish a connection and experience to lead individuals orient themselves towards the achievement of shared goal. Through stories, leader can evoke patterns of meaning that can give them considerable control over a given situation. Therefore, by interpreting IS endeavours undertaken by organizations as phenomena based on the management of meaning performed though story-telling and narrative, sufficient emphasis would be placed on the development of alternative practices through which organized corporate actions can be initiated and continued.

As it occurs in the relationship between IS publication and story-telling as alternative writing genre, we believe action research could play a key mediating role in the proposal of story-telling as alternative IS practices. Indeed, a number of synergies between action research, story-telling and narrative exist at a practical level (see Table 2).

Action research is a type of activity designed to engage, and so are story-telling and narrative. It is constructed with people, it is research undertaken *with* others, and as such it implies a collaborative relationship, where the purpose of engagement is to obtain the different but yet complementary perspectives of collaborators for understanding the problem domain [11]: this is fully aligned with story-telling's and narrative's aim – both as a writing genre and as a practice – to depict multiple perspectives and involve peers in the solution-crafting process. Being attentive, intelligent, reasonable, and responsible are required capabilities for both action research and

Table 2. Advantages and disadvantages of story-telling and narrative as alternative genres in IS practice.

Advantages	Disadvantages
• Provision of an instrument used by the storyteller/leader to evoke patterns of meaning in order to exerting control • Stimulation of empathy in the target listener (manager, employee, customer, supplier, user) • Anticipation and enablement of change management • Enablement of a paradigm shift in change management, from "user resistance" to "communication resistance" • Provision of a "communicational path" towards organizational transformation, to: - guarantee holism - provide a multifaceted and original description of the issues - resolve conflicts - close the manager-employee gap - facilitate smoother transitions - lower diffusion and cultural barriers - facilitate organizational communication of and commitment to the project - foster engagement, active participation, motivation and involvement of human resources and stakeholders at all level - include all individuals, groups or out-groups - enhance participation in the design and customization process of IS - realign employees' expectations on IS - possibly shorten project implementation length and reduce resources allotted to transformation management • Enhance the acculturation and open mindedness of employees (collateral benefit)	• Attribution of a positive value to the concepts of vagueness and uncertainty, hardly realizable in practical actions • Need for a capable storywriter/storyteller • Need for an attentive, intelligent, reasonable, and responsible action researchers to act as facilitator and narrator • Resistance of the conservatives and traditionalists, reluctant to employ unusual languages • Waste of resources in coding the rules of the game, the new language and the process' outcomes • Difficult transferability, translation and univocal interpretation of messages • Cultural risk of excluding clusters of key users, left behind or left aside because of the use of a communication tool they either do not like, do not understand or are too shy to use • Difficult applicability to global, multicultural companies

story-telling [39]. Action research is "genuine research" [39], due to the fact that it can meet requirement standards of rigorous inquiry within the realm of practical knowing and has the potential for enriching both scientific and practical knowing: therefore, this method's rigour and soundness can enhance story-telling's scientific and practical contribution. And lastly, a strong parallelism is present between the role of the action researcher and that of the writer/narrator of story-telling and narrative: due to her or his third-party role of facilitator, the action researcher is the most suitable quasi-omniscient narrator for IS-related stories, so as to guarantee holism and comprehensiveness through an broader perspective on the events occurring; again, this concluding synergy applies to both narrative's writing and practical domains.

As a result, action research in its quest for collaborative solutions could both *act* by means of story-telling and narrative practices, and *preach, promote and spread* such practices among the company's human resources.

Advantages and disadvantages of story-telling and narrative as alternative genres in IS practice (with possible impacts for many studies, e.g. [40–47]) are summarized in Table 3.

Table 3. Synergies between action research (AR) and the genres of story-telling (S) and narrative (N).

- AR is designed to enable engagement, participation of the client is incentivized, and an exchange relationship is assumed; S/N aim at stimulating empathy and involvement in the reader/listener
- AR is constructed with people, is done with others, it has an inherent collaborative nature to provide a multidimensional description of the problem domain; S/N aim at depicting multiple perspectives and involve peers in the solution-crafting process
- In applied fields such as organization development (and IS is a lever for organizational development), AR is extremely useful to investigate complex phenomena from the inside, establishing strong communication flows with clients and participant; S/N can serve as an organizational development language based on dialogue and social discourse
- Being attentive, intelligent, reasonable, and responsible are required capabilities for both AR and S/N
- Rigor and soundness of AR as an established qualitative research methodology can enhance S/N scientific contribution
- The Action Researcher is best suited to take on the role of S/N facilitator and quasi-omniscient narrator, to ensure holism and comprehensiveness

4   Conclusions

In this manuscript, we have presented an implementation of story-telling and narrative as alternative genres for writing IS publications. We argue that the incremental introduction of these genres, their principles and their features would be beneficial to IS research, as it would enable a revisited and unconventional representation of IS themes that extends the boundaries of canonical genres. In parallel, thanks to the peculiarity of the case we have been involved in – which is, fundamentally, a story on the use of stories on information systems implementation – we claim that story-telling and narrative are also powerful instruments supporting IS practice.

Story-telling hence abridges IS publication and practice, since it represents both the object and the means of communication of the study. We propose that the alternative genres investigated possess the power to frame both the writing and the practical domains of IS: in the former, their core value lies in conveying a multifaceted meaning of IS studies, while creating empathy in the reader, inducing a negotiation of diverging perspectives and avoiding the exclusion risk related to the usage of technical language;

while in the latter, they can serve as supporting instruments to engage human resources, resolve conflicts and enable change.

In this inherent link between IS publication and practice enabled by the properties of story-telling and narrative, we also recognize a mediating role of action research. On the one hand, since the research activity is part of the researcher's own human experiences and memories, consistently with [8] such activity should be quite naturally reported through narrated stories. On the other, action researchers can achieve their practical outcomes in IS projects by both using and sponsoring the use of story-telling and narrative communication practices.

Consistently with this finding, we propose the template on action research from [4] could be extended to explicitly include the element of "Narration", based on a properly reinterpreted set of narrative's principles and features.

With this compromising proposal, we wish not to deny the value of narrative as a possibly stand-alone genre for scientific publications: however, we believe a smoother migration from the *status quo* of IS publication – this migration being achieved through a gradual inclusion of the narrative genre's principles among the principles and structure of canonical action research writing [48] – would reduce resistance, facilitate accreditation and stimulate adoption of the alternative genre. An incremental inclusion that leverages the methodological protocols and approaches found in action research theory should also facilitate narrative accrual, catalysing the development of an IS body of knowledge based on stories and narrations. This open issue may represent an opportunity for future research endeavours.

It is our hope that our proposals will breathe new life into IS publication and writing styles, as well as provide a fresh perspective to look at IS practice.

Indeed, story-telling narrative constitute both a way of constructing human plights and a guide for using mind [8], which could be significantly helpful in the fascinating process of IS publication writing, and, relatedly, in applying IS as a practice.

References

1. Rowe, F.: Towards a greater diversity in writing styles, argumentative strategies and genre of manuscripts. Eur. J. Inf. Syst. **20**, 491–495 (2011)
2. Rowe, F.: Toward a richer diversity of genres in information systems research: new categorization and guidelines. Eur. J. Inf. Syst. **21**, 469–478 (2012)
3. Yetim, F.: Acting with genres: discursive-ethical concepts for reflecting on and legitimating genres. Eur. J. Inf. Syst. **15**(1), 54–69 (2006)
4. Mathiassen, L., Chiasson, M., Germonprez, M.: Style composition in action research publication. MIS Q. **36**(2), 347–363 (2012)
5. Duff, D.: Modern Genre Theory. Longman-Lavoisier, Paris (2000)
6. Avital, M., Mathiassen, L., Schultze, U.: Alternative genres in information systems research. Eur. J. Inf. Syst. **26**(3), 240–247 (2017)
7. Walsham, G.: Interpreting Information Systems in Organizations. Wiley, Chichester (1993)
8. Bruner, J.: The narrative construction of reality. Crit. Inq. **4**, 1–21 (1991)
9. Snowden, D.J.: The art and science of story or 'are you sitting uncomfortably?' part 1: gathering and harvesting the raw material. Bus. Inf. Rev. **17**(3), 147–156 (2000)

10. Cobley, P.: Narrative (The New Critical Idiom). Routledge, Milton Park (2001)
11. Coghlan, D., Brannick, T.: Doing Action Research in Your Own Organization. SAGE Publications, London (2005)
12. Vogler, C.: The moral of the story. Crit. Inq. **34**(1), 5–35 (2007)
13. Mckee, R., Fryer, B.: Story-telling that moves people. Harvard Bus. Rev. **81**(6), 51–55 (2003)
14. Thompson, K.: Story-Telling in the New Hollywood: Understanding Classical Narrative Technique. Harvard University Press, Boston (1999)
15. Clandinin, J., Connelly, M.: Narrative and Story in Practice and Research. Educational Resources Information Center (ERIC) (1989). http://files.eric.ed.gov/fulltext/ED309681.pdf
16. Boje, D.M.: The story-telling organization: a study of story performance in an office-supply firm. Adm. Sci. Q. **2**, 106–126 (1991)
17. Cuc, A., Ozuru, Y., Manier, D., Hirst, W.: On the formation of collective memories: the role of a dominant narrator. Mem. Cogn. **34**(4), 752–762 (2006)
18. Heikkinen, H.L.T., Huttunen, R., Syrjälä, L.: Action research as narrative: dive principles for validation. Educ. Action Res. **15**(1), 5–19 (2007)
19. Yin, R.: Case Study Research: Design and Methods. Sage Publishing, Thousand Oaks (2003)
20. Eisenhardt, K.M., Graebner, M.E.: Theory building from cases: opportunities and challenges. Acad. Manag. J. **50**(1), 25–32 (2007)
21. Kettinger, W., Grover, V.: Toward a theory of business process change management. J. Manag. Inf. Syst. **12**(1), 9–30 (1995)
22. Guha, S., Grover, V., Kettinger, W., Teng, J.: Business process change and organizational performance: exploring an antecedent model. J. Manag. Inf. Syst. **14**(1), 109–144 (1997)
23. Akkermans, H., Van Helden, K.: Vicious and virtuous cycles in ERP implementation: a case study of interrelations between critical success factors. Eur. J. Inf. Syst. **11**(1), 35–46 (2002)
24. Hong, K., Kim, Y.: The critical success factors for ERP implementation: an organizational fit perspective. Inf. Manag. **40**, 25–40 (2002)
25. Wei, H.L., Wang, E.T.G., Ju, P.H.: Understanding misalignment and cascading change of ERP implementation: a stage view of process analysis. Eur. J. Inf. Syst. **14**(4), 324–334 (2005)
26. Avital, M., Vandenbosch, B.: SAP implementation at metalica: an organizational drama. J. Inf. Technol. **15**(3), 183–194 (2000)
27. Myers, M.: Qualitative research in information systems. Manag. Inf. Syst. Q. **21**, 241–242 (1997)
28. Schein, H.: Process consultation, action research and clinical inquiry: are they the same? J. Manag. Psychol. **10**(6), 14–19 (1995)
29. Rapoport, R.: Three dilemmas of action research. Hum. Relat. **23**(6), 499–513 (1970)
30. Schultze, U., Avital, M.: Designing interviews to generate rich data for information systems research. Inf. Organ. **21**(1), 1–16 (2011)
31. Pearce, B., Pearce, K.: Extending the theory of the coordinated management of meaning (CMM) through a community dialogue process. Int. Commun. Assoc. **10**(4), 405–423 (2000)
32. Novak, M.: "Story" and Experience. In: Narrative and Story in Practice and Research. Routledge, Milton Park (1989)
33. Ghezzi, A.: Revisiting business strategy under discontinuity. Manag. Decis. **51**(7), 1326–1358 (2013)
34. Hensel, J.: Once upon a time. Meeting Professionals International, One+ (2010). http://www.mpiweb.org/Magazine/Archive/US/February2010/OnceUponATime

35. Doty, E.: Transforming Capabilities: Using Story for Knowledge Discovery & Community Development. National Story-telling Network, Albany (2003). http://storytellingin organizations.com/members2/EDotyTransformingCapabilities.pdf

36. Delgado, R.: Story-telling for oppositionists and others: a plea for narrative. Mich. Law Rev. **87**(8), 2411–2441 (1989)

37. Swap, W., Leonard, D., Shields, M., Abrams, L.: Using mentoring and story-telling to transfer knowledge in the workplace. J. Manag. Inf. Syst. **18**(1), 95–114 (2001)

38. Den Hartog, D., Koopman, P.: Leadership in organizations. In: Handbook of Industrial, Work & Organizational Psychology, pp. 166–187. Sage Publications (2011)

39. Coghlan, D.: Action research: exploring perspectives on a philosophy of practical knowing. Acad. Manag. Ann. **5**(1), 53–87 (2011)

40. Ghezzi, A., Dramitinos, M.: Towards a future internet infrastructure: analyzing the multidimensional impacts of assured quality internet interconnection. Telematics Inform. **33** (2), 613–630 (2016)

41. Ghezzi, A., Cortimiglia, M., Frank, A.: Strategy and business model design in dynamic telecommunications industries: a study on italian mobile network operators. Technol. Forecast. Soc. Chang. Part A **90**, 346–354 (2015)

42. Ghezzi, A., Balocco, R., Rangone, A.: A fuzzy framework assessing corporate resources management for the mobile content industry. Technol. Forecast. Soc. Chang. **96**, 153–172 (2015)

43. Ghezzi, A., Cortimiglia, M., Frank, A.: Business model innovation and strategy making nexus: evidences from a cross-industry mixed methods study. R&D Manag. **46**(3), 414–432 (2016)

44. Ghezzi, A., Balocco, R., Rangone, A.: Technology diffusion theory revisited: a regulation, environment, strategy, technology model for technology activation analysis of mobile ICT. Technol. Anal. Strateg. Manag. **25**(10), 1223–1249 (2013)

45. Dell'Era, C., Ghezzi, A., Frattini, F.: The role of the adoption network in the early market survival of innovations: the italian mobile VAS industry. Eur. J. Innov. Manag. **13**(1), 118–140 (2013)

46. Balocco, R., Ghezzi, A., Bonometti, G., Renga, F.: Mobile payment applications: an exploratory analysis of the italian diffusion process. In: Proceedings of the 2008 7th International Conference on Mobile Business, Barcelona, Spain, 7–8 July 2008, pp. 153–163. IEEE (2008)

47. Ghezzi, A., Renga, F., Balocco, R.: A technology classification model for mobile content and service delivery platforms. In: Filipe, J., Cordeiro, J. (eds.) ICEIS 2009. LNBIP, vol. 24, pp. 600–614. Springer, Heidelberg (2009). doi:10.1007/978-3-642-01347-8_50

48. Davison, R., Martinsons, M., Kock, N.: Principles of canonical action research. Inf. Syst. J. **14**(1), 65–86 (2004)

The Stuttgart IT Architecture for Manufacturing

An Architecture for the Data-Driven Factory

Laura Kassner[1]([✉]), Christoph Gröger[1,2], Jan Königsberger[1], Eva Hoos[1],
Cornelia Kiefer[1], Christian Weber[1], Stefan Silcher[1,3], and Bernhard Mitschang[1]

[1] Graduate School of Excellence Advanced Manufacturing Engineering,
University of Stuttgart, Nobelstraße 12, 70569 Stuttgart, Germany
{laura.kassner,jan.koenigsberger,eva.hoos,
cornelia.kiefer}@gsame.uni-stuttgart.de,
{christoph.groeger,christian.weber}@ipvs.uni-stuttgart.de
[2] Robert Bosch GmbH, Robert-Bosch-Platz 1, 70839 Gerlingen-Schillerhöhe,
Germany
[3] eXXcellent solutions gmbh, Heßbrühlstraße 7, 70565 Stuttgart, Germany

Abstract. The global conditions for manufacturing are rapidly changing towards shorter product life cycles, more complexity and more turbulence. The manufacturing industry must meet the demands of this shifting environment and the increased global competition by ensuring high product quality, continuous improvement of processes and increasingly flexible organization. Technological developments towards smart manufacturing create big industrial data which needs to be leveraged for competitive advantages. We present a novel IT architecture for data-driven manufacturing, the Stuttgart IT Architecture for Manufacturing (SITAM). It addresses the weaknesses of traditional manufacturing IT by providing IT systems integration, holistic data analytics and mobile information provisioning. The SITAM surpasses competing reference architectures for smart manufacturing because it has a strong focus on analytics and mobile integration of human workers into the smart production environment and because it includes concrete recommendations for technologies to implement it, thus filling a granularity gap between conceptual and case-based architectures. To illustrate the benefits of the SITAM's prototypical implementation, we present an application scenario for value-added services in the automotive industry.

Keywords: IT architecture · Data analytics · Big data · Smart manufacturing · Industrie 4.0

1 Introduction

The manufacturing industry is changing under the influence of increased global competition: product life cycles become shorter, products and processes become more complex, production conditions become more turbulent. Manufacturing

© Springer International Publishing AG 2017
S. Hammoudi et al. (Eds.): ICEIS 2016, LNBIP 291, pp. 53–80, 2017.
DOI: 10.1007/978-3-319-62386-3_3

companies can only succeed in this shifting environment if they ensure high product quality, continuous improvement of processes and flexible organizational structures [1].

Initiatives such as Industrie 4.0 [2] and Smart Manufacturing [3] promote the digitalization of manufacturing operations and the use of cyber-physical systems (CPS) [4] to enable the vision of decentralized, self-controlling, self-optimizing products and processes [5]. These developments are supported especially by the rise of the internet of things. Increasingly, large amounts of heterogeneous industrial data, that is, *big industrial data* [6], are created across the entire product life cycle. These data include both structured and unstructured portions, for instance, machine sensor data on the shop floor, product usage data, customer complaints data from social networks or failure reports written by service technicians. One central challenge in Industrie 4.0 is the exploitation of these data to extract valuable business insights and knowledge from them [7]. Sample fields of application for the exploitation of big industrial data are product design optimization, manufacturing execution and quality management.

The predominant manufacturing IT architecture in practice is the information pyramid of manufacturing [8] (see Fig. 1). It fails to enable comprehensive data exploitation because it has several limitations, as reported in [9]: (1) complex point-to-point integration of heterogeneous IT systems limits a flexible integration of new data sources; (2) strictly hierarchical aggregation of information prevents a holistic view for knowledge extraction; (3) isolated information provisioning for the manufacturing control level and the enterprise control level impedes employee integration on the factory shop floor.

This work is an extension of [9]. We build on the concept of the *data-driven factory* developed therein, which is recapitulated in Sect. 2. In this work, we put a stronger focus on the industry-near, use-case-driven IT architecture for the data-driven factory, the *Stuttgart IT Architecture for Manufacturing (SITAM)* which overcomes the insufficiencies of the traditional information pyramid of manufacturing, presented in Sect. 4. The SITAM enables *service-oriented integration*, *advanced analytics* as well as *mobile information provisioning*, which are central requirements of the data-driven factory in order to exploit big industrial data for competitive advantages. The general introduction of the architecture (Sect. 4) and the description of the prototype and application scenario (Sect. 6) are presented as in [9].

In extension of [9], we have added the following new contributions:

1. A detailed analysis of existing reference IT architectures for smart manufacturing and Industrie 4.0 in Sect. 3.
2. An analysis of existing technologies for the core layers and components of SITAM in Sect. 5.
3. A more elaborate evaluation of the SITAM architecture in comparison with existing reference architectures and with respect to available technologies as well as the use case in Sect. 7.

2 Motivation: A Data-Driven Factory for Leveraging Big Industrial Data

In this section, we first analyze the limitations of the traditional information pyramid of manufacturing with respect to big industrial data in Sect. 2.1, then present the concept of the data-driven factory [9] in Sect. 2.2. Further details on the data-driven factory can be found in [9].

2.1 Limitations of the Information Pyramid of Manufacturing

The information pyramid of manufacturing, also called the hierarchy model of manufacturing, represents the prevailing manufacturing IT architecture in practice [10]. It is used to structure data processing and IT systems in manufacturing companies and it is standardized in ISA 95 [8]. In a simplified version, the information pyramid is comprised of three hierarchical levels (see Fig. 1): the *enterprise control level* refers to all business-related activities and IT systems, such as enterprise resource planning (ERP) systems, the *manufacturing control level* focuses on manufacturing operations management especially with manufacturing execution systems (MES) and the *manufacturing level* refers to the machines and automation systems on the factory shop floor.

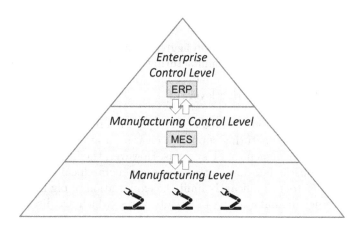

Fig. 1. Information pyramid of manufacturing [9].

Data processing in the information pyramid is based on three fundamental principles [10]:

- *Central automation* to control all activities top-down starting from the enterprise control level
- *Information aggregation* to condense all data bottom-up starting from the manufacturing level

– *System separation* to allow only IT systems at adjacent levels to directly communicate with each other.

The digitalization of manufacturing operations as well as the massive use of CPS lead to big industrial data, i.e., enormous amounts of heterogeneous industrial data at all levels of the information pyramid and across the entire product life cycle [6]. For instance, besides huge amounts of structured machine data and sensor data resulting from the shop floor, there are unstructured data on service reports and customer opinions in social networks. Exploiting these data, that is, extracting valuable business insights and knowledge, enables comprehensive optimization of products and processes [7]. For instance, customer satisfaction can be correlated with product design parameters using CAD data and CRM data or root causes of process quality issues can be analyzed using machine data and ERP data.

However, data processing according to the information pyramid of manufacturing prevents comprehensive data exploitation due to the following major technical limitations (L_i):

– L_1: Central automation and system separation lead to a *complex and proprietary point-to-point integration of IT systems,* which significantly limits a flexible integration of new data sources across all hierarchy levels [11].
– L_2: Strictly hierarchical information aggregation leads to *separated data islands* preventing a holistic view and strong analytics for knowledge extraction [6].
– L_3: Central control and information aggregation lead to *isolated information provisioning* focusing on the manufacturing control level and the enterprise control level and thus impede employee integration through information provisioning on the manufacturing level [12].

To conclude, the function-oriented and strictly hierarchical levels of the information pyramid of manufacturing support a clear separation of concerns for the development and management of IT systems. However, the information pyramid lacks flexibility, holistic data integration and cross-hierarchical information provisioning. These factors significantly limit the exploitation of big industrial data and necessitate new manufacturing IT architectures, which are discussed in the following section.

2.2 The Data-Driven Factory

The data-driven factory [9] is a holistic concept to exploit big industrial data for competitive advantages of manufacturing companies. For this purpose, the data-driven factory addresses central economic challenges of today's manufacturing (Westkämper [1]), particularly agility, learning ability and employee orientation.

The data-driven factory takes a holistic view on all data generated across the entire product life cycle, including both structured data and unstructured data, i.e. data with a relational schema as well as text, audio, video and image data without such a schema. In contrast to earlier integration approaches, especially Computer Integrated Manufacturing [13], the data-driven factory does *not* aim at totally automating all operations and decision processes but explicitly integrates employees in order to benefit from their knowledge, creativity and problem-solving skills.

From a manufacturing point of view, the data-driven factory is defined by the following core characteristics (see Fig. 2):

- The data-driven factory enables *agile manufacturing* (Westkämper [1]) by exploiting big industrial data for proactive optimization and agile adaption of activities.
- The data driven factory enables *learning manufacturing* [14] by exploiting big industrial data for continuous knowledge extraction.
- The data driven factory enables *human-centric manufacturing* [15] by exploiting big industrial data for context-aware information provisioning as well as knowledge integration of employees to keep the human in the loop.

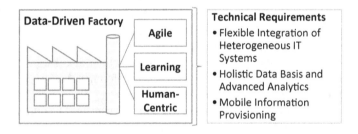

Fig. 2. Characteristics and technical requirements of the data-driven factory [9].

Based on the above characteristics and taking into account the limitations of the information pyramid of manufacturing (see Sect. 2.1), we have derived the following technical core requirements (R_i) for the realization of the data-driven factory (see Fig. 2):

- R_1: *Flexible integration of heterogeneous IT systems* to rapidly include new data sources for *agile* manufacturing, e.g., when setting up a new machine
- R_2: *Holistic data basis and advanced analytics* for knowledge extraction in *learning* manufacturing, e.g., to prescriptively extract action recommendation from both structured and unstructured data
- R_3: *Mobile information provisioning* to ubiquitously integrate employees across all hierarchy levels for *human-centric* manufacturing, e.g., including service technicians in the field as well as product designers

In order to realize these requirements, a variety of IT concepts and technologies has to be systematically combined in an overall IT architecture. Since the information pyramid of manufacturing lacks flexibility, holistic data integration and cross-hierarchical information provisioning ($\mathbf{R}_1$-$\mathbf{R}_3$), we develop a novel manufacturing IT architecture that enables the data-driven factory.

The data-driven factory leverages big industrial data for agile, learning and human-centric manufacturing. In this way, it creates new potentials for competitive advantages for manufacturing companies, especially with respect to efficient and simultaneously agile processes, continuous and proactive improvement as well as the integration of knowledge and creativity of employees across the entire product life cycle.

3   Reference Architectures for Smart Manufacturing and Industrie 4.0

We did a comprehensive literature analysis on recent architectural approaches for IT-based manufacturing. An overview of recent reference architectures can be found in [16,17]. As result, we have identified three major groups of work:

- *Abstract frameworks for Industrie 4.0 and Smart Manufacturing,* which represent meta models and roadmaps for standardization issues, especially the Reference Architectural Model Industrie 4.0 (RAMI, [18]) as well as the SMLC framework for Smart Manufacturing [3].
- *Cross-domain-spanning reference architectures*, which also target the manufacturing industry, e.g. the Industrial Internet Reference Architecture (IIRA) [19] and the Industrial Data Space (IDS) [20].
- *Concrete manufacturing IT architectures,* which structure IT components and their relations in and across manufacturing companies on a conceptual level, especially Vogel-Heuser et al. [10], Minguez et al. [11], Holtewert et al. [21], Papazoglou et al. [22].

In the following we discuss the identified types of reference architectures and analyze them with respect to the technical core requirements identified in Sect. 2.2.

R_1: *Flexible Integration of Heterogeneous IT Systems*
The above frameworks are defined on a significantly higher abstraction level than the information pyramid of manufacturing. Decomposed to its full structure, the pyramid contains a lot of additional hierarchical layers condensed to a reasonable minimum in the examined reference architectures [8]. The RAMI includes just a few layers of the equipment hierarchy model as dimensional perspective, which are extended by the layers product and connected world [18]. In [19], the IIC defines an Industrial Internet System by its technologies like manufacturing execution systems and programmable logical controllers which in turn are functionally related to the layers of the information pyramid of manufacturing. To solve data integration issues, they suggest a service-oriented architecture which includes a flexible method to combine services via metadata references at run-time to allow for dynamical composition in order to provide a real-time

response to changes in the environment [19]. The ZVEI [18] defines the concept of an administrative shell for I4.0 components, which contains a resource manager to expose services like OPC-UA[1] to other components. This administrative shell serves as digital representation for real-world assets on the shopfloor and allows integration with other administrative shells through a service-oriented architecture. To conclude, the common core of the above IT architectures is a service-oriented architecture (SOA) [23] in order to enable a flexible integration of IT systems – i.e. IT services – across all hierarchy levels [11,21].

R_2: *Holistic Data Basis and Advanced Analytics*
In [10], the need for a common data model standardizing the interfaces and the data of the IT services is underlined. In [22], a knowledge repository is part of the architecture. In contrast, the IIC defines complex event processing and advanced analytics as part of multiple hierachical layers of the industrial internet system to meet different processing requirements, e.g. edge analytics in close proximity to the place where the data is required for realtime processing. Integration techniques like syntactical and domain transformation are addressed, but not discussed in detail. [20] propose an industrial data space for the industry to exchange and integrate data across enterprise borders in a secure manner. For the integration, vocabulary and schema matching are used, as well as knowledge database management. However, the integration concepts of these reference architectures are very abstract and don't provide further details. A holistic data model or technique to integrate data is still missing.

R_3: *Mobile Information Provisioning*
In [20–22], a marketplace with IT services is proposed in addition. These services are offered via apps in [20,21]. However, concrete approaches for displaying tailored information from integrated data sources on mobile devices to support the information needs of workers are not discussed, nor are the particular challenges of mobile data provisioning addressed.

Table 1 shows an overview of the existing IT architectures for Smart Manufacturing and Industrie 4.0 evaluated against the requirements of the data-driven factory. All in all, these existing manufacturing IT architectures mainly address the limitation of a complex and proprietary point-to-point integration of IT systems in the information pyramid of manufacturing and enable the flexible integration of heterogeneous IT systems (R_1) by defining a service-oriented architecture. At the moment, only the IIRA includes a holistic data basis and advanced analytics (R_2) to allow for knowledge extraction in learning manufacturing. However, they still lack mobile information provisioning (R_3) to address isolated information provisioning. Our concept of the data-driven factory and the SITAM architecture address all three limitations. The SITAM provides a detailed structure in order to serve as an implementation guideline and describes a holistic approach as detailed in the following sections.

---

[1] https://opcfoundation.org/about/opc-technologies/opc-ua/.

Table 1. Evaluation of IT architectures for smart manufacturing and industrie 4.0 against the requirements of the data-driven factory. (● fulfilled; ◐ partly fulfilled; ○ not fulfilled.)

	R_1 integration	R_2 analytics	R_3 mobile
RAMI [18]	●	○	○
SMLC [3]	●	○	○
IIRA [19]	●	●	○
IDS [20]	◐	◐	◐
Vogel-Heuser et al. [10]	●	◐	○
Minguez et al. [11]	●	○	○
Holtewert et al. [21]	●	○	◐
Papazoglou et al. [22]	●	◐	○

4 SITAM: Stuttgart IT Architecture for Manufacturing

The SITAM architecture [9] is a conceptual IT architecture enabling manufacturing companies to realize and implement the data-driven factory. The architecture is based on the results and insights of several research projects we have undertaken in cooperation with various industry partners, particularly from the automotive and the machine construction industry.

In the following, we present an overview of the SITAM architecture in Sect. 4.1 and detail its components in Sects. 4.2–4.6.

4.1 Overview

The SITAM architecture (see Fig. 3) encompasses the entire product life cycle: *Processes*, *physical resources*, e.g., CPS and machines, *IT systems* as well as *web data sources* provide the foundation for several layers of abstracting and value-adding IT.

The *integration middleware* (see Sect. 4.2) encapsulates these foundations into services and provides corresponding data exchange formats as well as mediation and orchestration functionalities.

The *analytics middleware* (see Sect. 4.3) and the *mobile middleware* (see Sect. 4.4) build upon the integration middleware to provide predictive and prescriptive analytics for structured and unstructured data around the product life cycle and mobile interfaces for information provisioning.

Together, the three middlewares enable the *composition of value-added services* for both human users and machines (see Sect. 4.5). In particular, services can be composed ad-hoc and offered as mobile or desktop apps on an *app marketplace* to integrate human users, e.g., by a mobile manufacturing dashboard with prescriptive analytics for workers. The added value from these services feeds back into the product life cycle for continuous proactive improvement and adaptation.

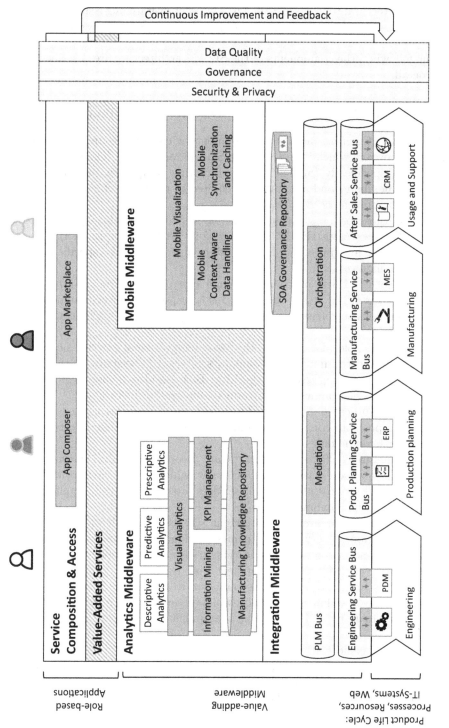

Fig. 3. Overview of the Stuttgart IT Architecture for Manufacturing (SITAM) [9].

Cross-architectural topics (see Sect. 4.6) represent overarching issues relevant for all components and comprise *data quality, governance* as well as *security and privacy*.

In the following, the components of the SITAM architecture are described in greater detail.

4.2   Integration Middleware: Service-Oriented Integration

The SITAM's *integration middleware* represents a changeable and adaptable integration approach which is based on the SOA paradigm [23]. The integration middleware is specifically tailored to manufacturing companies, providing the much needed flexibility and adaptability required in today's turbulent environment with a permanent need of change.

To enable those benefits, it builds on a concept of hierarchically arranged *Enterprise Service Buses* (ESBs) following [24]. Each one of these ESBs is responsible for the integration of all applications and services of a specific phase of the product life cycle.

All phase-specific ESBs are connected via a *superordinate Product-Lifecycle-Mana gement-Bus* (PLM Bus). The PLM Bus is responsible for communication and mediation between phase-specific busses as well as for the orchestration of services.

This concept enables, for example, the easier integration of external suppliers without opening up too much of a company's internal IT systems to them by just "plugging" their own ESB into the PLM Bus. Besides, it also reduces the complexity by abstraction over the introduced integration hierarchy.

A dedicated sub-component providing real-time capabilities is used in the manufacturing phase to connect CPS and other real-time machine interfaces to the overall ESB compound.

The ESB hierarchy effectively abstracts and decouples technical systems and their services into a more business-oriented view, which we call *value-added services*. Value-added services use the basic services providing access to application data, orchestrate and combine them.

This decoupling also evens out different speeds in the development and change of applications or services. Companies often face the problem of having to integrate, e.g., legacy mainframe applications with modern mobile apps, which inherently have very different development speeds. By decoupling business-oriented services from the technical systems/services, each application can be developed separately and at its own pace, while the integration middleware handles all transformations and mediations that might be necessary to maintain compatibility.

Each phase-specific ESB also utilizes its own *phase-specific data exchange format* to handle the different requirements of each phase. For example, engineering has to be able to exchange large amounts of data, e.g., CAD models, whereas manufacturing requires the quick exchange of a large amount of smaller data chunks, e.g., MES production data. Aftersales on the other hand needs to handle both large CAD data as well as small, lightweight data structures, e.g., live car data.

The separation into different phase-specific ESBs allows each department or business unit to make use of specialized data exchange formats tailored to phase-specific needs.

To sum up, the hierarchical composition of phase-specific ESBs across the entire product life cycle and the changeable service-oriented abstraction of IT systems address requirement R_1 (flexible integration of heterogeneous IT systems) of the data-driven factory.

4.3   Analytics Middleware: Advanced Analytics

The analytics middleware is service-oriented and comprises several manufacturing-specific analytics components which are crucial for a data-driven factory: The *manufacturing knowledge repository* for storing source data and analytics-derived insights, *information mining* on structured and unstructured data, *management of key performance indicators* (KPIs), and *visual analytics*. The analytics middleware includes functionalities for descriptive, predictive and prescriptive analytics, with prescriptive analytics being a novel introduction which provides actionable problem solutions or preventative measures before critical conditions lead to losses [25]. In providing *integrative, holistic* and *near-real time analytics* on big industrial data of all data types, the SITAM analytics middleware transcends the analytics capabilities of existing approaches (see Sect. 2). This significantly contributes to the learning and agile characteristics of the data-driven factory.

Source data are extracted using predefined ETL functions from the integration middleware. Integrated data of structured and unstructured type from around the product life cycle are stored in the *manufacturing knowledge repository* along the lines of [26] for maximum integration, minimum information loss and flexible access. Over the course of the product life cycle, this repository is enriched with various knowledge artefacts, e.g., analytics results like data mining models, business rules and free-form documents such as improvement suggestions. To store structured and unstructured source data in a scalable manner, the repository combines SQL and NoSQL storage concepts. It also includes the functionality for flexibly creating semantic links between source data and knowledge artefacts to support reasoning and knowledge management (see [26]).

The *information mining* component can be subdivided into classical data mining and machine learning tools for structured data on the one hand, and tools for various types of unstructured data – text, audio, video – on the other hand.

We will discuss text analytics [27] in more detail since its use in a framework for integrative data analytics is novel and since text data harbor a wealth of hitherto untapped knowledge. Typically, text analytics applications have been focused on one isolated unstructured data source and one analytical purpose, without integrating the results with analytics on structured data and with the disadvantage of information loss along the processing chain [28].

To secure flexibility of analytics and easy integration of data from different sources, we propose a set of basic and custom text analytics toolboxes, including domain-specific resources for the manufacturing and engineering domains and on an individual product domain level. This type of toolbox is similar to the generic and specific text analytics concepts proposed in [28]. Value-added applications of these text analytics tools fall into two main categories: (1) information extraction tasks and (2) direct support of human labor through partial automation. For example, presenting the top ten errors for a specific time span based on text in shop floor documentation is an information extraction task which helps workers gain insights into weaknesses of the production setup. Using features of text reports, for example occurrences of particular domain-specific keywords, to predict the likelihood of certain error codes which a human expert must manually assign to these text reports, constitutes an example of a direct support analytics task (see [29] for an implementation and proof of concept of this use case within the SITAM architecture).

Information mining can then be applied to discover knowledge, which is currently hidden in a combination of structured data and extracts from unstructured data. For example, process and machine data from the shop floor can be matched up with timestamps and extracted topics or relations from unstructured error reports to discover root causes for problems which have occurred. Real-time process data from the shop floor can be compared to historical data to discover indicators for problematic situations and prescribe measures for handling them, for example speeding up a machine when a delayed process has been discovered.

In order to constitute the backbone of a truly data-driven factory, information mining has to be conducted near real-time, on a variety of data sources as-needed, and manufacturing processes, sales, delivery, logistics and marketing campaigns have to adjust to meet the prescriptions derived from analytics results.

The *management of key performance indicators* is another important component and can be greatly improved by readily available and flexible analytics on a multitude of data sources. Instead of being an off-line process conducted by the executive layer based on aggregated reporting data, KPI management can become a continuous and pervasive process, as data analytics feedback loops are in place for all processes around the product life cycle and at any level of the process hierarchy.

Finally, the analytics middleware also includes *visual analytics* for data exploration through human analysts: This type of analytics mainly combines information mining and visualization techniques to present large data sets to human observers in an intuitive way, allowing them to make sense of the data beyond the capabilities of analytics algorithms. Thereby, visual analytics keep the human in the loop according to human-centric manufacturing.

Thus, the analytics capabilities of our reference architecture for the data-driven factory transcend those of related conceptual work in several aspects: (1) They include prescriptive, not just predictive or descriptive analytics, (2) they fully integrate structured and unstructured data beyond the manufacturing process, (3) they stretch across the entire product life cycle and provide a holistic view as well as holistic data storage, and (4) they are decentralized yet integrative, since analytics services are combined as needed to answer questions or supervise processes and keep the human in the loop. Advanced analytics mostly contribute to the fulfillment of requirement R_2, but also R_3 and R_1 of the data-driven factory.

4.4   Mobile Middleware: Mobile Information Provisioning

The mobile middleware enables mobile information provisioning and mobile data acquisition by facilitating the development and integration of manufacturing-specific mobile apps. Mobile apps [30] are running on smart mobile devices, such as smartphones, tablets, and wearables, and integrate humans into the data-driven factory. Due to their high mobility, workers on the shop floor have to have access to the services of the factory *anywhere and anytime*, e.g., viewing near real-time information or creating failure reports on-the-go, supported by the mobile devices' cameras and sensors. Workers can also actively participate in the manufacturing process, e.g., they can control the order in which products are produced. Furthermore, mobile apps offer an intuitive *task-oriented touch-based* design and enable users to consume only relevant data. Mobile devices also allow for the collection of new kinds of data, e.g., position data or photos. This enables new kinds of services such as context-aware apps and augmented-reality apps [31].

However, the development of mobile apps differs from the development of stationary applications due to screen sizes, varying mobile platforms, unstable network connections and other factors. In addition, manufacturing-specific challenges arise [31], e.g., due to the complex data structures as well as the high volume of data. In contrast to existing approaches (see Sect. 3), the mobile middleware addresses these manufacturing-specific needs.

The mobile middleware comprises three components: (1) mobile context-aware data handling, (2) mobile synchronization and caching as well as (3) mobile visualization.

The *mobile context-aware data handling* component provides manufacturing-specific context models describing context elements and relations, e.g., on the shop floor, as well as efficient data transfer mechanism so that only relevant data in the current context is transmitted to the mobile device. For instance, a shop floor worker specifically needs information on the current machine he is working at.

The *mobile synchronization and caching* component supports offline usage of mobile apps. This is important because a network connection cannot always be guaranteed, particularly on the factory shop floor. The component offers mechanisms to determine which data should be cached using context information provided by the context models.

The *mobile visualization* component provides tailored visualization schemas for manufacturing data, e.g., for CAD product models. For example, it provides a visualization schema to represent a hierarchical product structure and to browse it via touch gestures. Various screen sizes and touch-based interaction styles are considered.

To sum up, the mobile middleware enables the integration of the human by supporting the development and integration of mobile apps. This is done by offering manufacturing-specific services for data handling and visualization. Thus, by addressing requirement R_3 (mobile information provisioning), the mobile middleware contributes to the human-centric characteristic of the data-driven factory, i.e., keeping the human in the loop.

4.5 Service Composition and Value-Added Services

The service-based and integrative nature of the SITAM architecture allows it to provide value-added services in several ways. We define *value-added services* as services which provide novel uses and thus create value by transcending the limitations of the information pyramid of manufacturing (see Sect. 2.1): By providing flexible interfaces for data and service provisioning (addressing limitation L_1), by integrating, analyzing and presenting data from several phases around the product life cycle (addressing limitation L_2) and by providing access to information in all the contexts in which it is needed and in which the traditional model may fail to do so (addressing limitation L_3). The value-added services offered in the SITAM architecture cut across the architectural layers, packaging and combining functionalities of the integration middleware, the analytics middleware and the mobile middleware.

In the SITAM architecture, services are composed and adapted *on the basis of user roles* and the information needs and permissions associated with them. For example, a shop floor worker receives detailed alerts related to the process step he is responsible for, whereas his production supervisor is concerned with the aggregated state of the entire manufacturing process across all process steps.

Ad-hoc *service composition* is enabled by the *app composer*. The app composer offers this functionality for users in all roles, regardless of their educational background or their ability to code. For example, data sources and analytics services can be mashed up and composed via drag-and-drop in a graphic user interface. Atomic or composed services can then be offered and distributed as apps in the *app marketplace* for all types of devices, both stationary and mobile.

Since there is very little in the way of dedicated service composition frameworks to build on, we are in the process of developing an implementation for clean and easy service composition, including a graphic user interface for non-technical users. We take inspiration from mashup platforms, such as [32], and app generator tools, such as [33].

To sum up, flexible service composition contributes to the fulfillment of requirement R_1 (flexible integration of heterogeneous IT systems) and the provisioning of composed services as mobile apps helps to fulfill requirement R_3 (mobile information provisioning) of the data-driven factory.

4.6   Cross-Architectural Topics

Security and privacy, governance and *data quality* are overarching topics which must be considered at all layers of the architecture: at the data sources, in analytics and mobile middleware as well as in the applications. In the following, we focus on *SOA governance* and *data quality* as they require specific concepts for the data-driven factory. For general security and privacy issues in data management, we refer the reader to [34].

The governance of complex service-oriented architectures is often neglected in existing manufacturing IT architectures, such as [22], even though a lack of governance is one of the main reasons for failing SOA initiatives [35].

SOA governance covers a wide range of aspects (a list of key aspects can be found in [36]). With more and more systems being integrated – especially CPS, but also for example social media services – it is becoming difficult to keep track of planned changes to those systems and services. For this reason, service change management and service life cycle management governance processes track and report those changes to service consumers and providers, governed for example via consumer and stakeholder management processes.

When setting up those governance processes, it is important to keep them as lightweight and unobtrusive as possible in order to minimize complexity and managerial effort. To support this, the SITAM architecture contains a central *SOA Governance Repository,* which is built on a specific SOA governance meta model described in [36]. The SOA Governance Repository contains service data as well as operations data, spanning and providing support during all phases of the service life cycle, and therefore also supporting novel software development concepts like DevOps.

Apart from SOA governance, the *need for high quality data* is a direct consequence of the concept of the data-driven factory. A data quality framework for the data-driven factory needs to enable data quality measurement and improvement (1) near-real-time (2) at all analysis steps from data source to user (3) for all types of data accumulating in the product life cycle, especially structured data as well as unstructured textual, video, audio and image data.

Existing data quality frameworks, e.g., [37,38], fail to satisfy these requirements. Hence, we translate these requirements into an extended data quality framework, which allows a flexible composition of data quality dimensions (e.g., timeliness, accuracy, relevance and interpretability) at all levels of the SITAM architecture (see [38] for an example list of data quality dimensions). Furthermore, we define sets of concrete indicators considering data consumers at all levels, from data source to user, and we allow for near real-time calculation of data quality (e.g., the confidence or accuracy of machine learning algorithms, language of text and speech, author of data sources and the distribution of data points on a timeline). This makes the quality of data and of resulting analytics results transparent at all levels and therefore enables holistic data quality improvement.

To sum up, we have seen that SOA governance and data quality are crucial factors across all layers of the SITAM architecture. A flexible composition of

IT systems and services can be offered using service-oriented architectures. But complex service-oriented architectures are prone to fail without systematic SOA governance. Besides, a holistic data quality framework forms the basis to measure and improve data quality from data source to user, including the generated analytics results.

5 Technologies for SITAM

In the following, we review technologies suited for the implementation of the SITAM architecture. We focus on the middleware components which provide the core functionalities of the SITAM and on data quality controls as an important prerequisite for data-driven manufacturing with strong analytics. We first address technologies for each of the middlewares in Sect. 5.1 for integration, Sect. 5.2 for analytics and Sect. 5.3 for mobile. We then discuss technologies for assessing data quality as a central cross-architectural topic in Sect. 5.4.

5.1 Integration

The *integration middleware* layer of the SITAM consists of several components: (1) The service bus hierarchy, (2) mediation components for communication between the different life cycle phases, (3) an orchestration component and (4) the SOA Governance Repository. This chapter presents possible technologies to implement these components.

The goal of the service bus hierarchy is to structure the services into multiple, phase-specific integration environments, tailored to the respective needs of the phase (cf. Sect. 4.2). To realize this, basically any off-the-shelf Enterprise Service Bus can be used as they all provide the necessary functionalities. Options range from proprietary products such as IBM's Integration Bus[2] or the Oracle Service Bus[3] to open source alternatives such as the WSO2 Service Bus[4]).

Communication between the services as well as the different phases can be realized with a number of standardized technologies and protocols like SOAP over HTTP, SOAP over Message Queue or REST. For machine-to-machine communication, protocols like OPC-UA[5] and MQTT[6] exist, which also support real-time data exchange.

The phase-specific data exchange formats introduced in Sect. 4.2 can be defined in a protocol-independent format which then can be translated into different representations, e.g. XML Schema[7] or JSON Schema[8]. These exchange

---

[2] http://www-03.ibm.com/software/products/en/ibm-integration-bus.
[3] http://www.oracle.com/technetwork/middleware/service-bus/overview/index.html.
[4] http://wso2.com/products/enterprise-service-bus/.
[5] https://opcfoundation.org/developer-tools/specifications-unified-architecture.
[6] http://docs.oasis-open.org/mqtt/mqtt/v3.1.1/os/mqtt-v3.1.1-os.html.
[7] https://www.w3.org/TR/xmlschema11-1/.
[8] http://tools.ietf.org/html/draft-zyp-json-schema-04.

formats can also rely on existing definition formats like STEP [39] or JT Open [40], which are both used for the exchange of CAD data. The mediation component guaranteeing the communication between different life cycle phases can be realized programmatically as deployable Java artifacts or, in case XML-based formats are used, via Extensible Stylesheet Language Transformations (XSLT[9]).

To orchestrate atomic services into value-added services, workflows described using the Business Process Execution Language (BPEL[10]) can be used. If the composite service requires advanced logic, a workflow can be combined with additional program logic.

The SOA repository helps to manage all services and SOA artifacts across the complete product life cycle. There are several products available, among others IBM's WebSphere Service Registry and Repository[11] or WSO2's Governance Registry[12]. Unfortunately, existing products don't fulfill the requirements for a comprehensive SOA governance approach [36], which necessitates the development of a custom-tailored solution. As database backend a traditional relational database system can be used as well as a NewSQL database [41] or a triple store. The repository could be implemented either as a client/server or as a web-based system.

5.2 Analytics

The analytics layer of the SITAM requires a number of technical components. These components are typically organized in an integrated analytical tool stack. For such stacks, the Lambda Architecture [42] is becoming the de-facto standard in industry practice for scalable and robust analytical tool stacks and therefore represents the basis for an implementation of the analytics layer of SITAM. The Lambda Architecture mainly differentiates between components for batch data processing to store and analyze historic data in-depth with rather high latency and components for stream data processing for near-real-time data analysis of current data. In the following, we briefly describe the application of the Lambda Architecture to realize SITAMs analytics layer and highlight major tools.

With respect to batch data processing, the basis is a data lake approach on top of Hadoop[13] to implement the manufacturing knowledge repository, with structured, unstructured and semi-structured portions and semantic linking between related data. An alternative option would be a combination of a relational database and a NoSQL system, e.g. a content management system, for scenarios which do not need a massive scale-out. In both cases, semantic relations can be implemented either as relational or as NoSQL links, e.g., using a graph-based approach (see [26]).

Considering the SITAM's components for information mining, KPI management and visual analytics, the Apache data processing family also provides

---

[9] https://www.w3.org/TR/xslt.
[10] http://docs.oasis-open.org/wsbpel/2.0/OS/wsbpel-v2.0-OS.html.
[11] http://www-03.ibm.com/software/products/en/wsrr.
[12] http://wso2.com/products/governance-registry/.
[13] https://hadoop.apache.org/.

libraries for scalable batch machine learning and data mining, e.g., with Apache Mahout[14] and SparkR[15]. Further, there are a number of free and commercial data mining toolkits and libraries for structured data analytics and reporting, some of which also include libraries for preprocessing unstructured text data. Toolkits such as WEKA[16], KNIME[17] or RapidMiner[18] offer graphical interfaces for rapid data exploration and prototypical analytics design. Only some of them also allow integration into custom applications.

Apart from various linguistic preprocessing tasks which are already integrated into structured data mining libraries, there exist several dedicated frameworks for text analytics. GATE, the General Architecture for Text Engineering[19], and Apache UIMA[20], the Unstructured Information Management Architecture are both widely used in research and industry projects and provide capabilities for building full text processing pipelines with all processing steps, from reading in data sources, through standard preprocessing steps and custom-built analytics components, to outputting results in various data formats.

These batch components are complemented by stream processing components for near-real-time analytics. Tools for this include various options from the open source world focusing on massively scalable processing of data streams, e.g., Apache Spark Streaming[21] or Apache Storm[22]. In addition, there are classical commercial stream data processing platforms, e.g. IBM InfoSphere Streams[23] or Oracle Streams[24], which typically provide more enhanced functions for analyzing data streams but lack scalability in comparison with their open source counterparts.

5.3   Mobile

Different technologies are available for mobile visualization, context-aware data provisioning and mobile synchronization.

With respect to mobile visualization, we distinguish between native and web app development of mobile apps. Native apps are developed for a specific mobile platform such as iOS[25] or Android[26]. There are libraries and frameworks for native apps to support and facilitate the development of user interfaces. The

---

[14] http://mahout.apache.org/.
[15] https://spark.apache.org/docs/latest/sparkr.html.
[16] http://www.cs.waikato.ac.nz/ml/weka/.
[17] https://www.knime.org/.
[18] http://rapidminer.com/.
[19] https://gate.ac.uk/.
[20] http://uima.apache.org/.
[21] https://spark.apache.org/streaming/.
[22] https://storm.apache.org/.
[23] http://www-03.ibm.com/software/products/en/ibm-streams.
[24] http://www.oracle.com/technetwork/testcontent/streams-oracle-streams-twp-1282 98.pdf.
[25] https://developer.apple.com/.
[26] https://developer.android.com/index.html.

main purpose is to provide uniform user interface and interaction design according to their style guide. However, they are often limited to standard visualization such as lists and menu bars. More complex visualizations have to be developed individually for the respective use cases. There are also lots of frameworks supporting the development of web apps. They are not restricted to any style guide and can be used to develop responsive design which fits multiple devices. Popular frameworks, especially for mobile usage, are angular.js[27] and jQuery[28]. Complex visualization for web apps can be supported by dedicated frameworks for complex visualization such as d3.js[29] or rappid.js[30].

Context-aware data provisioning requires the management of context data and store them into a context model. There are several different approaches to model context based on key-value, logic-based, ontology, rule-based, or graphical model [43]. A review of context models to support context-aware provisioning can be found in [44].

Mobile synchronization requires local storage on the mobile devices. For native apps, light-weight databases such as SQLITE[31] can be used. For web apps, HTML5 provides local storage in key-value format[32]. For example, the chrome browser provides the Index db API to manage local offline storage[33].

5.4   Data Quality

For the implementation of the data quality layer, technologies which allow the measurement and improvement of structured as well as unstructured data are needed. Many commercial toolkits dedicated to the quality of structured data exist, but open source toolkits are rare (e.g. the DuDe tool[34] for duplicate detection and OpenRefine[35], a tool for cleaning and transforming structured data). Neither open source nor commercial toolkits are available for unstructured data. In Sect. 4.6 we mentioned concrete indicators for the quality of structured and unstructured data, such as the confidence of machine learning algorithms, language of text and speech and the distribution of data points on a timeline. Here, we provide concrete technologies which can be used to measure data quality based on these indicators. The *confidence* of the tools in the natural language processing library OpenNLP[36] can be retrieved for each classification decision. For automatic detection of the *language of texts*, e.g., LibTextCat[37], which is

---

[27] https://angularjs.org/.
[28] https://jquery.com/.
[29] https://d3js.org/.
[30] http://jointjs.com/.
[31] https://www.sqlite.org/.
[32] http://www.w3schools.com/html/html5_webstorage.asp.
[33] https://developer.chrome.com/apps/offline_storage.
[34] http://hpi.de/naumann/projects/data-quality-and-cleansing/
       dude-duplicate-detection.html.
[35] http://openrefine.org/.
[36] https://opennlp.apache.org/.
[37] http://software.wise-guys.nl/libtextcat/.

a C library, or the associated versions in other programming languages such as Java or Python can be used. *Outliers* are a well-studied task in the field of data quality and can be detected for example using the programming language R and the Rlof package[38].

6 Prototype and Application

In the following, we present current work on the realization of the SITAM architecture in a prototypical implementation in Sect. 6.1. Moreover, we introduce a real-world application scenario from the automotive industry using the SITAM architecture in Sect. 6.2 in order to illustrate its benefits for a number of value-added services.

6.1 Prototypical Implementation

Our current prototype covers core components in every layer of the SITAM architecture, in particular with respect to analytics, governance, mobile and repository aspects. In the following, we sketch major solution details and technologies we utilized. The latter were chosen from the large available pool of free and open source software to underline the broad applicability of the SITAM architecture and make the implementation easily adaptable to various industrial real-world settings.

The *integration middleware* relies on WSO2's Enterprise Service Bus, to realize the hierarchical ESB structure as well as the orchestration of basic services and mediation between phase-specific ESBs as described in [24]. As all interfaces are based on standards, the ESB hierarchy can also be heterogeneous, allowing to select different products from different vendors that might better support certain phase-specific requirements. Services within the prototype are implemented as either conventional SOAP web services or REST services. Data exchange formats are described as XSD documents and stored in the SOA Governance Repository. The repository itself relies on semantic web technologies, mainly the Resource Description Framework (RDF[39]), and provides a web-accessible as well as a Web Service interface as described in [45]. The use of those technologies allows for example the use of semantic reasoning to detect new dependencies or missing information within the repository.

In the *analytics middleware*, the manufacturing knowledge repository is implemented as a federation of a relational database and a NoSQL system – we used the content management system Alfresco CMS[40] – to store structured and unstructured data. These systems are integrated by a specific link store using a graph database such as Neo4j[41]. The information mining component includes

---

[38] https://cran.r-project.org/web/packages/Rlof/.
[39] https://www.w3.org/TR/rdf11-concepts/.
[40] https://www.alfresco.com/.
[41] https://neo4j.com/.

tools from the Apache UIMA framework[42] for unstructured data analytics, with the uimaFit extension[43] for on-the-fly analytics service composition. Structured data mining capabilities are taken from the WEKA data mining workbench[44]. On this basis, manufacturing-specific predictive and prescriptive analytics are realized using various data mining techniques, especially decision tree induction and text categorization, as described in [26, 29, 46], respectively.

Regarding the *mobile middleware*, we implemented several *mobile apps*, e.g., a mobile analytics dashboard for shop floor workers [26] and a mobile product structure visualizer for engineers. We have implemented native apps for Android and for Windows as well as platform independent web apps using standardized web technology such as HTML5.

An *app marketplace* and a graphical interface for intuitive access to the *app composer* are currently under development.

6.2 Use Case: Quality Management and Process Optimization in the Automotive Industry

To demonstrate the concept of the data-driven factory as well as the SITAM architecture, we have cooperated with an OEM to develop a real-world application scenario for the automotive industry. The scenario focuses on quality management and process optimization as critical success factors for OEMs especially in the automotive premium segment. An overview of all involved components and participants can be seen in Fig. 4.

An automotive manufacturer collects *big industrial data*, including structured sales and machine data, sensor and text data around the product life cycle. These data originally reside in isolated databases; for instance, text reports about product and part quality from development, production and aftersales are all gathered via different IT systems. To ensure a realistic representation of source data and processes, on the one hand, we take advantage of publicly available data sources, such as the records of automotive complaints covering the US market and maintained by the NHTSA[45]. On the other hand, we make use of anonymized data and internal knowledge resources of our industry partner.

On this basis, the SITAM architecture is applied to exploit these data for quality management and process optimization. In the following, we give an overview of representative value-added services and role-based apps across the product life cycle which are enabled by the SITAM architecture (see Fig. 4). We focus on car paint quality as a recurring example (all data samples in the following are fictitious for reasons of confidentiality).

During product development and testing, quality data are collected through the mobile *dev Q app* by engineers and test drivers on the go, including text reports and image material. The *aftersales Q app* is used to collect aftersales

---

[42] http://uima.apache.org/.

[43] https://code.google.com/archive/p/uimafit/.

[44] http://www.cs.waikato.ac.nz/ml/weka/.

[45] http://www.nhtsa.gov/NCSA.

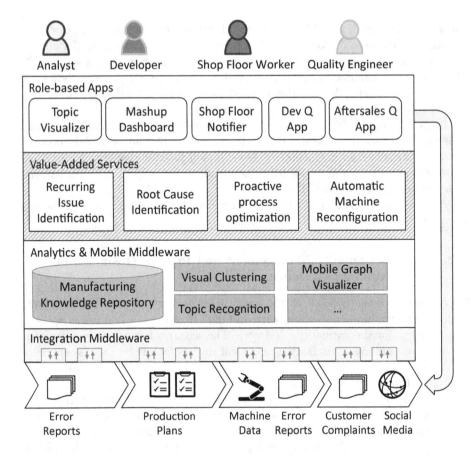

Analyst   Developer   Shop Floor Worker   Quality Engineer

Fig. 4. Value-added services and role-based apps in the application scenario [9].

quality data for the warranty and recovery process of damaged car parts in the form of unstructured text reports (e.g., "customer states that car paint is coming off after washing", "flaking paint on fender during extreme summer heat"). It has different profiles for quality engineers (whose primary task is the definition of new error codes), for quality expert workers (whose task it is to assign error codes to damaged parts) and for executives (who are interested in comparing aggregated error code data over time). In addition, quality data come in the form of *customer complaints* and via *social media* crawling services.

After aggregating these data into the manufacturing knowledge repository via the integration middleware, *topic recognition* on the text data is performed as an information mining step. The topics (e.g., "paint flaking – heat", "paint damage – washing") are presented to a human *analyst* via *visual clustering* to pick the most pressing ones or perform minor reclassification. This constitutes a value-added service of *recurring issue identification* and is performed via the *topic visualizer app,* which makes use of the *mobile graph visualizer* from the mobile middleware.

Next, the problem topics are combined with historical data from the production phase, especially machine data, shop floor environment data, and structured error counts for *root cause identification* (e.g., elevated humidity in the paint shop leading to a lower quality of paint and a higher risk of flaking when exposed to harsh environmental conditions). This analytics step is executed in an analytics and data *mashup dashboard* app, where data sources and analytics algorithms are combined ad-hoc, but can also be stored for recurring use.

Identified root causes and condition patterns serve as input for *proactive process optimization.* It makes use of prescriptive analytics to automatically identify potentially problematic situations (e.g., critical humidity in paint shops) during process execution and recommend actions to on-duty workers through a *shop floor notifier* app (e.g., to air the paint shops to decrease humidity) or trigger *automatic machine reconfiguration* (e.g., increasing air conditioning and heating to decrease humidity).

7 Evaluation and Benefits

This section evaluates the benefits of the SITAM architecture with respect to the requirements of the data-driven factory as well as in contrast to the reference architectures described in Sect. 3.

The application scenario from Sect. 6.2 allows us to analyze the fulfillment of the technical requirements of the data-driven factory and contrast it with the traditional information pyramid of manufacturing.

In the scenario, diverse systems across the product life cycle, such as machines, social media sources as well as sensors, are encapsulated as services and are uniformly represented in the SOA governance repository to ease integration and access in the integration middleware. By this service-oriented abstraction, the SITAM architecture enables a flexible integration of heterogeneous data sources as well as a flexible service composition fulfilling requirement R_1. This enables *agile manufacturing,* the first characteristic of the data-driven factory. Accessible service-based and role-based information provisioning also works towards keeping the human in the loop (*human-centric manufacturing*).

To merge structured and unstructured data from different life cycle phases, e.g., aftersales quality data and machine data in the application scenario, all data are integrated in the manufacturing knowledge repository of the analytics middleware. Moreover, predictive and prescriptive analytics are used to derive action recommendations for process optimization according to the application scenario. Thus, the SITAM architecture provides a holistic data basis encompassing the product life cycle as well as advanced analytics for knowledge extraction fulfilling requirement R_2. This analytics capability provides functionalities for *learning manufacturing,* such as learned improvements for the quality-optimal design of both processes and products. It also is a prerequisite for agile process adaptations (*agile manufacturing*), such as the near real-time adaptation of production conditions to prevent known product quality issues.

In the application scenario, various mobile apps support seamless integration of employees, e.g., for data acquisition by test drivers using the dev Q app or for notifications of shop floor workers using the shop floor notifier. The mobile middleware facilitates the development of such manufacturing-specific apps using predefined manufacturing context models as well as specific visualization components, especially for product models. These apps can be easily deployed on various devices using the app marketplace. In this way, the SITAM architecture enables mobile information provisioning and fulfills requirement R_3 of the data-driven factory to ubiquitously integrate employees across all hierarchy levels. Thus, it provides the framework for *human-centric manufacturing* in keeping the human expert in the loop through data provisioning and data gathering.

The SITAM architecture thus enables flexible system and data integration, advanced analytics and mobile information provisioning and thus fulfills all technical requirements (R_1–R_3) of the data-driven factory.

Table 2. Comparison of the SITAM to types of IT architectures for smart manufacturing and Industrie 4.0 (● fulfilled; ◐ partly fulfilled; ○ not fulfilled.)

	Abstract frameworks for Industrie 4.0 and Smart Manufacturing	Cross-domain-spanning reference architectures	Stuttgart IT Architecture for Manufacturing	Concrete manufacturing IT architectures
Integration (R_1)	●	◐	●	●
Analytics (R_2)	○	◐	●	◐
Mobile (R_3)	○	◐	●	◐
Granularity	———————————————————————————————————→			
Reference architecture	●	●	●	○
Concrete implementation	○	○	●	●

Table 2 shows the evaluation of the three groups of architectures described in Sect. 3 and the SITAM against the three requirements of the data-driven factory as well as in terms of granularity and concreteness. We find that the SITAM fills an important granularity gap: It provides both a full reference architecture and concrete recommendations for implementation. We have also included a discussion of technologies suited for the realization of its individual components in Sect. 5 where we point out which technologies already exist and which need to be further developed before they can be used in an industry context. In contrast, the abstract frameworks and the cross-domain-spanning reference architecture provide only the reference architecture and the concrete architectures provide only implementation details. None of the other architectures for smart manufacturing fulfills all requirements of the data-driven factory or addresses all the limitations of the information pyramid of manufacturing. Most notably, the SITAM excels over other architectures in its capability to keep the human in the loop, particularly in three areas: (1) data integration, where the hierarchy of ESBs provides maximum flexibility for including and accessing data sources as needed; (2) analytics with its particular focus on including unstructured data sources and visualizing intermediate results; and (3) mobile with its enormous impact on tailored data provisioning and active human participation.

8   Conclusion and Future Work

In this article, we have presented in detail the Stuttgart IT Architecture for Manufacturing (SITAM) [9] which (1) flexibly integrates heterogeneous IT systems, (2) provides holistic data storage and advanced analytics covering the entire product life cycle, and (3) enables mobile information provisioning to empower human workers as active participants in manufacturing. We have given an overview of technologies which are required for the implementation of the SITAM and pointed out concrete examples of infrastructures and toolboxes which can be used, as well as identified gaps in the technology landscape where more work is needed. We have compared the SITAM against major reference architectures for smart manufacturing and Industrie 4.0 and found that it surpasses them in several points, the most important ones being the integration of the human worker and the concrete technological recommendations.

We have prototypically implemented core components of the SITAM architecture in the context of a real-world application scenario concerned with quality and process management in the automotive industry. Our conceptual evaluation shows that the SITAM architecture enables the realization of the data-driven factory and the exploitation of big industrial data across the entire product life cycle.

Acknowledgements. The authors would like to thank the German Research Foundation (DFG) as well as Daimler AG for financial support of this project as part of the Graduate School of Excellence advanced Manufacturing Engineering (GSaME) at the University of Stuttgart.

References

1. Westkämper, E.: Towards the Re-industrialization of Europe: A Concept for Manufacturing for 2030. Springer Science & Business Media, Heidelberg (2013)
2. MacDougall, W.: Industrie 4.0: Smart Manufacturing for the Future (2014)
3. Davis, J., Edgar, T., Porter, J., Bernaden, J., Sarli, M.: Smart manufacturing, manufacturing intelligence and demand-dynamic performance. Comput. Chem. Eng. **47**, 145–156 (2012)
4. Shi, J., Wan, J., Yan, H., Suo, H.: A survey of cyber-physical systems. In: 2011 International Conference on Wireless Communications and Signal Processing, Piscataway, NJ, pp. 1–6. IEEE (2011)

5. Brettel, M., Friederichsen, N., Keller, M., Rosenberg, M.: How virtualization, decentralization and network building change the manufacturing landscape: an industry 4.0 perspective. Int. J. Sci. Eng. Technol. **8**, 37–44 (2014)
6. Kemper, H.G., Baars, H., Lasi, H.: An integrated business intelligence framework. closing the gap between IT support for management and for production. In: Rausch, P., Sheta, A.F., Ayesh, A. (eds.) Business Intelligence and Performance Management. Advanced Information and Knowledge Processing, pp. 13–26. Springer, London (2013). doi:10.1007/978-1-4471-4866-1_2
7. Gölzer, P., Cato, P., Amberg, M.: Data processing requirements of industry 4.0 - use cases for big data applications. In: Proceedings of the 23rd European Conference on Information Systems (ECIS), Paper 61 (2015)
8. ISA: Enterprise-Control System Integration. ANSI/ISA 95.00.01-2000, Instrument Society of America (2000)
9. Gröger, C., Kassner, L., Hoos, E., Königsberger, J., Kiefer, C., Silcher, S., Mitschang, B.: The data-driven factory. Agile, learning and human-centric manufacturing. In: Proceedings of the 18th International Conference on Enterprise Information Systems (ICEIS), Scitepress (2016)
10. Vogel-Heuser, B., Kegel, G., Bender, K., Wucherer, K.: Global information architecture for industrial automation. Automatisierungstechnische Praxis **51**, 108–115 (2009)
11. Minguez, J., Lucke, D., Jakob, M., Constantinescu, C., Mitschang, B.: Introducing SOA into production environments - the manufacturing service bus. In: Sihn, W., Becker, T., Kolev, I. (eds.) Proceedings of the 43rd CIRP International Conference on Manufacturing Systems (CMS), pp. 1117–1124. Neuer Wissenschaftlicher Verlag, Wien (2010)
12. Bracht, U., Hackenberg, W., Bierwirth, T.: A monitoring approach for the operative CKD logistics. wt Werkstattstechnik Online **101**, 122–127 (2011)
13. Groover, M.P.: Automation, Production Systems, and Computer-Integrated Manufacturing, 3rd edn. Prentice Hall, Upper Saddle River (2008)
14. Hjelmervik, O.R., Wang, K.: Knowledge management in manufacturing: the soft side of knowledge systems. In: Wang, K., Kovacs, G.L., Wozny, M., Fang, M. (eds.) PROLAMAT 2006. IIFIP, vol. 207, pp. 89–94. Springer, Boston (2006). doi:10.1007/0-387-34403-9_10
15. Zuehlke, D.: Smart factory - towards a factory-of-things. Ann. Rev. Control **34**, 129–138 (2010)
16. Weyrich, M., Ebert, C.: Reference architectures for the internet of things. IEEE Softw. **33**, 112–116 (2016)
17. EFFRA: Platforms for connected factories of the future. Technical report, Communications Networks, Content and Technology Directorate-General DG CONNECT, A3 and European Factories of the Future Research Association (EFFRA) (2015)
18. VDI/VDE, ZVEI: Reference Architecture Model Industrie 4.0 (RAMI4.0). Technical report, Plattform Industrie 4.0 (2015)
19. Lin, S.W., Miller, B., Durand, J., Joshi, R., Didier, P., Chigani, A., Torenbeek, R., Duggal, D., Martin, R., Bleakley, G., King, A., Molina, J., Schrecker, S., Lembree, R., Soroush, H., Garbis, J., Crawford, M., Harper, E., Raman, K., Witten, B.: Industrial internet reference architecture. Technical report 1.7, Industrial Internet Consortium (2015)
20. Otto, B., Auer, S., Cirullies, J., Jürjens, J., Menz, N., Schon, J., Wenzel, S.: Industrial Data Space - Digitale Souveränitt für Daten. Fraunhofer-Gesellschaft zur Förderung der angewandten Forschung e.V, Technical report (2016)

21. Holtewert, P., Wutzke, R., Seidelmann, J., Bauernhansl, T.: Virtual fort knox - federative, secure and cloud-based platform for manufacturing. In: Cunha, P.F.D.C. (ed.) Economic Development and Wealth through Globally Competitive Manufacturing Systems, Procedia CIRP., Red Hook, NY, Curran, vol. 7, pp. 527–532 (2014)
22. Papazoglou, M.P., van den Heuvel, W.J., Mascolo, J.E.: A reference architecture and knowledge-based structures for smart manufacturing networks. IEEE Softw. **32**, 61–69 (2015)
23. Erl, T.: Service Oriented Architecture: Principles of Service Design. The Prentice Hall Service-oriented Computing Series from Thomas Erl. Prentice Hall, Upper Saddle River (2008)
24. Silcher, S., Dinkelmann, M., Minguez, J., Mitschang, B.: Advanced product lifecycle management by introducing domain-specific service buses. In: Cordeiro, J., Maciaszek, L.A., Filipe, J. (eds.) ICEIS 2012. LNBIP, vol. 141, pp. 92–107. Springer, Heidelberg (2013). doi:10.1007/978-3-642-40654-6_6
25. Evans, J.R., Lindner, C.H.: Business analytics: the next frontier for decision sciences. Decis. Line **43**, 4–6 (2012)
26. Gröger, C., Schwarz, H., Mitschang, B.: The manufacturing knowledge repository. consolidating knowledge to enable holistic process knowledge management in manufacturing. In: Hammoudi, S. (ed.) Proceedings of the 16th International Conference on Enterprise Information Systems, Lisbon, Portugal, 39–51 April 2014, pp. 27–30. [S.l.], SciTePress (2014)
27. Aggarwal, C.C., Zhai, C.: An introduction to text mining. In: Aggarwal, C.C., Zhai, C. (eds.) Mining Text Data, pp. 1–10. Springer, New York (2012)
28. Kassner, L., Gröger, C., Mitschang, B., Westkämper, E.: Product life cycle analytics - next generation data analytics on structured and unstructured data. In: Teti, R. (ed.) 9th CIRP Conference on Intelligent Computation in Manufacturing Engineering - CIRPICME 14, Procedia CIRP., Red Hook, NY, Curran, vol. 33, pp. 35–40 (2015)
29. Kassner, L., Mitschang, B.: Exploring text classification for messy data: an industry use case for domain-specific analytics. In: Pitoura, E., Maabout, S., Koutrika, G., Marian, A., Tanca, L., Manolescu, I., Stefanidis, K. (eds.) Proceedings of the 19th International Conference on Extending Database Technology (EDBT), OpenProceedings.org, pp. 491–502 (2016)
30. Clevenger, N.C.: IPad in the Enterprise: Developing and Deploying Business Applications. Wiley, Indianapolis (2011)
31. Hoos, E., Gröger, C., Mitschang, B.: Mobile apps in engineering: a process-driven analysis of business potentials and technical challenges. In: Teti, R. (ed.) 9th CIRP Conference on Intelligent Computation in Manufacturing Engineering - CIRPICME 14, Procedia CIRP., Red Hook, NY, Curran, vol. 33 (2015)
32. Daniel, F., Matera, M.: Mashups: Concepts, Models and Architectures. Data-Centric Systems and Applications. Springer, Heidelberg (2014)
33. Francese, R., Risi, M., Tortora, G., Tucci, M.: Visual mobile computing for mobile end-users. IEEE Trans. Mob. Comput. **15**, 1033–1046 (2015)
34. Whitman, M.E., Mattord, H.J.: Principles of Information Security, 3rd edn. Thomson Course Technology, Boston (2007)
35. Meehan, M.: SOA adoption marked by broad failure and wild success (2008)
36. Königsberger, J., Silcher, S., Mitschang, B.: SOA-GovMM: a meta model for a comprehensive SOA governance repository. In: Joshi, J.B.D. (ed.) Proceedings of the 2014 IEEE 15th International Conference on Information Reuse and Integration, Piscataway, NJ, pp. 187–194. IEEE (2014)

37. Sebastian-Coleman, L.: Measuring Data Quality for Ongoing Improvement: A Data Quality Assessment Framework. Elsevier Science, Burlington (2013)
38. Wang, R.Y., Strong, D.M.: Beyond accuracy: what data quality means to data consumers. J. Manag. Inf. Syst. **12**, 5–33 (1996)
39. International Organization for Standardization: Industrial Automation Systems and Integration (1994)
40. International Organization for Standardization: Industrial Automation Systems and Integration - JT File Format Specification for 3D Visualization (2016)
41. Stonebraker, M.: Newsql: an alternative to NoSql and old SQL for new OLTP apps. Commun. ACM (2011)
42. Marz, N., Warren, J.: Big Data: Principles and Best Practices of Scalable Realtime Data Systems. Manning Publications Co., Greenwich (2015)
43. Nalepa, G., Bobek, S.: Rule-based solution for context-aware reasoning on mobile devices. Comput. Sci. Inf. Syst. **11**, 171–193 (2014)
44. Bolchini, C., Curino, C.A., Quintarelli, E., Schreiber, F.A., Tanca, L.: A data-oriented survey of context models. ACM SIGMOD Rec. **36**, 19 (2007)
45. Königsberger, J., Mitschang, B.: A semantically-enabled SOA governance repository. In: Proceedings of the 2016 IEEE 17th International Conference on Information Reuse and Integration. IEEE (2016)
46. Gröger, C., Schwarz, H., Mitschang, B.: Prescriptive analytics for recommendation-based business process optimization. In: Abramowicz, W., Kokkinaki, A. (eds.) BIS 2014. LNBIP, vol. 176, pp. 25–37. Springer, Cham (2014). doi:10.1007/978-3-319-06695-0_3

Pivot-Based Similarity Wide-Joins Fostering Near-Duplicate Detection

Luiz Olmes Carvalho[1,2(✉)], Lucio Fernandes Dutra Santos[1,3],
Agma Juci Machado Traina[1], and Caetano Traina Jr.[1]

[1] Institute of Mathematics and Computer Sciences, University of São Paulo,
São Carlos, SP, Brazil
luiz.olmes@ifmg.edu.br, {agma,caetano}@icmc.usp.br
[2] Federal Institute of Minas Gerais, Belo Horizonte, MG, Brazil
[3] Federal Institute in the North of Minas Gerais, Montes Claros, MG, Brazil
lucio.santos@ifnmg.edu.br

Abstract. Monitoring systems targeting to improve decision making in emergency scenarios are currently benefiting from crowdsourcing information. The main issue with such kind of data is that the gathered reports quickly become too similar among themselves. Hence, too much similar reports, namely near-duplicates, do not add valuable knowledge to assist crisis control committees in their decision making tasks. The current approaches to detect near-duplicates are usually based on a twofold processing, where the first phase relies on similarity queries or clustering techniques, whereas the second and most computationally costly phase refines the result from the first one. Aimed at reducing that cost and also improving the ability of near-duplication detection, we developed a framework model based on the similarity wide-join database operator. This paper extends the wide-join definition empowering it to surpass its restrictions and provides an efficient algorithm based on pivots that speeds up the entire process, whereas enabling to retrieve the most similar elements in a single-pass. We also investigate alternatives and propose efficient algorithms to choose the pivots. Experiments using real datasets show that our framework is up to three orders of magnitude faster than the competing techniques in the literature, whereas it also improves the quality of the result in about 35%.

Keywords: Similarity search · Similarity join · Query operators · Wide-join · Near-duplicate detection

1 Introduction

Emergency/crisis situations such as fire, flood, traffic accidents, attacks or natural disasters can threaten life, environment and properties. Consequently, great efforts are being made to develop systems aimed at reducing injuries and financial losses in crises situations. Existing solutions employ ultraviolet, infrared

The authors are grateful to FAPESP, CNPQ, CAPES and Rescuer (EU Commission Grant 614154 and CNPQ/MCTI Grant 490084/2013-3) for their financial support.

© Springer International Publishing AG 2017
S. Hammoudi et al. (Eds.): ICEIS 2016, LNBIP 291, pp. 81–104, 2017.
DOI: 10.1007/978-3-319-62386-3_4

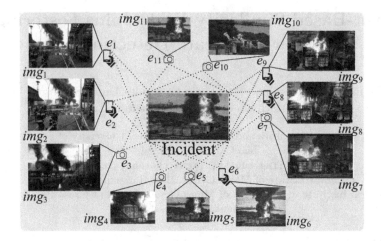

Fig. 1. Taking photos of an emergency scenario: industrial plant on fire.

sensors and surveillance cameras [1] to monitor events. However, to be useful for that purpose, those devices must be installed near to the prospected emergency places, and forecasting all the possible crisis situations in a particular region is seldom feasible.

Further, surveillance cameras can provide visual information of wider spaces. When associated with the increasing popularity of tablets and smartphones with good quality cameras and other mobile devices, they may lead to better solutions to map crisis scenarios and allow speeding up planning emergency actions to reduce losses. For instance, seizing the opportunity to take such information into account, the Rescuer[1] Project is developing an emergency-response system to assist Crisis Control Committees during an emergency situation. It provides tools that allow witnesses, victims and the rescue staff to gather emergency information based on images and videos sent from the incident place using a mobile crowdsourcing framework.

Crowdsourcing data can provide a large amount of information about the emergency scenario, but it often leads to a large amount of records very similar among themselves too. For instance, let us consider the occurrence of an event such as a building on fire or a serious incident in an industrial plant. As the eyewitnesses register the event with their smartphones many and repeatedly times, several pictures become copies almost identical to others. In the image retrieval context, the images too similar to each other with only smooth variations imposed by the devices or the capture conditions (resolution, illumination, cropping, rotation, framing) are called *near-duplicates* [2,3].

As a real example, Fig. 1 depicts a 9 days-long fire occurred in an industrial plant at Santos, Brazil, in April 2015. As shown in Fig. 1, eyewitnesses e_1, e_2 and e_3 took photos from the same perspective of the burning industrial

---

[1] Rescuer: Reliable and Smart Crowdsourcing Solution for Emergency and Crisis Management - <http://www.rescuer-project.org>.

plant, whereas e_4, e_5 and e_6 took photos from another side of the scenario and the same happened to eyewitness e_7, e_8 and e_9, and e_{10} and e_{11}. Too much similar images from the same perspectives (near-duplicates) may not improve the decision making support. In this example, each image subset $\{img_1, img_2, img_3\}$, $\{img_4, img_5, img_6\}$, $\{img_7, img_8, img_9\}$ and $\{img_{10}, img_{11}\}$ forms near-duplicates. Therefore, it is more useful *to remove* the near-duplicates, fostering more diversified results presenting a holistic vision about the incident, such as using only the subset $\{img_1, img_6, img_8, img_{10}\}$.

On the other hand, sometimes it is interesting to *retrieve* and *return* the near-duplicate elements. In the aforestated example (Fig. 1), law enforcement officers and investigators may be interested in the near-duplicate images. Although the near-duplicate elements may be not useful for non-expert people, those professionals usually see things differently and are trained to recognize small details among the images that can contribute to the investigation.

Near-duplicate image detection has attracted considerable attention in multimedia and database communities [2–6]. However, to the best of our knowledge, the near-duplicate detection is yet an open problem, with no consolidated technique able to accomplish such task in terms of both efficiency and efficacy. Most of the approaches to detect near-duplicate images rely on executing a twofold processing, described as follows:

1. *Building phase*: it aims at retrieving a candidate set of near-duplicate elements. It can use every individual image in the dataset as a similarity query center to retrieve the images most similar to each one [4,5], or employ clustering-based techniques [2].
2. *Improvement phase*: it processes and refines the candidate set, removing false positives. The main differences among the distinct methods are in this phase. Most of them sacrifices the computational efficiency to enhance the result efficacy.

Considering the scenario depicted in Fig. 1, it is reasonable to consider that any crowdsourcing framework like Rescuer can be "flooded" with a large amount of images. In that case, employing a twofold technique usually takes too much time to generate the first perspective about the incident scene and the situation may already be changed and aggravated when this result is achieved.

As a possible solution, recent approaches [5,7] consider using well-known searching operators from both the database and information retrieval areas, namely *similarity joins* and *wide-joins*, to detect near-duplicate elements. Similarity joins [8] obtain pairs of elements similar among themselves, assuming each pair corresponds to the near-duplicate candidates obtained by the building phase. However, those retrieval operators were applied only to detect near-duplicate elements in data represented by tokens, as in [5], but they were not explored in general domains such as images. In their turn, wide-joins [7] are designed to retrieve the overall most similar pairs, leading to an inherent combination of building and improvement phases in their processing. However, wide-joins process two distinct sets, while the near-duplicate detection task must combine a set with itself.

Although employing join-based techniques may improve performance, they require computing the similarity among every pair of images received. As the amount of elements is usually large, the situation becomes similar to the first alternative. Therefore, both alternatives present drawbacks when applied to emergency control systems.

In order to overcome the shortcomings and enable near-duplicate image detection for emergency scenarios efficiently, we introduce a framework model based on the similarity range wide-join database operator. The main contributions of such framework are summarized as follows:

- *The self-range wide-join operator*: we extended the wide-join definition to enable the operator to process a single relation, so as to enlarge its usability as a unary operator.
- *Pivot-based algorithm*: we introduce an optimized algorithm based on pivots to speed up processing similarity wide-join, prioritizing early result generation, as required by emergency-based support systems.
- *Single-pass computation*: our proposed framework enables to detect near-duplicates in a single, atomic operation, with no need for a further computationally costly improvement step.

A basic self-range wide-join operator was described in [9]. In this paper we extend the aforestated contributions with several improvements, as follows:

- We provide an extended description of our framework architecture and capabilities.
- We present four variations of our core similarity range wide-join algorithm, useful for emergency control systems.
- We design the range wide-join operator fully integrated to the relational model and complying with the relational theory.
- We discuss how the choice of pivots can affect the performance and propose three efficient alternatives to select them.
- We perform scalability, performance and answer quality evaluations using two real datasets. The results show that our proposal is at least two orders of magnitude faster than existing techniques, whereas always returning a high-quality answer.

The rest of this paper is organized as follows: Sect. 2 describes the main concepts and related work. Section 3 introduces our framework to detect near-duplicate images, the definition and algorithms for the self wide-join. Section 4 presents experimental evaluation of our technique and discusses the main results. Finally, Sect. 5 summarizes the main achievements and outlines future steps.

2   Background

This Section overviews the main concepts and the works related to ours regarding image representation (Sect. 2.1), near-duplicate object detection (Sect. 2.2) and evaluation of similarity queries, including the similarity joins (Sect. 2.3). The main symbols employed along the paper are summarized in Table 1.

Table 1. Symbols.

Symbol	Meaning
ξ	Similarity threshold
$\mathbb{D}$	Data domain
d	Distance function / metric
$\mathfrak{F}$	Feature extractor method
f	Feature value
h	Number of pivots p_i
img	An image
k, κ, m, n	Integer values
n	Cardinality of the dataset
p_i	Pivot i
$\mathsf{S}, \mathsf{S}_1, \mathsf{S}_2$	Attributes subject to a metric
$\mathsf{T}, \mathsf{T}_1, \mathsf{T}_2$	Relations
t, t_1, t_2, t_i, t_j	Tuples
$t[\mathsf{S}]$	The value of attribute S in tuple t
v	Feature vector

2.1 Feature Extraction and Image Representation

Aiming at enabling retrieval by content and near-duplicate detection, images are compared according to a similarity measure. To evaluate the similarity, images are represented by an n-dimensional array of numerical values, called *feature vector*, that describes their content. The features are numerical measurements of visual properties.

The algorithms responsible for processing images and obtaining their features are known as *feature extractors methods*. For each data domain there are specific features to be considered and, in the case of images, the *off-the-shelf* extractors capture features based on colors (e.g. histograms), texture (e.g. Haralick features) and/or shape (e.g. Zernike Moments) [10].

The evaluation of the similarity measure between two feature vectors is performed by a *metric*. Formally, given a feature vector space $\mathbb{D}$ (the data domain), a distance function $d : \mathbb{D} \times \mathbb{D} \mapsto \mathbb{R}^+$ is called a *metric* on $\mathbb{D}$ if, for all $x, y, z \in \mathbb{D}$, there holds:

- $d(x, y) \geq 0$ (non-negativity)
- $d(x, y) = 0 \Rightarrow x = y$ (identity of indiscernibles)
- $d(x, y) = d(y, x)$ (symmetry)
- $d(x, y) \leq d(x, z) + d(z, y)$ (triangle inequality)

The pair $\langle \mathbb{D}, d \rangle$ is called a *metric space* [11]. We use the metric space theory as the mathematical model to enable performing similarity queries, and hence detecting near-duplicate elements.

2.2   Near-Duplicate Detection

Several techniques for near-duplicate detection rely on the Bag-of-Visual Words (BoVW) model [2,3]. That model represents the features as *visual words* and the image representation consists of counting the words to create an histogram. However, BoVW reliability for duplicate detection is small, as it does not capture the spatial relationship existing among the extracted features.

Aimed at surpassing this drawback, studies like [3] combined the spatial information with the BoVW local descriptors. However, local descriptors yet generate feature vectors of varying dimensionality, which is troublesome to represent in metric spaces, requiring high-costly metrics.

Other approaches considered to spot near-duplicates are hash functions and the Locality Sensitive Hashing (LSH) [6,12]. Hash functions fail to represent data that must be retrieved by similarity, because small differences in the images leads to distinct hash representations. However, LSH circumvents this problem by retrieving approximate result sets. In the same line, weighted min-Hash functions improve the image representation, but once they are usually based on bag-of-words, they present the same drawbacks of the other technique [13]. Moreover, unlike those techniques, we are interested in accurate answers.

Still worth to mention is the "Adaptive Cluster with k-means" technique (ACMe) [2]. It applies clustering algorithms to group near-duplicate images in a twofold process. It starts clustering the dataset using the k-means algorithm. Subsequently, the coherence of the obtained clusters are checked to determine the need of recursively processing each cluster. The result is then refined using local descriptors. This is a highly expensive technique that requires the Improvement phase. Moreover, as the k-means algorithm is sensitive to outliers, our intuition is that better quality result might be achieved replacing it with k-medoids. Surpassing the existing drawbacks in algorithms that have an improvement phase, our proposal extends similarity joins to speed up the detection of near duplicates without post-processing the image database.

2.3   Similarity Join

Similarity joins are database operators that combine the tuples of two relations T_1 and T_2 so that each retrieved pair $\langle t_1 \in T_1, t_2 \in T_2 \rangle$ satisfies a similarity predicate θ_s. The similarity conditions most employed in similarity joins generate the similarity range join and the k-nearest neighbor join [8].

Assume that each relation has an attribute $S_1 \subseteq T_1$ and $S_2 \subseteq T_2$, both sampled from the same metric domain $\mathbb{D}$. Given a maximum similarity threshold ξ, the *similarity range join* retrieves the pairs $\langle t_1, t_2 \rangle$, $t_1 \in T_1$ and $t_2 \in T_2$, such that $d(t_1[S_1], t_2[S_2]) \leq \xi$. Given an integer value $k \geq 1$, the *k-nearest neighbor join* retrieves $k * |T_1|$ tuples $\langle t_1, t_2 \rangle$ such that the attributes S_2 of t_2 are one of the k values most similar to the values of S_1 in t_1 [7].

A third type of similarity join is often described in the database literature [8]: the *k-distance join*. It retrieves the k pairs $\langle t_1, t_2 \rangle$ having the most similar values $t_1[S_1]$ and $t_2[S_2]$. This operator can be described as a particular case of the similarity *wide-join* [7]. Wide-joins retrieve the most similar pairs in general sorting the tuple internally, which allows them to be processed both efficiently and complying with the relational theory.

Similarity joins can be used to perform several tasks, including near-duplicate detection. For this last purpose, however, similarity joins have been explored only over data represented as tokens, using metrics such as the Edit or Hamming distance, as in [5]. Our proposal considers other data domains and allows using other metrics as well, such as the Minkowski (L_p) family over image domains.

Likewise, similarity wide-joins have been restricted to operate over two distinct relations. As that operator retrieves the most similar pairs in general, when both inputs are same relation $T = T_1 = T_2$, it always returns pairs where both elements are the same. The self-range wide-join discards the self-pairs and seizes the optimization opportunities that can be exploited when processing elements from the same relation.

3   Near-Duplicate Detection

Detecting near-duplicates on multimedia repositories plays an important role in presenting a more useful result, as returning images too much similar not only poses a negative impact on the retrieval time, but generally it also reduces the users' browsing experience. Imposing users to interactively analyze near-duplicates until obtaining the desired result is annoying, and requires a lot of time that would be more wisely employed specially when handling emergency scenarios. Moreover, those problems may lead to users giving up the query, assuming that the dataset does not contain the expected answer.

Following, we present a novel framework to detect near-duplicates (Sect. 3.1) and an extension of the similarity wide-join definition, which greatly reduces such drawbacks (Sect. 3.2). Last but not least, Sect. 3.3 presents the basic approach to implement our proposed wide-join extension and Sect. 3.4 details an optimized version based on pivots to achieve an efficient computation.

3.1   The Framework Architecture

The proposed framework is composed of two modules: the Feature Extractor module and the Near-Duplicate Detection module, organized according to Fig. 2.

The Feature Extractor module processes images such as in a content-based image retrieval system, representing them as n-dimensional arrays. Formally, the Feature Extractor module receives as input an image repository $C = \{img_1, \ldots, img_m\}$ with m images, takes each individual image img_i and submits it to an special algorithm – the feature extrator method ($\mathfrak{F}$) (Sect. 2), which extracts the visual features $v_i = \mathfrak{F}(img_i)$ of each image $img_i \in C$. Each v_i is a feature vector $\langle f_1, \ldots, f_n \rangle$, where n is the number of features extracted by $\mathfrak{F}$ and each f_i is a numeric value representing the visual properties of the image. The features depend on the kind of visual aspect considered, like color, shape, texture, etc., as discussed in Sect. 2.1. Its result are the m Feature Vectors, which

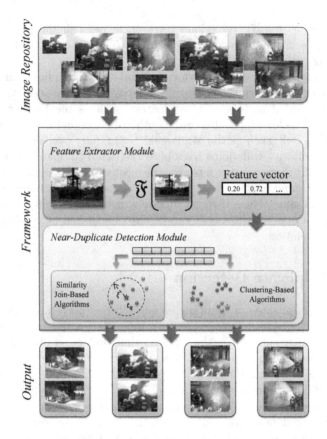

Fig. 2. The architecture of the framework for near-duplicate detection.

are stored as the S attribute in relation T such that $T[S] = \{v_1, \ldots, v_m\}$, and the corresponding images are stored as another attribute in T.

The second module – Near-Duplicate Detection – is the core module of our framework. It receives as input the collection of m feature vectors and can perform either a Similarity Join-based or a Clustering-based near-duplicate detection. Although our main focus is the similarity-join approach, the competitor methods were implemented in the cluster-based part. Both kinds of algorithms compare the feature vectors according to a distance function or metric. The detection based on a similarity join executes our specialized similarity join operator (described in Sect. 3.2) over T, employing two user-defined parameters that allows tuning the comparison to follow the user's perception of when image pairs can be considered near-duplicates. The Cluster-based detection processes T using either the original Adaptive Cluster with k-means (ACMe - Sect. 2) or our Adaptive Cluster with k-medoids variation (ACMd - Sect. 4). The framework returns the resulting image pairs detected by each algorithm as near-duplicates, allowing comparing both techniques. Our proposal allows the users to either remove, preserve or return the near-duplicates, according to their interests.

3.2 The Self Similarity Wide-Joins

The similarity join operators, such as the range join and the k-nearest neighbor join, present several shortcomings. Both of them return result sets whose cardinality is often too high, which leads to many more pairs of elements than users really need or expect. The large result set usually includes pairs truly similar, as well as pairs holding a low or even questionable degree of similarity. Therefore, to fulfill the near-duplicate task, the result of a similarity join must be further processed in order to exclude the pairs whose similarity measure is doubtful.

The k-nearest neighbor join is also troublesome, because it does not assure an equivalent similarity among the k-th nearest pairs from distinct elements. Thus, given two vectors $v_i = t_i[\mathsf{S}]$ and $v_j = t_j[\mathsf{S}]$, the distances ξ_i and ξ_j from v_i to its k-nearest neighbor – let it be v_{ik} – and from v_j to its k-nearest neighbor – let it be v_{jk} – are uncorrelated. In this way, for a given $k \geq 1$, a pair $\langle v_i, v_{ik} \rangle$ may be a near-duplicate whereas the pair $\langle v_j, v_{jk} \rangle$ may be not. Hence, looking at the range ξ variation in the k-neighbors becomes the main focus of our investigation.

Our proposal is that the resulting pairs of a similarity range join must have the similarity between their component elements evaluated and subsequently ranked so that the top-ranked ones correspond to the near-duplicate elements. Such kind of processing can be efficiently achieved by extending the similarity join operator called range wide-join (Sect. 2).

Wide-joins were designed to compute the similarity join between two relations and retain only the globally most similar elements. The near-duplicate detection requires combining a set with itself, but wide-joins do not comply with such processing, once the most similar pairs will also include combinations of each element with itself, distorting the result.

For this purpose, we employ a tailored version of the wide join operator, namely the *self range wide-join*, that atomically performs (i) the similarity evaluation over the *same set or relation* and (ii) the retrieval of the most similar elements in general. Those two operations intrinsically coupled as a single operator enable retrieving the pairs of elements considered as near-duplicates in a single-pass, avoiding further processing in a refinement phase.

Formally, let $\mathbb{D}$ be a data domain, $d : \mathbb{D} \times \mathbb{D} \mapsto \mathbb{R}^+$ be a metric over $\mathbb{D}$, T be a relation, $\mathsf{S} \subseteq \mathsf{T}$ be an attribute subject to the metric d with values sampled from $\mathbb{D}$, ξ be a maximum similarity threshold and κ be an upper bound integer value. The *self similarity range wide-join* is given by Definition 1.

Definition 1 (Self Similarity Range Wide-join.) *The self similarity range wide-join* $\boxed{\bowtie_{(\mathsf{S},\xi,\kappa)}\mathsf{T}}$ *is a similarity range join where both left and right input relations* T_1 *and* T_2 *are the same relation* T, *and returns at most* κ *pairs* $\langle t_1, t_2 \rangle \, | \, t_1, t_2 \in \mathsf{T}$ *overall, such that* $t_1 \neq t_2$, $d(t_1[\mathsf{S}_1], t_2[\mathsf{S}_2]) \leq \xi$ *and the returned pairs are the* κ *closest to each other. It is expressed in relational algebra according to* (1).

$$\bowtie_{(S,\xi,\kappa)} T \equiv$$

$$\pi_{\{T_1,T_2\}}\left(\sigma_{(ord \leq \kappa)}\left(\pi_{\{T_1,T_2,\mathcal{F}(d(t_1[S_1],t_2[S_2])) \to ord\}}\left(\rho_{(S/S_1)}(T/T_1)\overset{d(t_1[S_1],t_2[S_2]) \leq \xi}{\bowtie}\rho_{(S/S_2)}(T/T_2)\right)\right)\right) \tag{1}$$

The self similarity range wide-join is a *unary* operator (it takes one relation) that internally performs a range join $\left(\overset{d(t_1[S_1],t_2[S_2]) \leq \xi}{\bowtie}\right)$, sorts the intermediate result by the dissimilarity among the tuples and returns the top-κ pairs $\langle t_i, t_j \rangle$ of most similar elements in T. Function $\mathcal{F}$ is an aggregate function that receives the distances between the attributes $t_1[S_1]$ and $t_2[S_2]$ and generates the ordinal classification of those dissimilarity values as an attribute *ord* that exists only during the operator execution. This transient attribute is used to select the pairs most similar and then discarded in the final projection.

As seen in (1), the self similarity range join relies on the maximum threshold ξ to filter the candidate pairs and compose the answer. This operation is related to the building processing phase, where two images a and b are *possible* near-duplicates *iff* the dissimilarity between them is at most the threshold ξ, that is, $d(a,b) \leq \xi$.

The internal similarity join is influenced by the data distribution. Each attribute S_1 of the tuple pairs $\langle t_1, t_2 \rangle$ can be combined with varying quantities of values in S_2. Thus, the internal join retrieves pairs in a large range of distances, but only the closest pairs truly correspond to near-duplicate elements. The greater the distance among S_1 and S_2, the smaller the confidence that the pair is a near-duplicate.

Sorting the self-similarity among the pairs is related to the improvement phase of a near-duplicate retrieval process. As it is internally performed by the wide-join, no further processing is required. In addition, that step also solves a frequent issue occurring in traditional similarity joins: how to define ξ. Once the self-range wide-join sorts the pairs and filters just the closest, the ξ parameter can be overestimated without adversely affecting the quality of the final answer. Moreover, when compared to the clustering alternative, the self similarity range wide-join operator improves both the query answer quality and the execution performance, as it was confirmed with the experiments reported in Sect. 4.

3.3   Considerations About the Algorithms

The straightforward algorithm to compute the similarity range wide-join implements the sequence of operations following the similarity range join of (1). In order to process the internal similarity join, this algorithm follows a nested-loop strategy, once this is the generic way to compute similarity joins using any type of data. This main procedure is called the "Nested-Loop Wide-Join" and is depicted in Algorithm 1.

Algorithm 1. NESTED-LOOP WIDE-JOIN($\mathsf{T}_1, \mathsf{T}_2, \xi, \kappa$).

---

1 $Q \leftarrow \varnothing$;
2 **for** $i \leftarrow 1$ **to** $|\mathsf{T}_1|$ **do**
3   **for** $j \leftarrow 1$ **to** $|\mathsf{T}_2|$ **do**
4          $dist \leftarrow d(t_i[\mathsf{S}_1], t_j[\mathsf{S}_2])$;
5   **if** $t_i \neq t_j \wedge dist \leq \xi$ **then**
6   **if** $|Q| \leq \kappa$ **then**
7                  $Q \leftarrow Q \cup \{\langle t_i, t_j \rangle\}$;
8   **else**
9                  $q \leftarrow argmax_{\langle t_i, t_j \rangle \in Q} d(t_i[\mathsf{S}_1], t_j[\mathsf{S}_2])$;
10   **if** $dist < d(q[\mathsf{S}_1], q[\mathsf{S}_2])$ **then**
11                     $Q \leftarrow Q - \{q\}$;
12                     $Q \leftarrow Q \cup \{\langle t_i, t_j \rangle\}$;

13 **return** Q;

Following Definition 1, Algorithm 1 receives the same relation T for both inputs T_1 and T_2: the set of features vectors obtained by the Feature Extractor Module. Steps 2 to 3 of Algorithm 1 execute a nested-loop to compare each pair of images. Step 5 corresponds to the building phase of a near-duplicate task, where the candidate images t_i and t_j (ensuring $t_i \neq t_j$) are paired and included in the result set Q whenever they are dissimilar by at most the threshold ξ. The next step verifies if pair t_i and t_j truly corresponds to a near-duplicate. Until the result set Q does not contain κ pairs most similar in general (step 6), t_i and t_j are combined and included into Q. Thereafter, Q is checked in step 8 to verify if the pair q obtained in step 9 corresponds to images less similar than t_i and t_j (step 10) and, if so, the pair q is replaced by the new pair $\langle t_i, t_j \rangle$. When Algorithm 1 finishes, the result relation Q contains the near-duplicate elements. Considering $n = |\mathsf{T}|$, Algorithm 1 performs n^2 pairwise comparisons in order to achieve the final answer.

Nevertheless, still following a strategy based on nested-loops, self similarity range wide-joins can be implemented in a way more efficient than the sequence following the similarity range join of (1), optimized in relation to the Nested-Loop Wide-Join (Algorithm 1).

By analyzing the iterations of the outer loop, Algorithm 1 starts comparing image t_1 with images $t_2, t_3, ..., t_n$ in the inner loop. When the outer loop gets the next image t_2, the inner loop compares t_2 (outer) with t_1 (inner) again. Taking into account that both input relations T_1 and T_2 are the same and also considering the symmetry property of metric spaces (Sect. 2), two distinct elements must be compared only once, avoiding unnecessary distance calculations. Algorithm 2, which we call the Half Nested-Loop Wide-Join, applies the symmetry property to reduce the amount of comparisons and employs a priority queue to hold the final answer and speed up processing.

Usually, the traditional range wide-join should perform n^2 distance computations, because the input relations can be distinct. However, Algorithm 2 (steps

Algorithm 2. HALF NESTED-LOOP WIDE-JOIN(T, ξ, κ).

```
 1  Q ← ∅;
 2  for i ← 1 to |T| − 1 do
 3      for j ← i + 1 to |T| do
 4          dist ← d(t_i[S], t_j[S]);
 5          if dist ≤ ξ then
 6              if |Q| ≤ κ then
 7                  Q ← Q ∪ {⟨⟨t_i, t_j⟩, dist⟩};
 8              else
 9                  q ← argmax_{⟨⟨t_i,t_j⟩,dist⟩∈Q}(dist);
10                  if dist < d(q[S_1], q[S_2]) then
11                      Q ← Q − {q};
12                      Q ← Q ∪ {⟨⟨t_i, t_j⟩, dist⟩};

13  return Q;
```

2 and 3) requires only a half of them due to the symmetry property. Notice that the inner loop starts in the position immediately subsequent to the position the outer loop started. Therefore, a first improvement is that it is necessary to compute only $n(n-1)/2$ distances. Also, it is not necessary to check the equality of two elements anymore, as performed in step 5 in Algorithm 1.

Continuing Algorithm 2, the κ most similar pairs qualifying as near-duplicates (steps 5–6) are added into a priority queue Q in step 7. The priority parameter is the similarity distance: a greater distance corresponds to a higher priority for removal. After κ pairs were obtained, the current pair $\langle t_i, t_j \rangle$ replaces the highest priority element q in step 9 whenever it is more similar than q, as verified in step 10. Thus, the second improvement is obtained by truncating the sorting operation, as $\mathcal{F}$ in (1) can be incrementally performed by the priority queue, which avoids the cost of sorting the total whole amount of pairs or overflowing memory with too many elements. When the procedure finishes, the priority queue Q already contains the near-duplicate images.

Finally, besides exploring the symmetry property, we designed a third improvement to execute a self-similarity range wide-join. The trick here is based on the triangle inequality property (Sect. 2), using pivot elements in order to prune the in-list search space and further reduce the number of distance computations. Using pivots are described in the next subsections.

3.4 Pivot-Based Similarity Wide-Joins

The main idea to prune the search space with pivots when performing a nested-loop algorithm works as follows. Considering an element t_i in the outer loop, the inner one will compare t_i with each t_j in the rest of the dataset to check if $d(t_i[S], t_j[S]) \leq \xi$. However, considering the existence of h reference elements p_j (pivots) in the search space, it is possible to define an area (intersecting hyper-rings) surrounding t_i and each covering region limited by ξ to each pivot p_j, so

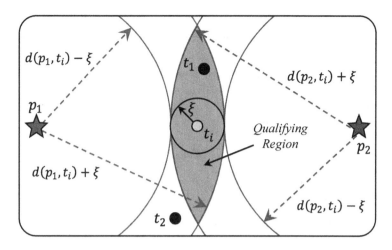

Fig. 3. Pivot-based strategy to prune the search space.

only the elements t_j inside this area should be compared, drastically reducing the number of distance calculations.

For an arbitrary and small number $h \ll n$ of pivots chosen among the available element in the database, this technique first compute the distance between each element $t_i[\mathsf{S}]$ to each pivot p_j. Therefore, each element is filtered by its distance to each pivot p_j. Notice that, in this step, only $h * n$ distance computations were performed, where $n = |\mathsf{T}|$.

The next step performs the similarity join. Each element t_i is compared to each elements t_j that is not filtered out by the pivots comparisons, and when they are closer than the similarity threshold ξ, the pair is included in the answer. To prune comparisons, it is first verified if t_j is within the qualifying area of t_i regarding to each pivot, assuring that for each pivot p_j the conditions defined in (2) and (3) simultaneously hold.

$$d(p_j, t_j) \geq d(p_j, t_i) - \xi \tag{2}$$

$$d(p_j, t_j) \leq d(p_j, t_i) + \xi \tag{3}$$

For instance, Fig. 3 depicts elements t_i, t_1 and t_2 in a search space with two pivots p_1 and p_2. Suppose that element t_i is the currently analyzed element. Element t_2 in Fig. 3 satisfies conditions (2) and (3) with respect to the pivot p_1, i.e., t_2 is within the hyper-ring delimited by the pivot p_1. However, when analyzed in relation to the pivot p_2, t_2 does not satisfy (3), thus it is guaranteed that t_2 is outside the intersection area among the two hyper-rings. Therefore, the distance between t_i and t_2 does not need to be computed, once the pivots ensure $d(t_i[\mathsf{S}], t_2[\mathsf{S}]) > \xi$ and t_2 is pruned.

However, still considering Fig. 3, element t_1 holds conditions (2) and (3) with respect to both pivots and thus it must be compared with t_i. Notice that although t_1 is within the qualifying area defined by the two pivots, it is not

Algorithm 3. PIVOT-BASED WIDE-JOIN$(\mathsf{T}, \xi, h, \kappa)$.

```
1  Q ← ∅;
2  P ← Pivots(h, T);
3  for x ← 1 to number of blocks of T do
4      for y ← x to number of blocks of T do
5          load block x to memory;
6          load block y to memory;

7          i ← 1;
8          while i < number of elements in block x do
9              j ← i;
10             if x = y then
11                 └ j ← j + 1;

12             while j < number of elements in block y do
13                 if (2) and (3) simultaneously hold for all pivot pⱼ ∈ P then
14                     dist ← d(tᵢ[S], tⱼ[S]);
15                     if dist ≤ ξ then
16                         if |Q| ≤ κ then
17                             | Q ← Q ∪ {⟨⟨tᵢ, tⱼ⟩, dist⟩};
18                         else
19                             q ← argmax₍⟨tᵢ,tⱼ⟩,dist⟩∈Q(dist);
20                             if dist < d(q[S₁], q[S₂]) then
21                                 Q ← Q − {q};
22                                 └ Q ← Q ∪ {⟨⟨tᵢ, tⱼ⟩, dist⟩};

23 return Q;
```

within the range area of t_i, so the real distance must always be computed for every non-pruned element.

For those elements within the qualifying region, the number of additional distance computations is based on the data distribution and cannot be exactly predicted beforehand. However, the worst and highly improvable situation occurs when all the n elements in the database lie within the qualifying area. In this case, it is necessary to perform, for each element t_i, n distance computations, which leads to a total of $np + n(n-1)/2$ calculations. Similar to the nested-loop case, due to the symmetry property of the metric (Sect. 2), at most a half of all the distance computations are required.

Nevertheless, it is very uncommon and easily avoidable to have all the dataset in the qualifying area. Notice in Fig. 3 that using $h = 3$ and putting a third pivot next to element t_2 can substantially reduce the qualifying area, and thus restricting it to almost the coverage region of t_i.

The opposite situation occurs when no element qualifies. In that case, there is no additional distance computation besides the initial $n \cdot h$ already calculated. In average, the number of distance computations can be estimated as the arithmetic mean among the best and worst cases, which leads the required number

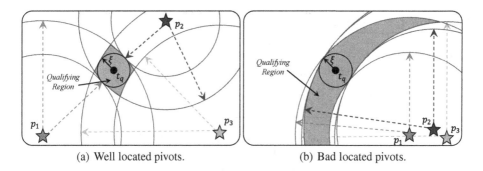

(a) Well located pivots.   (b) Bad located pivots.

Fig. 4. Choice of pivots.

of distance calculations to be significantly less than $nh + (n - 1)/4$, already including the $n \cdot h$ initial calculations.

Similarity wide-join based on pivots can be implemented in external memory following the block nested-loop approach presented as Algorithm 3. Like Algorithm 2, it also relies on a priority queue Q (step 1) in order to achieve the sorting step of similarity wide-joins. In step 2, h pivots are chosen among the elements in T. Heuristics on how the pivots should be chosen (procedure `Pivots()`) are presented later. Steps 3–6 iterate over the blocks where the tuples are stored. The nested-loop (steps 8–12) iterates over the elements inside the blocks. In order to avoid combining a element with itself, the condition in step 10 increments the start position of the inner loop, assuring the symmetry property.

For each pivot picked in step 2, expressions (2) and (3) must simultaneously hold (step 13). Notice that the distance between the elements and the pivots can be precomputed and stored when reading the elements in the loops of steps 8–12. Step 13 means that the analyzed tuple t_j is within the qualifying hyper-ring defined by the pivots. The pertinence of t_j to the region covered by t_i is then checked in steps 14–15, where an additional distance computation need to be performed. Steps 15–22 are similar to the corresponding ones in Algorithm 2 (steps 6–12), where κ elements are selected and the algorithm checks for possible replacements of the most similar pairs of images.

The choice of pivots in Step 2 plays an important role in the performance and pruning capability of Algorithm 3. The optimal and desired situation is the pivots are chosen in a way that the intersection of hyper-rings generated covers a region so small as possible. Once only the elements inside that intersection region are compared during the join operation, the smaller the intersection region the lower the probability it contains too many elements to be compared, leading to a reduced amount of distance calculations.

For instance, Fig. 4 illustrates two scenarios containing a search space with 3 pivots, the currently analyzed element t_q and the hyper-ring projected by each pivot. In Fig. 4(a), the pivots are disposed in a way that the intersection region of their hyper-rings is slightly larger than the region with distance ξ from t_q. In this case, the pivots are well located and every element complying with expressions (2) and (3) are almost certainly more similar to t_q than the threshold ξ and,

---

Algorithm 4. PIVOTS(h, T) - RANDOM.

---
1 $P \leftarrow \varnothing$;
2 **for** $i \leftarrow 1$ **to** h **do**
3      $newPivot \leftarrow$ random element in $\{T - P\}$;
4      $P \leftarrow P \cup \{newPivot\}$;
5 **return** P;

---

therefore are part of the answer. In a different way, Fig. 4(b) shows the pivots disposed very close to each other, which leads to an intersection qualifying region much larger than the area of distance ξ from t_q. Hence, most of the elements in that qualifying region must be compared to t_q, but only a few of them will in fact satisfy the condition $d(t_q, t_j) \leq \xi$ (Algorithm 3, step 14), which increases the number of distance computations and reduces the scalability of the algorithm.

A straightforward technique to choose pivots is to randomly pickup h distinct elements. This procedure, shown as Algorithm 4, starts with an empty set P of pivots and selects other ones among the set $T \setminus P$, i.e., the elements that were not chosen yet (step 3). The complexity of Algorithm 4 is linear in the number of pivots and despite its simplicity, it generally perform a good choice of pivots. However, it does not guarantee to avoid the situation illustrated in Fig. 4(b).

An improvement of Algorithm 4 aiming at avoiding similar occurrences such as in Fig. 4(b) is to force pivots to be far among themselves. One way to achieve this result is to consider that random pivots cannot be paired in the join operation. Thus, for any pair of pivots p_i, p_j, the distance between them must be greater than the similarity threshold, i.e., $d(p_i, p_j) > \xi$. Algorithm 5 implements this main idea. It starts with a random element in the list of pivots (step 1) and, for each new chosen pivot (steps 2–3), it checks if the new pivot is far apart of the elements in P by at least ξ (step 4).

Although both Algorithms 4 and 5 are quite faster due to their random choosing strategy, the pivots are fixed for all comparisons performed. Thus, as the outer loop (Algorithm 3 – step 8) pass by distinct elements t_i, the hyper-ring defined by each pivot varies and so does the qualifying region. In this manner, a set P of pivots can lead to a good situation similar to the one shown in Fig. 4(a) for a given t_1, but for the other elements $t_{\{2,3,\dots\}}$, it is prone to produce the undesired behavior seen in Fig. 4(b).

As a solution to this shortcoming, the pivots should be selected near the "border" of the dataset, in a way that the distances among them to the elements

---

Algorithm 5. PIVOTS(h, T, ξ) - SEPARATED PIVOTS.

---
1 $P \leftarrow$ random element in $\{T\}$;
2 **for** $i \leftarrow 1$ **to** $h - 1$ **do**
3      $newPivot \leftarrow$ random element in $\{T - P\}$;
4   **if** $d(newPivot, p) > \xi$ *for all pivot* $p \in P$ **then**
5          $P \leftarrow P \cup \{newPivot\}$;
6 **return** P;

Algorithm 6. PIVOTS(h, T) - EXTREME PIVOTS.

1   $f_{min}[1..n] \leftarrow t_1[\mathsf{S}]$;
2   $f_{max}[1..n] \leftarrow t_1[\mathsf{S}]$;
3   **foreach** $t \in \mathsf{T}$ **do**
4 | $f[1..n] \leftarrow t[\mathsf{S}]$;
5 | **for** $i \leftarrow 1$ **to** n **do**
6 | | $f_{min}[i] \leftarrow \texttt{min}(f_{min}[i], f[i])$;
7 | | $f_{max}[i] \leftarrow \texttt{max}(f_{max}[i], f[i])$;

8   **for** $i \leftarrow 1$ **to** h **do**
9 | **for** $i \leftarrow 1$ **to** $n - 1$ **do**
10 | | $newPivot[\mathsf{S}[i]] \leftarrow c \mid c < f_{min}[i] \vee c > f_{max}[i]$;
11 | $P \leftarrow P \cup \{newPivot\}$;

12 **return** P;

---

in the dataset are as larger as possible. Retrieving the elements really lying in the border of the space implies in computing all element pairs and then picking the most distant ones. This task would be not useful, once computing all pairs corresponds to the basic nested-loop join operation. Thus, although Algorithms 4 and 5 choose pivots among the elements in T, the pivots do not have to necessarily belong to the dataset. So, following we introduce a new method (Algorithm 6) to choose good pivots lying beyond the region where the elements in T are disposed.

Algorithm 6 starts with two arrays f_{min} and f_{max} that contain respectively the minimum and maximum values of each dimension of the images features vectors. Steps 3–7 compare the values of each dimension with the current minimum and maximum ones and performs possible replacements in order to choose the extreme values along the dimensions. Once the range of each dimension is obtained, the next step is to choose h pivots whose coordinates of each dimension are outside the computed range, that is, extreme points regarding to those in the dataset. Thus, in steps 9–10, each dimension of pivot $newPivot$ is assigned with a random value c such that c is lesser (or greater) than the minimum (or maximum) value of the corresponding dimension. Hence, this strategy enables choosing pivots defining a good qualifying region to reduce the number of comparisons performed for each element t_i processed in the join operation.

4   Experiments

This section reports experiments performed using our framework to detect near-duplicate images. The goal is to evaluate the proposed self range wide-join technique in terms of both the computational performance and the answer quality, targeting prioritizing those aspects as required for an emergency monitoring system.

4.1   Experiment Setup

The results were performed on a real dataset – `Fire` – composed of 272 images of fire incidents. Those images are a sample of the Rescuer dataset and were obtained from an emergency situation simulation, held in an Industrial Complex. The dataset was previously labeled by domain experts and 25 distinct incident scenes were recognized. The images were submitted to the Color Layout [14] extractor, which generated 16 features. The L_2 (Euclidean) metric was employed to evaluate the vector distances.

We implemented four variations of the self-range wide-join algorithm. The first is the similarity Wide-Join using the Nested-Loop approach (WJNL - Algortihm 1), which is a self version of the baseline found in the literature [7]. The second variation employs a HAlf nested-loop (WJHA - Algorithm 2), where the intention is to perform less distance computations than the previous one. In the two next variations, the Wide-Join operator was implemented according to the pivot strategy of Algorithm 3 using the Extreme Pivots (WJEP) procedure (Algorithm 6) and the Separate Pivots (WJSP) procedure (Algorithm 5).

We set the number of pivots to 25 in our four self-range wide-join variations and compared them with two cluster-based techniques. The first is the Adaptive Cluster with k-means (ACME - Sect. 2) [2]. Also, once k-means is sensitive to outliers and often computes "means" that do not correspond to real dataset images, we implemented a third method that is an ACME variant that replaces the k-means with the k-medoids algorithm and called it ACMD [9], in order to better analyze the answer quality. When necessary, the parameter ξ was set to retrieve about 1% of the total number of possible pairs.

The experiments were executed in a computer with an Intel® Core™ i7–4770 processor, running at 3.4 GHz, with 16 GB of RAM, under the GNU Linux distribution Ubuntu 14.10. All methods were implemented in C++ using the same framework to enable fair comparisons. Each technique was evaluated with respect to both the total running time (Sect. 4.2) and the answer quality (Sect. 4.3), as described following.

4.2   Performance Experiment

Figure 5(a) presents the total running time of the six approaches evaluated. The reported time corresponds to the execution of the Near-Duplicate Detection Module only, as the feature extraction was performed only once to provide data to all six methods. In this experiment, WJEP was the fastest technique, executing 65.26% faster than the nested-loop version of wide-joins (WJNL) and 2 and 3 orders of magnitude faster than ACME and ACMD, respectively.

Such behavior occurs due to the fact that both ACME and ACMD cluster the dataset and recursively redistribute the elements following a hierarchical approach for the improvement phase, until the coherence of each cluster does not exceed a maximum value, computed during the process. In addition, to achieve the result, an improvement phase based on local features is usually required,

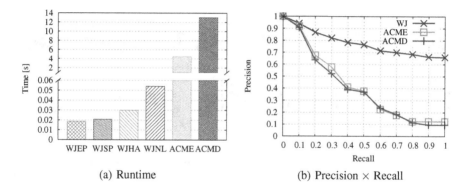

(a) Runtime   (b) Precision × Recall

Fig. 5. Performance and quality analysis: the `Fire` dataset.

which contributes to increase the computational cost of those approaches. Distinctly, the wide-joins perform a single pass computation that embodies the building and the improvement phases into an atomic, optimized operation.

Both ACME and ACMD require a parameter k to execute their core clustering algorithms, the k-means and k-medoids, respectively. Nevertheless, they returned a number of clusters greater than k, because the clusters obtained in the building phase are subdivided according to their coherence values. For the `Fire` dataset, those techniques achieved the better results when k was set to values between 20 and 30. Distinctly, the wide-join methods were able to achieve the result without the need of several executions in order to find the better parameter adjustments.

This experiment remarkably shows that approaches based on the Relational Algebra are much faster than those based on clustering techniques. Moreover, as shown in the next section, the algebra-based approaches achieve better results and do not require any parameters, freeing the users from the burden of chose them.

4.3 Result Quality Evaluation

To analyze the result quality, we evaluated how accurate is the result returned by each approach. In order to enable fair comparisons among the distinct algorithms, we computed Precision and Recall (P × R) curves. Evaluating P × R is a common technique used for information retrieval evaluation. Precision is defined as the rate of the number of relevant elements retrieved by the number of retrieved elements. Recall is given as the rate between the number of relevant elements retrieved by the number of relevant elements in the database. In P × R plots, the closer a curve to the top, the better the corresponding method.

It is worth remembering that all the self-range wide-join variations return exactly the same answer. Thus the four curves obtained by every wide-join variation are identical, only varying their run time.

(a) Query sample

(b) Self-range wide-join

(c) Adaptive cluster with *k*-means

(d) Adaptive cluster with *k*-medoids

Fig. 6. Near-duplicates obtained by the three evaluated methods for the query center shown.

Therefore, for this experiment, a generic wide-join approach is compared to the two cluster-based ones. Figure 5(b) shows the P × R curves achieved by the three approaches. Our self range wide-join method achieved the larger precision for every recall amount. It was, in average, 35.14% more precise than ACME and 36.78% than ACMD. After retrieving all relevant images in the dataset (recall of 100%), the wide-join consistently obtained 66.00% of precision in the result, whereas the competitor techniques achieved a maximum precision of 12.50%.

In order to show the gain of precision obtained, Fig. 6 samples the images considered as near-duplicates by the three techniques. Again, the wide-join variations were omitted once they compute the same result. For an image randomly chosen as query center (Fig. 6(a) – the 10th image with label 13), Fig. 6(b) shows the near-duplicates retrieved by the self range wide-join operator. As it can be seen, they have the same label and are in fact related to the query, recognizing even images with zoom and rotations.

Figures 6(c) and (d) show the clusters obtained by the ACME and ACMD, respectively. Both are from the clusters where the query image (Fig. 6(a)) is located. As it can be noted, both methods retrieved false positives, where the existence of false positives contributed to decrease the precision of ACME and ACMD. Although ACME theoretically leads to worse clusters than ACMD, as the seeds of *k*-means are not real images whereas the medoids are, the precision difference among both was in average only 1.63% (see Fig. 5(b)).

The superior quality of the answer of the self wide-join operator when compared to the cluster-based methods shown in Fig. 5(b) is explained by the fact that the clusters are generated based on centroids or medoids seeds, and the remaining elements are allocated according to their distances to those seeds. The cluster elements are analyzed only in relation to the seeds, ignoring the relationship among themselves. This fact leads to retrieving some images that are distinct among themselves but similar to their seed, as illustrated in Figs. 6(c) and (d). In its turn, the self wide-join method establishes a "pairing relationship" among the elements, avoiding such drawback and increasing the answer quality, as also observed in Fig. 6(b).

Notice that Fig. 6 shows the images *spoted as near-duplicates* by each of the three techniques. According to the user interest, those near-duplicates can be

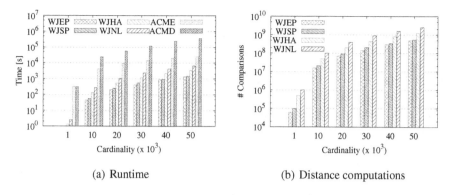

(a) Runtime   (b) Distance computations

Fig. 7. Scalability analysis: `Aloi` dataset.

either removed from the final answer of the framework so as to provide a more informative result set, or returned, allowing to analyze similar occurrences.

4.4   Scalability Analysis

The `Fire` dataset contains real images from an emergence scenario, but it contains a small number of images. Thus, we evaluated the scalability of our technique employing the `Aloi` dataset[2]. It contains images of 1000 objects rotated from $0°$ to $360°$ in steps of $5°$(72 images per object, which we assume to be near-duplicates) giving a total of 72,000 distinct images. The Color Moment extractor [15] was employed to represent the images and generated 144 features, which were compared using the L_2 metric.

For the scalability evaluation, we shuffled the `Aloi` dataset and varied the cardinality of the submitted data in several executions of our framework. Figure 7(a) depicts the total run time of each algorithm. The self range wide-join based on Extreme Pivots (WJEP) was again the fastest method. It was in average 17.24%, 66.15% and 82.76% faster than WJSP, WJHA and WJNL, respectively. When compared with the cluster-based techniques, WJEP was again 2 and up to 3 orders of magnitude faster than the ACME and ACMD, respectively. For example, for a cardinality of 10,000 objects, WJEP execution took 44 s while ACME took 1.18 h and AMCD took 6.61 h. Even the slowest implementation of the wide-join – the WJNL – was faster than the cluster-based ones, taking 4.39 min to calculate the answer.

In order to understand the results depicted in Fig. 7(a) and the potential of our proposed framework, suppose that an event containing twenty or thirty thousand people (e.g., in a soccer stadium, music show, etc.) and the occurrence of an incident. If a crowdsourcing systems receives at the same time an amount of 10,000 pictures of the incident, our proposal generates the first perspectives of the scene in less than 1 min, enabling a rescue control team to take actions almost immediately, whereas the competitor techniques will spend hours.

---

[2] <http://aloi.science.uva.nl> Access: July 4, 2016.

Finally, Fig. 7(b) compares the four similarity wide-join techniques with respect to the number of distance computations performed to achieve the result. The self range wide-join with extreme pivots (WJEP) executed in average 22.30% less distance calculations than WJSP, confirming our initial hypothesis that pivots lying out of the range of coordinates of the dataset generate a reduced qualifying region and improve the pruning capability of the Algorithm 3. Also, WJEP performed in average 68.61% and 84.30% less comparisons than WJHA and WJNL, respectively. Nevertheless, it is important to highlight that the four techniques obtained the same final result, but WJEP was able to use less computational resources.

Figure 7 shows that as the cardinality increases, the cluster-based methods need to process more and more elements in the building phase. However, the coherence value is not used in this phase, forcing the next one (the refinement phase) to need more iterations to subdivide the clusters and ensure that the coherence is maintained. Distinctly, the wide-join perform a one-pass strategy. The increased cardinality also turns the process more costlier, but in a much less pronounced way as compared to the cluster-based ones. Moreover, to avoid performing distance calculations among every pair, as occurs with WJNL, the wide-joins that uses pivots prune more comparisons, helping to reduce the running time.

4.5 Experiment Highlights

In a general way, there are three main reasons explaining why the introduced self-similarity range wide-join technique overcomes its competitors:

- *Single-pass computation*: usually, the near-duplicate detection is divided into two phases. The wide-join operator precludes a refinement phase. As aforestated, a single-pass execution allows to reduce the cost of the entire process in at least 2 orders of magnitude.
- *Efficient prune technique*: a pruning technique based on pivots enables the proposed WJEP algorithm to evaluate a reduced amount of element-to-element comparisons. The pivots delimit small space regions for analysis, allowing to discard many elements that surely will not be part of the answer. Also, this strategy reduces the number of distance computations in about 69% in relation to the traditional nested-loop approach.
- *Similarity relationship between elements*: unlike the cluster-based methods, that computes the proximity of an element to a group, the self wide-join operator establishes a similarity relationship between each distinct pair of elements. It avoids the dissimilarity found in two elements lying in opposite sides of a cluster, which increases the answer quality in about 35% in relation to the existing approaches.

5 Conclusion

Near-duplicate detection plays an important role in several real applications. For instance, emergency-based frameworks based on crowdsourcing data can benefit from those techniques in order to enhance the processing and decision making support on large sets of upcoming images.

This paper introduced a framework model to detect near-duplicates using the Relational Algebra-based similarity wide-join operator as its core. The framework is composed of two modules. The first one generates a computational representation and mapping of each images into a metric space. The second is in charge of detecting the near-duplicate elements using the self wide-join operator that was introduced in this paper. Thus, our main contribution is the self-range wide-join operator: an improved version of the wide-join that computes similarity by combining a relation with itself and exploiting the optimizations that such combination generates.

Our technique is general enough to be applied over any dataset in a metric space, but we focused its application for an emergency-based application. In emergency scenarios, it is common that the eyewitnesses gather large amounts of photos and videos about the incident. Existing monitoring systems can benefit from those crowdsourcing information, aiming at improving decision making support. However, as the information increases and its elements tend to become too similar among themselves, it is imperative to provide efficient techniques to properly handle near-duplicates.

We optimized the wide-join algorithm to scan the search space relying on pivots and proposed three algorithms to make their choice. Using two metric space properties to prune elements allowed to achieving a large performance gain when compared to the existing solutions. The experiments executed using two real datasets showed that our proposed wide-join-based framework is able not only to improve the near-duplicate detection performance by at least 2 and up to 3 orders of magnitude, but also to improve the quality of the results when compared to the previous techniques.

Our approaches are really useful for real applications. For example, suppose that an incident occurs during an event containing twenty or thirty thousand people (e.g., in a soccer stadium, a music show, etc.), leading a crowdsourcing system to suddenly receive several thousands of pictures of the incident. If the crowdsourcing system is based on a competitor technique, it will spend hours before generating the first perspectives of the scene. If it is based on our proposed technique, it will generate the first perspectives in less than 1 min, really helping the rescue control team to take immediate actions.

References

1. Chino, D.Y.T., Avalhais, L.P.S., Rodrigues Jr., J.F., Traina, A.J.M.: Bowfire: detection of fire in still images by integrating pixel color and texture analysis. In: Proceedings of 28th Conference on Graphics, Patterns and Images, pp. 1–8 (2015)
2. Li, J., Qian, X., Li, Q., Zhao, Y., Wang, L., Tang, Y.Y.: Mining near-duplicate image groups. Multimedia Tools Appl. **74**, 655–669 (2015)
3. Yao, J., Yang, B., Zhu, Q.: Near-duplicate image retrieval based on contextual descriptor. IEEE Sig. Process. Lett. **22**, 1404–1408 (2015)

4. Carvalho, L.O., Santos, L.F.D., Oliveira, W.D., Traina, A.J.M., Traina Jr., C.: Self similarity wide-joins for near-duplicate image detection. In: Proceedings of 2015 IEEE International Symposium on Multimedia, pp. 237–240 (2015)
5. Xiao, C., Wang, W., Lin, X., Yu, J.X., Wang, G.: Efficient similarity joins for near-duplicate detection. ACM Trans. Database Syst. **36**, 15:1–15:41 (2011)
6. Wang, X.J., Zhang, L., Ma, W.Y.: Duplicate search based image annotation using web-scale data. Proc. IEEE **100**, 2705–2721 (2012)
7. Carvalho, L.O., Santos, L.F.D., Oliveira, W.D., Traina, A.J.M., Traina Jr., C.: Similarity joins and beyond: an extended set of binary operators with order. In: Amato, G., Connor, R., Falchi, F., Gennaro, C. (eds.) SISAP 2015. LNCS, vol. 9371, pp. 29–41. Springer, Cham (2015). doi:10.1007/978-3-319-25087-8_3
8. Silva, Y.N., Aref, W.G., Larson, P.A., Pearson, S., Ali, M.H.: Similarity queries: their conceptual evaluation, transformations, and processing. VLDB J. **22**, 395–420 (2013)
9. Carvalho, L.O., Santos, L.F.D., Oliveira, W.D., Traina, A.J.M., Traina Jr., C.: Efficient self-similarity range wide-joins fostering near-duplicate image detection in emergency scenarios. In: Proceedings of 18th International Conference on Enterprise Information Systems, vol. 1, pp. 81–91 (2016)
10. Sonka, M., Hlavac, V., Boyle, R.: Image Processing, Analysis, and Machine Vision. Cengage Learning, Boston (2014)
11. Searcóid, M.Ó.: Metric Spaces. Springer, Heidelberg (2007). doi:10.1007/978-1-84628-627-8
12. Bangay, S., Lv, O.: Evaluating locality sensitive hashing for matching partial image patches in a social media setting. J. Multimedia **1**, 14–24 (2012)
13. Chum, O., Philbin, J., Zisserman, A.: Near duplicate image detection: min-hash and tf-idf weighting. In: British Machine Vision Conference, pp. 1–10 (2008)
14. Kasutani, E., Yamada, A.: The MPEG-7 color layout descriptor: a compact image feature description for high-speed image/video segment retrieval. In: Proceedings of 8th International Conference on Image Processing, pp. 674–677 (2001)
15. Stricker, M., Orengo, M.: Similarity of color images. In: Proceedings of 3rd Conference on Storage and Retrieval for Image and Video Databases, pp. 381–392 (1995)

Artificial Intelligence and Decision Support Systems

Combination of Interaction Models
for Multi-Agents Systems

Richardson Ribeiro[1]([✉]), Douglas M. Guisi[1], Marcelo Teixeira[1],
Eden R. Dosciatti[1], Andre P. Borges[2], and Fabrício Enembreck[3]

[1] Department of Informatics, Federal University of Technology of Paraná,
Pato Branco, Brazil
{richardsonr,dguisi,marceloteixeira,
edenerd}@utfpr.edu.br
[2] Department of Informatics, Federal University of Technology of Paraná,
Ponta Grossa, Brazil
apborges@utfpr.edu.br
[3] Graduate Program in Computer Science,
Pontifical Catholic University of Paraná, Curitiba, Brazil
fabricio@ppgia.pucpr.br

Abstract. In this paper we present an interaction technique for coordinating agents that use rewards generated by Reinforcement Learning algorithms. Agents that coordinate with each other by exchanging rewards need mechanisms to help them while they interact to discover action policies. Because of the peculiarities of the environment and the objectives of each agent, there is no guarantee that a coordination model can converge them to an optimal policy. One possibility is to take advantage of existing models so that a mechanism that is less sensitive to the system variables emerges. The technique described here is based on three models previously studied in which agents (i) share learning in a predefined cycle of interactions, (ii) cooperate at every interaction and (iii) cooperate when an agent reaches the goal-state. Traffic scenarios were generated as a way of validating the proposed technique. The results showed that even when the computational complexity was increased the gains in terms of convergence make the technique superior to classical Reinforcement Learning approaches.

Keywords: Multi-Agents Systems · Interaction model · Reinforcement Learning

1 Introduction

In a Multi-Agent System (MAS), agents need to interact and coordinate in order to carry out tasks. Coordination between agents can help to avoid problems with redundant solutions, inconsistency of execution, resource waste and deadlock [13], enabling learning-based coordination models to solve complex problems involving social and individual behaviors [21].

In addition to being able to learn, an agent in an MAS must be able to cooperate with other agents in the system in order to attempt to solve problems that require locally unknown knowledge or that could compromise the agent's performance. In this way, sharing agent expertise (usually in terms of *action policies*) becomes essential to

© Springer International Publishing AG 2017
S. Hammoudi et al. (Eds.): ICEIS 2016, LNBIP 291, pp. 107–121, 2017.
DOI: 10.1007/978-3-319-62386-3_5

converge to a global behavior that satisfies a certain specification or simply solves a particular problem.

An alternative to sharing an agent's expertise among multiple agents is to use specific computational paradigms that maximize performance based on reinforcement parameters (rewards or punishments) applied to agents as they interact with the environment. Learning based on paradigms of this kind is called Reinforcement Learning (RL) [7, 14].

RL algorithms, such as Q-learning [17], can be used to discover the optimal action policy for a single agent when it repeatedly explores its state-space. A major concern that arises from this action-policy-discovering approach is that it tends to suffer from large state-spaces because of *state-space explosion* problems. In such cases, RL involving multiple agents has proved to be a promising strategy as it modularizes the whole problem and implements action policies locally [8].

The idea behind the implementation of local policies is to discover a global action plan generated by combining agents' local knowledge. When this approach leads to the best global action plan, the policy π is said to be optimal (π^*) and corresponds to the highest rewards received by the agents.

In this paper we integrate coordination models for multiple agents using RL techniques. Our approach collects "good" features from individual approaches in the literature and integrates them into a single framework that can then be used to establish optimized information-sharing strategies for multiple agents. The preliminary results allow the performance of the integrated model to be compared with the performance of each model used in the framework. In general, the convergence rate among agents was substantially better than in the other cases.

The remainder of this paper is organized as follows. In Sect. 2, the state of the art is presented, some coordination methods for learning in Multi-Agent Systems are described, the Q-learning algorithm is reviewed and interaction models are summarized. In Sects. 3 and 4, details of the proposed method and the environment used to evaluate it are discussed, and numerical results illustrating the performance of the proposed method are presented. In Sect. 5, real-world applications are discussed. The conclusions are given in Sect. 6.

2 Learning in Multi-Agent Systems

Multi-agent Reinforcement Learning, in which multiple agents are involved in the solution of a complex task in a common environment, has been the subject of a considerable amount of research over the last decade. Unlike learning in an environment with a single agent, learning in an MAS assumes that the relevant knowledge is not locally available in a single agent, making it is necessary to coordinate the whole process [1, 19, 20]. One way for an agent to coordinate its actions is by interacting with other agents, changing and evolving their coordination model.

Coordination by interaction involves combining the efforts of a group of agents in the search for solutions to global problems [3]. Interaction can be considered the set of behaviors that result when a group of agents act to satisfy their goals and consider constraints imposed by resource limitations and individual skills. There is a significant body of literature on learning from interactions [11, 18] and collective or social learning [9].

In learning problems involving RL, interaction depends basically on a structure that enables communication among agents so they can share their accumulated rewards, immediately reinforcing the transition system. With this in mind, [2] created an interaction model that calculates rewards based on the individual satisfaction of neighboring agents in which agents continuously emit a level of personal satisfaction during the learning process. Adopting a different approach, [12] developed a learning strategy in which agents are able to remember information they have accumulated so they can reuse it later. This method has been tested on colored mazes, and reports confirm that it has a positive impact on jumpstarts and reduces the total learning cost compared with conventional Q-learning.

Ribeiro and Enembreck [9] combined theories from different fields to build social structures for state-space searches based on the way interactions between states occur and reinforcements are generated. They used social measures to guide exploration and approximation processes. Their experiments showed that identifying social behavior that incorporates interaction between agents within the social structure helps to improve the coordination and optimization process and yields results that are statistically more significant.

Integrating different methods into a single improved generic coordination model is usually challenging, especially because of the wide range of problems and the amount of knowledge about the problem domain required. Furthermore, in an MAS, conflicting values for cumulative rewards can be generated, as each agent uses only local learning values [3]. Collective learning assumes that the relevant knowledge is acquired when rewards are shared, intensifying the relationship between agents.

2.1   Reinforcement Learning

In RL an agent is given a reward or punishment by the environment in response to its actions [7]. This type of learning has been extensively investigated in the literature [4–6, 15, 16, 21] as part of efforts to find solutions to NP-hard problems.

We introduce briefly the Markov decision process (MDP) used to formalize the RL problem. An MDP is a tuple (S, A, $\beta_{s,s'}^a$, R), where S is a finite set of environmental states that can consist of a variable sequence of *states* = <$x_1, x_2, ..., x_y$>. An episode is a sequence of actions $a \in A$ that leads the agent from an initial-state to a goal-state. $\beta_{s,s'}^a$ is a function that indicates the probability that the agent arrives in state s when an action a is applied in state s'. Similarly, $R_{s,s'}^a$ is the reward received whenever the transition $\beta_{s,s'}^a$ occurs.

An RL agent must learn a policy $Q: S \rightarrow A$ that maximizes its expected cumulative reward, where $Q(s, a)$ is the probability of selecting action a in state s'. The optimal policy must satisfy Bellman's equation for each state $s \in S$:

$$Q(s,a) = R(s,a) + \gamma \sum \beta(s,a,s') \times \max Q(s',a) \tag{1}$$

where β is the weight of the values of future rewards and $Q(s, a)$ is the expected cumulative reward given that action a is executed in state s [14]. To reach an optimal policy, an agent that uses an RL algorithm must iteratively explore the state space $(S \times A)$, updating the cumulative rewards and storing these in a table Q. The Q-learning algorithm proposed by [17] converges to an optimal policy by applying the following update rule (Eqs. 2 and 3) after a time step t:

$$V = \gamma \max Q_t(s_{t+1}, a_{t+1}) - Q_t(s_t, a_t) \tag{2}$$

$$Q_{t+1}(s_t, a_t) \leftarrow Q_t(s_t, a_t) + \alpha[R(s_t, a_t) + V] \tag{3}$$

where V is the utility value of performing an action a in state s, and $\alpha \in [0, 1]$ is the learning rate. In dynamic environments it is desirable to use strategies because a satisfactory policy may no longer be appropriate after a change in the environment. When a strategy, such as ε-greedy, is used, the agent selects an action with the greatest Q value with probability $1 - \varepsilon$. In previous experiments with the Q-learning algorithm (Ribeiro *et al.* [8]), we found that the agent was not able to converge in dynamic environments during training (see Sect. 3) so we used an important property of the Q-learning algorithm, namely, that actions can be chosen using a random exploration strategy determined by ε. The state transition is given by Eq. 4:

$$\pi(s) = \begin{cases} argmaxQ(s, a), & \text{if } q > \varepsilon \\ a_{random}, & \text{otherwise} \end{cases} \tag{4}$$

where q is a random value with uniform probability in $[0, 1]$, ε $(0 \leq \varepsilon \leq 1)$ is a parameter that defines the exploration trade-off (the greater the value of ε, the smaller the probability of a random choice) and a_{random} is a random action selected from the possible actions in state s. Here, the ε-greedy exploration strategies were able to estimate better rewards and come up with new action policies.

In this paper, Q-learning is used to generate and evaluate partial and global action policies. By applying Q-learning, a policy can be found for each agent. However, if similar agents interact in the same environment, each agent has its own MDP, and optimal global behavior cannot be determined by local analysis. Thus, in an environment involving several agents, the goal is to select the actions of each MDP at time t so that the total of the expected rewards for all agents is maximized.

2.1.1 Reinforcement Learning with Multiple Shared Rewards

In RL algorithms with shared rewards, one agent's actions can produce a policy that has an effect on all individuals and eliminate their idiosyncratic behavior. Rewards are shared by agents through a partial action policy (Q_i). Usually, such policies contain partial information (learning values) about the environment but communicate with a central structure to share rewards in an integrated way in order to maximize the sum of the partial rewards obtained during the learning process. When policies $\pi_1,...,\pi_x$ are integrated, a new policy π^+ can be generated, where π^+ denotes the best rewards acquired by agents during the learning process.

Ribeiro *et al.* [8] showed how agents exchange information during learning. When the supervisor agent receives rewards from other agents, the following process occurs: on reaching goal state g by a lower-cost path, agent$_i$ uses a model to share the rewards with other agents. The reward of a partial policy π_1 can be used to upgrade the overall policy π^+, further influencing how other agents update their knowledge and interact with the environment.

Ribeiro *et al.* [8] also described the function that shares these rewards. This sharing can be accomplished in three ways, all of which involve internal sharing using Q-learning. The best rewards from each agent are sent to π^+, forming a new policy with the best rewards acquired by agent$_i$, which can be socialized with other agents.

Algorithm 1. Learning Algorithm.

Algorithm Shared_Rewards (I, model)

Learning table: Q_i, Q^*, π

```
01      π ← 0 ;
02      Foreach agent i ∈ I do:
03         Foreach state s ∈ S do:
04         // initializing learning values
             Foreach action a ∈ A do:
```

05
$$\hat{Q}_i(s,a) \leftarrow 0 \;;$$

```
06            Endfor
07         Endfor
08      Endfor
09      t ← 0;
10      Foreach agent i ∈ I do:
11         While not cooperate(t, model, Q*, Qi, π ) do:
12            t ← t + 1;
13            Choose state s ∈ S, action a ∈ A
              Update:
```

14
$$V \leftarrow \gamma \max_{a_{t+1}} \hat{Q}_t(s_{t+1},a_{t+1}) - \hat{Q}_t(s_t,a_t) \;;$$
$$\hat{Q}_{t+1}(s_t,a_t) \leftarrow \hat{Q}_t(s_t,a_t) + \alpha \left[R(s_t,a_t) + V \right] \;;$$

```
15         Endwhile
16      Endfor
17      Foreach agent i ∈ I do:
```

18
$$\hat{Q}_i(s,a) \leftarrow \pi \;;$$

```
19      Endfor
20      End
```

A policy is considered optimal when the agent is able to find the goal-state with the lowest possible cost, i.e., a cost similar to that provided by the supervisor agent (A* algorithm).

The interaction models for cooperative RL presented in [8] are summarized below (i, ii, iii). The cooperative RL algorithm, the other algorithms and the elements formalizing the RL models are detailed in [8].

(i) Discrete Model: Agents share learning in a predefined cycle of interactions c. Cooperation in this model occurs as follows: the agent accumulates rewards it obtained as a result of its actions during the learning cycle. At the end of the cycle, the agent sends the values of π_i to π^+. An agent shares its reward if and only if it improves the efficiency of the other agents in the same state.

(ii) Continuous Model: Agents cooperate at every transaction $T_{s,s'}^a$. Cooperation in the continuous model occurs as follows: if $s \neq g$, then every action performed by the agent generates a reward value, which is the sum of the accumulated reinforcements for all players in action a in state s. The goal is to accumulate the greatest rewards in π_i so that these can be shared at each interaction.

Algorithm 2. Cooperation model.

Algorithm cooperate (t, model, Q*, Q$_i$, π)
---
c: number of cycles
```
01      Switch (model):
02       Case "discrete":
03        If t mod c == 0 then
04            π ← update_policy(Q*, Qi, π )
05        Endif
06       Case "continous":
07        If s ≠ g then
08                r ← Σ Qi(s,a) ;
                    i=1
09            Q (s,a) ← r ;
                i
10            π ← update_policy (Q*, Qi, π );
11        Endif
12       Case " Objective-driven":
13        Se s == g then
14                r ← Σ Qi(s,a) ;
                    i=1
15            Q (s,a) ← r ;
                i
16            π ← update_policy (Q*, Qi, π );
17        Endif
18       Endswitch
19       Return( π )
```

(iii) Objective-driven Model: Unlike in the discrete model, cooperation in the objective-driven model occurs when the agent reaches the goal state, i.e., $s = g$. In this case, the agent interacts and accumulates reward values. This is necessary because in this model the agent shares his rewards only when the goal state is reached. When the agent reaches the goal state, the reward value is sent to π^+. If the reward value for the state improves the overall efficiency, then the agents share the reward. This shows that even when unsatisfactory rewards are shared (because of a lack of interaction), the agent is able to adapt his behavior without adversely affecting global convergence.

The cooperative RL algorithm, the other algorithms, and the elements formalizing the RL models are detailed in Algorithms 1–3. Figure 1 summarizes the learning process with the models in an activity diagram that uses such algorithms.

The following definitions are used in these algorithms:

- a set of states $S = \{s_1,...,s_m\}$;
- a set of agents $I = \{i_1,..., i_x\}$;
- a set of policies $\pi = \{\pi_1,..., \pi_x\}$, where π_i represents the policy of the agent i;
- a reward function $st(S) \rightarrow ST$ where $ST = \{-1, -0.4, -0.3, -0.2, -0.1\}$;
- a discrete time step $t = 1, 2, 3,...., n$;
- a learning cycle c, where $c < n$;
- a set of actions $A = \{a_1,..., a_n\}$, where each action is executed at time step t;
- a learning table $\hat{Q} : (SxA) \rightarrow \Re$, that define an policy π_i;
- a coordination method set Model = {discrete, continuous, objective-driven};
- a function *cooperate*, that defines the stop condition and cooperation models;
- a function *cost*: $cost(s,g) = \sum_{s \in S}^{g} 0.1 + \sum_{s \in S}^{g} st(S)$ used to calculate the cost of an episode (path s initial state to the goal state g) based on the current policy;
- a optimal policy (Q*) estimated with a supervisor algorithm (A*);

Algorithm 3. Update_policy.

Algorithm update_policy (Q*, Q$_i$, π)	
01	**Foreach** state $s \in$ S **do:**
02	**If** cost(Q$_i$,s) $\leq$ cost(Q*,s) **do**
03	$\pi \leftarrow \hat{Q}_i(s,a)$;
04	**Endif**
05	**Endfor**
06	**Return** (π)

Figure 1 shows the activity diagram that uses the Algorithms 1–3.

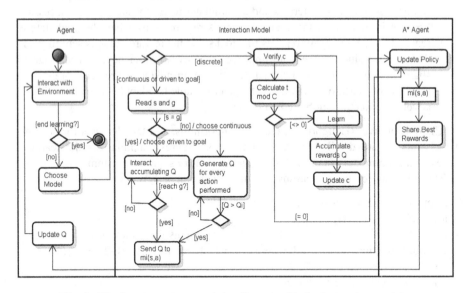

Fig. 1. The learning process activity diagram with the interaction models.

3   Integrated Interaction Model

In RL based on shared rewards, it is common to discover intermediate action policies that do not help to achieve a certain goal. In fact, knowledge exchange among agents may lead to intermediate action plans that do not immediately help agents converge. As each agent constantly updates its own learning, all agents must be aware of all updates taking place and of each agent's rewards.

Using the previously presented approaches for agent coordination based on shared rewards, there is no guarantee that the action plans will converge. While policies with initially mistaken states and values are improved by rewards shared by other intermediate policies, improving the π^+ function, the opposite is also possible, i.e., initially interesting policies with high rewards may become less attractive during execution of a given policy.

In order to overcome this inconvenience (local maximum), we integrated interaction models for multi-agent coordination, combining features of the discrete, continuous and objective-driven models previously presented. By analyzing the results obtained using these models, we found that the behavior of π^+ changes as a function of the number of interactions of the algorithms, the number of episodes involved in the problem and the cardinality of the set of agents used. This can be seen in Fig. 2, which shows the results of coordination models in a 400-state environment with 5 and 10 agents.

The proposed model captures the best features from each individual interaction model at every interaction in the coordination process. New action policies are

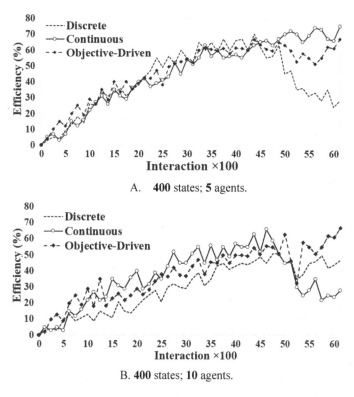

A. **400** states; **5** agents.

B. **400** states; **10** agents.

Fig. 2. Coordination models [8].

discovered without delaying the learning process, reducing the probability of conflicts between actions from different policies.

Technically, the model can be summarized as follows: at every interaction in the Q-learning process, the agent's performance is obtained from each interaction model. This is used to build a *learning table*, here referred to as IM-π^+ (Integrated Model). When the model update condition is reached, the agent starts its learning process using the best performance calculated from the learning tables in the interaction models. The learning is then transferred to IM-π^+, which will therefore always contain the best rewards from the discrete, continuous and objective-driven models.

Algorithm 4 shows how the discrete, continuous and objective-driven interaction models are integrated. For every learning iteration, the agent's performance is compared with the interaction models used. When a given model returns a superior performance, this learning is transferred to IM-π^+, which represents the current action policy of the integrated model.

In the next section, a simulation environment for assessing the efficiency of the proposed model is presented.

Algorithm 4. Combined model integration.

```
Algorithm Combined model integration
(s,a): model state/action;
Q_M_D: discrete model learning table;
Q_M_C: continuous model learning table;
Q_M_O: objective model learning table;
01    for each instance of (s,a) do
02        IM-π⁺ ← max(Q_M_D, Q_M_C, Q_M_O);
03    end for;
04    return IM-π⁺
```

4 Experimental Results

To evaluate the proposed approach we used a simulation environment composed of a state-space representing a traffic structure through which agents (drivers) try to find a route in an empirical scenario with a grid-world structure. The structure has an initial state s_{init}, an objective state g and a set of actions $A = \{\uparrow$ *(forward)*, $\rightarrow$ *(right)*, $\downarrow$ *(back)*, $\leftarrow$ *(left)*$\}$. A state s is a pair (X,Y), which defines the position on the X and Y axes, respectively. A status function $st: S \rightarrow ST$ maps traffic situations (rewards) to states, such that $ST = \{-0.2$ *(free route)*; -0.3 *(low congestion)*; -0.4 *(high congestion or unknown)*; -0.5 *(very high congestion)*; -1.0 *(blocked)*; 1.0 $(g)\}$.

Agents simulate routes that are available for drivers, and the global goal is to produce an action policy (a combination that maps states and actions) that can determine the best route connecting s_{init} to g. The global action policy is defined by determining step by step which action $a \in A$ should be performed at each state $s \in S$. After an agent's move (transition/interaction) from a state s to a state s', it knows whether or not the action was positive, as it recognizes the set of rewards shared by the other models. The reward for a given transition $T^a_{s,s'}$ is denoted by $st(s')$.

The results described in this section allow the performance of the proposed model and those of the discrete, continuous and objective-driven interaction models to be compared. The parameters used in the integrated model are the same as those used for the individual models: $y = 0.95$, $\alpha = 0.3$ and $\varepsilon = 0.9$.

To evaluate the performance of the model, we used different arbitrarily generated scenarios (Fig. 3) in an attempt to reproduce situations that resembled real-world situations as closely as possible. The agents are randomly positioned in the state-space. When an agent reaches the goal state, it is randomly positioned in another state s until the stopping criterion (a maximum number of interactions) is satisfied.

Learning with the algorithm was repeated twenty times for each scenario since it was found that doing experiments in one environment alone using the same inputs could lead to a variation in the results computed by the algorithm as agent actions are probabilistic and the values generated during learning are stochastic variables. The action policy determined by an agent can therefore vary from one experiment to another. The efficiency reported in this section is the mean of all the experiments in

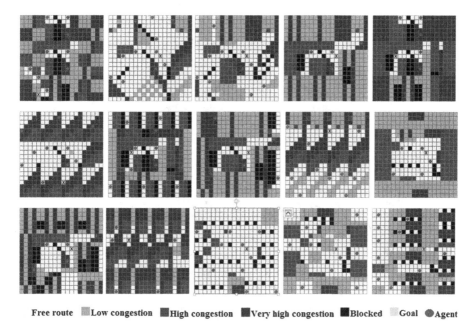

Free route ▨Low congestion ■High congestion ■Very high congestion ■Blocked ▢Goal ●Agent

Fig. 3. Samples of simulated scenarios (Download simulator: http://paginapessoal.utfpr.edu.br/ marceloteixeira/downloads-1/list-of-available-downloads/QLearning.zip). The agents have a visual field depth of 1 in the grid world.

each scenario. Twenty replications were sufficient to evaluate the algorithm's efficiency as the quality of the policies did not change significantly (see Table 1).

Although the problem simulated here could be deemed somewhat simplistic, it should be remembered that a total of s states can generate a large solution space, in which the number of possible policies is $|A\|^s|$. The results shown below provide a comparison of the proposed model and the other methods using 3, 5 and 10 agents in an environment composed of 100, 256 and 400 states. The efficiency of the models (the Y axis in the graphs) is based on the number of correct hits by an agent during each interaction. A correct hit occurs when the agent finds the goal-state with its costs optimized using the evaluation methodology for RL algorithms introduced in [10].

Figures 3, 4 and 5 show that the integrated model was more efficient than the other models individually. In general, it was superior in any interaction phase and substantially reduced the number of interactions needed to find an appropriate action policy.

Table 1. Variation in the results computed by the algorithm (standard deviation).

Grid world	Number of agents		
	3	5	10
(10 × 10)	±1.9%	±2.8%	±5.2%
(16 × 16)	±2.8%	±3.9%	±5.8%
(20 × 20)	±3.9%	±4.4%	±6.5%

118   R. Ribeiro et al.

Table 2. Overall comparative analysis.

State-space	Number of agents		
	3	5	10
100	18.5%	27.1%	36.9%
256	19.4%	24.9%	32.6%
400	15.2%	25.3%	34.2%

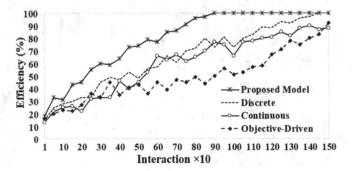

Fig. 4. 100 states and 10 agents.

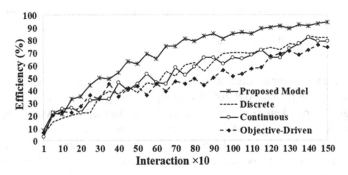

Fig. 5. 256 states and 10 agents.

Thus, with the proposed model, the agent's learning is smoother and converges more rapidly to a satisfactory action policy (Figs. 4, 5).

For experiments in environments with 100 states (see Table 3), the number of interactions was reduced on average by 22.8% when 3 agents were used; by 26.7% with 5 agents; and by 35.1% with 10 agents. For environments with 256 states, the corresponding figures were 21.1%, 21.9% and 32.7%, while for environments with 400 states, they were 17.4%, 22.9% and 29.1%. Table 2 shows the improvement in efficiency achieved with the integrated model using the most efficient of the three individual models (the continuous model) as reference.

The overall improvement achieved with the integrated model when the different numbers of agents and state-spaces tested were taken into account was of the order of 27.8%.

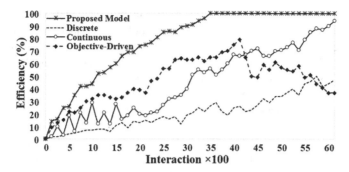

Fig. 6. 400 states and 10 agents.

Table 3. Comparison of number of interactions according to the number of agents.

State-space	Reduction in number of interactions according to the number of agents			
	Reference*	3 *vs* Reference	5 *vs* Reference	10 *vs* Reference
100	1000	22.8%	26.7%	35.1%
256	1500	21.1%	21.9%	32.7%
400	5000	17.4%	22.9%	29.1%

*The reference value corresponds to the result when the continuous interaction model is used.

5   Discussions: Real-World Applications

Case 1: The model proposed in this paper has been tested in scenarios in which it was possible to control all the environmental variables. In many real-world problems, you cannot always control the factors that affect the system, such as external variables to the environment. With the promising results of the model presented in this article, we started to adapt this model to a real case to support the daily decisions of the poultry farmer. In this problem, the agent of the system is used to generate action policies, in order to control the set of factors in the daily activities, such as food-meat conversion, amount of food to be consumed, rest time, weight gain, comfort temperature, water and energy to be consumed, etc. The main role of the agent is to perform a set of actions to consider aspects such as productivity and profitability without compromising bird welfare. Initial results show that, for the decision-taking process in poultry farming, our model is sound, advantageous and can substantially improve the agent actions in comparison with equivalent decision when taken by a human specialist. In the moment, we are evaluating the performance of the agent when handling specific management situations; checking the performance of the algorithm to process variations of scenario; and changing the set of attributes used to generate the rules, which can make them less susceptible to influence. Such statements are objects of study for future research.

Case 2: We also intend to adapt the model for use in optimization problems associated with smart–grids, paying particular attention to problems in which failure recovery is essential to restore service in distributed electrical power systems. Systems that can recover from failures independently are known as self-healing systems. An alternative for a self-healing system to emerge is to adapt Reinforcement Learning methods as a way of maximizing the system's objective functions. We found that the model described in this paper can be used as a tool to aid system recovery by helping to reconfigure the devices used to prevent and allow power flow in a network (distribution systems) as a way of ensuring satisfactory power distribution and optimizing loss parameters, maintenance etc. Furthermore, coordination of reward-based agents can be improved and scalability problems reduced, allowing combinatorial optimization problems typically found in power distribution systems to be solved.

6 Conclusions

This paper proposes an integrated model that improves coordination in Multi-Agent Systems by combining features from existing interaction models. The method accelerates convergence of agents' action policies by the order of 27.8% and overcomes important drawbacks observed in earlier approaches [8].

The proposed approach aims to improve the way agents share information with each other. In order to transmit and receive information, agents share a cooperative, coordinated interaction model that generally leads to improved action policies. The kernel for establishing optimized information-sharing strategies for multiple agents is therefore the interaction model.

The performance gains for agents that cooperate using the proposed integrated model stem from the fact that $IM\text{-}\pi^+$ is generated from learning values discovered in a collaborative way. This interaction between agents can result in more efficient policies, leading the agents to optimal solutions. Another benefit is the substantial reduction in the number of interactions needed to generate action plans. Nevertheless, it should be noted that the number of messages exchanged between agents increases exponentially with the number of agents and the size of the state-space. This is an important issue and will be investigated in future studies.

Acknowledgment. This research was supported by the Araucária Foundation and the National Council for Scientific and Technological Development (CNPq) under grant numbers 378/2014 and 484859/2013-7, respectively.

References

1. Chakraborty, D., Stone, P.: Multiagent learning in the presence of memory-bounded agents. Auton. Agent. Multi-Agent Syst. **28**(2), 182–213 (2014)
2. Chapelle, J., Simonin, O., Ferber, J.: How situated agents can learn to cooperate by monitoring their neighbors' satisfaction. ECAI **2**, 68–78 (2002)

3. DeLoach, S.A., Valenzuela, J.L.: An agent-environment interaction model. In: Padgham, L., Zambonelli, F. (eds.) AOSE 2006. LNCS, vol. 4405, pp. 1–18. Springer, Heidelberg (2007). doi:10.1007/978-3-540-70945-9_1

4. Devlin, S., Yliniemi, L., Kudenko, D., Tumer, K.: Potential-based difference rewards for multiagent reinforcement learning. In: Proceedings of the 2014 International Conference on Autonomous Agents and Multi-agent Systems, AAMAS 2014, Richland, SC, pp. 165–172 (2014)

5. Efthymiadis, K., Kudenko, D.: Knowledge revision for reinforcement learning with abstract MDPs. In: Proceedings of the 2015 International Conference on Autonomous Agents and Multiagent Systems, AAMAS 2015, Richland, SC, pp. 763–770 (2015)

6. Grzes, M., Hoey, J.: Efficient planning in R-max. In: The 10th International Conference on Autonomous Agents and Multiagent Systems, AAMAS 2011, Richland, vol. 3, pp. 963–970 (2011)

7. Kaelbling, L.P., Littman, M.L., Moore, A.P.: Reinforcement learning: a survey. J. Artif. Intell. Res. **4**, 237–285 (1996)

8. Ribeiro, R., Borges, A.P., Enembreck, F.: Interaction models for multiagent reinforcement learning. In: 2008 International Conference on Computational Intelligence for Modelling Control Automation, pp. 464–469 (2008)

9. Ribeiro, R., Enembreck, F.: A sociologically inspired heuristic for optimization algorithms: a case study on ant systems. Expert Syst. Appl. **40**(5), 1814–1826 (2013)

10. Ribeiro, R., Enembreck, F., Koerich, A.L.: A hybrid learning strategy for discovery of policies of action. In: Sichman, J.S., Coelho, H., Rezende, S.O. (eds.) IBERAMIA/SBIA - 2006. LNCS, vol. 4140, pp. 268–277. Springer, Heidelberg (2006). doi:10.1007/1187 4850_31

11. Ribeiro, R., Ronszcka, A.F., Barbosa, M.A.C., Enembreck, F.: Updating strategies of policies for coordinating agent swarm in dynamic environments. In: Hammoudi, S., Maciaszek, L.A., Cordeiro, J., Dietz, J.L.G. (eds.) ICEIS, vol. 1, pp. 345–356 (2013)

12. Saito, M., Kobayashi, I.: A study on efficient transfer learning for reinforcement learning using sparse coding. Autom. Control Eng. **4**(4), 324–330 (2016)

13. Stone, P., Veloso, M.: Multiagent systems: a survey from a machine learning perspective. Auton. Robots **8**(3), 345–383 (2000)

14. Sutton, R.S., Barto, A.G.: Reinforcement Learning: An Introduction. MIT Press, Cambridge (1998)

15. Tesauro, G.: Temporal difference learning and TD-Gammon. Commun. ACM **38**(3), 58–68 (1995)

16. Walsh, T.J., Goschin, S., Littman, M.L.: Integrating sample-based planning and model-based reinforcement learning. In: Fox, M., Poole, D. (eds.) AAAI. AAAI Press (2010)

17. Watkins, C.J.C.H., Dayan, P.: Q-learning. Mach. Learn. **8**(3), 272–292 (1992)

18. Xinhai, X., Lunhui, X.: Traffic signal control agent interaction model based on game theory and reinforcement learning. In: International Forum on Computer Science Technology and Applications, IFCSTA 2009, vol. 1, pp. 164–168 (2009)

19. Xuan, P., Lesser, V.: Multi-agent policies: from centralized ones to decentralized ones. In: Proceedings of the 1st International Joint Conference on Autonomous Agents and Multiagent Systems, Part 3, pp. 1098–1105 (2002)

20. Zhang, C., Lesser, V.: Multi-agent learning with policy prediction. In: Proceedings of the 24th AAAI Conference on Artificial Intelligence, Atlanta, pp. 927–934 (2010)

21. Zhang, C., Lesser, V.: Coordinating multi-agent reinforcement learning with limited communication. In: Ito, J., Gini, S. (eds.) Proceedings of the 12th International Conference on Autonomous Agents and Multiagent Systems, pp. 1101–1108 (2013)

Development of Escape Route System for Emergency Evacuation Management Based on Computer Simulation

Denis Shikhalev[1]([⊠]), Renat Khabibulin[1], Ulrich Kemloh[2], and Sergey Gudin[1]

[1] The State Fire Academy of EMERCOM of Russia,
B. Galushkina str. 4, 129366 Moscow, Russia
evacsystem@gmail.com
[2] Jülich Supercomputing Center, Forschungszentrum Jülich GmbH,
Wilhelm-Johnen-Straße, 52428 Jülich, Germany

Abstract. In this article we propose a safest path route choice algorithm which determines the safest path directions for pedestrians in case of fire. We also propose an escape route system for emergency evacuation management. The model and the algorithms are implemented in an open source framework (JuPedSim) which is a research platform to simulate pedestrian dynamics. The proposed algorithm allows the even distribution of the evacuees to all available emergency exits. We simulate the evacuation of a shopping centre and show that the application of the algorithm can reduce the total evacuation time up to 63% depending on the settings of the algorithm. Based on those results we elaborate an escape route system for emergency evacuation. The system includes three modules and can be operated in several modes. The designed system allow not only significantly to reduce the evacuation time but also to ensure people's safety during evacuation.

Keywords: Pedestrians dynamics · Evacuation strategies · Safest evacuation routes · Escape route system · Computer simulation

1 Introduction

In the last few decades, large fires in shopping malls were the reason of many people's death. A few of them are listed below:

- December 25, 2000. A fire occurred in a central shopping Centre (Luoyang, China). The fire killed 309 people;
- August 01, 2004. A fire occurred in a supermarket (Asunción, Paraguay). The fire killed 464 people;
- May 28, 2012. A fire occurred in a Villagio Mall (Doha, Qatar). The fire killed 19 people, including 13 children.

One of distinguishing features of shopping malls is the uneven distribution of people in the building. It can influence the evacuation process and lead to an unbalanced use of emergency and exits routes. Studies shows that a significant number of

© Springer International Publishing AG 2017
S. Hammoudi et al. (Eds.): ICEIS 2016, LNBIP 291, pp. 122–139, 2017.
DOI: 10.1007/978-3-319-62386-3_6

people are usually gathered in supermarkets and shops of home appliances compared to other shops of a shopping mall.

An analysis of some existing escapes route systems from different countries [1] showed that only a third of the systems were able to determine the direction of the escape routes using a scientifically founded method. The studies of many authors [2–5] indicate the following problems in the area of evacuation management in shopping malls:

- Uneven distribution of people inside shopping malls;
- Management problems in the evacuation process, done by the staff of shopping malls;
- Lack of information about possible (available) evacuation directions.

Therefore, the lack of both models and algorithms of information and analytical support for evacuation management lead to the fact that a decision maker cannot objectively evaluate the whole range of hazards and determine the safest routes for people during an emergency evacuation. To solve these problems, a mathematical model of a safest path route algorithm was developed. The algorithm is used to calculate the safest path for people in a danger zone, and to direct them to a safer area [6]. In a first estimation the model showed a positive impact on the evacuation time and overall on the people's safety during evacuation simulations [6]. Nevertheless, it is needed to complete a full estimation of all features of the model as well as determine the best combination of models parameters for evacuation simulations.

In this paper we consider the results of evacuation simulations using the algorithm. Simulations were performed using the Jülich Pedestrian Simulator, JuPedSim [7] with various numbers of people and different objects. The results of simulations are used while a decision support system for emergency evacuation is being developed.

This work is structured as follow:

In the second section we introduce the model and the algorithm. In the third section, we present computer simulations and analyses. The development of the decision support system for emergency evacuation is shown in the fourth section. Some concluding remarks and directions of future work are given in the last section.

2 Description of the Safest Path Route Algorithm

The safest path route algorithm is applied for calculation of the safest path for people from different points of a building to the exterior of the building. Originally the safest path route algorithm was created for a shopping mall. The main tasks of the algorithm are to calculate a safest route and direct people to a goal (current or newly defined). The algorithm of Floyd-Warschall [8] was applied for calculating the safest path to the nearest gate. In its normal application the Floyd-Warschall's algorithm finds the shortest path between all pairs of edges in a graph. A physical distance is used as the weight of the edges. For our task, we used a complex criterion φ as the weight of the edges. φ is calculated using Eq. 1:

$$\varphi = \sqrt{\alpha \cdot (a_i)^2 + \beta \cdot (b_i)^2 + \gamma \cdot (l_i)^2} \qquad (1)$$

at:

$a \to$ min, i = 1,...,n
$b \to$ min, i = 1,...,n
$l \to$ min, i = 1,...,n

where:

a – an obstruction criterion;
b – a timeliness criterion;
l – a length criterion.
α, β, γ – the weight coefficient at a, b, l.

The obstruction criterion is determined by the ratio of the people's density on a section of the escape route network, to the maximum people's density that does not cause adverse effects to humans. The timeliness criterion is directly linked to fire hazards (high temperature, a large amount of smoke, low visibility, toxic products of combustion etc.). The length criterion is the relative length of the current section. It is calculated as the ratio of current escape route length, to the maximal escape route length in a building. The coefficients (α, β, γ) are added to regulate the importance of the individual criteria. More details about the criterions and manners of its computing are found in previous work [6].

Under sections of escape route, we consider the crossing of two (or more) escape routes in the corridors of a shopping mall. Hence a section of an escape route corresponds to an edge in the graph of a shopping mall, and the crossing place of two (or more) escape routes corresponds to a vertex.

We used the JuPedSim simulator for computer implementation of the algorithm. The Generalized Centrifugal Force Model (GCFM) is applied into the simulator to simulate an evacuation process [9]. GCFM belongs to the class of forces based models [10] and describes the movement of people at the operational level [11] i.e. defines basic rules for the pedestrians such as acceleration, braking and stop. Motion of the pedestrians is determined by a so-called "social power" [10]. The calibration of the basic parameters of GCFM (attractive and repulsive forces, the size of the semi-axes of the ellipse depending on the density and velocity of the people flow etc.) were performed in [12, 13]. Verification and validation of the GCFM, as well as a more detailed description is given in [9, 14, 15].

At each step of the simulation, the evacuees are guided with the shortest path, to the nearest emergency exit in the building i.e. a shortest path route algorithm (*ShPA*) is used to determine the shortest escape route (Fig. 1).

However, there is a need to change the *ShPA* with regards to the problem of determining the safest evacuation routes. For this purpose, a safest path route algorithm (*SaPA*) was developed (Fig. 2).

An update frequency (*UF*) was added into the *SaPA* for the possibility of regulating how often the algorithm will be refreshed. Thus, a *UF* value of 5 means that the safest

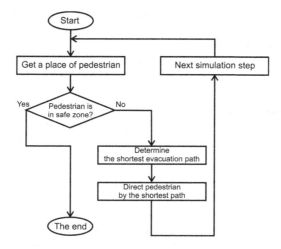

Fig. 1. The shortest path route algorithm (*ShPA*).

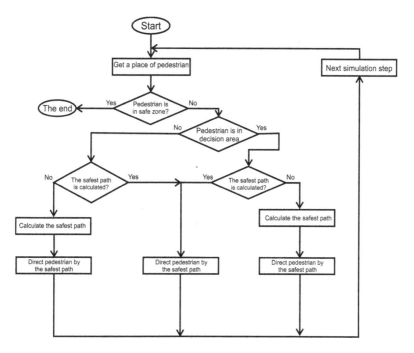

Fig. 2. The safest path route algorithm (SaPA).

path will be calculated once for every 5 s and the direction of movement will also be updated (in the decision areas) every 5 s.

The shortest path is given for all evacuees in an initial stage (pre-evacuation). Then the safest path is computed for each node (decision area) according to the *UF*. In other words, the decision area is a place where two or more routes crossed. It is possible from this place (decision area), to direct the pedestrians by a new path, for example, by using a dynamic indicator [16]. If a current path is not a safest path anymore, a re-routing will happen in the decision area. The safest path route algorithm was implemented into JuPedSim as a separate module and it can be chosen from other routing algorithms such as a quickest or shortest path algorithms.

The main purpose of simulation is to evaluate the effectiveness of the safest path route algorithm. This evaluation is done by comparing the performance of the shortest path route algorithm and the safest path route algorithm. Thus, the following research problems should be solved during simulation:

- How are the a-criteria and b-criteria changed in the process of evacuation and under what values does the process of re-routing happens?
- Which are the effects of re-routing pedestrians?
- How do weight coefficients affect the course of the evacuation process?
- How does the update frequency affect the course of the evacuation process?
- When is it advisable to apply the safest path route algorithm?

To answer these questions, it is necessary to conduct a preliminary assessment of the adequacy of the developed algorithm. From there, we perform a computer simulation of the evacuation process on the topology of an existing shopping mall, as an example.

3   Simulation and Analysis

In this section we provide simulation results and its analysis.

3.1   Preliminary Assessment

Several simulations at the T-junction of escape routes (Fig. 3) were carried out within a preliminary assessment of the *SaPA* as well as on the abstract model of the building (Fig. 4).

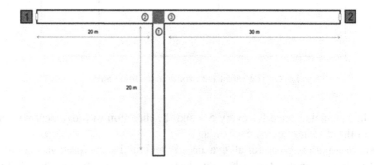

Fig. 3. Objects of simulation within a preliminary assessment – T-junction.

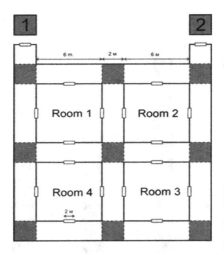

Fig. 4. Objects of simulation within a preliminary assessment – abstract model of the building.

Simulation results at the T-junction identified one of the features of the *SaPA*: the safest path route algorithm behaves as the shortest path route algorithm when there are no congestions or high-density of pedestrians.

It was also found that the usage of weight coefficients has an impact on the time of re-routing during evacuation. Weight coefficients (0,9-0,1) lead to the re-routing that occurs both with few and many pedestrians. In addition, weight coefficients of 0,6-0-0,4 allow to re-route flows when we have a high number of pedestrians. Moreover, re-routing occurs only at the maximum configured number of people in simulation (250 per., 6.25 pers./m^2 in a case when the weights are not applied).

Re-routing moments and duration of re-routing become longer when the value of a-criterion is increased.

The results obtained in the T-junction simulations led us to several conclusions:

- The safest path route algorithm behaves as the shortest path route algorithm in the case where there are no congestions or high-density of pedestrians;
- The application of weight coefficients influences the course of the evacuation process where the escape routes sections are of different geometrical size.
- In order to achieve the minimal evacuation time and prevent pedestrians' congestions, it is necessary to increase the importance of the a-criteria. Reducing the importance of a-criteria leads to an increase in evacuation time;
- It is possible to control a moment of re-routing of evacuation flows by applying different weight coefficients.

After simulations at the T-junction we continue in the abstract model (Fig. 4). Simulation results in the abstract model allow us to formulate the following facts.

Firstly, for uneven distribution of people during evacuation, the *SaPA* can immediately distribute pedestrians evenly to the emergency exits. This in turn significantly affects the evacuations time. Efficiency of the *SaPA* (Fig. 5) reduces when there is an uneven distribution of people. Efficiency is the ratio of evacuation time with the *SaPA* to evacuation time with the *ShPA*.

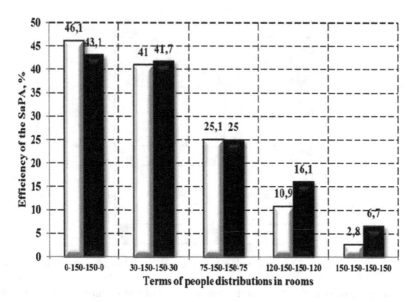

Fig. 5. Efficiency distribution of the *SaPA* depending on terms of people distributions. (0-150-150-0 value corresponds to the people distribution in rooms 1, 2, 3 and 4, respectively (Fig. 4)). White - scenario 1, black - scenario 2.

Secondly, there is a negative efficiency of the *SaPA* at 4%. This happened in the case where we had an uneven distribution of a small number of people (up to 50 people). Having reviewed the evacuation process in decision area, a reason of the negative efficiency of the *SaPA* was found. This is due to the update frequency of the *SaPA* which was equal to 1. There were many re-routing of pedestrians while they followed the decision areas (geometric size of decision area is 2 m by 2 m). Pedestrians were sometimes directed to different exits. This in turn, had to slow down the speed of pedestrians and as a result, increase the evacuation time.

Thus, an optimal value of the update frequency should be investigated and determined. The simulation results in the abstract model led us to conclude these facts:

- Weight coefficients do not play any role when there are two identical routes (by both geometric characteristics and number) from the decision area to the exit;
- The *SaPA* update frequency of 1 has a negative impact on evacuation process given a small number of pedestrians;
- The *SaPA* directs pedestrians by routes which are not using during evacuation but are available.

3.2 Simulation of a Shopping Mall

After preliminary assessment we performed simulations in a shopping mall. The plan is shown in Fig. 6. The color represents the decision areas. Some geometric characteristics of the evacuation exits and evacuation route sections in the front of evacuation exits are shown in Table 1.

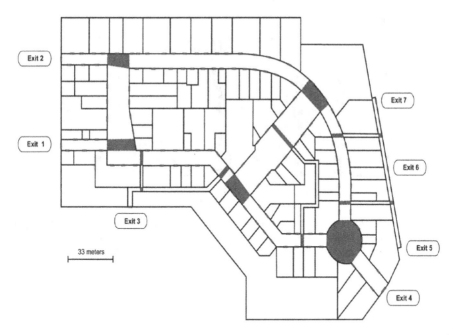

Fig. 6. Layout of shopping mall.

The number of people in evacuation simulation was chosen in the rate of 1 person per 1 m^2 of retail premises (the total number of evacuees is 2609). The influence of the update frequency on the evacuation process was considered in the first series of simulation. The simulation results are shown in Fig. 7.

Analysis of Fig. 7 shows that for many people, the closest emergency exit is №7, but based on its geometrical characteristics, it is not preferable because of its small width (See Table 1). However, most of the pedestrians were distributed between exits 1, 2, 4 which are preferable due to their geometrical dimensions (exit width).

Table 1. Geometric characteristics of the evacuation exits.

№	Parameter	Evacuation exit						
		1	2	3	4	5	6	7
1	Width, m	3,0	3,0	1,5	4,0	2,0	2,0	2,0
2	Width of evacuation route section in the front of evacuation exit, m	6,4	6,4	2,0	10,1	2,2	2,2	2,2

It is more clearly shown in Figs. 8 and 9. Almost all pedestrians were evacuated by using the *SaPA* after 300 s (Fig. 8). At the same time there are people's jams when using the *ShPA* (Fig. 9).

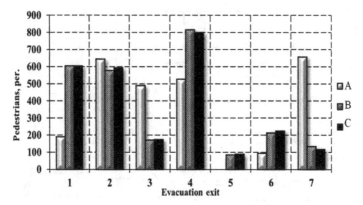

Fig. 7. People distribution to emergency exits. A - *ShPA*; B - *SaPA* with update frequency equal 5 (result of minimal evacuation time); C - *SaPA* with update frequency equal 13 (result of maximal evacuation time).

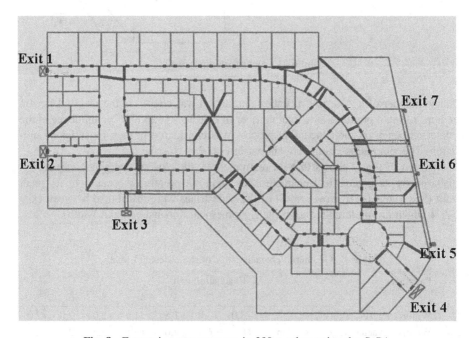

Fig. 8. Evacuation process stage in 300 s. when using the *SaPA*.

Thus, the direction of all pedestrians to the shortest emergency exits is not always justified and often leads to a significant increase of total evacuation time. Application of the *SaPA* allows to reduce evacuation time up to 63% depending on the update frequency of the algorithm.

The assessment of the update frequency of the algorithm showed that the preferred frequency is 5. That is why the frequency used for further studies will be 5. The

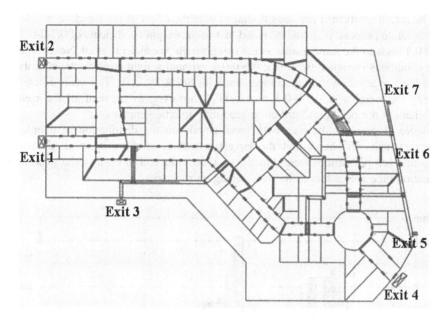

Fig. 9. Evacuation process stage in 300 s. when *ShPA* is used.

simulation results in the *T*-junction suggest that using different weight coefficients can reduce the evacuation time. An analysis of the effect of weight coefficients on the pedestrian's distribution to emergency exits was conducted in the next stage of the simulation. The results are shown in Fig. 10.

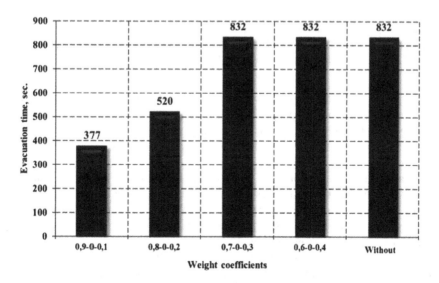

Fig. 10. Weight coefficients vs. evacuation time.

The results confirmed previous findings about the effect of the weight coefficients on evacuation process. It should be noted that using weight coefficients of 0.7-0-0.3 or 0,6-0-0,4 leads to the same results as not using weight coefficients at all. Nevertheless, these conditions (weights: 0,7-0-0,3; 0,6-0-0,4; without weight coefficients) contribute to reducing evacuation time in comparison with *ShPA* by 21%. The main difference between the weights of 0,7-0-0,3 or 0,6-0-0,4, however, as between all the weight coefficients is the people's distribution according to emergency exits.

Figure 11 presents the data with more details on the distribution of people to emergency exits. It shows that the largest reduction of the evacuation time was achieved when pedestrians were directed to wider exits and in contrast the maximum evacuation time was achieved by overloading narrow exits.

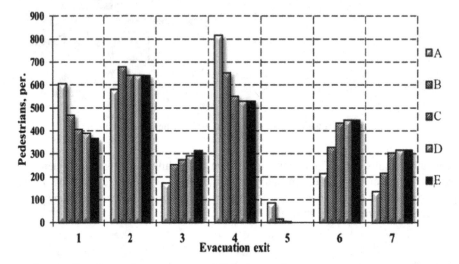

Fig. 11. The pedestrian distribution to emergency exits depending on the weights. A - weight coefficients are 0,9-0-0,1. B - weight coefficients are 0,8-0-0,2. C - weight coefficients are 0,7-0-0,3. D - weight coefficients are 0,6-0-0,4. E - without weight coefficients.

It was also interesting to consider the fairly frequent assertion of researchers in the field of human behavior, that people in case of a fire will follow the escape routes they used to get into the building [3–5]. It is likely that visitors enter a building on the gate leading from the metro stations, parking places, etc. Corresponding exits are 1, 2 and 4 in Fig. 6.

To carry out the simulation exits (3, 5, 6 and 7) are blocked, because it is unlikely that they can be used by most pedestrians entering the building. Different cases were simulated and investigated particularly when all of the exits (1, 2 and 4) are opened and then when one of the exits is blocked. The simulation results for different positions of the emergency exits are shown in Fig. 12.

The simulation results show that the direction of all pedestrians through the main evacuation exits can significantly reduce the evacuation time. For the last part of the simulation we elaborated four evacuation strategies:

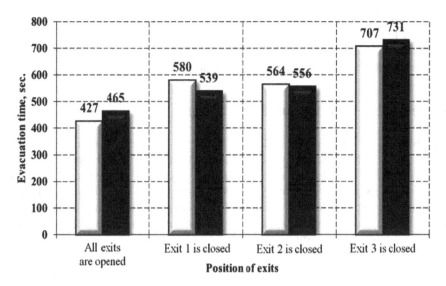

Fig. 12. Dependence of the evacuation time to an algorithm (*SaPA* vs. *ShPA*). White – *SaPA*. Black – *ShPA*.

- Strategy 1. Applying the *SaPA* with weight coefficients equal 0,9-0-0,1 provided that all exits are opened;
- Strategy 2. Applying the *SaPA* with weight coefficients equal 0,9-0-0,1 provided that only the main exits are opened;
- Strategy 3. Applying the *ShPA* provided that all exits are opened;
- Strategy 4. Applying the *ShPA* provided that only the main exits are opened.

Figure 13 shows the simulation results with the aforementioned strategies. Minimal evacuation time was achieved when the strategy 1 was chosen. The SaPA is still preferable than the ShPA only if main emergency exits are available. However, for

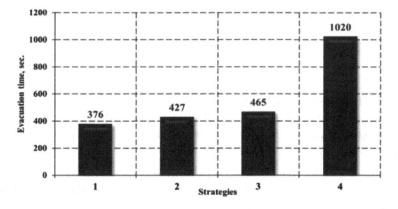

Fig. 13. Ratio of evacuation time to an evacuation strategy.

cases where the only possibility is to direct people through the shortest path, it is necessary to use strategy 4.

Obtained results shown an effectiveness of proposed algorithm. However an experimental assessment is required for its application in a real evacuation process.

4 Development of Escape Route System

The need for the development of Escape Route System for Emergency Evacuation Management (ERS) is defined by the several reasons. First of all, existing escape route systems are more oriented on voice alarm than evacuation management. Secondly, decision makers cannot objectively evaluate evolving situation during emergency evacuation in case of a fire due to a deficit of information (about the course of evacuation, people distribution in building, fire spreads etc.) and physiological features (including stress, time pressure).

4.1 Aim, Task and Structure

The aim of *ERS* is to ensure people's safety during emergency evacuation in case of a fire. To reach this aim, at least, implementation the following tasks are required:

- Definition of all available safest evacuation routes:
    - getting necessary information for calculating;
    - safest routes calculation in a building;
- Indication of the safest routs to all participants (staff and evacuees):
    - positioning of dynamic indicator in a safe direction;
    - update a safe direction when a newly safest route is identified;
- Evacuation process control:
    - evacuation process and fire spreading control by special devices;
    - take a decision if necessary.

A structure of the escape route system is based on the tasks assigned to it. The structure is presented in Fig. 14.

The diagram shows the basic modules of escape route system. The modules are discussed below.

Computing Module. This module is designed for calculation the safest evacuation routes. The *SaPA* has been developed [6] for this task. This model allows the assessment of the safety path evacuation of people in case of fire, and in real time to evenly distribute the flow of evacuation in a safe direction to evacuation exits. This model was presented in Sect. 2. Results of evaluation have shown that the use of the proposed algorithm can reduce the evacuation time up to 63% depending on the chosen frequency of the algorithm. The calculated routes are transferred to a management module.

Management Module. The objective of the module is to inform pedestrians and staff about the safe directions and direct to it. Analysis of existing dynamic indicators has

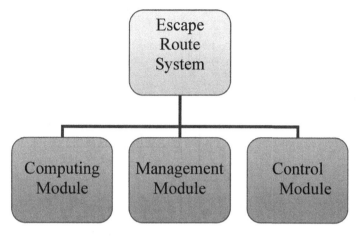

Fig. 14. Structure of escape route system.

showed its shortcomings [1]. A dynamic indicator was developed based on conducted analysis. The dynamic indicator allows updating a safe direction in real time based on information from computing module. A patent for utility model was received on the dynamic indicator. This way, the dynamic indicator can be used in the management module.

Control Module. Nowadays widely spread means of control are video cameras which are mainly intended for the control of public order. Assuming the video cameras as a means of control of evacuation process, the prerequisite is the installation of video cameras in each section of an escape route, which carried out the computation of the parameters in the mathematical model. Applying the video cameras, decision maker would always have information on emerging situations which could happen on escape routes. Decision makers can immediately "block" a section of escape route in the case of some critical situations that can be seen with video cameras. It will lead to re-routing of pedestrians flows and consequently avoid such place.

4.2   Functions and Algorithms

A functional process of *ERS* was elaborated according to the aim and the tasks of this system. The process is shown in Fig. 15.

The *ERS* is in constant contact with the external environment (fire detectors, CCTV etc.) through communication channels and permanently update information. The *ERS* begin to perform its functions in case of a fire and the beginning of an evacuation process. An algorithm of interaction between decision-makers and *ERS* is shown in Fig. 16.

The information about the location of the fire and about people's distribution inside of building are entered to the computing module in case of a failure of one or more fire detectors. The computing module calculates the complex criterion φ and defined safe escape routes from each room in the building to outside based on *SaPA*.

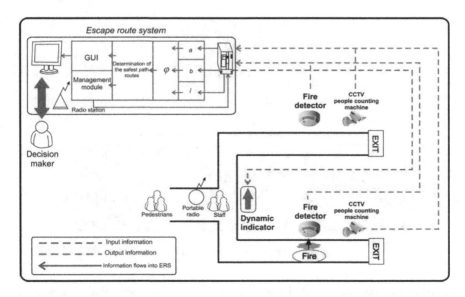

Fig. 15. Functional process of escape route system operations.

Information about safe escape routes is displayed on the decision makers PC and also supplied to the management module which switches each dynamic indicator to point to the safest direction.

Information is also transmitted to the staffs (on radio channels) who are involved in the evacuation. The information transmission process is represented in Fig. 17. Operation of the system is carried out till the end of the evacuation process and information about the features of the evacuation process is transmitted to a remote source. This information can later be used for assessment of staff and evacuees actions and for studies.

The designed system can be operated in several modes: daily activities mode (for getting information about the parameters of pedestrians in the building etc.) and emergency mode (for emergency evacuation management as well as for direct fire-fighter brigade to a fire place and/or to a place where pedestrians are blocked). The *ERS* can also be used for people's training for action during evacuation process.

The possibilities of decision maker are expanding with a such a system. The information load is also greatly reduced when making decisions during the evacuation process.

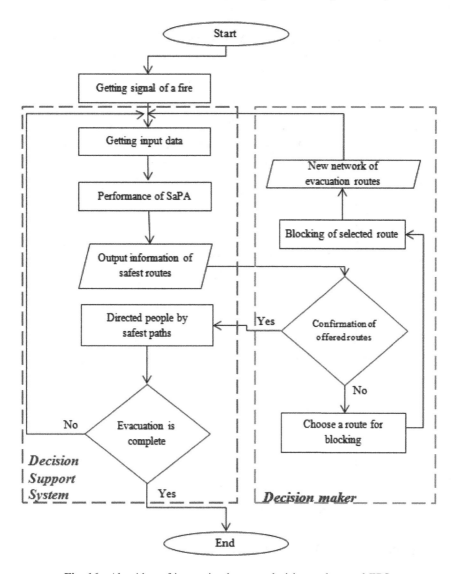

Fig. 16. Algorithm of interaction between decision-makers and ERS.

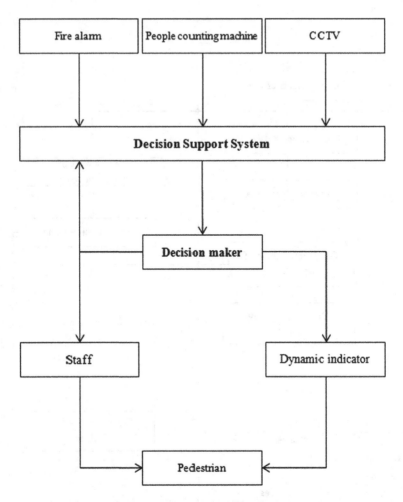

Fig. 17. Information transmission process.

5 Conclusions and Future Work

In this paper we presented the results of full assessment of the safest path route algorithm in the framework of evacuation simulations. It was found that the weights of 0,9-0-0,1 should be applied to prevent congestions during evacuations, when the density is high. For the algorithm, an update frequency of 5 should be chosen to timely direct the pedestrians to safe evacuation paths. The algorithm is suitable for cases when there are no widely dispersed emergency exits, uneven distribution of evacuation flows to the exits as well as to prevent congestions of high density during the evacuation.

In this contribution we designed an escape route system which will allow not only significantly to reduce the evacuation time but also to ensure people's safety during evacuation. It should be noted that the developed system can be used as a source of relevant information about the patterns and characteristics of people's movement. The results show the effectiveness of the proposed algorithm. However an experimental assessment is required for its application in a real evacuation process. The following phenomena should be investigated within the frame of an experimental assessment:

- people's reaction to dynamic indicators;
- do pedestrians follow the routes which would be offered;
- how staff responsible for evacuation organization will operate with dynamic indicators.

References

1. Shikhalev, D., Khabibulin, R.: Escape route systems at shopping malls. Fire Explos. Saf. J. **22**, 61–65 (2013)
2. Carattin, E.: Wayfinding architectural criteria for the design of complex environments in emergency scenarios. In: Advanced Research Workshop Proceedings, pp. 209–222. Universitad de Cantabria, Spain (2011)
3. Kobes, M., Helsloot, I., Vriesc, B., Posta, J.: Building safety and human behavior in fire: a literature review. Fire Saf. J. **45**, 1–11 (2010)
4. Samochine, D.A.: Towards an understanding of the concept of occupancy in relation to staff behaviour in fire emergency evacuation of retail store. Ph.D. thesis. University of Ulster, Belfast (1995)
5. Sandberg, A.: Unannounced evacuation of large retail-stores. An evaluation of human behavior and the computer model Simulex. Technical report, Lund University (1997)
6. Shikhalev, D., Khabibulin, R., Kemloh U.: Development of a safest path algorithm for evacuation simulation in case of fire. In: Proceedings of IV International Conferences on Agents and Artificial Intelligence, pp. 685–690 (2014)
7. Kemloh Wagoum, A.U., Chraibi, M., Zhang, J.: JuPedSim: an open framework for simulating and analyzing the dynamics of pedestrians. In: 3rd Conference of Transportation Research Group of India (2015)
8. Floyd, R.: Algorithm 97: shortest path. Commun. ACM **5**, 345 (1962)
9. Chraibi, M., Seyfrid, A., Schadschneider, A.: Generalized centrifugal force model for pedestrian dynamics. Phys. Rev. E **82**, 046111 (2010)
10. Helbing, D., Molnar, P.: Social force model for pedestrian dynamics. Phys. Rev. E **51**, 4282–4286 (1995)
11. Hoogendorn, S.P., Bovy, P., Daamen, W.: Microscopic pedestrian wayfinding and dynamics modelling. In: Pedestrian and Evacuation Dynamics, pp. 123–154 (2002)
12. Burghardt, S.: Analyse und vergleichende Untersuchung zum Fundamentaldiagramm a Treppen. Masterthesis. Bergische Universität Wuppertal (2009)
13. Meunders, A.: Kalibrierung eines Mikroskopischen Models für Personenströme zur Anwendung im Project Hermes. Masterthesis. Bergische Universität Wuppertal, Wuppertal (2011)
14. Chraibi, M.: Validated force-based modeling of pedestrian dynamics. Ph.D. thesis. Forschungszentrum Jülich, Jülich (2012)
15. Kemloh, U.: Route choice modeling and runtime optimization for simulation of building evacuation. Ph.D. thesis. Forschungszentrum Jülich, Jülich (2013)
16. Shikhalev, D., Khabibulin R.: Patent (in Russia) on December 27, 2013 № 136212 «Dynamic indicator» (2013)

Event Monitoring System to Classify Unexpected Events for Production Planning

Andrés Boza$^{(\boxtimes)}$, Faustino Alarcón, M.M.E. Alemany,
and Llanos Cuenca

Research Centre on Production Management and Engineering (CIGIP),
Universitat Politècnica de València, Valencia, Spain
{aboza,faualva,mareva,llcuenca}@cigip.upv.es

Abstract. Production planning prepares companies to a future production scenario. The decision process followed to obtain the production plan considers real data and estimated data of this future scenario. However, these plans can be affected by unexpected events that alter the planned scenario and in consequence, the production planning. This is especially critical when the production planning is ongoing. Thus providing information about these events can be critical to reconsider the production planning. We herein propose an event monitoring system to identify events and to classify them into different impact levels. The information obtained from this system helps to build a risk matrix, which determines the significance of the risk from the impact level and the likelihood. A prototype has been built following this proposal.

Keywords: Production planning · Event management · Decision making · Information system

1 Introduction

The production planning is one of the key functions in a company. Planning deals with finding plans to achieve some goal [1] and production planning is a partial planning approach for a particular function of a company [2]. Production planning also usually covers the allocation of activities to factory departments, which is a typical scheduling task. Production planning uses information to generate processing routes and to find what raw material should be ordered and when [1]. The production planning basically involves finding the most efficient way to use production resources in order to fulfill the demand requirements with regard to quality, quantity and delivery date.

Once production-planning decisions have been made and planning is ongoing, unexpected events can appear. Any cause (e.g. machine breakdowns or changes in firm orders) that endangers current production plan validity could lead to re-generating the entire plan [3]. However, making a new plan can be complex and time consuming when there is a lot of information to use (big bill of materials or a great variety of products). But, the main difficulty is to adapt the ongoing production plans, which produces that often no changes are made [4]. The conception and implementation of appropriate information and communication systems is a basic condition for identifying critical incidents [5]. In this sense, Sacala et al. [6] indicate that data collected from sensors must trigger a chain of events leading to changes within enterprise business process, collaboration mechanism or organizational framework. Such changes can be achieved in terms of simple sense-act enterprise behaviour (direct link between sense and act) or more complex sense-plan- act approach (decision level). Hence the first objective of an event monitoring system is to sense production information about a real-time environment and to detect events.

Enterprises normally use tools that provide them with information to make decisions. According to [7], Decision Support Systems (DSSs) are designed to use decision makers' own insights and judgments in an *ad hoc*, interactive analytical modeling process, which leads to a specific decision. So an event monitoring and management system should interact with DSSs to manage events that might affect previously made decisions. It should act as a supra-system that gather the necessary information to identify when previous decisions are still valid or need to be reanalyzed. Thus traditional DSS configuration should be extended to treat event management by a monitoring and management system, which monitors internal and external information [8]. This event information can also be represented in the form of rules, such as IF–THEN. These rules include events (or signals) that can alter the plans (IF…) and also the warning signal in each case (…THEN…). For example, IF a priority and very important customer order comes AND the production planning is just launched THEN a warning signal must be trigged, which may advise re-planning. This set of rules represents an expert system: it contains information obtained from a human expert, which is represented in form of rules [9].

According to the ISO/Guide 73:2009 [10], risk is the combination of the probability of an event and its consequences when exploiting any vulnerability. So, once events are identified, the associated risks can also be estimated. We propose herein a monitoring software application, based on rules, that detects unexpected events in production planning and identify risks produced by these events. In order to explain our purpose in this paper: Sect. 2 reviews problems in production planning in the literature; Sect. 3 deals with event management; Sect. 4 defines expert decision support system based on the literature; Sect. 5 explains our proposal to monitor and classify events; Sect. 6 offers a prototype of this proposal; Sect. 7 present the conclusions drawn from this approach.

2 Incidences in Production Planning

The occurrence of certain unexpected events or incidences, for example, a broken machine or a huge order may invalidate the ongoing production plan. In the literature, authors have dealt with these problems in different ways. Chan et al. [11] indicate that frequent changes in the current schedule may lead to disturbances in production, and may result in lateness orders or increased production costs. Weinstein and Chung [12] explain that when production equipment displays signs of failure, or they occur after, this may adversely affect both production plan integrity and product quality. Poon et al. [13] explain that in the actual manufacturing environment, shop floor managers face numerous unpredictable risks in day-to-day operations, such as defects in supplies of components or raw materials, or errors, failures and wastage in various production processes. Baron and Paté-Cornell [14] indicate that during the manufacturing process, unexpected interruptions appear, which could be accidents, machine breakdowns or human errors. In a cookie factory case, Van Wezel et al. [4] study planning flexibility and classify events according to their source: (a) Customer (e.g. rush order, change in order volume, or earlier/later delivery date); (b) Product (e.g. raw material out of stock, too little or too much stock of end product(s), or product sent back); (c) Process (e.g. setup/cleaning time variation, more/less waste, or higher/lower production speed; (d) Machines/staff (e.g. long disruptions, shortage or surplus capacity, or variation in run-in times). All these planning problems need to be managed and it is necessary to decide how to deal with these events. The objective is to minimize the impact caused in the whole company.

A proper management of these problems requires an identification and enumeration of them, including a study of where, how and when can appear. Furthermore, their detection is a very important task. If the detection of the event is slow, the troubles will be bigger. In this sense, new technologies based on the Industry 4.0 concept like Internet of Things can help in this purpose. Once an event occurs in a company, event information is stored in the system and analysis information is delivered. With this information, decision-makers decide what action must to take to solve the problem A quicker identification of relevant events is necessary to make a quicker analysis of their consequences. SAP [15] highlights how value diminishes as time elapses between when data is first captured and when an action or decision is triggered. Of course, this analysis must include not only a short-term point of view, but also the consequences for the ongoing production planning.

3 Event Management

Shamsuzzoha et al. [5] state that an event can be defined as an incident or occurrence that might evolve from either internal or external sources of operations within the network. An event can be identified assessing if a deviation of the current status as compared the planned one exists. Events should be viewed on a real-time basis. For achieving this, automated event-detection systems are usually necessary. But an event monitoring is more than an event-detection system. Boza et al. [8] indicate that an event monitoring system is a part of an event management system. Event management provides systems with a proactive response to business events, anticipating and planning solutions before damage is produced.

The literature includes various authors who deal with event management not only for a company but also for business networks, such as Virtual Organizations [16] or Collaborative Networks [17]. Baron and Paré-Cornell [14] provide an analytical and dynamic link between the Risk Management System and the long-term productivity and safety performance of the physical system. Barash et al. [18] propose a decision support tool for the business impact analysis and improvement of the incident management process in IT support organization. Bartolini et al. [19] present an approach to assess and improve the performance of an IT support organization in managing service incidents based on the definition of a set of performance metrics and a methodology. This guided analysis allows users to find the root causes of poor performance and to decide about the corrective actions to be taken. Liu et al. [20] develop an approach for modeling event relationships in a supply chain through Petri nets as a formalism for managing events. Söderholm [21] aims to outline different categories of unexpected events that appear in projects as a result of environmental impacts and how these are dealt with. Bearzotti et al. [22] present an agent-based approach for the Supply Chain Event Management problem, which can perform autonomous corrective control actions to minimize the effect of deviations in the plan currently underway.

The impact of an event can be positive or negative, representing the last one a risk. Events implying some risks are priority to be notified with the aim of their properly management assessment and response. The urgency of an event conditions the event notification process. This aspect leads to the necessity of classifying events in order to manage the unexpected events. Distinct classifications based on different criteria can be found in the literature: according to its impact [23], according to its supporting [24] and according to specific groups given by the company [20, 21]. Only one of these research made a monitoring system to detect events [22]. But all these approaches require an expert engineer to define the rules.

A very accepted classification of events is according to their impact in the organization on a scale from 1 to 5, where 1 represents the least level and 5 the strongest [5]. Knowing the severity of the event, risk can be identified by the occurrence likelihood of this event. Thus a risk matrix can be used to classify events. This matrix has several categories, "probability," "likelihood" or "frequency", for its columns and several categories, "severity," "impact" or "consequences", for its rows. It associates a recommended level of risk, urgency, priority or management action with each row-column pair; that is, with each cell [25].

These risk matrices have been widely praised and adopted as simple effective approaches to risk management. According to Cox [25], their main advantages are that they provide: (1) a clear framework for the systematic review of individual risks and portfolios of risks; (2) convenient documentation for the rationale of risk rankings and priority setting; (3) relatively simple inputs and outputs, often with attractively colored grids; (4) opportunities for many stakeholders to participate in customizing category definitions and action levels; (5) opportunities for consultants to train different parts of organizations on "risk culture" concepts at different levels of detail. So the risk matrix is an appropriate tool to classify events.

4   Expert Decision Support System

DSSs are normally used as a tool to make decisions when faced with certain problems. They are defined as computer systems that deal with a problem where at least some stage is semi-structured or unstructured. A computer system can be developed to deal with the structured portion of a DSS problem, but decision makers' judgment must consider the unstructured part, to hence constitute a human-machine problem-solving system [26]. The primary purpose of DSSs is to help decision-makers develop an understanding of the ill-structured complex environment represented by the model [27].

When an organization has a complex decision to make or a problem to solve, it often turns to expert for advice. The experts it selects have specific knowledge about and experience in the problem area. Expert systems attempt to mimic human experts' problem-solving abilities [28]. Turban and Watkins [29] described the Expert System like a computer program, which includes a knowledge base that contains an expert's knowledge for a particular problem domain, and a reasoning mechanism for propagating inferences on the knowledge base. The benefits generated by expert systems include [30]: (1) less dependence on key personal; (2) facilitating staff training; (3) improving the quality and efficiency of decision making; (4) transferring the ability of making decisions. Integrating an Expert System into DSSs helps obtain more benefits. These benefits can be used in several dimensions [29]: Expert Systems contribution, DSS contribution, and the synergy resulting from the DSS/ES combination.

5 Proposal of an Event Monitoring System to Classify Unexpected Events for Production Planning

Given the advantages of the Expert DSS presented in the previous section, we propose an Event Monitoring System (EMS) based on an Expert DSS, which identifies and classifies events (CE) that have an impact on ongoing production planning and interact with the DSS used in production planning (PP) systems, dubbed as EMS-CE-PP. Expert knowledge is necessary to identify and classify potential events by their impact level. Depending on its likelihood and impact level, the system indicates the seriousness of the event in the previously shown standard risk matrix. This likelihood can be estimated by the system, counting the number of times that an event appears.

The proposed expert DSS does not use an Expert System like an intelligent program, which automatically makes a decision, but uses it like a support system for decision makers.

5.1   Event Monitoring System (EMS) Framework

Some enterprises generate their production planning with DSSs that use mathematical models (Model-Driven DSS). The decisions made with these Model-Driven DSSs can be affected by different events. A significant set of events to be identified includes those that affect the planning generated by these Model-Driven DSSs. The mathematical models used in these DSSs are written in modeling languages, such as Modeling Programming Language (MPL). So it is possible to extract parameters and decision variables from these models that can be affected by events. The parameters and decision variables form a set of attributes of the models.

This is the starting point for our proposal, where an expert in production planning systems selects the set of attributes that require a control. These attributes will be used to make rules. A rule is a condition defined by the decision maker to identify the events: if this condition goes into effect, an event alert appears. These rules are made by the expert, a person with high knowledge about event detection in production. This expert is usually the decision maker.

The objective of these rules is to identify changes in the production system to reconsider the current production planning generated by the DSSs between each re-planning period. The current information about the production systems can be significantly different from the previous information used by the DSSs when the current planning was generated. Ultimately, the objective is to know if the ongoing production planning is still valid or it is necessary a new production planning before its term.

This proposal extends the DSS proposed by Boza et al. [31, 32], which includes three phases: (1) model and attributes selection: experts select decision models and the attributes (of these models) that can be affected by events; (2) criteria creation and visualization: experts create alert criteria about previously selected attributes; (3) execution: validation of the alert criteria conditions executed manually or automatically. Our proposal herein extends the previous proposal to include the event classification and risk identification based on the risk matrix. This information allows the decision-maker reconsider the current production planning. The following paragraphs review these phases and detail our proposal.

5.2   Model and Attributes Selection

An expert in production planning systems selects the mathematical models used in the planning production decision system to analyze the alert criteria on them. After selecting the models, experts can identify the model's parameters and decision variables to create the alert criteria to identify events. These selected attributes must have impact into the production planning and its variation can produce a modification in the production decisions. For example: variation in demand or machine setup times.

5.3   Criteria Creation and Visualization

Alert criteria can be defined according to the selected attributes and a classification of the events can be made. We propose using five impact levels for each criterion: Extremely Serious Level, Serious Level, Substantial Level, Moderate Level and Low Level. Each level is achieved according to a logical operation formed by constants, attributes and functions. Alerts are triggered when a true value appears in these logical operations. Constants are values that are introduced directly by the expert; attributes are the previously selected parameters and decision variables; functions are operations formed by attributes and constants, such as addition, averages, etc.

Enterprise information is dynamic, so any unexpected development of an attribute should be analyzed. In order to consider this development in the alert criteria, it is necessary the *current* and/or *previous* values for each attribute in the alert criteria; i.e., attributes values are taken from the current production system state and/or from the previous state (when the production planning was made). Thus, decision makers introduce rules (using logical conditions) to identify events. Table 1 shows combinations in these logical conditions (A -logical condition- B).

Alert criteria can also be defined for *particular* objects (e.g. the demand limit value of a specific product), or from a *general* perspective, (e.g. the demand limit value of all the products).

Table 1. Possible combinations of logical operation to criteria creation.

A	Logical condition	B
Current attribute value		Previous attribute value
Current or previous attribute value		Constant value
Current or previous attribute value		Function result
Function result		Constant value
Function 1 result		Function 2 result

5.4 Execution

After creating the alert criteria, decision makers can use the Event Monitoring Systems to evaluate the situation with these criteria. This evaluation can be made automatically (e.g. by time intervals: hourly, daily or weekly) or manually. During these evaluations, the EMS-CE-PP checks the criteria (using the rules previously introduced) with the enterprise information, and as a result, events can be detected and decisions makers are alerted.

5.5 Event Impact Classification

Decision makers obtain new information after each execution. This information shows detected events related with each criterion and the impact level that produces that event. Also, the information about the number of occurrences of the event is stored to have historical information in order to obtain the likelihood and calculate the risk.

The impact of the event had been indicated previously by the expert and the likelihood is estimated by the system with the information of previous executions. This information allows decision makers to identify the impact of the event in order to evaluate the situation, try to solve the problem and, if necessary, change the ongoing production planning, and to obtain information about the event risks.

5.6 EMS-CE-PP Main Components Relationships

This section shows the main components and their relationships included in this proposal

An UML use case diagram identifies the interactions between an actor (role) and a system. In this case, a use case diagram has been included to show the relationship between the users (Expert and Production Planning Decision Maker) and the expected functionalities (Fig. 1).

Furthermore, Figs. 2 and 3 present the previous and the proposal situation. Figure 2 shows the initial situation where DSSs are used to make production planning decisions. Figure 3 displays the main components included in the event monitoring system framework proposed.

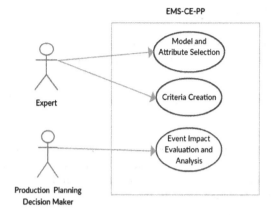

Fig. 1. EMS-CE-PP use case diagram.

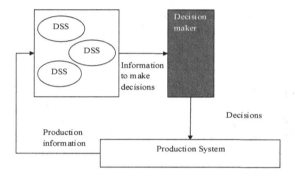

Fig. 2. DSSs used to make production planning (initial situation).

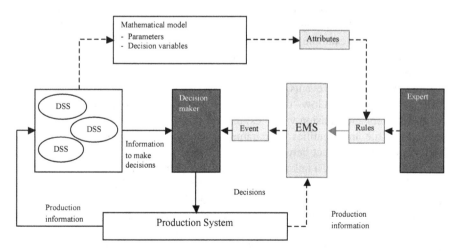

Fig. 3. The event monitoring system framework.

6   EMS-CE-PP Prototype

An Event Monitoring System prototype to Classify Events to reconsider the Production Planning was developed using Java libraries. The main elements used in the application were:

- Mathematical models used for the DSS to propose the production planning. The mathematical models have been defined in Mathematical Modeling Language (MPL).
- Databases with information about production. These databases include information about the current situation of the production system and the previous information of the production system when the DSS proposed the production planning.
- An internal database which includes the knowledge database.

The internal database has four main tables: *attributes* table to save the attributes of the model selected by the user; a *criteria* table, which stores the criteria created by decision makers; an *execution criteria* table, which saves information on execution (if execution is automatic or manually, interval time, etc.). Once execution has been run, the results are saved in the *results* table, which saves the information on each alert criterion (attributes values, event significance, event frequency, etc.).

6.1   Model and Attributes Selection

The scenario for this prototype is a company that generate its production planning with Model-Driven DSSs that use MPL (Mathematical Programming Language). MPL is an advanced modelling system that allows the model developer to formulate complicated optimization models in a clear, concise and efficient way. Models developed in MPL can then be solved with any of the multiple commercial optimizers available on the market today. MPL includes an algebraic modelling language that allows the model developer to create optimization models using algebraic equations [33]. Due to the fact that MPL is an structured language, it can be read easily for information systems. The Fig. 4 shows a basic example of an MPL file.

Every company can use its own set of MPL files, so it is possible to extract parameters and decision variables used in these models, and then, identifying those which can be affected by events.

The EMS prototype allows the user to select MPL files in order to load the attributes (parameters and decision variables) used in this model. Thus, the EMS prototype read the MPL file and identifies the parameters and decision variables included in the model. An expert can select between these attributes, which will be used to create the alert criteria. Furthermore, a link must be created between the attribute and the database (table and column) that contain their values. Figure 5 shows and example of selection of attributes, in this case, the attributes of "product" are showed.

The criteria creation form includes name, criteria operands, the logic operation to be performed with these operands, the impact level and a description. Also, some attribute characteristics need to be identified: (1) the attributes data in the criteria can be obtained

```
{   Planning.mpl   }

{   Aggregate production planning for 12 months   }


TITLE
    Production_Planning;

INDEX
    product = 1..3;
    month   = (January,February,March,April,May,June,July,
               August,September,October,November,December);

DATA
    price[product]                :=  (105.09, 234.00, 800.00);
    Demand[month,product]         :=  1000 DATAFILE(demand.dat);
    ProductionCapacity[product]   :=  1000 (10, 42, 14);
    ProductionCost[product]       :=  (64.30, 188.10, 653.20);
    InventoryCost                 :=  8.8 ;

DECISION VARIABLES
    Inventory[product,month]      ->   Invt
    Production[product,month]     ->   Prod
    Sales[product,month]          ->   Sale

MACRO
    Revenues  := SUM(product,month: price * Sales);
    TotalCost := SUM(product,month: InventoryCost * Inventory
                                  + ProductionCost * Production);
MODEL

    MAX    Profit = Revenues - TotalCost ;

SUBJECT TO
    InventoryBalance[product,month]  ->  IBal :
    Inventory = Inventory[month-1] + Production - Sales ;

BOUNDS
    Sales  < ProductionCapacity ; Inventory[month="January..November]" < 90000 ;
    Inventory[month="December]" ; END
```

Fig. 4. Basic example of MPL file [33].

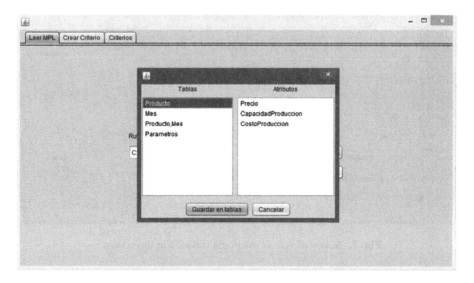

Fig. 5. Example of attribute selection.

from *current* values or *previous* values; (2) the alert criteria is general or for a particular object (Fig. 6). This information is stored in the internal database with the set of criteria to be checked (Fig. 7).

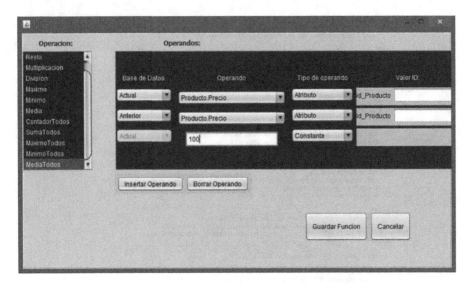

Fig. 6. Selection of the criteria operands.

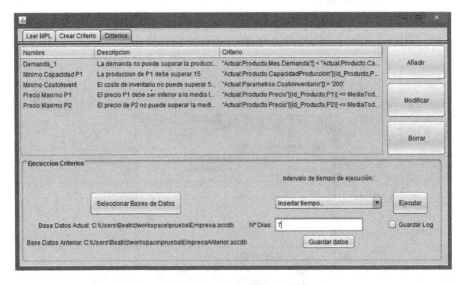

Fig. 7. Screen of the set of criteria included in the system.

6.2   Execution

Periodical or manual monitoring can be made using the EMS-CE-PP prototype. The event monitoring system obtains information from the production databases in order to evaluate the criterion previously defined. This evaluation of each criterion allows identifying the impact levels for each criterion: Extremely Serious Level, Serious

Level, Substantial Level, Moderate Level and Low Level. If an alarm appears in several levels for the same criterion, it is stored the most serious level (Fig. 8).

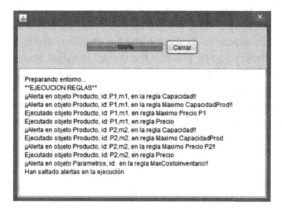

Fig. 8. Example of execution.

6.3 Event Impact Classification

The information is presented like a criterion list. A warning icon appears and indicates that an alarm occurs in this criterion. Production information is shown in white, yellow or red according to the impact level. This information can be evaluated for the decision-makers to reconsider the validity of the current production planning (Fig. 9).

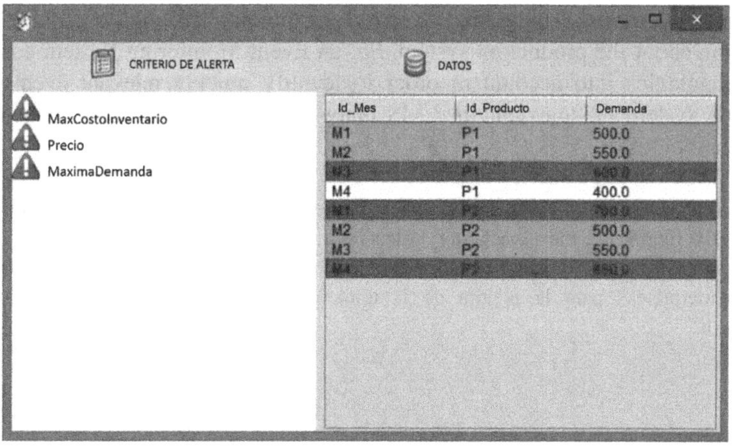

Fig. 9. Example of event impact classification. (Color figure online)

7 Conclusions

Production planning prepares the production area of the company for a future production scenario. This complex decision-making process requires an important volume of data and they can change when the production planning has been launched. Thus, unexpected events can appear while these plans are ongoing, which could have a major or minor impact on these ongoing plans. If the impact is major, it can force a change to be made in the established planning.

This research proposes an Event Monitoring Software Application based on an expert system to identify the events and to classify them according to their impact level on production planning. Experts with high knowledge about production planning can create production system alert criteria. In this way, decision makers can monitor these events and check if there are any unexpected events that impact in the ongoing production planning.

This proposal presents some advantages: (i) own creation of impact criteria (rules) according to each production system to classify events; (ii) connection with the DSS models used in the production planning and the production information system; (iii), information to alert decision makers to decide whether to change production plans or not.

An Event Monitoring System prototype to Classify Events and reconsider the Production Planning has been presented. The scenario for this prototype is a company that generate its production planning with Model-Driven DSSs that use MPL (Mathematical Programming Language).

A line for future research is to evaluate the economic impact of the events. A cost/benefits analysis could provide further information to the decision makers. Another area for future research is to identify the hierarchical decision levels in production planning and define different sets of criteria at each planning system level. Lastly, new Internet of Things and Sensor Technologies are able to provide further information about the production system. So, an Event Monitoring System could take these technologies into account in order to identify quickly relevant events in the Production System and to extend the EMS analysis with new information gathered with these technologies.

Acknowledgements. This research has been carried out in the framework of the project GV/2014/010 funded by the Generalitat Valenciana (Identificación de la información proporcionada por los nuevos sistemas de detección accesibles mediante internet en el ámbito de las "sensing enterprises" para la mejora de la toma de decisiones en la planificación de la producción).

References

1. Barták, R.: On the boundary of planning and scheduling: a study (1999)
2. Buzacott, J.A., Corsten, H., Gössinger, R., Schneider, H.M.: Production Planning and Control: Basics and Concepts. Oldenbourg Wissenschaftsverlag, München (2012)

3. Özdamar, L., Bozyel, M.A., Birbil, S.I.: A hierarchical decision support system for production planning (with case study). Eur. J. Oper. Res. **104**(3), 403–422 (1998)

4. Van Wezel, W., Van Donk, D.P., Gaalman, G.: The planning flexibility bottleneck in food processing industries. J. Oper. Manag. **24**(3), 287–300 (2006)

5. Shamsuzzoha, A.H., Rintala, S., Cunha, P.F., Ferreira, P.S., Kankaanpää, T., Maia Carneiro, L.: Event monitoring and management process in a non-hierarchical business network. In: Intelligent Non-hierarchical Manufacturing Networks, pp. 349–374. Wiley, Hoboken (2013)

6. Sacala, I.S., Moisescu, M.A., Repta, D.: Towards the development of the future internet based enterprise in the context of cyber-physical systems. In: 19th International Conference on Control Systems and Computer Science, CSCS 2013, pp. 405–412 (2013)

7. Chen, K.C.: Decision support system for tourism development: system dynamics approach. J. Comput. Inf. Syst. **45**(1), 104–112 (2004)

8. Boza, A., Alemany, M.M.E., Vicens, E., Cuenca, L.: Event management in decision-making processes with decision support systems. In: 5th International Conference on Computers Communications and Control (2014)

9. Liao, S.-H.: Expert system methodologies and applications–a decade review from 1995 to 2004. Expert Syst. Appl. **28**(1), 93–103 (2005)

10. ISO: 73: 2009: Risk management vocabulary. International Organization for Standardization (2009)

11. Chan, F.T.S., Au, K.C., Chan, P.L.Y.: A decision support system for production scheduling in an ion plating cell. Expert Syst. Appl. **30**(4), 727–738 (2006)

12. Weinstein, L., Chung, C.-H.: Integrating maintenance and production decisions in a hierarchical production planning environment. Comput. Oper. Res. **26**(10–11), 1059–1074 (1999)

13. Poon, T.C., Choy, K.L., Chan, F.T.S., Lau, H.C.W.: A real-time production operations decision support system for solving stochastic production material demand problems. Expert Syst. Appl. **38**(5), 4829–4838 (2011)

14. Baron, M.M., Pate-Cornell, M.E.: Designing risk-management strategies for critical engineering systems. IEEE Trans. Eng. Manag. **46**(1), 87–100 (1999)

15. SAP AG: SAP AG 2014. Next-Generation Business and the Internet of Things. Studio SAP | 27484enUS (14/03) (2014)

16. Carneiro, L.M., Cunha, P., Ferreira, P.S., Shamsuzzoha, A.: Conceptual framework for non-hierarchical business networks for complex products design and manufacturing. Procedia CIRP **7**, 61–66 (2013)

17. Vargas, A., Cuenca, L., Boza, A., Sacala, I., Moisescu, M.: Towards the development of the framework for inter sensing enterprise architecture. J. Intell. Manuf. **26**, 55–72 (2016)

18. Barash, G., Bartolini, C., Wu, L.: Measuring and improving the performance of an IT support organization in managing service incidents, pp. 11–18 (2007)

19. Bartolini, C., Stefanelli, C., Tortonesi, M.: SYMIAN: analysis and performance improvement of the IT incident management process. IEEE Trans. Netw. Serv. Manag. **7**(3), 132–144 (2010)

20. Liu, R., Kumar, A., van der Aalst, W.: A formal modeling approach for supply chain event management. Decis. Support Syst. **43**(3), 761–778 (2007)

21. Söderholm, A.: Project management of unexpected events. Int. J. Proj. Manag. **26**(1), 80–86 (2008)

22. Bearzotti, L.A., Salomone, E., Chiotti, O.J.: An autonomous multi-agent approach to supply chain event management. Int. J. Prod. Econ. **135**(1), 468–478 (2012)

23. Baron, M.M., Pate-Cornell, M.E.: Designing risk-management strategies for critical engineering systems. IEEE Trans. Eng. Manag. **46**(1), 87–100 (1999)

24. Bartolini, C., Stefanelli, C., Tortonesi, M.: SYMIAN: analysis and performance improvement of the IT incident management process. IEEE Trans. Netw. Serv. Manag. **7**(3), 132–144 (2010)
25. Cox Jr., L.A.: What's wrong with risk matrices? Risk Anal. Int. J. **28**(2), 497–512 (2008)
26. Shim, J.P., Warkentin, M., Courtney, J.F., Power, D.J., Sharda, R., Carlsson, C.: Past, present, and future of decision support technology. Decis. Support Syst. **33**(2), 111–126 (2002)
27. Steiger, D.M.: Enhancing user understanding in a decision support system: a theoretical basis and framework (2015). http://dx.doi.org/10.1080/07421222.1998.11518214
28. Turban, E., Aronson, J., Liang, T.-P.: Decision Support Systems and Intelligent Systems, 7th edn. Pearson Prentice Hall, Upper Saddle River (2005)
29. Turban, E., Watkins, P.R.: Integrating expert systems and decision support systems, **10**, 121–136 (1986)
30. Cohen, D., Asín, E.: Sistemas de información para los negocios: un enfoque de toma de decisiones. McGraw-Hill, New York City (2001)
31. Boza, A., Cortés, B., Alemany, M.M.E., Vicens, E.: Event monitoring software application for production planning systems. In: Cortés, P., Maeso-González, E., Escudero-Santana, A. (eds.) Enhancing Synergies in a Collaborative Environment. Springer, Heidelberg (2015). doi:10.1007/978-3-319-14078-0_14
32. Boza, A., Alarcón, F., Alemany, M.M.E., Cuenca, L.: Event classification system to reconsider the production planning. In: Proceedings of the 18th International Conference on Enterprise Information Systems, pp. 82–88 (2016)
33. Maximal Software: What is MPL? (2016). http://www.maximalsoftware.com/mpl/what.html

Router Nodes Placement Using Artificial Immune Systems for Wireless Sensor Industrial Networks

Pedro Henrique Gouvêa Coelho[(⊠)], Jorge Luís Machado do Amaral,
José Franco Machado do Amaral, Luciane Fernanda de Arruda Barreira,
and Adriano Valladão Barros

State University of Rio de Janeiro, FEN/DETEL, Rua São Francisco Xavier, 524,
Sala 5001E, Maracanã, Rio de Janeiro, RJ 20550-900, Brazil
{phcoelho,jamaral,franco}@uerj.br,
lucianebarreira@yahoo.com.br,
adriano_vbarros@yahoo.com.br

Abstract. The present work is concerned with the placement of router nodes in industrial environments for wireless sensor networks applications making use of artificial immune systems ideas. The motivation for using artificial immune systems lies on the properties of uniqueness, distributed sensing, learning and memory efficiency of such systems enabling the transmission of data from sensors to the gateway efficiently. As a matter of fact, that efficiency deals with a low rate of failure and other aspects such as minimizing retransmission issues done by the routers. The chosen criteria to be met are embedded in the so called affinity function which acts as an objective function. The router nodes positioning are accomplished in two modules which uses the immune systems concepts and related ideas. Different scenarios are considered for the presented examples based on oil and gas configurations and for criteria defined in the affinity function.

Keywords: Artificial immune systems · Node placement · Wireless sensor networks

1 Introduction

The advances in wireless networking technology offer a great opportunity for wireless connectivity of field devices both in oil and gas and other chemical processing plants. The requirements of a field network include real-time support for mixed traffic, availability, security, reliability and scalability in a harsh industrial environment. These conditions have to be fulfilled by any wireless network in order to operate. Safety, reliability, availability, robustness and performance are of paramount importance in the area of industrial automation. The network cannot be sensitive to interference nor stop operation because of an equipment failure, nor can have high latency in data transmission and ensure that information is not misplaced [1–3].

Wireless Sensor Networks are technically a challenging system, requiring expertise from several different areas. Thus, the information concerning important design criteria

© Springer International Publishing AG 2017
S. Hammoudi et al. (Eds.): ICEIS 2016, LNBIP 291, pp. 155–172, 2017.
DOI: 10.1007/978-3-319-62386-3_8

is often scattered. Additionally, characteristics for the industrial automation applications are usually stricter than the other domains, since the failure of the communication system may lead to loss of production or even lives.

Main advantages of wireless technology are reduced installation time of devices, no need of cabling structure, cost saving projects, infrastructure savings, device configuration flexibility, cost savings in installation, flexibility in changing the existing architectures, possibility of installing sensors in hard-to-access locations and others. Amongst the various challenges which are associated with the use of wireless communication, data security and interference are the most important issues. Data security issues are related to the use of wireless for transportation of vital process information and that requires the incorporation of data encryption and advanced security measures. As far as interference aspects are concerned, the use of license free radio channel for communication is susceptible to interference from other nearby sources operating in the same band. If the ISM for Industrial, Scientific and Medical band is to be used for communication, then it requires network coordinator to continuously assess the channel status to ensure reliable communications. Moreover, in industrial automation environment, data transmission in a wireless network may face interference generated by other electrical equipment, such as walkie-talkies, other wireless communication networks and electrical equipment, moving obstacles (trucks, cranes, etc.) and fixed ones (buildings, pipelines, tanks, etc.). In an attempt to minimize these effects, frequency scattering techniques and mesh or tree topologies are used, in which a message can be transmitted from one node to another with the aid of other nodes, which act as intermediate routers, directing messages to other nodes until it reaches its final destination. This allows the network to get a longer range and to be nearly fault tolerant, because if an intermediate node fails or cannot receive a message, that message could be routed to another node. However, a mesh network also requires careful placement of these intermediate nodes, since they are responsible for doing the forwarding of the data generated by the sensor nodes in the network to the gateway directly or indirectly, through hops. Those intermediate nodes are responsible for meeting the criteria of safety, reliability and robustness of the network and are also of paramount importance in the forwarding of data transmission. They could leave part or all the network dead, if they display any fault [7]. Most solutions to the routers placement solve this problem with optimization algorithms that minimize the number of intermediate router nodes to meet the criteria for coverage, network connectivity and longevity of the network and data fidelity [8, 9].

This work uses an artificial immune systems based procedure, inspired on the human immune system, applied to the described router nodes placement problem. In [5] and [10] the authors report the procedure but the present work stresses the affinity function flexibility in terms of a multiobjective function which enables the inclusion of several objectives in a weighted fashion way. Several cases studies are included in the present work and a particular case study shows an example of modifying the affinity function so that three different paths are guaranteed from each node to the gateway. The algorithms based on immune networks have very desirable characteristics in the solution of this problem, among which we can mention: scalability, self-organization, learning ability and continuous treatment of noisy data [10].

The present work is divided into four sections. Section 2 discusses briefly artificial immune systems. Section 3 presents the application of artificial immune systems to the nodes placement problem and Sect. 4 discusses case studies results and conclusions.

2 Immune Systems Concepts

The immune system is a biological mechanism for identifying and destroying pathogens within a larger organism [13]. Pathogens are agents that cause disease such as bacteria, viruses, fungi, worms, etc. Anything that causes an immune response is known as an antigen. An antigen may be harmless, such as grass pollen, or harmful, such as the flu virus. In other words disease-causing antigens are called pathogens. So the immune system is designed to protect the body from pathogens. In humans, the immune system begins to develop in the embryo. The immune system begins with hematopoietic, (i.e. blood-making from Greek) stem cells. These stem cells differentiate into the major players in the immune system e.g. granulocytes, monocytes, and lymphocytes. These stems cells also differentiate into cells in the blood that are not connected to immune function, such as erythrocytes e.g. red blood cells, and megakaryocytes for blood clotting. Stem cells continue to be produced and differentiate throughout our lifetime. The immune system is usually divided into two categories–innate and adaptive–although these distinctions are not mutually exclusive. The innate subsystem is similar in all individuals of the same species, whereas the adaptive subsystem depends on the experience of each individual i.e. exposure to infectious agents. The innate immune response is able to prevent and control many infections. Nevertheless, many pathogenic microbes have evolved to overcome innate immune defenses, and so to protect ourselves against these infections, we have to call in the more powerful mechanisms of adaptive immunity. Adaptive immunity is normally silent, and responds or adapts to the presence of infectious microbes by becoming active, expanding, and generating potent mechanisms for neutralizing and eliminating the microbes. The components of the adaptive immune subsystem are lymphocytes and their products. The most notable cells of adaptive immunity are lymphocytes. There are two main classes of lymphocytes. B lymphocytes, named so, because they mature in the bone marrow, secrete proteins called antibodies, which bind to and eliminate extracellular microbes. T lymphocytes, which mature in the thymus, and function mainly to combat microbes that have learned to live inside cells where they are inaccessible to antibodies. The normal immune system has to be capable of recognizing virtually any microbe and foreign substance that one might encounter, and the response to each microbe has to be directed against that microbe. The substances that are recognized by these lymphocytes are called antigens. The immune system recognizes and directs responses against a massive number of antigens by generating a large number of lymphocytes, each with a single antigen receptor. Therefore, there are about 10^{12} lymphocytes in an adult, and it is estimated that these are able to recognize at least 10^7–10^9 different antigens [13]. Thus, only a few thousand lymphocytes express identical antigen receptors and recognize the same antigen. The antigen receptors of B cells are membrane-bound antibodies, also called immunoglobulins, or Ig. Antibodies are Y-shaped structures [13]. The tops of the Y recognize the antigen and, in B cells, the tail of the Y anchors the molecule in the plasma membrane. Antibodies are capable of recognizing whole microbes and macromolecules as well as small chemicals. These could be in the circulation e.g. a bacterial toxin, or attached to cells (e.g. a microbial cell wall component. The antigen receptors of T cells are structurally similar to antibodies, but T cell receptors (TCRs) recognize only small peptides that are displayed on specialized peptide-display molecules [13]. Although the immune system is capable of recognizing millions of foreign antigens, it usually does not react against one's own, i.e. self, antigenic substances. This is because lymphocytes that happen to express receptors for self-antigens are killed or shut off when they recognize these antigens. This phenomenon is called self-tolerance, implying that we tolerate our own antigens and the breakdown of this process yields in autoimmune diseases. When one antibody binds to other material, the lymphocyte carrying it, is stimulated to reproduce by cloning, this is known as Clonal selection principle. Genes coding lymphocytes have a mutation rate above normal, one mutation per cell division, on average, leading to what is known as somatic hypermutation. Clonal selection and hypermutation increases affinity between antibodies and antigens. There are three steps for an Artificial Immune System (AIS). First, find a representation of the components i.e. artificial equivalents to cells and antigens. Second, define affinity functions between components in order to quantify interaction among them. Third, write a set of immune algorithms that control system behavior. Why would a computer scientist get the trouble to study immune systems? Immune systems are massively parallel information processing mechanisms and are incredibly effective examples of distributed systems built from diverse components which are constantly being renewed. So that may inspire better computer security systems, for example, because of their adaptiveness, they can train themselves to react to new threats. Moreover they are error—tolerant, so that small mistakes are not fatal, and also self-protecting.

2.1 Metaphors of the Immune System

The main algorithms that implement the artificial immune systems were developed from metaphors of the immune system: the mechanism of negative selection, the theory of immune network and the clonal selection principle.

The function of the negative selection mechanism is to provide tolerance to self-cells, namely those belonging to the organism. Thus, the immune system gains the ability to detect unknown antigens and not react to the body's own cells. During the generation of T-cells, which are cells produced in the bone marrow, receptors are generated by a pseudo-random process of genetic arrangement. Later on, they undergo a maturation mechanism in the thymus, called negative selection, in which T cells that react to body proteins are destroyed. Thus, only cells that do not connect to the body proteins can leave the thymus. The T cells, known as mature cells, circulate in the body for immune functions and to protect it against antigens.

The theory of immune system network considers several important aspects like the combination of antibodies with the antigens for the early elimination of the antigens. Each antibody has its own antigenic determinant, called idiotope. In this context, Jerne [14] proposed the Immune Network Theory to describe the activity of lymphocytes in an alternative way. According to Jerne [14], the antibodies and lymphocytes do not act alone, but the immune system keeps a network of B cells for antigen recognition. These cells can stimulate and inhibit each other in various ways, leading to stabilization of the network. Two B cells are connected if they share an affinity above a certain threshold and the strength of this connection is directly proportional to the affinity they share.

The clonal selection principle describes the basic features of an immune response to an antigenic stimulus, and ensures that only cells that recognize the antigen are selected to proliferate. The daughter cells are copies or clones of their parents and are subject to a process of mutation with high rates, called somatic hypermutation. In the clonal selection the removal of daughter cells are performed, and these cells have receptors that respond to the body's own proteins as well as the most suitable mature cell proliferation, i.e., those with a greater affinity to the antigens [13].

3   Router Nodes Positioning

Router Nodes positioning has been addressed in the literature by several researchers. Cannons et al. [4] proposed an algorithm for positioning router nodes and determine which router will relay the information from each sensor. Gersho and Gray [6] proposed one to promote the reliability of wireless sensors communication network, minimizing the average probability of sensor transmission error. Shi et al. [11] propo-sed a positioning algorithm of multi-router nodes to minimize energy consumption for data transmission in mobile ad hoc network (MANET - Mobile Ad Hoc Network). The problem was modeled as an optimization clustering problem. The suggested algorithm to solve the problem uses heuristic methods based on the k-means algorithm. More recently Lanza-Gutiérrez and Pulido [12] proposed an study on how to efficiently deploy relay nodes into previously established static Wireless Sensor Netwoks, with the purpose of optimizing two relevant factors for the industry: average energy consumption of the sensors and average for router nodes placement based on genetic algorithm which minimizes the number of nodes required for network.

The use of wireless sensor network in industrial automation is still a matter of concern with respect to the data reliability and security by users. Thus, an appropriate node positioning is of paramount importance for the wireless network to meet safety, reliability and efficiency criteria.

Positioning of nodes is a difficult task, because one should take into account all the obstacles and interference present in an industrial environment. The gateway, as well as the sensors generally have a fixed position near the control room. But the placement of router nodes, which are responsible for routing the data, generated by the sensors network to the gateway directly or indirectly, is determined by the characteristics of the network.

The main characteristics of wireless sensor networks for industrial automation differ from traditional ones by the following aspects: The maximum number of sensors in a traditional wireless network is on the order of millions while automation wireless networks is on the order of tens to hundreds; The network reliability and latency are essential and fundamental factors for network wireless automation. To determine the number of router nodes and define the position in the network, some important aspects in industrial automation should be considered. It should be guaranteed:

(1) redundant paths so that the system be node fault-tolerant;
(2) full connectivity between nodes, both sensors and routers, so that each node of the network can be connected to all the others exploring the collaborative role of routers;
(3) node energy efficiency such that no node is overwhelmed with many relaying information from the sensors;
(4) low-latency system for better efficiency in response time;
(5) combined attributes for industrial processes to avoid accidents due to, for example, high monitored process temperature;
(6) self-organization ability, i.e. the ability of the network to reorganize the retransmission of data paths when a new sensor is added to the network or when a sensor stops working due to lack of power or a problem in wireless communication channel.

All these factors must be met, always taking into consideration the prime factor security: the fault tolerance. In the end of the router nodes placement, the network of wireless sensors applied to industrial automation should be robust, reliable, scalable and self-organizing.

The positioning of router nodes in industrial wireless sensor networks is a com-plex and critical task to the network operation. It is through the final position of routers that one can determine how reliable, safe, affordable and robust the network is.

In the application of immune systems to router nodes positioning reported in this work, B cells that make up the immune network will be composed by a set of sensor nodes and a set of router nodes. The sensor nodes are located in places where the plant instrumentation is required. These nodes have fixed coordinates, i.e. they cannot be moved. For security to be guaranteed it is necessary to have redundant paths between these nodes and the gateway. The set of router nodes will be added to allow redundant paths. The position of these nodes will be changed during the process of obtaining the final network. The stimulation of the B cells, corresponding to the set of routers, is defined by the affinity degree among B cells in the training of the network. In this work, the role of the antigen is viewed more broadly as the entity that stimulates B cells. Thus, the function of the antigen takes into consideration possible missing paths to critical sensors, the number of times that a router is used and its proximity to sensors. The modeling of B cells affinity is the weighted sum of the three criteria that the positioning of each router will answer. The criteria are: fault degree of each router, number of times each router is used depending on the path and number of sensor nodes neighboring to each router.

3.1   The Router Nodes Algorithm

In the proposed algorithm, process dynamics can be divided into two processes: network pruning and cloning, and node mutation of the network routers.

In the pruning process, n_p router nodes that during a certain time failed to become useful to the network will be removed from it. The cloning process is responsible for generating n_c clones of router nodes that were over stimulated. The clones may suffer mutations of two kinds:

(i) Hypermutation – for positioning new elements in the network which are inversely proportional to the degree of stimulation of the router node selected;
(ii) Net Mutation – for positioning the new information into the network in order to assure the new clones are neighbors of the selected clone [16].

After the inclusion of the new router nodes, a stop condition is performed. If the condition is not met, all routers undergo an action of repulsive forces, generated by obstacles and routers for other nodes, followed by attractive forces created by critical sensor nodes. Those critical nodes are the ones that do not meet the minimum number of paths necessary to reach the gateway. The actions of repelling potential fields have the function of driving them away from obstacles, to allow direct line of sight for the router network nodes to increase the reliability of transmission and also increase the distance among the routers to increase network coverage. On the other hand, the attractive potential fields attract routers to critical sensors, easing the formation of redundant paths among sensors and the gateway. After the action of potential fields, from the new positioning of routers, a new network is established and the procedure continues until the stopping criterion is met.

The algorithm proposed in this work deals with a procedure based on artificial immune networks, which solves the problem of positioning the router nodes so that every sensor device is able to communicate with the gateway directly and or indirectly by redundant paths.

Figure 1 shows the main modules of the algorithm. The first module is called immune network, and the second, is called potential fields (i.e. positioning module) containing elements used in positioning sensor networks using potential fields [15].

The immune network module performs an algorithm that can be described by the following steps:

– Creation: Creation of an initial set of B cells to form a network.
– Evaluation: Determination of the B cells affinity to calculate their stimulation.
– Pruning: Performs the resource management and remove cells that are without resources from the network.
– Selection: Selects the most stimulated B cells to be cloned.
– Cloning: Generates a set of clones from the most stimulated B cells.
– Mutation: Does the mutation of cloned cells.

In the stage of creation, an initial set of routers is randomly generated to initiate the process of obtaining the network, and the user can specify how many routers to place it initially.

In the evaluation phase, a network which is represented by a graph is formed with sensor nodes and router nodes. From this graph, values of several variables are obtained that will be used to calculate the affinity. Examples of such variables are the number of paths that exist between each sensor and the gateway, the number of times that a router is used on the formed paths, etc.

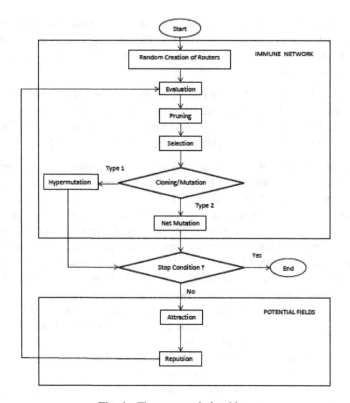

Fig. 1. The proposed algorithm.

It should be stressed that the affinity value is calculated for each router and comprises three parts. The first part provides the degree of fault of each network router - this affinity is the most important of all. It defines the value or importance each router has in the network configuration. This is done as follows: a router is removed from the network, and the number of paths that remain active for the sensors send information for the gateway is evaluated. If the number of active paths remaining after the node removal is small, the router node needs another nearby router to reduce their degree of fault.

Furthermore, if the node suffers battery discharge or hardware problems, other paths to relay information should be guaranteed until the problem is solved.

The second part relates to the number of times that each router is used in paths that relay the information from the sensors to the gateway. The greater the number of times it is used, more important is that router.

The third part relates the number of sensor nodes neighboring to each router – one can say that the more sensor nodes neighbors, the greater the likelihood that it will become part of the way that the sensor needs to transmit your message to the gateway.

4   Examples and Conclusions

Case studies were simulated in a 1×1 square scenario. The cloning procedure considered that only the router with higher affinity would be selected to produce three clones in each generation. For each case study 10 experiments were carried out that demonstrated the algorithm's ability to create at least two redundant paths to get the information from any sensor to the gateway.

Two set of results will be presented. The first set does not consider obstacles which are treated in the second set.

4.1   Case Studies with No Obstacles

Two configurations were considered to demonstrate the functionality of the proposed algorithm. The configurations used in the simulation were motivated by oil & gas refinery automation applications.

The first one called PosA consists of five network nodes, where node 1 is the gateway and nodes 2, 3, 4 and 5 are fixed sensors. The gateway has direct line of sight with all the network nodes as shown in Fig. 2.

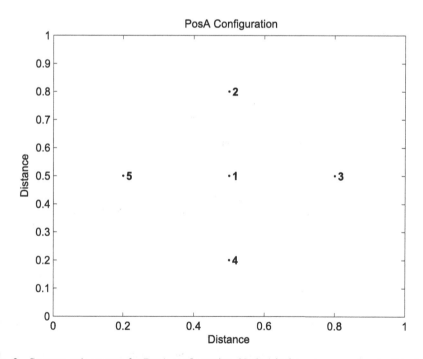

Fig. 2. Sensors and gateway for PosA configuration. Node 1 is the gateway and nodes 2 to 5 are the sensors.

The second one (PosB) considers a network with nine nodes, where node one is the gateway and the others are fixed sensors. As in configuration PosA, PosB has direct line of sight with all the network nodes as shown in Fig. 3. For both configurations it will be considered that there is no connectivity among them, i.e. the distance between them will be greater than their operating range.

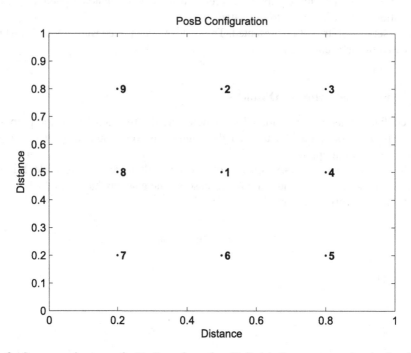

Fig. 3. Sensors and gateway for PosB configuration. Node 1 is the gateway and nodes 2 to 9 are the sensors.

For the case studies simulations considered, the goal is to get any two paths for each sensor to transmit the monitored sensor data to the gateway node in the case study 1 and three for the case study 2. The operating range is 0.2, and 0,1 for cases studies 1 and 2 respectively i.e. for both configurations there is no connectivity between any sensor and the gateway.

Table 1 describes the parameters used in the case study 1. After completion of ten experiments, the best network configuration can be seen in Fig. 4, and the consolidations of the tests are shown in Table 2.

Figure 4 also shows that one of the paths from sensor node 3 to the gateway shows three jumps (3-7-8-1) i.e. the information had to be relayed by two routers to reach the gateway node. Regarding the degree of fault, all eight routers have 20% degree of fault tolerance. This means that 80% of the paths from the sensors to the gateway continue to exist even after the removal of a node. With respect to the maximum number of routers used in terms of paths, the router node 8 is used twice in the paths 3-8-1 and 3-7-8-1. Consequently, this router will have a greater battery consumption than the others,

Table 1. Case study 1. PosA configuration parameters.

Simulation parameters	Values	Method
No. of generations	50	-
Initial no. of routers	10	-
Mutation operator as indicated in Fig. 1	-	Hypermutation (Type 1)
Affinity	-	Fault degree

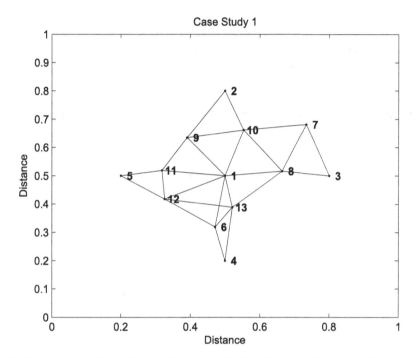

Fig. 4. Best router nodes positioning for case study 1 in PosA configuration. Node 1 is the gateway, nodes 2 to 5 are the sensors, and nodes 6 to 13 are the router nodes.

Table 2. Network performance for case study 1. PosA configuration.

Network	Min.	Average	Max.	Standard deviation
Number of nodes	13	13.7	15	0.67
Number of routers	8	8.7	10	0.67
Number of critical sensors	0	0	0	-
Number a router is used	1	2.1	3	0.57

which could make it stop working and be disconnected from the network. But even if that happens, there will still be a path (3-7-10-1) for node 3 to communicate to the gateway.

Case study 2 considers configuration PosB for the sensors and gateway. Table 3 shows the parameters used in the case study 2 simulations. The goal now is to assure at

Table 3. Case study 2. PosB configuration parameters.

Simulation parameters	Values	Method
No. of generations	90	-
Initial no. of routers	10	-
Mutation operator as in Fig. 1)		Net mutation (Type 2)
Affinity	-	Fault deg., no of times a rout is used, no of neighbor sensors

least three paths for each sensor and gateway, but now the affinity criteria consider fault degree, number of times a router is used and number of neighbor sensors. After ten experiments the best network configuration is shown in Fig. 5 and the network performance is seen in Table 4. Table 4 indicates that even using a low number of initial routers the algorithm was able to reach a positioning result meeting the goals and avoided again critical nodes.

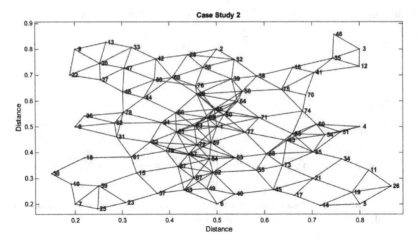

Fig. 5. Best router nodes positioning for case study 2 in PosB configuration. Node 1 is the gateway, nodes 2 to 9 are the sensors, and nodes 9 onwards are the router nodes.

Table 4. Network performance for case study 2. PosB configuration.

Network	Min.	Average	Max.	Standard deviation
Number of nodes	83	87.7	92	2.87
Number of routers	74	78.7	83	2.87
Number of critical sensors	0	0	0	-
Number a router is used	4	4.7	6	1.23

Figure 5 also shows that nodes 3,5, 7 and 9 in the paths 3-48-35-41-75-56-80-1, 5-26-11-34-65-85-71-1, 5-14-17-45-55-53-72-1, 7-25-23-37-67-84-69-1, 7-10-30-18-81-79-61-1, 9-22-27-46-44-66-89-1 and 9-13-33-42-68-29-80-1, features seven hops to the gateway. That means that the information sent by these devices will be delayed when received by the gateway node, since it will need to be relayed through six intermediate nodes. Regarding to the degree of fault, the intermediate nodes 35 and 41 has 19% degree of fault, and all the other routers have an index less than 19%. Regarding to the maximum number of routers used in terms of paths, router nodes 89 is used four times in the paths (2-28-68-29-89-1, 2-52-39-64-89-1, 9-22-27-46-44-66-89-1 e 8-36-78-24-89-1). As far as the number of sensors to neighboring routers is concerned, none of the 89 routers had over one neighbor sensor, indicating that the power consumption of the devices will be the same, increasing the life time of the network devices.

4.2 Case Studies with Obstacles

Two configurations with obstacles were considered to illustrate the proposed router nodes positioning algorithm in environments with obstacles.

The first configuration (PosC) comprises two circular obstacles with a radius of 0.1, and five nodes, in which node 1 is the gateway and the others are sensor nodes. Initially, the gateway has not direct line of sight with sensor nodes 3 and 5 and is not connected, i.e. out of range, to any of the network nodes, as depicted in Fig. 6.

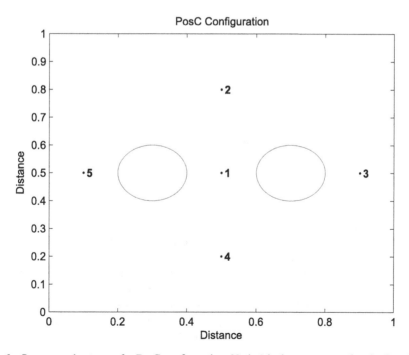

Fig. 6. Sensors and gateway for PosC configuration. Node 1 is the gateway and nodes 2 to 5 are the sensors.

The second configuration (PosD) has eight obstacles: three circular ones have radius of 0.05, another circular one has radius 0.15 and four rectangular obstacles with different sizes. Besides, the gateway is node 1 and nodes 2 to 8 are the seven sensor nodes. Initially, the gateway has not direct line of sight to any of the sensor nodes and is not connected to any network node as it is out range to the other nodes. Moreover, sensor nodes have also not a direct line of sight with each other and are also not connected as they are out of range with each other too. Figure 7 shows the PosD configuration.

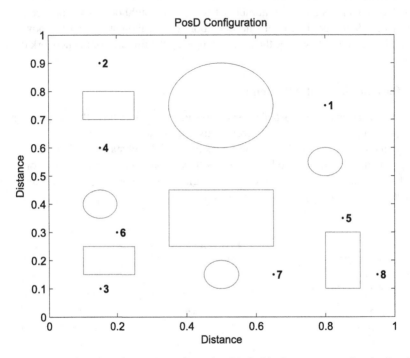

Fig. 7. Sensors and gateway for PosD configuration. Node 1 is the gateway and nodes 2 to 8 are the sensors.

In this section, case studies 3 and 4 are considered using the configurations PosC and PosD.

For case study 3, the network configuration is cross shaped, the operating range of the network nodes is 0.2 and the positioning procedure lead to two disjoint paths for the sensors send data to the gateway.

Case study 4 uses configuration PosD and considers the same operating range as in the case study 1, 0.2, and three disjoint paths are required.

Tables 5 and 7 show the used parameters for case studies 3 and 4 respectively.

Figure 8 shows the best configuration obtained from the 10 experiments. Table 6 shows the network performance for case study 3.

Table 5. Case study 3. PosC configuration parameters.

Simulation parameters	Values	Method
No. of generations	30	-
Initial no. of routers	10	-
Mutation operator (as indicated in Fig. 1)		Net mutation (Type 2)
Affinity	-	Fault degree, number of times a router is used and number of neighbor sensors

Table 6. Network performance for case study 3. PosC configuration.

Network	Min.	Average	Max.	Standard deviation
Number of nodes	19	19.9	22	0.99
Number of routers	14	14.9	17	0.99
Number of critical sensors	0	0	0	-
Number a router is used	2	2	2	0

Table 7. Case study 4. PosD configuration parameters.

Simulation parameters	Values	Method
No. of generations	100	-
Initial no. of routers	10	-
Mutation operator (as indicated in Fig. 1)		Net mutation (Type 2)
Affinity	-	Fault degree, number of times a router is used and number of neighbor sensors

It can be seen in Fig. 8 that the sensor nodes 3 and 5 in the paths 3-16-17-20-1, 3-19-7-10-1, 5-13-11-18-1 and 5-12-14-15-1 show four jumps to the gateway. This means the data sent by these devices suffer a delay when received by the gateway, since it will need to be relayed through three intermediate nodes. With respect to the degree of fault, the intermediate nodes 7, 10, 11, 12, 13, 14, 16, 17 and 19 have a 30% degree of fault, and the other router nodes have an index lower than 30%. So 70% of the paths from the sensors to the gateway, continue to exist even after the removal of a node.

Figure 9 shows the best configuration out of ten experiments for case study 4 and Table 8 shows the network performance for case study 4.

Figure 9 indicates that for sensor nodes 3 and 6, the paths 3-20-22-24-7-40-63-53-36-1, 3-50-49-61-4-52-15-56-39-1 and 6-58-61-4-60-31-15-37-26-1 show nine hops to the gateway. This means that the data sent by these devices suffer a delay in the gateway, since it will need to be relayed by eight intermediate nodes. With respect to the degree of fault, the router node 32 have 21% degree of fault, and the other router nodes have an index lower than 21%. This means that 79% of the paths from the sensors are still present even after a node removal.

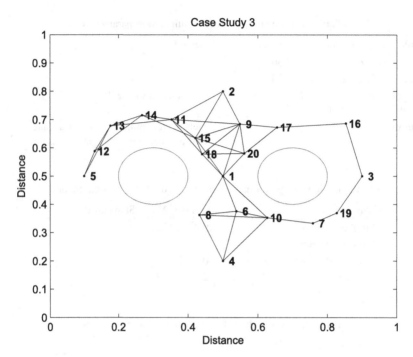

Fig. 8. Best router nodes positioning for case study 3 in PosC configuration. Node 1 is the gateway, nodes 2 to 5 are the sensors, and nodes 6 to 20 are the router nodes.

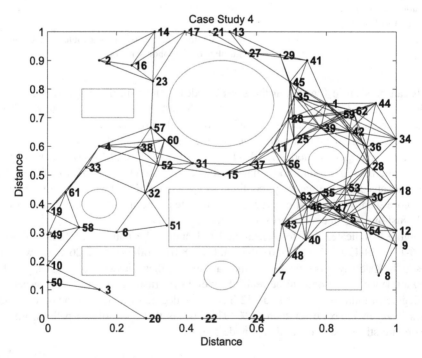

Fig. 9. Best router nodes positioning for case study 4 in PosD configuration. Node 1 is the gateway, nodes 2 to 8 are the sensors, and nodes 9 to 63 are the router nodes.

Table 8. Network performance for case study 4. PosD configuration.

Network	Min.	Average	Max.	Standard deviation
Number of nodes	59	60.50	63	1.18
Number of routers	51	52.50	55	1.18
Number of critical sensors	0	0	0	-
Number a router is used	5	5.4	8	0.97

This work proposed a positioning algorithm for router nodes in wireless network using immune systems techniques. It should be stressed that the affinity function, which acts as an objective function, is made flexible enough to incorporate several objectives in a weighted fashion. The weights as well as the criteria could be combined so that the resulted wireless sensor network can have different characteristics meeting a group of desired criteria for different solutions and environments.

The procedure creates redundant paths to the data collected by the sensors to be sent to the gateway by any two or more paths, meeting the criteria of degree of failure, the number of retransmission by routers and number of sensors to neighboring routers. In other words the method allows each criterion to be enabled at a time or even to be combined with adjustable weights. The affinity function, which works as an objective function, is multi-objective, so several other objectives could be jointly considered.

References

1. Zheng, J., Lee, M.J.: A comprehensive performance study of IEEE 802.15.4. In: Sensor Network Operations, Chapter 4, pp. 218–237. IEEE Press/Wiley InterScience (2006)
2. Jämsä-Jounela, S.L.: Future trends in process automation. Annu. Rev. Control **31**(2), 211–220 (2007)
3. Moyne, J.R., Tilbury, D.M.: The emergence of industrial control, diagnostics, and safety data. Proc. IEEE **95**(1), 29–47 (2007). IEEE Press
4. Cannons, J., Milstein, L.B., Zeger, K.: An algorithm for wireless relay placement. IEEE Trans. Wirel. Commun. **8**(11), 5564–5574 (2006). IEEE Press
5. Coelho, P.H.G., do Amaral, J.L.M., do Amaral, J.F.M., de Arruda Barreira, L.F., Barros, A.V.: Applying artificial immune systems for deploying router nodes in wireless networks in the presence of obstacles. In: Cordeiro, J., Hammoudi, S., Maciaszek, L., Camp, O., Filipe, J. (eds.) ICEIS 2014. LNBIP, vol. 227, pp. 167–183. Springer, Cham (2015). doi:10.1007/978-3-319-22348-3_10
6. Gersho, A., Gray, R.M.: Vector Quantization and Signal Compression. Springer, Heidelberg (1992)
7. Hoffert, J., Klues, K., Orjih, O.: Configuring the IEEE 802.15.4 MAC layer for single-sink wireless sensor network applications, Technical report (2007). http://www.dre.vanderbilt.edu/~jhoffert/802_15_4_Eval_Report.pdf
8. Youssef, W., Younis, M.: Intelligent gateways placement for reduced data latency in wireless sensor networks. In: ICC 2007 International Conference on Communications, Glasgow, pp. 3805–3810 (2007)
9. Molina, G., Alba, E., Talbi, E.G.: Optimal sensor network layout using multi objective metaheuristics. J. Univ. Comput. Sci. **15**(15), 2549–2565 (2008)

10. Coelho, P.H.G., do Amaral, J.L.M., do Amaral, J.F.M., de Arruda Barreira, L.F., Barros, A.V.: Further developments on router nodes positioning for wireless networks using artificial immune systems. In: Proceedings of the 18th International Conference on Enterprise Information Systems, pp. 99–105 (2016)
11. Shi, Y., Jia, F., Hai-Tao, Y.: An improved router placement algorithm base on energy efficient strategy for wireless network. In: ISECS International Colloquium on Computing, Communication, Control and Management (CCCM2009), pp. 421–423. (2009)
12. Lanza-Gutiérrez, J.M., Pulido, J.A.G.: Studying the multiobjective variable neighbourhood search algorithm when solving the relay node placement problem in wireless sensor networks. Soft Comput. **20**, 67–68 (2016)
13. Castro, L.N., Timmis, J.: Artificial Immune Systems: A New Computational Intelligence Approach. Springer Science & Business Media, Heidelberg (2002)
14. Jerne, N.K.: Towards a network theory of the immune system. Ann. Immunol. (Inst. Pasteur) **125**, 373–389 (1974)
15. Howard, A., Mataric, M.J., Sukhatme, G.S.: Mobile sensor network deployment using potential fields: a distributed, scalable solution to the area coverage problem heuristics. In: Asama, H., Arai, T., Fukuda, T., Hasegawa, T. (eds.) Distributed Autonomous Robotic Systems 5. Springer, Tokyo (2002)
16. Poduri, S., Pattem, S., Krishnamachari, B., Sukhatme, G.: Controlled Deployments of Sensor Networks (2006, in Press)

Information Systems Analysis and Specification

Moving Towards Agility in an Ordered Fashion

Ilia Bider[(✉)] and Oscar Söderberg

DSV, Stockholm University, Stockholm, Sweden
ilia@dsv.su.se, oscar.soderberg88@gmail.com

Abstract. The paper suggests a new method of transiting from Traditional Software Development (TSD) to Agile Software Development (ASD) called non-disruptive transition. The novelty of the method consists of allowing to complete the major transition steps to the agile "mindset" while remaining in the frame of an already established TSD process. The method is being developed using a knowledge transformation perspective to identify the main features of ASD mindset and how it differs from the one of TSD. More specifically, it uses a version of Nonako's SECI model to represent software development. To analyze the current mindset and plan the movement to the mindset that is more agile, the paper suggests using a process modelling technique that considers the software development process as a complex socio-technical system. The paper also discusses external conditions that might hinder going all the way to becoming agile and require the transition to stop, and how to become agile while developing complex systems.

Keywords: Agile · Software engineering · Tacit knowledge · Knowledge · Transformation · SECI · Design Science

1 Introduction

1.1 Formulating a Problem

Agile Software Development (ASD) has appeared as a reaction on the increasing rate of changes in system requirements, e.g. see [1]: "requirements change at rates that swamp traditional methods". Since 15 years from its inception, ASD from a niched development methodology, mainly used for the web development, made its way to becoming one of the mainstream methodologies. This leads to organizations that use a traditional phase-based methodology become more willing to move to ASD.

Due to the essential difference between the Traditional Software Development (TSD) and ASD, a transition from one to another is quite difficult and includes a number of challenges and pitfalls that are reported in research papers [2, 3] books [4], and practitioners blogs [5]. The main challenge here is that an ASD team requires having a "mindset" that differs from the one of a TSD team, see a popular explanation of the difference in [6].

There are a number of books, such as, [3], that suggest methods for transiting from TSD to ASD. However, following these methods presumes that a decision to complete

S. Hammoudi et al. (Eds.): ICEIS 2016, LNBIP 291, pp. 175–199, 2017.
DOI: 10.1007/978-3-319-62386-3_9

such a transition has been made, and risks attached to it have been understood. In addition, a decision on which brand of Agile, e.g. XP, or SCRUM, to try needs to be taken quite early in the transition process.

Understanding the transition risks and making a right for the given situation choice of the agile practice requires experience. Thus, such a transition has better chances for success if it is led by an experienced person, e.g. an agile coach. Even in this case, there is no guarantee of success. What is more, even if the transition was successful in the end, it could cause a disruption of the existing development process for quite long time. If the existing process does not work, taking the risk and introducing the disruption is fully justified. However, if the process works satisfactory, there could be doubts whether it make sense to jump into the unknown taking the risks and going through the disturbances without knowing whether a better development process will emerge after the transition has been completed.

In connection to the deliberations above, a question arises whether it is possible to gradually transit from TSD to ASD with the minimum disruption of the existing development process? In other words, the question is whether there already exists a method of non-disruptive transition to ASD, and if not, whether such method can be devised. Ideally, such a method should improve the existing development process even before the full transition cycle has been completed. It should be also possible to delay taking the decision on which brand of ASD to use, and even stop the transition at some point being satisfied with what has been achieved, and not taking risks of going farther.

1.2   Overview of a Solution

This paper is a report on on-going research aimed at answering the question posed in Sect. 1.1. To the best of our knowledge, no non-disruptive method of transition to ASD can be found in the research or practical literature. Therefore, our way of finding an answer whether a non-disruptive transition to agile is possible is by using Design Science (DS) [7] for developing and testing in practice such a method.

According to the case studies reported in the literature, e.g. [2, 3], the biggest issue when transiting to ASD is acquiring the agile mindset by the development team. The latter requires all team members to acquire a set of skills that might not be necessary in the existing TSD. For example, social and communication skills are mandatory for all members of the ASD team, so that all of them can meet and talk to the stakeholders. The main focus of our design work is directed to acquiring the agile mindset and a set of skills that is required for it.

To design a method that leads to changing the current mindset of a team to a more agile mindset, we need to:

1. Find a basis on which to identify the main features of the agile mindset and in what way it differs from the mindset of a more traditional team.
2. Find a way of mapping (modelling) the mindset of a team so that the distance between the current mindset and the targeted one (agile) can be measured, and a plan of actions aimed at shortening this distance can be developed.

As far as the first goal on the list is concerned, the most commonly used framework for this kind of goals is Agile Manifesto [8]. However, we consider it too vague and allowing multiple interpretations, which leads to misunderstandings and heated discussions in the agile community [9] (see also critique of Agile Manifesto in [10]). We need a more "scientific" basis for developing a non-disruptive method of transition to agile. For this end, we have chosen a framework suggested in [11, 12] that compares TSD and ASD projects from the knowledge transformation perspective. Based on this comparison, [11, 12] define the essence of the difference between TSD and ASD and set requirements on the structure of the agile project, its team, relationships with the customer and tools used in the project. The results from [11, 12] do not contradict Agile Manifesto, but rather more clearly underline the main features of ASD and the difference between TSD and ASD.

As far as the second goal on the list is concerned, there are a number of methods for evaluating and measuring the current level of agility, see for example [13]. However, mostly, these methods rely on Agile Manifesto when determining what the agile mindset is, which we have rejected. Furthermore, they are meant to be used when a decision on transition to ASD has been made and the transition process is on the way. They also disregard the current structure of the development process accepted in the given organization. Thus, it is difficult to use these methods before the transition has been started and at the early stages of the transition. Based on the reasons above, we consider that the existing methods of evaluating the level of agility do not fit the task of creating a method of non-disruptive transition to agile.

In this work, we have designed our own technique of mapping (modelling) the mindset of the development team suitable for planning steps for advancing the current mindset towards the agile one. The technique is based on the business process modelling suggested in [14, 15], called step-relationship modelling in [14]. The step-relationship modeling uses a system view on the business process, considering it as a number of components (or steps) connected with each other via various relationships. The step-relationship modelling focuses on depicting these relationships and their properties. When adopting step-relationship modelling for our purpose, we concentrated on relationships between the teams that man the components/steps of the given system development process.

One of the main activities in a Design Science (DS) research project is testing the new solution (or artifact), which is a method in our case, in at least one real situation. DS does not set a restriction on when in the course of the research project such test needs to be started, e.g. after the design has been finished or in parallel with the design. In our case, the research was conducted in parallel with investigating a business case in the IT department of an insurance company. This department was interested in adopting a non-disruptive approach of moving towards agility, and it was also used as a test bed for the method. The test is far from being completed; it was run up to the department management understood our non-disruptive method and became prepared for completing their first step on the way to agility.

The rest of the paper is structured in the following way. Section 2 gives a brief overview of the research methodology and knowledge base used in this research. Section 3 presents the proposed method. Section 4 gives more details on our research process and discusses the test completed so far. Section 5 discusses amendments needed for transiting to agile while developing complex software systems. Section 6 analyzes the difference between our non-destructive method of transition to agile and already existing methods, using the method from [4] as an example. Finally, in Sect. 7, we summarize the results achieved and draw plans for the future.

2   Research Background

2.1   The Project History and Methodology

This research has been initiated by the management of an IT department in a large insurance company expressing their interest in transition to a more agile development process. The management did not possess much knowledge on the essence of ASD, or its various brands. They were interested in an approach that included minimum risks and gave a possibility to learn the essence of ASD on the way, while allowing to delay the decision of which particular brand/practice of ASD to adopt. The literary study, part of which is presented in Sect. 1, has shown that there are a number of practical methods of transition to agile. Nevertheless, none of them was particularly suitable for the requirements that came from the IT department. These requirements were reformulated into the question of "whether it is possible to gradually transit from TSD to ASD with the minimum disruption of the existing development process?" posed in Sect. 1.1 To answer this question, we decided to develop a "non-disruptive" method of transition to agile.

The development of our method follows the pattern of Design Science (DS) research [7, 16], which is related to finding new solutions for problems known or unknown. To count as a design science solution, it should be of a generic nature, i.e. applicable not only to one unique situation, but to a class of similar situations. DS research can be considered as an activity aimed at generating and testing hypotheses for future adoption by practice [17].

The development of our method ran in parallel with the investigation of the business case of the IT department in the insurance company. More exactly, we investigated and modelled the structure of the development process in the department including the skills of the process participants and the ways they communicated with each other. The activities were carried out through interviews with representatives of various phases in the process, and studying internal documentation.

One of the key activity in a DS project is implementation and verification of a generic solution, or artefact in terms of [7], in at least one situation. This activity is also referred to as demonstration or proof of concept in the literature devoted to methodology of DS [7]. The demonstration phase in this research is a continuation of our case study. More exactly, we worked out a suggestion on the first steps of transition to agility for the IT department; and it was accepted by the management. More details on this activity are presented in Sect. 4.

As has already been mentioned in Sect. 1, we used existing theoretical frameworks as a knowledge base when developing our method. As we do not expect that these frameworks are known to the reader, in the next subsections, we give a short overview of them.

2.2   Agility from the Knowledge Transformation Perspective

In this section, we give a short summary of TSD and ASD models built based on the knowledge transformation perspective presented in [11, 12]. These models, in their own turn, are built based on the SECI model [18]. SECI stays for Socialization – Externalization – Combination – Internalization, and it explains the ways of how knowledge is created in an organization while being transformed from the tacit form (in the heads of the people) to the explicit one (e.g. on the paper) and back. The difference between tacit and explicit knowledge was first introduced my Michael Polanyi, see, for example, [19].

The cycle of knowledge creation consists of the following four steps or phases represented in Fig. 1.

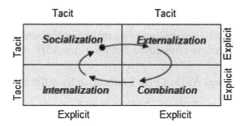

Fig. 1. SECI diagram of knowledge creation.

1. The cycle starts with *Socialization*, where tacit knowledge is transferred from the heads of one group of people to others via informal means, such as conversations during the coffee breaks, meetings, observations, working together, etc.
2. The next phase is *Externalization*, which is the conversion of knowledge from the tacit form into the explicit one, e.g. a model of situation.
3. The third phase is *Combination*, which is transforming the externalized (explicit) knowledge in a new form using existing knowledge, e.g. solution design principles.
4. The last phase is *Internalization*, which is converting the explicit knowledge, e.g. a solution, in the tacit knowledge of people who will apply this knowledge to any situation that warrants it.

Applying ideas from SECI to software development, [11, 12] designed two models of knowledge transformation in software development projects, one - for Traditional Software Development (TSD), and another - for Agile Software Development (ASD). Both are presented in Fig. 2. In both cases, the knowledge transformation cycles starts with tacit knowledge possessed by stakeholders on problems/needs to be solved/satisfied by a new software system. The next step common for both models is embedment when the knowledge on a solution becomes embedded in the system that is considered by its users as a whole possessing its own behavior. The last step in the knowledge transformation in both models is adoption – transforming the knowledge embedded in the system into the tacit knowledge of the system's users on how to use this system in various working situations.

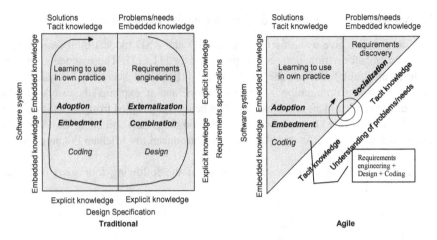

Fig. 2. Left – ECEA model (Externalization-Combination-Embedment-Adoption) for TSD. Right - SEA model (Socialization-Embedment-Adoption) for ASD. Adapted from [11].

The models for TSD and ASD in Fig. 2 substantially differ in the following aspects:

1. The nature of the first phase in ASD differs from that of TSD. It consists in transferring tacit knowledge on the problem and needs from the stakeholders to the development team. This phase corresponds to *Socialization* in Fig. 2. Also, *Design* and *Coding* are merged into one phase Embedment. This can be defined as the first motto of agility: "Avoid or delay explication of knowledge as much as possible. Ideally go from tacit knowledge directly to the embedded one."
2. In addition, one big cycle is substituted by many smaller and shorter ones. The system is built iteratively starting with the basic functionality. During the exploitation of the basic system, better understanding of the needs is acquired, which is converted in adding details to the system in the next iterations. In other words, the second motto of agility can be defined as: "Develop and introduce in practice as little as possible as soon as possible, and build upon it in the following iterations"

Based on the analysis of the knowledge transformation models for TSD and ASD, [11, 12] identifies 6 properties of the development process that differentiate TSD and ASD; these are presented in Table 1. The first three properties, *team*, *user involvement* and *agreement*, belong to the social perspective of system development, while the second three properties, *core system*, *architecture* and *tools*, belong to the technical perspective of system development. We will be using these differentiating properties when developing our non-disruptive method later in Sect. 4.

2.3 Step-Relationship Model

A step-relationship model represents a business process as a (relatively) small number of steps [14], or functional components [15], connected with each other through various types of relationships. Each type of relationships, i.e. a relation in a mathematical sense, represents a separate view of the model.

Table 1. Properties that differentiate ASD from TSD.

#	ASD	TSD
1	One *team* consisting of "universal" members	Several specialized *teams*
2	*Stakeholders involvement* during the duration of the project	*Stakeholders involvement* during the *Externalization* and *Adoption* phases
3	Non-contractual *agreement* based on trust	*Contractual* agreement is possible
4	Possibility to identify and agree on a *core system* that can be expanded in consequent iterations	Not mandatory, but can be employed.
5	*Architecture* aimed at expansion	*Architecture* aimed at fulfilling the identified requirements
6	Employing *high-level tools*, e.g. domain-specific languages, development platforms, libraries	Not mandatory – low level, and universal tools can be employed

There are two ways of representing a relationships type, graphical and matrix. In the graphical form, the steps/components are presented as rectangles (boxes), while arrows between the rectangles show relationships between the corresponding steps/functional components. Labels inside the rectangles name the steps, while labels on the arrows give additional characteristics to the relationships. As an example, Fig. 3 represents output-input relationships in a sample software development process. Each arrow shows formalized output of one step/component serving as an input to another step/component.

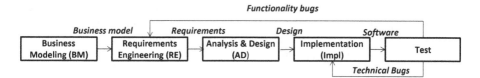

Fig. 3. Graphical presentation of relationships.

In the matrix form, a relationships type is represented as a square matrix where both columns and rows correspond to steps/components of the process. A sell (a,b) where a is a column and b is a row is reserved for describing a relationship of the given type between step a and step b, if any exists. As an example, Table 2 presents the same output-input relationships type as Fig. 3, but in the matrix form. More examples of relationships in the graphical and matrix forms are presented in Sect. 3.

3 Designing a Method

3.1 Creating a Single Team

There are several essential properties of ASD that need to be achieved in order to successfully transit to agile. When developing our method, we assume that at least

Table 2. An example of presenting relationships in the matrix form.

	BM	RE	AD	Impl	Test
Business Modeling (BM)					
Requirements Engineering (RE)	Model				Bugs
Analysis and design (AD)		Reqs			
Implementation (Impl)			Design		Bugs
Test				Software	

some of them can be achieved without essentially changing the current process. We also assume that it is possible to somehow measure the progress achieved on the way.

According to the first row in Table 1, ASD has a single development team of members that could do all kind of work in the process, including talking to the stake-holders and programming. This is not mandatory for TSD, where separate specialized nonintersecting teams can complete the job. Also, in a single ASD team, all members communicate with each other frequently, which is not required in TSD. In TSD, informal communication in the frame of the development process may concentrate inside each specialized team, while the formal output-input channels are used for passing over the job between the teams, as is represented in Fig. 3, and Table 2.

The two properties of (a) having specialized teams and (b) lack of communication between the teams are related to each other. A narrow specialization may create a hinder for communication due to differences in professional jargons and culture.

Based on the deliberation above, we have identified two properties of the development process that need to be measured and improved, in the first hand, when transiting to ASD. These are: (a) intensity of communication between the teams, and (b) ability of members of one specialized team to do the job assigned to the other teams. These two properties can be represented via relationships between the teams manning the steps. Technically, these relationships can be represented with the help of two matrixes: (a) the *communication intensity matrix*, and (b) the *cross-competency matrix*, as is discussed in the next subsections.

Increasing Communication Intensity

An example of the *communication intensity matrix* for the model in Fig. 1 is presented in Table 3. A cell (a,b) in the communication intensity matrix, where a stays for a column and b for a row, defines the intensity of communication between teams of steps a and b initiated by team a. Interpretation of the values in the cells depends on the level of separation between the teams, e.g. one site or multiple sites. In the example presented in Table 3, communication are supposed to take place in the form of meetings, were *High* means daily communications meetings. *Average* means 3 times a week, *Low* means once a week. Empty cells outside the diagonal mean that no communication happens between the corresponding teams.

Note that the communication intensity matrix is aimed at characterizing the intensity of communication between the specialized teams, assumption being that inside the teams their members communicate/collaborate in a natural way. If this is not true, the diagonal of the matrix can be used for representing communication intensity inside the teams.

Table 3. An example of a communication intensity matrix.

	BM	RE	AD	Impl	Test
Business Modeling (BM)		High	Average		Low
Requirements Engineering (RE)	High		Average	High	Low
Analysis and design (AD)	High	High		High	
Implementation (Impl)	Low		Average		High
Test	Low	Low	Average	High	

The communication intensity matrix can be used for both depicting the communi-cation intensity in the current state and planning for increasing the communication intensity. The latter can be done by changing values of some cells in the matrix to reflect the goal of increasing communication intensity. To facilitate the planning work, we have transferred some information from the output-input matrix, see Table 2, to the communication intensity matrix in Fig. 3. More specifically, we make the borders of cell (a,b) thick in all cases where cell (a,b) is not empty in the output-input matrix. The latter means that the column step a *produces* a formalized input for the row step b, e.g. design specification. In addition, we made the background of cell (a,b) grey in case cell (b,a) is nonempty in the output-input matrix (Table 2). The later means that the column step b *receives* formalized output from the row step b.

Formally, the result of adding thick borders and grey background means that the matrix presented in Table 3 is a merger of a "pure" intensity communication matrix (without thick borders and grey background) with the simplified output/input matrix (the content of the cells in the latter is not represented in the merger) and a transposition of the latter. The merged communication extensity matrix is more convenient for planning the next step of transition to agile as described below.

One can expect that communication should be more extensive between the steps that are connected with an output-input relationship. Formalized outputs, like requirements or a design specification, in a software development process cannot be made totally formal, and they need interpretation from the receiving team. Misinterpretation can lead to a wrong system being delivered to the customer. The thick border represents the needs of informal explanation of the formalized output when it is being transferred to the receiving team. The grey background represents the need for communication between the receiving team and the producing team while the former is doing their part of work. Even when the receiving team gets the informal explanations on their formalized input, there can be a need to verify their understanding from the originator of the input. For example, the designers may need to contact the requirements engineers later on when they start converting certain requirements into design. In [14], this type of backward communication is called week dependencies, while [15] refer to them as to feedback links.

Summarizing the above, when planning the next goal in intensifying the communication between the teams, it is worthwhile to start intensification that corresponds to cells with thick borders or grey background. For example, the next goal for the

Table 4. Next step in communication intensity.

	BM	RE	AD	Impl	Test
Business Modeling (BM)		High	Average		Low
Requirements Engineering (RE)	High		**High**	High	Low
Analysis and design (AD)	High	High		High	
Implementation (Impl)	Low		**High**		High
Test	Low	Low	Average	High	

situation presented in Table 3, could be the one described in Table 4, where the difference is presented in bold. The difference consists of intensifying forward communication between *Analysis & Design* and *Implementation*, and backward communication between *Analysis & Design* and *Requirements Engineering*. Note that such measure makes sense even for improving the already existing process without aiming at becoming fully agile.

Increasing Cross-Competency.
While the communication intensity matrix can be considered as a tool of intensifying internal communication in the future single team, the cross-competency matrix can be considered as a tool for achieving "universality" of its members (see the first row in Table 1). An example of such a matrix is presented in Table 5. In this matrix a cell (*a*, *b*), where *a* stays for a column and *b* for a row, defines the percentage of the team *a* members that have working knowledge on the tasks completed by team *b*. An empty non-diagonal cell means 0%. Here, having working knowledge on a specific task means that a person in question has some practical experience of this task..

As with the communication intensity matrix, we add to this matrix some information from the output-input matrix in the form of thick borders around cells and grey background. This information is aimed at helping to plan the next step of transition to agile. Marked cells should be targeted for increasing cross-competence in the first place, as this can decrease the risks of misinterpretation of the formalized inputs and misunderstanding in communications. Such measure might be helpful even for improving the existing process.

An example of the next planned step for the situation presented in Table 5 is presented in Table 6, where the difference is presented in bold. The difference consists of increasing cross-competency of the Requirements Engineering and Implementation teams.

As cross-competency requires *working* knowledge of the tasks completed by other teams, it is not enough just to send people to a training course. The proper way of achieving cross-competency in cell (*a,b*) in the frame of the existing software development process is to send some people from team *a* to work in team *b* for some time. This can degrade the overall performance in the beginning, but this one-time cost is

Table 5. An example of cross-competency matrix.

	BM	RE	AD	Impl.	Test
Business Modeling (BM)		50%	75%		
Requirements Engineering (RE)	75%		75%		50%
Analysis and design (AD)	75%				
Implementation (Impl)	50%	50%	75%		50%
Test	50%				

Table 6. Next step in achieving cross-competency.

	BM	RE	AD	Impl	Test
Business Modeling (BM)		50%	75%		
Requirements Engineering (RE)	75%		75%		50%
Analysis and design (AD)	75%	50%		50%	
Implementation (Impl)	50%	50%	75%		50%
Test	50%			50%	

worth taking, as increase in cross-competency minimizes the risk of producing the wrong software (see deliberation above).

When planning increase in cross-competency for *Implementation* step in other teams, it is worthwhile to consider row 6 in Table 1 that refers to using high-level tools. This property has not been introduced for the sake of creating a single team of "universal" members, but for being able to complete development loops in a speedy manner. However, having high-level development tools may also help in acquiring programming skills by people without technical education. So, if such tools are not already employed, it could be advantageous to start transition from low-level programming to using high-level tools before increasing competency in programming in other teams.

3.2 Avoiding Explication of Knowledge

As was discussed in Sect. 2.2, one of the ASD principles is to delay or avoid explication of knowledge, ideally, by going from the tacit understanding of problems/needs to building software. This implies skipping creating detailed requirements and design specifications. More specifically, requirements are left on the tacit level as a general understanding/image of the problems and needs, while design is done via proper structuring of the code. The latter could be facilitated by using high-level development tools, like domain specific languages or component libraries.

Avoiding explicit requirements and design does not mean that these activities are excluded; they are done on the tacit level. To reach the level of proficiency when requirements and design are done on the tacit level is difficult, if ever possible, without obtaining skills in both requirements engineering and design. Obtaining these skills by all team members in the frame of the existing phase-based process has already been discussed in Sect. 3.1.

The next question is how to shorten the time period from the first contact with the customer to starting producing executable code while still remaining in the frame of a traditional software development project. We believe that this can be achieved by gradual transition from sequential execution of the steps of the development process to the semi-parallel execution. The latter means starting the design before all require-ments are discovered, and starting coding before all design specifications are created.

The current level of parallelism can be represented in a graphical form as a timeline intensity diagram [15]. An example of such a diagram that corresponds to Fig. 3 is presented in Fig. 4. The difference between Figs. 3 and 4 is that in Fig. 4, the shapes representing steps do not have rectangular form. The upper border of the shape can be of any form representing the increase/decrease in the amount of work being done at certain moments of time. The intensity of work can be increasing or decreasing with time, or can be first increasing and then decreasing or vice versa (not illustrated in Fig. 4). In addition, the step shapes in Fig. 4 are placed in the order they are executed. If some steps run partly in parallel, the projections of their shapes on the time axes will intersect. In the example of Fig. 4, there are two occasions of the parallelism, namely (1) step *Analysis & Design* runs partly in parallel with *Implementation*, and step *Implementation* runs partly in parallel with *Test*.

Timeline intensity diagram can be used for planning the next goal for transition to agile in the same way as communication intensity and cross-competency matrices are used, see Fig. 5.

In the example of Fig. 5, all steps run partially in parallel, which is rather a radical change when starting from Fig. 4. If such a transition is too difficult to complete in one go, then smaller goals can be set in between, e.g. where only two new steps run in parallel.

Working in parallel means that formalized output is delivered to the next step in portions. This requires understanding of how the formalized output is used by the next step so that each portion is relatively independent and can be successfully used by the team of the next step for producing its own formalized output. Thus parallel execution requires certain degree of cross-competency on behave of the output producer. In addition, it requires efficient communication channels between the steps. Parallel execution of steps in software development bares a risk that the already produced portion of the given step output, e.g. requirements, can be negated when the work progresses. If this "negated" portion has already been sent to the next step, e.g. design, and is under processing of this step's team, then the information on the negation should be immediately made available for this team. Getting this information can stop or postpone their activities related to the questionable portion of the requirements. Note that with an experienced team, the advantages of running in parallel, e.g. shorten time, overweight the risks described above.

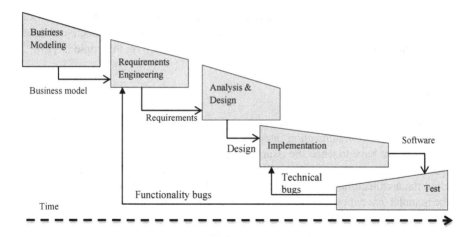

Fig. 4. An example of timeline intensity diagram.

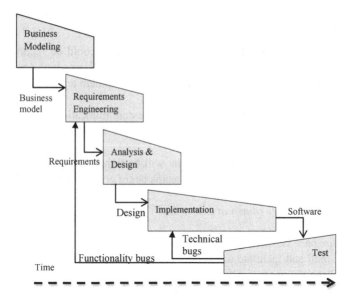

Fig. 5. An example of timeline intensity diagram to be achieved.

Summarizing the deliberation above, transition to parallel execution of two steps should be planned when a certain degree of cross-competency and communication intensity between these steps has already been achieved.

It is also worthwhile to mention that portioning of the output needs to take into account architectural considerations. Portions that are sent first need to be significant for building a skeleton of the architecture, and portions that are sent later should be relatively independent of each other and should not considerably affect the architecture.

Another consideration related to parallel execution of phases concerned collaboration tools to support the development process. They need to provide an effective channel for communication between the teams, see detailed discussion on this topic in [14].

3.3   Practical Guidelines

In the previous part of this section we have discussed three issues that can help in transition to agile: communication intensity, cross-competency and parallel execution. Furthermore, we have touched the issue of high-level development tools that facilitates both achieving cross-competency, and excluding explicit design. In addition, we have touched the architectural issues that need to be taken care of when planning transition to the parallel execution of phases. We have also shown that all these issues are interconnected and should be considered together when planning transition to agile. In this subsection, we will summarize the discussion above and discuss the order in which the steps to agility are undertaken. The order depends on the specific situation at hand, thus the suggestions below should be considered only as guidelines that need to be tuned to a specific situation. Also, the order does not mean sequentiality, the steps can be implemented in parallel.

1. *Transition to using high-level development tools*. This could be recommended as the first step if these kinds of tools are not already in use. Using high-level tools will make it easier to less technical members of the development team to understand and get competence of the implementation phase.
2. *Increasing cross-competence*. This will facilitate communication between the teams participating in different phases, as it will be easier for them to understand each other.
3. *Increasing communication intensity*. This will facilitate transition to parallel execution of phases, as members of various teams begin getting more knowledge on the progress achieved in other teams
4. *Employing architecture aimed at expansion*. This will help to minimize the time for each iteration
5. *Planning for core system and incremental expansion*. This will make each delivery relatively small and facilitate transititing to parallel execution and excluding design and formal requirements engineering.
6. *Increasing parallelism in execution of phases*. This will make it possible to involve stakeholders in verification of decisions taken during the development. Parallel execution ensures that a new portion of software is produced in a speedy fashion, and could be demonstrated and discussed with the stakeholders.
7. *Involving stakeholders for functional software testing*. This could be started early in the development cycle and conducted until the delivery
8. *Excluding design phase*. This can be done by design team directly using the high level development tools adopted by the team.
9. *Excluding formal requirement elicitation*. At this steps, the requirements are started to be captured on the tacit level with consequent expression them into software

systems to be shown to the stakeholders for verification. In practical terms, formal requirements can be substituted by user stories.

3.4 Stopping the Transition Before Becoming Fully Agile

A method of transition to ASD presented in this section does not require full implementation. In some situations, becoming fully agile might be impossible due to the conditions outside the control of the development team. For example, a customer might insist on preparing full requirements and using them in contractual agreement. This will prevent implementation of Step 9 from Sect. 3.3. Other steps can still be implemented in this situation, except that starting parallel execution of other phases may become risky if signing of the contract for system development in not ensured.

Adopting our proposal for transition to ASD allows the team to decide on what steps to implement and where to stop based on their specific situation. What is more, they can decide on different stop points for different customers.

4 Research Process and Results of Testing

As has already been discussed in Sect. 2.1, development of our non-disruptive method of transition to agile was conducted in parallel with a case study in the IT department of a large insurance company. The first phase of the study was connected to the development of the method, and the second phase with testing it.

The first phase was completed based on the internal process documentation and semi-structured interviews with representatives of different teams engaged in the development process. The template for the interviews is presented in Appendix. In total, 10 people have been interviewed according to this template. Each interview took about 20 to 30 min. The interviewees had various roles, such as project leader, project manager, system developer, test leader, development support, some of them having more than one role simultaneously. The set of interviewees was defined in coordination with the management of the IT department.

Based on the information obtained, it was decided that the three most important aspects that needed to be mapped when describing the current state of affairs were communication intensity, cross-competency and timeline intensity. The step relationship modelling technique [14, 15] was chosen for representing these aspects. The concept of the timeline diagram was already known from [15], while the communication intensity matrix and cross-competency matrix were designed during the current project.

Based on the internal documentation and information from the interviews, a model of the current development process was produced. This model is closed to the one presented in Figs. 3 and 4, and Tables 2, 3 and 5, except that one step from the original model is omitted. The structure of the communication intensity and cross-competency matrixes in the original model were somewhat simpler than what is presented in Tables 3 and 5. More exactly, the details that came from merging with the output-input matrix were absent; they were added when we worked on this paper.

The test phase of the case study consisted of: (a) suggesting the next desired state of the development project, which roughly corresponds to the one presented in Tables 4 and 5 and Fig. 5, and (b) presenting the suggestions to the IT department management. The goal of the test phase was twofold, namely, to check

1. Whether the method could be understood by people not very familiar with agile practices.
2. Whether they can accept concrete suggestions based on this method, provided that they are approved by the higher management. This check (approximately) corresponds to "readiness to use" in Technology Acceptance Model (TAM) [20].

The check has been completed by presenting the method and an action plan based on it to the management of IT-department that consisted of 4 persons. After the presentation, an interview has been conducted with each person based on the following 4 questions/topics:

1. Based on the presentation, have you understood what kind of organizational changes the transition to agile will require?
2. Based on the presentation, have you understood the action plan for movement towards a more agile development process?
3. Based on the presentation, are you prepared to submit the action plan to the upper/higher management for approval?
4. Based on the presentation, are you prepared to set the suggested plan in action if approved by the higher management?

For the questions 1, 2 and 4 the answers were on the positive side from all respondents. When answering question 3, some respondents expressed doubts whether just presenting the action plan to the higher management is enough to influence the approval. However, all of them agreed that such a presentation makes sense. The doubts on influencing the decisions were connected to the plan itself not explaining the benefits to be obtained. However, another opinion was that presenting the action plan could initiate discussions that would lead to understanding the benefits. Anyway, the discussion around the third topic explicated the needs to explain the benefits achieved even before the full transition to agile has been completed. This served us as a motivation to insert the discussion on such benefits in various places of this paper.

Summarizing the lessons learned about our non-disruptive method of transition to agile from the case study, we can state that:

1. It is possible to model the current state of the development process and suggest a plan of actions for transition to agile.
2. The method is understandable for the professionals in software development not familiar with the details of agile practices. What is more, the plan of actions based on the method is considered to be "doable", and could be accepted for implementation, provided the approval of the higher management is obtained. Though, th are some doubts that such approval is easy to obtain, presenting the plan of action to the higher management might initiate a discussion that could lead to its acceptance.

The lessons above were obtained based only on one case study. However, from our practical experience, the IT department in the study is just an ordinary software development organization, and there is no reason to suggest that the lessons learned will substantially differ when the method is applied to another organization of the same kind.

In short, we consider the check for "readiness to use" as completed with positive results. On its own, such a check does not guarantee that an organization can actually execute a plan of actions developed based on the method. However, we consider this check encouraging enough for continuing the efforts of further developing and testing the method.

5 Agility in Complex Projects

The method of transition to an agile mindset presented in Sect. 3 has been developed in relation to a "classical" agile model where a relatively small and flat team can complete the whole project. For developing complex system, this may not be possible; some team structure might need to be imposed on the project even when transiting to ASD. In this section, we will consider an example when a deviation from the "flat" team is warranted, and discuss how to deal with this kind of situations when transiting to agile.

One of the steps in transition to ASD suggested in Sect. 3 is adopting high-level development tools instead of programming in a low-level programming language, like Java. A tool can be in form of a high-level domain specific language, a library of functions or classes, or a system development platform, like Ruby-on-Rails [21]. Not for all projects such a tool can be found from a third party (a vendor, or the Open Source community). Even when a somewhat suitable tool is found, it may need adjustment and extension. Both cases warrant creating an additional project inside the main project, which we refer to as tools development project.

To ensure that the main project follows ASD, the tools development project needs to be also driven in an agile manner. The connection between the two projects is illustrated in Fig. 6 that shows that the tools development project runs and is to be synchronized with the embedment phase of the main project. The developers engaged in the main project – the users of the tools become stakeholders of the tool development project. Dependent on the complexity of the system and the tool(s), the tools development project may share the main project team or get a completely different team.

Defining the core systems and iterations in the tools development project needs to be synchronized with the core system and iterations of the main project. The priority is given to the tools features that are needed for the main developers to start their work. In general, iterations in the tools development project should be shorter than in the main project, and more or less follow the idea of continues delivery [22].

Even when the main and tools development projects share (fully or partly) the same development team, they need to be kept separate, as they have different characteristics. For example, the main project can develop a system with high intensity of user-interactions, why the tools development project is about more technical systems. Note that the technical character of the tools development project does not exclude that it also uses high-level development tools, e.g. parsers, or tools for compiler development.

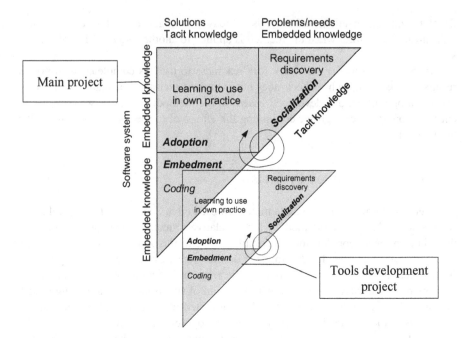

Fig. 6. Nested agile projects.

An example considered above represents a case of what could be called vertical integration of agile software projects. Though, we have not succeeded in finding scientific literature on the vertical integration of agile projects, such integration does happen in practice. More specifically, the first author of this paper has experience of this kind of nested projects both as a tools developer and as a main project developer who used tools created in a tools development project. Besides being suitable for integrating a tools development project into the main project, vertical integration could be suitable for developing multilayered systems in situations when the previous layer provides a platform for building the next layer.

Vertical integration of agile projects is not the only way of structuring complex agile projects. In case of a software system consisting of a number of semi-autonomous sub-systems that have some degree of interactions between them, a horizontal integration on the agile projects can be necessary. This, for example, is the case of hardware-near software development where the structure of software system reflects the component structure of hardware. This was, for example, the case in projects investigated in [15, 23]. A horizontal integration may be required for developing a multilayered system that consists of relatively independent interacting layers, e.g. presentation layer, business rules layer, etc. The details of horizontal integration of software projects are outside the scope of this paper; they constitute a topic of our future research.

6 Understanding the Difference

Though all methods of transiting to agile take into consideration the needs of acquiring the agile mindset, they approach the transitions in different ways. In this section, we will explain how our non-disruptive method of becoming agile differs from that of others. This is done by comparing our method with the one described in [4], the preference being made based on the fact that this method has a scientific background in form of dissertation [13].

The essence of the approach suggested in [4] is defined in the recommended sequence of steps it suggests for transiting to agile:

1. Assess your organization to determine where you should begin adding agility.
2. Obtain executive support for the move to a more agile process. You can use the readiness assessment to quantify the value of bringing in agile and identify the risks you must manage during migration.
3. Get the development team involved in the migration process to ensure buy-in. You do this by establishing a core team.
4. Identify a coach or consultant to help you with your migration. They will train the core team on agile and help you with other adoption aspects.
5. Develop a clear understanding of your current processes by documenting them.
6. Review your current process, and look for areas that can be shifted to more agile methods. Focus on areas with the most potential for improvement and the most value to the customer and your organization. The readiness assessment will also help with this task.
7. Outline a custom process based on the findings in step 6.
8. Try the new process on a pilot project.
9. Review the findings after the pilot, make changes, and continue to scale out your new methodology.

The assessing phase related to step 1 is completed by determining the following characteristics of the organizational environment:

1. *Management style*. Whether a collaborative or a command-control relation exists between managers and subordinates. The management style indicates whether management trusts the developers and vice versa.
2. *Manager buy-in*. Whether management supports or resists having a collaborative environment.
3. *Power distance*. Whether people are intimidated by/afraid to participate and be honest in the presence of their managers.
4. *Developer buy-in*. Whether the developers are willing to plan in a collaborative environment.

The assessment itself is done by conducting interviews or having a survey that includes questions with a fixed set of answers on the Likert scale, e.g.:

"Regardless of your personal preferences, as a manager you actively encourage team work over individual work." Answers: *Strongly Disagree, Tend to Disagree, Neither Agree nor Disagree, Tend to Agree, Strongly Agree.*

As we can see from the description, the focus here is on **changing the development process**. The skills needed for the agile mindset are acquired during training by a coach or consultant chosen in Step 4 during the pilot project (Step 8). Also, the first three important steps consist of ensuring support from both management and developers for transiting to an agile methodology. The amount of efforts for this phase is determined by the assessment of the organizational environment, including assessment of the existing organizational culture. As we can see from the description above, neither assessment, nor steps descriptions pay much attention to the acquiring skills that constitutes the agile mindset. Presumption is that they are to be obtained on the way when the collaborative environment and the right management style have been established.

In difference from the method shortly described above, the focus of the non-disruptive method is on **acquiring a set of skills** that constitutes the agile mindset. Presumption here is that obtaining the skills will facilitate creating a collaborative environment. For example, if all members of the development team have practical (albeit limited) experience of all phases of the development, arranging right level of communication intensity will be relatively easy. The focus on skills does not mean that the process remains the same. For example, changing the timeline intensity to provide more parallelism will require substantial change in the development process.

Another difference consists of the **level of understanding** of the essence of the agile development that is required for initiating the transition. As we can see from the description of steps in the method from [4], a considerable amount of efforts should be invested for reaching this understanding before doing something in practice. In the non-disruptive method, such level of understanding of the agile concepts is not required before starting the transition. Small localized steps could be plan, the essence of which would be easily understood by both the management and the development team, e.g. acquiring skills that the neighboring teams possess. Another example, of localized change is transiting to using the high-level development tools which will mainly concern the implementation team. The changes escalates when more radical steps are undertaken, like going to parallelism, but by that time, hopefully, the team members have the necessary skills for undertaking these steps.

From the business process perspective, the approach from [4] follows the traditional, **workflow view** on a business process as a partially ordered sequence of activities/steps/tasks for achieving some goal [24]. In short, a process is defined as a sequence of activities that can be quite complex and include parallel brunches, decision points and cycles. This is how the method of transition to agile from [4] has been built – a number of steps (activities) with detailed instruction of how to complete them illustrated by examples from practice.

The non-disruptive method of transition to agile is built based on the **state-oriented view** on business processes [25]. The latter considers a business process instance as a point moving in a multi-dimensional state-space towards a goal. A goal, in this case, is represented by some region, e.g. a surface in the state space. Such presentation of a process is quite usual in the field of physical process control, but is rarely used for controlling business processes. A process description using the state-oriented view, besides the structure of the state space, needs to provide:

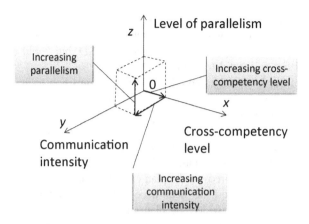

Fig. 7. The state space for the non-disruptive method of transition to the agile.

- means for measuring current position of the process in the state space, and
- rules on where and how to move from a given position in the state space. These rules could be non-deterministic, providing the people who run the process with the flexibility to make a decision based on their experience and knowledge of the process environment. The rules can take the form of recommendations "move in a certain direction" or negative recommendations – "do not take this path".

In a simplified way, the state space for our transition process is represented in Fig. 7. The x-axis represents the level of cross-competency, where zero means no cross-competency between the teams. The y-axis represents the communication intensity, where zero means that the teams do not communicate except through the formalized output/input. The z-axis represents the level of parallelism, where zero means no two teams work in parallel in the frame of the same process instance. Movements in the state space could be completed along axes, as illustrated in Fig. 7, or diagonally.

The diagram in Fig. 7 is a simplification, as points on the axes cannot be represented by numbers but are complex constructs that are represented by matrixes as in Tables 3, 4, 5 and 6, and time-line diagrams, as in Figs. 4 and 5. The presentation of the non-disruptive transition is done in this paper in accordance to the state-oriented view – how to measure the position and how to plan the next moves.

7   Conclusion

Though ASD becomes more and more popular, transition to agile still seems problematic according to the scientific and practice-oriented literature. The main reason for it, in our view, is that such a transition represents a major organizational change for a software development organization. It is well known that any organiza-tional change is difficult to complete due to an organization, as a system, always resists any change. According to [26], one of the important condition for successful organizational change is stability. A method of transition to ASD suggested in this paper provides this condition for an organization with a well-functioning TSD process. Such an organization does not need to "jump" on a radical pass to ASD, but could use the existing process as a tool for successful transition to ASD.

To the best of our knowledge, no other method of transition to agility is based on the idea of using the current well-functioning process as a platform for stepwise transition to agility. In our view, exploiting such an idea is worth trying, and this paper shows that a method for stepwise transition to ASD could be developed, at least, theoretically. While the suggested method might not be the best or an optimal one, the initial test shows that it is understandable for the management of a typical software development organization. Moreover, the plan of actions designed for this organization based on the suggested method has been accepted by the middle management who were ready to implement it provided the plan would be approved by the higher-level management. More tests and further development are required to confirm the validity of our method. However, the results achieved so far (including the initial test) look encouraging.

Our method for transition to agility exploits three types of measurements that can be used to determine the level of agility achieved while the organization is still following TSD: communication intensity, cross-competency, and the level of parallelism. These are easy to understand measures, and as our test case shows, they can be obtained through interviewing people working in the project. These measurements can be used independently whether the organization wants to transit to agility in disruptive or non-disruptive manner. These measurements could be also of use for improving the existing process without having the goal of becoming fully agile.

Our method for transition to ASD, including measuring the level of agility, has been developed based on a theoretical view that considers a software development process as a knowledge transformation activity [11, 12]. This view represents a new way of understanding agility, which in its own turn needs validation and testing. The current work could be also considered as an additional to [11, 12] confirmation of the usefulness of the knowledge transformation view on software development.

As has been shown in Sect. 5, transiting to ASD while developing complex software systems adds an additional dimension to the transition process. Initial analysis shows that it is possible to make transition even in such cases, provided a proper structure for the parallel running projects could be found.

Our plans for the future include further development and testing of the stepwise method for transition to agility, as well as dissemination of results, especially among practitioners. The latter activity is considered as an important one in the Design Science research [7]. The reason for its importance is that the researchers themselves have no possibility to fully test a new design, aside of conducting demonstration in few cases. The real test can be completed only when (and if) the industry adopts the method so that more test cases become available for studying.

Acknowledgements. The authors are in debts to the management and developers of the IT department of the insurance company who initiated this research and spent their time answering interview questions, and listening, discussing and accepting our suggestions. The authors are also thankful to the anonymous reviewers and to the ICEIS 2016 conference participants whose comments and questions helped us to improve this paper.

Appendix

This appendix presents a template used in semi-structured interviews (translated from Swedish). The questions in the template served only as an introduction to the topics of interest, an open discussion always followed after the topic had been introduced.

1. Group 1: Introduction and working environment in general
   (a) What is your position/role in the organization?
   (b) How does your ordinary working day look like? Which regular tasks do you complete?
   (c) Does your organization use any kind of analysis when planning an organizational change?
   (d) Does your organization have a support center which provide the information support, education, tools, answers questions, etc.?
   (e) Does your organization use any kind of "hybrid solution", where the agile and traditional methods are combined?
2. Group 2: Communication between teams and roles
   (a) How the team to which you belong communicates with colleagues that belong to other teams? Who initiates communication? Does it work well? What is input/output of such communication?
   (b) With which other teams and roles do you/your team communicates most frequently during a project?
   (c) With which other teams and roles do you/your team communicates least frequently or not communicates at all during a project?
3. Group 3: Team structure
   (a) How does the team structure looks like in the projects in which you participate?
4. Group 4: Cross-competency
   (a) What is you experience of other roles in software development project in addition to the role/position you hold today?
   (b) What is physical layout of your office? Is it team/project based or role/position based?
   (c) How the flow of activities in the projects in which you participate looks like? Is it more of a waterfall nature or there is an inclination to agile?

References

1. Highsmith, J., Orr, K., Cockburn, A.: E-Business Application Delivery, pp. 4–17. www.cutter.com/freestuff/ead0002.pdf2. Accessed 2000

2. Conboy, K., Coyle, S., Wang, X., Pikkarainen, M.: People over process: key challenges in agile development. IEEE Softw. **28**(4), 48–57 (2011)
3. Hajjdiab, H., Taleb, A.: Adopting agile software development: issues and challenges. IJMVSC **2**(3), 1–10 (2011)
4. Smith, G., Sidky, A.: Becoming Agile. Manning, Greenwich (2009)
5. Hunt, A.: The Failure of Agile. http://blog.toolshed.com/2015/05/the-failure-of-agile.html. Accessed 2015
6. Love, K.: Waterfall vs Agile: Baseball vs Soccer? https://www.linkedin.com/pulse/waterfall-vs-agile-baseball-soccer-kristin-love. Accessed July 2016
7. Peffers, K., Tuunanen, T., Rothenberger, M.A., Chatterjee, S.: A design science research methodology for information systems research. J. Manag. Inf. Syst. **24**(3), 45–78 (2007)
8. Agile Alliance: Manifesto for Agile Software Development. http://agilemanifesto.org/. Accessed 2001
9. Weaver, M.: Do you agree or disagree that Scrum is not Agile? http://www.linkedin.com/groups/Do-you-agree-disagree-that-81780.S.52354777. Accessed 2011
10. Conboy, K., Fitzgerald, B.: Toward a conceptual framework of agile methods: a study of agility in different disciplines. In: Proceedings of the 2004 ACM Workshop on Interdisciplinary Software Engineering Research, Newport Beach, pp. 37–44 (2004)
11. Bider, I.: Analysis of agile software development from the knowledge transformation perspective. In: Johansson, B., Andersson, B., Holmberg, N. (eds.) BIR 2014. LNBIP, vol. 194, pp. 143–157. Springer, Cham (2014). doi:10.1007/978-3-319-11370-8_11
12. Bider, I.: Can the systems perspective help in attaining success in software engineering projects? Inquiry into the area of applicability for agile software development. In: Jacobson, J., Lawson, H. (eds.) Software Engineering in the Systems Context: Addressing Frontiers, Practice and Education, pp. 423–466. College Publications, London (2015)
13. Sidky, A.: A structured approach to adopting agile practices: the agile adoption framework. Ph.D. thesis. In: Digital Library and ARchives. http://scholar.lib.vt.edu/theses/available/etd-05252007-110748/. Accessed 2007
14. Bider, I., Perjons, E.: Design science in action: developing a modeling technique for eliciting requirements on business process management (BPM) tools. Softw. Syst. Model. **14**(3), 1159–1188 (2015)
15. Bider, I., Otto, H.: Modeling a global software development project as a complex socio-technical system to facilitate risk management and improve the project structure. In: Proceedings of the 10th IEEE International Conference on Global Software Engineering (ICGSE), forthcoming, Ciudad Real, Spain (2015)
16. Baskerville, R.L., Pries-Heje, J., Venable, J.: Soft design science methodology. In: DERIST 2009, pp. 1–11 (2009
17. Bider, I., Johannesson, P., Perjons, E.: Design science research as movement between individual and generic situation-problem-solution spaces. In: Baskerville, R., De Marco, M., Spagnoletti, P. (eds.) Designing Organizational Systems. An Interdisciplinary Discourse, pp. 35–61. Springer, Heidelberg (2013)
18. Nonaka, I.: A dynamic theory of organizational knowledge creation. Organ. Sci. **5**(1), 14–37 (1994)
19. Polanyi, M.S.: Knowing and Being. University of Chicago, Chicago (1969)
20. Davis, F.: Perceived usefulness, perceived ease of use, and user acceptance of information technology. MIS Q. **13**(3), 319–340 (1989)
21. Rails. http://rubyonrails.org/. Accessed Aug 2016
22. Humble, J., Farley, D.: Continuous Delivery Reliable Software: Releases through Build, Test, and Deployment Automation. Pearson Education, Upper Saddle River (2010)

23. Bider, I., Karapantelakis, A., Khadka, N.: Building a high-level process model for soliciting requirements on software tools to support software development: experience report. In: Short Paper Proceedings of the 6th IFIP WG 8.1 Working Conference on the Practice of Enterprise Modeling (PoEM 2013), CEUR, Riga, Latvia, vol. 1023, pp. 70–82 (2013)
24. Hammer, M., Champy, J.: Reengineering the corporation: a manifesto for business revolution. HarperBusiness, New York (1993)
25. Khomyakov, M., Bider, I.: Achieving workflow flexibility through taming the chaos. In: Patel, D., Choudhury, I., Patel, S., de Cesare, S. (eds.) OOIS 2000, pp. 85–92. Springer, Heidelberg (2000)
26. Regev, G.: Fundamental systems thinking concepts for is engineering: balancing between change and non-change. In: CAiSE2015. http://sched.co/2OGV. Accessed 2015

Linking Knowledge Mapping and Lessons Learned in a Research and Development Group: A Pilot Study

Erivan Souza da Silva Filho[1(✉)], Davi Viana[1,2], Jacilane Rabelo[1],
and Tayana Conte[1]

[1] USES Research Group, Instituto de Computação,
Universidade Federal do Amazonas, Manaus 69077, Brazil
{essf,jaci.rabelo,tayana}@icomp.ufam.edu.br,
davi.viana@ufma.br
[2] Coordenação do Curso de Engenharia da Computação,
Universidade Federal do Maranhão, 1966, São Luís, Brazil

Abstract. In Software Engineering, Knowledge Mapping is a process to discover aspects or meanings through the analysis of relationships between artifacts or people. However, to create a knowledge map, we need a process for capturing and analyzing data, so that we can extract information that reflects those aspects. In this paper, we propose a knowledge mapping process that generates a knowledge map and a set of knowledge profiles considering each mapped member. We developed a new technique by improving existing techniques in literature. In addition, we planned and performed a pilot study in a Research and Development (R&D) group. In this paper, we present our findings regarding the application of the proposed technique and the analysis of the knowledge map for that group. Additionally, we generated links between the knowledge profiles and collected lessons learned for one of the projects that was performed by this R&D group.

Keywords: Knowledge management · Post-mortem Analysis · Knowledge mapping · Knowledge map

1 Introduction

The main asset of Software Companies is knowledge. Thus, it is necessary to manage this knowledge and use their experiences in development activities [1]. In any industrial or academic environment, there are people who have knowledge, and it may be of interest to promote such knowledge management [2].

Knowledge management is the process of creating, validating, representing, distributing and applying knowledge [3]. Knowledge management also refers to identifying and increasing the collective knowledge in an organization to help it become more competitive [4].

The goal of these efforts is to provide members of the organization with the knowledge they need to maximize their effectiveness, thus improving the efficiency of the organization [5]. The environment or territory in the context of knowledge

S. Hammoudi et al. (Eds.): ICEIS 2016, LNBIP 291, pp. 200–224, 2017.
DOI: 10.1007/978-3-319-62386-3_10

management is not geographical, but intellectual [6], where we need techniques that seek to represent the main aspects of that environment.

One of the techniques in Knowledge Management that seeks to represent these aspects is Knowledge Mapping. Knowledge mapping is a process of surveying, assessing and linking the information, knowledge, competencies and proficiencies held by individuals and groups within an organization [7].

The result of a mapping is a Knowledge Map that shows the relationships among the procedures, concepts and skills, which provides easy and effective access to sources of knowledge [8]. The main purpose and benefit of a knowledge map are to show people from within the company where to go when they need knowledge [8].

This paper presents a process of knowledge mapping that aims at representing the flow of the employees' knowledge within software organizations. We combined some approaches in order to create such process. This paper also describes the results of a pilot study in which the proposed process was applied in a Research and Development (R&D) group. Additionally, we have extended the results from our Knowledge Mapping process in our previous study with a Post-mortem Analysis.

The remainder of this paper is organized as follows. Section 2 presents our theoretical reference. Section 3 presents the developed knowledge mapping process. Section 4 shows planning process of the pilot study. Section 5 discusses the results obtained in the pilot study and Sect. 6 shows the results of our knowledge mapping process linked with the lessons learned from a previous study. Finally, Sect. 7 presents our conclusions and future work.

2 Theoretical Reference

Individual knowledge is necessary for the development of knowledge within an organization [3]. Knowledge within an organization is a collection of knowledge, experiences and information, which people or groups employ to carry out their tasks [9]. This section shows the theoretical reference and the main concepts for this work.

2.1 Knowledge Management

Human resources are the main assets of many companies where knowledge has to be preserved and passed from the individual to the organizational level, enabling continuous improvement and learning [10]. Companies generally understand Knowledge as how information is encoded with a high proportion of human value-added, including perception, interpretation, context, experience, wisdom, and so on [11].

Davenport and Prusak [12] made a distinction between data and information. Data is a group of distinct facts and goals related to events. Information aims at changing the way in which the receiver perceives something, exercising some impact on his/her judgment and behavior.

Nonaka and Takeuchi [13] states that knowledge, unlike information, is about beliefs and commitment, and characterize it into two types: explicit and tacit. Explicit or codified knowledge can be articulated in formal or textual language. Tacit knowledge is the personal knowledge, incorporated to the individual experience, and that involves intangible factors (e.g. personal beliefs, perspectives and value systems).

Knowledge Management is a method that simplifies the process of sharing, distributing, creating and comprehending a company's knowledge [14]. Its goal is to solve problems regarding the identification, localization and usage of knowledge [15].

A prerequisite for the strengthening of knowledge management is a good understanding of how knowledge flows within the organization [1]. The identification of the knowledge flow shows us the way on which new concepts and ideas are spread, which can be useful to facilitate changes in management initiatives [16]. One of the applied techniques for searching and defining organizational knowledge flow is knowledge mapping.

2.2 Knowledge Mapping

Knowledge mapping is a process, method, or tool made for analyzing knowledge in order to discover characteristics or meanings, and view knowledge in a comprehensible and transparent manner [17]. The purpose of knowledge mapping is to seek a better orientation in a given domain and access knowledge from the right people at the right time [2].

One of the advantages of knowledge mapping includes the freedom to organize without restriction, meaning that there are no limits to the number of ideas and connections that can be made [18]. Knowledge mapping usually takes part of Knowledge Audit processes and methodologies.

Elias et al. [19] define Knowledge Audit (KA) as the identification, analysis and evaluation of the activities, processes and practices for managing the knowledge that a company already has.

Knowledge Audit is used to provide an investigation into the organization's knowledge about the health of knowledge [19], identifying and understanding the knowledge needs in organizational processes.

Meanwhile, by using Knowledge Mapping techniques would show a logical structure of relationships between tacit human knowledge and explicit knowledge in documents [2]. The result of knowledge mapping is a knowledge map.

2.3 Knowledge Map

Knowledge Map is a diagram that can represent words, ideas, tasks, or other items linked to and arranged in radial order around a central key word or idea [18]. Furthermore, it is an interactive and open representation that organizes and builds structures and procedural knowledge used in the pursuit of exploration and problem solving [7].

Knowledge maps also provide a holistic view of knowledge resources [8]. Eppler [6] distinguishes five types of Knowledge Maps, shown in Table 1. The five maps can be combined to generate new mapping techniques.

Table 1. Types of knowledge maps [6].

Name	Description
Knowledge source maps	These are maps that structure a population of experts from a company through search criteria, such as their knowledge domain, proximity, length of service or geographical distribution
Knowledge asset maps	This type of map visually describes the storage of knowledge of a person, a group, a unit or an organization
Knowledge structure maps	It is the overall architecture of a knowledge domain and shows how parts relate to each other. It assists managers in understanding and interpreting a specialized field
Knowledge application maps	It shows what kind of knowledge must be applied at certain stages of the design process or in a specific business situation. It answers the question of which people are involved in an intensive knowledge process, such as auditing, consulting, research or product development
Knowledge development maps	These maps can serve as development pathways or visual learning which provide a common corporate vision for organizational learning

2.4 Related Work

There are different techniques to map organizational knowledge, and each technique can use a set of tools, approaches, objectives and specific characteristics [17]. In the following paragraphs, we show the main works that served as the theoretical basis for our mapping proposal.

Hansen and Krautz [1] proposed using Rich Pictures (mechanism that uses pictograms for representation) as a technique to map the flow of organizational knowledge. The methodology consists of two large main stages: preparation phase and mapping phase.

- Preparation Phase: Based on the collected data, (s)he created an initial map of the organization.
- Mapping phase: It results in a knowledge map that describes actors and knowledge flow, as well as key features of the organization.

Kim et al. [20] defined that a map is composed of two main components: diagrams that are graphical representations of components; and specifications, which are descriptions of the components. The authors also suggested creating a profile of the extracted knowledge, establishing a structure representing the characteristics of the mapped knowledge.

According to Kim et al. [20], knowledge maps should achieve:

1. Formalization of all the knowledge inventories in the organization;
2. Perception of the relationship between knowledge;
3. Efficient Navigation of knowledge inventories;
4. Promotion of socialization/outsourcing of knowledge by connecting the experts' domains with knowledge explorers.

Eppler [6] has developed five steps that must be performed to design and build a Knowledge Map. These are:

1th. Step: To identify the knowledge-intensive processes, problems or issues within the organization. The resulting map should focus on improving the intensive knowledge.
2th. Step: To deduce the sources of knowledge, assets or relevant process elements or problems.
3th. Step: To codify these elements in a way that it makes them more accessible to the organization.
4th Step: To integrate this codified knowledge or documents information in a visual interface that allows the user to navigate or search for it.
5th Step: To provide means for updating the Knowledge Map. A Knowledge Map is as good as the links it provides. If these links are outdated or obsolete, the map is useless.

The mapping techniques found in the literature show some approaches focusing on the flow of knowledge within the organization and the definition of knowledge sources. However, improved techniques may be applied to represent participants' knowledge based on knowledge flow.

Finally, Elias et al. [21] proposed a methodology to identify and analyze knowledge flows in work processes. Such stages are:

1. To identify the main documents and people involved in the process;
2. To analyze the knowledge sources identified in the first step;
3. To identify how the knowledge and sources are involved in the activities performed in the process;
4. To analyze to find the problems that could be affecting knowledge flows identified.

The purpose of this paper is to integrate and improve these previous methods and generate a set of profiles of the participants in a software project team. From the data of these profiles, we can verify what is the most used knowledge by participants.

3   Process of Knowledge Mapping in Software Teams

Our Process of Knowledge Mapping is mainly based on the work of Hansen and Kautz [1], since their method allows enhancements or modifications. Furthermore, the work by Kim et al. [20] contributes to the profiling strategy and the work by Eppler [6] contributes to the definition of the steps to build the knowledge maps.

The main objective of the map is to find the core competencies of the participants based on their interaction with other team members and with sources of knowledge. The procedure of the Knowledge mapping consists of two phases:

- **Data Collection Phase:** The data that will compose the Knowledge Map will be collected. The collected data can come from two sources in the organization: the project or organization. Regardless of the origin, this phase will organize the data that will be employed to build a map of the structure;

- **Mapping Phase:** It is the organization of the data and the construction of the Knowledge Map. According to Table 1, the produced map is classified as a Knowledge Source Map, showing the sources of explicit (websites, books or documents) and tacit (participants) knowledge. Moreover, a profile for each participant will be produced, indicating his/her main accessed knowledge.

The moderator of the Knowledge Mapping Process can play many roles such as facilitator (during the data collection phase) or map developer (during the mapping stage).

3.1 Data Collection Phase

The purpose of the data collection phase is to extract the necessary information to create the Knowledge Map, as shown in Fig. 1.

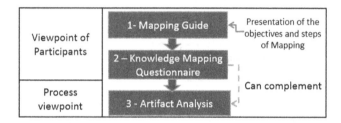

Fig. 1. Activities of the data collection stage from the Knowledge Mapping process.

1. The Mapping Guide is a presentation showing the participants which activities they will do during the meeting. The purpose of the presentation is to support the facilitator of the meeting and present a practical visual guide to participants;
2. We apply the questionnaire to the participants who will create the Knowledge Map;
3. Analyzing Artifacts. The purpose of this activity is to see how organizations or group view the participants and to triangulate the facts with the questionnaire information.

We describe these activities in the following subsections.

3.1.1 Presentation of the Mapping Guide

The Mapping Guide should be presented to the participants of the meeting before the questionnaire. The structure of the presentation follows the following steps:

- Presentation of the Facilitator and his role for the group;
- Explanation of what is tacit and explicit knowledge;
- Brief explanation of Knowledge Management (optional);
- Brief explanation of what is Knowledge Mapping (if this is the first mapping);
- Presentation of the questionnaire structure;
- Presentation of the activity guides to the participants;

- Presentation of the questions on Knowledge Mapping.

Knowing the question of the knowledge mapping helps us to focus on the knowledge that we want and to capture accurate information, aiming to avoid extracting information that has nothing to do with the knowledge we demand.

3.1.2   Knowledge Mapping Questionnaire

The Knowledge Mapping questionnaire has a logical structure that seeks to find three aspects: what activities the participant exerted during the execution of the project, what or who (s)he researched to acquire knowledge and who (s)he helped.

Participants must be left free to consult each other, and they must have available resources to consult when they have questions while filling out the questionnaire. The reason for using these resources is that some people may not be able to remember some relevant information.

The first part of the Knowledge Mapping survey (see Fig. 2) is related to the **Applied Topic of knowledge** of the activities (s)he carried out. The purpose of this information is to know what knowledge (s)he applied.

> **Based on the activities you performed in the project:**
> **Which topics knowledge did you applied to your activities?**
> *Sample topics: Programming C, Personas creation, Case Study, Apache configuration, etc.*

Fig. 2. Field to describe which activities were conducted.

The field in Fig. 3 is related to **Who/What (s)he consulted** to carry out his/her activities. The participant may indicate if (s)he consulted a person or an artifact and they should describe the name of the consulted person or artifact in the "Name of Person or Artifact" field. Then s/he must complement with a brief description regarding what was consulted. Some fields present different sizes because it might be possible that the participant has more than one consult to a device or person.

> **Which people or artifacts did you consulted during the project?**
> *Example artifact: starckoverflow (website) Project Document (Doc), Learn C in 24 hours (Book), Practical guide in C (pdf).*
>
> **Name of Person or Artifact:**
> **Brief description of consultation(s):**

Fig. 3. Field to describe the consults that were performed.

Finally, the participant must inform in the field shown in Fig. 4 **Which people (s) he helped** during his/her activities. Based on this and the previous field, we can triangulate the information aiming to find the flow of knowledge among participants and to know what kind of knowledge takes place among them.

Which people have you helped and shared some knowledge during the project?
Name of Person: Brief description of help (s):

Fig. 4. Field where the participant informs who (s)he helped.

3.1.3 Artifact Analysis

The artifact analysis is defined as the analysis of information from project-related documents that may be potential sources of knowledge. Its purpose is to explicit knowledge sources that will integrate the knowledge map.

3.2 Mapping Phase

The mapping phase will analyze the collected data in the data collection phase and will generate the knowledge map of the project team. Initially, we organize all the collected data on a table, as shown in Fig. 5. Then, we produce the representation of the knowledge map sources (either by using physical materials with a whiteboard or through digital tools). Finally, we will generate the profile of each participant.

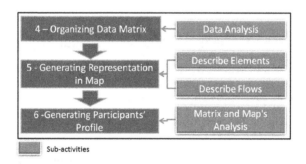

Fig. 5. Activities from the Knowledge Mapping phase.

3.2.1 Organizing the Data Matrix

Mapping questionnaires are analyzed at this stage and the moderator, who is implementing the Knowledge Mapping process, should examine each of them as (s)he carries out the parallel activities of this phase.

In the actors-artifacts relationship (where the actors are the participants), we organize all the data in a table following the format in Fig. 6. In the horizontal lines, we insert all the names of the project participants that have been mentioned in the fields "who you consulted" and "who you helped" from the questionnaires.

The columns are filled with the same name of the participants defined horizontally. After dividing the "artifacts", we can enter the names of the mentioned artifacts by any participant within the questionnaires.

Actors	Participant 1	Participant N	Artifacts	Artifact 1 (Type)
Participant 1		Id 1		Id 2
Participant N				

Plan1   Plan2

Fig. 6. Structure of actors-artifact in the data matrix.

While reading what artifacts were mentioned by the participants in the question-naire, we should avoid duplication and then generalize when two participants refer to the same artifact. For example, two participants can mention the Stackoverflow online forum of questions and answers differently, where one says "**Search Stackoverflow forum**" while another says "**stackoverflow.com**". Both participants refer to the same artifact, the Stackoverflow forum, so we will not insert two different columns for it. Instead, we can name the same column as "**Stackoverflow (website)**", where the parentheses in keyword help identifying what this artifact is.

After finishing to fill out the table, the cells are filled with an identifier of the description of the consulted information by the participant. For this, we will use a table for supporting where we will store the consult description gathered in the fields "who you consulted" and "who you helped" from the questionnaires. It is exemplified in Fig. 7.

Id	Relationship description	Helped (<) /Consulted (>)	Participant
1	Description of Id 1	<	Participant 1
2	Description of Id 2	>	Participant 2

Plan1   Plan2

Fig. 7. Structure to assist description of relationships.

Finally, we have the name of the participants horizontally, while what they accessed (whether it is other participants or artifacts) is shown vertically.

3.2.2 Generating Representations in Map

The representation on the map can be done by a support tool which must have the following characteristics:

- Change colors or pictures of the node;
- Create edges between nodes;
- Assign weights and Text on the edges;
- Assign texts to the nodes.

After choosing the tool to be used, the activities of the process of knowledge mapping creation are initiated.

Based on the Data Matrix information built in the previous activity, we will perform the following steps to build the map:

1. Write what project members are;
2. Write what the artifacts informed by the participant are;
3. Center map members and leave the artifacts at the edges;
4. Insert an edge between nodes, namely between a member and an artifact, or between members;
5. Assign which or what are the relationships from such edge, based on the auxiliary table of the Data Matrix called Relationship Description;
6. Repeat from step 4 until all edges are created;
7. Document the map and its version.

After that, it is estimated that this map shows which members consult others and about what, and what artifacts are found during a project. It is recommended the review of the map by a second person in order to avoid omissions or errors.

3.2.3   Generating Participants' Profile

The profile of the participants is a representation indicating what skills or competencies (s)he is applying. They reference not only what (s)he informs, but what other participants inform. The map should also show how we can find him/her, what knowledge (s)he masters, what his/her sources of knowledge are and with whom (s)he communicates.

To generate the participant's profile, we will use the Data Matrix information, the analysis of the artifacts and the Knowledge Map as basis looking for:

- What are the main topics of knowledge (s)he employed in his/her activities?;
- What sources of knowledge does (s)he use?;
- What people has (s)he worked with or had some knowledge flow?.

This information will fill the items about the participant's profile in Fig. 8.

Participant Name	<The full name entered by the participant.>
Position or Role	<Position or role of participant.>
Email	<Participant contact E-mail.>
Telephone	<Participant contact number.>
Keywords of major skills	
<Keywords that describe he/she skills. The keywords are the codes identified below.>	
Knowledge sources	
<What sources of explicit knowledge he/she consult based on the knowledge map.>	
People whom (s)he is related in the map	
<Which people the participant has a knowledge transfer based on knowledge map.>	
Worked projects within the Group	
<Project works within the research group.>	
Knowledge flow	
<The topics of knowledge informed by the participants.>	
Knowledge in...	
<Knowledge flow code.>	<Full description of flow.>

Fig. 8. Capturing information about artifacts used by a participant.

The fields **Name, E-mail, Position or Role**, and **Telephone** are extracted from the information previously collected. The information from the Knowledge Sources field will be collected analyzing the data matrix based on the columns of the artifacts that the user entered. As shown in Fig. 9, we use the participant's line and check the column of the artifacts used by him/her. This will be the information that will compose the field.

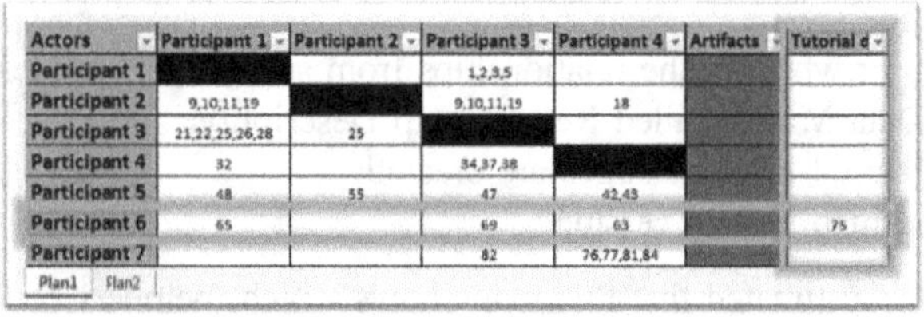

Actors	Participant 1	Participant 2	Participant 3	Participant 4	Artifacts	Tutorial d
Participant 1			1,2,3,5			
Participant 2	9,10,11,19		9,10,11,19	18		
Participant 3	21,22,25,26,28	25				
Participant 4	32		34,37,38			
Participant 5	48	55	47	42,43		
Participant 6	65		69	63		75
Participant 7			82	76,77,81,84		

Plan1 Plan2

Fig. 9. Capturing information about artifacts used by a participant.

The **people to whom (s)he is related in the map** field will consist of all participants and people outside the project with whom the participant had any knowledge flow. In addition to identifying the participants, we assign weights according to the total sum of the flows between two participants, as seen in Fig. 10.

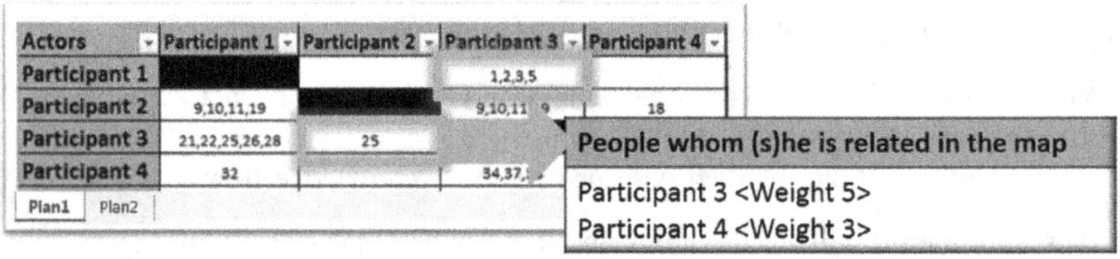

Fig. 10. How to identify people connected to a participant.

Regarding the **Worked projects within the Group** field, this information will be extracted based on the analysis of the artifacts. In case that there is no identification, the field is filled with "None identified".

The **Participant Knowledge Topics** is the information that participants provided in the knowledge topic field of carried out activities in the questionnaire research, Subsect. 3.1.2. After entering the information, we will generate codes for what was inserted. In addition, two descriptions may belong to the same code and thus increase the weight of this information, as seen in Fig. 11.

Knowledge flow will be the cross analysis of the Data Matrix for each participant (see Fig. 12). The reason is that while the row shows just what the participant said, the column complements what others have reported about him/her. The Id (identifier) and his name should be placed in sequence in the field to be codified in the future.

After entering all the flows belonging to the participant, we will code with words that identify a concept or represent these flows (see Fig. 12). The **Knowledge in …**

Participant Knowledge Topics		
Review of material on Molic interaction modeling; Mockups together with Molic (diagrams); Case studies; Inspection techniques for Molic diagrams; TAM (Technological Acceptance Model).		
Molic (3)	•	Review of material on Molic interaction modeling;
	•	Mockups together with Molic (diagrams);
	•	Inspection techniques for Molic diagrams.
TAM (1)	TAM (Technological Acceptance Model.	
Case studies (1)	Case studies.	

Fig. 11. Knowledge topics of a participant.

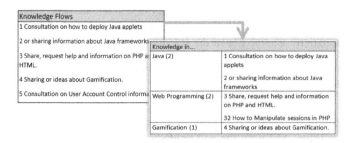

Fig. 12. How to identify people connected to a participant.

field will be composed of all the coding of flows. Some encodings may have more than one flow, and the flow may belong to more than one coding.

It is recommended the execution of codification by someone with knowledge of the organizational culture. Thus, the creation of codes is closer to reflect the reality of the organization.

4 Pilot Study in a Research and Development Group

The focus of the pilot study is to conduct a feasibility study of the Knowledge Mapping process. The primary purpose of a feasibility study is not to find a definitive answer, but to create a body of knowledge about the application of the technology [22].

As a result, we gain knowledge regarding if the process we are developing is feasible, if it produces a consistent result while identifying its limitations which, according to Shull *et al.* [23], allows: (1) the refinement of technology; and (2) the generation of new hypotheses on the application (in this case, the process of Knowledge Mapping) to be investigated in future studies.

The pilot study was applied in a software engineering and usability research group, which is formed by six Ph.D. candidates and four master students working on research and development in the areas of Software Engineering and Human- Computer Interaction. Thus, there are representatives of the population and, because it is a pilot study, we sought first to carry out the study within the research group and then evaluate in an industrial environment. The focus of the knowledge map was to find information related to types of knowledge that participants had applied or were applying in their research or in R & D (Research and Development) projects.

4.1   The Steps of the Pilot Study

The pilot study followed three steps detailed below.

1. Preparation: Contains the pilot study design, the creation of instruments and training of possible applicators of activity of Data Collection;
2. Implementation: The group in which the proposed technology would be applied attends a meeting in order to collect data. In this case, the Knowledge Mapping process;
3. Analysis and generation of results: The collected information will go through the data analysis of the Knowledge Mapping process.

By running the pilot study, we can verify the main aspects required for the application of the proposed technology (the process of mapping of knowledge) and analyze its limitations to evolve it in the future.

Instrumentation. For the pilot study, the following instruments that supported the whole process were developed:

- Approach manual: a Knowledge Mapping process manual was prepared explaining step by step how to apply and generate a knowledge map, how to collect data, which tools to use and what the end products of the process would be.
- Knowledge Mapping Questionnaire: a questionnaire that aims to capture key information needed to generate the knowledge map and profiles of the participants.
- Presentation of the Mapping Guide: a presentation guide that supports the moderator when applying the questionnaire and participants during the data collection. The presentation consists of 12 slides that show the objectives of the data collection, the structure of the questionnaire and a behavior guide for participants to follow during the session.

Guest Researcher. A researcher with no relation to the research was asked to administer the questionnaire to the participants. At a meeting, the author of the proposal presented the research objectives, the guide of the approach and the tools (questionnaire and presentation) for the guest researcher.

Additionally, we collected suggestions from the invited researcher to better conduct the experiment, which allowed gathering initial feedback for the improvement of the technical instrumentation. After the transfer of information, the execution of the study was scheduled with the group of participants.

4.2   Knowledge Mapping Results

In this phase, we plan and prepare all the instrumentation and contact the people that are necessary for the implementation of the Knowledge Mapping process. The main purpose of the preparation is to address threats to validity. Based on the recommendations by Wohlin *et al.* [24], the following threats were addressed:

- Internal validity (Instrumentation): This is the effect caused by the artifacts used in the execution of the experiment. In the case of a poorly-planned experiment, its results will be negatively affected. Thus, a second researcher reviewed the artifacts created by the author process.
- Construct validity (Expected Experimenter): The author of the knowledge mapping process can consciously or unconsciously cause bias in the results of a study based on what (s)he expects the results of the experiment will be. When implementing the experiment, we asked another researcher with no involvement in this research to apply the process. However, in the analysis phase and the generation of results, the author of the process performed the analysis.
- External validity (interaction of participants and treatment): It occurs when a sample does not represent the population we want to generalize. The focus of the process is to map software project teams. We chose a research group and R & D (Research and Development) projects due to convenience and the similarity of their themes and situations.

4.3   Execution

Execution is the application of knowledge mapping questionnaire with the participants that will create the knowledge map. The questionnaire was printed and distributed to participants with no time limit to fill it out, and we allowed the interaction among them. The guest researcher assumed the role of facilitator, which sought to conduct all data collection and answer questions from the participants.

The participants took around thirty minutes to answer the questionnaire. The author of the proposal was absent during the execution process of the data collection in order to avoid any bias in the pilot study. After finishing the execution, the data was delivered to the author of the process for analysis.

4.4   Knowledge Mapping Results

We explain the performed data analysis in this section. The results are related to the knowledge map of the team and the profiles of participants. For the execution of this phase, we did not invite another researcher, because the process needed a closer analysis from the authors of the proposal.

At this stage, all the Knowledge Mapping phase must have been executed, as described in Subsect. 3.2, for the activities of **Organizing Data Matrix** and **Generating Representation in Map**.

For the **Generating Participant's Profile** activity, which is the analysis and creation of all profiles, there is no reliable estimate to be informed due to the improvement of the technique while performing the activity. We explain the results of this pilot study in the following section.

5 Results of Knowledge Mapping Process

This section presents the results of the implementation of the Knowledge Mapping process. In addition, lessons learned and results of the implementation of the knowledge mapping process are presented.

5.1 Knowledge Mapping Results

As presented in Sect. 4.3, in the execution of the study, we employed a printed questionnaire (Subsect. 3.1.2) with ten participants in an R & D (Research and Development) group. Ten questionnaires were analyzed in the mapping stage. A spreadsheet was used to support the creation of the Data Matrix.

For the matrix, two tabs have been created. The first one shows the connections between participants with participants or artifacts, as described in Subsect. 3.2.1. A sample result can be seen in Fig. 13.

Actors	Participant 1	Participant 2	Participant 3	Participant 4	Participant 5	Participant 6	Participant 7	Participant 8	Participant 9	Participant 10
Participant 1			1,2,3,5		6			8	7	4
Participant 2	9,10,11,19		9,10,11,19	18					18,14,15,20	16,17
Participant 3	21,22,25,24,28	25			23,24,27				27,19	30,31
Participant 4	32		34,37,38				33	35,36		39
Participant 5	48	55	47	42,43					54	46,53
Participant 6	65		69	63	66,74		64	71	68	59,60,61,62,72,73
Participant 7			82	76,77,81,84				79		78,80
Participant 8				85						
Participant 9		96	99	100			100	57		94,95
Participant 10	111		106,110	104,108,114	117	107	104,108		104-110-113-115-11	

Plan1   Plan2

Fig. 13. First tab of the data matrix.

The second tab stores the description Ids generated in each cell. Moreover, it stores the participant's name and if the data is going in or out Fig. 14).

Id	Description	Helped(<)/ Consulted (>)	Participant
1	Help in the division or material for interaction modeling	<	Participant 1
2	Sharing information on technical proposals for inspection Mo	<	Participant 1
3	Sharing and request help information about GT and TAM.	<	Participant 1
4	Sharing ideas about gamification.	<	Participant 1
5	Consultation on TAM's information and GT	>	Participant 1
6	Consultation on statistical test information	>	Participant 1
7	Consultation on technical ideas for inspection	>	Participant 1
8	Consultation on statistical tests and English	>	Participant 1

Plan1   Plan2

Fig. 14. Second tab of the data matrix.

Then, we generated the graphical representation of the Knowledge Map based on the steps described in Subsect. 3.2.2. We applied the NetMiner 4.2.1 tool due to its ease of use. The generated result can be seen in Fig. 15.

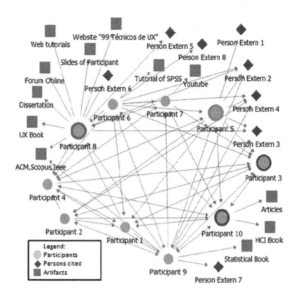

Fig. 15. Map generated by NetMiner (available at: http://www.netminer.com). (Color figure online)

The map elements were created based on the Data Matrix. As recommended in the approach's manual, participants were centralized on the map and indicated people or artifacts were allocated at the edges of the map.

Knowledge maps can provide a set of knowledge sources and flows. In addition, managers can use this information for decision-making. However, it is important to carry out a systematic analysis of such knowledge maps to reveal relevant insights of the organization [25]. Consequently, we applied Social Network Analysis (SNA) to systematically investigate some aspects of knowledge flow depicted by the knowledge maps.

In the map, we identified two central connectors. The central connectors are people with whom other participants interact more [26], they are the participants from 3 to 10 (green circle with a blue border in Fig. 15). Participant 5 is classified as Border Key [26], which communicates with more people outside the network and serves as an ambassador between the network's internal and external knowledge.

We can check the level of reciprocity that is the similarity between the entries of two participants [27]. The strongest connections are between the participants 1 and 3, followed by the participants 9 and 10.

Additionally, we can analyze that Participant 8 behaves like a person with the most access to artifacts (Red border in Fig. 15). Moreover, Participant 5 (Orange border in Fig. 15) is the person who consults the higher number of people within the network, which may be an indicator that (s)he had the current highest level of learning.

After creating the knowledge map graphically and in the matrix, we analyzed and generated the profiles of the participants based on the steps of Subsect. 3.2.3. We define the key words that represent the main competences of each participant and using such information, we identified his/her and the group's main knowledge. Figure 16 presents a profile created for one of the participants.

Participant Name	Participant 10
Position or Role	PhD student
E-mail	XXX
Telephone	XXX
Keywords of major skills	
Systematic Literature Review (6), Paper Writing (4), Statistical Analysis (3) Usability (3) Pilot Study (3), Modeling themes (3), Review proposal (3).	
Knowledge sources	
ACM,Scopus,Ieee,Books of HCI	
People whom (s)he is related in the map	
Participant 9 < Weight 7>	
Participant 6 < Weight 7>	
Participant 4 < Weight 4>	
Participant 3 < Weight 4>	
Participant 3 < Weight 3>	
Participant 5 < Weight 3>	
Participant 2 < Weight 2>	
Participant 1 < Weight 2>	
Worked projects within the Group	
None Identified	

Fig. 16. Profile from a participant.

Finally, we produced the two main products of the Knowledge Mapping process: the group's knowledge map and a set of profiles for each participant.

Group leaders received the data for analysis and assessment. Moreover, the analysis of the participants, based on the maps and in the matrix, includes: who accessed other participants, who accessed more artifacts, which participants had the strongest connection (edges or knowledge flow) and what the strongest knowledge domain of the group was.

5.2 Lessons Learned from the Knowledge Mapping Process

We requested the participants to answer the questionnaires based on the main question of the mapping. Thus, the questionnaire words and examples should be according to the defined mapping question.

The participants must be free to communicate with each other, so that they can easily retrieve information when filling out the questionnaires. Research on books, websites or document names should be allowed for a richer filling of the questionnaire.

During the mapping step, the matrix was modified based on the original idea with respect to the field describing the relations. A column with the name of the participants was inserted to provide a better way of identifying who owned that description in a bigger data set.

Once completing the knowledge map, we started the creation of the profiles from the participants. In the beginning, the first version of the proposed structure did not work to generate the profile of the participants. This was due to the lack of a review process of the results for filling fields correctly.

Improvements in the participants' profile form were: (1) The structure has been redesigned to display necessary information from each participant profile. (2) A knowledge technique for identifying the applied knowledge of the participants was defined to analyze the flow of knowledge among the participants. (3) The steps of the analysis and profile creation activities have been rewritten. The main goal for such change is that others can properly apply the process without help or interference of the authors of the process. Next, we have extended the studies by linking the results of the pilot study with the lessons learned generated by a Post-mortem Analysis process from our previous study.

6 Linking Lessons Learned from Post-mortem Analysis and Knowledge Mapping Profiles

Post-mortem Analysis (name given to Retrospective Analysis) is the activity of gathering lessons learned that can be organized for a project in a final stage or finished stage [28]. According to Scott and Stålhane [29], during a Post-mortem Analysis, the participants of an ongoing or finished project are reunited and they are asked to identify: (a) which aspects of the project went well and must be repeated, and (b) which aspects of the project went wrong and must be avoided.

The R&D group participated in a software development project for a system focusing on supporting the daily care of the elderly. For that project, in our previous work [30], we collected lessons learned for each of its Sprints. Four members of the R&D group that participated of the Knowledge Mapping process also participated in the project.

A total of 37 lessons learned were collected in three Post-mortem meeting and they were generated and stored in a knowledge codification document called SABC-Pattern [31]. The structure of the document in which the lessons learned were stored contained:

- **Title:** the lesson's name and a brief description;
- **Situation:** a detailed description of the situation or a question that the lesson learned tried to solve;
- **Cause of the Problem:** a detailed description of what caused the problem;
- **Consequence(s) of the Problem:** a description of the consequences of the problem. In other words, what happened after the problem occurred;
- **Action:** a detailed description of the solution to the problem, (i.e. it highlights an activity that was performed to solve the problem);
- **Benefit:** a detailed description containing the effects (positive and/or negative) caused by the action;
- **Keyword:** a set of keywords that identify the lesson;
- **Relationship to other lessons:** this item lists the identification code of other lessons that are related to the currently described lesson;

- **Context:** this item characterizes the environment in which the action was executed. The context can be described in terms of:
  - **Project Type:** description of the project type (development project, maintenance project, or both);
  - **Project Size:** description of the project size (small project, medium project, large project, or project of any size);
  - **Project Phase:** indication of the project phase (requirements elicitation, requirements analysis, project, implementation, testing, deployment, management activities, supporting activities, others);
  - **Date of the Creation of the Lesson: this item** displays the date/time of the lesson learned. It is employed to support the actions of the user;
- **Responsibility/Role from the Creator of the Lesson:** description of the responsibility/role of the person who created the lesson;
- **Related Domain:** description of the domain in which the lesson can be applied;
- **Other Relevant Information:** description of other information that the lesson's creator judges necessary, for instance, examples of its use, known user and pictures.

After the creation and storage of the lessons learned, we combined them with the participants' knowledge profiles that were generated by the Knowledge Mapping Process (see Sect. 5). Such combination allowed us to create a hierarchical structure called Knowledge Model (see Fig. 17).

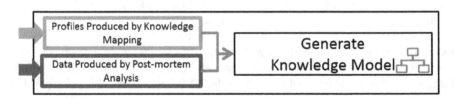

Fig. 17. Process to generate the knowledge model of the R&D group.

The Knowledge Model is a hierarchical structure that represents the products that were produced by the practitioners who have learned the stored lessons from a project and who have a knowledge profile. This model was built to contain three levels (Fig. 18):

1. The first level refers to the organization's software projects with their stored lessons learned and all mapped knowledge profiles;
2. The second level refers to the software projects that were carried out by the organization, including the number of knowledge profiles and lessons learned related to them;
3. The third level refers to the knowledge topics from each software project and the knowledge profiles that are related to them.

In the following section, we present how we created a relationship between the lessons learned and the knowledge profiles in order to generate the Knowledge Model.

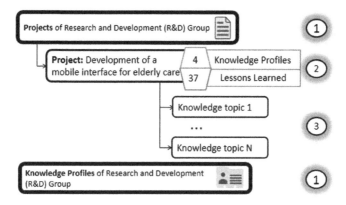

Fig. 18. Levels of the knowledge model.

6.1 Creation of the Knowledge Model for the Research and Development Group

The participants' Knowledge Profiles represent some indications of what skills or competencies they have. A set of profile keywords (regarding major skills, see Fig. 8) represents those indications and can be related with a keyword field of the lesson learned document according to the structure of the SABC-Pattern shown in the previous section.

We present four steps for generating the Knowledge Model of the project from the R&D group: (1) we create a file for the project called "Interface Design of Mobile Applications", such file is necessary to represent the collected experiences of the project; (2) we review the lessons learned and the keywords' field from the SABC-Pattern; (3) we generate knowledge topics for each group of similar lessons learned; and (4) we analyze each codified experience created through the Post-mortem Analysis and we identified topics to similar codified experiences by checking the keywords.

To represent the Knowledge Model, we developed a web portal in order to provide access to the relevant knowledge for the members of the R&D project. Figure 19 shows one of the screens of such Web portal.

Members from the R&D group can see which knowledge topics exist for a specific project and what knowledge profiles are available. These knowledge profiles are the same ones generated in Sect. 5. After that, we evaluated the web portal with the four project members. For this evaluation we applied a feedback questionnaire with the project members to retrieve their impressions and opinions and evaluate the usefulness of the proposed knowledge model. The results are shown in the next section.

6.2 Knowledge Model's Results

We applied a feedback questionnaire in order to gather the impressions and opinions regarding the proposed Knowledge Model. Table 2 shows the relationship between the participants who answered the feedback questionnaire (and who also participated of the

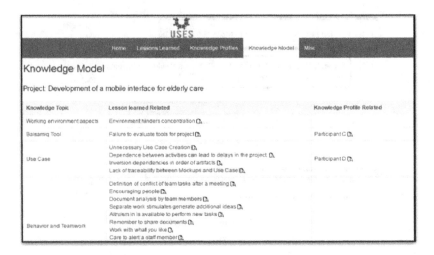

Fig. 19. Knowledge model web portal.

Table 2. Relationship of the participants of the Knowledge Mapping process and project.

Participant of the Knowledge Mapping process	Participant of the R&D group project
Participant 1	**Renamed to Participant A**
Participant 2	Did not participate in the project
Participant 3	Did not participate in the project
Participant 4	**Renamed to Participant B**
Participant 5	Did not participate in the project
Participant 6	Did not participate in the project
Participant 7	Did not participate in the project
Participant 8	**Renamed to Participant C**
Participant 9	**Renamed to Participant D**
Participant 10	Did not participate in the project

project) with the participants of the Knowledge Mapping Process. The project participants are the same who evaluated the Knowledge Model and answered the feedback questionnaire.

Table 3 shows the feedback questionnaire that we applied in the Knowledge Model evaluation. Next, we presented the results from our evaluation.

Q1: All participants stated that they were able to visualize the lessons learned. However, there were some improvement suggestions such as adding links to the knowledge profile or displaying more information.

"*...when selecting the codified experiences, it is not clear what type of project generated the experience. I believe that a column with this information should be created (...) I also suggest describing if a particular lesson learned was resolved in project*" Participant A.
"*I can go to the page and see the lessons. It would be interesting if you had a link for when you click the item, to go straight to the page of the lessons learned (and other items as well), to make the search faster*" Participant B.

Table 3. Feedback questionnaire of the knowledge model.

Id	Question
Q1	Can you check what are the lessons learned from a group project based on the Knowledge Model? Please comment
Q2	If you wanted to find some stored knowledge or wanted to locate any person related to a certain kind of knowledge you have doubt about, would you use the Knowledge Model as a reference guide? Why?
Q3	In your opinion, which were the positive and negative aspects of the Knowledge Model?
Q4	Would you change anything regarding the Knowledge Model? Any suggestions for improving it?

Q2: Three participants stated that they would check the Knowledge Model again and one participant would not check it due to the lack of a search engine. However (s)he stated that the information was useful.

> *"I will apply the Knowledge Model because it is possible to see the knowledge profile of each group member. I suggest that it describes the update date of each knowledge profile."* Participant A
> *"No. The information was useful but the search is difficult. I cannot easily find the information"* Participant C.

Q3 and Q4: In terms of positive aspects, the participants cited that the relationship of the profiles from the encoded experiences had useful information about the project and that they could be used in other projects. Regarding negative aspects, there is a lack of a search engine tool, lessons learned are not detailed and the names of the fields are very similar.

> *"Positive aspects of the Knowledge Model: it is a practical way to view this kind of information [knowledge information] and it contains useful information to be observed in other projects."* Participant D.
> *"Positive aspects: Project Information. Project summary. Aspects of the people and lessons learned. Negative aspects: Lessons Learned are summarized and not detailed and I cannot easily find things."* Participant C
> *"[The knowledge model] could have a section with applied technologies, for example: personas, use cases, molic, balsamiq tool, and others."* Participant B.

7   Conclusions and Future Work

The Knowledge Mapping process presented in this paper maps a group of participants and creates knowledge profiles for each participant. The profiles generated by the knowledge mapping and lessons learned can be collected by a Post-mortem process are related in the form of a hierarchical structure named Knowledge Model. Also, we carried out a pilot study where it we found out that this Knowledge Mapping process is feasible. Finally, we also evaluated the implementation of the Knowledge Model web portal.

The Knowledge map of the R&D group presents the connections that a participant has with each knowledge source, either being explicit (websites, books, and others) or tacit (access to people). Also, it is possible to check how and what kind of knowledge is flowing between the participants. A social network analysis was performed, showing the kind of participants that are present in the group.

Knowledge profiles display basic information on how to find the participant in the organization. They also show complex information such as with whom (s)he is connected to on the map and what activities (s)he performs. A profile also displays indicators of the main competences a participant has in the group by using the information that other participants check from him/her.

A Knowledge Model relates the knowledge profiles produced by the Knowledge Mapping Process with the lessons learned resulting from the Post-Mortem Analysis Process [30]. The goal is to provide software teams and the organization with a structure that allows finding what participants are associated with a particular knowledge topic, providing a learning analysis.

The advantages found to justify the creation of a knowledge map in our study are the following:

- To check what main competences a participant is in fact executing. Based on such information, we can verify if (s)he is doing something for which (s)he was assigned to, or if there are any mistakes in the execution of his/her activities;
- To check for anomalies in the knowledge flow of a participant. Perhaps a participant is researching a source of knowledge that does not fit into his/her role. It can mean a learning signal or an irregularity;
- To check if the flow of information between members is happening. In an integrated team, we can see through a map if two members are or not interacting when they should be. For example, the analyst responsible for gathering requirements and the developer;
- To identify the current knowledge in a group or software team. Based on the identified keywords within the profiles, we can draw conclusions from what knowledge the group or team is employing and which members have higher scores in such knowledge.

The importance of choosing appropriate keywords in the knowledge profiles impacts the creation of the knowledge model. Without propor keywords, it is very difficult to relate the documents with the lessons learned. The same applies to the documents of lesson learned within the Post-mortem Analysis.

The advantages found for justifying the creation of a knowledge model in the study are:

- To relate the knowledge profile of participants with the lessons learned of the software projects;
- To check what knowledge may not be (or is not being) learned in a software project, or to analyze what knowledge may have been learned by a participant;
- To check what experiences a participant produces or to find out what experiences were not produced in a software project.

Finally, as future work, we intend:

- To apply the Knowledge Mapping Process in a Case Study with software projects teams;
- To analyze if knowledge already acquired in the company can supply the knowledge mapping process;
- To verify the quality of the Knowledge Mapping questionnaire and if there is any information that cannot be captured to generating knowledge profiles;
- To automate the data analysis process and the creation of profiles;
- To compare the Knowledge Mapping with the network analysis techniques such as Social Network Analysis; and
- To apply the Knowledge Mapping Process in the Knowledge Audit Process performed by Elias *et al.* [19].

Acknowledgements. We would like to thank the support granted by CAPES; by FAPEAM through processes: 062.00600/2014 and 062.00578/2014. We would like to thank all the subjects who participated in this study.

References

1. Hansen, B.H., Kautz, K.: Knowledge mapping: a technique for identifying knowledge flows in software organisations. In: Dingsøyr, T. (ed.) Software Process Improvement. EuroSPI 2004. LNCS, vol. 3281. Springer, Heidelberg (2004). doi:10.1007/978-3-540-30181-3_12
2. Krbálek, P., Vacek, M.: Collaborative knowledge mapping. In: Proceedings of the 11th International Conference on Knowledge Management and Knowledge Technologies, pp. 1–29. ACM (2011)
3. Bhatt, G.D.: Knowledge management in organizations: examining the interaction between technologies, techniques, and people. J. Knowl. Manag. **5**(1), 68–75 (2001)
4. Alavi, M., Leidner, D.E.: Review: knowledge management and knowledge management systems: conceptual foundations and research issues. MIS Q. **25**(1), 107–136 (2001)
5. Mitchell, S.M., Seaman, C.B.: A knowledge mapping technique for project-level knowledge flow analysis. In: International Symposium on Empirical Software Engineering and Measurement (ESEM), pp. 347–350. IEEE (2011)
6. Eppler, M.J.: Making knowledge visible through intranet knowledge maps: concepts, elements, cases. In: Proceedings of the 34th Annual Hawaii International Conference on System Sciences, pp. 189–205 IEEE (2001)
7. Anandarajan, I., Akhilesh, A.K.: An exploratory analysis of effective indo-Korean collaboration with intervention of knowledge mapping. In: Proceedings of the 4th International Conference on Intercultural Collaboration, pp. 129–132. ACM (2012)
8. Balaid, A.S.S., Zibarzani, M., Rozan, M.Z.A.: A comprehensive review of knowledge mapping techniques. J. Inf. Syst. Res. Innov. (JISRI) **3**, 71–76 (2013)
9. Vasconcelos, J.B., Seixas, P.C., Lemos, P.G., Kimble, C.: Knowledge management in non-governmental organizations: a partnership for the future. In: Proceedings of the 7th International Conference Enterprise Information Systems (ICEIS), USA, pp. 1–10 (2005)
10. Lindvall, M., Rus, I., Sinha, S.S.: Software systems support for knowledge management. J. Knowl. Manag. **7**(5), 137–150 (2003)
11. Davenport, T.H., Völpel, S.C.: The rise of knowledge towards attention management. J. Knowl. Manag. **5**(3), 212–222 (2001)

12. Davenport, T.H., Prusak, L.: Working Knowledge: How Organizations Manage What They Know. Harvard Business School Press, Boston (1998)
13. Nonaka, I., Takeuchi, H.: The Knowledge-Creating Company. Oxford University Press, New York (1995)
14. Bjørnson, F.O., Dingsøyr, T.: Knowledge management in software engineering: a systematic review of studied concepts, findings and research methods used. Inf. Softw. Technol. 5(11), 1055–1068 (2008)
15. Lindvall, M., Rus, I.: Knowledge management in software engineering. IEEE Softw. 19(3), 26–38 (2002)
16. Gourova, E., Toteva, K., Todorova, Y.: Audit of knowledge flows and critical business processes. In: Proceedings of the 17th European Conference on Pattern Languages of Programs, pp. 1–10. ACM (2012)
17. Jafari, M., Akhavan, P., Bourouni, A., Roozbeh, H.A.: A framework for the selection of knowledge mapping techniques. J. Knowl. Manag. Pract. 10(1), 1–9 (2009)
18. Nada, N., Kholief, M., Metwally, N.: Mobile knowledge visual e-learning toolkit. In: Proceedings of the 7th International Conference on Advances in Mobile Computing and Multimedia, pp. 336–340. ACM (2009)
19. Elias, O.M.R., Rose-Gómez, C.E., Vizcaíno, A., Martienz-Garcia, A. I.: Integrating current practices and information systems in KM initiatives: a knowledge management audit approach. In: Proceedings of the International Conference on Knowledge Management and Information Sharing (KMIS), pp. 71–80 (2010)
20. Kim, S., Suh, E., Hwang, H.: Building the knowledge map: an industrial case study. J. Knowl. Manag. 7(2), 34–45 (2003)
21. Elias, O.M.R., García, A. M., Vara, J. F., Vizcaíno, A., Soto, J. P.: Knowledge flow analysis to identify knowledge needs for the design of knowledge management systems and strategies: a methodological approach. In: Proceedings ICEIS 2007-9th International Conference on Enterprise Information Systems, pp. 492–497 (2007)
22. Mafra, S.N., Barcelos, R.F., and Travassos, G.H.: Aplicando uma metodologia baseada em evidência na definição de novas tecnologias de software. In: Proceedings of the 20th Brazilian Symposium on Software Engineering (SBES), vol. 1, pp. 239–254 (2006). (in Portuguese)
23. Shull, F., Carver, J., Travassos, G.H.: An empirical methodology for introducing software processes. ACM SIGSOFT Softw. Eng. Notes 26(5), 288–296 (2001)
24. Wohlin, C., Runeson, P., Höst, M., Ohlsson, M.C., Regnell, B., Wesslén, A.: Experimentation in Software Engineering. Springer Science & Business Media, Heidelberg (2012)
25. Kelvin, C., Liebowitz, J.: The synergy of social network analysis and knowledge mapping: a case study. Int. J. Manag. Decis. Mak. 7(1), 19–35 (2005)
26. Cross, R., Prusak, L.: The people who make organizations go-or stop. Harv. Bus. Rev. 80(6), 104–112 (2002)
27. Tichy, N.M., Tushman, M.L., Fombrun, C.: Social network analysis for organizations. Acad. Manag. Rev. 4(4), 507–519 (1979)
28. Dingsøyr, T.: Postmortem reviews: purpose and approaches in software engineering. Inf. Softw. Technol. 47(5), 293–303 (2005)
29. Scott, L., Stålhane, T.: Experience Repositories and the Postmortem. In Wissensmanagement, pp. 79–82 (2003)
30. Silva Filho, E.S., Conte, T., Viana, D.: Applying knowledge codification in a post-mortem process - a practical experience. In: 17th International Conference on Enterprise Information Systems (ICEIS), vol. 2, pp. 153–165. Barcelona (2015)
31. Rabelo, J., Viana, D., Santos, G., Conte, T.: Using pattern-PABC to coding knowledge: an experimental study. In: XIII SBQS, pp. 13–27 (2014). (in Portuguese)

Agile-Similar Approach Based on Project Crashing to Manage Research Projects

Dorota Kuchta[1], Pierrick L`Ebraly[2], and Ewa Ptaszyńska[1(✉)]

[1] University of Science and Technology,
Wyb. St. Wyspianskiego 27, 50-370 Wroclaw, Poland
{dorota.kuchta,ewa.ptaszynska}@pwr.edu.pl
[2] Ecole Nationale des Ponts et Chaussees,
Cite Descartes, 6-8 Avenue Blaise Pascal, 77455 Champs-sur-Marne, France
plebraly@gmail.com

Abstract. Research projects are an integral part of each university's activity. Recently many theorists and practitioners have started to consider how such projects should be managed (e.g. [13]). They analyse if it is better to use traditional project management (TPM) or agile project management (APM). In this paper we propose agile-similar approach based on project crashing and stakeholder analysis to manage research project. First we present a theoretical introduction. Then we present a model for the proposed approach and its Linear Programing (LP) implementation. Finally we present an example of using the proposed model and we formulate conclusions.

Keywords: Project management · Project crashing · Linear programming · Decision-making tools · Research projects

1 Introduction

Recently we have been dealing with two types of project management approaches [17] - traditional approaches and agile approaches. Simplifying, it can be said that the main difference between them is that in the traditional approach the project scope, deadline and budget are essentially known at the beginning and the project management methods aim at realizing this scope while in the agile approach, the scope, and even the objective tend to change during the project realisation and the project management methods are aimed at helping the project team to adapt the project and its realisation to the changing objective. However, the two approaches cannot be isolated from each other. Recently, researchers have noticed the need to compare and combine the two approaches. Kosztyn in [10] proposes a matrix-based approach to project planning and describes a generic algorithm that builds schedules for both agile and traditional project management approaches. Spundak in [15] compares both approaches and suggests that a mixed approach may be needed in the future as we have been facing a more and more varied spectrum of project types and, to use his words, methodology should be adapted to the project and not vice versa. This paper continues this line of research, as it allows introduction of agile elements into traditional project management. In Figs. 1 and 2 both approaches (traditional and agile) are described; the upper part of triangle

© Springer International Publishing AG 2017
S. Hammoudi et al. (Eds.): ICEIS 2016, LNBIP 291, pp. 225–241, 2017.
DOI: 10.1007/978-3-319-62386-3_11

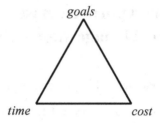

Fig. 1. Short term approach, agile approach.

represents objectives while the lower parts represent the chosen set of constraints. These are widely inspired by a similar representation found in [10].

Figure 1 presents agile approach. A simple way to understand agile approach is to see it in terms of maximizing goals in a fixed time and cost environment.

Figure 2 presents traditional approach. Traditional planning focuses on reaching fixed goals while trying to minimise time and cost; which implies solving a time-cost trade-off problem.

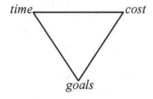

Fig. 2. Long term approach, traditional approach.

In this paper we will present an approach to introduce an agile element into traditional approach (Fig. 3).

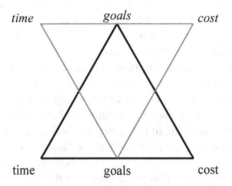

Fig. 3. Mixing both approach.

The approach we propose here allows modification in the project short-term objectives in order to deal with another major aspect of project planning – project stakeholder satisfaction.

Our proposal is motivated by the fact that the stakeholders play a growing role in project management. In a competitive environment it is important to keep in mind that a major criterion for project success is client satisfaction [3]. This aspect is made clear in the agile approach to project management, where the client and other stakeholders are allowed to change his expectancies between every sprint as to the project expected outcome. Thus, the aim of our proposal is to allow the client and other stakeholders to influence the project realisation in the traditional approach to a greater degree than it is usually done. We blend in the traditional approach to project management the idea taken from agile management of regular meetings, where stakeholders should be "made as happy as possible" [2].

In traditional project management minimizing cost or time, or more often achieving an optimal cost-time trade-off [4] is a common goal and has been tackled by different methods, including neural networks [7]. Linear programming models have been used for a long time to model the dependencies in the project network and their consequences for the project schedule. The crashing model is a well-known model in formal traditional project management, i.e. [1]. Traditional project crashing is a method for shortening project duration by reducing the duration of project activities situated on the critical path. It allows, in the scheduling phase, to decide which project activities should be crashed shortened at a cost in order to achieve a desired project completion time while keeping the cost minimal (or to find the earliest possible completion time given a global budget for activities shortening, a problem that is outside of the scope of this article).

In traditional project management we also have to observe certain dependencies between activities (like those of the "finish-start" type"), which are defined in the planning stage of the project. But in some cases, especially in case of research projects, it may be possible to give up certain dependencies, for a certain cost, in order to finish earlier activities of higher value for certain stakeholders. Such decisions (about crashing or giving up certain dependencies) should be taken dynamically, in an agile way - adapting to the continuously changing needs of stakeholders and the current situation in the project.

The objective of the paper is thus to propose a model supporting a trade-off between traditional and agile project management. We retain the traditional way of project planning, but we allow the traditional plan to adapt itself to the stakeholders wishes and needs during project realisation. In order to build up the model, we propose to complete the crashing model with a measure of stakeholder satisfaction, implemented through regular meetings with the specific stakeholders, as well as with the possibility to pay for giving up certain dependencies between activities in order to increase the stakeholders' satisfaction.

This paper gives a LP model which should help deciding which activities should be crashed and which dependencies given up (for a certain cost) to ensure the stakeholder is satisfied throughout the project realisation, and not only after project completion, to the highest possible degree at the minimal cost in a budget and time limited environment.

The proposed set of constraints provide time and money limits trough-out the project evolution, as well as a reward system to encourage early satisfaction of stakeholder's needs.

The proposed model and its usefulness is verified using a case study of a real world research project.

2 Stakeholders in Research Projects

In this section the definitions of research project, stakeholder, meeting, project end date, crashing and precedence relationship between activities are presented.

Lock in [14] classified projects into four main groups: production, economic, technical and research. He states that research projects require huge capital investments and they are characterized by high level of uncertainty.

Definition 1. *A research project is a systematic investigation to establish scientific theories or hypothesis which is performed by scientists (organised in a project team) at universities.*

Successful management of research projects most often depends on the ability of Project Manager to plan and coordinate the surveys. Based on [11, 12] we can state that many researchers do not formally manage their projects what causes a lot of problems with project execution. The starting point for managing project effectively is to know what we are trying to achieve (project objectives), how we are going to achieve project goals (research methods), what we need to achieve project goals (project resources), who will be involved in achieving project goals (project stakeholders).

Definition 2. *A project stakeholder is a person or an organization who/which is involved in the project.*

Note that there could be many stakeholders involved in the project and different stakeholders may have conflicting interests [9].

In research projects we can identify the following project stakeholders:

1. Project manager.
2. Project team.
3. University administration (central level).
4. University authorities (central level).
5. University administration (lower level, i.e. Department).
6. University authorities (lower level, i.e. Department).
7. Scientists.
8. Institution financing the project (i.e. National Science Centre).

Inappropriate management of project stakeholders can lead to communication issues within the project and interpersonal conflicts. Therefore every Project Manager of research project during project planning should examine who the stakeholders are, analyse the relationships between stakeholders and understand the impact of specific stakeholders on the project. Final analysis of stakeholders in research projects should be taken into account when project is being planned (schedule preparation).

Definition 3. *A meeting is a point in time at which the stakeholder has access to the state of the project, and thus is able to measure the state of advancement of the project according to its own criteria. Having taken knowledge about the current project state, it is possible that after the meeting the stakeholder changes its priorities, induce more resources for the future of the project or even redefines the project.*

Meetings are important in that they are the tools that allow stakeholders to *have insight and impact on the project. In the planning stage we try to model the stakeholder* ongoing satisfaction after each meeting according to the information possessed in this moment, but after each meeting the stakeholder has the right to change its mind, which implies the model must be reapplied to the unaccomplished part of the project with changed parameters each time the stakeholder express a change in priorities.

Definition 4. *A project end date is the furthest possible date at which the project stops. Three reasons may cause a project to stop: project completion, when no further activities are to be completed, the end of the current planning horizon for the project, that is, a new planning phase needs to be planned later before this point so the project can carry on, or the decision to give up on the project because it has taken too long to give expected results.*

For some projects, end date considered as a hard deadline is quite unsatisfactory, as the project outcome is not clearly perceived at the beginning of the project. In this case, the project end date should be referred to as the planning horizon and the role of the finish activity is modified as project success does not require any given activity to be completed.

Definition 5. *A project crashing is a method for shortening project duration at minimum cost.*

It allows to decide which project activities should be shortened in order to achieve a desired project completion time while keeping the cost minimal. Crashing an activity means to reduce its duration by allocating more resources to it.

Definition 6. A *weak precedence relationship between activity b and activity a is a relationship which can be removed. Removing activities dependency results in increasing respective costs but also increasing the satisfaction of project stakeholders at the same time.*

Research project are connected with a high level of uncertainty so that relationships between activities will be frequently changed.

3   Proposed Model

3.1   Basic Definitions

A project P can be broken down in a number of activities that can be either activities or events, an event being an activity of zero duration by opposition to an activity which has to be performed [8]. In the rest of this paper we will use the word activity. For the purpose of this model, we suppose that each activity and event is performed at most once in the course of the project. Two additional dummy events are added to provide the beginning and the completion of the project. Let $V = [\![0, N+1]\!]$ be the set of activities [9].

For each of these activities we define a base duration and cost, using notations that are consistent with those proposed. This is done by introducing vectors $D \in \mathbb{N}^V$ and $C \in \mathbb{R}^V$, where D_i and C_i are respectively the duration and the cost of performing activity i. Additionally each activity can be crashed by devoting more resources to it. This increases the total cost to perform the activity. We introduce vectors $D^C \in \mathbb{N}^V$ and $C^C \in \mathbb{R}^V$ as, respectively, the maximal crashing duration (i.e. by how many days we can maximally shorten the activity) and the daily cost of crashing activities (the cost of shortening a given activity by one day).

Crashing cost is always positive, and we have $0 \le D_i^C \le D_i$ for each activity. If $D_i^C = D_i$ then we say the activity can be externalized. Another concern that has to be addressed is the relationship between activities. For this purpose, we introduce a graph A in which each arc indicates that the predecessor activity must be completed before starting the successor activity. Unlike Brucker in [6] we will not introduce waiting times between two activities, as those can be modelled by adding additional dummy activities with a fixed duration between activities that need to be separated, which means that the graph A can be seen as a subset of $V \times V$, at the cost of over-dimensioning the set V.

Actual starting times are kept in a variable vector $t \in \mathbb{N}^V$ and actual crashing times are kept in a variable vector $c \in \mathbb{N}^V$.

In every project some dependencies between activities can be removed. Therefore we introduce a graph S which is a subgraph of graph A and presents weak dependencies between activities. If (a, b) is present in the subgraph S then (a, b) can be removed from graph A with a fixed payment. Matrix S^C represents respective fixed costs of removing dependencies.

3.2   The Linear Programming Model Proposed – a General Description

Three different objectives have to be taken in account in order to plan a project: reaching goals, as perceived by the client, the time needed to do so and the money used to do so. However, these are all dependent on each other and for this reason, as described above, past approaches made some of them constraints and other objectives. It is also important to take into account, as mentioned above, the objective of stakeholders satisfaction which is absent in classical crashing models.

On the one hand, our model focuses on two resources: time (the project completion time), and money (budget available for crashing activities and carrying activities), to reach a fixed goal. What is more, we keep track of project's achievement throughout the duration of the project by introducing meetings with the stakeholders to take into account their satisfaction at different points during the project, because we assume that the specific stakeholder, though interested in the development of the project, does not need to be aware of every activity but rather has knowledge about the state of a project at a number of given times (meetings) during the project.

In order to address the three objectives: early completion time, minimal cost and maximal ongoing stakeholders satisfaction, we decided:

- to make the time objective a constraint - a project deadline will be imposed;
- to make the cost objective both a model objective (the total cost of activities crashing should be minimal) and a constraint: in each consecutive period between two meetings with the stakeholders there is a budget available for carrying out activities, including crashing;
- to make the stakeholder satisfaction a model objective. For this reason, the objective function will focus on money.

Thus, our model will have two objectives: the total cost of crashing the activities (minimised) and the satisfaction of the stakeholders throughout project realisation (maximised). The latter objective is difficult to express in a formal way and to measure, as it is immaterial. We have decided to measure it in monetary units - project planners will be asked to express the stakeholder satisfaction in terms of value. This translation is crucial, as it will play an important role when we combine the objectives, which will be discussed later on. The problem of expressing consumer satisfaction in monetary units will be discussed further in the next subsection.

To account for time-wise gain in this objective function, bounties are awarded for early activity completion. These bounties are awarded for each activity if the given activity is started before the j-th meeting with the stakeholder. For this we introduce $W \subset \mathbb{N}$ the set of meetings and $E \in \mathbb{N}^W$ the vector of meeting dates. B_i^j is the bounty awarded for activity i if it has completed before meeting j. For the purpose of calculation, we use a matrix $B' \in \mathbb{R}^{V \times W}$ where $B^{tj} = B^j - B^{j+1}$. This comes in handy as we can now attribute a bounty for meeting j without checking whether or not we already gave a bounty for week $j - 1$. However, it can be noted that activities that are not valued by the stakeholder, or activities that need to be completed in order to have a value for the stakeholder, must be treated with caution. In the first case no bounty should be awarded for the activity, and, in the second case, bounties should be awarded for an event that depends on and only on the completion of the activity. It needs to be remembered that bounties are not used to congratulate a team on its fast work, but to represent the value-added of having the stakeholder implied in the development. For this reason, bounties should be calculated based on their capacity to get the stakeholder further involved in the project. We obtain a bi-criteria linear programming problem, which can be solved in many ways. Here we assume the weighting approach with equal weights given to both objectives, but of course the approach to solving the bi-criteria problem could be changed, either by modifying the weights or by using a different method to combine the criteria. As mentioned above, resources availability for activities crashing is limited in time which is modelled using a fixed budget limit for each interval between two meetings, M_j. We use a construction similar to the one used for B' to deduct a matrix M' which can then be used to account for staying in the budget during intervals $[0..j]$.

A variable has to be introduced to denote whether activity i has started before meeting j. This variable matrix is noted (o_i^j) and calculated dynamically. In objective function we also minimise costs of removing dependencies between activities. Therefore we introduce a binary variable p to denote whether precedence relationship is respected.

3.3 The Linear Programming Model Proposed – Mathematical Formulation

In this subsection we will present the mathematical formulation of the model described in the previous section. Below we present a Table 1 summing up all notations used to this point.

This leads us to introduce the following LP model:

$$\text{Min cost}: \sum_{i\in V}(C_i^c * x_i - \sum_{j\in W} o_i^j * B_i^j) + \sum_{(i,j)\in S} p_i^j * S_i^{C_j} \tag{1}$$

$$\forall i, j\in S, \forall k\in W, -z_{ik}^j + p_i^j + o_i^k \leq 1 \tag{2}$$

$$\forall i, j\in S, \forall k\in W, 2 * z_{ik}^j - p_i^j - o_i^k \leq 0 \tag{3}$$

$$\forall k\in W, \sum_{iV} o_k^i * C[i] + \sum_{(i,j)S} z_{ik}^j * S_i^j \leq m[k] \tag{4}$$

$$\forall i\in V, x_i \leq D_i^C \tag{5}$$

$$y_0 = 0 \, and \, y_{n+1} \leq T_{end} \tag{6}$$

$$\forall (i,j)\in A\backslash S, y_j - y_i + x_i \geq D_i \tag{7}$$

Equation (1) is the objective function and Eqs. (2)–(7) represent constraints. Constraints (2) and (3) are introduced in order to link variables p and z. Constraint (4) refers to budget limits in the timespan between two meetings. Constraint (5) refers to maximum crashing durations of specific activities. Constraint (6) refers to starting and ending time of the project. Constraint (7) refers to the order of activities. Note that in Eq. (1) different objectives were accounted for in an equation. The sum here is used because matrix B can always be normalized to be of the same order of magnitude as the costs in the project, as it is used there and only there. However, the decision of whether or not to normalize the bounty matrix has to be taken when this matrix is filled: in some situations the benefits of showing early results to the stakeholder are not commensurable to the crashing costs involved, and, in these cases, no crashing should occur. On the other hand, sometimes costs are not an issue if the stakeholder can have early results, for example while handling a project designed at resuming production for a much larger manufacturing scheme, only early delivery should be valued.

Table 1. Notations previously introduced.

Name	Type	Notes
N	Natural number	The number of activities to be performed throughout the project, including dummy activities
V	Subset of $\mathbb{N}$	Project activities, including start and finish activities
A	Subset of $V \times V$	Activity dependency graph. If (a, b) is present in the graph then b depends on a to start
S	Subgraph of A	Weak dependency graph. If (a, b) is present in the subgraph S then (a, b) can be removed from graph A with a fixed payment
W	Subset of $\mathbb{N}$	Meetings
D	Element in $\mathbb{N}^V$	Vector of the base durations in time unit for each activity
D^C	Element in $\mathbb{N}^V$	Vector of the maximum crashing durations
C	Element in $\mathbb{R}^V$	Vector of the base costs for each activity
C^C	Element in $\mathbb{R}^V$	Vector of the crashing cost per time unit for each activity
S^C	Element in $\mathbb{R}^S$	Hollow matrix of the respective costs of removing a dependency
MT	Element in $\mathbb{N}^W$	Vector indicating the times on which meetings take place
$Tend$	Natural number	Hard limit for project completion (note this can also denote the project planning horizon)
B (B')	Element in $\mathbb{R}^{V \times W}$	Matrix of the bounties handed out for completing a given activity before a given meeting
M (M')	Element in $\mathbb{R}^W$	Vector used to represent budget limits in the span between two meetings
y	Variable in $\mathbb{N}^V$	Calculated starting time
x	Variable in $\mathbb{N}^V$	Calculated crash duration
o	Variable in $\{0, 1\}^{V \times W}$	Binary indicating whether an activity is started before a given meeting
p	Variable in $\{0, 1\}^S$	Binary variable indicating whether a precedence relationship is respected
z	Variable in $\{0, 1\}^S$	Binary variable indicating whether a precedence relationship is respected in the k-th time interval

4 Example

In this section we go through a few cases in which the introduced model results in a different schedule chosen for the project development than in a classical approach. Due to the limited space in this article we present only a brief example of a project. The proposed linear programming model has been implemented in a free editor GUSEK (GLPK Under SciTE Extended Kit) and tested on a selected research project performed by Wroclaw University of Science and Technology. The main goal of the analysed project is to identify success and failure factors of research projects with particular emphasis on projects performed at universities, based on the example of Poland and France.

Identifying success and failure factors of projects is a popular problem in the scientific literature of project management, i.a. [5, 8, 10, 18]. Research projects at universities represent very specific type of project, i.a. [15, 16] therefore they require dedicated research.

In the analysed project the following activities were identified:

1. Preparing IT tools to support project realization.
2. Collecting contacts among stakeholders of research projects in Poland.
3. Collecting contacts among stakeholders of research projects in France.
4. Studying literature.
5. Conducting a survey among stakeholders of research projects in Poland.
6. Performing interviews with specific stakeholders of research projects in Poland.
7. Conducting a survey among stakeholders of research projects in France.
8. Performing interviews with specific stakeholders of research projects in France.
9. Organizing workshops with specific stakeholders of research projects in Poland.
10. Organizing workshops with specific stakeholders of research projects in France.
11. Preparing research results.

Based on the identified activities we can create a project schedule (represented as Project Network Diagram or Gantt Chart). The schedule will be however different from the point of view of different project stakeholders.

In the analysed project we can outline two main project stakeholders:

- project team consisting of scientists,
- National Science Centre.

Figure 4 presents Project Network Diagram and Fig. 5 presents Gantt Chart which are defined from the point of view of project team. In the diagrams the red colour represents critical activities in the project.

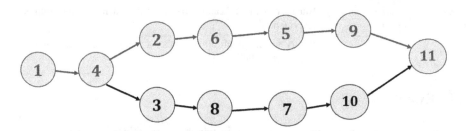

Fig. 4. Project Network Diagram from the point of view of project team.

However, if we take into account the point of view of the second major stakeholder in our project which is NCN (Narodowe Centrum Nauki – National Science Centre), the schedule will look different when the project team allows to remove some dependencies between the activities. In the analysed case the project team identified the following weak precedence graph: S = (1, 4), (3, 8), (4, 2), (4, 3). National Science Centre required the project could not last longer than 20 months. If some dependencies

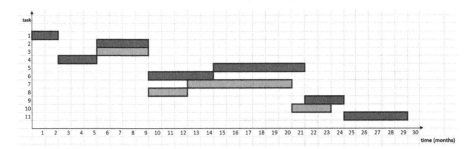

Fig. 5. Gantt Chart from the point of view of project team. (Color figure online)

between the selected activities are removed then the activities can be realised in parallel. Thanks to this fact the time of project execution will be shortened and there will be a possibility to get bounties from the stakeholder (National Science Centre) because of increasing its satisfaction. The facts described above were input to the model from Sect. 3 and the solution is presented in Fig. 6 in the form of Project Network Diagram and in Fig. 7 in the form of Gantt Chart.

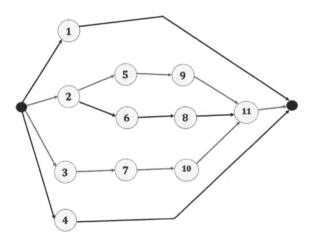

Fig. 6. Project Network Diagram after including the requirements of National Science Centre.

But this is not the final schedule version because in the next steps the meetings (*M1–M4*) with other project stakeholders and project crashing are also considered.

Based on schedule presented in Figs. 6 and 7 another important input data to the model in the analysed case of research project were collected. They are presented in Table 2.

Base durations for each activity (D), maximum crashing durations (D^C), base costs for each activity, crashing costs per time unit for each activity (C), bounties handed out for completing a given activity before a given meeting $(B_i^1, B_i^2, B_i^3, B_i^4)$, dates of

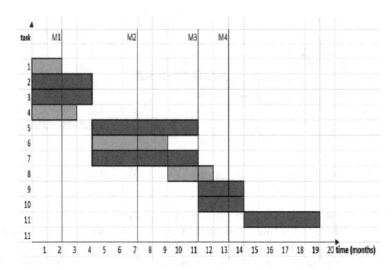

Fig. 7. Gantt Chart after including the requirements of National Science Centre.

Table 2. Input data.

V	Pred.	D	C	D^C	C^C	B_i^1	B_i^2	B_i^3	B_i^4
0	∅	0	0	0	0	0	0	0	0
1	{0}	2	2000	1	1000	0	0	0	0
2	{0}	4	500	1	200	0	0	0	0
3	{0}	4	500	1	200	0	0	0	0
4	{0}	3	500	1	200	500	0	0	0
5	{2}	7	5000	1	1500	0	0	0	0
6	{2}	5	2000	2	1000	0	2000	0	0
7	{3}	7	5000	1	1500	0	0	0	0
8	{6}	3	3000	1	1000	0	2000	1000	0
9	{5}	3	6000	1	0	0	0	0	7000
10	{7}	3	10000	1	0	0	0	0	0
11	{9, 10}	5	7000	0	0	0	0	0	0
12	{11}	0	0	0	0	0	0	0	0
W	MT								
1	2								
2	7								
3	11								
4	13								
S	S^C								
(6,8)	1500								

meetings with specific stakeholder of the project (*MT*), dependencies which can be removed (*S*) and costs of removing a dependency (S^C) were estimated by the Project Manager of the analysed research project. In this case there were no budget limits in the span between meetings (*M*).

The first important meeting (M1) in our project takes place in the second month. This is a scientific seminar not only for the project team but also for other scientists from the university. At the seminar the concept of the project is presented. From the point of view of scientists participating in the seminar the important outcome of this meeting is building the common understanding of its idea that definitely must be supported by the analysis of the literature. That is why we can state that we should crash activity 4. In traditional project management approach activity 4 will never be crashed if its length is smaller than activity 2 or 3. But in this case we get a greater reward if we shorten activity 4. $B_4^1 = 500\,PLN$ (all bounties are presented in Table 2) is the bounty rewarded for completing activity 4 before starting the meeting M1, specified by Project Manager. For scientists activity 4 is much more important than having a tool to manage our project (activity 1) or how many contacts among stakeholders of research projects we have (activities 2, 3). Moreover if scientists are properly understanding the subject of our project, they will better support our research by answering questions in interviews (activities 6, 8) or filling in survey questionnaires (activities 5, 7). Based on this example we can observe that in some cases it is worth crashing a shorter activity before the meeting, while leaving longer activity uncompleted after the meeting. Such decisions are specific for agile approach. In the example above, a completed activity 4 is shown to the stakeholders (scientists) while other activities, which are not important to the scientists, are not crashed even though they are cheaper to crash than activity 4.

The second meeting (M2) in our project takes place in the seventh month. After three months of performing activities 5, 7 the survey team expects the results from the interviews (activity 6) because they can help to determine the final version of the questionnaire for stakeholders in Poland and France.

Therefore the activity 6 should be shortened to 3 months. Project Manager defined that for completing activity 6 before starting M2 the rewarded bounty is $B_6^2 = 2000\,PLN$. In this case the model indicated to remove a dependency between activity 6 and activity 8. Initially it was established that these two activities will be performed by one team which first conducts the interviews with Polish scientists and then the interviews with French scientists. Based on model results the Project Manager decided to create two separate teams: the first for the interviews with Polish scientists and the second for the interviews with French scientists. Therefore activity 6 and activity 8 could be executed in parallel. As a consequence activity 8 was finished before the second meeting (M2) in the 7th month and the third meeting (M3) in the 11th month. The third meeting is a meeting with Rector of Wroclaw University of Science and Technology to report progress in the project and may bring additional bounty. Project Manager defined that the bounties for completing activity 8 before starting meeting M2 and M3 are respectively: $B_8^2 = 2000\,PLN$ and $B_8^3 = 1000\,PLN$.

The fourth meeting (M4) in our project takes place in the thirteenth month when we have to report progress in our project to National Science Centre. This is the example of crashing activities in series. Activity 9 cannot be performed until activity 5 is completed. In traditional approach crashing the project is done by crashing the cheapest-to-crash activity situated on the critical path. However, when 5 and 9 have comparable crashing costs, crashing 5 to meet the deadline is preferable, even when the crashing cost for 5 is slightly higher than the crashing cost for 9. Crashing early is important in time-constrained projects as it gives room for the possible last-minute crashing of final activities. That could not be done in the case when these activities are already crashed to their minimum length. In our case we crash activity 9 before the fourth meeting with National Science Centre because of the two reasons:

- activity 5 cannot be shortened any more,
- Project Manager defined that for completing activity 9 before starting meeting M4 the rewarded bounty is $B_9^4 = 7000\ PLN$. It is because of the fact that National Science Centre is more interested in the results of Polish workshops than in results of surveys.

Table 3 presents results obtained by solving the given model. Figure 7 shows the updated schedule, including the changes described above. In Fig. 7 dashed stroke and light colour mean old activities and continuous stroke and saturated colour mean updated activities (Fig. 8).

Table 3. Results.

V	x_i	y_i	o_i^1	o_i^2	o_i^3	o_i^4
0	0	0	1	1	1	1
1	0	0	1	1	1	1
2	0	0	0	1	1	1
3	0	0	0	1	1	1
4	1	0	1	1	1	1
5	0	4	0	0	1	1
6	2	4	0	1	1	1
7	0	4	0	0	1	1
8	0	4	0	1	1	1
9	1	11	0	0	0	1
10	0	11	0	0	0	0
11	0	14	0	0	0	0
12	0	19	0	0	0	0

We have seen in the analysed case that the model can render in a systematic manner decisions that make sense from the point of view of satisfying selected project stakeholders during the project realisation but are not the choice that would have been retained by a traditional crashing. This allows for better project planning in an environment where stakeholders stay present throughout project execution and may influence it and its perception. In the analysed case the proposed approach would positively influence the satisfaction of the following stakeholders:

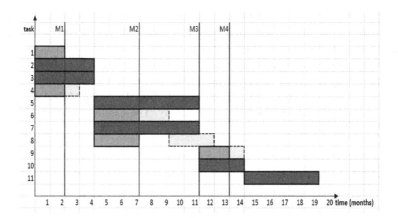

Fig. 8. Updated Gantt Chart.

1. Scientists – because of completing activity 4 before starting meeting M1.
2. The survey team – because of completing activity 6 before starting meeting M2.
3. Rector of the Wroclaw University of Science and Technology – because of completing activity 8 before starting meeting M3.
4. National Science Centre – because of completing activity 9 before starting meeting M4.

The proposed model has also its weaknesses. The more input data we have, the more accurate model we get. This can cause problems for the projects where no input would be available. Our future work will focus on the dependencies between the input dataset size and the accuracy of the estimations. Another future work is to examine more complicated relationships between the parameters of our model (e.g. non linear relationships between crashing cost and crashing duration) as well as to investigate the accuracy of our model on projects of different sizes and number of available resources.

5   Conclusions

Recently we have been dealing with two types of project management approaches: traditional and agile. A simple way to understand agile approach is to see it in terms of maximising goals in a fixed time and cost environment. Whereas traditional approach focuses on reaching fixed goals while trying to minimise time and cost which implies solving a trade-off problem between time and cost. Based on the results obtained in this paper we can state that research projects should be managed by using adaptive approach. The project manager of research project should be prepared for frequent changes in the schedule. Moreover the main stakeholders should be taken into account in determining the schedule. Stakeholders in research projects have a huge impact on project results. Therefore the project manager should carefully analyse what is better: to increase costs, crash the activity and gain stakeholders satisfaction or to keep costs at a constant level without including stakeholders satisfaction. It is also important to analyse the relationships between the activities (if some relationships between activities can be cancelled to rapidly accelerate project execution). Based on the analysis of several research projects we could see that sometimes it is really profitable to cancel relationships between some activities. One case study is shown in Sect. 3 of this paper. Another case study relates to the research project which goal was to develop a model of cost management for universities based on Activity Based Costing (ABC) and to carry out its pilot implementation at a selected university. The following main stakeholders were identified in that project:

- project manager,
- project team,
- financing institution,
- rector of University,
- University Finance and Accounting Office.

In the analysed research project there were problems with access to research data. An agreement for surveys was signed by Rector but afterwards it turned out that the administration (Finance and Accounting Office) did not agree to share financial data. The research had to be carried out at another university where no research was done, thus only teaching activities were able to be examined, which meant a severe limitation of the project scope. In the analysed case the accurate analyses of all project stakeholders and the analyses of relationships between activities were missing. Activities "obtaining agreement of Rector" and "obtaining agreement of Finance and Accounting Office" should be performed in parallel rather than one after another.

References

1. Abbasi, G.Y., Mukkatash, A.M.: Crashing PERT networks using mathematical programming. Int. J. Proj. Manage. **9**, 181–188 (2011)
2. Al-Taani, R.H., Razali, R.: Prioritizing requirements in agile development: a conceptual framework. Procedia Technol. **11**, 733–739 (2013)
3. Al-Tmeemy, S.H., Abdul-Rahman, H., Harun, Z.: Future criteria of success of building projects in Malaysia. Int. J. Proj. **29**, 337–348 (2010)
4. Alba, E.: Software project management with GAs. Inf. Sci. **177**(11), 2380–2401 (2007)
5. Blumer, Y.B., Stauffacher, M., Lang, D.J., Hayashi, K., Uchida, S.: Non-technical success factors for bioenergy projects-Learning from a multiple case study in Japan. Energy Policy **60**, 386–395 (2013)
6. Brucker, M.N.P.: Resource-constrained project scheduling: notation, classification, models, and methods. Eur. J. Oper. Res. **112**(1), 3–41 (1999)
7. Dohi, S.O.T., Nishio, Y.: Optimal software release scheduling based on artificial neural networks. Ann. Softw. Eng. **8**, 167 (1999)
8. Elkadi, H.: Success and failure factors for e-government projects: a case from Egypt. Egypt. Inf. J. **14**(2), 165–173 (2013)
9. Freeman, R.E.: Strategic Management: A Stakeholder Approach: Pitman Series in Business and Public Policy. Harpercollins, College Div, New York (1984)

10. Kosztyn, Z.T.: Exact algorithm for matrix-based project planning problems. Expert Syst. Appl. **42**(9), 4460–4473 (2015)
11. Kuchta, D., et al.: Success and failure factors of R&D projects at universities. In: R&D Management Conference "From Science to Society: Innovation and Value Creation", Cambridge, UK (2016)
12. Kuchta, D., Ptaszyńska, E.: Using risk register in research projects. In: EDULEARN16 Proceedings, Barcelona, Spain (2016)
13. Kuchta, D., Skowron, D.: Classification of R&D projects and selection of R&D project management concept. R&D Management **46**(5), 831–841 (2016)
14. Lock, D.: Project Management. Gower Publishing Ltd., Farnham (2007)
15. Luglio, F., Bertazzoni, N.: Research management in higher education institutions: a process management experience in Italian Universities. In: Connecting Science with Society - The Role of Research Information in a Knowledge-Based Society - 10th International Conference on Current Research Information Systems, CRIS 2010 (2010)
16. Powers, L.C., Kerr, G.: Project Management and Success in Academic Research. Realworld Syst. (2009). https://ssrn.com/abstract=1408032
17. Wysocki, R.K.: Effective Project Management: Traditional. Agile Extreme, Wiley (2014)
18. Zou, W., Kumaraswamy, M., Chung, J., Wong, J.: Identifying the critical success factors for relationship management in PPP projects. Int. J. Proj. Manage. **32**(2), 265–274 (2014)

Guidelines for Web Application Designers:
A Meta-Model, a Grammar, and a Tool

Anh Do Tuan[1], Isabelle Comyn-Wattiau[1,2(✉)],
and Samira Si-saïd Cherfi[1]

[1] CEDRIC-CNAM, 292 Rue Saint Martin, 75141 Paris Cedex, France
anhdtl@gmail.com, {wattiau, samira.cherfi}@cnam.fr
[2] ESSEC Business School, 1 Av Bernard Hirsch, 95021 Cergy Cedex, France

Abstract. Web application developers are not all experts. Even if they use methods such as UWE (UML web engineering) and CASE tools, they are not always able to make good decisions regarding the content of the web application, the navigation schema, and/or the presentation of information. Literature provides them with many guidelines for these tasks. However this knowledge is disseminated in many sources and not structured. In this paper, we perform a knowledge capitalization of all these guidelines. The contribution is threefold: (i) we propose a meta-model allowing a rich representation of these guidelines, (ii) we propose a grammar enabling the description of existing guidelines, (iii) based on this grammar, we developed a guideline management tool. Future research will consist in enriching the UWE method with this knowledge base leading to a quality based approach. Thus, our tool enriches existing UWE-based Computer Aided Software Engineering prototypes with ad hoc guidance.

Keywords: Web application design · Guideline · Meta-model · Quality characteristic · Knowledge capitalization · Grammar · Tool

1 Introduction

Companies develop and maintain complex web sites that allow them to communicate easily and dynamically with their customers, suppliers, partners, etc. In 2008, according to Krigsman, 24% web projects fail to be delivered within budget and 5% were unable to confirm the final cost of their web development project [1]. Moreover, 21% fail to meet stakeholder requirements and nearly a third of web based projects (31%) were not delivered within the agreed timescales [1]. More recently, a research, conducted by McKinsey and the University of Oxford on more than 5400 IT projects, concluded that 45% of large projects are over budget, 7% are over time and 56% delivered less value than predicted [2]. The reasons vary: unclear objectives, lack of business focus (missing focus), shifting requirements, technical complexity (content issues), unaligned team, lack of skills (skill issues), unrealistic schedule, reactive planning (execution issues) [2], inconsistent stakeholder demands, and insufficient time or budget [1].

Web sites and web applications are in fact software applications. In this sense, the classical application methodologies may be used manually or with the help of computer

© Springer International Publishing AG 2017
S. Hammoudi et al. (Eds.): ICEIS 2016, LNBIP 291, pp. 242–260, 2017.
DOI: 10.1007/978-3-319-62386-3_12

aided software engineering (CASE) tools. However, the very specific nature of these applications led to the proposition of more dedicated approaches. Indeed, during the two last decades, research in Web Engineering brought a rich contribution composed of methods and techniques to support Web applications development. These methods such as UWE, WebML, or others are generally founded on a model-driven development paradigm, and provide models and transformation rules to handle several web applications' aspects such as data, navigation, interaction, and presentation. However and despite the research and the tooling efforts, very few developers adopt these methods and many continue to apply ad-hoc practices.

The main reason is that these approaches suffer from lack of guidance. Even if web application designers refer to these approaches, they do not have sufficient knowledge and help in implementing them efficiently. As a consequence, the resulting applications are neither user-friendly nor easy to maintain.

We argue that the current approaches are well structured. However they need to be enriched with guidelines helping designers in the numerous decisions they have to make during the web application development. Therefore, we have collected the different sets of guidelines proposed in the literature and organized them along different dimensions. In particular, this structure allows us to link the guidelines with the quality objectives (maintainability, performance, functionality, security, etc.) and with the relevant steps of the web application design (content design, navigation design and presentation design).

This article is organized as follows. Section 2 describes how we collected and selected the guidelines, and a short experiment we conducted on how methods and guidelines are followed in websites construction. Based on the survey conclusions, Sect. 3 motivates and describes our research question. Section 4 describes the meta-model we propose in order to represent the guidelines in a useful way. Section 5 analyses the set of resulting guidelines. Section 6 is dedicated to the grammar we propose for guideline descriptions. Section 7 sketches the prototype we developed for guideline management. Section 8 is dedicated to related works on guidelines. Finally, the last section concludes and sketches future research directions.

2 An Experiment on Guideline Usage

Before defining the research question, we performed a quick inventory on how well web design best practices and guidelines are followed by existing websites. The objective was (i) to analyze whether existing practices and guides are used and (ii) identify how to facilitate their adoption and hence avoid ad hoc approaches. Thus, we first collected 475 guidelines from several sources and confronted them with three websites: the web site of our university department (deptinfo.cnam.fr), the website of a French newspaper (lemonde.fr) and a well-known e-commerce web site (amazon.fr). We first describe briefly the collected guidelines and then their verification on the three websites.

2.1 Collecting the Guidelines

World Wide Web Consortium (W3C) is the main international standards organization for the World Wide Web. This consortium puts together around 400 organizations. They developed Web Content Accessibility Guidelines (WCAG) with the goal of proposing a single shared standard for web content accessibility that meets the needs of individuals, organizations, and governments (Web Accessibility Initiative). Two versions of WCAG were published until now. The first one was introduced in 1999. It contains 14 large guidelines. Each main guideline is composed of atomic guidelines addressing the same topic. The second version was published in 2008. It contains 12 guidelines organized into four categories, targeting four desirable characteristics of websites: perceivable, operable, understandable, and robust.

WCAG defines three levels of conformance, respectively A, AA and AAA. Some of the related guidelines could be automatically checked whereas others require manual checking. Authors in [3] conducted a case study on Irish websites showing that web designers are aware of web accessibility but they concentrate their efforts on ensuring validation of automatically controlled checkpoints and ignore those requiring additional manual testing.

The guidelines of WCAG focus only on accessibility. Thus, we collected other guidelines which address all the characteristics of web site quality. The literature contains guidelines for specific web sites (for children for instance) as well as rules available for all sites.

Identifying the Relevant Sources. For collecting guidelines from literature effectively, we use some keywords when searching, such as "website guideline", "guideline for website", "guideline security web application" in title and content of document, from main electronic libraries and databases in computer science: IEEE Xplore, Springer, ScienceDirect, ACM, and DBLP. As an example, based on the keywords "web" and "guideline", we have 1273 results from IEEE, 273 results from Science-Direct and 168 results from DBLP. With Springer and ACM, we have much more results in many domains, so we had to refine the results and choose results with high relevance (as computed by the search engines). Then we defined inclusion criteria for selecting sources (primary studies) and rejecting the other ones. The inclusion criteria are presented in the table below (Table 1).

We found several guideline lists published since 2000. However, these documents are sparse and address many domains. One objective is to gather them, categorize, and model guidelines. Thus they will be more usable for supporting web application

Table 1. Inclusion criteria.

Criterion	Description
C1	The study focuses on guideline definition for web sites
C2	The study mentions quality characteristics of web sites
C3	The paper is recent, i.e. published since 2000
C4	The paper proposes original guidelines (does not only mention guidelines from other studies)

developers. Some guidelines are general and others are dedicated to specific domains: education, international, or for particular ages (children or seniors). As an illustration, the guidelines of AgeLight Company are divided in six categories: layout and style, color, text, general usability testing, accessibility and disabilities, user customization [4]. Web sites for old people are the research object of a number of studies [5, 6]. Meloncon et al., in contrast, concentrated on guidelines for children [7]. Maguire focused on e-commerce international sites [8]. Some papers focused on the charac- teristics of quality directly, such as [9] which targeted portability and efficiency. [10] capitalizes on the 14 guidelines from WCAG, so we did not collect them. Finally, we took into account fourteen sources. Their analysis is described below.

Extracting the Appropriate Guidelines. Our systematic search followed by a scan of sources allowed us to exhibit fourteen papers containing relevant guidelines. The next step consisted in studying all the guidelines and selecting the helpful guidelines. In each source of guidelines, we found some obsolete guidelines or some recommenda- tions which were out of our scope. For example, in [11], guidelines in the last part (part 18), such as "Use an iterative design approach" or "Solicit test participants' comments" were not selected, since they are too general or dedicated to testing. So we eliminated them from the list.

We found 14 sources with 475 guidelines. The number of guidelines of each source is presented in Table 2. In some cases, we split some guidelines, hence the number of selected guidelines may be higher than the number of guidelines proposed in the paper.

Some sources propose general guidelines. Others are more specific. For example [12] concentrates on web forms or [9] focuses on portability and efficiency.

Table 2. Source, number and scope of guidelines.

Source	Proposed guidelines	Selected guidelines	Scope
[4]	53	35	General
[12]	20	20	General but concentrating on web forms
[5]	7	10	Old people/medical information
[9]	17	15	General/focusing portability and efficiency
[11]	196	209	General
[13]	9	9	Blind people
[14]	13	14	General
[8]	20	8	International sites
[7]	21	11	Children
[15]	50	49	General
[16]	11	11	General
[17]	20	20	General
[6]	31	31	Old people
[18]	7	8	Universities

Some guidelines are too complex, so we had to divide them into two parts or more. For example the guideline for images in [9] is separated into two atomic guidelines: "The preferred use of JPEG and GIF images" and "The resolution of image should be set correctly inside the tags".

2.2   Analyzing the Guidelines Usage

To analyze how well the guidelines are applied in practice, we defined four levels namely: Yes, No, Partial and NN. Yes means that the site satisfies completely the guideline, No means that this site does not satisfy it, Partial means that this site partially meets the guideline and NN means that "We don't know", since either the guideline cannot be applied to the site or we don't have enough information. The result is synthesized at Fig. 1. Each guideline obtains the grade 1, 0.5, 0 point for Yes, Partial and No respectively. After applying all guidelines to the three websites, each guideline obtains a grade between 3 and zero or is equal to NN. Thus, 206 guidelines are verified on the three selected sites (totalizing 3 points). 33 guidelines reach 2.5, 46 guidelines obtain 2 points. 60 guidelines obtain between 0.5 and 1.5. 47 guidelines obtain 0, meaning that they are not respected on the three selected sites. But let us remind that 3 guidelines are dedicated to international or children sites, and thus are not required in the three tested web sites. Besides them, there are 83 guidelines obtaining the NN value. For guidelines which have NN value, many of them are related to the security aspects. To check if they are fulfilled, we require the admin authority, so we cannot conclude about these guidelines.

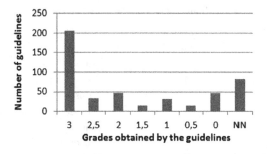

Fig. 1. The distribution of guideline grades.

As an illustration, the guideline G115 "considering both levels: 'high' and 'low' of cultural context for satisfying both viewpoints" or G176 "Limit navigational topics" are not relevant for the three web sites. Others may be irrelevant, such as G217 "Inform users of long download times" or G247 "Limit homepage length" since we had high speed connection for our tests.

Figure 2 compares the scores obtained by the three websites if we consider the rule: the more guidelines the web site complies with, the better score it obtains. deptinfo. cnam.fr obtains the score of 264.5 while lemonde.fr obtains 287 points. Finally,

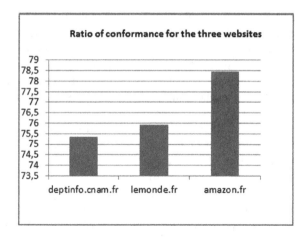

Fig. 2. Results for the three websites.

amazon.fr is the best one with score of 300.5. However, deptinfo.cnam.fr has 124 NN guidelines, whereas lemonde.fr has only 97 NN guidelines and amazon.fr has 92 NN guidelines, so if we compare ratios, deptinfo.cnam.fr achieves 75.3%, lemonde.fr 75.9% and amazon.fr is the highest with 78.5%.

These figures show that either these guidelines are not considered as references or these websites still face quality problems. As an example, let us mention G345 "Provide auto-tabbing functionality" for increasing users' convenience and G362 "Using photographs of people" for increasing users' reliability. The three websites are not aligned with these two guidelines. That means that these guidelines which were validated through complex processes are not sufficiently known by web site designers.

3   Research Questions

From the mid of 1990s, methods and approaches have been created for helping developers to build web applications more easily and constructively. The Object-Oriented Hypermedia Design Method (OOHDM) was one of the first methods proposing a rigorous process from requirements elicitation to implementation including navigational and interface design [19]. The method relies on object-oriented principle and proposes notation mainly derived from UML. The transition from models to specification is not supported and thus requires a considerable effort.

The Web Modelling Language (WebML) is a model driven web engineering method dedicated to data-intensive web applications [20]. WebML is one of the most used web engineering methodologies. It is supported by a development framework, Ratio5 [21] that is fully integrated to the Eclipse framework. Several extensions of the first version have been proposed offering a rich modelling approach for developers. However, the method relying very few on standards, it led to a proliferation of proprietary notations increasing the method complexity.

The UML-based Web Engineering (UWE) methodology [22] is a model-driven Web Engineering approach. It relies heavily on UML and is extensively related to standards. The model driven orientation allows generating platform specific implementation through dedicated transformation rules. Model driven approaches are based on four levels of abstraction: the computer independent model (CIM), the platform independent model (PIM), the platform specific model (PSM), and the code. Some methods address only the CIM level, other methods focus on PIM level. In the same way, some methods deal with the transformation of CIM to PIM (e.g. NDT, OOWS), others address the transformation of PIM to PSM (e.g. WebML, UWE) and others incorporate the transformation of PSM to code (e.g. OOHDM, UWE) [23]. Even if these methods offer a real support, they are still not used by practitioners probably since they are complex and they do not provide designers with sufficient guidance.

We argue that most methods do not provide their users with sufficient guidance in the design and development process. Either in the same approaches or in other sources, researchers propose many guidelines in order to help designers and developers. These guidelines may be very helpful to support them.

Thus the research question we address in this paper may be defined as follows: "How to structure all the existing guidelines helping website designers to understand and apply them?" To answer this question the experiment presented in Sect. 2 helped us to elicit the main characteristics of these guidelines. We then defined a meta-model allowing us to represent this knowledge. Finally we categorized the selected guidelines based on our meta-model. This categorization aims to facilitate their reuse. Then we defined a grammar enabling to model all these guidelines and serving as a basis for our guideline management prototype. This prototype, described below, is a first answer to our second research question: "Can we help the web application designers by providing them with a tool for managing literature guidelines enriched with their guidelines?"

4 Guideline Capitalization: A Model-Based Approach

In the literature, we find different ways to describe guidelines: in [9], they are represented by three attributes: Category, Name and Content. Meanwhile in [24], a guideline has three parts: design/application solutions, objective and description. We argue that this descriptive information is not sufficient to facilitate the reuse of guidelines by web application designers. In particular, the latter must find easily the guidelines using different criteria. For example, in case of designing a web application for blind people: which recommendations do they have to take into account? If developers want mainly to facilitate the maintainability of the web application: which guidelines aim at this objective? Etc.

We first propose a model helping capitalizing and structuring the guidelines. The meta-model is depicted at Fig. 3.

Following the general description of patterns for decision processes [25], we propose to link each guideline with the following categories:

- The source where the guideline was found,
- The quality characteristics and sub-characteristics that the guideline addresses,

- The problem it aims to solve,
- The solution proposed,
- The particular domain concerned if any,
- The lifecycle aspect, meaning which web application model (content model, navigation model, presentation model) it deals with.

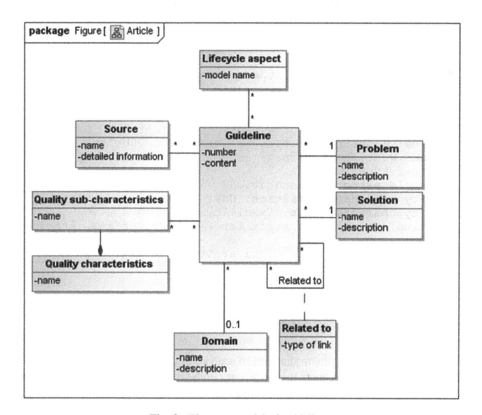

Fig. 3. The meta-model of guidelines.

This structure will constitute a knowledge base for automatic reuse through a web application design tool. The meta-model is represented as a UML class diagram at Fig. 3. The *related to* relation between guidelines allows us to represent potential links between guidelines. Thus the attribute *type of link* may take the values "in contradiction with", "specializes" or "similar to".

Each guideline solves a problem; however several guidelines may tackle the same problem. The solution of the guideline describes the rules to be applied. As explained above, in our process, we split some guidelines such that each resulting guideline recommends one and only one solution. The domain may be general or it may be a specific one. The quality characteristics (functional suitability, performance/efficiency, compatibility, usability, reliability, security, maintainability, portability) and sub-characteristics refer to ISO25010 for software quality. For space reasons we may not list all of them. Some guidelines are common to several sources, hence the multiplicity of the relation here is many-to-many. Finally, the lifecycle aspect consists of three elements: Content, Navigation, and Presentation.

In order to illustrate, let us describe the guideline G37: "For body copy, the recommended faces for the web, in order of preference, are Verdana, Arial and Helvetica. The browser should use Verdana first; if it is not available, use Arial and then Helvetica. If none are available, use another Sans serif font".

```
Number: #37
Content: For body copy, the recommended faces for the
web, in order of preference, are Verdana, Arial and
Helvetica. The browser should use Verdana first; if it
is not available, use Arial and then Helvetica. If none
are available, use another Sans serif font.
Problem: Choosing appropriate font for a website
Domain: web for university (even if it can also apply
to other types of site)
Lifecycle aspect: Presentation
Quality sub-characteristics: User interface aesthetics
Quality characteristic: Usability
Solution: Choose Sans serif font, namely Verdana, Arial
and Helvetica.
Source: (Carnegie Mellon University)
```

5 Guidelines Analysis

In this section, we provide the reader with an analysis of the guidelines according to the different dimensions of our meta-model. Let us remind that our selection process led to the creation of a set of 475 guidelines (the guidelines can be found at http://deptinfo.cnam.fr/ ∼ wattiaui/Guidelines.html).

If we analyze them from the lifecycle dimension (Content/Navigation/Presentation), we counted 203 guidelines for Presentation, 291 guidelines for Content and only 40 guidelines for Navigation. Some guidelines address more than one model. Hence the total exceeds 475 (Fig. 4).

The 475 guidelines were mapped with quality sub-characteristics. Some guidelines are mapped with several sub-characteristics. The characteristic Usability, with sub-characteristics Operability and User interface aesthetics, is the most involved one. It is easy to explain since many papers address interface aspects (User interface aesthetics) and aim to build easy-to-use interfaces (Operability).

Many guidelines are about font (G37, G42, G49, G50, etc.) and color (G6, G8, G39, G41, G86, G185, G186, etc.) of websites. White is the color which is not recommended (G9, G39, G189, etc.).

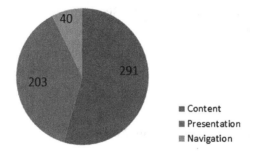

Fig. 4. Percentage of guidelines per lifecycle aspect.

We can detect some contradictory guidelines, since some guidelines aim at different goals. In the guidelines of a university (Carnegie Mellon University) the documents should be opened in new windows (G35), probably for legal responsibilities. It is opposite to guideline G101 [4] which recommends not to open external links in new windows, since it can cause user distracting.

Guideline G37 recommends using only Sans-serif font, but meanwhile G85 accepts serif font in web site for printing.

Some guidelines are dedicated to different types of users, but finally they have same contents. As an illustration, Sun et al. [6] focused on website for old people; meanwhile Meloncon et al. [7] concentrated on web applications for children. Old people and children are two types of users which have some specific characteristics in comparison with others (e.g. not being able to understand complex content).

The guideline about Security of web applications in MSDN of Microsoft (Microsoft Developer Network) contains about 50 sections. Many of them address Integrity (prevent unauthorized access) (in 38 sections) and Confidentiality (data are accessible only to those authorized) (in 18 sections). This is due to the fact that Integrity and Confidentiality are important for web applications which are designed for many kinds of users and also are the targets of attacks.

Among the eight quality characteristics, Compatibility is not mentioned at all, since guidelines focus on the site itself, and not on the relation of the site with other sites or other applications (scope of Compatibility).

6   Guideline Description Grammar

The previous sections of the paper capitalized on guidelines found in the literature. In order to facilitate their acquisition and to enrich them, we propose to structure each guideline as a sentence. These sentences must use the natural language (English here) but they must be easy to understand by referring only to simple structures. To define such structures, we propose a grammar in this section. We based our grammar on Pohl's four rules [26] which allow designers to document scenarios:

- Rule 1: Use the present tense
- Rule 2: Use the active voice

- Rule 3: Use the subject-predicate-object (SPO) sentence structure
- Rule 4: Avoid modal verbs

However, the rule 4 is adequate for scenarios but not for guidelines which actually have to contain different modalities defined using modal verbs. Thus, we applied only the first three rules.

6.1   Guideline Grammar Backus-Naur Notation

Based on these three rules, we screened the whole literature guidelines and built a grammar using an inductive process. This grammar is presented with Backus-Naur Form. Backus-Naur notation (more commonly known as BNF or Backus-Naur Form) is a formal way to describe a language, which was developed by John Backus (Fig. 5). It is used to define the grammar of a language formally, so we can use it for describing

```
<guideline> ::= <first part> <main part> <complement
part>
<first part> ::= <modal verb> | <modal verb> 'not' |
'do not' | Ø
<modal verb> ::= 'should'| 'must' | 'have to'
<main part> ::= <verb> <main part complement>
<main part complement> ::= <main part complement>
<comma> | <adjective>* <noun phrase> <adverb>*
<complement part> ::= <preposition> <body of
complement> | Ø
<comma> ::= ','
<noun phrase> ::= <determiner> <pre-modifier> <noun>
<complement of noun phrase> | <determiner> <pre-
modifier> <noun> <post-modifier>
<body of complement> ::= <clause> | <gerund phrase>
<clause> ::= <noun phrase> <verb phrase>
<gerund phrase> ::= <gerund> <complement of gerund
phrase>
<complement of gerund phrase> ::= <noun> | <pronoun> |
<adverb>
<gerund> ::= <verb>'-ing'
<determiner> ::= 'a'|'an'|'the'
<pre-modifier> ::= <adjective> | <noun> | Ø
<post-modifier> ::= <adverb> | <prepositional phrase> |
<clause>
<complement of noun phrase> ::=  <prepositional phrase>
| <clause>
<verb phrase> ::= <verb> | <auxiliary verb> <gerund> |
<auxiliary verb> <past participle verb> |<modal verb>
<verb>
<prepositional phrase> ::= <preposition> <noun> |
<preposition> <pronoun>
```

Fig. 5. BNF description of the guideline grammar.

our grammar of guidelines [27]. A guideline is composed of three components: the first part, the main part, and the complement part.

The first part is a modal verb (must, have to, should) depending on the level of the recommendation. It is optional. The guideline may be expressed as a negative sentence. The main part of the sentence is composed of a verb and a complement. The main part complement may be composed of several parts with adjectives, noun phrases and adverbs. Finally, the sentence may contain a complement part. The verb may be any verb of the dictionary. A closed list of already used verbs is proposed, but it is an open list. In the same way, the sentence may contain prepositions, adjectives, nouns, adverbs, pronouns, auxiliary verbs, and past participle verbs.

6.2   Pre-processing of Raw Guidelines

When collecting guidelines from literature, we performed a pre-processing of guidelines which did not satisfy the grammar we proposed. We divided long guidelines into several shorter guidelines. We transformed some guidelines, for example the relative position of elements of clauses in order to follow the rules of the grammar, while preserving their meanings.

The simplest form of guidelines is Verb + Noun. An example is guideline 20: "Provide a site-map". A more sophisticated form is guideline 17: "Do not use a deep hierarchy and group information into meaning categories".

The guideline "Left justified text, text line should not be long" was split into two guidelines: "Justify left text" and "Do not use long text line".

Thus, we harmonized the guidelines extracted from the literature in order to facilitate their understanding and their appropriation by web application designers. In the following section, we describe the tool making these guidelines available.

7   Prototype Description

We propose to make the guidelines available through a web tool allowing web application designers to add, query, and verify guidelines. The prototype of this tool is described below. It contains three modules for respectively adding, verifying and, querying guidelines.

7.1   Add Guidelines

The first module allows the user to enter new guidelines. The basic syntax of the sentence is made available through a screen form (Fig. 6). One example is adding guideline 73: "Should not create primary colors by mixing other colors". We choose "Should" from modal verbs, tick "not", choose "create" in verb list (or can add new verbs not in the list), choose "primary" from adjective list, add "colors" in the Noun phrase box. There is no adverb in this guideline. The complement is "by mixing other colors", so we choose "by" from "linking words" and "mixing other colors" in the complement box.

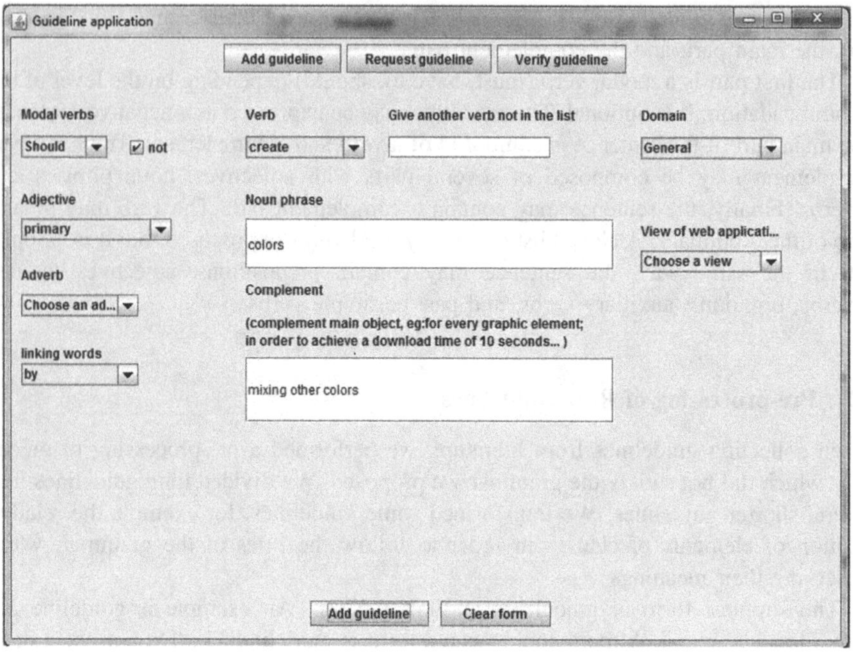

Fig. 6. Adding a new guideline.

We choose the button "Add guideline" and this guideline is inserted into the pending list. We turn into the "Verify guideline" part.

7.2   Verify Guidelines

In the first version of the prototype, the verification process is limited to finding existing similar and/or contradictory guidelines and presenting them to the user. The similar and/or contradictory guidelines are extracted by comparing the different components of the sentence based on Levenshtein distance [28]. The prototype lists all existing guidelines whose distance's value passing defined threshold. Here, we chose a threshold equal to 0.5. The guideline is in the pending list and we select the button "Find similar guidelines" (Fig. 7). The result appears in the below box: the only similar guideline is itself: this guideline is new and we can accept it (Fig. 8).

As an illustration, we can add another guideline which is similar to this guideline. It is "Should not create secondary colors by mixing many colors". The result box lists two results: the first is the guideline 73 we've just added before with the distance 0.81 and the second is the guideline to be added. After comparing it with guideline 73, we can accept the new guideline (Fig. 9).

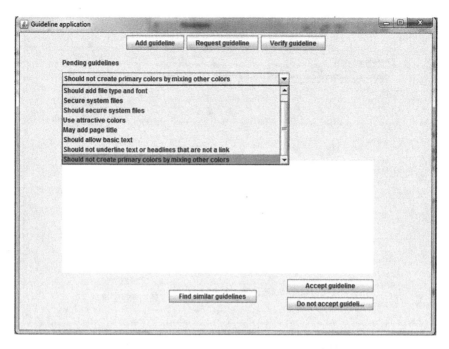

Fig. 7. Check guidelines.

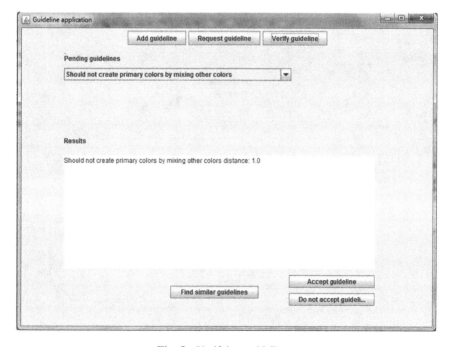

Fig. 8. Verifying guidelines.

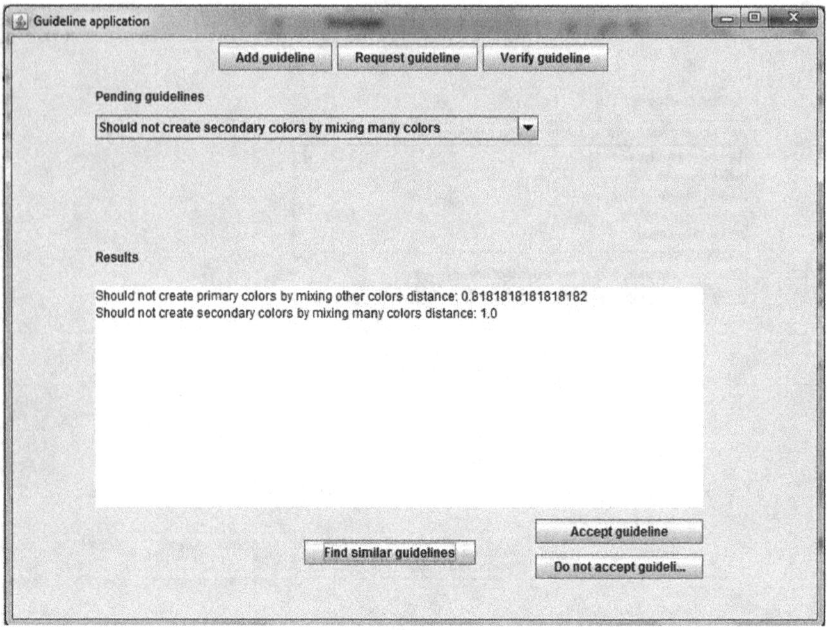

Fig. 9. Verifying guidelines: another example.

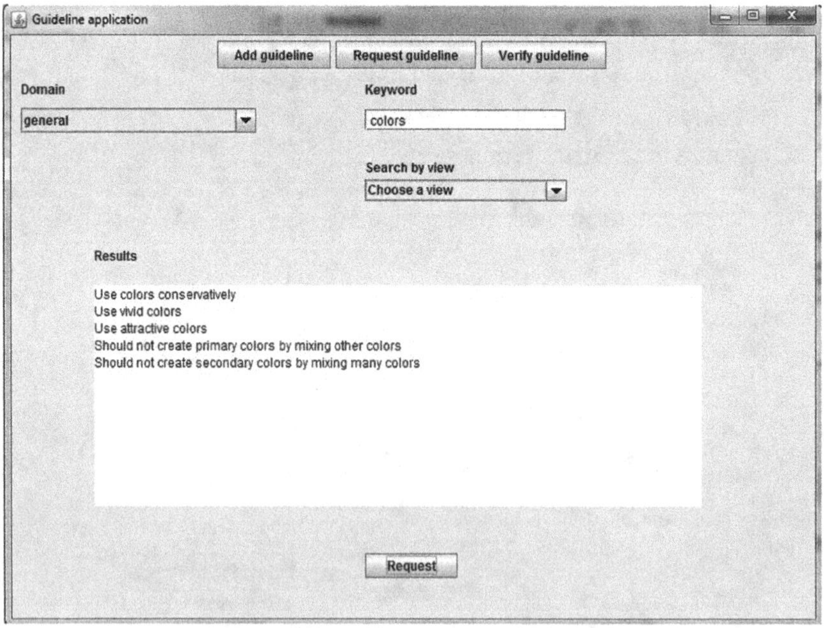

Fig. 10. Querying the guideline database.

7.3   Request Guideline

With the "Request guideline" function, we can query the guideline base using between one and three criteria, which are the domain (general, children, etc.), the view (presentation, content, navigation), and a keyword (a word contained in the guideline). Figure 10 shows the result when only the keyword color is entered.

8   Related Works

In this section, we synthesize the literature on guidelines for web site design. We organized this state of the art in two categories: first the approaches which propose guidelines and, second, the approaches which involve such guidelines.

8.1   Design for Guidelines

One of the most famous works delivering guidelines for web site design is Web Accessibility Initiative (WAI) of W3C [29]. It is a collection of standards, guidelines, and techniques for making accessible products in four categories: websites, authoring tools, browsers, and web applications. Each category has a bunch of guidelines for constructing web design and for improving accessibility. Other sources of guidelines were listed above in this paper and enrich considerably the W3C recommendations.

Khlaisang is an example of research illustrating how these guidelines may be either validated or elicited [30]. The author developed user interface guidelines and a prototype for evaluating educational service websites. Based on source sites of Thailand Cyber University Project (TCU), he studied the use of sites, the website structure, the user interface design and conducted usability tests of the site. Resulting from these experiments, he presented a model of suitable website for TCU service. Starting from this website, model, he designed and developed a prototype of site. The paper also mentions similar approaches.

8.2   Design by Guidelines

Besides works creating guidelines, other works used existing guidelines for proposing ways to improve quality of websites.

Leuthold et al. [13] designed enhanced text user interfaces for blind Internet users. Starting from the guidelines of web content accessibility guidelines (WCAG), they proposed enhanced text user interface (ETI) helping blind users in spending less time to complete tasks, making fewer mistakes and expressing greater satisfaction when surfing the website. This system contains nine guidelines. For blind users, this system is more usable than normal GUI.

Another work building on WCAG guidelines is [31]. Using e-learning as an example, they propose a framework that guides web authors and policy makers in addressing accessibility at a higher level, by defining the context in which a Web resource will be used and considering how new alternatives may be combined to enhance the accessibility of the web site.

After a brief description of the 14 guidelines of WCAG (version 1), Radosav et al. discussed the choice of colours for adjusted web design [10]. They classified colours into several groups and concluded that colours, which cannot be differentiated by people with colour discrimination disability, should not be placed next to each other.

For space reasons, we cannot provide a more detailed literature review. As a conclusion, research in this field is prolific and aims at (i) proposing guidelines for web site designers, (ii) enriching existing ones, (iii) implementing guidelines into more comprehensives approaches, (iv) evaluating guidelines through experiments. To the best of our knowledge, we did not find any paper proposing a meta-model, a grammar, and a tool allowing web application designers to put together the different guidelines as a first step for their reuse in an automatic way.

9   Conclusion and Future Research

The companies grasp the importance of having usable and efficient web applications. Thus, their development and maintenance is of high importance. The academic literature on the subject contains hundreds of guidelines aiming at helping web site designers. The research question we addressed in this paper may be expressed as follows: How to structure the existing guidelines helping website designers in order to facilitate their application? As a first contribution, we defined a meta-model allowing us to describe each guideline with six dimensions: the problem it addresses, the solution it proposes, the lifecycle aspect it deals with, the target quality characteristics, the source it comes from, the potential links (similarity, contradiction, specialization) with other guidelines. Our search and selection process allowed us to define 475 such guidelines and to feed our meta-model with them. This required the mapping of them with the relevant quality sub-characteristics. As a first evaluation of these guidelines, we checked whether they were compliant with three very different web sites. Second, we proposed a grammar for homogenizing the guideline description. Finally, we developed a prototype allowing us to store such guidelines and providing users with simple access to the guidelines as well as the possibility to enrich them with new guidelines.

This research suffers from some limitations. Thus, it is rather easy to check the contradiction between guidelines attached to the same quality characteristics and/or sub characteristics. However, contradictions may also occur between guidelines associated with different quality characteristics. Moreover, some guidelines may become obsolete due to new technical opportunities. It is not easy to ensure an easy update of guidelines.

Future research will explore three directions: first, the implementation of these guidelines in a CASE tool implementing UWE web application design method; second, a validation of the approach through an experiment with web site designers, in order to evaluate how the guidelines help them when using the CASE tool; third, we would like to build an audit tool for automatically checking the quality of web applications thanks to our guideline database.

Acknowledgments. We want to thank the colleagues who helped us improve our paper, by their comments during the ICEIS presentation.

References

1. Krigsman, M.: www.zdnet.com/article/research-25-percent-of-web-projects-fail/
2. Bloch, M., Blumberg, S., Laartz, J.: Delivering large-scale IT projects on time, on budget, and on value. McKinsey Financ. Number **45**(Winter), 28–35 (2013)
3. Trulock, V., Hetherington, R.: Assessing the progress of implementing web accessibility-an irish case study. In: 10th International Conference on Enterprise Information Systems (ICEIS), pp. 105–111 (2008)
4. AgeLight LCC: Interface design guidelines for users of all ages. Technical report (2001)
5. Xie, B., Watkins, I., Huang, M.: Making web-based multimedia health tutorials senior-friendly: design and training guidelines. In: iConference Seattle, Washington, USA, pp. 230–237 (2011)
6. Sun, Z., Zhao, Y.: The preliminary construction of accessibility design guidelines of learning website for old people. In: International Workshop on Education Technology and Computer Science, pp. 612–615 (2010)
7. Meloncon, L., Haynes, E., Varelmann, M., Groh, L.: Building a playground: general guidelines for creating educational web sites for children. Tech. Commun. **57**(4), 398–415 (2010)
8. Maguire, M.C.: Guidelines on website design and colour selection for international acceptance. In: Marcus, A. (ed.) DUXU 2011. LNCS, vol. 6769, pp. 162–171. Springer, Heidelberg (2011). doi:10.1007/978-3-642-21675-6_19
9. Chiuchi, C.A., de Souza, R.C.G., Santos, A.B., Valêncio, C.R.: Efficiency and portability: guidelines to develop websites. In: Software Engineering and Knowledge Engineering, Miami Beach, USA, pp. 37–41 (2011)
10. Radosav, D., Karuovic, D., Markoski, B., Ivankovic, Z.: Guidelines on accessible web portal design. In: 2011 IEEE 12th International Symposium on Computational Intelligence and Informatics (CINTI), pp. 297–302 (2011)
11. U.S. Department of Health and Human Services: U.S. General Services Administration. Research-Based Web Design & Usability Guidelines (2006)
12. Bargas-Avila, J.A., Brenzikofer, O., Roth, S.P., Tuch, A.N., Orsini, S., Opwis, K.: Simple but crucial user interfaces in the world wide web: introducing 20 guidelines for usable web form design. In: Matrai. R (ed.) User Interfaces. InTech (2010)
13. Leuthold, S., Bargas-Avila, J.A., Opwis, K.: Beyond web content accessibility guidelines: design of enhanced text user interfaces for blind internet users. Int. J. Hum Comput Stud. **66** (4), 257–270 (2008)
14. Lokman, A.M., Noor, N.L.M., Nagamachi, M.: ExpertKanseiWeb: a tool to design kansei website. In: Filipe, J., Cordeiro, J. (eds.) ICEIS 2009. LNBIP, vol. 24, pp. 894–905. Springer, Heidelberg (2009). doi:10.1007/978-3-642-01347-8_74
15. Microsoft Developer Network: Chapter 4 - design guidelines for secure web applications. https://msdn.microsoft.com/en-us/library/ff648647.aspx
16. Ministry of Community and Social Services of Ontario: Making your website more accessible. Queen's Printer for Ontario (2012). http://www.mcss.gov.on.ca/en/mcss/publications/accessON/accessible_websites/toc.aspx
17. Ozok, A., Salvendy, G.: Twenty guidelines for the design of Web-based interfaces with consistent language. Comput. Hum. Behav. **20**(2), 149–161 (2004)

18. Carnegie Mellon Universit: Web guidelines. http://www.cmu.edu/marcom/brand-guidelines/print-web-products/web/index.html
19. Schwabe, D., Rossi, G.: The object-oriented hypermedia design model. Commun. ACM **38**(8), 45–46 (1995)
20. Ceri, S., Fraternali, P., Bongio, A.: Web modeling language (WebML): a modeling language for designing Web sites. Comput. Netw. **33**(1), 137–157 (2000)
21. Acerbis, R., Bongio, A., Brambilla, M., Butti, S.: WebRatio 5: an eclipse-based CASE tool for engineering web applications. In: Baresi, L., Fraternali, P., Houben, G.-J. (eds.) ICWE 2007. LNCS, vol. 4607, pp. 501–505. Springer, Heidelberg (2007). doi:10.1007/978-3-540-73597-7_44
22. Hennicker, R., Koch, N.: A UML-based methodology for hypermedia design. In: Evans, A., Kent, S., Selic, B. (eds.) UML 2000. LNCS, vol. 1939, pp. 410–424. Springer, Heidelberg (2000). doi:10.1007/3-540-40011-7_30
23. Aragon, G., Escalona, M.J., Lang, M., Hilera, J.: An analysis of model-driven web engineering methodologies. Int. J. Innov. Comput. Inf. Control **9**(1), 413–436 (2013)
24. Ekberg, J., Ericson, L., Timpka, T., Eriksson, H., Nordfeldt, S., Hanberger, L., Ludvigsson, J.: Web 2.0 systems supporting childhood chronic disease management: design guidelines based on information behaviour and social learning theories. J. Med. Syst. **34**(2), 107–117 (2010)
25. Harrison, N.B., Avgeriou, P., Zdun, U.: Using patterns to capture architectural decisions. IEEE Softw. **24**(4), 38–45 (2007)
26. Pohl, K.: Requirements Engineering - Fundamentals, Principles, and Techniques. Springer, Heidelberg (2010). pp. I-XVII, 1-813. ISBN 978-3-642-12577-5
27. Marcotty, M., Ledgard, H.: The World of Programming Languages. Springer, Berlin (1986). p. 41 and following (1986)
28. Yujian, L., Bo, L.: A normalized Levenshtein distance metric. IEEE Trans. Pattern Anal. Mach. Intell. **29**(6), 1091–1095 (2007)
29. Web Accessibility Initiative (WAI): Web Content Accessibility Guidelines (WCAG) Overview (2008). http://www.w3.org/WAI/intro/wcag
30. Khlaisang, J.: Research-based guidelines for evaluating educational service website: case study of thailand cyber university project. Procedia – Soc. Behav. Sci. **174**, 751–758 (2015)
31. Sloan, D., Heath, A., Hamilton, F., Kelly, B., Petrie, H., Phipps, L.: Contextual web accessibility, maximizing the benefit of accessibility guidelines. In: W4A 2006 Proceedings of the 2006 International Cross-Disciplinary Workshop on Web Accessibility (W4A): Building the Mobile Web: Rediscovering Accessibility?, pp. 121–131 (2006)

A New Mechanism to Preserving Data Confidentiality in Cloud Database Scenarios

Eliseu C. Branco Jr.[✉], José Maria Monteiro, Roney Reis,
and Javam C. Machado

Federal University of Ceara, Fortaleza, CE, Brazil
{ecastelob,monteiro,roneyreis,javam}@lsbd.ufc.br

Abstract. A cloud database is a database that typically runs on a cloud computing platform. There are two common deployment models: users can run databases on virtual machines hosted and managed by a infrastructure as a service provider, or they can purchase access to a database service, maintained by a software as a service provider, without physically launching a virtual machine instance for the database. In a database service, application owners do not have to install and maintain the database themselves. Instead, the database as a service provider takes responsibility for installing and maintaining the database, and application owners pay according to their usage. Thus, database services decrease the need for local data storage and the infrastructure costs. Nevertheless, hosting confidential data at a database service requires the transfer of control of the data to a semi-trusted external provider. Therefore, data confidentiality is an important concern from cloud service providers. Recently, three main approaches have been introduced to ensure data confidentiality in cloud services: data encryption; combination of encryption and fragmentation; and fragmentation. Besides, other strategies use a mix of these three main approaches. In this paper, we present i-OBJECT, a new mechanism to preserve data confidentiality in database service scenarios. The proposed mechanism uses information decomposition to split data into unrecognizable parts and store them in different cloud service providers. Additionally, i-OBJECT is a flexible mechanism since it can be used alone or together with other previously approaches in order to increase the data confidentiality level. Thus, a user may trade performance or data utility for a potential increase in the degree of data confidentiality. Experimental results show the potential efficiency of i-OBJECT.

Keywords: Data confidentiality · Cloud database · Information decomposition

1 Introduction

Cloud Computing moves the application software and databases to large data centers, where data management may not be sufficiently trustworthy. Cloud storage is an increasingly popular class of services for archiving, backup and sharing

© Springer International Publishing AG 2017
S. Hammoudi et al. (Eds.): ICEIS 2016, LNBIP 291, pp. 261–283, 2017.
DOI: 10.1007/978-3-319-62386-3_13

data. There is an important cost-benefit relation for individuals and small organizations in storing their data using cloud storage services and delegating to them the responsibility of data storage and management [1]. Despite the big business and technical advantages of the cloud storage services, the data confidentiality concern has been one of the major hurdles preventing its widespread adoption.

The concept of privacy varies widely among countries, cultures and jurisdictions. So, a concise definition is elusive if not impossible [2]. For the purposes of this discussion, privacy is "the claim of individuals, groups or institutions to determine for themselves when, how and to what extent the information about them is communicated to others" [3]. Privacy protects access to the person, whereas confidentiality protects access to the data. So, confidentiality is the assurance that certain information that may include a subject's identity, health, lifestyle information or a sponsor's proprietary information would not be disclosed without permission from the subject (or sponsor). When dealing with cloud environments, confidentiality implies that a customer's data and computation tasks are to be kept confidential from both the cloud provider and other customers [4].

Recently, three main approaches have been introduced to ensure the data confidentiality in cloud environments: (a) data encryption, (b) combination of encryption and fragmentation [5], and (c) fragmentation [1]. However, in this context, it is in fact crucial to guarantee a proper balance between data confidentiality, on one hand, and other properties, such as, data utility, query execution overhead, and performance on the other hand [6,7].

The first approach, denoted by data encryption, consists in encrypting all the data collections. This technique is adopted in the database outsourcing scenario [5]. Actually, encryption algorithms presents increasingly lower costs. Cryptography becomes an inexpensive tool that supports the protection of confidentiality when storing or communicating data [5]. However, dealing with encrypted data may make query processing more expensive [1,5]. Some techniques have been proposed to enabling the execution of queries directly on encrypted data (remember that confidentiality demands that data decryption must be possible only at the client side) [6]. These techniques associate with encrypted data indexing information on which queries can be executed. The mainly challenger for indexing methods is the trade off between precision and privacy: more precise indexes provide more efficient query execution but a greater exposure to possible privacy violations [6,8]. Besides, the solutions based on an extensive use of encryption suffer from significant consequences due to loss of keys. In the real scenarios, key management, particularly the operations at the human side, is a hard and delicate process [6]. The security of cryptography techniques is based on the computational difficulty of mathematical problems. Any breakthrough in solving such mathematical problems or increasing the computing power can render a cryptography technique vulnerable.

The second approach, called combination of encryption and fragmentation, uses encryption together with data fragmentation. It applies encryption only on the sensitive attributes and splits the attributes with sensitive association into several fragments, which are stored by different cloud storage services [5]. In other words, sensitive association constraints are solved via fragmentation, and encryption is limited to those attributes that are sensitive by themselves. Thus, a single cloud service provider cannot join these fragments for responding queries. Therefore, these techniques must also be accompanied by proper query transformation techniques defining how queries on the original data are translated into queries on the fragmented data. Besides, splitting the attributes with sensitive association into some fragment is a NP-hard problem [6,7].

The third approach, denoted by fragmentation, does not use cryptography. In this approach, the sensitive attributes remains under the client's custody while the attributes with sensitive association are split into several fragments, which are stored by different cloud storage services [1]. It is important to note that this approach has the same drawbacks discussed previously (for the combination of encryption and fragmentation approach) regarding to query execution [6,7].

In this paper, we present i-OBJECT, a new approach to preserve data confidentiality in cloud storage services. The science behind i-OBJECT uses concepts of the Hegel's Doctrine of Being. The proposed approach is based on the information decomposition to split data into unrecognizable parts and store them in different cloud service providers. The proposed approach does not use public cryptography keys. So, i-OBJECT does not require setting up and maintenance of public key management infrastructure, which involves a handsome financial budget. In this sense, i-OBJECT is a low cost approach, which can be used by small and medium enterprises. Besides, i-OBJECT is a flexible mechanism since it can be used alone or together with other previously approaches in order to increase the data confidentiality level. Thus, a user may trade performance or data utility for a potential increase in the degree of data confidentiality. Experimental results show the potential efficiency of the i-OBJECT.

The remain of this paper is organized as follows. Sections 2 and 3 presents the proposed approach, called i-OBJECT. Experimental results are presented in Sect. 4. Next, Sect. 5 addresses related works. Finally, Sect. 6 concludes this paper and outlines future works.

2   A Decomposition-Based Approach for Data Confidentiality

The proposed approach for ensuring data confidentiality in cloud environments, denoted i-OBJECT, was designed for transactional data. In this environments, reads are much more frequent than write operations. Thus, i-OBJECT needs to be fast to decompose a file and much faster to recompose a file stored in the cloud.

Figure 1 has shown the i-OBJECT stakeholders. In this context, we have 5 actors: a customer, you want to store their private data in the public cloud, three providers of cloud storage services and a Trusted Third Party (TTP) that

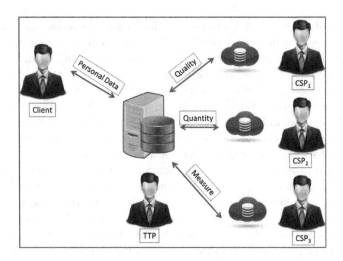

Fig. 1. i-OBJECT stakeholders.

is responsible for processing i-OBJECT algorithms and control communications between the client and cloud providers.

In the following, we describe the system restrictions and assumptions.

System Assumptions. We assume that quality, quantity and measure data will be stored into three different clouds. The users must be identified and authenticated to access the data stored in the cloud. We assume that users establish authenticated channels with the servers. Cloud providers should ensure the availability and integrity of data and they are considered honest, curious, that is, properly execute the protocols, but are interested in inferring the data and analyze the flow of messages received during the protocol in order to learn information about the data.

System Restrictions. We assume that there exists a secure network infrastructure that allows participants in the protocol perform mutual authentication and establish encrypted communication channels.

The i-OBJECT approach was inspired by the German philosopher Hegel's work, according to which an object has three fundamental characteristics [9]: quality, quantity and measure. From this idea, we developed the concept of information object (see Definition 1). From this concept, we have developed the processes to: (i) fragment a file in a sequence of information objects and (ii) decompose each information object in its properties (quality, quantity and measure).

The i-OBJECT approach has three phases: data fragmentation, decomposition and dispersion, which will be discussed later. Figure 2 shows an overview of the i-OBJECT approach.

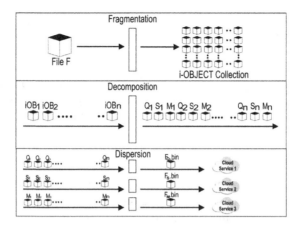

Fig. 2. i-OBJECT approach overview.

2.1 The Fragmentation Phase

Fragmentation phase consists in splitting an input file **F** in a sequence of n chunks, where each chunk has 256 bytes. Each chunk is denoted information object, **i-OBJECT** for short (see Definition 1).

Then, we can represent a file **F** as an ordered set $\{iOBJ_1, iOBJ_2, \cdots, iOBJ_n\}$ of information objects (**iOBJs**). According to [9], an information object has three properties that define it: Quality, Quantity (or Size) and Measure, denoted from now on by **Q**, **S** and **M**, respectively.

Definition 1 (i-OBJECT). *An information object, i-OBJECT for short, is a piece of 256 sequential bytes from a file.*   ◇

In order to illustrate the iOBJ definition, consider a file $F = <b_1, b_2, \cdots, b_{612}>$, where b_i is a byte. Thus, the file F is splitted in 3 information objects ($iOBJ_1$, $iOBJ_2$ and $iOBJ_3$), where $iOBJ_1$ has the first 256 sequential bytes (from $<b_1$ to b_{256}), $iOBJ_2$ has the second 256 sequential bytes (from $<b_{257}$ to b_{512}) and $iOBJ_3$ has the last 100 sequential bytes (from $<b_{513}$ to b_{612}).

2.2 The Decomposition Phase

The decomposition phase receives as input a file F, represented as an ordered set $\{iObj_1, iObj_2, \cdots, iObj_n\}$ of i-OBJECTs and decomposes F in three files: Fq.bin, Fs.bin and Fm.bin, which represent, respectively, F's quality, quantity and measure. It is important to highlight that the knowledge of one of these three files (or parts) does not reveal any information about the other 2 files (or parties). More specifically, the knowledge about **Q** (Fq.bin) reveals which bytes are present in F, but does not reveal the order in which these bytes are willing, nor the frequency of occurrence of them in the F. The knowledge about **S** (Fs.bin) reveals whether the bytes present in the F occurs only once or more than once, but does not disclose what are these bytes or their positions in F. Finally, the knowledge about $\mathbf{M}$ (Fm.bin) reveals the positions occupied by the bytes into F, but does not disclose what the bytes, neither their frequency of occurrence. In this sense, data confidentiality is ensured by decomposing each information object (iOBJ) in its three fundamental characteristics (Q, S and M) and coding them using one characteristic such as encryption key from the others. For example, to generate S we use Q as an encryption key and to generate M we use S as an encryption key. The decomposition phase has 5 steps, that will be present next.

Step 1: Generating the Quality, Quantity and Measure Properties. In order to understand the decomposition phase, it is necessary to formally define the quality, quantity and measure properties. These definitions are presented next.

Definition 2 (Quality). *Quality is the set of diverse bytes that composes a particular i-OBJECT. Let $iObj_k$ be an i-OBJECT, $Q(iObj_k)$ denotes the quality property of the $iObj_k$. $Q(iObj_k)$ is a ordered vector containing the m diverse bytes present in $iObj_k$. More formally, $Q(iObj_k) = \{b_1, b_2, b_3, \cdots, b_m\}$ such that $1 \leqslant b_i \leqslant 256$ and $i \neq j \rightarrow b_i \neq b_j$, where b_i is a byte present in $iObj_k$.* ◇

Definition 3 (Quantity). *Quantity is an array containing the number of times that each distinct byte appears in a specific i-Object. Let $iObj_k$ be an i-OBJECT, $S(iObj_k)$ denotes the quantity property of the $iObj_k$. $S(iObj_k)$ is a vector containing, for each different byte b_j (representing a ASCII Symbol) present in $Q(iObj_k)$ the number of times that b_i appears in $iObj_k$. More formally, $S(iObj_k) = \{s_1, s_2, s_3, \cdots, s_m\}$ such that $1 \leqslant s_i \leqslant 256$, where s_i represents the number of times that b_i appears in $iObj_k$.* ◇

Definition 4 (Measure). *Measure is a two-dimensional array containing, for each diverse byte that composes a particular i-OBJECT, a vector with the positions where this byte occurs in the i-OBJECT. Let $iObj_k$ be an i-OBJECT, $M(iObj_k)$ denotes the measure property of the $iObj_k$. $M(iObj_k)$ is a two-dimensional array containing, for each different byte b_j present in $Q(iObj_k)$, an array m_{b_j} storing the positions in which the byte b_j appears in $iObj_k$. More formally, $M(iObj_k) = \{m_{b_1}, m_{b_2}, \cdots, m_{b_m}\}$, such that, $m = 256$ and $1 \leqslant size(m_{b_i}) \leqslant 256$.* ◇

Given a file F, where $F = \{iOBJ_1, iOBJ_2, \cdots, iOBJ_n\}$. Initially, the decomposition phase consists in extracting, for each iOBJ $iOBJ_k$, where $1 \leqslant k \leqslant n$ and $iObj_k \in F$, the properties $Q(iOBJ_k)$, $S(iOBJ_k)$ and $M(iOBJ_k)$.

Next, the proposed approach combines the quality values for all iOBJs in the set $\{iOBJ_1, iOBJ_2, \cdots, iOBJ_n\}$ and creates a file called Fq.bin. After this, the i-OBJECT approach combines the quantity values for all iOBJs in the set $\{iObj_1, iObj_2, \cdots, iObj_n\}$ and creates a file denoted by Fs.bin. Finally, the proposed approach combines the measure values for all iOBJs in the set $\{iObj_1, iObj_2, \cdots, iObj_n\}$ and creates a file called Fm.bin (see Fig. 2).

In order to illustrate how an iOBJ $iOBJ_k$ is decomposed into its three basic properties (Q, S and M) consider the following example, denoted Example 1.

Example 1. Consider an information object $iOBJ_k$ containing the following text: "Google dropped its cloud computing prices and other vendors are expected to follow suit, but the lower pricing may not be the key for attracting enterprises to the cloud. When Enterprises comes to cloud, they're more concerned about privacy and security".

Note that $iOBJ_k$ contains 31 diverse bytes, where each byte represents an ASCII symbol. So, the quality property of the $iOBJ_k$ is a vector with 31 elements, we show the ASCII code and symbol as follows:

$Q(iOBJ_k) = \{32(\text{space}), 34("), 39('), 44(,) 46(.), 69(E), 71(G), 87(W), 97(a), 98(b), 99(c), 100(d), 101(e), 102(f), 103(g), 104(h), 105(i), 107(k), 108(l), 109(m), 110(n), 111(o), 112(p), 114(r), 115(s), 116(t), 117(u), 118(v), 119(w), 120(x), 121(y)\}$.

Thereby, the quantity property of the $iOBJ_k$ is also a vector with 31 elements:

$S(iOBJ_k) = \{40, 2, 1, 2, 1, 1, 1, 1, 8, 3, 13, 10, 28, 2, 4, 6, 11, 1, 7, 4, 12, 21, 9, 18, 10, 21, 8, 2, 2, 1, 5\}$.

One should carefully observe the relationship between quality and quantity properties. Note that, for example, the character "space" (ASCII 32), the first element in $Q(iOBJ_k)$, denoted by $Q(iOBJ_k)_1$, appears 40 times in the $iOBJ_k$, and the character "y" (ASCII 121), the last element in $Q(iOBJ_k)$, denoted by $Q(iOBJ_k)_{31}$, occurs 5 times in the $iOBJ_k$.

In this scenario, the measure property of the $iOBJ_k$ is a two-dimensional array containing 31 arrays, as follows:

$M(iOBJ_k) = \{\{7, 15, 19, 25, 35, 42, 46, 52, 60, 64, 73, 76, 83, 89, 93, 97, 103, 111, 115, 119, 122, 126, 130, 134, 145, 157, 160, 164, 171, 176, 188, 194, 197, 204, 212, 217, 227, 233, 245, 241\}, \{0, 255\}, \{209\}, \cdots, \{114, 129, 208, 253, 240\}\}$.

Observe that, for example, the character "y" (ASCII 121), the 31st element in $Q(iOBJ_k)$, occurs 5 times ($Q(iOBJ_k)_{31} = 5$) in the $iOBJ_k$, in the positions 114, 129, 208, 253 and 240, which are represented by the last array in $M(iOBJ_k)$. Therefore We extract the quality, quantity and measure properties from a specific i-OBJECT $iOBJ_k$. The next task in this step consists in create bit arrays to represent $Q(iOBJ_k)$, $S(iOBJ_k)$ and $M(iOBJ_k)$.

Initially, from the array $Q(iOBJ_k)$, the proposed strategy generates a bit array, denoted by $Q_{BA}(iOBJ_k)$, to represent $Q(iOBJ_k)$. $Q_{BA}(iOBJ_k)$ is created as following.

A particular $iOBJ_k$ may contain a maximum of 256 distinct bytes. Then, $Q_{BA}(iOBJ_k)$ is a 256-bit length array. Each position in $Q_{BA}(iOBJ_k)$ represents a byte, in an ordered manner. If a particular byte occurs in $iOBJ_k$, the position corresponding to its ASCII decimal code in $Q_{BA}(iOBJ_k)$ will store a bit 1, otherwise will store a bit 0. The $Q_{BA}(iOBJ_k)$, created from the $Q(iOBJ_k)$ illustrated at Example 1, is shown as follows.

$Q_{BA}(iOBJ_k) = \{\mathbf{0}, 0, 0, 0, 0, 0, 0, 0, 0, 0, 0, 0, 0, 0, 0, 0, 0, 0, 0, 0, 0, 0, 0, 0, 0, 0, 0, 0, 0, 0, 0, 0, \mathbf{1}, 0, \mathbf{1}, 0, 0, 0, 0, \mathbf{1}, 0, 0, 0, 0, \mathbf{1}, 0, \mathbf{1}, 0, 0, 0, 0, 0, 0, 0, 0, 0, 0, 0, 0, 0, 0, 0, 0, 0, 0, 0, 0, 0, \mathbf{1}, 0, \mathbf{1}, 0, 0, 0, 0, 0, 0, 0, 0, 0, 0, 0, 0, 0, 0, 0, 0,$

1, 0, 0, 0, 0, 0, 0, 0, 0, 0, 1, 1, 1, 1, 1, 1, 1, 1, 1, 0, 1, 1, 1, 1, 1, 1, 0, 1, 1, 1, 1, 1, 1, 1, 1, 0, 0, 0, 0, 0, 0}.

Note that $Q_{BA}(iOBJ_k)_1 = 0$ because the first character in the ASCII Table is the symbol "null" and it is not present in the $iOBJ_k$ shown at the Example 1. Besides, observe that $Q_{BA}(iOBJ_k)_{32} = 1$ because the 32nd symbol in the ASCII Table is the character "space" and it is present in the $iOBJ_k$.

Next, from the array $S(iOBJ_k)$, the proposed strategy generates a bit array, denoted by $S_{BA}(iOBJ_k)$, to represent $S(iOBJ_k)$. $S_{BA}(iOBJ_k) = \{bit_1, bit_2, bit_3, \cdots, bit_q\}$ such that, q is the quantity of diverse bytes present in $iOBJ_k$, that is, q is equal to the length of $Q(iOBJ_k)$. Each bit in $S_{BA}(iOBJ_k)$ characterize an element of the $Q(iOBJ_k)$. So, the first element in $S_{BA}(iOBJ_k)$ characterize the first element in $Q(iOBJ_k)$, and so on. If the byte b_i occurs only once in the $iOBJ_k$, the position i in the $S_{BA}(iOBJ_k)_i$ will store the bit 0, otherwise it will store the bit 1. The array S_{BA} has 256-bit length to support iOBJs with 256 different bytes.

The $S_{BA}(iOBJ_k)$, created from the $S(iOBJ_k)$ illustrated at Example 1, is shown as follows.

$S_{BA}(iOBJ_k) = \{$**1**, 1, 0, 1, 0, **0**, 0, 0, 1, 1, 1, 1, 1, 1, 1, 1, 1, 0, 1, 1, 1, 1, 1, 1, 1, 1, 1, 1, 1, 0, 1}.

Note that, $S_{BA}(iOBJ_k)_1 = 1$ because the 1st element at $Q(iOBJ_k)$ is the character "space" and it occurs 40 times n $iOBJ_k$. Besides, observe that $S_{BA}(iOBJ_k)_6 = 0$ because the 6th element at $Q(iOBJ_k)$ is the character "E" and it appears just one time in $iOBJ_k$ shown at the Example 1.

The two-dimensional array $M(iOBJ_k)$ will be transformed into a one-dimensional array, denoted $M_{ALL}(iOBJ_k)$ containing all elements present in $M(iOBJ_k)$. It's important to note that $M_{ALL}(iOBJ_k)$ will always contain 256 different numbers (0 to 255). So, the $M_{ALL}(iOBJ_k)$ is illustrated at Example 1, is shown as follows.

$M_{ALL}(iOBJ_k) = \{$7, 15, 19, 25, 35, 42, 46, 52, 60, 64, 73, 76, 83, 89, 93, 97, 103, 111, 115, 119, 122, 126, 130, 134, 145, 157, 160, 164, 171, 176, 188, 194, 197, 204, 212, 217, 227, 233, 245, 241, 0, 255, 254, 209, 203, 88, 170, 177, 1, 172, 43, 61, 113, 135, 139, 228, 242, 238, 90, 229, 120, 20, 26, 39, 69, 107, 140, 165, 189, 198, 218, 221, 248, 239, 8, 14, 24, 45, 56, 72, 169, 202, 244, 226, 6, 13, 40, 50, 54, 63, 65, 68, 71, 96, 101, 121, 125, 128, 146, 149, 155, 163, 174, 180, 186, 192, 207, 211, 216, 222, 247, 225, 131, 77, 4, 34, 144, 110, 49, 95, 124, 162, 206, 173, 16, 32, 38, 86, 106, 108, 142, 153, 184, 251, 236, 127, 5, 21, 79, 80, 98, 199, 166, 28, 112, 213, 191, 33, 44, 55, 109, 116, 143, 147, 175, 178, 220, 243, 224, 2, 3, 10, 22, 27, 47, 57, 75, 78, 81, 99, 117, 132, 159, 167, 190, 196, 200, 214, 230, 219, 11, 12, 29, 36, 67, 104, 151, 234, 182, 9, 37, 51, 58, 62, 102, 105, 133, 138, 150, 152, 181, 183, 210, 215, 223, 250, 235, 18, 41, 59, 84, 154, 156, 185, 187, 246, 193, 17, 31, 48, 70, 74, 87, 92, 94, 118, 123, 136, 137, 141, 148, 158, 161, 179, 195, 205, 252, 232, 23, 30, 85, 91, 168, 201, 249, 231, 237, 53, 100, 82, 66, 114, 129, 208, 253, 240}.

Step 2: Measure Anonymization. The measure elements represent the positions occupied by quality bytes sets. The values of each set were arranged in ascending order by reversing the positions of the last 2 bytes to indicate the end of the assembly. The analysis of the elements of $\mathbf{M}_{ALL}$ could reveal values of $\mathbf{S}_{BA}$ to the attacker. To prevent disclosure of this information the elements of $\mathbf{M}_{ALL}$ are permuted using Q_{BA} and S_{BA} like sort keys, generating MP_{ALL}.

$$MP_{ALL} = \begin{pmatrix} M_{ALL}(iOBJ_k)_1 & \cdots & M_{ALL}(iOBJ_k)_{256} \\ Q_{BA}, S_{BA}(iOBJ_k)_1 & \cdots & Q_{BA}, S_{BA}(iOBJ_k)_{256} \end{pmatrix}$$

Step 3: Quality and Quantity Anonymization. The bits of Q_{BA} and S_{BA} are permuted using MP_{ALL} like sort key, generating QP_{BA} and SP_{BA}. This procedure is done so that the quality and quantity of information is hidden and can only be revealed when are satisfied with the information measure.

$$QP_{BA} = \begin{pmatrix} Q_{BA}(iOBJ_k)_1 & \cdots & Q_{BA}(iOBJ_k)_{256} \\ MP_{ALL}(iOBJ_k)_1 & \cdots & MP_{ALL}(iOBJ_k)_{256} \end{pmatrix}$$

$$SP_{BA} = \begin{pmatrix} S_{BA}(iOBJ_k)_1 & \cdots & S_{BA}(iOBJ_k)_{256} \\ MP_{ALL}(iOBJ_k)_1 & \cdots & MP_{ALL}(iOBJ_k)_{256} \end{pmatrix}$$

Step 4: Reducing the Measure Property. In this step, from the array $MP_{ALL}(iOBJ_k)$, the proposed strategy generates two bit arrays, denoted $MP_{GEN}(iOBJ_k)$ and $MP_{GROUP}(iOBJ_k)$, to represent $MP_{ALL}(iOBJ_k)$. These two bit arrays are created as following:

1. $MP_{GEN}(iOBJ_k) = MP_{ALL}(iOBJ_k) \bmod 32$
2. $MP_{GROUP}(iOBJ_k) = MP_{ALL}(iOBJ_k)/32$

The i-OBJECT strategy classifies the elements of $MP_{ALL}(iOBJ_k)$ into 32 groups (0 to 31) of 8 elements (0 to 7). $MP_{GEN}(iOBJ_k)$ stores the values of groups and $MP_{GROUP}(iOBJ_k)$ stores the values of elements.

The next task in this step consists in reducing the size of $MP_{GROUP}(iOBJ_k)$ from 768 to 512 bits, to save disk space, generating $MP_{KEY}(iOBJ_k)$. Note that, each sequence of eight elements in $MP_{GROUP}(iOBJ_k)$ is a combination of 8 different numbers (0 to 7). So, we can encode this permutation to a Lehmer code [10], compressing to $\log(8!) = 16$ bits, saving 8 bits for each set of 8 elements of $MP_{GROUP}(iOBJ_k)$. How $MP_{GROUP}(iOBJ_k)$ has 32 groups of 8 elements, this procedure saves 256 bits in the total.

Step 5: Generating the Output Files. In this step, the output files **Fq.bin**, **Fs.bin** and **Fm.bin** are created. In order to create the **Fq.bin** file, we concatenate $QP_{BA}(iOBJ_k)$ for all iOBJs in the set $\{iOBJ_1, iOBJ_2, \cdots, iOBJ_n\}$. In order to create the **Fs.bin** file, we concatenate $SP_{BA}(iOBJ_k)$ for all iOBJs in the set $\{iOBJ_1, iOBJ_2, \cdots, iOBJ_n\}$. In order to create the **Fm.bin** file, we concatenate $MP_{GEN}(iOBJ_k)$ with ($MP_{KEY}(iOBJ_k)$ xor $QP_{BA}(iOBJ_k)$ xor $SP_{BA}(iOBJ_k)$) for all iOBJs in the set $\{iOBJ_1, iOBJ_2, \cdots, iOBJ_n\}$.

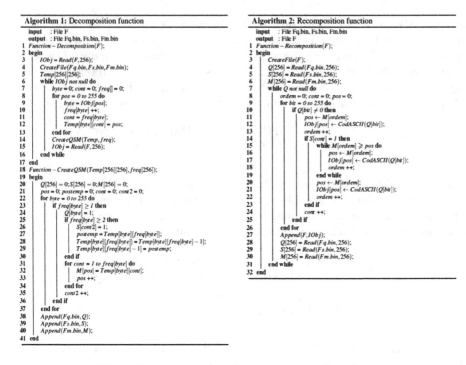

Fig. 3. Decomposition and recomposition algorithms.

It is important to note that, these XOR operations are necessary to hide the information of $MP_{GROUP}(iOBJ_k)$ and prevent the recomposition of $MP_{ALL}(iOBJ_k)$.

The Decomposition Algorithm. The decomposition algorithm is performed in two stages. (Figure 3) The first step (lines 1 to 17) obtains the information of the bytes ordinal positions (M) of $iObj_k$ (Q) and stores it in a two-dimensional vector temp [256] [256] (line 12), where the first dimension of the vector represents the decimal value of the byte and the second dimension is a list of the positions occupied by the byte's occurrence in $iObj_k$. The second step of the process (lines 18 to 41) generates three vectors containing the Q and S information, where each element of these sets is represented by one bit, and a byte vector M, which contains the positions grouped in ascending order of Q elements. In groups with more than one element, the two last elements are made to reverse its positions to indicate the end of the group.

2.3 Dispersion Phase

In the dispersion phase, the files **Fq.bin**, **Fs.bin** and **Fm.bin** are spread across different cloud storage service providers. So, i-OBJECT requires that these three files will be isolated between themselves. The information in one of these three files are insufficient to restore the original data file **F**.

2.4   The Recomposition Process

The steps of the data stored in the cloud recovery process are as follows: recovery of Fq.bin binary files, Fm.bin and Fs.bin, restoration of iOBJs and reassembly of data The details of these steps are described below:

The recovery of the files can occur sequentially or in parallel. The recomposition of iOBJs must start upon receipt of Fq files, Fs and Fm.

The Fq.bin and Fs.bin files are read in sequence and processed in 256-bit chunks. The Fm.bin file is read sequentially and processed in chunks of 224 bytes, and 160 bytes corresponding to $MP_{GEN}(iOBJ_k)$(M) and 64 bytes relating to $MP_{KEY}(iOBJ_k)$. The following operations are performed:

1. The elements of $MP_{KEY}(iOBJ_k)$ are decrypt: $MP_{KEY}(iOBJ_k)$ $=$ $MP_{KEY}(iOBJ_k)$ xor $QP_{BA}(iOBJ_k)$ xor $SP_{BA}(iOBJ_k)$.
2. The elements of $MP_{KEY}(iOBJ_k)$ are converted from Lehmer codes to permutations of 8 elements to recreate the vector $MP_{GROUP}(iOBJ_k)$.
3. The vectors $MP_{GROUP}(iOBJ_k)$ and $MP_{GEN}(iOBJ_k)$ are used to recover $MP_{ALL}(iOBJ_k)$, that is used to unscramble $QP_{BA}(iOBJ_k)$ and $SP_{BA}(iOBJ_k)$, producing $Q_{BA}(iOBJ_k)$ and $S_{BA}(iOBJ_k)$.
4. Vectors $Q_{BA}(iOBJ_k)$ and $S_{BA}(iOBJ_k)$ are used to unscramble the vector $MP_{ALL}(iOBJ_k)$ generating $M_{ALL}(iOBJ_k)$.
5. Finally, $M_{ALL}(iOBJ_k)$, $Q_{BA}(iOBJ_k)$ and $S_{BA}(iOBJ_k)$ are used to recover $iOBJ_k$.

The Recomposition Algorithm. The recomposition algorithm receives as input the files $F_q.bin$, $F_s.bin$ and $F_m.bin$ and restores the original file F. (Figure 3) The files are read sequentially in blocks of 256 bits (Q and S) and 256 bytes (M) (lines 4 to 6) so that the rebuilding of elements Q, S and M starts. The algorithm goes through the sample space of Q elements (0 to 255), identifying bytes exist in $iObj_k$ (line 11) and if they occur one time or more than once (S) (line 15) to then retrieve positions occupied by these bytes and insert them in vector $iObj_k$ (rows 18 and 22).

3   Security Considerations

Our security model stores files Fq.bin, Fs.bin and Fm.bin in cloud servers within different domains, both physically and administratively. According to [11], physical dispersion of storage servers, along with the careful choice of the number of servers and the amount of fragments needed for recovery of files, reduces the chances of an attacker to obtain the necessary pieces to restore files and is enough to make the system safe.

In order to analyze the security level of the i-OBJECT strategy, consider a hypothetical scenario where the file Fq.bin is stored in a provider CSP_1, Fs.bin is stored in another provider CSP_2 and Fm.bin is stored in a different provider CSP_3. Now, we discuss the effort that an internal attacker has to restore the original file from Fq.bin, Fs.bin or Fm.bin, whereas the attacker has unrestricted access to cloud servers of one of the providers and can recover one of the files.

3.1   The Attacker Model

We proposed an adversarial model in which the data owner O is honest, the client C may be malicious, and the server S is assumed to be honest-but-curious and not to collude with clients. Specifically, the cloud server acts in an honest fashion and correctly follows the designated protocol specification. However, it is curious to infer and analyze data (including index) in its storage and message flows received during the protocol so as to learn additional information. These assumptions are common in the literature (see, e.g., [12,13]) and are well justified in a cloud setting, since it is of predominant importance for service providers to keep a good acceptability, which discourages them from clearly misconduct, while they may have an incentive in passively collection sensitive information given the economic interest of personal data.

3.2   Quality and Quantity Security

According to Shannon, a secrecy system is defined abstractly as a set of transformations of one space (the set of possible messages) into a second space (the set of possible cryptograms), to enciphering with a particular key. The transformations are supposed reversible [14].

In this case, a secrecy system is a set of transformations of one set of elements into another, there are one natural combining operations which produce a third system from two given systems. This combining operation is called the product operation and corresponds to enciphering the message with the first secrecy system R and enciphering the resulting cryptogram with the second system S, the keys for R and S being chosen independently. This total operation is a secrecy system whose transformations consist of all the products of transformations in S with transformations in R. The probabilities are the products of the probabilities for the two transformations. It is shown that secrecy systems with these combining operations form essentially a linear associative algebra with a unit element, an algebraic variety that has been extensively studied by mathematicians [14].

Following, the security operations of i-OBJECT technique, related to the Quality information, are described:

1. extract and sort in ascending order the different bytes of iOBJ and represent this information using a 256-bit array (system R_1);
2. perform permutation operation of the bits using Q_{BA} as key elements of Measure MP_{ALL} (system S_1).

This gives a resultant operation T_1 which we write as a product $T_1 = R_1 S_1$. R_1 has 256-bits keys, that are chosen with probabilities $p_1\ p_2\ p_3...p_{256}$ and S_1 has 256-byte keys with probabilities $p_1'\ p_2'\ p_3'...p_{256}'$. As each byte can be present or not into $iOBJ_k$, the probability of the attacker hit if the byte exists in iobj is $p_i = 1/2$ for $1 \leqslant i \leqslant 256$.

Even as any byte can hold any position of 1st up to 256th in $iOBJ_k$, the probability of the attacker hit what is the byte position in iobj is $p_j' = 1/n$, for $1 \leqslant j \leqslant 256$, where **n** is the number of positions available in $iOBJ_k$.

$P(S_1)$ is the probability of an attacker, who does not has the Fq.bin file, find the vector Q_{BA}. $P(R_1)$ is the probability of an attacker, that has the Fq.bin file, find the vector Q_{BA}. This calculation refers only to one iOBJ:

$$P(S_1) = \prod_{i=1}^{256} p_i = 1/2 \times 1/2 \times 1/2 \cdots \times 1/2 = 1/2^{256} \approx 1/10^{77}$$
$$P(R_1) = \prod_{j=1}^{256} p_j = 1/256 \times 1/255 \times 1/254 \times \cdots \times 1/2 \times 1 = 1/256! \approx 1/10^{506}$$

Since $P(R_1) > P(S_1)$, it is concluded that the fact that the CSP_1 have the Fq.bin file doesn't improve its chances of discover the information of iOBJ Quality feature.

Following, the security operations of i-OBJECT technique, related to the Quantity information, are described:

1. extract information from the frequencies of occurrence of the diverse bytes in iOBJ and represent this information using a 256-bit array (system R_2);
2. exchange the elements of quantity, using the elements of Measure as vector index ordering of MP_{ALL} (system S_2).

This gives a resultant operation T_2 which we write as a product $T_2 = R_2 S_2$. R_2 has q-bits keys, where q is the length of Q, that are chosen with probabilities $p_1\ p_2\ p_3...p_q$ and S_2 has 256-bytes keys with probabilities $p_1'\ p_2'\ p_3'...p_{256}'$. As the frequencies of the different bytes may be equal to 1 or greater than 1, $p_i = 1/2$ to $1 \leqslant i \leqslant q$. As the same key MP_{ALL} is used to permutation of the Quantity and Quality elements, $P(R_2) = P(R_1)$.

$P(S_2)$ is the probability of an attacker, who does not have the Fs.bin file, find the vector S_{BA}. $P(R_2)$ is the probability of an attacker, that has the Fs.bin file, find the vector S_{BA}. This calculation refers only to one iOBJ:

$$P(S_2) = \prod_{i=1}^{q} p_i = 1/2 \times 1/2 \times 1/2 \cdots \times 1/2 = 1/2^q$$
$$P(R_2) = 1/256! \approx 1/10^{506}$$

Since $P(R_2) > P(S_2)$, it is concluded that the fact that the CSP_2 have the Fs.bin file doesn't improve its chances of discovering the information of iOBJ Quality feature.

3.3 Measure Security

The data of Measure (M) is stored in MP_{GEN} and MP_{KEY} arrays into Fm.bin file. The vector MP_{KEY} is encrypted by an XOR operation with QP_{BA} and SP_{BA}. For CSP_3 recover M, he would have to calculate QP_{BA} and SP_{BA}, which are stored in CSP_1 and CSP_2 respectively.

Following, the security operations of i-OBJECT technique, related to the Measure, are described:

1. extract and sort in ascending order the positions of iOBJ's bytes, group by Q elements (system R_3).
2. exchange the elements of Measure (M_{ALL}), using the elements of Q_{BA} and S_{BA} as index order to generate MP_{ALL} (system S_3).

3. Anonymize the MP_{ALL} elements generating the vectors MP_{GEN} and MP_{GROUP}.
4. Encrypt the 64-byte MP_{GROUP} through XOR operation with a key **K** formed by the 32 bytes of QP_{BA} and 32 bytes of SP_{BA} (system V_3).

This give a resultant operation T_3 which we write as a product $T_3 = R_3 S_3 V_3$. R_3 and S_3 have 256-bytes keys, that are chosen with probabilities p_1 p_2 $p_3...p_{256}$ and p_1' p_2' $p_3'...p_{256}'$ and V_3 has one **K** key with probability $p_1^* = 1/2^{512}$. $P(S_3) = P(R_3) = 1/256! \approx 1/10^{506}$.

$P(S_3)$ is the probability of an attacker, who does not have the Fm.bin file, find the vector M_{BA}. $P(R_3) \times P(V_3)$ is the probability of an attacker, that has the Fm.bin file, find the vector M_{BA}. This calculation refers only to one iOBJ:

$$P(R_3) \times P(V_3) = 1/2^{512} \times 1/10^{506} =\approx 1/10^{154} \times 1/10^{506} \approx 1/10^{660}$$

Like $P(R_3) \times P(V_3) > P(S_3)$, it is concluded that the fact that the CSP_3 have the Fm.bin file doesn't improve its chances of discover the information of iOBJ Measure feature.

The degree of data confidentiality is based on the difficulty of the attackers to reconstruct the i-OBJECTS from one of these three files, Fq.bin, Fs.bin or Fm.bin. Besides, i-OBJECT is a flexible mechanism since it can be used alone or together with other previously approaches (such as encryption algorithms like AES, DES or 3-DES) in order to increase the data confidentiality level.

3.4   Data Confidentiality Considerations

The data confidentiality in the proposed approach stems from the fact that the files Fq.bin, Fs.bin and Fm.bin are stored in different cloud providers, which are physically and administratively independent. According to [11], physical data dispersion in different storage servers, along with the careful choice of the number of servers and the amount of fragments needed for restore the original files, reduces the chances of an attacker and is enough to make a system safe. So, in i-OBJECT, the degree of data confidentiality is based on the difficulty of the attackers to reconstruct the i-OBJECTS from one of these three files, Fq.bin, Fs.bin or Fm.bin. Besides, i-OBJECT is a flexible mechanism since it can be used alone or together with other previously approaches (such as encryption algorithms like AES, DES or 3-DES) in order to increase the data confidentiality level.

4   Experimental Evaluation

In order to show the potentials of i-OBJECT, several experiments have been conducted. The main results achieved so far are presented and discussed in this section. Thus, we first provide information on how the experimentation environment was set up. Thereafter, empirical results are quantitatively presented and qualitatively discussed.

4.1   Experimental Setup

We implemented i-OBJECT and the other data confidentiality approaches using C and Java. In order to run these approaches we have used a private cloud computing infrastructure based on OpenStack. Figure 4 shows the architecture used in the experiments, which contains two kinds of virtual machines: the client node and the data storage nodes. The client, a Trusted Third Party (TTP), runs the i-OBJECT algorithms: decomposition and recomposition. The data storage nodes (called VM1, VM2 and VM3) emulate three different cloud storage service providers. We assume that the data nodes provide reliable content storage and data management but are not trusted by the client to maintain data privacy.

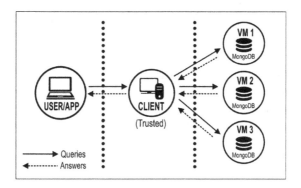

Fig. 4. Experimental architecture.

Each data storage node has the following configuration: Ubuntu 14.04 operating system, Intel Xeon 2.20 GHz processor, 4 GB memory and 50 GB disk. The client is a Intel Xeon 2.20 GHz processor, 4 GB memory and 40 GB disk capacity, running a Windows Server 2008.

Besides this, each data storage node has a MongoDB instance with default settings. MongoDB is an open source, scalable, high performance, schema-free, document oriented database. We opted to use the MongoDB because it is one of the most used database in cloud computing environments and exists opportunities for improvement its security and privacy. MongoDB supports a binary wire-level protocol but doesn't provide a method to automatically encrypt data. This means that any attacker with access to the file system can directly extract the information from the files [15].

In order to evaluate the i-OBJECT efficiency, we have used a document collection, synthetically created, which contains files (documents) with different sizes. Each file has four parts (or attributes), which have the same size. These attributes are: curriculum vitae (A1), paper text (A2), author photo (A3) and paper evaluation (A4).

4.2   Test Results

In this section, we present the results of the experiments we carried out. For evaluate the i-OBJECT efficiency, we have used two metrics: the input and output times. The input time is defined as the total amount of time spent to process a file F and generates the data that will be send to the cloud storage service providers. The output time is defined as the total amount of time spent to process the data received from the cloud storage service providers in order to remount the original file F. It is important to highlight that the time spend in the communication process, to send and receive data to the cloud providers do not composes neither the input nor the output time. We have evaluated different file sizes (2^{18}, 2^{20} and 2^{22} bytes). For each distinct file size, we have used 10 files and computes the average time for decomposes and recomposes these files. To validate the i-OBJECT approach, we have evaluated four different scenarios, which will be discussed next.

Scenario 1: Encryption Algorithms. The first scenario was running with the aim of compare the most popular symmetric cryptographic algorithms: AES, DES and 3-DES. It is important to note that, in this experiment, the Input Time matches the Encryption Time (the spent time to encrypt a file F) and Output Time matches the Decryption Time (time necessary to decrypt a file F). So, in this scenario, the client receives a file F from the user, encrypt it, generating a new file F_e, and sends F_e to VM1. Figure 5 shows the encryption time for the algorithms AES, DES and 3-DES. Next, the client receives the encrypted file F_e from VM1, decrypt it, generating the original file F and sends F to the user. Figure 5 shows the decryption time for the algorithms AES, DES and 3-DES. Note that, for files with size of 2^{16} bytes these three algorithms presented the same encryption time, while AES and DES presented the same decryption time.

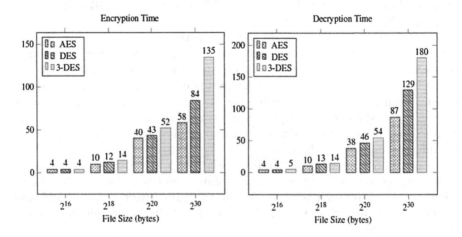

Fig. 5. Scenario 1: encryption and decryption time.

However, for files with sizes of 2^{18}, 2^{20}, and 2^{30} bytes AES outperforms DES and 3-DES, for both encryption and decryption.

Scenario 2: Data Confidentiality Approaches. In the second scenario, we compared the i-OBJECT approach with the three main approaches to ensure the data confidentiality in cloud environments: (a) data encryption, (b) combination of encryption and fragmentation, and (c) fragmentation (see Sect. 1) [6,7].

In order to run the approaches (b), combination of encryption and fragmentation, and (c), fragmentation, it is necessary to define which attributes are sensitive, besides to identify the sensitive association between attributes. Moreover, splitting the attributes with sensitive association into some fragment is a NP-hard problem [6,7].

Thus, we have assumed that each document has four attributes: curriculum vitae (A1), paper text (A2), author photo (A3) and paper evaluation (A4). Besides, we supposed that there is a set C of sensitive association constraints, with the following constraints: $C_1 = \{A1\}$, $C_2 = \{A2\}$, $C_3 = \{A2, A4\}$, $C_4 = \{A1, A3\}$. So, the attributes A_1 and A_3 are considered sensitive and must be encrypted in approaches (b) and (c). The constraint $C_3 = \{A2, A4\}$ indicates that there is a sensitive association between A2 and A4. The constraint $C_4 = \{A1, A3\}$ indicates that there is a sensitive association between A1 and A3, and these attributes should be stored in different servers in the cloud. Based on the set C of confidentiality constraints, a set P of data fragments was generated, as following: (i) the approach (b), combination of encryption and fragmentation, produced the fragments $P_1 = \{A1, A4\}$ and $P_2 = \{A2, A3\}$; and (ii) the approach (c), fragmentation, formed the fragments $P_3 = \{A1, A3\}$, $P_4 = \{A2\}$ and $P_5 = \{A4\}$.

It is important to emphasize that the time necessary to define the set of fragments (fragments schema) for splitting the attributes with sensitive association, that is a NP-hard problem, was not considered in this experiment. Furthermore, for the approach (a), data encryption, we have used the AES algorithm, since it presented best results in the first scenario.

In this experiment, we considered performance with respect to the following metrics: (i) Input Time and (ii) Output Time. These metrics change a little according to the used data confidentiality approach.

Input Time is computed as following:

- Approach (a), data encryption: time to encrypt a file F using AES, generating a file F_e. The file F_e will be send to VM1;
- Approach (b), combination of encryption and fragmentation: time to encrypt A_1 and A_3, plus the time to generates P_1 and P_2. Where, A_1 and P_1 will be send to VM1, while A_3 and P_2 will be send to VM2.
- Approach (c), fragmentation: the time to generates P_3, P_4 and P_5. Where, P_3 will be send to VM1, P_4 to VM2 and P_5 to VM3.
- i-OBJECT Approach: time to decompose a file F into $F_q.bin$, $F_s.bin$ and $F_m.bin$. Where, $F_q.bin$ will be send to VM1, $F_s.bin$ to VM2 and $F_m.bin$ to VM3;

Output Time is computed as following:

- Approach (a), data encryption: time to decrypt a file F_e using AES, generating the original file F;
- Approach (b), combination of encryption and fragmentation: time to decrypt A_1 and A_3, plus the time to join A_1, A_3, P_1 and P_2 in order to remount the file F;
- Approach (c), fragmentation: the time to join P_3, P_4, P_5 and the sensitive attributes stored in the client;
- i-OBJECT Approach: time to recompose a file F from $F_q.bin$, $F_s.bin$ and $F_m.bin$.

Figure 6 shows the input time for the evaluated approaches. Note that i-OBJECT approach has a performance slightly worse than Data Encryption (AES). Fragmentation approach outperforms the other approaches, for all file sizes. On the other hand, the last two approaches, Encryption/Fragmentation and Fragmentation, need to define the set of fragments (fragmentation schema) for splitting the attributes with sensitive association. However, how we have used a fixed example, the time necessary to define the fragmentation schema was not computed. In part, this explains the better results obtained by these two approaches.

Figure 6 shows the output time for the evaluated approaches. Note that i-OBJECT outperforms all the other approaches, for all file sizes. It is important to highlight, for the file size of 2^{22} bytes, i-OBJECT is 88 s slower than the Fragmentation approach in the input phase, that is, to process and a file F before sending it to the cloud storage service provider. However, for the same file size, i-OBJECT is 48 s faster than the Fragmentation approach. So, for a complete cycle of file write and read, i-OBJECT is just 40 s slower than the Fragmentation approach. Then, if the user writes F one time and reads F two times, i-OBJECT is 8 s faster than Fragmentation approach. Thus, i-OBJECT outperforms all the other previous approach in scenarios where the number of reads is at least twice larger than the number of writes, which is expected real databases and cloud storage environments.

Scenario 3: Using I-OBJECT Together with Previous Approaches. In the third scenario, we evaluated the use of i-OBJECT together with previous approaches. We believe that i-OBJECT can be used together with other data confidentiality approaches in order to improve their data confidentiality levels.

Figure 7 shows the input time for the evaluated approaches. In this chart, the first bar shows the input time to i-OBJECT (that is, the time to decompose a file F); the second bar represents the input time to apply the Data Encryption approach and, after that, the i-OBJECT (that is, the time to encrypt a file F, producing a new file F_e, plus the time to decompose F_e); the third bar indicates the input time to apply the Encryption/Fragmentation approach and, next, the i-OBJECT; finally, the fourth bar denotes the input time to apply the Fragmentation approach and then the i-OBJECT. Then, we can argue that

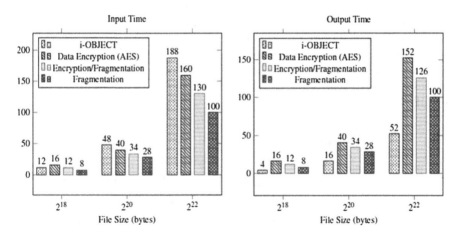

Fig. 6. Scenario 2: input and output time.

i-OBJECT is a flexible approach, in the sense that it can be used together with previous approaches, in order to improve their data confidentiality level. The results presented in Fig. 7 show that this strategy provides a small increase in the input time, while providing a high gain in the data confidentiality. Figure 7 shows that the output time overhead has a similar behavior that input time.

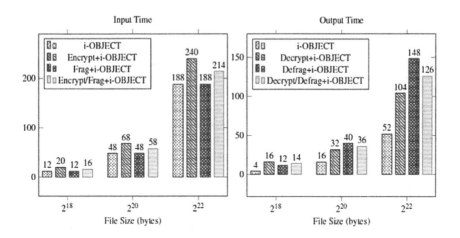

Fig. 7. Scenario 3: input and output time.

Scenario 4: Improving Data Confidentiality in I-OBJECT. In the fourth scenario, we evaluated some strategies to improve the data confidentiality in the i-OBJECT approach. The first strategy consists in encrypt the files $F_q.bin$ and

$F_s.bin$, the second strategy consists in encrypt only the file $F_q.bin$ and the third strategy consists in encrypt just the file $F_s.bin$.

Figure 8 show, respectively the input and output time with and without the use of these strategies. Note that the strategy of encrypting just the file $F_q.bin$ provides a low overhead, while greatly increases the data confidentiality level of the i-OBJECT approach.

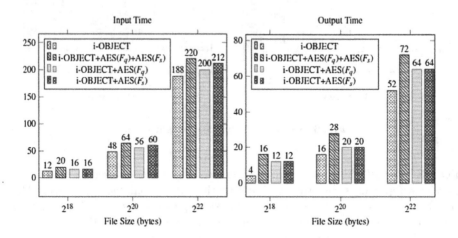

Fig. 8. Scenario 4: input and output time.

Storage Space Considerations. In the i-OBJECT approach, a file F is decomposed into three files (Fq.bin, Fs.bin and Fm.bin), which are dispersed (sent) to three different cloud providers. The experimental results showed that the size of these files represent, respectively, 12.5%, 12.5% and 90% of the original file size. So, adding these values, the proposed approach provides an overhead of 15% in the disk space utilization. This drawback is minimized since the cloud storage services are designed to store a large quantity of data.

5   Related Work

A significant amount of research has recently been dedicated to the investigation of data confidentiality in cloud computing environment. Most of this work has assumed the data to be entirely encrypted, focusing on the design of queries execution techniques [5]. In [8] the authors discuss different strategies for evaluating the inference exposure for encrypted data enriched with indexing information, showing that even a limited number of indexes can greatly favor the task for an attacker wishing to violate the data confidentiality provided by encryption.

The first proposal proposing the storage of plaintext data, while ensuring a series of privacy constraints was presented in [16]. In this work, the authors suppose data to be split into two fragments, stored on two honest-but-curious service providers, which never exchange information, and resorts to encryption any time these two fragments are not sufficient for enforcing confidentiality constraints. In [1,5], the authors address these issues by proposing a solution that first split the data to be protected into several (possibly more than two) different fragments in such a way to break the sensitive associations among attributes and to minimize the amount of attributes represented only in encrypted format. The resulting fragments may be stored at different servers. The proposed heuristic to design these fragments present a polynomial-time computation cost while is able to retrieve solutions close to optimum. In [17], the authors propose an efficient graph search based method for the fragmentation problem with confidentiality constraints, which obtains near optimal designs.

The work presented in [1] proposes a novel paradigm for preserving data confidentiality in data outsourcing which departs from encryption, thus freeing the owner from the burden of its management. The basic idea behind this mechanism is to involve the owner in storing the sensitive attributes. Besides, for each sensitive association, the owner should locally store at least an attribute. The remainder attributes are stored, in the clear, at the server side. With this fragmentation process, an original relation R is then split into two fragments, called F_o and F_s, stored at the data owner and at the server side, respectively. [12] extends the "vertical fragmentation only" approach and proposes use horizontal fragmentation to filter out confidential rows to be securely stored at the owner site. [18] proposes an approach based on data fragmentation using graph-coloring technique wherein a minimum amount of data is stored at the owner. In [19] the authors present SPARSI, a theoretical framework for partitioning sensitive data across multiple non-colluding adversaries. They introduce the problem of privacy-aware data partitioning, where a sensitive dataset must be partitioned among k untrusted parties (adversaries). The goal is to maximize the utility derived by partitioning and distributing the dataset, while minimizing the total amount of sensitive information disclosed. Solving privacy-aware partitioning is, in general, NP-hard, but for specific information disclosure functions, good approximate solutions can be found using relaxation techniques.

In [6] the authors discuss the main issues to be addressed in cloud storage services, ranging from data confidentiality to data utility. They show the main research directions being investigated for providing effective data confidentiality and for enabling their querying. The survey presented in [7] addressed some approaches for ensuring data confidentiality in untrusted cloud storage services. In [20], the authors discuss the problems of guaranteeing proper data security and privacy in the cloud, and illustrate possible solutions for them.

6   Conclusion and Future Work

In this paper, we presented i-OBJECT, a new approach to preserve data confidentiality in cloud services. The proposed approach uses fragmentation, information decomposition and dispersion to split data into unrecognizable parts and store them into distributed hosts in the cloud. i-OBJECT is low cost approach suitable for small and medium enterprises. Besides, i-OBJECT is a flexible mechanism since it can be used alone or together with other previously approaches in order to increase the data confidentiality level. Thus, a user may trade performance or data utility for a potential increase in the degree of data confidentiality.

Experimental results showed the efficiency of i-OBJECT, which can be used with any kind of file and is more suitable for files larger than 256 bytes, files with high entropy and environments where the number of read operations exceeds the number of writes. As a future work, we intend to evaluate i-OBJECT performance with other data types and using different cloud configurations, including public and mixed clouds.

Acknowledgments. This Research was partially supported by LSBD/UFC and CNPQ - Brazil. We acknowledge that this work is a partial result of the Automatic Management of Cloud Databases project supported by CNPq (MCTI/CNPq 14/2014 - Universal) under grant number 446090/2014-0.

References

1. Ciriani, V., De Capitani di Vimercati, S., Foresti, S., Jajodia, S., Paraboschi, S., Samarati, P.: Keep a few: outsourcing data while maintaining confidentiality. In: Backes, M., Ning, P. (eds.) ESORICS 2009. LNCS, vol. 5789, pp. 440–455. Springer, Heidelberg (2009). doi:10.1007/978-3-642-04444-1_27
2. Clarke, R.: Introduction to dataveillance and information privacy, and definition of terms (1999)
3. Camenisch, J., Fischer-Hübner, S., Rannenberg, K.: Privacy and Identity Management for Life. Springer, Heidelberg (2011). doi:10.1007/978-3-642-20317-6
4. Zhifeng, X., Yang, X.: Security and privacy in cloud computing. IEEE Commun. Surv. Tutor. **15**, 843–859 (2013)
5. Ciriani, V., Vimercati, S., Foresti, S., Jajodia, S., Paraboschi, S., Samarati, P.: Combining fragmentation and encryption to protect privacy in data storage. ACM Trans. Inf. Syst. Secur. **13**, 22:1–22:33 (2010)
6. Samarati, P., di Vimercati, S.D.C.: Data protection in outsourcing scenarios: issues and directions. In: Proceedings of the 5th ACM Symposium on Information, Computer and Communications Security. ASIACCS 2010, pp. 1–14. ACM (2010)
7. Joseph, N.M., Daniel, E., Vasanthi, N.A.: Article: survey on privacy-preserving methods for storage in cloud computing. In: IJCA Proceedings on Amrita International Conference of Women in Computing - 2013 AICWIC, pp. 1–4 (2013). (Full text available)
8. Ceselli, A., Damiani, E., Vimercati, S.D.C.D., Jajodia, S., Paraboschi, S., Samarati, P.: Modeling and assessing inference exposure in encrypted databases. ACM Trans. Inf. Syst. Secur. (TISSEC) **8**, 119–152 (2005)
9. Hegel, G.: The Encyclopedia Logic, vol. 1. Hackett, Indianapolis (1991). (Geraets, T.F., Suchting, W.A., Harris, H.S. (trans.))
10. Barbay, J., Navarro, G.: Compressed representations of permutations, and applications (2009). arXiv preprint: arXiv:0902.1038
11. Resch, J.K., Plank, J.S.: AONT-RS: blending security and performance in dispersed storage systems. In: Proceedings of FAST-2011: 9th Usenix Conference on File and Storage Technologies, February 2011

12. Wiese, L.: Horizontal fragmentation for data outsourcing with formula-based confidentiality constraints. In: Echizen, I., Kunihiro, N., Sasaki, R. (eds.) IWSEC 2010. LNCS, vol. 6434, pp. 101–116. Springer, Heidelberg (2010). doi:10.1007/978-3-642-16825-3_8

13. Ning, C., Cong, W., Ming, L., Kui, R., Wenjing, L.: Privacy-preserving multi-keyword ranked search over encrypted cloud data. IEEE Trans. Parallel Distrib. Syst. **25**, 222–233 (2014)

14. Shannon, C.E.: Communication theory of secrecy systems*. Bell Syst. Tech. J. **28**, 656–715 (1949)

15. Okman, L., Gal-Oz, N., Gonen, Y., Gudes, E., Abramov, J.: Security issues in NoSQL databases. In: 2011 IEEE 10th International Conference on Trust, Security and Privacy in Computing and Communications (TrustCom), pp. 541–547 (2011)

16. Aggarwal, C.C.: On k-anonymity and the curse of dimensionality. In: Proceedings of the 31st International Conference on Very Large Data Bases, pp. 901–909. VLDB Endowment (2005)

17. Xu, X., Xiong, L., Liu, J.: Database fragmentation with confidentiality constraints: a graph search approach. In: Proceedings of the 5th ACM Conference on Data and Application Security and Privacy, CODASPY 2015, pp. 263–270. ACM (2015)

18. Krishna, R., Sayi, T., Mukkamala, R., Baruah, P.K.: Efficient privacy-preserving data distribution in outsourced environments: a fragmentation-based approach. In: Proceedings of the International Conference on Advances in Computing, Communications and Informatics, ICACCI 2012, pp. 589–595. ACM (2012)

19. Rekatsinas, T., Deshpande, A., Machanavajjhala, A.: SPARSI: partitioning sensitive data amongst multiple adversaries. Proc. VLDB Endow. **6**, 1594–1605 (2013)

20. Samarati, P.: Data security and privacy in the cloud. In: Huang, X., Zhou, J. (eds.) ISPEC 2014. LNCS, vol. 8434, pp. 28–41. Springer, Cham (2014). doi:10.1007/978-3-319-06320-1_4

Investigating the Identification of Technical Debt Through Code Comment Analysis

Mário André de Freitas Farias[1,2(✉)], José Amâncio Santos[3],
Marcos Kalinowski[4], Manoel Mendonça[2],
and Rodrigo Oliveira Spínola[5,6]

[1] Federal Institute of Sergipe, Lagarto, Sergipe, Brazil
mario.andre@ifs.edu.br
[2] Federal University of Bahia, Salvador, Bahia, Brazil
manoel.g.mendonca@gmail.com
[3] State University of Feira de Santana, Feira de Santana, Bahia, Brazil
zeamancio@gmail.com
[4] Fluminense Federal University, Rio de Janeiro, Brazil
kalinowski@ic.uff.br
[5] Fraunhofer Project Center at UFBA, Salvador, Bahia, Brazil
rodrigoospinola@gmail.com
[6] Salvador University, Salvador, Bahia, Brazil

Abstract. In order to effectively manage technical debt (TD), a set of indicators has been used by automated approaches to identify TD items. However, some debt items may not be directly identified using only metrics collected from the source code. CVM-TD is a model to support the identification of technical debt by considering the developer point of view when identifying TD through code comment analysis. In this paper, we investigate the use of CVM-TD with the purpose of characterizing factors that affect the accuracy of the identification of TD, and the most chosen patterns by participants as decisive to indicate TD items. We performed a controlled experiment investigating the accuracy of CVM-TD and the influence of English skills and developer experience factors. We also investigated if the contextualized vocabulary provided by CVM-TD points to candidate comments that are considered indicators of technical debt by participants. The results indicated that CVM-TD provided promising results considering the accuracy values. English reading skills have an impact on the TD detection process. We could not conclude that the experience level affects this process. We identified a list of the 20 most chosen patterns by participants as decisive to indicate TD items. The results motivate us continuing to explore code comments in the context of TD identification process in order to improve CVM-TD.

Keywords: Contextualized vocabulary · Technical debt · Code comment · Controlled experiment

1 Introduction

The Technical Debt (TD) metaphor reflects the challenging decisions that developers and managers need to take in order to achieve short-term benefits. These decisions may not cause an immediate impact on the software, but may negatively affect the long-term

S. Hammoudi et al. (Eds.): ICEIS 2016, LNBIP 291, pp. 284–309, 2017.
DOI: 10.1007/978-3-319-62386-3_14

health of a software system or maintenance effort in the future [1]. The metaphor is easy to understand and relevant to both technical and nontechnical practitioners [2, 3]. In this sense, its acceptance and use have increased in software engineering researches.

In order to effectively manage TD, it is necessary to identify TD items[1] in the project [4]. Li *et al.* [5], in a recent systematic review, reported that code quality analysis techniques have frequently been studied to support the identification of TD. Automatic analysis tools have used software metrics extracted from the source code to identify TD items by comparing values of software metrics to predefined thresholds [6]. Although these techniques have shown useful to support the automated identification of some types of debt, they do not cover human factors (e.g., tasks commented as future work) [7, 8]. Thus, large amounts of TD that are undetectable by tools may be left aside. In this sense, pieces of code that need to be refactored to improve the quality of the software may continue unknown. To complement the TD identification with more contextual and qualitative data, human factors and the developers' point of view should be considered [9].

In this context, Potdar and Shihab [8] have focused on code comments aiming to identify TD items. Therefore, they manually read more than 101 K code comments to detect those that indicate a self-admitted TD. These comments were analyzed to identify text patterns that indicate a TD. In the same way, Maldonado and Shihab [10] have read 33 K code comments to identify different types of debt using the indicators proposed by [11]. According to the authors, these patterns can be used to manually identify TD that exists in the project by reading code comments. However, it is hard to perform such a large manual analysis in terms of effort and the process is inherently error prone.

Farias *et al.* [9] presented a Contextualized Vocabulary Model for identifying TD (CVM-TD) based in code comments. CVM-TD uses word classes and code tags to provide a set of TD terms/patterns of comment (a contextualized vocabulary) that may be used to filter comments that need more attention because they may indicate a TD item. CVM-TD was evaluated through an exploratory study on two large open sources projects, jEdit and Lucene, with the goal of characterizing its feasibility to support TD identification from source code comments. The results pointed that the dimensions (e.g. Adjectives, Adverbs, Verbs, Nouns, and Tags) considered by the model are used by developers when writing comments and that CVM-TD can be effectively used to support TD identification activities.

These promising initial outcomes motivated us to evaluate CVM-TD further with other projects. Therefore, in this paper we extend the research of Farias *et al.* [9] with an additional study to analyze the use of CVM-TD and the contextualized vocabulary with the purpose of characterizing its overall accuracy when classifying candidate comments and factors that influence the analysis of the comments to support the identification of TD in terms of accuracy.

We address this research goal by conducting a controlled experiment to investigate the overall CVM-TD accuracy and the influence of the English skills and developer experience factors. We analyzed the factors against the accuracy by observing the

---

[1] The term "TD item" represents an instance of Technical Debt.

agreement between each participant and an Oracle elaborated by the researchers. We compared the accuracy values for the different factors using statistical tests.

We also analyzed the agreement among the participants. These aspects are decisive to understand and validate the model and the contextualized vocabulary. Our findings indicate that CVM-TD provided promising results considering the accuracy values. The accuracy values of the participants with good reading skills were better than the values of the participants with medium/poor reading skills. We could not conclude that the experience level affects the accuracy when identifying TD items through comment analysis. The results indicate that 89.21% of the TD comments that were chosen by Oracle were also chosen by at least 50% of all participants. We also observed that, on average, the participants identified many comments that were filtered by the vocabulary and selected as a TD indicator by Oracle. This means that the vocabulary proposed by CVM-TD helped the participants to comprehend and identify comments that may point out TD items. We also identified the 20 most chosen patterns by participants as decisive to indicate TD items.

The remainder of this paper is organized as follows. Section 2 presents relevant literature reporting on technical debt identification approaches and the use of comments in source code. Section 3 describes the planning of the controlled experiment. Section 4 presents its operation. The results are presented in Sect. 5. Next, we have a discussion section. Finally, Sect. 7 concludes the paper.

2   Background

2.1   Code Comments Mining

Comments are an important software artifact which may help to understand software features [12]. Code comments have been used as data source in some research [12, 13].

In [13], the authors analyzed the purpose of work descriptions and code comments aiming to discuss how automated tools can support developers in creating them.

Storey *et al.* [12] analyzed how developers deal with software maintenance tasks by conducting an empirical study investigating how comments may improve processes and tools that are used for managing these tasks.

In fact, comments have been used to describe issues that may require future work, emerging problems, and decisions taken about those problems [13]. These descriptions facilitate human readability and provide additional information that summarizes the developer context [9].

Therefore, code comments are considered a vital documentation used in maintenances. They complete the general documentation of a system and are a conventional way for developers keep documentation and code consistently up to date [14].

Despite of the existence of different syntaxes and types of comments according to the programming language, they are usually divided into two categories: (i) inline comments, which only permit the insertion of one line of comment, and (ii) block comments, which permit the insertion of several lines. Developers write comments in a sublanguage of English using a limited set of verbs and tenses, and personal pronouns are almost not used [15].

According to Steidl et al. [14], the comments within these categories can be classified in seven different types:

- **Copyright Comments:** notes that include information about the copyright or the license of the source code file. They are usually found at the beginning of each file;
- **Header Comments:** give an overview about the functionality of the class and provide information about the class author, the revision number, or the peer review status.
- **Member Comments:** describe the functionality of a method/field, being located either before or in the same line as the member definition. This type of comment is similar to header comments.
- **Inline Comments:** describe implementation decisions within a method body. This type was named as the same description of the category of comments presented above.
- **Section Comments:** this comments address several methods/fields together belonging to the same functional aspect.
- **Code Comments:** contain commented out code which is source code ignored by the compiler. Often code is temporarily commented out for debugging purposes or potential later reuse.
- **Task Comments:** are a developer note containing a to-do statement, a note about a bug that needs to be fixed, or a remark about an implementation hack.

In this work we are interested only in the **inline comments** and **task comments** types because they can describe the developer's feeling about open tasks in the project and the risk of causing problems if not done in the future.

2.2 Using Code Comments to Identify TD

More recently, code comments have been explored with the purpose of identifying TD [8–10, 16].

Potdar and Shihab [8] analyzed code comments to identify text patterns and TD items. They read more than 101 K code comments. Their findings show that 2.4–31.0% of the files in a project contain self-admitted TD. In addition, the most used text patterns were: (i) "is there a problem" with 36 instances, (ii) "hack" with 17 instances, and (iii) "fixme" with 761 instances.

In another TD identification approach, Maldonado and Shihab [10] evolved the work of Potdar and Shihab [8] proposing four simple filtering heuristics to eliminate comments that are not likely to contain technical debt. For that, they read 33 K code comments from source code of five open source projects (Apache Ant, Apache Jmeter, ArgoUML, Columba, and JFreeChart). Their findings showed that self-admitted technical debt can be classified into five main types: design debt, defect debt, documentation debt, requirement debt, and test debt. According to the authors, the most common type of self-admitted TD is design debt (between 42% and 84% of the classified comments).

In the same sense, Bavota and Russo [16] performed a replication of the work of Potdar and Shihab [8]. Their study reported an empirical analysis conducted on 159 software projects to investigate the diffusion and evolution of TD. The authors mined commits and code comments using the patterns proposed by [8] and carried out a qualitative analysis. Their results show that the diffusion of TD in OSS projects is, on average, 51 instances per system, the TD instances have a long survivability, on average, more than 1,000 commits, and have an increasing trend over the projects lifetime.

In an another approach, Farias *et al.* [9] proposed the CVM-TD. CVM-TD is a contextualized structure of terms that focuses on using word classes and code tags to provide a TD vocabulary, aiming to support the detection of different types of debt through code comment analysis. To evaluate the model and quickly analyze developers' comments embedded in source code, the *eXcomment* tool was developed. This tool extracts and filters candidate comments from source code using the contextualized vocabulary provided by CVM-TD.

This research provided preliminary indication that CVM-TD and its contextualized vocabulary can be effectively used to support TD identification (the whole vocabulary can be found at https://goo.gl/TH2ec5). However, the factors that may affect its accurate usage are still unknown. In this work, we focused on characterizing CVM-TD's accuracy and some of these factors.

3   Study Planning

3.1   Goal of Study and Research Questions

This study aims at investigating the following goal: "Analyze the use of CVM-TD with the purpose of characterizing its overall accuracy and factors affecting the identification of TD through code comment analysis, with respect to accuracy when identifying TD items from the point of view of the researcher in the context of software engineering master students with professional experience analyzing candidate code comments of large software projects". More specifically, we investigated five Research Questions (RQ). The description of these RQs follows.

RQ1: Do the English reading skills of the participant affect the accuracy when identifying TD through code comment analysis?

Considering that non-native English speakers are frequently unaware of the most common terms used to define specific parts of code in English [17], this question aims to investigate whether a different familiarity with the English language could impact the identification of TD through code comment analysis. In order to analyze this variable, we split the participants into levels of "good English reading skills" and "medium/poor English reading skills". This question is important to help us to understand the factors that may influence the analysis of comments to identify TD.

RQ2: Does the experience of the participant affect the accuracy when identifying TD through code comment analysis?

Experience is an important contextual aspect in the software engineering area [18]. Recent research has studied the impact of experience on software engineering experiments [19]. Some works have found evidence that experience affects the identification of code smells, and that some code smells are better detected by experienced participants rather than by automatic means [20]. Considering this context, this question aims to discuss the impact of the participants' experience on the identification of TD through code comment analysis. To analyze the variable, we classified the participants into three levels considering their experience with software development: (i) high experience, (ii) medium experience, and (iii) low experience. This question is also important to help us to understand the factors that may influence the analysis of comments to identify TD.

RQ3: Do participants agree with each other on the choice of comments filtered by CVM-TD that may indicate a TD item?

With this question, we intend to investigate the contribution of CVM-TD in the TD identification process and how many and what comments had high level of agreement. That is, what comments point out to a TD item. This question will also allow us to analyze the agreement among the participants about the candidate comments that indicate a TD item. We conjecture that high agreement on the choice of comments filtered by CVM-TD evidences its relevance as a support tool on the TD identification.

RQ4: Does CVM-TD help researchers on select candidate comments that point to technical debt items?

With this question, we intend to investigate if the contextualized vocabulary provided by CVM-TD points to candidate comments that are considered indicators of technical debt by researchers. This question will also allow us to investigate the contribution of CVM-TD to support the TD identification process.

RQ5: What were the most chosen code comment patterns by participants as decisive to indicate a TD item?

In this question, we intend to investigate which patterns were considered more decisive to help participants on identifying comments that report a situation of TD. For each comment marked as yes, the participants highlighted the part of the comment that was decisive for their answer. The answer for this question will allow us to classify the most decisive patterns and closing a feedback cycle expanding the vocabulary by inserting new patterns.

3.2   Participants

The participants of the study were selected using convenience sampling [21]. Our sample consists of 21 software engineering master students at the Federal University of Sergipe (Sergipe-Brazil) and 15 software engineering master students at the Salvador University (Bahia-Brazil). We conducted the experiment in the context of the Empirical Software Engineering Course.

In order to classify the profile of the participants and their experience in the software development process, a characterization form was filled by each participant before the experiment. The questions were about professional experiences, English reading skills, and specific technical knowledge such as refactoring and programming languages. The result of the questionnaire showed that participants had a heterogeneous experience level, but all had some experience on software projects.

The participants were classified into three experience levels (high, medium and low) regarding the experience variable and the classification proposed by [18], which is presented in Table 1. We discarded the category E1 because there were not any undergraduate students as participants. We considered low experience for participants related to the categories E2 and E3. The participants related to the category E4 were considered as having medium experience, and, finally, we considered the participants related to category E5 as having high experience.

Table 1. Classification of the experiences of participants.

Category	Description	Experience levels
E1	Undergraduate student with less than three months of recent industrial experience	–
E2	Graduate student with less than three months of recent industrial experience	Low
E3	Academic with less than three months of recent industrial experience	Low
E4	Any person with recent industrial experience between 3 months and two years	Medium
E5	Any person with recent industrial experience for more than two years	High

When considering the English reading skills, the participants were classified into two levels (good and medium/poor). We had 4 participants with poor English reading skills and 21 participants with medium. Despite these participants have been selected as medium/poor English, they may understand short sentences like code comments in English. Table 2 shows the characterization of the participants.

Table 2. Distribution of the participants.

Group	Participants by experience level			Participants by English reading level	
	High	Med	Low	Good	Med/Poor
G1 (12)	4	3	5	1	11
G2 (12)	3	5	4	5	7
G3 (12)	4	5	3	5	7
Total (36)	11	13	12	11	25

The participants were split into three groups. Each group had 12 participants with approximately the same levels of experience. This strategy provides a balanced experimental design. The design involved each group of participants working on a different set of comments (experimental object) and permits us to use statistical test to study the effect of the investigated variables. We adopted this plan to avoid an excessive number of comments to be analyzed by each participant.

3.3 Instrumentation

Forms. The experimental package is available at https://goo.gl/DdomGk. We used slides for the training and four forms to perform the experiment:

Consent Form: the participants authorize their participation in the experiment and indicate to know the nature of the procedures which they have to follow.

Characterization Form: contains questions to gather information about professional experiences, English reading skills, and specific technical knowledge of participants.

Data collect Form: contains a list of source code comments. During the experiment, the participants were asked to indicate, for each comment, if it points to a TD item.

Feedback Form: in this form, the participants may write their impression on the experiment. We also asked the participants to classify the training and the level of difficulty in performing the study tasks.

Software Artifact and Candidate Comments. We gathered and filtered comments from a large and well-known open source software (ArgoUML). The project is written in Java with 1,846 files. In choosing this project, we considered the following criteria: being long-lived (more than ten years), having a satisfactory number of comments (more than 2,000 useful comments).

To be able to extract the candidate comments from the software that may indicate a TD item, we used *eXcomment*. We were only interested in comments that have been intentionally written by developers [9].

Once the comments were extracted, we filtered the comments by using terms that belong to the vocabulary presented in [9]. A comment is returned when it has at least one keyword or expression found in the vocabulary. We will call these comments 'candidate comments'. At the end, the tool returned 353 comments, which were listed in the collect data form in the same order in which they are in the code. This is important because comments that are close to each other can have some relationship.

3.4 Analysis Procedure

We considered three perspectives to analyze accuracy:

(i) Agreement between each participant and the Oracle: In order to investigate RQ1 and RQ2, we adopted the accuracy measure, which is the proportion of true results (the comments chosen in agreement between each participant and the Oracle) and the total number of cases examined (see Eq. 1).

$$
\begin{aligned}
accuracy = (num\,TP + num\,TN)/ \\
(num\,TP + num\,FP + num\,TN + num\,FN)
\end{aligned}
\tag{1}
$$

TP represents the case where the participant and the Oracle agree on a TD comment (comment that points to a TD item). FP represents the case where the participant disagrees with the Oracle on the selected TD comment. TN occurs when the participant and the Oracle agree on a comment that does not report a TD item. Finally, a FN happens when the participant does not mark a TD comment in disagreement with the Oracle.

The definition of the Oracle, which represents an important aspect of this analysis process, was performed before carrying out the experiment. We relied on the presence of three specialists in TD. Two of the specialists did, in separate, the indication of the comments that could point out to a TD item. After, the third specialist did a consensus process for the set of the chosen comments. All this process took one week.

(ii) **Agreement among the Participants:** To analyze RQ3, we adopted the Finn coefficient [22]. The Finn coefficient is used to measure the level of agreement among participants. In order to make the comparison of agreement values, we adopted classification levels, as defined by [23], and recently used by [20]: slight, for values between 0.00 and 0.20; fair (between 0.21 and 0.40); moderate (between 0.41 and 0.60); substantial (between 0.61 and 0.80); and almost perfect (between 0.81 and 1.00) agreement.

(iii) **TD Comments selected by Oracle and Participants:** To analyze RQ4, we investigated the candidate comments that point to TD items selected by the Oracle and participants. We also identified and analyzed the false positives (*i.e.*, comments that do not report a TD item).

(iv) **The most chosen Patterns by Participants as decisive to indicate a TD item:** To answer the RQ5, we analyzed the patterns that were chosen by participants as decisive patterns to identify a TD item through code comments analysis.

3.5 Pilot Study

Before the experiment, we carried out a pilot study with a computer science Ph.D. student with professional experience. The pilot took 2 h and was carried out in a Lab at the Federal University of Bahia (Bahia-Brazil). We performed the training at first hour, and next the participant performed the experimental task described in the next section. The participant analyzed 83 comments and selected 52 as TD comments.

The pilot was used to better understand the procedure of the study. It helped us to evaluate the use of the data collection form, the necessary time to accomplish the task and, mainly, the number of comments used by each group. Thus, the pilot study was useful to calibrate the time and number of comments analyzed.

4 Operation

The experiment was conducted in a classroom at Federal University of Sergipe, and at the Salvador University, following the same procedure.

The operation of the experiment was divided into different sessions. A week prior to the experiment, the participants filled the consent and characterization form. The training and experiment itself were performed at the same day. For training purposes, we performed a presentation in the first part of the class. The presentation covered the TD concepts and context, as well as the TD indicators [11] and how to perform a qualitative analysis on the code comments. This training took one hour.

After that, a break was taken. Next, each participant analyzed the set of candidate comments, extracted from ArgoUML, in the same room where we performed the training. They filled the data collection form pointing out the initial and end time of the task. For each candidate comment listed in the form, the participants chose "Yes" or "No", and their level of confidence on their answer. Besides, for each comment marked as yes, they should highlight the piece of text that was decisive for giving this answer.

The participants were asked to not discuss their answers with others. When they finished, they filled the feedback questionnaire. A total of three hours were planned for the experiment training and execution, but the participants did not use all of the available time.

4.1 Deviations from the Plan

We did not include the data points from participants who did not complete all the experimental sessions in our analysis since we needed all the information (characterization, data collection, and feedback). Thus, we eliminated 4 participants.

Table 3 presents the final distribution of the participants. The value in parentheses indicates the final number of participants in each group. In each of the groups G1 and G3, a participant was excluded because of not filling the value of confidence. In group G2, a participant was excluded because he did not analyze all comments and another was excluded because did not mark the text in the TD comments.

Table 3. Final distribution of the participants among groups.

Group	Participants by experience level			Participants by English level	
	High	Medium	Low	Good	Med/Poor
G1 (11)	4	3	4	1	10
G2 (10)	2	5	3	5	5
G3 (11)	3	5	3	5	6
Total (32)	9	13	10	11	21

5 Results

In this section, we present the results for each RQ.

RQ1: Do the English reading skills of the participant affect the accuracy when identifying TD through code comment analysis?

In order to investigate the impact of the English reading level skills on the TD identification process, we calculated the accuracy values for each participant with

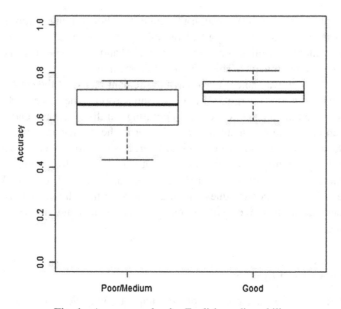

Fig. 1. Accuracy value by English reading skills.

respect to the Oracle. Figure 1 shows a box-plot illustrating the accuracy distribution. It is possible to note that the participants with good English reading skills had the lowest dispersion. It indicates that they are more consistent in the identification of TD comments than the participants with medium/poor English reading skills. Moreover, the accuracy values of the participants with good reading skills are higher than the values of the participants with medium/poor reading skills. However, the median accuracy of the participants with medium/poor reading skills is 0.65. This means that the participants with this profile were able to identify comments that were pointed out as an indicator of a TD item by the Oracle.

We also performed a hypothesis test to reinforce the analysis of this variable. To do this, we defined the following null hypothesis:

H0: The English reading skills of the participant do not affect the accuracy with respect to the agreement with the Oracle.

We ran a normality test, *Shapiro-Wilk*, and identified that the distribution was normal. After that, we ran the *t-test*, a parametric test, to evaluate our hypotheses. We used a typical confidence level of 95% ($\alpha = 0.05$). As shown in Table 4, the p-value calculated (p = 0.02342) is lower than the α value. Consequently, we may reject the null hypothesis (*H0*).

Table 4. Hypothesis test for analysis of English reading.

	Shapiro-Wilk (normality test)		Parametric test
	Good	Medium/Poor	t-test
p-value	0.9505	0.9505	0.02342

We also evaluated our results regarding magnitude, testing the effect size measure. We calculate *Cohen's d* [24] to interpret the size of the difference between the distribution of the groups. We used the classification presented by Cohen [24]: 0 to 0.1: No Effect; 0.2 to 0.4: Small Effect; 0.5 to 0.7: Intermediate Effect; 0.8 and higher: Large Effect.

The magnitude of the result ($d = 0.814$) also confirmed that there is a difference (Large Effect) on the accuracy values with respect to both groups. This evidence reinforces our hypothesis and shows that the results were statistically significant.

In addition, we analyzed the feedback form and we highlighted the main notes at the following (translated to English): (i) *I had some difficulties to understand and decide about complex comments*; (ii) *I had the feeling that I needed to know the software context better*; (iii) *I believe some tips on English comments could help us to interpret the complex comments*. This data is aligned with our finding that indicates that English reading skills may affect the task of analyzing code comments to identify TD in software projects.

RQ2: Does the experience of participant impact the accuracy when identifying TD through code comment analysis?

In order to investigate the impact of the experience level on the TD identification process, we calculated the accuracy values for each participant with respect to the Oracle. We show the accuracy distribution by experience level of the participants in Fig. 2. From this figure, it is possible to note that the box-plots have almost the same level of accuracy regarding high, medium and low experience. Considering the medians, the values are very similar. Participants with high and low experience have

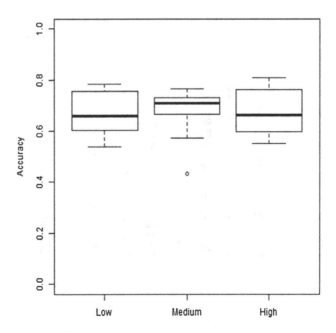

Fig. 2. Accuracy by participants' experience.

the same median value (0.66), whereas the median of participants with medium experience is moderately higher (0.71).

We also calculated the variation coefficient. This coefficient measures the variability in each level – that is, how many in a group is near the median. We found the coefficients of 12.91%, 13.17%, and 13.96%, for high, medium and low experience, respectively. According to the distribution presented by Snedecor and Cochran [25], the coefficients are low, showing that the levels of experience have homogeneous values of accuracy.

Finally, we performed a hypothesis test to analyze the experience variable. We defined the following null hypothesis:

H0: *The experiences of the participants do not affect his or her accuracy with respect to the agreement with the Oracle.*

After testing normality, we ran Anova, a parametric test to evaluate more than two treatments. The p-value calculated ($p = 0.904$) is bigger than α value. In this sense, we do not have evidences to reject the null hypothesis (*H0*).

From the analysis, we consider that the experience level did not impact the distribution of the accuracy values, i.e., when using CVM-TD, experienced and non-experienced participants show the same accuracy when identifying comments that point out to TD items. A possible interpretation of this result is that CVM-TD can be used by non-experienced participants.

RQ3: *Do participants agree with each other on the choice of comments filtered by CVM-TD that may indicate a TD item?*

Our analysis considered the number of comments per rate of participants that chose the comment. Figure 3 shows the ratios in the *X-axis* and the number of comments in

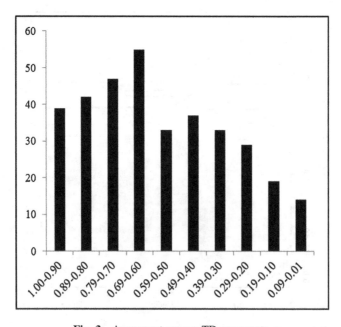

Fig. 3. Agreement among TD comments.

each interval in *Y-axis*. The ratio values are the proportion of "number of participants who choose the comment" and the "number of participants in the experiment group". For example, a comment from group G1 (the G1 has 11 participants) that was chosen by 10 participants has ratio = 0.91 (that is, 10/11).

We can note that all or almost all participants have chosen some comments as good indicator of TD, which means that these comments had high level of agreement and CVM-TD filtered comments that may really point out to TD item. Almost 40 comments have ratio intervals between 1 and 0.90. Some examples of such comments are:

```
"NOTE: This is temporary and will go away in a "future"
release (ratio = 1)";
"FIXME: this could be a problem...(ratio = 1) ";
"TODO:Replace the next deprecated call(ratio = 0.90) ".
"TODO: This functionality needs to be moved someplace
useful…(ratio = 0.90) ".
```

The whole set of these comments is available at https://goo.gl/fSaMj9.

On the other hand, considering the agreement among all participants identifying TD comments, we found a low coefficient. We conducted the Finn test to analyze the agreement in each group, considering all comments. Table 5 presents the agreement coefficient values. The level of agreement was 'slight' and 'fair' according to [23] classification.

Table 5. Finn agreement test.

	Finn	p-value	Classification levels
Group 1	0.151	3.23e−05	Slight
Group 2	0.188	5.74e−07	Slight
Group 3	0.265	8.34e−12	Fair

RQ4: Does CVM-TD help researchers on select candidate comments that point to technical debt items?

We analyzed the candidate comments identified by the Oracle as TD comments. Table 6 shows the number of comments identified by the Oracle. We observed that almost 60% of comments filtered by terms that belong to the vocabulary (candidate comments) proposed by Farias *et al.* [9] were identified as good indicators of TD by the Oracle.

Table 6. TD comments identified by the Oracle.

	Group 1	Group 2	Group 3
Number of candidate comments	123	124	106
Number of TD comments	68 (55.28%)	83 (66.94%)	58 (54.72%)

Regarding the average accuracy of all participants against the Oracle, the overall value is 0.673. On average, this shows that the participants archived good accuracy values. We also analyzed the dispersion of the set of values. The standard deviation (SD) is 0.087 which is considered a low value. In particular, the low SD indicates that the values do not spread too much around the average. That is, it indicates low dispersion of the accuracy values from the average. The box-blot in

Figure 4 represents the distribution of accuracy values for all participants. This figure shows that the values have a homogeneous distribution of accuracy.

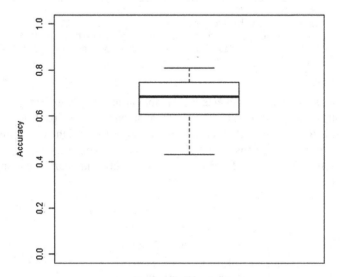

Fig. 4. The distribution of the accuracy values.

We can also see the accuracy distribution by each group of the participants in Fig. 5. From this figure, it is possible to note that the box-plots have almost the same level of accuracy. Considering the median, the values are very similar.

Next, we analyzed the number of TD comments chosen by participant and Oracle. Table 7 shows the TD comments identified by the Oracle and also by at least 50% of all participants in each group. This means that 66 comments were chosen by the Oracle and by at least 5.5 participants of the group 1. For group 2, 72 comments were chosen by Oracle and by at least 5 participants. While for group 3, 51 comments were chosen by Oracle and by at least 5.5 participants. The achieved results indicate that 89.21% of the TD comments that were chosen by Oracle were also chosen by at least 50% of all participants. The results indicate that the vocabulary helps the participants to identify comments that can point out to TD items.

We also analyzed the number of comments per rate of participants that chose the comments indicated by Oracle as a TD comment. Figure 6 shows the ratios in the *X-axis* and the number of comments in each interval in *Y-axis*. The ratio values are the proportion of *"number of participants who chooses a comment indicated as TD comment by Oracle"* and the *"number of participants in the experiment group"*. For

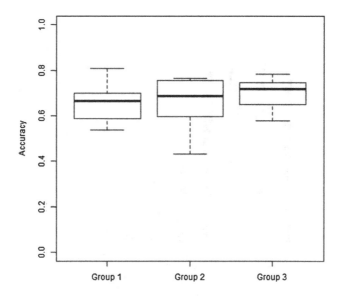

Fig. 5. Accuracy values by groups.

Table 7. TD comments identified by the Oracle and participants.

	Group 1	Group 2	Group 3
Number of candidate comments	123	124	106
Number of TD comments	71 (57.72%)	83 (66.94%)	58 (54.72%)
Number of TD comments chosen by participants and Oracle	66 (92.95%)	72 (86.74%)	51 (87.93%)

example, a comment from group G1 indicated as TD comment by the Oracle (G1 has 11 participants) that was chosen by 11 participants has ratio = 1.00 (that is, 11/11).

When looking at the number of comments reporting TD, it is possible to note that, on average, the participants identified many comments that were filtered by the vocabulary and selected as TD indicators by Oracle. This means that the vocabulary proposed by CVM-TD helped the participants to comprehend and identify comments that may point out TD items. More than 170 comments have ratio intervals equal or higher than 0.5.

In order to perform a deep analysis, we investigated a sample of these comments. From the analysis, let's consider the following comments:

Example comment #1 (ratio 1.00):

```
/* Install the trap to "eat" SecurityExceptions. *
NOTE: This is temporary and will go away in a "future"
release */
```

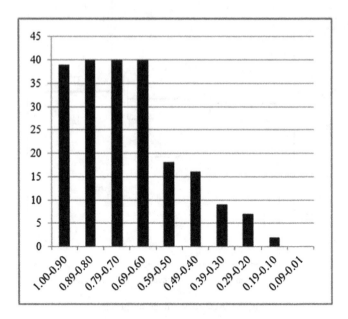

Fig. 6. Number of comments per rate of participants.

The above comment (#1) mentions issues in source code and highlights that a specific part of code is temporary and need to be removed in a future release. The comment has three patterns: *"the trap"*, *"NOTE: This is temporary"*, and *"future release"*. In other words, it was indicated as a comment reporting a TD item by Oracle and all participants.

Example comment #2 (ratio 0.92):

```
/* TODO: Why is this here? Who is calling this? @see
java.beans.VetoableChangeListener#vetoableChange(java.b
eans.PropertyChangeEvent) */
```

Example comment #3 (ratio 0.64):

```
// This is somewhat inconsistent with the design of the
constructor // that receives the root object by
argument. If this is okay // then there may be no need
for a constructor with that argument.
```

In comments #2 and #3, the developers describe situations correlated with violation of principles of good design, inadequate location of a method, and inconsistence with the design. We can see this context through the patterns *"Why is this here?"*, *"Who is calling this?"*, and *"inconsistent with the design"*. Besides these patterns, we can note the tag *TODO* reporting the need to revisit this code in future.

Example comment #4 (ratio 0.91):

```
/* TODO: needs documenting, why synchronized? */
```

Example comment #5 (ratio 0.82):

```
/* TODO: As currently coded, this actually returns all
BehavioralFeatures which are owned by Classifiers
contained in the given namespace, which is slightly
different than what's documented. It will not include
any BehavioralFeatures which are part of the Namespace,
but which don't have an owner. */
```

Comments #4 and #5 are examples that we consider as documentation debt. In the above comment, the developers describe the necessity for documentation and show their worries about the missing or inadequate documentation. Maybe this TD item could not be identified using only code-based metrics because the necessity of documentation cannot be measured only analyzing the source code.

Example comment #6 (ratio 0.82):

```
// The following debug line is now the single most
memory consuming // line in the whole of ArgoUML. It
allocates approximately 18% of // all memory allocated.
// Suggestions for solutions: // Check if there is a
LOG.debug(String, String) method that can // be used
instead. // Use two calls. // For now I (Linus) just
comment it out.
```

Comment #6 reports strategies that caused a very large processing consuming in the build process of the projects. The patterns *"most memory consuming"* and *"memory allocated"* may refer to build related issues that make a task harder, and more time/processing consuming unnecessarily.

Example comment #7 (ratio 0.91):

```
/* TODO: Replace the next deprecated call. This case is
complicated * by the use of parameters. All other Figs
work differently. */
```

In comment #7, the developers describe situations correlated with bad coding practices, deprecated code, and difficult to be maintained in the future. The patterns *"TODO: replace"*, *"deprecated"*, and *"case is complicated"* refer to the problems found in the source code which can negatively affect the quality of the code making it more difficult to be maintained in the future. They are examples of what we consider as code debt.

Example comment #8 (ratio 0.91):

```
/* TODO: The copy function is not yet completely
implemented - so we will have some exceptions here and
there.*/.
```

Comment #8 describes the lack of synchronism between optimal requirements specification and what is currently implemented. The pattern *"is not yet completely implemented"* indicates a requirement that are only partially implemented.

Some of these comments have patterns which report more clearly a situation related with the description of TD items, such as, *"TODO: this is temporary"*, *"inconsistent with the design"*, and *"TODO: needs documenting"*. We analyzed some of the top comments having ratio higher than 0.8. Table 8 lists the patterns identified by participants in these comments. Besides the fact that these comments have patterns that we considered to clearly identify TD, we can also see that many of them have more than one pattern reporting a TD context. This also helps indicating that the patterns can be used to filter comments describing a situation of TD.

Table 8. List of patterns identified by participants in these comments.

ID comment	Ratio	Identified patterns
17	1.00	the trap
		NOTE: This is temporary
		"Future" release
945	1.00	This is a bug
1005	1.00	TODO: This is probably not the right location
1064	1.00	FIXME: this could be a problem
26	0.91	TODO:
		Need to be in their own files?
		TODO: Why is this here?
44	0.91	Who is calling this?
		TODO: needs documenting
68	0.91	A temporary solution
122	0.91	Should be fixed
318	0.91	TODO: split into
485	0.91	Problems directly in this class
		Critic problem
		TODO: Replace
521	0.91	Deprecated
		This case is complicated
		Is there no better way?
549	0.91	TODO: implement this
835	0.91	TODO: ??
1227	0.91	Code is not used
		Why is it here?
		Causes dependency

Although the vocabulary allowed filtering good comments reporting TD, it also returned false positives. The Oracle and participants identified 141 comments, which were returned by the vocabulary, as comments that do not report a situation of TD, that is, they are false positives. This shows that 39.94% of the comments identified by our approach may have been misclassified by patterns of the vocabulary (353 comments were returned in total).

Some examples of these false positives follow:

Example comment #9:

```
// NOTE: This is package scope to force callers to use
ResourceLoaderWrapper
```

Example comment #10:

```
// Note that this will not preserve empty lines // in
the body
```

The *eXcomment* selected these candidate comments (#9 and #10) because of presence of the *"NOTE:"* but the comment only gives an overview of the information about the code implementation.

Example comment #11:

```
/* Now we have to see if any state in any statemachine
of * classifier is named [name]. If so, then we only
have to link the state to c. */
```

The pattern *"have to"* was interpreted as an open task verb reporting a task to be done but it only composes an expression describing the functionality of the code.

Example comment #12:

```
/* This is used in the todo panel, when "By Poster" is
chosen for a      * manually created todo item.*/
```

The pattern *"TODO"* made our tool and vocabulary selecting the comment as a candidate comment, while the term was used only to describe the name of a component.

Example comment #13:

```
/* This next line fixes issue 4276: */
```

The pattern *"fixes"* may suggest something to be fixed in the project but, in this case, the comment describes the opposite, a piece of the code fixing an issue.

This result indicates that the vocabulary and *eXcomment* need to be better calibrated to reduce the number of returned comments that do not report a situation of TD. With this in mind, we intend to perform a complementary investigation with the purpose of identifying the patterns that are more decisive to detect TD items.

RQ5: What were the most chosen code comment patterns by participants as decisive to indicate a TD item?

Table 9 shows the top 20 selected patterns. Column "Patterns" lists the patterns identified by participants, *"# of occurrence"* summarizes the number of times that a participant highlighted the patterns as important, and *"# of Participants"* summarizes the total of participants who have chosen the pattern as important to identify a TD item.

Table 9. Top 20 patterns more chosen by participants as decisive to indicate a TD item.

Patterns	# of occurrences	# of Participants
TODO	899	26
Need to	48	22
Remove	54	19
?	49	19
Replace	19	14
Is this needed?	15	14
Must be	22	13
Should be	20	12
Does not work!	18	12
Critic	21	11
Check	14	11
Fix	22	11
Why?	21	10
Cyclic dependency	10	10
This is a bug	10	10
Note	13	9
Move	13	9
Have to	12	9
Temporary	9	9
Probably redundant	9	9

The most selected pattern was *'Todo'*. It was chosen by 26 of 32 participants (81.25%), followed by *"need to"* selected by 22 participants (65.63%), *"remove"*, and *"Todo: Replace"* by 16 participants (50%). From the table, we can also see that several comment patterns have the tag *"Todo"*, such as *"Todo: This does not work!"* and *"Todo: Is this needed/correct?"*. The pattern *"Todo"* was identified as a decisive pattern in 899 cases by the participants. This highlights the importance of *"Todo"* for composing important patterns to identify TD through code comment analysis. Besides the pattern *"Todo"*, the patterns *"need to"*, *"remove"*, *"?"*, *"replace"*, *"Is this needed?"*, *"must be"*, *"should be"*, and *"does not work"* were also chosen as decisive patterns by the participants. The complete list is available at https://goo.gl/ZDxTmn.

Even though these results show that there are decisive patterns to identify a situation of TD, further investigations are needed for analyzing how much each pattern is decisive to identify TD. In this way, we intend to perform another experiment to widely analyze and classify all patterns by considering the importance level of the patterns to point out to a TD item.

6 Discussion

Our results suggest that the English reading level of the participants may impact the identification of TD through comment analysis. Participants with good English reading skills had accuracy values better than participants who have medium/poor English reading skills. On the other hand, participants with poor/medium English profile were able to identify a good amount of TD comments filtered by the contextualized vocabulary.

We also observed in the feedback analysis that some participants had difficulties to understand and interpret complex comments, and tips might help them with this task. We conjecture that some tips may support participants to make decision on the TD identification process. For instance, highlight the TD terms or patterns of comment from the contextualized vocabulary into the comments.

Considering the impact of experience on TD identification, we could not conclude that the experience level affects the accuracy. This can indicate that comments selected by the vocabulary may be understood by an experienced or non-experienced observer. This reinforces the idea that the TD metaphor aids discussion by providing a familiar framework and vocabulary that may be easily understood [26, 27].

Considering the agreement among participants identifying TD comments, the results revealed some comments pointed out as good indicator of TD, with high level of agreement. It may evidence the contribution of CVM-TD as a support tool on the TD identification. However, in general, the level of agreement between participants was considered low. We believe that this occurred due to the large amount of comments to be analyzed, and the amount of comments selected by the contextualized vocabulary that does not indicate a TD item. In this way, the level of agreement might rise whether the vocabulary is more accurate.

We noted that a high number of comments filtered by the CVM-TD was considered to indicate TD items. In view of the contribution of the CVM-TD to support TD identification, the results indicate that many comments that were chosen by Oracle were also chosen by participants as comments that may point out to a TD item. This means that the vocabulary proposed by CVM-TD helped the participants to comprehend and identify comments that may reporting a situation of TD.

These results provide preliminary indications that CVM-TD and the contextualized vocabulary can be considered an important support tool to identify TD item through code comments analysis. Different from code metrics-based tools, code comments analysis allow us to consider human factors to explore developers' point of view and complement the TD identification with more contextual and qualitative data. Both approaches may contribute with each other to make the automated tools more efficient.

The last aspect we analyzed was the patterns mostly chosen by participants as decisive to indicate a TD item. We identified a list of the top 20 patterns. We could note that there are patterns that are more decisive than others, but we need to perform further investigations on the patterns considering their importance level to identify a TD item.

6.1 Threats to Validity

We followed the checklist provided by Wohlin et al. [28] to discuss the relevant threats to this controlled experiment.

Construct Validity. To minimize the mono-method bias, we used an accuracy and agreement test to provide an indication of the TD identification through comment analysis. We selected the researchers that composed the Oracle. In order to mitigate the biased judgment on the Oracle, its definition was performed by three different researchers with knowledge in TD. Two of them selected the TD comments, and the third researcher did a consensus to decrease the bias. Finally, to reduce social threats due to evaluation apprehension, participants were not evaluated.

Another thread involves the definition of the proposed vocabulary. It is possible that the set of patterns and combinations used by our model and vocabulary are simply too many to be studied. An alternative would be to limit the studies to specific contexts and software domains. Another point is related to the imprecision in the filtering of candidate comments. Our results might be affected by false positives and false negatives returned by the vocabulary and the automatic filtering heuristic. To reduce this threat in next experiment, we intent to calibrate the vocabulary and *eXcomment* to reduce the number of comments that do not report a situation of TD.

Internal Validity. The first internal threat we have to consider is subject selection since we have chosen all participants through a convenience sample. We minimized this threat organizing the participants in different treatment groups divided by experience level.

Another threat is that participants might be affected negatively by boredom and tiredness. In order to mitigate this threat, we performed a pilot study to calibrate the time and amount of comments to be analyzed. To avoid the communication among participants, two researchers observed the operation of the experiment at all times. A further validity threat is the instrumentation, which is the effect caused by artifacts used for the experiment. Each group had a specific set of comments, but all participants used the same data collection form format. To investigate the impact of this threat in our results, we analyzed the average accuracy in each group. Group G1 has average value equal to 0.65. For group G2, the average value is equal to 0.66, and group G3 is equal to 0.69. From these data, it is possible to note that groups have almost the same level of average accuracy. It means that this threat did not affect the results.

External Validity. This threat relates to the generalization of the findings and their applicability to industrial practices. This threat is always present in experiments with students as participants. Our selected samples contained participants with different levels of experience. All participants have some professional experience in the software development process. It is an important aspect in mitigating the threat. A further threat is the usage of software that may not be representative for industrial practice. We used software adopted in the practice of software development as an experimental object to mitigate the threat.

Conclusion Validity. To avoid the violation of assumptions, we used normality test, Shapiro-Wilk, and a parametric test, the t-test, for data analysis. To reduce the impact of reliability of treatment implementation, we followed the same experimental setup on both cases.

7 Conclusion and Future Work

In this paper, we performed a controlled experiment to evaluate the CVM-TD aiming to characterizing its overall accuracy and factors that may affect the identification of TD through code comment analysis. Our results indicate that: (i) English reading skills affect the participants' accuracy; (ii) we could not conclude that the experience level impacts on understanding of comments to support the TD identification; (iii) concerning the agreement among participants, although we found low agreement coefficients between participants, some comments have been indicated with a high level of agreement; (iv) CVM-TD provided promising results concerning to the identification of comments as good indicator of TD by participants. The results indicate that 89.21% of the TD comments that were chosen by the Oracle were also chosen by at least 50% of all participants. The results indicate that the vocabulary helps the participants to identify comments that can point out to TD items.

Although the vocabulary has been used to filter good comments reporting TD, it also returned false positives. We identified that 39.94% of the comments automatically identified by our approach may have been misclassified by patterns of the vocabulary. This result indicates that the vocabulary and *eXcomment* need to be better calibrated to reduce the number of returned comments that do not report a situation of TD.

The results motivate us to continue exploring code comments in the context of the TD identification process to improve CVM-TD and the *eXcomment*. We believe that the vocabulary and the study findings on how code comment analysis supports the TD identification represent a significant contribution to the research community.

Future works include to: (i) perform further investigations for analyzing how much each pattern is decisive to identify TD, (ii) develop some features in *eXcomment* associated with the CVM-TD to support the interpretation of comments, such as "usage of weights and color scale to indicate the comments with more importance in TD context, and highlight the TD terms or patterns of comment into the comments", and (iii) evaluate the use of CVM-TD in projects in the industry.

Acknowledgements. This work was partially supported by CNPq Universal 2014 grant 458261/2014-9. The authors also would like to thank Methanias Colaço and André Batista for their support in the execution step of the experiment.

References

1. Izurieta, C., Vetrò, A., Zazworka, N., Cai, Y., Seaman, C., Shull, F.: Organizing the technical debt landscape. In: 3rd International Workshop on Managing Technical Debt, MTD 2012 – Proceedings, pp. 23–26 (2012)
2. Ernst, N.A., Bellomo, S., Ozkaya, I., Nord, R.L., Gorton, I.: Measure it? Manage it? Ignore it? Software Practitioners and Technical Debt. In: 10th Joint Meeting on Foundations of Software Engineering - ESEC/FSE 2015, pp. 50–60 (2015)
3. Alves, N.S.R., Mendes, T.S., Mendonça, M.G., Spínola, R.O., Shull, F., Seaman, C.: Identification and management of technical debt: a systematic mapping study. Inf. Softw. Technol. **70**, 100–121 (2016)
4. Guo, Y., Spínola, R.O., Seaman, C.: Exploring the costs of technical debt management – a case study. Empir. Softw. Eng. **1**, 1–24 (2014)
5. Li, Z., Liang, P., Avgeriou, P., Guelfi, N.: A systematic mapping study on technical debt and its management. J. Syst. Softw. **101**, 193–220 (2014)
6. Mendes, T.S., Almeida, D.A., Alves, N.S.R., Spínola, R.O., Mendonça, M.: VisMinerTD - an open source tool to support the monitoring of the technical debt evolution using software visualization. In: 17th International Conference on Enterprise Information Systems (2015)
7. Zazworka, N., Spínola, R.O., Vetro', A., Shull, F., Seaman, C.: A case study on effectively identifying technical debt. In: Proceedings of the 17th International Conference on Evaluation and Assessment in Software Engineering - EASE 2013, pp. 42–47. ACM Press, New York (2013)
8. Potdar, A., Shihab, E.: An exploratory study on self-admitted technical debt. In: IEEE International Conference on Software Maintenance and Evolution, pp. 91–100 (2014)
9. Farias, M.A.F., Silva, A.B., Mendonça, M.G., Spínola, R.O.: A contextualized vocabulary model for identifying technical debt on code comments. In: 7th International Workshop on Managing Technical Debt, pp. 25–32 (2015)
10. Maldonado, E.S., Shihab, E.: Detecting and quantifying different types of self-admitted technical debt. In: 7th International Workshop on Managing Technical Debt, pp. 9–15 (2015)
11. Alves, N.S.R., Ribeiro, L.F., Caires, V., Mendes, T.S., Spínola, R.O.: Towards an ontology of terms on technical debt. In: Sixth International Workshop on Managing Technical Debt (MTD), pp. 1–7 (2014)
12. Storey, M., Ryall, J., Bull, R.I., Myers, D., Singer, J.: TODO or to bug : exploring how task annotations play a role in the work practices of software developers. In: ICSE: International Conference on Software Engineering, pp. 251–260 (2008)
13. Maalej, W., Happel, H.-J.: Can development work describe itself? In: 7th IEEE Working Conference on Mining Software Repositories (MSR), pp. 191–200 (2010)
14. Steidl, D., Hummel, B., Juergens, E.: Quality analysis of source code comments. In: 21st International Conference on Program Comprehension (ICPC), pp. 83–92. IEEE (2013)
15. Etzkorn, L.H., Davis, C.G., Bowen, L.L.: The language of comments in computer software: a sublanguage of English. J. Pragmat. **33**, 1731–1756 (2001)
16. Bavota, G., Russo, B.: A large-scale empirical study on self-admitted technical debt. In: 13th Working Conference on Mining Software Repositories – MSR, pp. 315–326 (2016)
17. Lemos, O.A. de Paula, A.C., Zanichelli, F.C., Lopes, C.V.: Thesaurus-based automatic query expansion for interface-driven code search categories and subject descriptors. In: 11th Working Conference on Mining Software Repositories – MSR, pp. 212–221 (2014)

18. Host, M., Wohlin, C., Thelin, T.: Experimental context classification: incentives and experience of subjects. In: Proceedings of 27th International Conference on Software Engineering, ICSE 2005, pp. 470–478 (2005)
19. Salman, I., Misirli, A.T., Juristo, N.: Are students representatives of professionals in software engineering experiments? In: Proceedings of the 37th International Conference on Software Engineering (2015)
20. Santos, J.A.M., Mendonça, M.G., Pereira, C.: The problem of conceptualization in god class detection: agreement, strategies and decision drivers. J. Softw. Eng. Res. Dev. **2**, 1–33 (2014)
21. Shull, F., Singer, J., Sjoberg, D.: Guide to Advanced Empirical Software Engineering. Springer, London (2008). doi:10.1007/978-1-84800-044-5
22. Finn, R.H.: A note on estimating the reliability of categorical data. Educ. Psychol. Measur. **30**(1), 71–76 (1970). doi:10.1177/001316447003000106. ISBN 0013-1644
23. Landis, J.R., Koch, G.G.: The measurement of observer agreement for categorical data. Biometrics **33**, 159–174 (1977)
24. Cohen, J.: Statistical Power Analysis for the Behavioral Sciences, 2nd edn. Lawrence Earlbaum Associates, Hillsdale (1988). http://www.worldcat.org/isbn/-0805802835
25. Snedecor, G.W., Cochran, W.G.: Statistical Methods, 6th edn. Iowa State University Press, Ames (1967)
26. Spínola, R., Zazworka, N., Seaman, C., Shull, F.: Investigating technical debt folklore. In: 5th International Workshop on Managing Technical Debt, pp. 1–7 (2013)
27. Kruchten, P., Nord, R.L., Ozkaya, I.: Technical debt: from metaphor to theory and practice. IEEE Softw. **29**(6), 18–21 (2012)
28. Wohlin, C., Runeson, P., Höst, M., Ohlsson, M.C., Regnell, B., Wesslén, A.: Experimentation in Software Engineering: An Introduction. Kluwer Academic Publishers, Norwell (2000)

Software Agents and Internet Computing

A Platform for Supporting Open Data Ecosystems

Marcelo Iury S. Oliveira[1,2(✉)], Lairson Emanuel R. de Alencar Oliveira[2],
Glória de Fátima A. Barros Lima[2], and Bernadette Farias Lóscio[2]

[1] Academic Unit of Serra Talhada, Federal Rural University of Pernambuco,
Serra Talhada, PE, Brazil
marcelo.iury@ufrpe.br
[2] Center for Informatics, Federal University of Pernambuco, Recife, PE, Brazil
{miso,lerao,gfabl,bfl}@cin.ufpe.br

Abstract. In this article we present a platform, called DataCollector, which aims fostering of use and appropriateness of open data by different open data ecosystem actors. The DataCollector helps data consumers searching and consuming open data as well as allows data producers to easily register, update and refine their datasets. This platform also allows the collaboration between the actors by providing features to collect and manage feedback about the open data. The proposed platform was evaluated by its viability in cataloging 14 Brazilian open data portals, covering a total of 29,540 datasets. The preliminary results indicate the DataCollector offers a robust solution for cataloging and access to distributed datasets in multiple platforms for open data publication.

Keywords: Open data · Catalog · Meta-data · DCAT · Management · Standardization · Design

1 Introduction

In recent years, there has been a great movement in which governments, communities and institutions are publishing data with no restriction rules to share or re-use, also called Open Data. There is a vast amount of open data being published in a variety of domains, including: environment, cultural, science, and statics. The open data comes from governments, sensors (*e.g.*, fleet vehicles, roadway sensors and traffic lights) and scientific institutions.

The open data model promises significant benefits. For instance, it can be used to promote democratic premises, such as accountability and transparency, for public administrations [1,2]. It also has the potential to enhance the efficiency and the quality in science by increasing the opportunities for collaboration in research as well as in innovation.

The amount of open data available as well as their data consumer and producers are growing at fast pace. And often, all that data are underused or not used at all. Since it is recent movement, most of open data are not properly

© Springer International Publishing AG 2017
S. Hammoudi et al. (Eds.): ICEIS 2016, LNBIP 291, pp. 313–337, 2017.
DOI: 10.1007/978-3-319-62386-3_15

known [3]. Challenges in explore open data primarily relies on understanding of the data itself. Furthermore, it is important to evaluate available datasets according to quality metrics and the open data principals. Moreover, most of the open data initiatives are not sustainable and consequently end up not being properly used or forgotten. The lack of communication and cooperation between stakeholders, *i.e.* data producers and consumers, is one of the main obstacles to be faced by sustainable open data initiatives [4].

In this context, where open data comes from many sources and are created in an autonomous way, it becomes necessary to have an easy way to find and to combine these distributed data. Moreover, providing tools to perform high-level analysis on top of these data is also important requirement. While developers are more interested on the raw data, policy and decision makers will profit from the analysis tools. Furthermore, the creation of an Open Data Ecosystem to enable the communication between data producers and data consumers becomes a fundamental issue. The open data ecosystem involves stakeholders who interact with each other and may play more than one role. These roles define how they relate to produce and consume both data and solutions. [5] say that actors have yet to experience fully mutual interdependence and how to improve the cooperation and connection between them is a concern introduced in the ecosystem conceptualization.

Therefore, just opening the data is not good enough. According [4], it is important to create an ecosystem in which all the stakeholders are able to perform their roles. Considering this heterogeneity of stakeholders and the differences in the implementation of open data activities, turned out the importance to have a more precise definition of the actors roles and the relationship between them to improve the collaboration to produce innovation [4–6]. In this sense, an open data platform should be able to identify where the data comes from, who consume the data, how to able feedback to the producer and who are the sponsors that drive the promotion of open data initiatives.

In this article, we present a platform, called *DataCollector*, which aims fostering of use and appropriateness of open data by different open data ecosystem actors. The DataCollector helps data consumers searching and consuming of open data and related open data solutions. The DataCollector also allows data producers to easily register, update and refine their datasets. In addition, our proposal enables collaboration between the actors by providing features to collect and manage feedback about the open data. In this sense, the DataCollector also provides tools to perform datasets analysis. By using DataCollector, it is possible to visualize the domains of the datasets as well as the domains with higher number of datasets, for example. Other aspects like usage license and data formats can also be analysed. The DataCollector may be used to perform analysis about open data scenarios as well as to facilitate the automatic identification of relevant datasets for a given user or application. Considering the growing number of open data, these tasks become time consuming and therefore very expensive.

The proposed platform also offers an easy way to query data based on both graphical interfaces and remote access mechanisms, such as Web Services, which enable automated processing and facilitate searching activities. Finally, to promote interoperability, DataCollector uses the standardized vocabularies such as DCAT vocabulary (Data Catalog Vocabulary) [7] to describe its data catalog.

The remainder of this article is organized as follows. In Sect. 2 we discuss some related work. In Sect. 3, we present the Open Data Ecosystem. In Sect. 4, we present our Metadata Vocabulary. In Sect. 4 we present our Metadata Vocabulary. In Sect. 5 we present a general overview of the proposed solution, contextualizing the services and main components of the DataCollector. In Sect. 6 we present more details about the implementation of the DataCollector. In Sect. 7 we discuss the evaluation of our proposal and in Sect. 8 we present the final considerations and future work.

2   Related Work

The use of open data has grown substantially in the last years. In general, open data is available in catalogs, which provide an interface between who makes data available (publisher) to those interested in using them (consumers). Architectures and platforms for data cataloging, as well as the harvesting of data portals, have been the subject of some works reported in the literature or solutions available on the Web [8–12].

In this context, CKAN[1] and SOCRATA[2] are the main solutions currently adopted for open data cataloging. CKAN is an open source software, which provides support for the creation of data portals, as well as offers features for publishing, storage and management of datasets [13]. CKAN provides an Application Programming Interface (API) for automated access and has functionalities for data previewing, creation of graphs and maps and the searching of geolocated datasets. The Socrata, instead, is a proprietary solution based on cloud computing and Software as a Service paradigms. One of the main differentials of Socrata is the possibility of building more complete data visualizations (conditional formatting, graphs and maps) [10].

DataHub.io [9] is an open source platform for data management provided by the Open Knowledge Foundation and powered by CKAN. DataHub.io allows everybody to host their data and is also widely used to aggregate datasets published elsewhere in one place. Despite DataHub.io provides a single point to find datasets published in different sites, it strongly depends on the cooperation of users to publish data and it doesn't offer additional support for data analysis or datasets evaluation. PublicData.eu [11] and OpenDataMonitor.eu [12] have been proposed to offer access to multiple open data portals at the same time. These data platforms provide access to datasets published by governmental agencies all over Europe. In particular, the OpenDataMonitor also provides automated evaluation of datasets.

---

[1] http://www.ckan.org.
[2] http://www.socrata.com.

Different from the solutions mentioned above, the DataCollector may be instantiated to collect data about different sets of data portals, *e.g.*, it can be used to collect datasets from brazilian open government data portals, as well as it could be used to collect datasets from biological data portals. Besides collecting datasets, the DataCollector provides free access to its metadata and also allows performing analysis about the collected datasets.

It is worth mentioning the UrbanProfiler [8], which is a tool that automatically extracts detailed information about datasets to help datasets selection. UrbanProfiler aims to collect information to help data consumers to explore and understand the contents of a dataset. In a similar way, we also offer information about the datasets in order to help datasets identification and selection.

Despite its importance, the mentioned solutions do not have a precise definition of the actors that consume and produce open data [4]. Thus, it is important to have a more precise definition of the actors roles and the relationship between them to improve the collaboration to produce innovation.

There are also works that propose open data analysis scheme with regards to employed technological approaches [14], analytical frameworks for assessing economic, social and political values of open datasets [15] and open data metadata quality assessment framework [16]. There also studies that analyze open data repositories with regard to different aspects, such as Sunlight Foundation's Open Data Principals [17], potential benefits and risks of opening government data [18], and metadata quality [19]. Barbosa *et al.* [3] presented the most broad study that analyzed different aspects of American open data, including their contents and size, creation and update history, formats, and other important aspects to data integration and management perspective, such as characteristics of the schemata.

3   Open Data Ecosystem

The Open Data Ecosystem describe a self-organizing community of actors, interacting with each other in conjunction with information technologies resources like services, databases and portals. The perspective of Open Data Ecosystem research is providing methods and tools to achieve a set of objectives of the ecosystem (e.g., sustainability, accountability, innovation). Figure 1 shows our perspective for an Open Data ecosystem. The main actors of our model are: government, application developers, small and medium enterprises (SMEs), startups, civil society, universities, funding agencies and investors.

Each one of the actors would play at least one of the following roles: consumers, producers and sponsors. The producers producing and publishing open datasets as well as for providing solutions based on these datasets. The consumers consuming open datasets. The sponsors are responsible for supporting persons, organizations or communities financially or through the provision of products in order to promote open data initiatives and to develop open data innovation. The roles also can be specialized as intermediary and final. In the former case, an intermediary actor is a third party that offers intermediation of

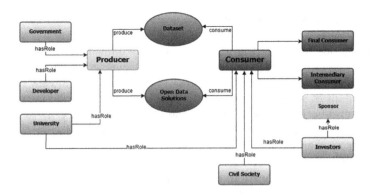

Fig. 1. Open data ecosystem.

the role between two parties. For instance, a developer can act as intermediary data consumer by producing developing an application to process datasets. The intermediary acts as a conduit for goods or services offered to the roles. Typically the intermediary offers some added value or eases the work of publishing or consume data. In its turns, the role is classified as final when is actor the last point in a data consumption or production process. For instance, a citizen acts as a final consumer do not share the results of his data consumption process to anyone.

In this context, the government publishes datasets, sponsors open data initiatives and consumes solutions produced by developers and research groups. The developers are intermediaries consumers and producers of solutions because they retrieve open datasets in order to develop innovative solutions. The university consumes datasets in order to improve and release them with better quality, consumes open data applications, hosts research groups that work producing innovative solutions in projects sponsored by investors, thus the university is considered a producer of solutions, final and intermediary consumer. The investors play the role of sponsoring. They sponsor projects in public and private initiatives, as universities and developers. The civil society plays the roles of indirect producer, final consumer and intermediary consumer, which requests demands, consumes solutions and consumes datasets in the format they are disclosed, respectively.

A service-based platform and a vocabulary to describe the open data ecosystems allow the creation of a knowledge base that will provide information about the actors and their relationships, results from their partnerships, areas of interest, solutions available and new demands. Also, inferences, recommendations and new data about open data ecosystems will be available on the knowledge base in order to raise productivity. Furthermore, a service-based platform will bridge the gap between the actors and build channels of communication between them in order to contribute for the sustainability of open data initiatives.

4   Metadata Vocabulary

As previously described, the DataCollector offers an unified view of open datasets
available in several open data portals or catalogs. Considering the heterogeneous
nature of the available data portals, in order to offer this uniform view it becomes
necessary adopt of a common data vocabulary to describe the data catalogs and
available datasets. In our work, we use the DCAT vocabulary [7] to overcome
metadata heterogeneity of the open datasets being catalogued.

DCAT is a vocabulary, proposed by the W3C, which seeks to facilitate interoperability between data catalogs. In general, vocabularies are used to classify
terms of a particular application, characterize possible relationships and define
restrictions on the use of these terms. Specifically, DCAT defines the concepts
and relationships used in the field of data catalogs. DCAT also incorporates
terms of other existing vocabularies, in particular, the *Dublin Core*[3] and *FOAF*[4].
Figure 2 presents the main classes of the DCAT.

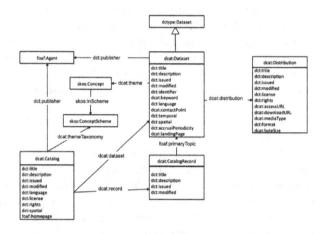

Fig. 2. DCAT model.

The central entity of the DCAT vocabulary is the Dataset, which is a collection of data, available for access or download in one or more formats [7]. Datasets
are described by general metadata, *e.g.* publication date, keywords, language [7],
and other information that makes it easier to discover and use dataset.

A single dataset may be available over different distributions to meet interoperability and usage requirements of different users. These distributions might
represent different formats of the dataset or different endpoints [7]. Examples
of distributions include a downloadable CSV file, an API or an RSS feed. Distributions are also described by metadata. The format property (*dct:format*),
for example, specifies data format used in the distribution. In order to ensure

---

[3] http://www.dublincore.org.
[4] http://www.xmlns.com/foaf/spec.

interoperability, the format should be a standard MIME type, like text/csv or application/json. The accessURL (*dcat:accessURL*) property determines a resource that gives access to the distribution of dataset, like a landingpage or a SPARQL endpoint. The downloadURL property (*dcat:downloadURL*) represents a file that contains the distribution of the dataset in a given format. Other relevant metadata about a distribution include the size of a distribution in bytes (*dcat:byteSize*) and the license (*dct:license*) under which the distribution is made available.

Finally, a Catalog is defined as a curated collection of metadata about datasets. Catalogs are also described by several properties, including: date of publication, date of modification, language used in the textual descriptions of datasets and the entity responsible for online publication of the catalog [7]. A record in a data catalog, describing a single dataset, is represented as an instance of the CatalogRecord class.

In our work, besides concepts offered by DCAT, we also use other vocabulary proposals to model feedback collected from data consumers about specific datasets. In general, data cataloguing solutions don't offer means to collect and to share feedback about datasets. However, gathering such information produces benefits for both producers and consumers of data, contributing to improve the quality of the published data, as well as to encourage the publication of new data.

The feedback data is modeled using two vocabularies developed by the W3C (World Wide Web Consortium): Dataset Usage Vocabulary[5] and Web Annotation Data Model[6]. The former one aims to define a vocabulary that offers concepts to describe how datasets published on the Web have been used as well concepts to capture data consumer's feedback and dataset citations. The later describes a structured model and format to enable annotations to be shared and reused across different platforms.

Figure 3 presents the main classes used to model feedback. *duv:Usagefeedback* allows to capture consumer's feedback in the form of annotations. As described in the Web Annotation Data Model [20], an Annotation is a rooted, directed graph that represents a relationship between resources, whose primary types are Bodies and Targets. An Annotation *oa:Annotation* has a single Body, which is a comment or other descriptive resource, and a single Target, which references the resource being annotated. In our context, the target resource is a dataset or a distribution. The body may be a general comment about the dataset, a suggestion to correct or to update the dataset, a dataset quality evaluation or a dataset rating. The property *oa:motivation* may be used to explicitly capture the motivation for a given feedback. For example, when the consumer suggests a dataset update then the value of oa:motivation will be "reviewing".

The *dqv:UserQuality Feedback* and *duv:RatingFeedback* are subclasses of *duv:UsageFeedback*. The first one allows consumers to evaluate a dataset based on

---

[5] http://www.w3.org/TR/vocab-duv/.
[6] http://www.w3.org/TR/annotation-model/.

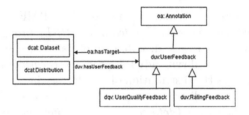

Fig. 3. Feedback model.

a grade or a star schema, for example. The second one allows to capture feedback about the quality of the dataset, like availability, consistency and freshness[7].

Feedback could be captured from data consumers by rating questionnaires, where users are asked to provide a value point on a fixed scale [21]. This interaction model could be viewed as a form of Web collaboration in such way that datasets evaluation is accomplished by engaging data consumers as "processors" to annotate datasets according to different classification taxonomies, such as data quality level or knowledge domain covered by the dataset's content. Moreover, a data consumer can also provide feedback annotations to fulfill missing metadata about datasets. Finally, a user may submit a report based on the problems they have witnessed when consuming the data. In general, the annotation model provides the user with an added value for little effort, because it facilitates finding a desirable dataset, as well as, becomes easier to find similar new resources that could be of interest [22].

Besides the feedback, we also captured descriptions of the applications that use the open data. Generally, it searches to capture the data that are used in an application, a description of what the application does and whats the problem it helps to solve. As in the feedback, it looks for to get a return about possible improvements in the dataset. To get these data, we use the APP-OD vocabulary, that was specified after an analysis of several portals that turned possible the register of applications and also uses of DCAT [23].

Figure 4 presents the main classes used to model applications. *app-od: Application* allows to capture the descriptions of the application, besides the license and date of creation. The datasets used to develop the application are captured by the *app-od:Consumes*. The *app-od:Platform* captures the different platforms, operational systems and urls to download the application. Its also captured data of who developed the application through the *app-od:Developer* class, that may be represented by an organization or a developer, and its category (domain) through the *app-od:Category* class.

5 DataCollector Architectural Overview

The DataCollector is a service-based platform that aims to provide storing, cataloging, searching and analysis services for open data initiatives. In order to

---

[7] http://www.w3.org/TR/vocab-dqv/.

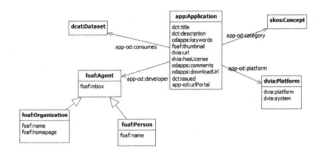

Fig. 4. Application model.

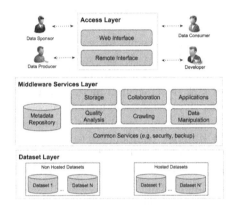

Fig. 5. DataCollector architecture.

achieve its goals, the DataCollector defines several loosely coupled modules that compose its logical architecture, as seen in Fig. 5 and described in the following.

The *Dataset Layer* is composed by the datasets managed by the DataCollector. The datasets are classified as non-hosted and hosted. While non-hosted datasets represent those ones that are directly accessed through their own producers, the hosted ones represent the datasets that are stored and accessed directly through the DataCollector. In the latter case, the data producer publishes its dataset using the storage service of DataCollector. It is indicated for those data producers that do not have technology infrastructure to publish its own datasets. Thus, providing a situation in which the producers don't need to worry about the software technology to open up their data.

The *Middleware Services Layer* provides services required to maintain datasets (*e.g.*, registry, update, analysis of datasets) as well as to manage actor profiles. This layer the following major services: *Storage, Crawling, Collaboration, Data Manipulation, Application, Quality Analysis, Applications* and other common services.

The *Storage Service* is responsible for storing datasets produced by the data producers and for managing their constantly growing. In order to provide storage at low cost, the DataCollector use a Peer-to-Peer (P2P) approach to harness the collective storage of individual computers connecting them in a collaborative fashion to provide mutual storage service. The potential of pooling commodity computing has been demonstrated by desktop grid computing systems that deliver sustained high-throughput computing required by several current applications [24]. Such approach for storage is desirable and made feasible since the capacity of modern hard disks has outgrown the needs of many users, leaving them with much idle storage space [25]. Moreover, a P2P storage service provides certain advantages over conventional centralized storage service. For example, compared to the conventional client-server model, P2P systems provide inherent scalability and availability of resources. They take advantage of redundancy of resources and build a coherent view of the system using decentralized, independent components.

The *Crawling Service* is responsible for collecting metadata from datasets and representing them according to the our metadata vocabulary (vf. Sect. 4). In general, metadata extraction is an automatic task. However, in cases such as lack of API access or lack of structured metadata, manual creation of metadata may be required. In these cases, the metadata creation is performed in a standardized manner in order to ensure the conformity and the metadata quality. It uses standardized *Wrapper* components to extract metadata from a given dataset. Given the heterogeneity of the data portals, it becomes necessary to have a specific wrapper for each portal. Therefore, subscribed sources need to provide a wrapper that implements communication and transformation functions from the original model to the DataCollector supported model. As there are prominent platforms for publishing open data (*e.g.* CKAN), a custom wrapper implementation may be reused among different datasets based on the same platform.

In order to maintain the freshness of the DataCollector catalog, the registered datasets should periodically be crawled to check for updates, including: inclusion of new datasets, removal of existing datasets and metadata updates. The Crawling Service can be configured to automatic periodic crawling sessions, in which datasets are periodically crawled to get fresh metadata. Furthermore, to deal with the dynamic behaviour of data producers, the Crawling Service also supports monitoring mechanisms to detect the unavailability of datasets.

The Crawlling Service is also responsible for processing the metadata extracted from the datasets. The processing tasks include metadata cleaning and loading. The concept of data cleaning was broadly used in data warehouse and data processing systems, which aims to clean up incomplete, erroneous and duplicated data [26]. In our context, the cleaning phase is responsible for fixing incorrect or missing metadata about datasets. For instance, the most frequent cleaning tasks are related to correct information about data format and the byte size of the dataset. Very often the extracted values of these metadata don't correspond to the expected value and, therefore, they need to be corrected. In this case, cleaning tasks are performed to ensure metadata values are correct with respect to the actual descriptions of the datasets, therefore promoting more accuracy. In the loading phase, all extracted metadata is stored in the *Meta-dataRepository.*

The *Quality Analysis Service* evaluates the registered datasets according different criteria. The criteria are evaluated using metrics that can be objective (*i.e.* can be calculated automatically) and subjective (*i.e.* when human intervention is required to evaluate the criteria). The evaluation criteria are performed at dataset instance level and includes the following criteria:

- Dataset size: refers to the total amount of data stored (*e.g.* 10 MB, 1 GB);
- Data format: concerns the data formats used to publish the data (*e.g.* JSON, XML);
- Data domain: describes the subject and features of interests (*e.g.* Education, Health, Finance, Mobility);
- Creation and update history: concerns the history of dataset changes over time;
- License information: refers to the type of data license adopted (*e.g.* Creative Commons, Open Data Commons Open Database License);
- Contactability information: concerns the information available to a data consumer as the data publisher's contact point (*e.g.* an email address or HTTP URL);
- Syntax and Structural Rules Adherence: refers to information about the dataset adherence to the syntax and structural rules;
- Field Naming Convention: refers to information about the quality and informativeness of the field names used to describe the dataset's content;
- Field Naming Convention: refers to information about the quality and informativeness of the field names used to describe the dataset's content;
- Schema Size: refers to number of fields of dataset;
- Sparseness: refers to proportion of empty fields in a dataset;

The aforementioned evaluation may be performed once, if the datasets are static, or repeated over time, if the datasets are dynamic and their content changes.

The *Collaboration Service* aims to facilitate the collaboration among open data actors, for instance enabling data consumers to evaluate datasets or fulfill missing metadata. The actors collaborate through the submission of structured feedback. Besides the classic way of giving feedback by adding a simple full text comment, structured feedback allows a more precise structured comment to a resource. This enables data consumers to directly fix an information about a dataset or to provide a patch to apply to correct datasets, for instance.

The *Data Manipulation Services* encompass the services necessary to archive and retrieve data from the hosted datasets. The *Applications Services* provides a model and environment for submitting open data solutions that are used to consume open datasets. Thus, the DataCollector also acts as a central repository for open data applications by easing the search of applications for data consumers. Finally, the *Common Services* encompass infrastructure services offered by the platform, such as security (in terms of user authenticity, confidentiality, and integrity) as well as dataset life cycle management. In particular, the dataset life cycle management operations are responsible for the registration and update of datasets managed by the platform. During the registration process, the DataCollector captures basic information from datasets, such as their Web address.

The *Web Interface* and the *Remote Interface* provide easy access to the open datasets as well as the DataCollector services for both humans and machines. The Web Interface provides visual abstractions over the DataCollector through Web dynamic pages that enables users to browse and discovery datasets. Users can use different dataset search mechanisms, such as keyword search mechanism as well as browsing by tags or related datasets. Moreover, it is also possible to select and visualize datasets with specific data formats or license, for example. The Web Interface aims to allow data visualization by different audiences with different needs and expectations. The Web Interface makes use of graphical components like maps and charts to enhance the experience for users.

The Remote Interface provides a HTTP-based API to enable metadata retrieval as well as to perform more advanced operations such as searching and filtering. Almost all DataCollector features are accessible via this API, which provides alternative access to a variety of clients, including other Java clients, Web crawlers and Web services. The default data exchange format is JSON. In its current version, lacks an authentication and access control system. Finally, the Remote Interface provides different remote front ends using several Web technologies such as Rest, XML-RPC and Web Services.

6   DataCollector Implementation

The implementation of the modules that compose the logical architecture of the DataCollector were the Java [8] and PHP[9] programming languages, Apache CxF[10] framework and MySQL[11] database management system. The Java programming language was used for implementing the middleware services and the remote interface. In its turns, the Web Interface was developed using PHP programming language. This combination of programming languages allows to leverage of the strengths of both language and also allow to deploy the DataCollector on several application servers, such as Apache and JBoss.

The *Metadata Repository* was implemented using MySQL[12], which is an open source relational database management system. The data access to the *Metadata Repository* is indirectly done through the Data Access Object (DAO) design pattern. DAOs are design patterns that provide access to data that is usually read or written from one or more databases [27]. The goal of this design pattern is to enhance software maintainability, providing an interface independent of the

---

[8] http://java.com.
[9] http://www.php.net.
[10] http://cxf.apache.org/.
[11] http://www.mysql.com.
[12] http://www.mysql.com.

underlying database technology. Therefore, a DAO pattern allows to replace the *Metadata Repository* solution without to recode all the Middleware services.

In general, the crawling process spends a lot of time waiting for responses to metadata retrieval requests. To reduce this inefficiency, the Crawling Service uses several *CrawlerWorkers* to crawl the registered datasets. In fact, *Crawler-Workers* are the ones that do the actual crawling work. The Crawling Service begins by retrieving the list of subscribed datasets and then it distributes crawling tasks among the different *CrawlerWorkers* instances. Datasets are crawled concurrently, which allows the *CrawlerWorkers* to achieve faster crawl speeds by not being limited by any particular datasets constraint, such as a very slow site.

Moreover, the *CrawlerWorkers* employ threads to fetch several datasets in parallel, avoiding to wait for a result to arrive before sending new requests. Making multiple requests at the same time is a well known approach to improve crawling performance [28]. Each dataset is enqueued in a shared queue to organize the metadata extraction process. After all available datasets are enqueued, the threads are used to fetch dataset metadata by removing a extraction task from the front of the queue. When the queue is empty, the *CrawlerWorker* has finished its work and updates the *MetadataRepository* with the processed metadata.

Quality Analysis Service uses series of *Counters* to gather metrics/statistics which can later be aggregated to produce statistics reports about different facets, such as number of datasets per given data format or total amount of data that covers education domain. Counters are incremented when certain internal condition is valid. In order to evaluate this condition, counters instances receives as input a dataset metadata. The behavior of Counter objects is defined by the following methods:

- *evaluateAndCount*: Increment a counter when a certain condition was evaluated to true;
- *evaluate*: Defines a function to evaluate if the counter need to be incremented;
- *count*: Defines how the counter must be incremented.

There are some predefined Counters and Custom counters can also be defined. The former ones are responsible to gather the analysis statistics presented in Subsect. 5. When all datasets are analysed, these counters are consolidated to produce a holistic view for the datasets and data producers.

Quality Analysis Service executes analysis process as presented in the Fig. 6. At first, it initialize all counter instances and then retrieves a list of all registered datasets. Finally, all of the counters evaluate each data set according their own conditions.

Users can access the main functionalities offered by the *DataCollector* through the Web interface provided by specific Web Pages, which were implemented with PHP open source technologies. In order to support Remote Interfaces, we have adopted the Apache CxF framework, a Web service stack from the Apache Software Foundation. Apache CxF allows a clean separation from remote front-ends to application implementation. Furthermore, both Web and

```
AnalysisAlgorithm :
    couters = initializeCounters();
    dataSourceList = retrieveDataSourceList();
    FOR EACH DataSource source IN dataSourceList DO
        datasetList = retrieveDatasetList(source);
        FOR EACH Dataset dataset IN datasetList DO
            FOR EACH Counter counter IN counters DO
                conter.evaluateAndCount(dataset);
            END
        END
    END
    RETURN counters;
```

Fig. 6. Analisys pseudocode.

Remote interfaces interact with the services provided by the *Metadata Layer* through a design pattern, called Facade, that provides a unified interface to a set of interfaces in a subsystem. The Facade module encapsulates the complexity of underlying modules within a single interface, therefore promoting loose coupling to the system.

Web Interface and Remote Interface have mechanisms to facilitate datasets discovery through faceted search using multiple criteria, including the name of the dataset, data domain, format and license. When the user chooses a dataset of interest, is possible to view the metadata available on the DataCollector about that dataset. In addition, when attempting to download the dataset, it is redirected automatically to the origin website. The Remote Interface use JSON as data exchange format and it employs a pagination-based iterator to deal with the large amount of data. Each request has four possible outputs: *help*, to describe the access possibilities; *next*, indicating the next page with 15 new records; *success*, indicating if the query was successful or not; and *result*, containing one *array* with all datasets found and are described in the our metadata vocabulary (vf. Sect. 4).

7   Evaluation

In order to validate the DataCollector and demonstrate its potential in a real-world scenario, we developed a Web portal, as a proof-of-concept, that concentrates datasets collected from 14 Brazilian open data portals. More details about this portal can be found at the following URL address: http://www.dadosabertosbrasil.com.br. This evaluation focus on the crawling, quality analysis and common services. The rest of the services will be evaluated in future studies.

We focus on Brazilian open data portals promoted by federal, state and municipal governments. The selection of open data portals was performed by an exploratory research on official portals of Brazilian states and its respective bigger cities. As a result, were collected data from the following open data portals:

– Brazilian Federal Government[13];

---

[13] http://dados.gov.br/.

- States: Alagoas[14], Federal District[15], Minas Gerais[16], Pernambuco[17], Rio Grande do Sul[18], and So Paulo[19];
- Capital: Curitiba[20], Fortaleza[21], Porto Alegre[22], Recife[23], Rio de Janeiro[24], and So Paulo[25].

7.1 DataCollector Quantitative Evaluation

In this scenario, the DataCollector enabled a unified view of several Brazilian open data portals and allowed the creation of a single point to access the datasets provided by them. Data consumers profit from this unified view because it becomes easier to search and select datasets distributed in multiple data portals. In its turns, data producers are able to monitor how datasets are being consumed and what problems are being notified about their datasets. In our initial evaluation, the application performance was not considered, but, in general, the response time was satisfactory. The initial crawling process spent few hours in a domestic computer. The entire analysis process take less than 1 min, and for most of datasets, it takes less than 3 seconds to show the metadata and charts. However, customized dataset search may take longer. Improving the performance through the use of materialized views and is one of our future works.

As most of the Brazilian data portals employs CKAN as platform to publish open data, a wrapper to extract metadata from CKAN was developed. This wrapper performs the following tasks: (i) obtains dataset metadata through the REST protocol; (ii) transforms JSON original data to the DataCollector metadata model. Any portal CKAN compliant can be easily integrated to the DataCollector by using the same wrapper.

After the dataset registration and the metadata extraction and transformation, it was possible to perform dataset faceted search and several analysis about the datasets available on the brazilian open data portals. Table 1 summarizes the analysis results.

---

[14] http://dados.al.gov.br/.
[15] http://www.dadosabertos.df.gov.br/.
[16] http://www.transparencia.dadosabertos.mg.gov.br.
[17] http://www.dadosabertos.pe.gov.br/.
[18] http://dados.rs.gov.br/.
[19] http://www.governoaberto.sp.gov.br/view/consulta.php.
[20] http://www.curitiba.pr.gov.br/conteudo/dados-abertos-consulta/1498.
[21] http://dados.fortaleza.ce.gov.br/catalogo/.
[22] http://datapoa.com.br/.
[23] http://dados.recife.pe.gov.br/.
[24] http://data.rio.rj.gov.br/.
[25] http://www.prefeitura.sp.gov.br/cidade/secretarias/desenvolvimento_urbano/dados_abertos/.

7.2   Dataset Characteristics

This section provides a general analysis covering several dataset characteristics, such as the number of instances, total amount of stored data, data formats, data domain, creation date and update history.

Number and Volume of Datasets. Referring to the number of datasets, we found out that the quantity is very diverse, ranging from 33 (Curitiba) to 16,623 (Rio de Janeiro City) datasets. While only 3 Portals provide more than 1 thousand datasets, half of the portals is very small and contains only a subset of government data. For a better understanding, Fig. 7(a) presents the proportion of number of datasets per portals.

Table 1. Dataset general analysis.

Data source name	Dataset count	Total dataset size	Dataset proportion with multiple distributions
Alagoas	1,167	12.8 MB	3.34%
Curitiba	33	239.5 MB	0.00%
Federal district	47	1.2 GB	0.00%
Fortaleza	642	234.9 MB	0.62%
Minas Gerais	40	230.5 MB	20.00%
Pernambuco	66	1.3 GB	100.00%
Porto Alegre	149	1.1 GB	0.67%
Recife	384	1.1 GB	14.84%
Rio de Janeiro (Cap.)	16,623	1.6 GB	0.07%
Rio Grande do Sul	162	1.4 GB	13.58%
So Paulo (Cap.)	37	2.0 GB	0.00%
So Paulo(Sta.)	119	725.9 MB	2.52%
Federal government	4,051	176.9 GB	35.74%

We also analyzed the size of the datasets, which ranges from some bytes to gigabytes of data. As expected, the biggest portal is the Federal Government portal containing 176.9 GB of data. In contrast, Alagoas provides only 12.8 MB of data, even though it has more than 1 thousand datasets. Moreover, the total size of some portals is heavily affected by small portion of files. The majority of datasets provided by So Paulo City contains less than 10 MB of data, whereas only one dataset has almost 1.5 GB. For a better understanding, Fig. 7(b) presents the distribution of datasets size. As we may observe, most of dthem are small - more than 80% of datasets have less than 10 MB. Only 48 datasets (0.18%) have more than 100 MB.

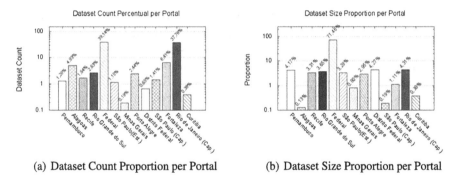

(a) Dataset Count Proportion per Portal   (b) Dataset Size Proportion per Portal

Fig. 7. Number and size of datasets per portal.

Table 2. Data format proportions.

Formats	Count proportion	Size proportion
csv	67.15%	21.84%
pdf	8.18%	0.11%
html	4.79%	0.01%
json	3.82%	0.07%
xml	3.52%	73.24%
shp	2.81%	1.71%
geojson	2.64%	2.14%
kml	2.58%	0.02%
txt	1.49%	0.10%
Other formats	2.08%	0.76%

Dataset Format. Numerous formats are being used, ranging from document and multimedia files, such as PDF and PNG, to structured types, such as XML and CSV. At least 47 different data formats were found during the analysis. Table 2 presents an overall proportion of the most representative data formats considering the number of occurrences and dataset size. Despite that, there is no standard data format and the large majority of datasets are distributed with structured formats (84.25%). Other datasets are published as documents (14.62%), and others formats (1.13%). Relatively fewer datasets are provided in more than one format. Pernambuco and Federal Government have a higher proportion of multiple dataset distributions (100% and 33.74%). Other portals like Minas Gerais, Rio Grande do Sul, and Recife provide, respectively, 20%, 14.84% and 13.58% of all your data in more than one format. In contrast, the remainder portals provide the majority of its datasets in only one data format.

Dataset Domain. Several topics and domains were identified, such as Education, Health, Finance and Mobility. To better understand the dataset domain landscape, Fig. 8 presents a word cloud containing the most frequent keywords. The most required topics are related to Geosciences, Statistics analysis, and Finance. However, this distribution is not the same for all portals. While in Porto Alegre and Recife Mobility is the dominant domain; in Pernambuco and Rio Grande do Sul, the most frequent domains are Employment and Education, respectively. Moreover, there is a lack of standardized terms to classify dataset domains. As a consequence, several different terms are used to represent the same concept, such as transportation and transit (Federal Government), mobility (Recife) and transit (Rio Grande do Sul).

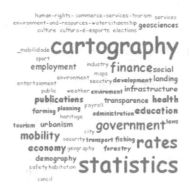

Fig. 8. Dataset domain word cloud.

Dataset Creation and Update History. The lifetime of the data portals was also analysed. As a result of this, we identified two main phases during the lifetime of Brazilian open data portals. First, the creation phase, when the data portal is created and an initial load with several datasets is performed. Second, the update phase, when new datasets are created or existing datasets are updated. In our analysis, we observe in the most cases instead of adding new information in already published dataset, the portals publish a new dataset with the new content.

7.3   Schema Analysis

Data schema is a broad term that determines how to organize data using syntactic rules and encoding mechanisms. The structure of data makes it easier to understand and permeates different aspects of data management. Although most of the datasets are published in (semi) structured formats, there are inherent issues that need to be tackled, such as lack of schema information, syntax or encoding errors, duplicated records and empty records. These issues can make difficult to process a dataset. In this section, we show our evaluation about dataset schemata considering the following criteria: Syntax and Structural Rules Adherence, Field Naming Convention, Schemata Size and Data Sparseness.

We focused on CSV data because it is the most used data format in Brazil. It is important to note that Curitiba does not provide any file in CSV format, whereas Fortaleza provides a large amount of datasets registered as simple TXT, but they are actually structured as CSV data format.

Syntax and Structural Rules Adherence. Despite CSV is commonly used as file format for exporting and importing data, there is no official standard for the CSV. In an attempt to standardize CSV files, W3C released the recommendation "Model for Tabular Data and Metadata on the Web" [29], which proposes an abstract model for tabular data and a non-normative guidance on how to parse CSV files. However, the most commonly accepted CSV standard is RFC 4180[26]. Based on this standard, we evaluated the presence of the header, the inconsistency in the number of fields, duplication of records and encoding problems. The results of our evaluation are summarized in Table 3.

An interesting result is that the majority of the portals provide more than 90% of their CSV datasets with the header. Although the use of header is optional, it contains names corresponding to the fields in the file, which can make easier to humans to understand the meaning of the data. Exceptions to this pattern are Fortaleza, So Paulo city, and Federal Government, which has the largest amount of datasets without a header. However, Federal Government has the largest set of metadata documentation describing its datasets and their schemata.

Table 3. CSV files analysis.

Portals	CSV files count			Files Proportions		
	Raw files	Compacted files	Presence of header	Inconsistent number of fields	Duplicated tuples	Quotation encoding error
Alagoas	3	0	100.00%	66.67%	0.00%	0.00%
Curitiba	23	0	95.65%	8.70%	43.48%	4.35%
Federal district	46	0	100.00%	8.70%	50.00%	8.70%
Fortaleza	378	0	8.73%	10.32%	0.53%	0.26%
Minas Gerais	22	0	100.00%	22.73%	18.18%	4.55%
Pernambuco	29	0	100.00%	0.00%	3.45%	0.00%
Porto Alegre	71	8	100.00%	0.00%	7.04%	1.41%
Recife	182	0	100.00%	1.10%	6.04%	0.00%
Rio de Janeiro (City)	15617	0	99.99%	1.69%	0.31%	0.10%
Rio Grande do Sul	93	33	100.00%	20.43%	16.13%	2.15%
So Paulo (City)	107	107	87.85%	45.79%	33.64%	0.00%
So Paulo(State)	204	196	100.00%	1.47%	39.22%	3.43%
Federal government	7205	6614	61.86%	14.30%	11.99%	2.07%

---

[26] http://www.rfc-base.org/rfc-4180.html.

Although there is a rule that states that a CSV file should contain the same number of fields for all the records, the evaluated portals do not properly meet this rule. Almost half of the portals provides datasets with variable (*i.e.* inconsistent) number of fields. The exceptions are So Paulo city and Pernambuco, which have no inconsistent number of fields in their files. However, more than half of datasets provided by Rio Grande do Sul (67.74%) has at least one line with inconsistent number of field.

With regard to duplicated records, half of the portals has fewer datasets with duplicated lines, while the other half presents more than 15% of their datasets presenting any duplication. Finally, fields that contain a special character (*e.g.* comma, breaking line code, or double quote), must be "escaped" by enclosing them in double quotes. Most of portals provide very small portion of datasets with quotation error.

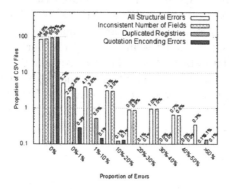

Fig. 9. Distribution of proportion of structural errors per dataset.

It is important to observe that this former analysis does not represent the amount of occurrences within the datasets. The Fig. 9 presents the proportion of structural errors in the CSV files for all portals. Interestingly, the great majority of files have no incidence of errors; for example, 84.8% of them have no error. In particular, at least 95.4% and 99.3% have no duplicated record or quotation error, respectively. Regarding an inconsistent number of fields, 2.5% of files have errors in between 10% and 50% of their registries. However, Federal District and So Paulo city have respectively almost 15% of their CSV files with different numbers of fields in between 10% and 75% of the existing registries.

Schemata Size. Another important analysis is the size of the dataset schemata (*i.e.* number of fields). This information allows us to have an initial idea of the size of the datasets with respect to the number of defined fields.

Figure 10(a) shows a distribution of the number of fields examined with respect to each portal. We can see that 5 of 13 portals have fewer datasets containing more than 150 fields. 94% of the datasets from the Rio de Janeiro portal have schemata with less than 20 fields. The Federal Government portal has a variation between 10 and 50 fields per schema, keeping the average around 20. The other portals provide the majority of their datasets containing from 10 to 20 fields. The exceptions, such as So Paulo city, Federal Government, Fortaleza and Rio de Janeiro portals, provide some CSV datasets with a wide number of fields, which can exceed 200 fields.

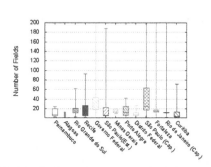

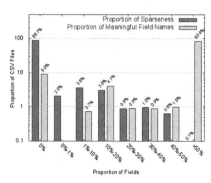

(a) Distribution of Number of Fields per Dataset by Portal

(b) Distribution of Proportion of Sparseness and Meaningful Field Names

Fig. 10. Distribution of sparseness and meaningful field names.

Field Naming Convention. Naming conventions for dataset schema attributes is a well-known good practice for the Database community [30]. Good names are particularly important for data consumers who need to find the objects they are looking for. Moreover, self-explanatory names are also helpful while integrating multiple datasets [31]. However, despite the recognized importance, the topic of giving good names to elements of a dataset is often heavily underestimated.

We evaluated the quality of dataset naming convention by checking the name of the CSV fields against a word list in a Portuguese dictionary[27]. For each CSV file, we measured the proportion of meaningful field names. Concatenated names, such as `public_education` or `criminal-statistics`, were first tokenized and then each token with more than three characters was checked in the word list dictionary.

Figure 10(b) presents the distribution of meaningful field names for all datasets. Interestingly, for most of the datasets (83.4%), at least 50% of their field names were presented in the dictionary. Only 9.7% of datasets have less than 10% of meaningful field names. Rio de Janeiro, Alagoas, and Federal Government are the ones with the highest amount of datasets with meaningful field names. However, the significant number of datasets provided by them influences the overall analysis, creating a biased result.

---

[27] http://voc.cplp.org/.

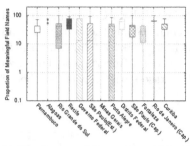 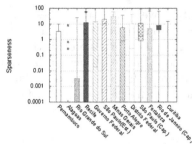

(a) Distribution of Proportion of Meaningful Field Names per Dataset by Portal

(b) Distribution of Proportion of Sparseness per Dataset by Portal

Fig. 11. Distribution of sparseness and meaningful field names.

Figure 11(a) presents the proportion of meaningful field names for each dataset. For instance, Minas Gerais, So Paulo state, and Alagoas have a low proportion of meaningful names, *i.e.* these portals provides a significant portion of datasets with less than 10% of their fields using meaningful names. It is important to highlight that these analysis represent a lower bound for good quality names, since some field names have words concatenated (*e.g.*, `citylocation` and `creationdate`) or have well-known acronyms (*e.g.* `lat` and `log` for geographic coordinates).

Data Sparseness. A sparse dataset typically has several empty or null value records. According to Barbosa *et al.* [3], null values represent missing data and a high proportion of nulls might indicate data quality problems. Another common sense perspective about sparse datasets is that it arises merely as the result of poor schema design. In order to evaluate the sparseness of datasets, we computed the number of null values and other empty common values such as "null", "unspecified", "unknown", or "N/A." for each one of the CSV files. Figure 10(b) summarizes our findings and presents the proportion of null values in overall datasets.

The great majority of CSV datasets (94.1%) have no empty or null value records. Among sparse datasets, 2.7% of them have sparseness between 0 and 0.1 (*i.e.* at most 10% of the values are null) and 2.1% have sparseness between 0.1 and 0.2. Nevertheless, there are datasets (0.4%) that have more than 40% of their values null. However, the sparseness distribution is not the same for all portals. To illustrate this, we show in Fig. 11(b) the dataset sparseness distribution per portals. Federal Government, Federal District, So Paulo city, and Rio de Janeiro have more than 10% of their CSV datasets with at least 10% of null values. For instance, Rio de Janeiro has 54 datasets with at least 50% of null values.

8   Conclusion and Future Works

The decentralized production of data and the absence of metadata hinder the Open Data initiatives. In this context, where Open Data comes from many sources and are created in an autonomous way, it becomes necessary to have an easy way to find and to combine these distributed data. In order to deal with some of the open issues and challenges identified during our research, we are developing the DataCollector platform, presented in this article, which aims to allow the cataloging and discovery of datasets available in open data portals, providing a single point of access for open datasets published in heterogeneous portals.

The presented platform enables automatic extraction of detailed metadata about the datasets and stores them in accordance with the standard vocabulary for data modeling catalogs. It also provides a set of procedures and mechanisms that allows dataset search using either Web graphic interfaces, as well as remote access mechanisms, such as Web Services, enabling the building of applications for recovery and automatic data processing.

A first evaluation was conducted by cataloging 14 Brazilian open data portals, covering a total of 29,540 datasets. Preliminary results indicate the DataCollector offers a friendly interface and a robust solution for cataloging and dataset access. Based on the services offered by the DataCollector, we could create a single point access to distributed Brazilian open government datasets, helping the identification of relationships between datasets as well as the dataset search. We could perform several analysis on these datasets and we found out several interesting information about the brazilian open data scenario.

The DataCollector is still under development and new features may be incorporated. As future works, we intend to improve the analysis support offered by the DataCollector with the implementation of a support decision module that allows the creation of OLAP (*Online Analytical Processing*) reports and offers *dashboard* panels for data visualization and data analysis. We also plan to improve the analysis with the inclusion of analysis based on the datasets schemas as well as on the data itself in order to evaluate aspects like data sparseness.

Acknowledgement. This work was partially supported by the Brazilian funding agency FACEPE (Fundação de Amparo à Ciência e Tecnologia do Estado de Pernambuco) under grant APQ-1088-1.03/15. The authors are indebted to the Brazilian Federal Agency for Support and Evaluation of Graduate Education (CAPES) and National Committee of Technological and Scientific Development (CNPq), for the scholarship of Marcelo Iury and Lairson Emanoel.

References

1. Vaz, J.C., Ribeiro, M.M., Matheus, R.: Dados governamentais abertos e seus impactos sobre os conceitos e práticas de transparência no Brasil. Cadernos PPG-AU/UFBA 9 (2011)

2. Goldstein, B., Dyson, L., Nemani, A.: Beyond Transparency: Open Data and the Future of Civic Innovation. Code for America Press (2013). http://beyondtransparency.org/pdf/BeyondTransparency.pdf
3. Barbosa, L., Pham, K., Silva, C., Vieira, M.R., Freire, J.: Structured open urban data: understanding the landscape. Big Data **2**, 144–154 (2014)
4. Gama, K., Lóscio, B.F.: Towards ecosystems based on open data as a service. In: ICEIS (2), pp. 659–664 (2014)
5. Heimstädt, M., Saunderson, F., Heath, T.: Conceptualizing open data ecosystems: a timeline analysis of open data development in the UK. In: Conference for E-Democracy and Open Governement, p. 245 (2014)
6. Shekhar, Satyarupa, M.C., Srimarga, I.: Creating an eco-system for open subnational governments: Lessons from a developing country perspective. In: Open Data Research Symposium (2015)
7. Maali, F., Erickson, J., Archer, P.: Data catalog vocabulary (DCAT). W3C recommendation, The World Wide Web Consortium (2014)
8. Ribeiro, D.C., Vo, H.T., Freire, J., Silva, C.T.: An urban data profiler. In: Proceedings of the 24th International Conference on World Wide Web Companion, International World Wide Web Conferences Steering Committee, pp. 1389–1394 (2015)
9. The OK Foundation: Datahub.io (2015)
10. Miranda, C.: Abra com simplicidade desmistificando os dados abertos (2015)
11. The OK Foundation: Publicdata.eu (2015)
12. Project C: Opendatamonitor.eu (2015)
13. van den Broek, T., Rijken, M., van Oort, S.: Towards open development data. Open for Change. Retrieved February 25 2013(2012)
14. Kalampokis, E., Tambouris, E., Tarabanis, K.: A classification scheme for open government data: towards linking decentralised data. Int. J. Web Eng. Technol. **6**, 266–285 (2011)
15. Ubaldi, B.: Open government data: towards empirical analysis of open government data initiatives. Technical report, OECD Publishing (2013)
16. Reiche, K.J., Höfig, E., Schieferdecker, I.: Assessment and visualization of metadata quality for open government data. In: Conference for E-Democracy and Open Governement, p. 335 (2014)
17. Sayogo, D.S., Pardo, T., Cook, M., et al.: A framework for benchmarking open government data efforts. In: 47th Hawaii International Conference on System Sciences (HICSS), pp. 1896–1905. IEEE (2014)
18. Kucera, J., Chlapek, D.: Benefits and risks of open government data. J. Syst. Integr. **5**, 30–41 (2014)
19. Umbrich, J., Neumaier, S., Polleres, A.: Towards assessing the quality evolution of open data portals. In: ODQ2015: Open Data Quality: from Theory to Practice Workshop, Munich, Germany (2015)
20. Sanderson, R., Ciccarese, P., Young, B.: Web annotation data model. W3C recommendation, The World Wide Web Consortium (2015)
21. Amatriain, X., Pujol, J.M., Oliver, N.: I Like It.. I Like It Not: evaluating user ratings noise in recommender systems. In: Houben, G.-J., McCalla, G., Pianesi, F., Zancanaro, M. (eds.) UMAP 2009. LNCS, vol. 5535, pp. 247–258. Springer, Heidelberg (2009). doi:10.1007/978-3-642-02247-0_24
22. Hotho, A., Jäschke, R., Schmitz, C., Stumme, G.: Information retrieval in folksonomies: search and ranking. In: Sure, Y., Domingue, J. (eds.) ESWC 2006. LNCS, vol. 4011, pp. 411–426. Springer, Heidelberg (2006). doi:10.1007/11762256_31

23. Oliveira, L.E.R.A., Lóscio, B.F.: Uma abordagem para captura de informações sobre aplicações que fazem uso de dados abertos. Revista Brasileira de Administração Científica **5**, 127–140 (2014)
24. Cirne, W., Brasileiro, F., Andrade, N., Costa, L.B., Andrade, A., Novaes, R., Mowbray, M.: Labs of the world, unite!!!. J. Grid Comput. **4**, 225–246 (2006)
25. Douceur, J.R., Bolosky, W.J.: A large-scale study of file-system contents. ACM SIGMETRICS Perform. Eval. Rev. **27**, 59–70 (1999)
26. Simon, A.: Data Warehouse Data Mining and OLAP. Wiley, Hoboken (1997)
27. Johnson, R.: Expert one-on-one J2EE design and development. Wiley, Hoboken (2004)
28. Boldi, P., Codenotti, B., Santini, M., Vigna, S.: UbiCrawler: a scalable fully distributed web crawler. Softw. Pract. Exp. **34**, 711–726 (2004)
29. Tennison, J., Kellogg, G.: Model for tabular data and metadata on the web. W3C recommendation, World Wide Web Consortium (W3C) (2015). https://www.w3.org/TR/tabular-data-model/
30. Coronel, C., Morris, S., Rob, P.: Database systems: design, implementation, and management. Cengage Learn. **9**, 15–17 (2009). http://bit.sparcs.org/~dinggul/tools/1423902017.pdf
31. Chua, C.E.H., Chiang, R.H., Lim, E.P.: Instance-based attribute identification in database integration. VLDB J. Int. J. Very Large Data Bases **12**, 228–243 (2003)

Ambient Assisted Living Systems: A Model for Reasoning Under Uncertainty

Alencar Machado[1,2(✉)], Vinicius Maran[1,3], Iara Augustin[2],
João Carlos Lima[2], Leandro Krug Wives[3],
and José Palazzo Moreira de Oliveira[3]

[1] Colégio Politécnico, Universidade Federal de Santa Maria, Santa Maria, Brazil
alencar.machado@ufsm.br, maran@inf.ufsm.br
[2] PPGI, Universidade Federal de Santa Maria, Santa Maria, Brazil
{august, caio}@inf.ufsm.br
[3] Instituto de Informática, Universidade Federal do Rio Grande do Sul,
Porto Alegre, Brazil
{wives, palazzo}@inf.ufrgs.br

Abstract. Ambient Assisted Living are equipped with ubiquitous technologies, and use sensors as their main element for environmental data collection, providing systems with updated information. Currently, there is a convergence combining systems for smart environments and uncertainty reasoning. Considering that the world population is aging, health-support issues are in evidence, and many dangerous situations concerning users in their living environment may arise. However, reasoning to detect situations taking into account uncertainty presents a great challenge. This paper describes a contextual model based on semantic web technologies that deals with uncertainty. This model may be used to detect unwanted situations with a certain grade of contextual uncertainty. The model was evaluated in scenario exhibiting the reasoning over uncertain data to predict unwanted or perhaps dangerous situations.

Keywords: Semantic web · Uncertainty · Smart environments · Probabilistic ontologies

1 Introduction

Homes are becoming intelligent environments able to assist people who live in it. These systems are planned to act according to the user profile, and with the complex physical environment, where objects are added, updated or moved. Moreover, the user profile also varies over time. For instance, users may suffer from different diseases during their lives, and these can affect the interaction with the objects of their residence. Also, cognitive problems, such as forgetfulness, can sometimes put the user into an unwanted or perhaps dangerous situation; for instance, forgetting the stove on after preparing a meal.

Systems for Ambient Assisted Living (AAL) need to interpret the context in which the user lives to be able to act in advance to some situation. Using ontologies to represent the contextual model is the most complete and expressive way to support

S. Hammoudi et al. (Eds.): ICEIS 2016, LNBIP 291, pp. 338–363, 2017.
DOI: 10.1007/978-3-319-62386-3_16

reasoning about the user context for intelligent systems [1, 2]. The ontologies have some constructors that support reasoning over the domain model. Some studies show contextual models for different domains [3, 4]. These efforts aim to model the user's context and provide support for systems making decisions about situations of interest. Some works try to support systems in reasoning about uncertainty [5–7]. These works present contextual models using ontologies that are implemented in Ontology Web Language – Description Logic (OWL-DL).

The main limitation for reasoning about uncertainty in OWL-DL is the conceptual foundation of DL, a subset of First Order Logic (FOL). FOL defines sentences that are always true logical statements about the domain to which they are representing [8, 9]. However, for systems that look for detection of situations and make decisions in real environments where data may have an error rate, low but present, it becomes imperative to support the detection of situations and provide decision-making on uncertain data. Also, the information obtained from sensors must be interpreted, and this interpretation is generally surrounded by uncertainty.

To manage these challenges, some research efforts try to manipulate information modelled in ontologies and submit this information to prediction algorithms using fuzzy logic, neural networks, or Bayesian networks [5]. These strategies have purely statistical results as the prediction is made without semantic information contained in the ontological representation. Consequently, it is necessary that the ontological contextual model represent the uncertainty about the context. Furthermore, there is a need to have native support for reasoning about uncertainty within the context model. This approach gives more possibilities to the detection of situations and allows decision making with incomplete information.

This paper presents a context model used for reasoning over uncertainty in smart environments. More specifically, we employed a Multi-Entity Bayesian Network (MEBN) for the developing of a semantic model to support the prediction of unwanted situations in smart environments. The model is evaluated through empirical experiments using a case study where an unwanted situation is simulated. In the case study described in this paper, we present the context supporting reasoning with uncertainty. It is shown as the model supports the automatic generation of Bayesian Networks in a given situation depending on the available evidence within the ontology.

This paper is organized as follows. Section 2 discusses the background and related work. Section 3 presents the model for developing the context of AAL with reasoning with uncertainty in smart environments. Section 4 describes the developed case study. Finally, Sect. 5 discusses our conclusions and future work.

2 Background and Related Work

User interaction with devices in a real-world environment is uncertain by nature. This communication is influenced by several factors, such as the knowledge that users have about using a device, their cognitive ability, and their humor, among others.

There are big challenges for the design of AAL systems. Currently, the context-aware field is consolidating systems for smart environments. Context can be understood as *"the environment in which the system operates"* [10]. Dey and Abowd

[11] characterize *context* as the situation of an entity in an environment. The concept of *situation* is utilized to characterize the state of the user environment.

Ye et al. [10] define *situation* as the abstraction of the events occurring in the real world that are derived from the context and hypotheses about how the observed context relates to factors of interest. Systems that manipulate the context detecting situations of interest through events generated by user's interaction must handle uncertainty to assist correctly users in their living environment.

2.1 Ambient Assisted Living

Ambient Assisted Living (ALL) has a very singular focus: users with physical or cognitive impairments. In particular, elderly people may suffer from various physical and cognitive disabilities developed over the years. The aging affects the human senses; the information processing capacity reduces the speed and precision movements, etc. As a result, older people lose their ability to perform effortlessly the daily activities. Thus, using household appliances, instead of facilitating the lives of citizens, can become a burden that increases the limitations of the elderly [12].

Therefore, AAL is the area of research in computing which is intended to provide environments that assist people who live in them, being sensitive to them and able to anticipate their needs and behaviors, providing complex networks of heterogeneous smart devices.

AAL can be defined as a sensitive and adaptable electronic environment that responds to people's actions to meet their needs, i.e., an intelligent system, customizable, aware of the context, adaptive and anticipatory user needs. These concepts include the whole environment, taking into account each object, associating their interaction with humans. Thus, it is the convergence of areas such as ubiquitous computing, sensor networks and artificial intelligence [12].

Ubiquitous computing, considers that the computing environment should not impose restrictions on the user to use it. It assumes that there must be an invisible and transparent computing environment, with intuitive interactions between users and computing facilitating its use by the end user. With the availability of wireless sensor networks infrastructure and long distance networks, various systems and prototypes have been developed to demonstrate how this paradigm can benefit specific applications, such as health and emergencies in smart hospitals, smart homes, entertainment and others.

In this work the focus is centered on smart homes, one of the subdomains of Ambient Intelligence that stands out [13]. The concept of smart home is linked to home automation, as well as used to define environments to assist people with cognitive problems, seeking to provide independent living. These houses are focused on the improvement of the quality of life, increasing user's independence levels, reducing the need for hospitalization by increasing the time people can live in their homes. Smart homes focused on personal assistance are linked to the AAL area. AAL uses environmental infrastructure and Intelligent Environments as essential tools to provide integrated solutions to support independent living of people in different contexts [12].

AAL covers interoperability concepts, products, and services that combine information and communication technologies to provide increased quality of life for the ordinary citizen. Among technologies that allow AAL, some take into account the modeling of sensors, services, recognition of activities and the detection of situations. [14] describe that systems to smart home environments directed to AAL are intelligent technologies able to follow citizens in their daily activities, monitoring risks to health or safety, issuing alerts to family or health care providers when specific situations occur.

Paganelli and Giulia [15] define smart homes as micro-ecosystems that are usually within the following features:

- Environments containing multiple physical types of equipment and furniture parts, electrical appliances, electronics and rooms providing living spaces;
- People who carry out various activities within the environment;
- Sensor devices, home electronics, and actuators that identify and act on the environment to provide adaptation to the behavior of the inhabitants;
- Assisted features that include health professionals, family members, middleware services and applications responding to events and situations.

In this article, the developed approach looks for supporting systems for assisted living environments linked to smart homes, and for this, the approach needs to be adapted to the characteristics described above. These features include home automation for personal assistance and directed to the needs (situations) involving the user and can act in advance because of the situations identified in their living environment. For computer systems to recognize the environment where they interact, sensitivity to user context becomes a critical issue.

2.2 Context Awareness

There is growing interest in the use of context-awareness and techniques for developing applications that are flexible, adaptable and able to act automatically on behalf of the user. According to [11], context is any information that can be used to characterize the situation of an entity. Entity is a person, a place or an object relevant to the interaction between the user and the application, including the user himself and the application. Thus, knowing the facts surrounding the user in an environment makes applications to interact and act more fruitfully on behalf of this user. Therefore, applications may be aware (sensitive) to the context, adapting automatically to changes in the environment and the current needs of users, without requiring their attention. These applications should explore environmental features such as user location, closeness to users, and time of day, among others.

For applications able to infer the environment and, consequently, identify the situation where the user is inserted, it becomes necessary to model the environment context, seeking to identify *things* existing in the environment and influencing the generation of information for applications.

2.2.1 Context Modeling

According to Henricksen and Induslka [16], context modeling is an essential element in building intelligent systems, wherein the degree of refinement and sensitivity of model determines the perception of the environment by the application. One of the main reasons why it becomes necessary to generate models for systems in smart environments is the fact that these environments are highly complex. Taking into account this prerogative and considering that the human capacity (intelligence) has a rational limit generating models to increase abstraction helps in understanding these environments. Therefore, modeling the context to identify things (physical or abstract objects) that exist in the environment is a necessary task for the development of context-aware systems.

Finally, Strang and Linnhoff-Popien [1] and Moore et al. [17] show that context-aware systems have high demands regarding distributed composition, partial validation, richness and quality of information, completeness and ambiguity, formalism and applicability level for existing environments. They compared models for the representation of context and concluded that ontology-based modeling reached the highest satisfaction among the listed requirements. So the next section discusses how to model context semantically.

2.2.2 Context Semantic Modeling

Due to the limited capacity of human reasoning of the and considering the complexity of the world, humans seek artifices to understand and communicate, so started using symbols to express themselves. People are prone to seek symbolic representation regarding a domain to help their understanding as well as to facilitate their communication.

Guarino [18] highlights that only a shared conceptualization (resulting of human communication) superimposed on the conceptual models, can decrease the distance between the existing human conceptualization and machines. It can be able to provide knowledge to generate context-aware systems and smart machines.

In Computing, ontologies are used to provide meta-knowledge to systems, seeking to make computer systems smarter. Ontologies provide a greater understanding of the domain in which systems must interact, sometimes giving reasoning ability to them. In this sense, according to Gruber [19], ontology is an explicit specification of a conceptualization. Brost [20] derived this definition describing ontologies as a *formal and explicit specification of a shared conceptualization*.

Poli and Obrst [21] propose that ontologies can be classified into lightweight and heavyweight. Lightweight ontologies use formal hierarchies and properties relationships. On the other hand, heavyweight ontologies, besides the characteristics of lightweight ontologies, also represent axioms and rules, using a knowledge representation language, and can be interpreted semantically by machines.

In this paper, lightweight ontology is built for AAL, but some rules and axioms were added. We define the ontology as lightweight because the model can have a lack of expression in some of its parts, especially those regarding the depth of the concepts. The semantic context modeling uses ontologies for representation and logical reasoning. According to Bettini et al. [2], it is used for multiple purposes: (i) to describe a complex entity context that cannot be represented by simple languages; (ii) to provide a more formal semantics for the context entities, creating the possibility of becoming distributed and integrated in the context of different sources; (iii) to evaluate the reasoning through tools that verify consistency and the set of relationships described in a domain.

Some developers focus on specific modeling properties and internal structures of concepts in individual domains, such as location, people, and computational entities, ignoring the common semantics relation that is the basis for their meaning. Thus, the task of understanding the meaning of the semantic relationships between entities of the context is at the application level, as well as the tasks for the detection of the inconsistency of context [10].

The formalization of an ontology-based context modeling is typically linked to the Ontology Web Language-Description Logic (OWL-DL), or some of it variations. More complex definition can be obtained using operators. It can be property restrictions that can force any or all of the values of a particular property belonging to a particular class, or they can force a property to have at least k values. Thus, context entities can be inferred by the inference engine, based on raw data collected by sensors, or other complex data context that can be represented by structures and OWL-DL expressions. This data typically includes information obtained from sociocultural user environment, complex user preferences regarding the adaptation of services and activities [2].

These issues make the semantic modeling responsible for the flexibility and handling complexity. It provides many advantages in processing capacity, such as automated processing, knowledge discovery, distribution, reuse, integration and sensitive assistance to situations. These characteristics ca be made through reasoning technique [22].

2.2.3   Reasoning About Context for Situation Treatment

Proactive systems in smart environments act on behalf of the user. One of the biggest problems of reactivity and proactivity in computer systems is to support appropriate, and satisfactorily user needs, without explicit or instructively demonstrate control over these requirements. Thus, it allows the user to maintain the perception of control over the environment. To gather this requirement, it was considered situation awareness as a key element to designing proactive systems. One of the main causes to reason about the context is the generation of information on a higher level of abstraction. Thus, it reduces the complexity of handling the dynamics of the context by detecting situations (current or future) that the user may be involved.

Situation-aware Systems for Smart Environments should not concentrate their focus on individual sensor data as the room where the user is, the heart rate or person's blood pressure; this information should be interpreted in high conceptual level as if the person is suffering a heart attack. These high-level concepts are called *situations*, which, in this paper, are abstractions of the states of the application's context of interest. A situation is defined as a set of context features that are invariant for a given time interval. These include capturing *what* and *how* situations must be recognized through which context elements.

In context-aware applications, situations are generated by low-level semantic interpretations. The adaptation in context-aware applications is caused by changes in the events production that characterize situations. For example, the change of a context value that produces an event can trigger adaptation if the context update generates events and changes the situation [13]. An event is an occurrence within a particular system or domain, it is something that has already happened, or it is contemplated to have occurred in this domain. Events can be modeled as simple or complex. Simple events are produced by some context entity such as, for example, sensors. Complex events are high-level in semantics hierarchy and usually correspond to a pattern (correlation between simple events).

In Fig. 1 we represent a scenario for health monitoring systems in AAL. At the bottom of the picture, sensors generate raw data, which can be aggregated into a set of domain entities and produce events. This context can be modeled in different ways to generate useful information (after reasoning) about a domain of interest.

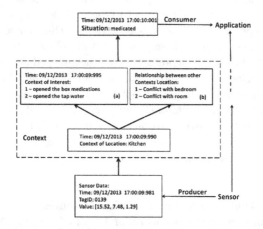

Fig. 1. Context aggregation for situations detection, adapted from [22].

For instance, in Fig. 1, the Interaction Context can be derived from the information produced by events such as *"patient opened the medicines box"* or *"patient opened the water tap"*. Similarly, its structure can predict if data are conflicting like, for example, in Fig. 1(b), where the relationship between Location Context predicts that, if the user's location is Kitchen, events that relate the user and are linked to the room or bedroom's location context are conflicting. Also in this picture, through abstraction of these contexts, it is possible to identify the situation where the user is in a medicated situation. We can notice that the production of events and detection of high-level situations are inherently influenced by uncertainty since the sources which support the production of this high-level information are prone to errors. Both the accuracy of the sensors as the own modeling (by humans) are sensitive to errors, so end up putting a percentage of uncertainty in the reasoning stage.

Reasoning about the context involves generating knowledge through the modeled environment. In this paper, we take into account reasoning rules through inference machines and probabilistic reasoning to predict situations through Multi-Entity Bayesian Networks. Thus, when using inference mechanisms based on rules, it is evidenced the current state of the environment and seeks to reflect such state in the model. The reasoning based on ontologies, using languages like OWL-DL, can be done through consistency of formalized modeling in the ontology, and by rules, such as for example, using Semantic Web Rule Language (SWRL) for generating new acquirements.

According to Bettini et al. [2], an inference engine may (i) automatically derive new knowledge about the current context and (ii) perform the detection of possible inconsistencies in context information. The ontological reasoning can be conducted to infer new context information based on classes and defined properties. The purpose for reasoning is to infer new context information typically deducted from high-level context (such as the current state of the environment or the user) through the low-level context (such as the location or instant messaging from user status). As the high-level context information are performed for longer periods, because they depend on a range of data produced by the lower layers, these contexts must be associated with a level of uncertainty, depending on the accuracy and information collected by sensors in a process of reasoning. Systems for smart environments incorporate these features, and, in the case of real environments, they are sensitive to uncertainty in the final result. Therefore, it is necessary to include methods that manipulate the uncertainty to enable proactive computing.

2.3 Reasoning with Uncertainty

Reasoning for the detection of situations and performing decision making with uncertain data comprises some shortcomings related to modeling about the modeler conception of the world. The modeling process may have misconceptions and possibly they will be addressed through ontology's consistency checks. Hence, this fact must be taken into consideration and can be treated through probabilistic reasoning.

The probabilistic reasoning might support the processing of uncertainty. It is possible to make predictions of future situations taking uncertainty into account. Many works that focus on the prediction phase have been published, and they present algorithms to identify the future with an acceptable accuracy.

Ontologies provide a range of features that search for representing the environmental context in a broad and expressive form. Context modeling using ontologies is currently done through the use of the Ontology Web Language (OWL). Among its variations (Lite, DL and Full), the most widely employed by the possibility of decidability is the Description Logics (DL). The interpretation of a theory determines the definition of each constant, predicate and symbolic function in relation to the area. Each symbolic constant denotes a particular entity; each predicate denotes a group containing entities to which the predicate holds, and each symbolic function is a function defined in the domain. The logical sequences of a set of axioms consist of sentences that are always true in all interpretations, also called *true sentences*. Because sentences are always interpreted as logical assertions, DL is not suitable for areas where there are uncertainties in relations among the concepts [9].

One way to model uncertainty is the use of probability, and a suitable model for existing domains is the Bayesian Networks (BN). These are Directed Acyclic Graphs representing a distribution function of joint probabilities of variables in a domain of interest. Each Bayesian network consists of nodes (random variables) and edges connecting these nodes. These links represent the influence from one node (ancestor) in relation to another node (successor) generating a directed arc. Each node has a Conditional Probability Table (CPT) to calculate the influence of a parent node "x" about its affected node "y", and the joint probability distribution is measured by the effect of every parent about a leaf node [23].

For Semantic Web applications, BNs have the potential to provide a powerful, compact structure for probabilistic inference mechanisms. However, BNs have some key limitations. The first is that the number of variables must be known in advance (i.e. number of nodes is fixed). However, many domains require reasoning about numbers and types of related entities, where the relationships among entities cannot be specified in advance or are uncertain. The second limitation is that the language used to determine BNs is not powerful enough to express significant problems with repeated structure. The third one is that a BN is a directed acyclic graph, and hence no native support for recursion is provided [8].

2.4 Probabilistic Ontologies

The area of probabilistic ontologies appeared with the objective of using the expressive power of the First-Order Logic and the treatment of uncertainty supported by Bayesian Networks. In general, there are two approaches to the generation of probabilistic ontologies. The first consists in representing uncertainty by probability values described as annotations, such as [24]. However, annotate ontology with numerical probability is not enough, and some information is lost with the lack of representation capturing the structural constraints and dependencies between nodes [9]. The second alternative consists of using a First-Order Probabilistic Language, which combines aspects of probabilistic representation with first-order logic [25].

According to Costa [26], a probabilistic ontology must be able to properly represent: the (i) types of entities that exist in the field; the (ii) properties of these entities; the (iii) relationships between entities; the (iv) processes and events happening with these entities; the (v) statistical regularities that characterize the domain; the (vi) inconclusive knowledge, or ambiguous and incomplete or unreliable related to domain entities; and (vii) uncertainty over all previous forms of knowledge. It should be noted that the term entity refers to any concept that can be described and reasoned in an application domain. Probabilistic ontologies are used to describe comprehensively the knowledge of a domain and associated uncertainty, structured and shareable, preferably in a format that can be read and processed by the computer.

Howard and Stumpter [25] compare those First-Order Probabilistic Languages about (i) aspects for handling uncertainty, (ii) structural support related to types of inheritance (iii) types of fields on which the language may represent and (iv) reasoning techniques on a group of entities and relationships. An overview of this comparison is presented in Table 1.

In Table 1, "attribute" means uncertainty about the attributes of entities and relationships; "numeric" indicates the uncertainty of numerical data entities in a domain;

Table 1. Languages for uncertainty representation. Adapted from [25].

		PRMs	MEBNs	OPRML
Uncertainty	Attribute	X	X	X
	Numeric	X	X	X
	Reference	X	X	X
	Identity	X	X	
	Existence	X	X	X
	Type		X	
Inheritance	Simple	X		X
	Multiple		X	
Domain	Static	X	X	X
	Recursive	X	X	X
	Dynamic		X	X

and "reference" means uncertainty about the relationship between domain entities. "Existence" means uncertainty about the existence (or not) of entities and their relationships in the area. "Types" mean when an entity of interest is identified, but it can be one or more of possible subtypes.

Table 1 compares Probabilistic Relational Models (PRMs), Object-Oriented Probabilistic Relational Modeling Language (OPRML) and Multi-Entity Bayesian Networks (MEBNs). Based on that comparison, we choose to use MEBN's to represent uncertainty. Also, an OWL extension was created through an upper ontology using Probabilistic Ontology Web Language (PR-OWL). That extension expresses a probability distribution on interpretations of any first-order theory. PR-OWL was designed to be interoperable with non-probabilistic ontologies. However, the probabilistic definitions of an ontology must to form a theory about the fragments of the complete or partial valid world [26].

2.5   Multi-Entity Bayesian Network

Multi-Entity Bayesian Network (MEBN), as proposed by [28] represents the world as composed of entities that have attributes and are associated with other entities. Knowledge about the attributes and their relationships are described as a collection of MEBN fragments (*MFrags*) organized in MEBN theories (*MTheories*). An *MFrag* represents a distribution of conditional probability for instances of random variables about their parent nodes in the same *MFrag*. An MEBN theory is a set of *MFrags* that collectively satisfy consistency constraints, ensuring the existence of a single joint probability distribution on instances of the random variables represented in each *MFrag*. MEBN integrates the semantics of the standard theoretical model of first-order logic with random variables, as formalized in Bayesian Networks [25].

Such as in a Bayesian Network (BN), one *MFrag* contains nodes that represent random variables arranged in a directed graph whose edges represent relations of direct dependence. An isolated *MFrag* can be compared with a standard BN with known values to their root nodes and local distributions of nodes that are not root. A node in an

MFrag may have a list of arguments in parentheses. These arguments are placeholders for authorities in the field [26]. According to [9], an *MFrag* consists of three types of nodes: resident, input and context. The resident nodes (object property in OWL-DL) have local distributions that define how their probabilities depend on the values of their parents in the graph. In a complete MEBN theory, each resident node has exactly one *MFrag* where their local distribution is set. The input and context nodes can influence the distribution of the resident nodes, but their distributions are set in their *MFrags*. Context nodes represent conditions that must be satisfied for the influences, and local distributions of an *MFrag* can be applied. These conditions are Boolean values, which may have true, false or absurd values.

An MEBN does not specify a model for the Conditional Probability Table (CPT). However, as in a default BN, CPT's summarize statistical regularities that characterize a domain. These regularities are captured and coded into a knowledge base using a combination of expert opinions and learning from observation. To better describe how it is possible to use an MEBN, a representation is exemplified below to support the diagnosis of a patient with symptoms of fever. The diagnosis takes into account that, if the patient has recently visited an area with a flu epidemic, this could be the cause. Otherwise, the patient has other viruses [27]. The ontology presented in Fig. 2 is encoded in OWL-DL and was developed using Protégé. The graphical representation was generated with the OntoGraf plugin. This ontology describes the concepts in a simplified form; it semantically represents that Patient has Diagnosis. The diagnosis instances are FluEpidemic and anotherVirus. Patients visiting the Region, which may or not have the presence of the flu epidemic at some point in time.

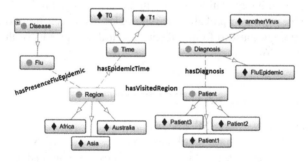

Fig. 2. Ontology to help in diagnosis, adapted from [27].

Using this ontology, it becomes possible to generate an MTheory for supporting the medical diagnosis for flu. Figure 3 shows that three MEBN fragments (Patient, Region, RegionVisited) were generated inside of MEBN Theory for Flu Diagnosis. This model was generated using PR-OWL with UnBBayes[1] software.

The MFrags describe: (i) the *MFrag RigionVisited* establishing the relationship between a patient and a specific area visited by him; (ii) the *MFrag Patient* describing

---

[1] http://unbbayes.sourceforge.net/.

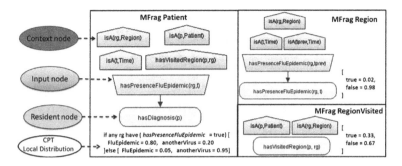

Fig. 3. MEBN theory to diagnosis of patient, from adapted [27].

the relationship between the patient and a region which may or may not be with influenza epidemic; (iii) the *MFrag Region* capturing the knowledge about the presence or not of influenza epidemic in a specific region in a given period of time.

A major limitation of conventional BN's is the lack of recursion. An extension such as Dynamic Bayesian Networks allows repeating the distribution of nodes over time. In MEBN, recursion can be represented by MFrags allowing influences between instances of the same random variable. For example, in the MFrag Region, using the context node, it is possible to observe the *t* variable, which represents the Time entity, and the *tprev* variable, which represents the previous step of *t*. Thus, using standard Bayesian Networks prediction algorithms, we can determine whether regions will have or not the presence of the influenza epidemic at a particular time. To allow recursive definitions, it must be ensured that a random variable cannot depend on, directly or indirectly, of its probability distribution. Otherwise, the Bayesian Network represented by this model could be a cyclic graph, violating the requirements of a Bayesian Network.

In Fig. 3, a repeatable pattern of knowledge that can be instantiated many times to form a Specific Situation Bayesian Network (SSBN). It can be seen as a template of fragments consisting of Bayesian Networks. The template is instantiated by binding their arguments to identify domain entities and create instances of random variables (ontology instance), feeding the model with evidence (findings).

Findings are a mechanism for incorporating observations into MEBN theories. From a logical point of view, the inclusion of evidence in an MTheory corresponds to the insertion of a new axiom in a first order logic. In other words, the MEBN logic is open, having the ability to incorrorate new axioms as evidence and updating the probabilities of all the random variables in a logical form. Therefore, MFrags are templates that can repeatedly be instantiated to form Specific Situation Bayesian Networks, and the random variables usually contain as arguments entity instances of an ontology that are instantiated in the process of generation of SSBNs. These are typical Bayesian Networks formed in response to a query to represent a situation in a knowledge domain.

As shown in Fig. 4, feeding the Patient Diagnosis MTheory with findings of the ontological model, it is possible to generate probabilistic models (SSBNs) which show specific situations of particular patients. The figure illustrates the probability of an

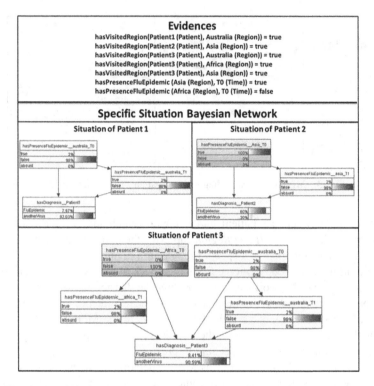

Fig. 4. Specific situation Bayesian Network and evidences adapted from [27].

individual having Flu Epidemic. The likelihood of patients having Flu increases (i) if they have visited or not a region, and (ii) if the area has registered flu epidemic at some point in time (recursivity), or (iii) if this information does not exist in evidence.

MFrags provide a flexible way to represent knowledge about particular interests within the domain of discourse. Another gain of expression is when these *knowledge patterns* aggregate. They form a coherent model of the discourse domain to generate instances in different situations. MEBN provides a compact way to represent repeated structures in Bayesian Networks. One of the positive points of this language is not being fixed regarding the number of variables and neither limited to random variables that represent instances of entities, which are dynamically instantiated.

For more information about MEBN and PR-OWL, we suggest reading the following works [9, 26, 28].

3   Dealing with Uncertainty in AAL Systems

Systems for smart environments need to know the user environment, and where necessary, implement assistance actions. Currently, the primary source for real-time data collection is sensors. They collect raw data without semantic characterization and with error rates adding uncertainty in the collected data. Therefore, it becomes necessary to consider this associated with data from other entities such as people, rooms' characteristics, and electrical networks state. It is possible to group data to generate useful information from a higher level, i.e., detecting of an environmental or user situation, as cold or emergency.

In this paper, the vision of the environment perceived by the system is obtained from the data captured by sensors; these inputs are aggregated with environmental contextual entities generating useful information. The actions triggered by the system for the environment are realized by Web services, which are associated with objects like smart phones, televisions, microwaves ovens, and others in the living environment. In Fig. 5 we present the information and decision flow.

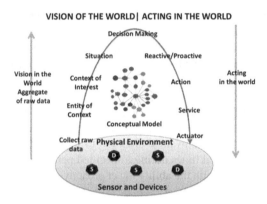

Fig. 5. Adapted from [29].

The system starts collecting raw data from sensors and aggregates the information associated with those entities to generate higher-level information that is used to characterize the state (*situation*) of the environment. With this characterization, the system can make a decision to act in the environment using the capabilities (*services*) provided by the available services, automating the environment according to the situations of interest and user preferences.

3.1   Issues for Ambient Assisted Living Systems

A availability of a large number of devices for interaction with the environment and the behavioral changes of people's profiles intensify numerous challenges in the conception of intelligent systems. One of the main challenges is to represent semantic relationships between things of the world, which sometimes are easily understood by humans, to be processed by machines in a same semantic level [30]. Simple features, such as the ones listed below become extremely complex to be managed by Ambient Assisted Living Systems (AALS):

- Physical objects, such as electronics and furniture, can be purchased or updated in a residence. They can often become invisible in relation to AALS, because there is no significant model to describe these objects, as well as being necessary to use sensors to collect data about them and the ability to be interpreted by the system. Currently, there is a variety of patterns for the low-level layer, where communication protocols are used to exchange data between different devices and systems. Nowadays, each manufacturer is generating its standard. Initiatives such as Bluetooth Health Device, ZigBee and others seek to minimize this heterogeneity;
- Factors such as the updating of objects' location inside a residence can put people with cognitive problems into unwanted situations not foreseen in the preliminary stages of the implementation of systems;
- Cognitive declines due to age increase over time and change the user behavior so that new unwanted situations may arise, and Ambient Assisted Living Systems need to adapt to these changes;
- Unwanted situations that are related to the user's health need a specialized team to model how it can be detected and how it should be handled. That requires a heterogeneous team of professionals continuously available, always analyzing the physical environment and the user's profile;
- Whenever unwanted situations arise in the environment, it is necessary to act to assist the user at this time. Reactive actions are the main behavior in user assistance, but they do not prevent an unwanted situation to happen. Thus, if an undesirable situation is detected several times during a specified period, it may be desirable that systems were developed with the ability to act proactively, seeking to anticipate and prevent the unwanted situation;
- To become proactive, an ability to predict future situations is necessary, but to make this feature possible, reasoning about uncertainty is a key factor, because the own common sense in predicting something in the near future is not guaranteed (uncertain).

These characteristics make new situations arise, situations involving the user or the physical environment. Considering the current dynamicity in physical environments, any middleware controlling ALL systems needs an extension of the ability to recognize different situations over time. These factors determine that the implementation of middleware systems for physical environments management become an extremely complex task.

The next section presents the model developed, which it seeks to address unwanted situations through reactive and proactive behaviors.

3.2 Ontology Network for AAL

Other works on situation-awareness for smart environments are directed to modeling concepts that relate to the situation itself, paying little or no attention to the modeling of other concepts of an intelligent environment. In this article, we try to approximate the home automation model (which essentially describes semantic relations between the structures of the physical environment) with the user model and higher-level information such as events, situations and actions.

For this, we have developed a network of ontologies for ALL. It has the role of being the knowledge base for middleware in AAL recognize the context of a physical environment. Thus, it promotes interoperability, seeking to offer more semantics to the middleware, supporting to identify the most appropriate actions to be carried forward to unwanted situations that may involve the user in their living environment.

According to [31], the development of networks of ontologies is based on the integration of existing ontologies encouraging modularity, reuse, and re-engineering of knowledge. They define some of the generic relationships that may be present in a network of ontologies, such as:

- Dependencies (imports): ontologies are related and dependent on each other. More precisely, to define their model, ontologies need to reference the definitions contained in other ontologies;
- alignment: different ontologies can implement the same concept in a variety of ways. Alignment is defined as the construction of an ontology formally specifies the union of the vocabulary between two other ontologies. Those ontologies sometimes may endure the conceptualization of the same area of interest or two areas that overlap.
- versioning: keeps track of different versions of the ontology, because the evolution of an ontology must be carefully monitored. It also deals with how different versions of an ontology can be comparable.
- modularization: big ontologies are difficult to handle, use and maintain. Modular ontology is the attempt to divide ontological models into self-contained and interconnected components. They can be considered independent, but are related to generating a broad conceptualization of a domain of interest.

Using these ideas, we created a network of ontologies that is comprehensive for the detection of unwanted situations in AAL, providing decision-making support for applications directed to the execution of reactive and proactive actions. It has the role of being the knowledge base for middleware in AAL recognize the context of a physical environment. It also promotes interoperability, offering more semantics to middleware, supporting the identification of the most appropriate actions to be carried forward to unwanted situations that may involve the user in their living environment.

The ontology network created was described with the Web Ontology Language using the Protégé software. The probabilistic fragments that make up the Reference Model for Systems to Predictive Situations-awareness in AAL were developed using the UnBBayes software. Intra networks relations were established with OWL-DL *owl: subclass* and *owl:import* resources and other relationships were implemented using the DOOR ontology.

The DOOR ontology is a methodology that defines a network structure. A key argument for modeling knowledge by the use of ontologies is their relatively easy reuse. In general, ontologies are not studied as isolated artifacts but have been seen as a set of ontologies that are explicitly or implicitly related to each other. In this context, the concept of ontology networks emerges.

3.3   Ontology Network for AAL

This section describes the entities of the environment that can be used by developers to build applications for AALS as a generic design. Thus, it allows these applications to recognize a particular environment. The conceptual model was defined through a network of related ontologies by a set of previously described meta-relationships. More specifically, each domain of knowledge involves the ontology itself on a network, and all ontologies of the network are related. In this design, some of the selected ontologies were not available online, and therefore it was necessary to re-develop them. In the cases where there were overlapping concepts, only one of the involved concepts was used.

The developed ontology network describes an AAL environment that supports an adaptive strategy based on the detection and prediction of situations to execute reactive and proactive actions. This network is modularized to cover different areas that create context. In this sense, we can cite: (i) the user ontology network that covers the user domain profile information; (ii) the physical ontology that covers the home automation domain information related to devices, features, states, communication protocols, location and organization; and (iii) the proactive ontology network, which covers situation, events and actions.

The complete ontology network for intelligent environments is presented in Fig. 6, where each type of meta-relationship is represented with a different type of arrows. In the developed network, some ontologies are related to other about the same domain. For these cases, the relationships are referred as (domain) inter-relationships. In Fig. 4, the dependency (*dependsOn*) between User and Domotic ontologies occurs because devices and users are located within a Domotic environment. The ontology of Services *dependsOn* Devices and Location, as devices are contextualized in a physical space according to the services provided by them in a particular location.

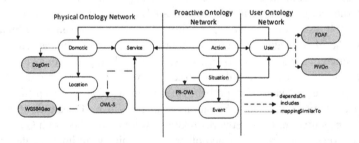

Fig. 6. Domain of the ontology network.

Actions *dependsOn* a specific situation and then interact with the environment consuming services embedded in the devices. The Event *dependsOn* Services used by Actions. When this happens, events are generated and update the information on the environment and can describe a new situation. The Situation *dependsOn* detected Events and information about the User, because a situation is modeled (i.e., is composed) with events to represent the situation of a user.

A simplified form of each network is presented in Fig. 7. This structure may be modified to incorporate new concepts, allowing the inclusion of new entities in different domains. The objective is to construct a model that describes an automated home environment, entirely controlled by a middleware to support a home care environment.

Analysing Fig. 7, the user performs *Actions* (*Human Action*). These result in *External* Events collected by the system. Events *start* and *finish* the *Current Situation* involving the user in the current time. The same events influence a *Predictive situation* that may require the *User* in the future.

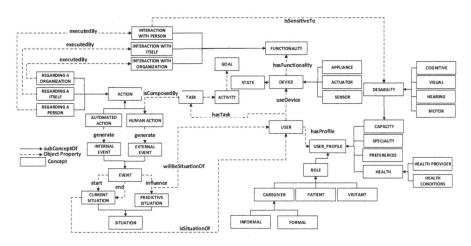

Fig. 7. Ontology network for AAL environments.

Using the information about *Current* and *Predictive Situation*, the system can select *Automated Actions* to handle situations of interest. For example, if is necessary to handle the situation including the interaction with a *User*, the system should choose an *Automated Action Type Regarding Person*.

This action will be performed by a functionality provided by a device of the type *Interaction with Person*. This functionality must be sensitive to the disability presented by the *User*. The *Automated Actions* produce *Internal Events*. Analyzing these events, the system can detect if the *Current* and *Future Situation* change or will change in relation to a *User*.

3.4   Reference Model for Predictive Situations in Smart Environments

To represent uncertainty in ontologies is not the same as to build a probabilistic system. In this particular case, the *probabilistic part* refers to the semantic relationships modeled using the PR-OWL settings that collectively form an MEBN theory. There is no need for all the relations of an ontology to be probabilistic. However, the parts modeled with the PR-OWL extension should form a valid MEBN theory. The semantic relationships that extend PR-OWL resources are shown in Fig. 8.

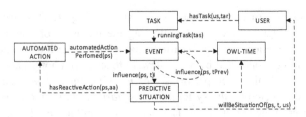

Fig. 8. Probabilistic ontology for the proactive domain.

In this picture, the probabilistic ontology for predictive situations is graphically represented. In this probabilistic ontology, the semantic relationships contain parameters derived from entity instances of the ontology. The definition of the semantic relationships with parameters is inherited from the PR-OWL model. In this case, the instances of entities are random variables that will feed the reference model to the *Predictive Situation* and form a valid theory. In this probabilistic ontology, events are affected when the user is involved in some *Task* running (*runningTask*(tar)) and *Automated Actions* taken in relation to a Predictive situation (*AutomatedActionPerformed (ps)*).

The recursion for the model is promoted by the Temporal Entity defined in the OWL-TIME ontology [32]. This concept can be used as a discrete concept, so representing subsequent steps orderable of *"T0"* to *"Tn"* rather than continuous scales. Therefore, an event can influence a predictive situation at an earlier time by the relationship *influence(ps, tPrev)* and influence a predictive situation at time *t*. The *willBeSituationOf(ps, t, us)* gives the probability of a Predictive situation *ps* on a time *t* involving user *us*. Therefore, it can perform prediction of a situation over time.

So the question that the probability part of the ontology must answer is: *"what is the likelihood of a situation at a specific time, involving the User in his living environment?"*

In Fig. 4 we show the MBEN reference theory for predictive situation-aware systems. Systems using this model can answer questions through the resident node *willBeSituationOf(ps, t, us)*. This reference model is a repeatable structure (template) that generates Bayesian Networks according to a user situation. The Specific Situation Bayesian Networks are generated according to the semantic relationships that are linked to the user's instance within the ontology. Therefore, at runtime, when there is a need to generate a Bayesian network, the structure of the network is dynamically generated according to the reference model and the user context that are represented in the ontology. The model is composed of fragments, described below, and the random variables related to the context nodes are the following: *"tas"* to task, *"us"* to User, *"aa"* for Automated Action, *"ev"* for Event, *"ps"* for Predictive Situation, and *"tPrev"* and *"t"* for orderable Discrete Times. The resident nodes will be described as <*resident node name*> = *{states}*.

The *Task* MFrag present the probability of a specific task being in execution in the environment, and this fact is represented by the runningTask*(tas)* = *{True, False}* resident node. The Automated Action *MFrag* presents the probability of an automated action being executed in relation to a predictive situation, and this fact is represented by the *automatedActionPerformed(ps)* = *{Automated Action}* resident node. The TaskU-ser *MFrag* describes, through the resident node *hasTask(us,tas)* = *{True, False}*, the probability of a user being involved in a task. The Predictive Situation *MFrag* generates the local probability distribution of a particular predictive situation involving a user at a specific time by the resident node *willBeSituationOf(ps, t, us)* = *{True, False}*. Such distribution is calculated through of the influence of the resident node *influence (ps, t)* = *{events}*, whereas the states of the resident node *influence* must be instances of events. So we can calculate the probability of a particular event happening while being affected by a task and an automated action. This context node applies the probability distribution that an Event influences a predictive situation in time *t*, when affected by the input nodes *runningTask(tas)*, *automatedAction Performed(ps)* and its distribution in a previous time *influence(ps, tPrev)*.

This reference model is a repeatable structure that instantiates specific Bayesian Networks according to existing evidence. The reasoning process on the Reference Model for Predictive situations is intended to the generation (queries) of Specific Situation Bayesian Network (SSBN). Determining the values (probability) of a set of queries, the system can refer to the likelihood of a situation being a situation of a User at a given moment in the future. Thus, the system has the possibility to choose the proactive actions to trigger in relation to the probability values generated by the *Specific Situation Bayesian Network.*

4   Case Study

A scenario is the complete description of a contextualized user's routine. This case study is based on a scenario that demonstrates how the probabilistic model described in this article could be applied in a smart environment. To analyze the proposed model, we have used a *Pervasive Application* and a prototype of the Situation as a Service (SIaaS) middleware described in [33]. Thus, the scenario described is typical of an AAL environment, consisting of an unwanted situation.

Different aspects of the user interaction with the objects of the residence are identified to generate events that can determine the beginning, the end or the influence of unwanted situations. These features result in the execution of proactive actions to handle situations. The scenario is intended to generate data for the detection of unwanted situations and to perform actions to deal with these situations, and to check the events generated (i.e., the effects of these actions).

Imagine John's, a 75 years old citizen who has some aging-associated diseases such as diabetes, hypertension, and lightweight dementia. John's residence consists of a living room and kitchen, among other spaces. This kind of patient tends to forget in what activity he is immersed. They commonly start an activity and forget that they were doing another (for instance, cooking and watching television), or even confuse the time of day and to go to sleep. Therefore, the family of John buys a Pervasive Application to assist John in his daily activities. According to Blasco et al. [12], older people are a group with the highest vulnerability to accidents, especially in their homes. The vast majority of domestic accidents are related to activities in the kitchen: utensils, cutlery, and appliances are the most dangerous utensils. As a result of these accidents, older people lose confidence in their abilities, lowering their self-esteem and, consequently, in many cases, deciding to live in a nursing home. Thus, the focus of this scenario is the activity of cooking, where John interacts with the stove device (task "use the stove").

To avoid problems, a smart stove was installed in John´s kitchen. This stove has the following features: (i) is able to identify the user (by the user digital); (ii) only after the user detection it may be turned on; (iii) has a proximity sensor; (iv) registers the time in which a person used or neared it; and (v) automatically turns off.

Therefore, imagine that John is watching television in the living room, but moves to the kitchen and decide to cook. John organizes the preparations, turns on the stove and put a pot on it. After, he listens interesting news on TV, so he backs into the living room, sitting on the sofa in front of the television, forgetting that he is using the stove. An application that seeks to assist users affected by the state of Senile in their daily activities should interfere in everyday life as little as possible.

Therefore, in this scenario, the application has an interest in being notified if John forgot the stove turned on, avoiding putting him and his family in an unwanted (dangerous) situation. So, the application can make the *decision for triggering proactive actions to manipulate the unwanted situation* (i.e., automatically turning off the stove after a few minutes). Table 2 presents the actions and events that may be produced in this scenario.

Table 2. Actions of appPervCook.

Actions
ac1: Warn User; **ac2:** Notify Caregiver that stove is turned on; **ac3:** Turn off the stove automatically
Events
ev1: User forgot stove on; **ev2:** Stove off; **ev2.1:** Sensor detected presence near to the stove

The *ev1* event starts the unwanted situation, and *ev2* and *ev2.1* finish the situation. The actions can be reactive or proactive. To handle that situation, a reactive behavior of the application could be to turn off the stove automatically, to alert the caregiver to perform this action, or to wait for more time. Regarding a proactive behavior, the application could have the ability to predict whether John, once the stove was turned on, will forget this action. This feature is allowed by the proposed *Reference Model for Predictive situation-aware system*. The local probabilistic distribution for each MEBN fragment must be generated with the help of an expert in Senile (in a real scenario), or by machine learning. This model can be filled with historical data of people affected by this disease, or even after John turned on the stove a few times (and forget to turn it off). Consequently allowing it to identify a behavioral pattern and determine the probability of John forgetting the stove on while using it. In the fictitious scenario, if John turns on the stove, there is a possibility of forgetting it. In Table 3, the distribution for each fragment MEBN is presented.

Table 3. Local probability distribution for resident nodes of appPervCook.

Resident: **automatedActionPerformed(ps)** [ac1 = **0.15**, ac2 = **0.5**, ac3 = **0.35**]	*Resident:* **runningTask(tas)** [true = **0.5**, false = **0.5**]
Resident: **willBeSituationOf** *(ps, t)* If any **ps** has (*influence* = ev1) [true = **0.99**, false = **0.01**] else If any **ps** has (*influence* = ev2) [true = **0.01**, false = **0.99**] If any **ps** has (*influence* = ev21) [true = **0.45**, false = **0.55**] else[true = **0.5**, false = **0.5**]	*Resident:* **hasTask** **(us, tas)** [true = **0.92**, false = **0.08**]

Resident: **influence (ps, t)**
If any **ps** has (*automatedActionPerformed* = ac1) If any **tas** has (*runningTask* = false)
[ev1 = **0.05**, ev2 = **0.35**, ev21 = **0.6**] else [ev1 = **0.75**, ev2 = **0.05**, ev21 = **0.2**]] else If any **ps**
has (*automatedActionPerformed* = ac2) If any **tas** has (*runningTask* = false) [ev1 = **0.02**,
ev2 = **0.38**, ev21 = **0.6**] else [ev1 = **0.45**, ev2 = **0.05**, ev21 = **0.5**]] else If any **ps** has
(*automatedActionPerformed* = ac3) If any **tas** has (*runningTask* = false) [ev1 = **0**, ev2 = **1**,
ev21 = **0**] else [ev1 = **0**, ev2 = **1**, ev21 = **0**]] else [ev1 = **0.34**, ev2 = **0.33** ev21 = **0.33**]

The resident node *runningTask(tas)* describes the probability that there is a running task in the environment. For this node, we used values that do not affect other nodes residents (50% true and 50% false). The node *hasTask(us, tas)* establishes that 92% of the time there running task the user is involved. The resident node *automatedActionPerformed(ps)* shows that the action to directly warn John (ac1) was executed 15% of the time. Also, to notify the caregiver (ac2) was executed 50% and to automatically turn off the stove (ac3) by 35%.

The local distribution to the resident node *influence(ps, t)* describes how *Automatically Executed Actions* and *Running Task* influenced the establishment of the Events "forgot stove turned on (ev1)", "Stove turned off (v2)" and "Sensor detected presence near to the stove (ev2.1)".

Therefore, if: (a) John is warned (ac1) and the task is not running, John forgets the stove turned on in 5% of cases; do not forget in 35%, and is near to the stove about 60%. If the task is running, John forgets the stove turned on in 75% of cases; does not forget in 5%, and there is presence near to the stove in 20% of cases. Otherwise, if (b) the caregiver is notified (ac2) and there is no running task, John forgets the stove on 2% of the time, do not forget about 38% and is near to the stove about 60%. If there is a running task, he forgets in 45% of the time, do not forget about 5% and is present about 50%. Finally, if (c) the stove is turned off automatically (ac3), in 100% of cases the stove is turned off (v2) and, for a default distribution, all events are distributed on average about 33.33%.

The resident node *influence(ps, t)* applies its local distribution probability into *willBeSituationOf(ps, t, us)* node at time *t*, so if John forgot the stove on (ev1), then about 99% of the cases the dangerous situation is valid, and only about 1% is false. If John turned off the stove (v2), then there is 99% of chance that a dangerous situation does not exist and, if a presence was detected near the stove (ev2.1), then there is a dangerous situation in 45% of the time. Thus demonstrating that even if someone neared the stove (checking or not the cooking activity), there is a probability of danger.

Using the structure of the reference model defined in Sect. 3.4 and the local probability distributions given in Table 4, the system can generate the Specific Situation Bayesian Network for the scenario as shown below. In Fig. 9, the T1 time (ontology instance) was added. Therefore, it was possible to determine that John will be involved in a Dangerous Situation at T1 with 46.4%.

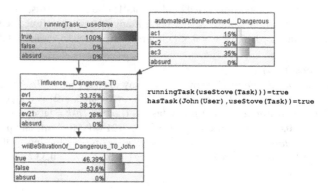

Fig. 9. SSBN at T0 and John using stove.

The difference between the two scenarios (T0 and T1) was small (about 0.01%) but it may be relevant depending on the interpretation of an expert on this kind of situation. Continuing our simulation, in Fig. 10 we present evidence that John, at T0, forgot the stove turned off (ev1), so in T1 there is a probability about 72.5% of chance that John will be in a Dangerous Situation at T1. After, we have added more evidence and the network was used to verify *the probability that John will be in a dangerous situation in T2*. In Fig. 11, the SSBN is presented with this evidence (axioms when applied in SSBN result in gray nodes) provided by the scenario. Therefore, the current time is T1, John is involved in the tasks *watching tv* and *using (the) stove*, these tasks comprise the cooking activity.

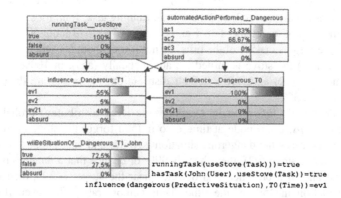

Fig. 10. SSBN from T0 to T1, John using stove and Ev1 detected at T0.

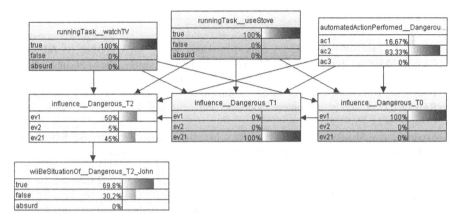

Fig. 11. SSBN with evidence.

The local probability distribution of Table 4 describes that if John is involved in some task, it is a positive influence to a dangerous situation. For instance, there is evidence that John at T0 forgot the stove on (ev1 = 100%) and in the current time (T1) the presence of some people near the stove was detected (ev21 = 100%). With this evidence, the system can calculate the likelihood of John be involved in a Dangerous Situation in T2. According to what is shown in Fig. 8, there is 69.8% of chance that John will be in a Dangerous Situation in T2.

5   Conclusions

Systems for intelligent environments may become proactive when technologies support the reasoning over uncertainty during runtime. These systems should be proactive and finely integrated with the needs of the inhabitants which living in the AAL environment. To the system be able to offer utility, usability and ubiquity, at the same time that provide management of the environment and interacts with the users, it is necessary to express situation awareness. Multi-Entity Bayesian Networks make these characteristics possible through the generation of Specific Situation Bayesian Networks. This paper presented a Reference Model for Predictive Situation-Awareness for giving dynamic support about reasoning over uncertainty for the detection unwanted situations with Multi-Entity Bayesian Network Theory. This model provides essential support for the prediction of situations in real world environments. The reference model enables Bayesian network structures as well as probability values for predictions to be generated at runtime. Therefore, the SSBN are produced at the moment that users are living in their residences. Ordinary Bayesian Networks are not dynamic this way because they need an expert to model their structures. The contributions of this paper include the use of Semantic Web Technologies for reasoning about uncertainty, as well as a reference model for predicting unwanted situations. Further work is the identification of a top ontology to increase the coverage context model and using the reference model for different scenarios.

References

1. Strang, T., Linnhoff-Popien, C.: A context modeling survey. In: Workshop on Advanced Context Modeling, Reasoning, and Management, UbiComp 2004 - The Sixth International Conference on Ubiquitous Computing, Nottingham, England (2004)
2. Bettini, C., Brdiczkab, O., Henricksen, K., Iindulzkad, J., Nicklase, D., Ranganathanf, A., Rriboni, D.: A survey of context modelling and reasoning techniques. Pervasive Mob. Comput. 6(2), 161–180 (2010)
3. Sixsmith, A., Meuller, S., Lull, F., Klein, M., Bierhoff, I., Delaney, S., Savage, R.: SOPRANO – an ambient assisted living system for supporting older people at home. In: Mokhtari, M., Khalil, I., Bauchet, J., Zhang, D., Nugent, C. (eds.) ICOST 2009. LNCS, vol. 5597, pp. 233–236. Springer, Heidelberg (2009). doi:10.1007/978-3-642-02868-7_30
4. Tazari, M.R., Furfari, F., Ramos, J.P.L., Ferro, E.: The PERSONA service platform for AAL spaces. In: Nakashima, H., Aghajan, H., Augusto, J.C. (eds.) Handbook of Ambient Intelligence and Smart Environments, pp. 1171–1199. Springer, New York (2010). doi:10.1007/978-0-387-93808-0_43
5. Coronato, A., De Pietro, G.: Situation awareness in applications of ambient assisted living for cognitive impaired people. Mob. Netw. Appl. 18(3), 444–453 (2013)
6. Rasch, K., Li, F., Sehic, S., Ayani, R., Dustdar, S.: Context-driven personalized service discovery in pervasive environments. World Wide Web 14(4), 295–319 (2011)
7. Forkan, A.R.M., Khalil, I., Tari, Z., Foufou, S., Bouras, A.: A context-aware approach for long-term behavioural change detection and abnormality prediction in ambient assisted living. Pattern Recognit. 48(3), 628–641 (2015)
8. Costa, P.C.G., Carvalho, R.N., Laskey, K.B., Park, C.: Evaluating uncertainty representation and reasoning in HLF systems. In: 2011 Proceedings of the 14th International Conference on Information Fusion (FUSION), pp. 1–8. IEEE (2011)
9. Laskey, K.: MEBN: a language for first-order bayesian knowledge bases. Artif. Intell. 172(2), 140–178 (2008)
10. Ye, J., Stevenson, G., Dobson, S.: A top-level ontology for smart environments. Pervasive Mob. Comput. 7(3), 359–378 (2011)
11. Dey, A., Abowd, G.: The context toolkit: aiding the development of context-enabled applications. In: Proceedings of the SIGCHI conference on Human factors in computing systems, Pittsburgh, Pennsylvania, US, pp. 434–441 (1999)
12. Blasco, R., Marco, Á., Casas, R., Cirujano, D., Picking, R.: A smart kitchen for ambient assisted living. Sensors 14(1), 1629–1653 (2014)
13. Ye, J., Dasiopoulou, S., Stevenson, G., Meditskos, G., Kontopoulos, E., Kompatsiaris, I., Dobson, S.: Semantic web technologies in pervasive computing: a survey and research roadmap. Pervasive Mob. Comput. 23, 1–25 (2015)
14. Chen, P.P.S.: The entity-relationship model—toward a unified view of data. ACM Trans. Database Syst. (TODS) 1(1), 9–36 (1976)
15. Paganelli, F., Giuli, D.: An ontology-based system for context-aware and configurable services to support home-based continuous care. J. IEEE Trans. Inf. Technol. Biomed. 15(2), 324–333 (2011)
16. Henricksen, K., Induslska, J.: Developing context-aware pervasive computing applications: models and approach. Pervasive Mob. Comput. 1(1), 37–64 (2006)
17. Moore, P., Hu, B., Zhu, X., Campbell, W., Ratcliffe, M.: A survey of context modeling for pervasive cooperative learning. In: First IEEE International Symposium on Information Technologies and Applications in Education, ISITAE 2007, Kunming, Yunnan, China, p. 16 (2007)

18. Guarino, N.: Formal ontologies and information systems. In: First International Conference (FOIS), Trento, Italia, June 1998
19. Gruber, T.R.: A translation approach to portable ontology specifications. Knowl. Acquis. **5** (2), 199–220 (1993)
20. Borst, W.N.: Construction of Engineering Ontologies for Knowledge Sharing and Reuse. Centre for Telematica and Information Technology, University of Tweenty, Enschede, The Netherlands (1997)
21. Poli, R., Obrst, L.: The interplay between ontology as categorial analysis and ontology as technology. In: Poli, R., Healy, M., Kameas, A. (eds.) Theory and Applications of Ontology: Computer Applications, pp. 1–26. Springer, Netherlands (2010). doi:10.1007/978-90-481-8847-5_1
22. Ye, J., Dobson, S., McKeever, S.: Situation identification techniques in pervasive computing: a review. Pervasive mob. comput. **8**(1), 36–66 (2012)
23. Friedman, N., Geiger, D., Goldszmidt, M.: Bayesian network classifiers. Mach. Learn. **29**(2–3), 131–163 (1997)
24. Yang, Y., Calmet, J.: Ontobayes: an ontology-driven uncertainty model. In: International Conference on Intelligent Agents, Web Technologies and Internet Commerce, pp. 457–463. IEEE (2005)
25. Howard, C., Stumptner, M.: A survey of directed entity-relation–based first-order probabilistic languages. ACM Comput. Surv. (CSUR) **47**(1), 4 (2014)
26. Costa, P.C.: Department of Systems Engineering and Operations Research, Bayesian Semantics for the Semantic Web, p. 312. George Mason University, Fairfax (2005)
27. Haberlin, R.: UnBBayes PR-OWL 2.0 Tutorial (2013). http://sourceforge.net/projects/unbbayes/files/UnBBayes%20Plugin%20Framework/Plugins/Probabilistic%20Networks/MEBN/PR-OWL2: Accessed 18 May 2016
28. Carvalho, R.N., Laskey, K.B., Costa, P.C.G.: PR-OWL 2.0 – bridging the gap to OWL semantics. In: Bobillo, F., et al. (eds.) UniDL/URSW 2008-2010. LNCS, vol. 7123, pp. 1–18. Springer, Heidelberg (2013). doi:10.1007/978-3-642-35975-0_1
29. Machado, A., Pernas, A.M., Augustin, I., Thom, L.H., Krug, L., Palazzo, J., De Oliveira, M.: Situation awareness as a key for proactive actions in ambient assisted living. In: Proceedings of the 15th International Conference on Enterprise Information, pp. 418–426 (2013)
30. Bellavista, P., Corradi, A., Fanelli, M., Foschini, L.: A survey of context data distribution for mobile ubiquitous systems. ACM Comput. Surv. **44**(4), 24 (2012)
31. Allocca, C., D'Aquin, M.: Door: towards a formalization of ontology relations. In. International Conference on Knowledge and Ontology Development, Proceedings of the International Conference on Knowledge and Ontology Development, Madera, pp. 13–20 (2009)
32. Hobbs, J.R., Pan, F.: An ontology of time for the semantic web. ACM Trans. Asian Lang. Inf. Process. (TALIP) **3**(1), 66–85 (2004)
33. Machado, A., Lichtnow, D., Pernas, A.M., Wives, L.K., de Oliveira, J.P.M.: A reactive and proactive approach for ambient intelligence. In: International Conference on Enterprise Information System, pp. 501–512 (2014)

Multi-model Service for Recommending Tourist Attractions

Alexander Smirnov[1,2], Andrew Ponomarev[1,2(✉)],
and Alexey Kashevnik[1,2]

[1] St. Petersburg Institute for Informatics and Automation of the RAS,
14th line, 39, St. Petersburg, Russia
{smir, ponomarev, alexey}@iias.spb.su
[2] ITMO University, Kronverksky, 49, St. Petersburg, Russia

Abstract. Tourist information support is very important due to the fact that a tourist has to make decisions in dynamic and unfamiliar environment. One of the popular types of tourist decision support is recommendations (of attractions to see, events, transportation routes, etc.). However, each of the classical approaches for making recommendations relies heavily on the availability of particular information. This paper proposes a multi-model approach to recommendation systems design in the domain of tourist information support. Specifically, it proposes to construct a recommendation system as a composition of loosely coupled modules, implementing both personalized and non-personalized methods of recommendations and a coordination module responsible for adaptation of the whole system to the specific tourist and situation context. The paper also presents some results on practical evaluation of the proposed models and an integration of the developed recommendation system into a mobile tourist guide (TAIS).

Keywords: Recommendation system · Tourism · Context-awareness · Collaborative filtering · Point-of-interest · Knowledge · Ontology

1 Introduction

Tourism has become one of the largest and fastest-growing economic sectors in the world. Despite occasional shocks, it has shown virtually uninterrupted growth. International tourist arrivals have increased from 527 million in 1995 to 1133 million in 2014. International tourism receipts earned by destinations worldwide have surged from US\$ 415 billion in 1995 to US\$ 1245 billion in 2014 [1]. Moreover, the number of international tourist arrivals worldwide is expected to increase by an average of 3.3% a year over the period 2010 to 2030 [1].

At the same time, there are some structural and behavioral changes in tourism highly connected to the development of Internet and Information Technologies. The increasing use of ICTs in tourism services allows tourists to take a more active role in the production of tourism products, being no longer satisfied with standardized products. The "postmodern tourist" with differentiated life-styles, individual motives and specific interests demands products tailored accordingly to stated preferences [2].

S. Hammoudi et al. (Eds.): ICEIS 2016, LNBIP 291, pp. 364–386, 2017.
DOI: 10.1007/978-3-319-62386-3_17

All that makes the problem of tourists' information support more actual than ever. Therefore, information (and search) services of all kinds that can help in collecting information about the trip being planned and provide tourist with information needed during the trip are becoming more and more popular. One of the functions typically provided by those services is recommendation of attractions based on tourist's preferences and current conditions (weather, transport, etc.).

Systems intended to mitigate a choice problem leveraging (implicit or explicit) subjective preferences received a name of "recommendation systems". The variety of techniques to build, deploy and assess this kind of systems separated into a specific research area in the mid-90s of XX century.

Approaches to build recommendation systems are usually classified according to the kind of input data that is used for recommendations. Most popular are two of them [3]: collaborative filtering and content-based. In the former one the only information that is available are ratings that users assigns to objects. In the latter, input information is formed by structured representation of items and a vector of user's ratings. There are several more approaches: demographic recommendation systems, knowledge-based recommendation systems, social-based recommendation systems, but they are less used.

Dependence on a specific type of information causes limitations in applying each of recommendation techniques. For example, collaborative filtering cannot be used when the number of ratings is small, but just after start of any recommendation system the set of ratings is usually empty, hence the so called "cold start" problem. Similarly, the structured representation of items needed for content-based methods might be available for one regions (in tourist recommender systems) and be missing for others.

This paper proposes multi-model approach, which prescribes creation of a family of recommendation modules, based on various principles and relying on different types of input information. Coordination of the modules and composing an aggregate recommendations list, taking into account current situation, is performed by a coordination module. Employed basic models range from knowledge-based fuzzy rules to collaborative filtering and coordination module leverages fuzzy inference to evaluate each basic model in the current context.

There is a prototype implementation of the recommendation service, functioning as a part of tourist information support system "TAIS – Mobile Tourist Guide" [4].

2   Recommendation Systems in Tourist Information Support

Key premises to employ recommendation systems in some domain are, first, abundance of choice complicating decision-making, and second, significant subjectivism in decision-making. Tourist in an unfamiliar environment (city, country) frequently face both of the premises: abundance of attractions to visit and uncertainty in which of them to visit to gain most positive experience from the stay. This explains the attention that is paid to tourist information support in recommendation systems community. Besides, social sciences research reveals the importance of decision support systems in tourism, caused by large number of aspects that need to be paid attention to: tourist mobility, high risk and uncertainty in unfamiliar environment, distributed nature of information sources and several other factors [5].

Main directions and achievements in tourist recommendation systems design are summarized in review papers [6] (systems before fall 2009) and [7] (2008–2014). These studies reveal that nowadays in tourist recommendation systems all modern recommendation techniques are used. Collaborative filtering, content-based and demographic ones are the most widely employed.

There is also another branch of research that may be relevant to tourist recommendation system community. It is media stream analysis, employed e.g. for point-of-interest (POI) detection (see, e.g., [8]). In some sense, this technique can be interpreted as an "open form" of collaborative filtering. Openness here means that this technique does not implement functionality of user's feedback collection typically present in recommendation systems; instead, it relies on some external feedback source, namely, social media event stream. A common idea of this kind of systems is that geo-tagged images are interpreted as some signs that a user who posted them enjoyed the place or view. Additional analysis can help make further inference, e.g., [8] try to distinguish images made by tourists (which are mostly relevant for making recommendations to tourists) from images made by local population by analysing attributes of the image poster's account in Flickr (the primary media event stream for that system). In [9] city attractions are visualized based on the analysis of images from photo sharing service. In [10] methods are proposed to detect actual events taking place in city based on the Twitter stream. Photo2Trip system [11, 12] makes step further; based on the analysis of sequences of geo-tagged photos from public photo sharing sites, Photo2trip identifies and recommends typical tourist trips.

To the best of authors' knowledge, there are no systems trying to integrate "classical" recommendation approaches (e.g., content-based, collaborative filtering) with emerging "open form" non-personalized recommendation techniques based on the social media event stream analysis.

3 Multi-model Approach for Recommendation Systems Design

As it was noted earlier, there is a set of well-known approaches to make recommendations. Main criterion for distinguishing between them is the kind of information used in the respective approach. Each existing approach inevitably bears some advantages and disadvantages. In the recommendation systems research specific consequences of disadvantages have received metaphorical (usually) names: "cold start problem", "grey sheep problem". The former one refers to impossibility of a recommendation system that is based solely on historical data, to make recommendations to new users (without any historical data associated with them) or recommend new items (not rated by any user yet). The latter one refers to difficulties in dealing with non-typical users. These problems on a higher level are consequences of incompleteness of input data and assumptions that are immanent to recommendation systems.

As each of the "pure" approaches to making recommendations is based on its own set of input data, it is natural to compensate paucity of information of one type (more difficult to obtain) by information of some other type, leveraging several "pure" approaches simultaneously. This is how hybrid recommendation systems work.

Hybridization may touch different levels of the system. For example, one of the most popular forms of hybridization is "collaboration via content" [13], which is based on collaborative filtering, but similarity measure between users is modified in such a way that it considers not only ratings, but also similarity of some semantic attributes of users. "Collaboration via content" is an example of "deep" hybridization as it transforms the algorithm of one of "pure" approaches, adding to it some new information. An example of "shallow" hybridization is an ensemble of recommendation systems that work independently with their results merged.

In this paper, recommendation system is built by similar "shallow" hybridization. The system includes several independent modules, each of them implementing one recommendation algorithm (mostly, "pure" ones, as they are more tried-and-tested). Along with recommendation modules, the system includes coordination module that merges recommendations generated by "pure" algorithms, using knowledge about their strong and weak sides and current situation. For example, if there are not so many ratings in the database, then recommendations of collaborative filtering module will likely be regarded as not reliable. Advantage of this modular construction is the simplicity of adding new recommendation modules – it requires mapping its input specification on the information model of the system and (in some cases) modifying the coordination module. Coordination module is intentionally designed as configurable.

Recommendation service provides POI recommendations on two levels: non-personalized and personalized. Personalized recommendations are usually preferable, but their generation requires information about user-item interactions. If this information is not available, the service falls back to non-personalized recommendations, that requires only aggregate information about item popularity. For example, if there is no information about users' preferences, then upon trip to St. Petersburg it is only possible to recommend popular tourist locations like Hermitage museum, Peter and Paul fortress, or St. Isaac's Cathedral, and these recommendations can be made only on the basis of the statistics of visiting. If, however, the user stated in her profile that she is interested in engineering, and it is known that she visited Centre Pompidou during her trip to Paris and enjoyed it, then it is possible to recommend Central Railway Museum, Central Museum of Communications, or Erarta Museum of Contemporary Art.

However, on both levels POI recommendation may, and usually should be context-aware. In the non-personalized recommendations level context-awareness stands for using a stratified and time-bound data for making recommendations. Non-context-aware non-personalized recommendations would be based on overall visiting statistics (actually, for all time). The simplest form of context-awareness in this case, would be making recommendations on yearly statistics data, which would help to identify and recommend places that are most popular now recently. The more elaborate form is making stratified samples, attributing visitors to days of week, months of year, country of origin etc. On the other hand, non-context-aware personalized recommendations are well-known classical collaborative filtering in the space of solely user-item ratings, or content-based methods matching users to some features of items. Context-awareness would usually mean attributing each rating set by the user to some kind of external conditions and limiting ratings used for recommendations to those, which are attributed to similar conditions.

3.1 Non-personalized Recommendations

For non-personalized recommendations that are most actual in the paucity of preferences data, the TAIS's attractions recommendation service leverages the publicly
available geo-tagged stream of events (photos and tweets). As it was discussed earlier,
non-personalized recommendations are based on visiting statistics data. There are three
potential sources of these data: (a) the data can be collected by the tourist application
itself (TAIS in this case); (b) the data can be queried for from be local authorities or
POI administration; (c) the data can be mined from the global stream of public data.
The source (a) is the most convenient as the data can be collected with all the needed
context attributes and in the most appropriate form and granularity, however, it requires
a huge number of users and cannot be employed by a newly created application. The
source (b) relies on the communication with external entities (local authorities and
museums administration) and is very laborious. It can be appropriate for a local
application, e.g. St. Petersburg local city guide, but hardly can be implemented for a
global recommendation service that should work in every location worldwide. Moreover, it is not suitable for recommending architectural POIs, publicly available
observation places, as there might be no administration to collect visiting statistics.
With all the drawbacks of (a) and (b) for making a globally active POI recommendation
service, the option (c) becomes viable. With the dissemination of camera and
GPS-equipped mobile devices, widening mobile internet coverage and the forming of
new information processing habits, publicly available stream of geo-tagged events is
becoming more and more affluent. There are many scientific publications showing
various ways of leveraging this live source of human activity: from events and opinion
detection to, a more relevant to the topic of this paper, POI detection and recommendation. However, this stream obviously bear some bias that must be taken into
account. E.g., it is produced by active users of social networks and owners of modern
smart-phones. Target users of mobile tourist guide are obviously a subset of
smart-phone owners, but actually not necessarily are active users of social networks, so
there still is a chance of biased inference.

In the working prototype of the recommendation service Flickr is used as a source
of geo-tagged photos. Each geo-tagged photo is interpreted as an evidence that some
user has visited certain geographical location. In contrast with classical recommendation systems, making photo doesn't express explicitly user's attitude to the object in the
frame. So, not necessarily making photo is equivalent to marking the place with "like"
or setting it a good rating. However, as the research on geo-tagged social media reveals,
geo-tags are concentrated around attractive landmarks and can be used to detect them.

One impediment caused by the way Flickr API is organized, is that it is relatively
easy to estimate the number of photos in the area, but getting the attributes (shot time,
date and precise location, poster's home location) of all the photos is impractically slow
due to the number of API calls required.

More precisely, the most useful from the purpose of this paper Flickr API call is
`flickr.photos.search`. This call returns a list of photos matching some criteria.

Criteria that can be specified as a parameter for this call include tags, visibility,
content type and many other, but the most relevant to this paper are:

- Minimum and maximum date the photo is taken.
- Bounding box (in geographic coordinates) to limit the area where photos are searched.

The result of this call provides not the complete information about the photos found, but rather their descriptors. For example, a call might return an XML document like this:

```
<photos page="1" pages="89"
        perpage="2" total="881">
   <photo id="2636"
          owner="47058503995@N01"
          secret="a123456" server="2"
          title="test_04" ispublic="1"
          isfriend="0" isfamily="0" />
   <photo id="2635"
          owner="47058503995@N01"
          secret="b123456" server="2"
          title="test_03" ispublic="1"
          isfriend="0" isfamily="0" />
</photos>
```

The most important information in this XML is total attribute of the photos element, corresponding to the number of photos satisfying the criteria specified in the call. To get an additional information about photos one has to use other API calls providing the unique identifiers of photos (attribute id of photo element). For example, to get exact geographic coordinates associated with the photo flickr. photos.geo.getLocation can be used.

The goal of the proposed system is to recommend interesting locations in the area unfamiliar to the user. Recommendation systems are usually based on some assumption that simplifies original recommendation problem and helps to build rigorous mathematical model. In case of non-personalized recommendations module, the assumption is that people tend to make and share photos of the places they find interesting and attractive. That is the same class of places that are usually recommended to the tourists visiting the area.

To fulfil the original goal there has to be a method and an algorithm to identify local clusters of photos taking into account that they are stored in Flickr photo sharing service and can be accessed only via Flickr API. It means that finding out precise coordinates of a photo is possible only by special query (one query for each photo), but it is also possible to easily (with one query) to find out the number of photos in a rectangular area.

Time required to execute an API call is high enough to make collecting precise coordinates of all photos impractical, therefore, local clusters should be approximately identified using aggregate data on rectangular areas.

All the examined region (currently, a city) is split into a number of rectangular areas forming grid with cell size of about 400×400 m (see Fig. 1). The size is influenced by the following factors. The bigger the cell is the less calls to the Flickr API are needed, and it reduces the time required to obtain data. On the other hand, large cells

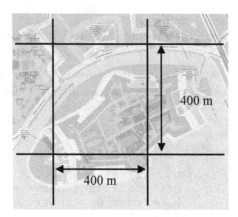

Fig. 1. Grid fragment example

bear too much uncertainty about actual location of interesting places. E.g. it is rather hard to find something interesting if all you know that it is somewhere in the square with side of 1 km. The selected size of 400 m presents one of possible compromises. It is large enough, but also can be examined in several minutes of walk.

For each of the cells it is possible to obtain the number of photos in the cell via Flickr API. Then, the task is to find some kind of "outstanding cells" of the resulting matrix. However, in general case, the number of such cells (even as large as 400 × 400 m) can be quite large. For example, the size of St. Petersburg and its suburbs is about 40 × 40 km, which results in 10000 cells and therefore 10000 calls to Flickr API. It may be acceptable for a system targeted to one city, but for universal system supporting many cities it becomes too time consuming and may result in blocking by Flickr for abusing.

Hence, there are two tasks:

1. To define a criterion for selecting cells as potentially interesting. It might be local maximum or something entirely different.
2. To develop a method for effective pruning of unnecessary calls to FlickrAPI (about the cells that most probably are not interesting according to the defined criterion).

For the first task, the proposed method is to find 10% of cells containing most photos. In other words, all cells belonging to the area being examined are sorted in descending order by the number of photos attributed to them. The first 10% of cells in this sequence are considered to contain some potentially interesting sites and are recommended to the user.

For the second task, the proposed method is to consider several layers of aggregation over the initial layer consisting of 400 × 400 m cells (layer 0). Each aggregated layer i also consists of square cells but the side of the cell of layer i twice as big as the side of layer $i - 1$ (see Fig. 2). Moreover, cell bounds in different layers are aligned in such a way that each cell of layer i consists of exactly four cells of layer $i - 1$. Photo counts of cells in aggregated layers can also be found out via Flickr API. Obviously, there is a simple relation between photo counts in different layers. Let all rows and

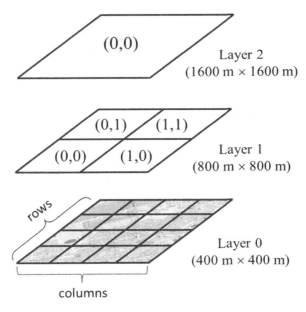

Fig. 2. Area representation

columns of cells in each layer i be numbered from 0 to $n^{(i)} - 1$. Let, also, $q_{i,j}^{(k)}$ denote the number of photos in the cell in row j and column i located in the layer k. Then, by the construction of the aggregate layers:

$$q_{c,r}^{(k)} = \sum_{j=0}^{1} \sum_{i=0}^{1} q_{2c+j,2r+i}^{(k-1)}.$$

As $q_{i,j}^{(k)} \geq 0$, then:

$$q_{2c+j,2r+i}^{(k-1)} \leq q_{c,r}^{(k)}, \quad j, i \in \{0, 1\}.$$

That gives an idea for possible pruning condition. If at some point of the search process we have identified the needed number of layer 0 cells (10% of the total number) and at the same time we have not evaluated all the cells in the layer 0, but have evaluated only cells of layers 1 and higher, and the respective values of that higher layer cells are less than the values of identified layer 0 cells, we can stop the search process.

So, the search procedure can be organized as a form of branch and bound search, when we start from the highest layer (say, 3rd, but it can be even 4th, depending on the actual size of the area being examined), evaluate all the values of $q_{i,j}^{(3)}$. Then pick a cell to branch (bc, br), and branching in this context means descending to the lower layer, and evaluating cells $q_{2*bc+i,2*br+j}^{(2)}$, $i, j \in \{0, 1\}$. Then again pick a cell to branch, and so on until values of the required number of layer 0 cells are known and the rest cell values (in any layer) are less than them.

The final thing to be defined is a heuristic to determine the cell to branch on (branching heuristic). This heuristic is important as it significantly affects the overall performance of the procedure. It should balance the necessity to evaluate the needed amount of layer 0 cells as soon as possible to reach the stop condition, and undesirability to evaluate many cells at all. Two heuristics are proposed and evaluated.

The first one (*PICK-MAX*) is to pick each time a cell with the highest number of photos no matter what layer this cell belongs.

The second one (*PICK-ADJ*) is to pick each time a cell with the highest normalized adjusted number of photos $a_{i,j}^{(k)}$, where adjusted number is defined by the following equation:

$$a_{c,r}^{(k)} = \frac{q_{c,r}^{(k)}}{4^k}.$$

The purpose of the adjustment is to equalize cells of different layers; for higher layers it corresponds to the expected number of photos in the layer 0 cells covered by this cell assuming uniform distribution of photos.

Algorithm 1. Interesting cells search.
Input:
- L – starting layer, $L >= 0$
- $n^{(L)}$ – the number of rows/columns in the starting layer, $n^{(L)} > 0$
  0: $Q \leftarrow \varnothing$
  1: $S \leftarrow \lfloor n^{(L)} * n^{(L)} * 4^L / 10 \rfloor$
  2: $R \leftarrow \varnothing$
  3: **for** $c \in n^{(L)}$ **do**
  4:   **for** $r \in n^{(L)}$ **do**
  5:     $Q \leftarrow Q \cup \{(c, r, L, count(c, r, L))\}$
  6: **while** True **do begin**
  7:   $(c, r, l, q^{(l)}_{c,r}) \leftarrow PICK\text{-}MAX(Q)$
  8:   **if** $|R| \geq S$ **and** $ordered(R)[S][4] > q^{(l)}_{c,r}$ **then**
  9:     **return** R
  10:   $(c, r, l, q^{(l)}_{c,r}) \leftarrow pick\_cell(Q)$
  11:   $Q \leftarrow Q \setminus \{(c, r, l, q^{(l)}_{c,r})\}$
  12:   **if** $l \neq 0$ **then begin**
  13:     **if** $|R| \geq S$ **and** $ordered(R)[S][4] > q^{(l)}_{c,r}$ **then**
  14:       **continue**
  15:     **for** $j \in \{0, 1\}$ **do**
  16:       **for** $i \in \{0, 1\}$ **do**
  17:         $Q \leftarrow Q \cup \{(2*c+j, 2*r+i, l\text{-}1,$
                      $count(2*c+j, 2*r+i, l\text{-}1))\}$
  18:   **else**
  19:     $R \leftarrow top(S, R \cup \{(c, r, l, q^{(l)}_{c,r})\})$
  20: **end**

In the Algorithm 1 Q is the queue of all cells that should be examined and either included to the result set R or pruned out. One element of Q is a tuple consisting of cell coordinates inside layer, layer number and the number of photos in the cell. S is the number of "interesting" layer 0 cells the algorithm is looking for. The algorithm depends on several functions, which are:

- $count(c, r, l)$ – function that evaluates $q_{c,r}^{(l)}$ via Flickr API;
- $pick\_cell(Q)$ – selects an element of Q according to the employed heuristic, either *PICK-MAX* or *PICK-ADJ*. These heuristics are also implemented as functions – *PICK-MAX(Q)* retrieves a cell with the greatest number $q_{c,r}^{(l)}$ from the queue Q, *PICK-ADJ(Q)* retrieves a cell with the greatest ratio $q_{c,r}^{(l)}/4^l$;
- $top(S, Q)$ – a function that returns S elements with the highest values $q_{c,r}^{(l)}$ from the Q, or the entire Q, if $|Q| \leq S$.

Lines 3–5 of the algorithm add all cells of the highest (starting) layer to the queue to examine them later.

Lines 6–20 form the main part of the algorithm. On each iteration of the cycle finish condition is checked. Expression "ordered(R) [S] [4] " means 4th element of the 4-tuple that is in the Sth position in the R ordered by descending (of the 4th tuple elements). If all queued elements are less than the best S known cells of layer 0, then the algorithm is stopped and R is returned. Otherwise, an element is picked according to one of the examined heuristics and either added to the result (if it is layer 0 cell) or decomposed to cells of lower layer.

The algorithm is provided in general form, however if *PICK-MAX* heuristic is employed, lines 10, 13, and 14 become unnecessary, as the cell with the largest count is selected in the line 7 to check the stop condition.

Obvious improvement of lines 15–17 is based on the relationship between counts of higher-level and lower-layer cells. If the count of an upper cell is known and counts of any three inner cells are known then the count of the fourth inner cell can be easily calculated without a call to FlickrAPI. The algorithm implementation used in experiments takes advantage of this improvement.

The algorithm depends on selection procedures from Q. Efficient implementation of these selection procedures can be based on heap data structure (see, e.g., [14]). However, as there are two criteria of ordering (photos number and adjusted photos number), there must be two heaps – one for each criterion – synchronized on modification.

To validate the whole idea that lies behind the interesting places identification, a following experiment was performed. Two different cities were selected: St. Petersburg, a big cultural center (Fig. 3) and Tyumen, a middle-sized regional center in Siberia. The rationale of selecting two cities was that the detection procedure may depend significantly on the city size or cultural status.

In each of the cities, five "experts" were selected. The experts had higher education, mostly technical, but no special cultural education or training. Among experts, there were both male and female, and they belonged to rather wide age group of 25–60 years old. Each expert had lived in the city he/she was asked about for at least five years.

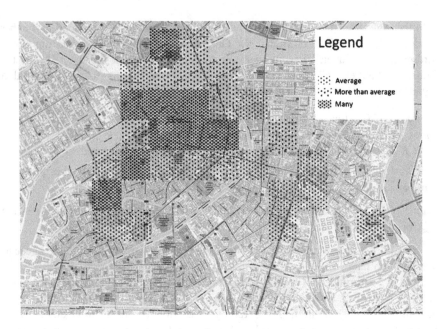

Fig. 3. Example statistics on the number of photos made by Flickr users in St. Petersburg in 2015.

Each of the experts was asked to mark areas on a city map that they would recommend to city visitors. Then cells of the layer 0 were detected corresponding to the marking of each expert. As cell sets selected by different experts were different, and there was no reason to prefer one expert opinion to another five joint etalon sets were constructed. The first etalon set contained the cells selected by at least one expert, the second one contained the cells selected by at least two experts and so on with the fifth set containing cells selected by all five experts. Sizes of the sets are shown in the Table 1.

Quality of the output produced by the proposed algorithm was evaluated by widely used in information retrieval measures precision and recall. In the context of the considered task, precision is the probability that randomly chosen cell retrieved by the algorithm is among cells, selected by the experts. Recall is much like the opposite, it is the probability that randomly chosen cell from the set, selected by experts, is actually found by the algorithm. Recall and precision for both cities are presented in the Table 2.

It can be seen, that in both cities recall is rather high, which means that the proposed method was able to detect most of the places that were selected by experts.

Table 1. Sizes of the joint etalon sets.

Set number	St. Petersburg	Tyumen
1	70	29
2	36	14
3	27	9
4	15	6
5	7	3
Number of cells in the area	576	256

Table 2. Quality measures of the proposed method.

Set number	St. Petersburg		Tyumen	
	Precision	Recall	Precision	Recall
1	0.68	0.56	0.6	0.52
2	0.52	0.83	0.4	0.71
3	0.40	0.85	0.32	0.89
4	0.22	0.87	0.2	0.83
5	0.12	1.0	0.12	1.0

Precision, on the other hand, is not as high, which means that the method detects many cells (places) which are not marked as recommended to visit by human experts. To some extent, it can be controlled by the parameter of the selection criterion, i.e. instead of 10% of the cells with most photos one can use 5% or even 1%. However, that will inevitably affect recall.

F1 score is widely used as a single quality measure instead of precision/recall pair:

$$F1Score = 2\frac{Precision * Recall}{Precision + Recall}.$$

In this paper, F1 score is used to check if the selection of top 10% (containing most photos) cells is adequate. For that purpose, F1 score of top n cells was evaluated on each etalon set for n ranging from 5 (five top cells of the area) to 10% of the area cells (57 for St. Petersburg and 25 for Tyumen). The results for St. Petersburg are in Fig. 4.

It can be seen from the figures, that stricter selection criteria will not improve overall quality (measured by F1 score).

For Tyumen, the results are worse than for St. Petersburg. Probably, that may be explained by the fewer active Flickr users, but further investigation needed.

To measure the efficiency of different branching heuristics the number of calls to Flickr API was assessed for values of selection criterion from 1% to 10%. The results

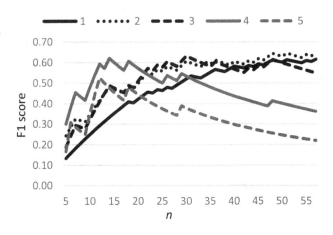

Fig. 4. F1 score for St. Petersburg.

are presented at Fig. 6. The experiment was performed in the St. Petersburg center area where the total number of cells was 576. It can be seen from the figure, that both branching heuristics give very similar results, *PICK-MAX* being not worse than *PICK-ADJ* for all tested selection criterion values (and sometimes slightly better). Absolute numbers of calls to Flickr API for detection of top 10% cells is about half of the number of cells (Fig. 5).

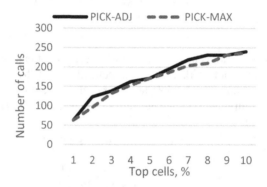

Fig. 5. Number of calls to Flickr API for different values of the selection criterion.

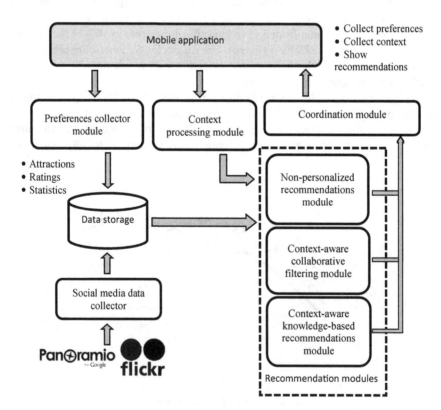

Fig. 6. Recommendation service architecture.

3.2   Personalized Recommendations

Personalized recommendations account for user's preferences and potentially are more accurate, however, they demand more information. Particularly, user preferences should be defined in some form. In the proposed service personalized recommendations are represented by context-aware collaborative filtering.

As TAIS application is targeted on the support of tourists during trip, it is important to differentiate between photos that are likely to be done during trip from those that are done, for example, at the work, after work and even during.

Context-Aware Collaborative Filtering. One of the promising directions to improve the predictive quality of recommendation systems in general (and collaborative filtering systems among them) is context-awareness [15]. The context describes conditions in which the user rates an object or asks for recommendations.

In the proposed tourist attraction information service the following context attributes are distinguished:

(a) time;
(b) company in which the user visited the attraction (alone, with a friend or with the family);
(c) weather (sunny, rainy, etc.).

Values are assigned to these attributes in mostly automated fashion. For example, the user opens the attraction evaluation screen being near to that particular attraction (according to the mobile device's GPS sensor). In this case the time attribute is filled in with the current time and current weather is queried from the context service. However, there is also a possibility to set the values of context attributes manually in the evaluation screen of the mobile application. It is convenient, for example, if a user wants to rate the attractions seen during the day upon returning to the hotel in the evening. To facilitate deferred evaluation the proposed system tracks attractions the user visits and shows unrated visited attractions in a special screen. The user does not have to assign values to each context attribute. If a context attribute is not given a value, it is assumed to have value "any".

There are three general approaches to take context into account in recommendation systems [15]: (a) contextual pre-filtering; (b) contextual post-filtering; (c) contextual modelling.

The advantage of the contextual pre-filtering and post-filtering approaches is that they are compatible with classical (not context-aware) recommendation algorithms. The context awareness in these approaches comes true by transformation of either input or output of the classical recommendation algorithm. In the contextual pre-filtering approach, the rating data that is not related to the context is filtered out before applying the recommendation algorithm. On the other hand, in the contextual post-filtering approach the resulting list of recommendations is ordered or filtered taking into account context values.

In the contextual pre-filtering approach all the ratings that are irrelevant to the context discarded from the rating matrix before the recommendation algorithm is applied. For example, if in some attraction recommendation service the context includes weather conditions, then making recommendations in a rainy day should not use ratings assigned in sunny days. This approach aggravates the important problem inherent to collaborative filtering systems – rating matrix sparsity. The main goal pursued by contextual pre-filtering methods is to take into account the context, but not let rating matrix to become too sparse.

In the proposed system the context generalization method [3] (one of the contextual pre-filtering methods) is used for taking context into account. In this method, the rating matrix is filtered not only by exact values of context attributes, but also by its possible generalizations. To use this method the context model has to support context generalization. In most general form, it means that at least one context attribute must be defined on a set with a strict partial order relation of generalization ($\rightarrow$). Let A be a set of attribute values and $a_i, a_j \in A$. Then notation $a_i \rightarrow a_j$ means that value a_j is a generalization of a_i. A context is usually represented by m attributes. Let $c = (c_1, ..., c_m)$ and $c' = (c'_1, ..., c'_m)$ are two contexts. We define c' as a generalization of c ($c \rightarrow c'$), iff there exists at least one $i \in \{1, ..., m\}$, such that $c_i \rightarrow c'_i$. We call context c incompatible with c', iff neither $c \rightarrow c'$ nor $c = c'$. In most cases, the generalization relation forms some kind of a hierarchy (or multiple hierarchies).

In the proposed system, the context generalization is enabled by following:

(a) The set of Time attribute values includes not only exact date and time values but also "any" value and aggregate values for each season, day type (working day or weekend) and time of day (morning, afternoon, evening). The generalization relation is defined naturally.

(b) The set of Company attribute values includes values "alone", "with friends", "with family" and "any". "Any" value is defined to be a generalization of any other value.

(c) The set of Weather attribute values includes values "sunny", "rainy", "cloudy", "snowy" and "any". "Any" value like in (b) is defined to be a generalization of any other value.

For example, the exact context could be (Time: "July 31, 2013 17:30"; Company: "with family"; Weather: "sunny"). This context can be generalized to (Time: "summer"; Company: "with family"; Weather: "sunny") or even to (Time: "summer"; Company: "any"; Weather: "any").

It is obvious that a context can be generalized in several ways and directions. In systems with many attributes and many levels of granularity of attributes, enumerating all possible context generalizations is a problem and various heuristics are used for picking appropriate generalizations [3]. In the proposed system, there are not so many possible generalizations, so all of them are enumerated through implicit directed graph traversal procedure. The nodes of this graph are attribute values and the arcs are generalization relations.

A user rates attractions on a five-point scale (1 – bad, 5 – excellent). The rating obtained from the user (raw rating) is normalized to reduce individual bias in assessment: some users tend to put relatively high ratings to all attractions, others in contrary tend to put relatively low ratings. Normalized rating $\tilde{r}_{uj}$ given by user u to attraction j is defined by formula:

$$\tilde{r}_{uj} = r_{uj} - \frac{1}{|K_u|+1}\left(3 + \sum_{k \in K_u} r_{uk}\right),$$

here, r_{uj} is raw rating of the attraction j given by user u, and K_u is a set of all attractions rated by user u. The idea of normalization is to shift from user-oriented five-point scale to calculations-oriented zero-centered scale. The sign of the normalized rating corresponds to general attitude of the user (whether it is positive or negative) and the absolute value of the rating corresponds to the strength of that attitude. The straightforward way to normalize ratings is to subtract scale average (i.e. "3") from each rating. It would work nice if users normally used all the range of five-point scale. However, most users in fact rate items using some subset of the scale, e.g., only "3", "4" and "5". In this case subtracting scale average would result in non-negative normalized ratings missing the fact that the user definitely likes items he/her rated "5" and probably doesn't like items rated "3". Hence, the normalization procedure should capture not only the scale characteristics but also the observed usage of this scale. Therefore, a popular method of normalization is subtracting average user rating from all his/her ratings. This method works well in most cases but have some subtle drawback which turns out when there are only a few ratings. For example, when the user rated only two items – both with "5" – then normalization over the average user rating would turn these ratings into zeroes. I.e. a priori notion of five-point scale with "5" as the best mark is lost in favor of adaptation to the observed usage of this scale. To alleviate this drawback in the proposed system we use slightly modified version of the normalization over the average user rating. During the normalization we add one fake rating of "3" (scale average) to the set of user ratings having a purpose to stick other ratings to the original notion of the scale. This modification is significant when there are a few ratings (in the example above two "5" ratings become positive) but its contribution to the normalized ratings vanishes as the number of users' ratings grows.

Attraction rating estimation for a given user is performed in two steps:

(1) a group of users with ratings similar to the given user's is determined;
(2) rating of attraction is estimated based on ratings of this attraction assigned by users of the group.

While building the list of recommendations, several possible generalizations of the context is used. For each context generalization ratings received in contexts incompatible with this generalization are not taken in to account.

User group is determined by k-Nearest Neighbours method (kNN). The similarity between users u and v is calculated as a cosine measure between normalized ratings vectors of users according to the following formula:

$$s_{uv} = \frac{\sum\limits_{i \in I_{uv}} \tilde{r}_{ui}\tilde{r}_{vi}}{\sqrt{\sum\limits_{i \in I_{uv}} \tilde{r}_{ui}^2}\sqrt{\sum\limits_{i \in I_{uv}} \tilde{r}_{vi}^2}}.$$

Here I_{uv} is a set of attractions rated by both users u and v.

Attraction rating estimation for the user is based on ratings of that attraction assigned by other users of the group with respect to their similarity to the user. It is calculated as a weighted average of normalized ratings among group members:

$$r_{uj}^* = \frac{\sum\limits_{v \in G} \tilde{r}_{vj} s_{uv}}{\sum\limits_{v \in G} |s_{uv}|},$$

here G is the group of the user.

Context-Aware Knowledge-Based Recommendations. This recommendations module uses the attractions data extracted from open internet services, tourist type and context data. It is driven by a knowledge base connecting tourist properties, attraction properties and context parameters. The advantage of this approach is that this module does not require ratings history and therefore, it can be used immediately after recommendation service deployment.

Problems of tourist industry development have received much attention in the scientific literature. From the point of this paper, the most valuable are attempts to build a tourist typology and link different types of tourists to their preferred types of activities during trip. One of the first papers proposing a typology like that was [16], with 4 types of tourists. Later, other typologies either for all the variety of tourists [17, 18], or for some subset of them were proposed [19, 20].

The knowledge-based recommendation module uses typologies, proposed in [18, 20], as Gibson and Yiannakis in [18] propose a typology with a greater differentiation (15 roles), which allows to specify preferences of each role more precisely. McKercher and Du Curos in [20] propose a cultural tourist typology, and cultural tourism is one of the focuses of this paper.

To fill the knowledge base the results of several scientific publications [21–23] were used linking types of tourists and their preferred activities.

Fuzzy logic is used to represent the properties of the tourist and of the situation. It is caused by the fact that crisp classifications rarely can be applied to cultural objects or people [18].

Linguistic variable is defined by a tuple (x, T, U, G, M), where x is a name of the variable, T – term-set, each element of which (a term) is represented as a fuzzy set on the universe U; G – syntactical rules of new terms construction, often in the form of a grammar; M – semantic rules, defining membership functions of fuzzy sets in T.

All the linguistic variables in the recommendation module can be divided into three groups:

1. Variables that describe a tourist type, according to [18, 20]. Their names are synthesized as prefix "*Type_*" followed by a type abbreviation (e.g., *Type_SNL* corresponds to "Sun Lover" type from [18]). Term-set for all these variables is a set T = {"Definitely true", "Likely true", "Likely not true", "Definitely not true"}, and a universe – $U = [0; 1]$.
2. Variable *Weather*, describing the weather in fuzzy linguistic terms.
3. Output variable *Recommend*, having term-set {"Definitely recommend", "Recommend", "Neither recommend or not", "Not recommend", "Definitely not recommend"}.

The recommendations are formed by a set of fuzzy rules involving statements with linguistic variables and crisp predicates using Mamdani-type inference (see, [24]). For example:

```
IF (Type_EDT IS "Definitely true" OR
        Type_PCT IS "Definitely true") AND
        ObjectType IS Museum AND
        FreeTime > 2 hours
    THEN
        Recommend IS "Definitely recommend"
```

3.3   Coordination Module

The goal of the coordination module is to merge results obtained by various recommendation modules based on their expected trustworthiness (which is related to the availability of the information crucial for the algorithm implemented by that particular module). Major criteria taken into account by the coordination module are:

- collaborative filtering module requires significant amount of user-item ratings;
- to receive recommendations with the help of collaborative filtering module, a user should express her preferences by making several ratings;
- non-personalized recommendations module can function only in the areas where social media stream is fairly intensive.

Therefore, each recommendation module has its own restrictions, and the coordination module assigns a degree of belief to each of the modules, based on evaluating these restrictions. Coordination module is also based on fuzzy inference. Linguistic variables used in its knowledge base can be divided into 4 groups:

1. User characteristics (a number of ratings set by the user, the number of user's "neighbours" in the collaborative filtering module).
2. Ratings database characteristics (RMSE – Root mean squared error, expected error of rating prediction by collaborative filtering module).
3. Context characteristics (photos in the region).
4. Output variable Belief.

Rule example:

```
IF RatingsByUser IS "Many" AND
        NeighborsOfUser IS "Many" AND
        RMSE IS NOT "High"
    THEN
        Belief IS "High"
```

Degree of belief to the recommendations provided by a module is obtained by applying rules to the module and defuzzification of the output variable. After that, recommendations provided by each of the modules are weighted according to the degree of belief, ranked, and shown to the user. Overall architecture of the recommendation service is shown in Fig. 2.

4 TAIS – Mobile Tourist Guide

TAIS is a mobile travel guide application based on Smart-M3 platform [25] implementing a smart space concept. That allows to significantly simplify further development of the system, to add information sources and services, and to make the system highly scalable. The key idea of this platform is that the formed smart space is device, domain, and vendor independent. Smart-M3 assumes that devices and software entities can publish their embedded information for other devices and software entities through simple, shared information brokers. Platform is open source and accessible for download at Sourceforge.

Implementation of TAIS application has been developed using Java KPI library. Mobile clients have been implemented using Android Java Development Kit. The application consists of a set of services [4] that interact with each other for providing the tourist recommendations about attraction that is better to see around. There are client application, attraction information service, recommendation service (described earlier in this paper), region context service, ridesharing service [26], and public transport service.

The main application screen is shown in Fig. 7, left screenshot. The tourist can see images extracted from accessible internet sources around, clickable map with his/her location, context situation (weather), and the best attractions around ranked by the recommendation service. When the tourist click to an attraction the following context menu is opened (see Fig. 7, right screenshot). The tourist can see detailed information about the chosen attraction (Fig. 8, left screenshot), browse attraction reaching path

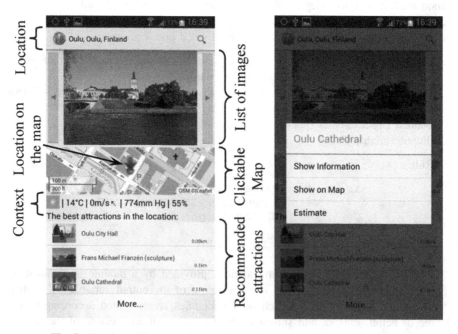

Fig. 7. Tourist guide screenshots: main screen, context menu with actions.

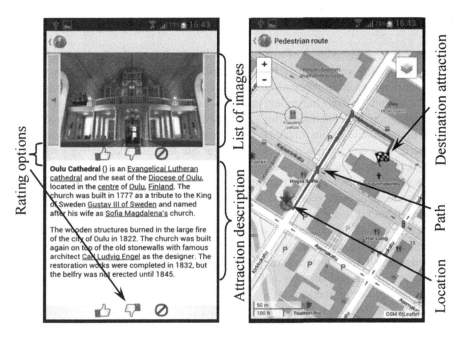

Rating options | List of images | Attraction description | Destination attraction | Path | Location

Fig. 8. Tourist guide screenshots: attraction details and route to the attraction.

that is proposed by the system route to an attraction (Fig. 8, right screenshot), and/or rate it (Fig. 8, left screenshot).

Detailed information about attraction contains a list of images that is associated with this attraction and it description. This information is extracted by the attraction information service from different internet sources (e.g., Wikipedia, Wikivoyage, and Panoramio are currently used).

The tourist has possibility to rate images using the following options: "like image", "dislike image", "this image is not applicable" to the attraction (see Fig. 8, left screenshot). Based on these ratings the recommendation service will re-order images for this or another tourist next time.

The tourist can browse the attraction reaching path by choosing "Show on the map" item in context menu (see Fig. 8, right screenshot). The routing service that is responsible for path finding uses OpenStreetMap-based web mapping service [27]. Routing service provides the tourist possibility to build pedestrian path, find fellow travelers who go to the same direction [26], and find public transport to reach chosen attraction.

Pressing "menu" button allows to search information for worldwide attractions by choosing another area (country, region, and city) and to access the settings page of the mobile tourist guide application. In the status bar, the tourist can search for attractions worldwide.

5 Conclusions

Motivated by the dependency of different recommendation approaches and techniques on the availability of particular types of input information, the paper proposes a multi-model approach for recommendation services for tourist domain. Its main idea is to create a family of recommending modules, each module implementing a specific recommendation model and requiring corresponding input (needed for that model). To merge and reconcile results obtained from these modules, a coordination module is introduced. It is designed to be highly configurable and uses declarative knowledge representation. In particular, it uses a fuzzy knowledge base that contains knowledge about how accurate recommendations of each module are expected to be in the current situation, and then, based on this knowledge it leverages fuzzy inference to weight the output of different modules.

The implemented modules are: a module for non-personalized recommendations based on the analysis of photo stream of a popular media sharing service, a module for knowledge-based recommendations, leveraging knowledge accumulated in tourism literature, and a collaborative filtering module. The evaluated accuracy of non-personalized recommendations via FlickR turned out to be high enough to detect most areas with popular tourist attractions.

The proposed approach is implemented in the recommendation service of "TAIS – Mobile Tourist Guide" system, developed under the EU program for cross-border e-tourism framework in Oulu Region and the Republic of Karelia (Development of Cross-Border e-Tourism Framework for the Program Region – Smart e-Tourism (European Community – Karelia ENPI CBC 2007–2013 Program, 2012–2014 – project KA322)).

Further work can be arranged in the following directions:

– Implementation of new recommendations modules (e.g., social recommendations, content-based, other models of collaborative filtering).
– Improving already implemented models, first of all, by considering context. For example, in the media stream based recommendations it can be fruitful to differentiate tourist photos from local citizens photos.
– Fine-tuning the knowledge base of the coordination module, based on the actual usage data.

Acknowledgements. The research was partially supported by grants # 14-07-00345, # 15-07-08092, # 16-07-00463 of the Russian Foundation for Basic Research and project 213 (program I.5P) of the Presidium of the Russian Academy of Sciences. This work was also partially financially supported by the Government of the Russian Federation, Grant 074-U01.

References

1. World Tourism Organization: UNWTO Tourism Highlights 2015 Edition (2015). http://www.e-unwto.org/doi/pdf/10.18111/9789284416899. Accessed 03 July 2016
2. Berka, T., Plößnig, M.: Designing recommender systems for tourism. ENTER, Cairo (2004). http://195.130.87.21:8080/dspace/handle/123456789/583. Accessed 03 July 2016

3. Adomavicius, G., Tuzhilin, A.: Toward the next generation of recommender systems: a survey of the state-of-the-art and possible extensions. IEEE Trans. Knowl. Data Eng. **17**(6), 734–749 (2005)
4. Smirnov, A., Kashevnik, A., Ponomarev, A., Shilov, N., Shchekotov, M., Teslya, N.: Smart space-based intelligent mobile tourist guide: service-based implementation. In: Proceedings of the 15th Conference of Open Innovations Association FRUCT, St. Petersburg, Russia, 21–25 April 2014, pp. 126–134. ITMO University Publisher House (2014)
5. Gretzel, U.: Intelligent systems in tourism: a social science perspective. Ann. Tour. Res. **38** (3), 757–779 (2011)
6. Kabassi, K.: Personalizing recommendations for tourists. Telemat. Inform. **27**(1), 51–66 (2010)
7. Borràs, J., Moreno, A., Valls, A.: Intelligent tourism recommender systems: a survey. Expert Syst. Appl. **41**, 7370–7389 (2014)
8. Han, J., Lee, H.: Adaptive landmark recommendations for travel planning: personalizing and clustering landmarks using geo-tagged social media. Pervasive Mob. Comput. **18**, 4–17 (2015)
9. Crandall, D.J., Backstrom, L., Huttenlocher, D., Kleinberg, J.: Mapping the world's photos. In: Proceedings of the 18th International Conference on World Wide Web, WWW 2009, pp. 761–770. ACM, New York (2009). ISBN 978-1-60558-487-4
10. Marcus, A., Bernstein, M.S., Badar, O., Karger, D.R., Madden, S., Miller, R.C.: TwitInfo: aggregating and visualizing microblogs for event exploration. In: Proceedings of the 2011 Annual Conference on Human Factors in Computing Systems, CHI 2011, pp. 227–236. ACM, New York (2011). ISBN 978-1-4503-0228-9
11. Lu, X., Wang, C., Yang, J.-M., Pang, Y., Zhang, L.: Photo2Trip: generating travel routes from geo-tagged photos for trip planning. In: Proceedings of the International Conference on Multimedia, MM 2010, pp. 143–152. ACM, New York (2010). ISBN 978-1-60558-933-6
12. Yin, H., Lu, X., Wang, C., Yu, N., Zhang, L.: Photo2Trip: an interactive trip planning system based on geo-tagged photos. In: Proceedings of the International Conference on Multimedia, MM 2010, pp. 1579–1582. ACM, New York (2010). ISBN 978-1-60558-933-6
13. Blanco-Fernández, Y., Pazos-Arias, J., Gil-Solla, A., Ramos-Cabrer, M., López-Nores, M., García-Duque, J., Fernández-Vilas, A., Díaz-Redondo, R.: Exploiting synergies between semantic reasoning and personalization strategies in intelligent recommender systems: a case study. J. Syst. Softw. **81**, 2371–2385 (2008)
14. Cormen, T.H., Leiserson, C.E., Rivest, R.L., Stein, C.: Introduction to Algorithms, 3rd edn. MIT Press, McGraw-Hill, Cambridge, Boston (2009)
15. Adomavicius, G., Mobasher, B., Ricci, F., Tuzhilin, A.: Context-aware recommender systems. AI Mag. **32**(3), 67–80 (2011)
16. Cohen, E.: Toward a sociology of international tourism. Soc. Res. **39**, 164–172 (1972)
17. Wickens, E.: The sacred and the profane: a tourist typology. Ann. Tour. Res. **29**(3), 834–851 (2002)
18. Gibson, H., Yiannakis, A.: Tourist roles: needs and lifecourse. Ann. Tour. Res. **29**(2), 358–383 (2002)
19. Mehmetoglu, M.: Typologising nature-based tourists by activity – theoretical and practical implications. Tour. Manag. **28**, 651–660 (2007)
20. McKercher, B., Du Cros, H.: Testing a cultural tourism typology. Int. J. Tour. Res. **5**(1), 45–58 (2003)
21. Pearce, P.L., Packer, J.: Minds on the move: new links from psychology to tourism. Ann. Tour. Res. **40**, 386–411 (2013)
22. Hannam, K., Butler, G., Paris, C.M.: Developments and key issues in tourism mobilities. Ann. Tour. Res. **44**, 171–185 (2014)

23. Park, H., Yoon, A., Kwon, H.: Task model and task ontology for intelligent tourist information service. Int. J. u- e- Serv. Sci. Technol. 5(2), 43–58 (2012)
24. Mamdani, E.H.: Application of fuzzy algorithms for the control of a simple dynamic plant. In: Proceedings of IEEE, pp. 121–159 (1974)
25. Honkola, J., Laine, H., Brown, R., Tyrkko, O.: Smart-M3 information sharing platform. In: Proceedings of ISCC 2010, pp. 1041–1046. IEEE Computer Society (2010)
26. Smirnov, A., Shilov, N., Kashevnik, A., Teslya, N.: Smart logistic service for dynamic ridesharing. In: Andreev, S., Balandin, S., Koucheryavy, Y. (eds.) NEW2AN/ruSMART - 2012. LNCS, vol. 7469, pp. 140–151. Springer, Heidelberg (2012). doi:10.1007/978-3-642-32686-8_13
27. Teslya, N.: Web mapping service for mobile tourist guide. In: Proceedings of the 15th Conference of Open Innovations Association FRUCT, Saint-Petersburg, Russia, 21–25 April 2014, pp. 135–143. ITMO University Publisher House (2014)

Human-Computer Interaction

Interactive Visualizations for Workplace Tasks

Tamara Babaian[✉], Wendy Lucas, Alina M. Chircu,
and Noreen Power

Bentley University, 175 Forest Street, Waltham, MA 02452, USA
{tbabaian,wlucas,achircu,npower}@bentley.edu

Abstract. Enterprise Resource Planning (ERP) systems pose usability challenges to all but the most sophisticated of users. One challenge arises from complex menu structures that hinder system navigation. Another issue is the lack of support for discovering and exploring relationships between the data elements that underlie transactions performed with the system. We describe two dynamic, interactive visualizations, the Dynamic Task Map and the Association Map, which were designed to assist users in ERP system navigation and data exploration activities. We present two laboratory studies comparing the use of these visual components to SAP interfaces. Results from an initial empirical evaluation revealed performance gains when using the visual components compared to the default SAP interface. A follow-up study showed users' overall preference for the visual interface, although no significant user performance differences were detected. User-reported mental effort associated with the visual interface was lower compared to the SAP table-based presentation.

Keywords: Dynamic visualizations · Interactive visualizations · Enterprise systems · ERP

1 Introduction

In the first issue of Interactions, Myers [1] wrote that "Time is valuable, people do not want to read manuals, and they want to spend their time accomplishing their goals, not learning how to operate a computer-based system." Over 20 years later, many Enterprise Research Planning (ERP) systems still stand between the users and their ability to achieve their work-related goals. Companies have learned the hard way that spending enormous amounts of time and money on ERP system training is a critical prerequisite for success. A case in point is the well-known ERP failure at Lumber Li-quidators, which was blamed in large part on insufficient attention to user training [2].

Even with considerable investments in training, there are no guarantees that implementing an ERP system will be successful and will lead to increased productivity. Experience has shown that poor usability characteristics are at least partly to blame. Massive menu structures, inadequate navigational guidance, limited task support, and complex interfaces are just some of the obstacles facing users of these systems [3–8].

The motivation for this research comes from the belief that it shouldn't require such vast resources on the part of the company or herculean efforts on the part of its employees for ERP usage to meet with success. Today's workers have become more

© Springer International Publishing AG 2017
S. Hammoudi et al. (Eds.): ICEIS 2016, LNBIP 291, pp. 389–413, 2017.
DOI: 10.1007/978-3-319-62386-3_18

demanding of their office software after having experienced user-friendly personal devices, and ERP software providers are paying increased attention to usability [2]. A recent Gartner report [9] notes that ERP vendors are looking to improve the user experience by applying social software approaches to building communication tools. This tactic, however, won't tackle the systemic causes of poor usability.

Interactive information visualizations, on the other hand, can directly impact the user experience by providing tools and techniques for, among other things, selecting, filtering, exploring, and connecting data items [10]. While such techniques are widely used by the visual analytics community [11], interactive visualizations are not prevalent in ERP systems.

In this paper, we present empirical studies of two interactive visualizations designed to aid ERP system users in navigation and data exploration tasks [12]. The Dynamic Task Map (DTM) helps users locate the desired functionality by providing dynamic, interactive visualizations of transactions performed with the system. It reveals common usage patterns by visualizing measures that reflect aggregate user activity, such as the frequency with which a task has been performed. The Association Map (AM) highlights associative relationships between master data entities selected by the user. It presents an easy to understand, aggregated view of data relationships that would otherwise need to be extracted from detailed reports.

In an initial exploratory study, ten participants, all of whom were novice users of SAP, performed a set of tasks with each of these components and answered questions related to those tasks. They performed those same tasks and answered the same questions using the corresponding interfaces in SAP, a market leader in enterprise application software [13]. The installation used was SAP ECC 6.0 with SAPGUI 7.40 for Windows. The participants also answered questions comparing their experiences with each of the visual interfaces to those with SAPGUI. All of the participants took less time and answered at least as many, and typically more, questions correctly with the visual interfaces than with SAPGUI. The vast majority also preferred the visual components.

Although users in the exploratory study performed significantly better when using a visualization, it is possible that the performance gains were due to the visual interfaces containing no data that was irrelevant to the tasks while the SAP interfaces displayed a significant amount of additional data. A follow-up study was conducted to more closely investigate user performance with and attitudes towards the AM visual interface under conditions in which both interfaces showed equivalent data. This study, with over 80 participants, revealed no significant differences in user performance on assigned tasks. The participants did, however, report less mental effort needed for solving tasks with the visualization compared to the table-based representations in SAP. The vast majority of users expressed their preference for the Association Map compared to SAP.

In the next section of this paper, we review related work. This is followed by a description of the visualization components under investigation. The exploratory user study setup is detailed, and results from that study are then presented and discussed. Next, the follow-up associations study and its findings are described and discussed. We conclude with a summary of findings and directions for future work.

2 Related Work

ERP usability issues have been documented in industry reports and articles as well as research studies (see, for example, [5, 14–16]). It has been readily acknowledged that these systems are typically difficult to use, particularly for novice users, and have very long learning curves. A study by Topi et al. [3] defined six categories of usability problems, including the identification of and access to the correct functionality, system output limitations, and overall system complexity. More recent studies confirm that the issues identified in this work still persist today [6–8].

Rather than tackle ERP usability issues directly, however, research has often focused on the "human factor." Hurtienne et al. [17] describe three ways for optimizing the fit between the user, the task, and the software. The first is adapting the business processes to the software (i.e., organizational change management). The second is user training, and the third is changing and adapting the software to the users and their tasks via customization. They note that while the first two approaches are critical for success, the third approach of customization is usually discouraged. Given that customization can be costly, time-intensive, and will typically need to be re-implemented in new releases, this is not surprising.

Having usability designed into the ERP system in the first place would be a far more preferable option. Integrating information visualizations into ERP interfaces is one way to work toward achieving this outcome. Parush et al. [18] found that graphical visualizations improved performance of ERP users on tasks of varying complexity in two different task domains: Purchasing and Production Planning and Control. Visualizations can better represent quantitative data, integrate data from multiple sources, and aid decision-making. More advanced visual-spatial displays can support multi-source integration, which is essential for ERP performance, and can improve user fit, which contributes to ERP success [19].

A survey of 184 users with different experience levels working with a variety of ERP systems revealed that being able to find the desired enterprise functionality is still a problem across all user experience levels [7]. They also found that the availability of useful and numerous visualizations can reduce user ratings of system complexity. Supplementary systems were found to provide more useful visualizations than ERP systems [8].

Recently, visualizations have gained popularity as tools for process navigation, discovery, and mining [20]. Hipp et al. [21] point out that being able to quickly and easily find process information during process execution is critical, yet most business processes are presented in a static way. Hipp et al. [22] present a navigation space for navigating over large process model collections and related process information. They have applied this approach to complex, real-world automotive process models in an application called Compass. A controlled user experiment validated the usefulness of their three-dimensional approach, which consists of semantic, geographic, and view dimensions, for navigating complex process model collections.

Outside of the ERP domain, studies indicate that complex decision problems in general can benefit from visualizations such as visual query interfaces, which are superior to text-based interfaces especially when larger data and solution sets are involved [23]. As the objective complexity of the task increases, however, decision-makers employ different problem-solving processes. This results in a more nuanced relationship between the information presentation format and task performance, with visualizations being better for some but not all complex tasks [24].

Despite the wealth of evidence regarding their potential benefits, visualizations have yet to be integrated in any significant way into commercial ERP systems. In the following pages, we present and evaluate visual components that take us a step closer to the goal of improving ERP usability via dynamic, interactive visualizations.

3 Artifacts

The two dynamic, interactive visualizations used in the study described in this paper are the Dynamic Task Map (DTM) and the Association Map (AM). The DTM was developed to assist users in ERP system navigation, while the AM supports data exploration activities. Both were implemented in D3 (see http://d3js.org). Earlier versions of these components were presented in [12].

3.1 Dynamic Task Map (DTM)

SAP, like other commercial ERP systems, includes a central menu structure called the SAP Easy Access Menu (see Fig. 1), which is displayed on the system's front page. Despite its name, this menu is so massive and unwieldy that most users tend to avoid it, preferring to navigate the system by memorizing transaction codes and entering them directly. The only way to locate a transaction directly within the SAP Easy Access Menu is by expanding the menu branches and browsing the expanded view. SAP has two separate search functions for finding a transaction's code and location within the SAP Easy Access Menu. These functions, however, are not integrated with the menu.

Within each transaction screen, there is a separate menu with related tasks, located on top of the transaction screen. All aforementioned menus are fixed, in that they do not change with the use of the system. SAP also provides a *Favorites* menu, which can be configured by the user.

The Dynamic Task Map (DTM) provides an alternative means for finding a transaction via a dynamic, interactive visualization of transactions and the links between them. These transactions and links, along with their associated properties, are derived from ERP system logs.

Each task in the DTM is depicted by a circular, blue node labelled with the task name, as shown in Fig. 2. The size of each node reflects the frequency with which that transaction has been performed. In the top left corner of DTM is a search interface, which locates transactions by name or by code. The visualization of all transactions does not display any links, as the resulting view would be too cluttered to be useful. Selecting a particular transaction, however, will cause the display to zoom in and make visible the links between that task and all transactions that typically co-occur or follow it, as shown in Fig. 3. These connections are computed dynamically from SAP's internal usage logs, thus representing the actual way people use the system.

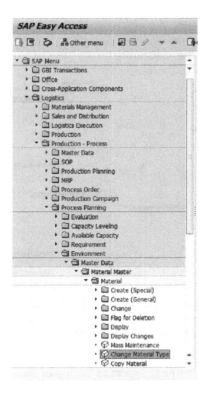

Fig. 1. SAP easy access menu expanded to locate the change material type transaction.

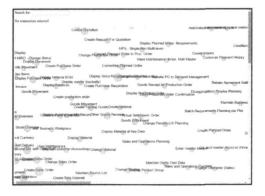

Fig. 2. DTM visualization of all transactions. No nodes are selected. The search box appears in the top left corner.

To select a transaction in DTM, the user can either click on the node representing it or type its name (partial or complete) or transaction code into a search box. Figure 3 shows what is displayed after the user has selected the "Change Material" transaction. As can be seen, The selected node appears in yellow and bears a larger label. The name

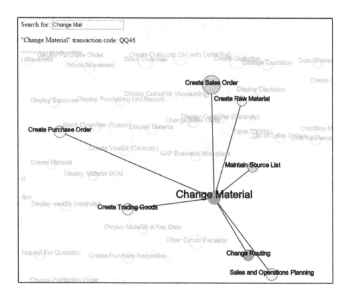

Fig. 3. Selected task (in yellow and with larger label) with connected tasks in varying shades of red to reflect frequency with which they co-occur or follow the selected task. The top left corner contains the search interface, the title, and the code of the selected transaction.

and transaction code for that node appear at the top of the visualization. Transaction codes can also be displayed by hovering the mouse over a node. Connected transactions are highlighted in red, with the intensity of the color reflecting the likelihood of that transaction following the selected one.

3.2 Association Map (AM)

Discovering relationships between master data elements in ERP systems can be a challenging process involving multiple steps. For novice users, even knowing where to begin can be problematic. Once the correct source document has been identified, extracting and interpreting data from a report designed to serve multiple purposes presents its own challenges.

The Association Map (AM) was designed to provide users with an intuitive interface for exploring many-to-many relationships. It extends the D3 concept map (http://www.findtheconversation.com/concept-map) by allowing the user to specify search parameters.

Figure 4 shows the visualization for exploring relationships between vendors, materials, and plants. Vendors are represented by blue circular nodes, plants by green circular nodes, and materials by brown rectangular nodes. Grey lines connect each vendor to every material it supplies and each plant to every material it stores. Each material can be supplied by multiple vendors and stored in multiple plants.

To zoom in on a particular entity, the user can either point the mouse at the node of interest or enter a search term. Pointing a mouse at a vendor node, for example, will

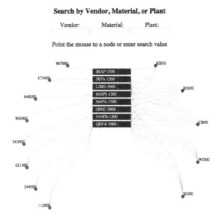

Fig. 4. AM visualization of vendor-plant-material relationships. The search interface appears at the top of the visualization.

display all plants using materials from that vendor, while entering a vendor identifier to the search interface will show all materials supplied by that vendor. Similarly, pointing at a plant node will show all materials stored by that plant, while entering a plant identifier to the search interface will show all vendors supplying materials to that plant. Figure 5 shows the results of pointing at PLANT KB00. Note that the nodes of vendors supplying materials used by that plant are enlarged. Figure 6 shows the resulting visualization when the user either points at the OPEC-9800 material or enters that name in the Material field of the search interface. Figure 7 shows the display after the user has specified a search on Plant KB00.

4   Exploratory User Study

In this section, we describe an experiment comparing visual interfaces presented in Sect. 3 with the navigation and association support interfaces in SAP. Comparisons are in terms of user performance and satisfaction.

4.1   Exploratory Study Setup

We recruited thirteen study participants from graduate students in a small business university. All students were taking a course that involved the use of SAP. Of the thirteen, ten completed the study according to the instructions provided to them. The three who significantly digressed from the instructions are not included in the analysis presented in this paper. A summary of the demographic data for the ten participants is presented in Table 1.

Our experiment included two independent parts: the Navigation study and the Associations study. Each of these studies included two component parts, one involving an interactive visualization and one involving SAP, as well as a questionnaire (see

Fig. 5. Selection of Plant KB00 from the search interface shows all materials stored by that plant.

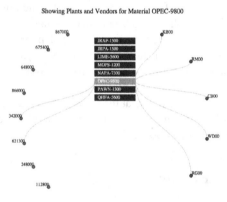

Fig. 6. Selection of material OPEC-9800 from AM search interface or by pointing at it in the AM visualization.

Fig. 8). For each component part, participants were first shown a two-to-four minute video tutorial introducing the specific tool that they would be using. After viewing the tutorial, they were asked to answer a set of questions, each of which required the participant to perform a specific task and, at the end of each task, to enter their answer. The tutorials did not provide answers to these task questions. Each study ended with a questionnaire regarding the user's perceptions of the interfaces they used in the study components.

As others have done before [5], we use a mix of quantitative and qualitative measures to capture data about the users' performance and experience. Correctness of responses and time spent answering each question are used as proxy measures for user effectiveness and efficiency with each of the interfaces (see Sect. 4.2.1). To allow direct comparison between SAP and the visualizations, the task questions in both the

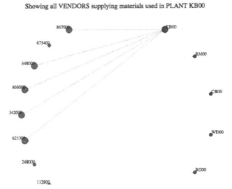

Fig. 7. Selection of Plant KB00 by pointing at its node in the AM visualization shows links to vendors supplying materials used by that plant.

Table 1. Demographic data.

Gender	Female: 3	Male: 7
Age	20–30: 8	>30: 2
Experience with SAP	<2 months: 6 Between 2 and 6 months: 4	

Navigation and Associations studies were based on data that was identical in structure but labelled differently. This made it impossible for participants to reuse the answers that they had found earlier.

The Navigation and Associations questionnaire responses, discussed in Sect. 4.2.2, provide a qualitative assessment of the users' relative satisfaction with the interfaces.

4.1.1 Navigation Study

Both the SAP and DTM components of the Navigation study presented users with five pairs of questions. These questions required finding and selecting a task with a specified name, followed by finding a task related (or in the case of DTM, linked) to the previous task, based on the task name or its description. Users were given an option to write 'skip' when they were unable to find the answer to the question after spending a few minutes trying. The SAP transaction search operations as well as the way to look for transactions and transaction codes in DTM were demonstrated in the Navigation tutorials (see Fig. 8). All participants had knowledge of the SAP menu gained in their previous course work.

The DTM for the study was based on the SAP usage logs from the course in which all participants were enrolled. The DTM included 180 transactions and 345 links. The number of different transactions presented by SAP in a production system is, of course, much larger than this, but limiting the size of the transaction set to a subset of transactions actually used in an organization is a deliberate part of the design of the DTM.

Part 1 -- Navigation study:	Part 2 -- Associations study:

1.1 DTM Navigation component
   • DTM tutorial (4 min.)
   • 10 task questions
1.2 SAP Navigation component
   • SAP Navigation tutorial (5.5 min.)
   • 10 task questions
1.3 Navigation questionnaire (3 questions)
	2.1 SAP Associations component
	   • SAP ME1P report tutorial (2.5 min)
	   • 6 task questions
	2.2 AM component
	   • AM tutorial (2.5 min)
	   • 6 task questions
	2.3 Associations questionnaire (3 questions)

Fig. 8. Components of the exploratory user study.

The different sizes of transaction sets have no bearing on the study results, as it would be impossible to find the answers to the task questions we presented in a reasonable time in either DTM or SAP without using the search tools, whose performance is not noticeably affected by the size of the transaction set.

Finding a task in DTM involved either using the search interface or clicking directly on a task circle. To verify that the correct task had been found, participants had to report the task code that was revealed when the task was selected. To find a task in SAP, users had to either locate it in the Menu or use SAP search transactions (SEARCH_USER_MENU or SEARCH_SAP_MENU). Similarly to DTM, users had to report the corresponding task code.

The transaction names in both the DTM and SAP tasks were nearly identical, with both based on SAP transaction names. The task codes in DTM were purposely different from those in SAP to prevent users from reusing the codes they discovered in the SAP part of the Navigation study in their responses in the DTM part.

4.1.2   Associations Study

The Associations study tasks asked participants to answer six questions regarding three entities: Vendors, Materials supplied by Vendors, and Plants using the Materials. The questions required different analyses of the data but did not substantially differ in complexity. For evaluation in SAP, we prepared a variant of the SAP Order Price History report (ME1P), which summarizes data from purchase orders in a textual form (see Fig. 9). The AM component visualized the same set of Materials, Plants, and Vendors as the report but used different names. The data included eight materials, eight vendors, and five plants involved in approximately 24 purchasing records. Each question asked the user to identify and report a set of items; for example: *"List vendor numbers of all vendors that supply materials that are used in Plant WD00."* The tutorial for AM demonstrated basic features of the visualization; the SAP tutorial briefly described the contents of the report.

To answer task questions using AM required that users select an appropriate item via clicking on it or by entering its name in the search interface and observing the linked items. The item names were then entered by the users in the spaces provided. To obtain the answers in SAP required inspecting the entire report. This process could be

Purchase Order Price History

🔲 🔍 Info Record

Info Rec. Vendor	Material	P.Org Plnt InfoCat
5300000000 106500	ORHB1500	US00 DL00 Standard

Date	Net Price	Curr.	Qty	Un	Order No.	Item	Variance
☐02/15/2016	25.00	USD	/ 1	EA	4500000000	00010	

Info Rec. Vendor	Material	P.Org Plnt InfoCat
5300000001 102000	ORWN1000	US00 MI00 Standard

Date	Net Price	Curr.	Qty	Un	Order No.	Item	Variance
☐02/15/2016	1,300.00	USD	/ 1	EA	4500000001	00010	

Fig. 9. A snapshot of two records in an SAP purchase order price history report used for comparison with AM.

simplified by the use of a selection function, available via the Ctrl-F keyboard shortcut or by clicking on the Find icon in the menu.

4.2   Analysis of Results

The analysis of user performance in the Navigation and Associations studies between SAP and the visualizations is presented next. The participants' responses regarding the usefulness of the visualizations, their preferences regarding the visualizations versus SAP, and suggested improvements are discussed in Sect. 4.2.2.

4.2.1   Quantitative Findings

Tables 2 and 3 summarize the results from the Navigation and Association studies, respectively. As shown in Table 2, all participants in the Navigation study were at least twice as fast at finding transactions in DTM compared to SAP. On average, the SAP interface required users spend three times as much time as with DTM. In terms of correctness, none of the users provided correct answers to all of the questions in SAP, whereas eight out of ten participants had perfect responses when using DTM. Overall, the SAP interface yielded a 49% correctness rate versus a 94% rate with DTM. 'Skip' answers, indicating the user had given up, are counted as incorrect here. Out of 51 incorrect answers with SAP, 29 were 'skips.' In the DTM category, there was one 'skip' answer.

As shown in Table 3 for the Associations study, users came up with answers an average of 2.6 times faster when using the Association Map. The correctness achieved with the use of the SAP report was approximately 67%, with two people out of 10 providing all correct answers. Using AM, correctness was 90%, with five out of ten participants entering perfect answers. There were no 'skip' answers with SAP and one with AM.

Table 2. Summary of the efficiency and effectiveness results of the navigation study.

	SAP Total Time (sec)	DTM Total Time (sec)	SAP/DTM time ratio	SAP corr. out of 10	DTM corr. out of 10	SAP/DTM corr. ratio
1	579	163	3.6	6	8	0.8
2	544	222	2.5	0	6	-
3	1266	346	3.7	8	10	0.8
4	615	208	3.0	2	10	0.2
5	455	200	2.3	6	10	0.6
6	482	245	2.0	8	10	0.8
7	1104	259	4.3	9	10	0.9
8	533	234	2.3	3	10	0.3
9	705	192	3.7	2	10	0.2
10	579	222	2.6	5	10	0.5
Ave	**686**	**229**	**3.0**	**4.90**	**9.4**	**0.6**
% correct answers				49	94	
% perfect answers				0	80	

Overall, the results demonstrate that across 20 cases involving 10 users and two different tasks, the interactive visualizations yielded greater (in 90% of cases) or equally accurate responses and required less time than SAP in all cases. The higher number of 'skip' responses in the SAP Navigation part indicates the particular difficulty users experience in locating transactions with this interface.

4.2.2 Qualitative Findings

After the participants completed the tasks in each of the two studies, they were asked to respond to a short questionnaire about their experiences. The three questions asked after the Navigation study are shown in Fig. 10, while the three asked after the Associations study appear in Fig. 11.

Navigation Study: Responses to the navigation questionnaire revealed that participants were generally pleased with DTM and typically preferred it to SAP. In response to **Question 1.1**, eight of the 10 participants replied that they would use DTM. The primary reason given was that it was much easier to find transaction codes than with SAP because you can see the connections between transactions. Participants also commented that DTM is intuitive and logical. Of the two dissenters, one said s/he would try it but had difficulty getting overlapping names to spread out. The other thought s/he would use it at first but would then likely switch to searching with SAP once s/he had more experience.

Table 3. Summary of the efficiency and effectiveness results of the associations study.

	SAP Assoc Time (sec)	AM Time (sec)	SAP/AM time ratio	SAP corr. out of 6	AM corr. out of 6	SAP/AM corr. ratio
1	373	240	1.6	5	6	0.8
2	507	191	2.7	3	6	0.5
3	622	293	2.1	6	6	1.0
4	606	78	7.8	4	5	0.8
5	280	175	1.6	1	5	0.2
6	320	90	3.5	5	5	1.0
7	351	150	2.3	6	6	1.0
8	353	206	1.7	2	5	0.4
9	621	428	1.4	3	4	0.8
10	246	193	1.3	5	6	0.8
Ave	428	205	2.6	4.00	5.40	0.7
% correct answers				66.7	90	
% perfect answers				20	60	

In comparing DTM to SAP (**Question 1.2**), nine participants strongly preferred DTM. Comments included that it was much easier to use, faster for searching, and more useful and intuitive. The one less enthusiastic comment was that neither DTM nor SAP are ideal for searching, but that DTM does provide better visualizations of steps and how they are connected.

Participants had many useful suggestions in response to **Question 1.3**, including having DTM remember and highlight the user's prior searches, spreading the transactions out more for easier reading, and adding logical groupings of nodes (such as production planning, inventory, etc.).

Associations Study: Responders to the associations questionnaire were also pleased with AM. In response to **Question 2.1**, the majority of participants commented on how easy it was to use for finding associated information. Seven would use AM with no qualifications given, one would use it but would prefer an excel report with pivoting, one would potentially use it, and another expressed concern about how crowded it might get when used with a full production system. Other comments included how well it organizes the information and how it "took away the tedious scrolling that SAP required."

The responses to **Question 2.2** were all positive, with eight participants noting that AM was much easier to use than SAP, one commenting on how it saves time, and another on how it is clearer and less "search-heavy."

1.1   Would you use the Dynamic Task Map for navigating to a desired transaction, if it were embedded within an ERP interface and if clicking on a transaction circle would open the transaction? Why or why not? 1.2   How would you compare the Dynamic Task Map to the way of finding transactions in SAP in terms of ease of use and usefulness? 1.3   Do you have any suggestions for improving the Dynamic Task Map interface?

Fig. 10. Navigation study questionnaire.

2.1   Would you use the Association Map for answering questions about plant-material-vendor associations if it were embedded within an ERP interface? Why or why not? 2.2   How would you compare the Association Map to the way of finding the same information in SAP in terms of ease of use and usefulness? 2.3   Do you have any suggestions for improving the Association Map interface?

Fig. 11. Associations study questionnaire.

Some of the suggestions in response to **Question 2.3** included preserving the view when the mouse moves away from an association and making the drill-down "sticky" so that the user can capture the information more easily, providing automatic report generation/file download from the selected associations, and improving support for searching over multiple fields.

4.3   Summary of Findings from the Exploratory Study

The analysis of the data from this study shows that for novice users performing common tasks, such as finding transactions or associations among master records, interactive visualizations considerably decreased task completion time and increased accuracy compared to traditional ERP interfaces. Notably, participants were introduced to DTM and AM at the time of the study, while the SAP interface was already familiar to them through prior coursework. The users' greater success rate at completing the tasks with visual interfaces that were previously unfamiliar to them suggests that interactive visualizations may enable novice users to complete more difficult tasks without the extensive training and experience with the system that would otherwise be required.

The qualitative data analysis suggests that even as users become more experienced with the system, they may still benefit from interactive visualizations. The visualizations presented here could incorporate more advanced options, such as grouping transactions in DTM together by business function and facilitating easier data download from AM for report generation. Such options would improve the fit between the user, the business needs, and the interface capabilities, which is an essential element of ERP implementation success [19, 25].

5   Follow-up Associations Study

To further investigate the differences in user performance with and attitudes towards traditional, table-based format representations of data and the Association Map, we performed a follow-up study. We customized the default SAP interface and altered the original AM interface so that the content presented by both interfaces in this study was identical, though presented in a different way. We call these two interfaces SAP-C (for a Customized version of SAP) and AM-N (for the New version of the AM).

5.1   Interfaces: SAP-C and AM-N

The customized SAP interface displaying Purchase Order Price history is shown in Fig. 12. Compared to the non-customized version shown in Fig. 9, SAP-C strips away the details of association not shown in the Association Map, showing each association instance as a single row of three values: Vendor, Material and Plant. Depending on which column is used for sorting the records, repeated values of either Material, Vendor or Plant are omitted. In contrast, the default interface used in the exploratory study (Fig. 9) for each association instance displays a small table with multiple cells containing additional details of the association.

The new AM interface, AM-N, includes four different views: one showing all associations and the remainder showing associations for a selected Vendor, Material, or Plant, respectively (see Figs. 13, 14, 15 and 16).

Throughout the remainder of this section, we refer to SAP-C and AM-N as SAP and AM for simplicity.

5.2   Follow-up Associations Study Setup

This study was conducted as part of the coursework in an undergraduate course on ERP configuration and a graduate course in Business Process Management, both of which involve the use of SAP. The design of the study was similar to the exploratory Associations study (see Sects. 4.1 and 4.1.2). Participants were asked to answer a set of nine questions, each of which required the performance of a specific task. At the end of each task, users entered their answer and also indicated how much mental effort was required to complete the task on a scale from 1 (very, very low) to 9 (very, very high). The study concluded with a questionnaire regarding the participants' perceptions of the interfaces they had used.

Differently from the exploratory study, half of the participants were first shown a two-to-four minute video tutorial introducing the specific tool that they would be using, while the remaining participants did not receive any training. The tutorials did not provide answers to the task questions. In order to minimize potential biases, the participants were randomly assigned to the training or non-training group; within each group, they were further randomly assigned to see either the AM interface or the SAP interface first.

List   Edit   Goto   Views   Environment   Settings   System   Help

Purchase Order Price History

Vendor	Material	Plant
122500	BOTL1500	HD00
122500		HD00
122500		HH00
122500		MI00
122500		SD00
122500	CAGE1500	HD00
122500		HH00
105500		MI00
122500		MI00
105500		SD00
122500		SD00
105500	CHAN1500	DL00
120500		HD00
103500	DXTR1500	DL00
103500		MI00
103500		SD00
101500	OHMT1500	MI00
101500		SD00
106500	ORHB1500	DL00
106500		HD00
123500	ORMN1500	HD00
123500		HH00
114500	RHMT1500	HD00
114500		HH00

Fig. 12. A screenshot of the SAP-C interface.

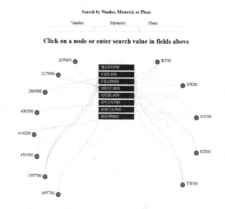

Fig. 13. AM-N interface showing all associations.

Of the hundred and six participants, eighty six completed the study according to the instructions provided, with 83 participants providing usable answers for each task question, and 86 providing usable answers to interface perception questions. Twenty responses that were incomplete or digressed significantly from the instructions were not included in the analysis presented below. A summary of the demographic data is presented in Table 4.

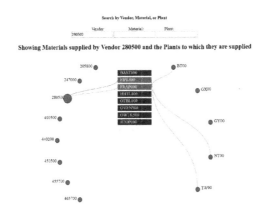

Fig. 14. AM-N interface showing associations for the selected vendor (on the left).

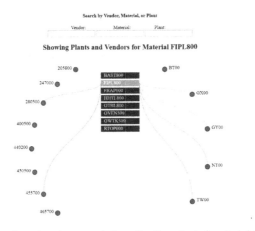

Fig. 15. AM-N interface showing associations for the selected material (in the middle).

5.3   Analysis of Results

Quantitative Findings. Tables 5 and 6 summarize the quantitative results from the follow-up Association study. To understand the data, a variety of analyses were performed using the R programming language.

As shown in Table 5, users took between 7 and 8 min on average to complete the tasks (across all nine questions) using either interface, with or without training. A visual inspection of this data indicates users without training took slightly less time using the AM interface, while users with training took slightly more time using this interface than with SAP. There seems to be more variability in the data in the non-training groups than in the training groups with either interface and more variability for the SAP interface than for AM, with or without training. To see if these differences are statistically significant, we ran t-tests as well as a series of general linear models with total time as a dependent variable and type of system (AM versus SAP), training, and

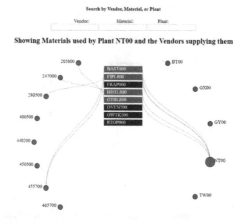

Fig. 16. AM-N interface showing associations for the selected plant (on the right).

Table 4. Demographic data for the follow-up association map study.

Gender	Female: 41	Male: 45
Age	21–24: 69	25–28: 17
Experience with SAP	<2 months: 44	
	Between 2 and 6 months: 26	
	Between 7 and 11 months:14	
	Between 1 and 2 years: 1	
	Over 2 years: 1	

Table 5. Summary of the efficiency and effectiveness results of the follow-up associations study.

	Total time to complete all 9 questions		Mean question time (across all 9 questions)		Number of correct answers (out of 9)		% of perfect answers (all 9 correct)	
	Average *(st dev)* across participants (sec)		Average *(st dev)* across participants (sec)		Average *(%)* across participants		% across participants	
	AM	SAP	AM	SAP	AM	SAP	AM	SAP
With training	448.62 *(196.18)*	444.65 *(280.69)*	49.85 *(54.48)*	49.41 *(78.26)*	8.40 *(93%)*	8.28 *(92%)*	55%	50%
Without training	466.57 *(228.97)*	471.95 *(360.24)*	51.84 *(55.70)*	52.44 *(79.99)*	7.86 *(87%)*	7.88 *(88%)*	40%	37%

Table 6. Summary of the mental effort results of the follow-up Association study.

	Mean mental effort (across 9 tasks)	
	Average *(st dev)* across participants (1–9 scale)	
	AM	SAP
With training	2.64*(1.65)*	3.28*(1.72)*
Without training	3.05*(1.77)*	3.73*(1.87)*

question (1–9) as independent variables. None of these more advanced tests indicated significant effects, with the exception of one test for a complex question in the non-training group. Based on this experiment, the time to complete the tasks is, therefore, similar for both SAP and AM, with or without training. Further testing will be required to understand if significant differences occur when users have to answer more complex questions.

The correctness achieved with the use of the SAP report was 92% with training and 88% without training, with 50% of the participants in the training group and 37% in the non-training group providing all correct answers. Using AM, correctness was 93% with training and 87% without training, with 55% of the participants in the training group and 40% in the non-training group providing all correct answers. Chi-square tests confirmed that correctness is significantly higher with training ($p = 0.006$) and when using the AM interface ($p = 0.0001$).

Furthermore, as shown in Table 6, the average value of the mental effort reported by users receiving no training (on a 1–9 scale, across all tasks) was 3.05 when using the AM interface and 3.73 when using the SAP interface. The average value of mental effort reported by users receiving training was slightly lower overall, with the AM interface still requiring less effort than the SAP interface (average of 2.64 vs 3.28). To see if these differences are statistically significant for each task, we ran a general linear model with mental effort as a dependent variable and type of system (AM versus SAP), training, and question characteristics (difficulty, answer length) as independent variables. The results indicate that mental effort is significantly lower for simple questions and for the training group, and significantly higher when using the SAP interface (with 0.001 significance for all these variables).

Qualitative Findings. The participants were asked to answer questions based on their experiences with SAP and AM after the task completion process. These questions included perceptions of the visual and interactive aspects of the two interfaces, perceptions of sorting and searching capabilities, ratings of the interfaces over various attribute ranges, selecting which interface would be preferred for future work, and short answer responses focused on comparing and evaluating the interfaces. Following are the findings from each of these categories of questions.

Perceptions of the Visual and Interactive Aspects: After completing the set of tasks using either of the systems, participants were asked to rate the following attributes with

Table 7. Comparison of visual and interactive aspects of SAP and AM interfaces.

Statement	Polarity	SAP		AM	
		Mean	SD	Mean	SD
The interface was complex	−	3.66	1.53	2.91	1.48
The interface was crowded	−	3.89	1.67	3.25	1.70
The interface was interactive	+	3.59	1.69	5.73	1.28
The interface displayed too much information	−	3.61	1.62	2.77	1.36

respect to the system that had just been used. A seven-point Likert scale ranging from 1 (disagree strongly) to 7 (agree strongly) was employed. Table 7 shows the results of this ranking. As can be seen, participants found that the SAP interface was more complex, more crowded, and displayed too much information as compared to the AM interface. The AM interface was found to be more interactive than that of SAP.

Sorting and Searching Capabilities: After completing the set of tasks with SAP, participants were asked if "The **sorting** feature of SAP was useful to me in answering the questions." Since AM does not have a sorting feature, participants were asked to rank the following statement after completing the set of tasks with that interface: "Having data presented in **sorted order** was useful to me in answering the questions." In both cases, participants were asked if the **search** feature of the particular interface was useful to them in answering questions. The choices available to users in answering all of these questions were 1 (I was not aware of this feature) followed by a Likert scale ranging from 2 (Disagree Strongly) to 8 (Agree Strongly).

More participants were unaware of the sorting and searching features of SAP vs. AM. The mean and standard deviation values for the sorting feature (SAP) and the sorted order of data (AM) shows there was not much difference in ratings of usefulness, with 5.58 M, 2.5 SD for SAP and 5.91 M, 2.07 SD for AM (note that the features being compared were not exactly the same). Among those who were aware of the searching features, far more participants found AM's search capability to be useful than SAP's (3.63 M, 2.3 SD for SAP, 5.91 M, 2.08 SD for AM).

Attribute Comparisons: Participants were also asked to rate the use of each interface for performing tasks along five perceived enjoyment dimensions [25] using a seven-point scale. The results of these ratings are shown in Table 8. The ratings for AM were higher than for SAP along all of these dimensions.

Interface Comparisons and Evaluations: Lastly, participants were asked 5 short answer questions, as shown in Fig. 17. Eighty-five of the 86 participants provided usable answers to all these questions.

In answering **Question 3.1**, eighty-one of the participants made positive comments about how the AM interface compares to SAP for finding information. "Interesting," "user-friendly," "visually appealing," and "easy to use" were some of the terms that were frequently used. Eleven participants described negative aspects of AM, including the lack of a sort function, limited search options, and a confusing presentation when links are tangled, making it less suitable for larger data sets. Two of those eleven had

Table 8. Ratings of SAP and AM interfaces for performing tasks along five dimensions.

Using the interface for task performance was	Polarity	SAP		AM	
		Mean	SD	Mean	SD
Unexciting (1) to exciting (7)	+	3.36	1.59	4.91	1.37
Dull (1) to neat (7)	+	3.38	1.77	5.34	1.40
Not fun (1) to fun (7)	+	3.23	1.60	4.92	1.38
Unappealing (1) to appealing (7)	+	3.66	1.70	5.31	1.42
Boring (1) to interesting (7)	+	3.33	1.65	5.06	1.56

3.1 How would you compare the Association Map to the way of finding the same information in SAP?

3.2 Assuming you have access to both the Association Map and the SAP interface, which one do you intend to use the next time you have to perform similar tasks? (choices of AM, SAP, or Undecided)

3.3 Please explain your answer to the above question regarding which interface you intend to use.

3.4 Do you have any suggestions for improving the Association Map?

3.5 Do you have any suggestions for improving the SAP interface?

Fig. 17. Short answer questions.

nothing positive to say about AM and felt that the results shown by SAP were clearer, while a third thought that both interfaces were confusing.

Eighteen participants had positive observations about SAP, including its suitability for working with large amounts of data, its sort feature, and the straightforward and professional way the results are presented. Thirty participants made negative comments about SAP, noting it was more difficult to use and confusing.

The following comment illustrates the overall perspective of many of the respondents: "Using the AM was a lot more interactive and dynamic. Using a more graphic way to represent the relationships as opposed to SAP made finding the information a lot easier. Also, the AM allowed for the searches to be broader than SAP. In SAP, for example, it is not as easy to search both a vendor and a plant in order to look for the materials. In SAP you have to do a lot of the work yourself when looking for different relationships or information."

In answering **Question 3.2** on system preferences, 73 participants chose AM, eight participants chose SAP, and five were undecided. The most common reasons given in **Question 3.3** for preferring AM focused on the interface being easy to use, requiring less effort, and being more visually appealing and fun. As summarized by one participant, "AM's interface is user-friendly and more appealing to the eyes. I liked the visible and clear search boxes. Also, with how the page was set up the vendor, material, and plant data was very easy to view and decipher. Using AM made the physical work and mental work I had to do in order to reach the answers much less." Several participants also commented on the interactive features of the AM interface and how the visualization helped them understand the relationships between the data elements.

Two of the eight participants who preferred SAP indicated a preference for AM in their answer to question 3 on intended use, and a third (confusingly) stated that "Because AM is more straightforward than SAP, I prefer SAP." Of the remaining five, two thought SAP was clearer, two noted its sorting feature, and one preferred it because s/he has used it before so is more familiar with it. Of the five undecided participants, one commented on liking SAP during prior use, one would need more experience with both, and the remaining three indicated that it would depend on the amount of data involved.

Sixty-eight participants offered suggestions for improving the AM interface in response to **Question 3.4**. These included expanding the search functionality, hiding all but the relevant data after a selection has been made, allowing data points to be draggable so that connections can be more easily viewed, revealing related information when an item is clicked, using additional color coding for differentiating between data elements and for highlighting links, allowing the user to specify the range of variables for limiting the amount of data displayed, and using straight rather than curved lines for clarity.

Sixty-nine participants offered suggestions for improving SAP in response to **Question 3.5**. These included removing repeated data after sorting, allow sorting on more than one field at a time, highlight the columns being sorted and indicate the sorting direction, make both sorting and searching functionality more obvious, provide single-click sorting capability, include visualizations of tabular data and make it more interactive (like AM), offer a "quick hide" option to remove excess information, color code the data for easier identification, highlight the more useful menu options, and streamline the number of menu items and label them more clearly.

5.4 Summary of Findings from the Follow-up Associations Study

The follow-up comparison study of AM versus a customized table-based SAP interface containing exactly the same content showed no advantage of either interface in terms of task completion time. The fact that the data in the SAP table all fit within one screen is important, because it implies that no scrolling was necessary. The users in our study were relative novices in SAP and were all exposed to AM for the first time. It is possible that for our novice users, the tasks reached the complexity at which spatial representations are not superior to other methods, or that our participants were making the types of accuracy/effort trade-offs identified in previous research [24].

In terms of user attitudes towards both interfaces, users reported that less mental effort was required when working with the visual interface than with the SAP table. They also largely preferred the visual interface to the tabular one, expressing it in free form comments as well as using a variety of measures of user satisfaction. Many participants attributed their preferences to less physical and mental work required for finding answers to questions using the Association Map. Study participants reported several opportunities for improving both interfaces.

6 Conclusions and Future Work

In this paper, we advance ERP usability research by investigating the use of interactive visualizations for navigation and association-related tasks in enterprise systems. Our results showed that novice users performed those tasks faster and at least as accurately when using DTM and AM visualizations than when using the default SAP interfaces. In a closer comparison of a tabular representation of associations within SAP versus the Association Map, users reported lower mental effort when working with the AM visualization, while performing with similar speed and accuracy. Users also over-whelmingly preferred the visual interfaces to the SAP alternatives. These results empirically corroborate the view expressed by users in surveys [7, 8] that useful visualizations decrease the complexity of ERP interfaces, enabling more productive use of the system.

The results of the studies presented here suggest that interactive visualizations are one way that ERP vendors can increase the usability of their products, which is becoming more and more important in today's ERP marketplace [2]. These visual-izations are more intuitive to learn and easier to use; they should therefore reduce the need for extensive and expensive training. The users' improved perception of the ERP system and greater confidence in their ability to perform the necessary tasks with it would likely lead to less resistance and increased acceptance of a newly implemented system. Last, but not least, DTM would potentially result in productivity improvements by reducing the time it takes to locate task interfaces.

The main limitation of our studies stems from the fact that our visualizations were implemented as standalone interfaces, while the SAP interfaces for the same tasks were embedded in the context of a larger system. Thus, some inefficiencies in performing tasks with SAP could be due to the users' attention being distracted by the numerous features of the interfaces. Another limitation is the novice status and the relatively young age of the study participants. Although a more diverse sample population would provide a more complete assessment of the benefits of interactive visualizations for different user groups, our sample is appropriate for initial usability studies targeted at novice, entry-level ERP users.

In future work, we plan to fine-tune and enhance the existing visualizations based on feedback from the study. We will use the improved interfaces to investigate the impact of different features on user performance and user perceptions in more detail and with a larger sample population.

Acknowledgements. We would like to thank Ren Zhang for his contributions to analyzing the data from the user studies.

References

1. Myers, B.: Challenges of HCI design and implementation. Interactions **1**(1), 73–83 (1994)
2. King, R.: SAP owns up to usability problem. The Wall Street Journal CIO Report (2012)

3. Topi, H., Lucas, W., Babaian, T.: Identifying usability issues with an ERP implementation. In: Proceedings of the International Conference on Enterprise Information Systems (ICEIS-2005), pp. 128–133 (2005)
4. Rettig, C.: The trouble with enterprise software. Sloan Manag. Rev. **49**(1), 21–27 (2007)
5. Scholtz, B., Cilliers, C., Calitz, A.: Qualitative techniques for evaluating enterprise resource planning (ERP) user interfaces. In: Proceedings of the 2010 Annual Research Conference of the South African Institute of Computer Scientists and Information Technologists, New York, pp. 284–293 (2010)
6. Parks, N.E.: Testing & quantifying ERP usability. In: Proceedings of the 1st Annual Conference on Research in Information Technology, New York, NY, USA, pp. 31–36 (2012)
7. Lambeck, C., Fohrholz, C., Leyh, C., Supulniece, I., Müller, R.: Commonalities and contrasts: an investigation of ERP usability in a comparative user study. In: 22nd European Conference on Information Systems, Tel Aviv, Israel (2014)
8. Lambeck, C., Fohrholz, C., Leyh, C., Müller, R.: (Re-) evaluating user interface aspects in ERP systems - an empirical user study. In: Proceedings of the 47th Hawaiian International Conference on System Sciences (2014)
9. Ganly, D., Montgomery, N.: Hype cycle for ERP. Gartner (2015)
10. Yi, J.S., Kang, Y., Stasko, J., Jacko, J.: Toward a deeper understanding of the role of interaction in information visualization. IEEE Trans. Vis. Comput. Graph. **13**(6), 1224–1231 (2007)
11. Pike, W.A., Stasko, J., Chang, R., O'Connell, T.A.: The science of interaction. Inf. Vis. **8**(4), 263–274 (2009)
12. Babaian, T., Lucas, W., Li, M.: Modernizing exploration and navigation in enterprise systems with interactive visualizations. In: Yamamoto, S. (ed.) HIMI 2015. LNCS, vol. 9172, pp. 23–33. Springer, Cham (2015). doi:10.1007/978-3-319-20612-7_3
13. Drobik, A.: IT Market Clock for ERP Platform Technology. Gartner (2015)
14. Babaian, T., Lucas, W., Xu, J., Topi, H.: Usability through system-user collaboration. In: Winter, R., Zhao, J.L., Aier, S. (eds.) DESRIST 2010. LNCS, vol. 6105, pp. 394–409. Springer, Heidelberg (2010). doi:10.1007/978-3-642-13335-0_27
15. Cooprider, J., Topi, H., Xu, J., Dias, M., Babaian, T., Lucas, W.: A collaboration model for ERP user-system interaction. In: Proceedings of HICCS 2010, pp. 1–9 (2010)
16. Lucas, W., Babaian, T.: Implementing design principles for collaborative ERP systems. In: Peffers, K., Rothenberger, M., Kuechler, B. (eds.) DESRIST 2012. LNCS, vol. 7286, pp. 88–107. Springer, Heidelberg (2012). doi:10.1007/978-3-642-29863-9_8
17. Hurtienne, M., Prümper, J., Rötting, M.: When enterprise resource planning needs software ergonomics: some typical scenarios. In: The 17th World Congress on Ergonomics, IEA 2009 (2009)
18. Parush, A., Hod, A., Shtub, A.: Impact of visualization type and contextual factors on performance with enterprise resource planning systems. Comput. Ind. Eng. **52**(1), 133–142 (2007)
19. Hong, K.-K., Kim, Y.-G.: The critical success factors for ERP implementation: an organizational fit perspective. Inf. Manag. **40**(1), 25–40 (2002)
20. van der Aalst, W.: Process Mining: Discovery, Conformance and Enhancement of Business Processes. Springer, Heidelberg (2011)
21. Hipp, M., Mutschler, B., Reichert, M.: Navigating in complex business processes. In: Liddle, S.W., Schewe, K.-D., Tjoa, A.M., Zhou, X. (eds.) DEXA 2012. LNCS, vol. 7447, pp. 466–480. Springer, Heidelberg (2012). doi:10.1007/978-3-642-32597-7_42

22. Hipp, M., Michelberger, B., Mutschler, B., Reichert, M.: Navigating in process model repositories and enterprise process information. In: IEEE 8th International Conference on Research Challenges in Information Science (RCIS 2014), pp. 1–12 (2014)

23. Speier, C., Morris, M.G.: The influence of query interface design on decision-making performance. MIS Q. **27**, 397–423 (2003)

24. Speier, C.: The influence of information presentation formats on complex task decision-making performance. Int. J. Hum.-Comput. Stud. **64**(11), 1115–1131 (2006)

25. Xu, J.D., Benbasat, I., Cenfetelli, R.T.: The nature and consequences of trade-off transparency in the context of recommendation agents. MIS Q. **38**(2), 379–406 (2014)

Participatory Icons Specification for Expressing Intentions in Computer-Mediated Communications

Julio Cesar Dos Reis[1(✉)], Cristiane Josely Jensen[2],
Rodrigo Bonacin[2,3], Heiko Hornung[1],
and Maria Cecília Calani Baranauskas[1]

[1] Institute of Computing, University of Campinas, Campinas, São Paulo, Brazil
{julio.dosreis,heiko,cecilia}@ic.unicamp.br
[2] Faculty of Campo Limpo Paulista, Campo Limpo Paulista, São Paulo, Brazil
cris_jensen3@hotmail.com, rodrigo.bonacin@cti.gov
[3] Center for Information Technology Renato Archer, Campinas, São Paulo,
Brazil

Abstract. Web-mediated conversations require treating intentions more explicitly. Literature lacks adequate design methods and interactive mechanisms to support users in the sharing of intentions. This research assumes that icons representing emotions play a central role as means for aiding users to convey intentions in communication tasks. This article proposes a method to specify emoticons for representing the users' intentions, named "*intenticons*". The work explores Speech Act Theory and Semiotics in a conceptual framework to structure classes of intentions. We conduct participatory activities to experiment the method with 40 users. The obtained *intenticons* were evaluated with a different set of users to reveal their effectiveness. The obtained results suggest the feasibility of the method to select and enhance emoticons for intention expression. Evaluations point out that most of the achieved *intenticons* indicate an acceptable degree of representativeness for the intention classes.

Keywords: Icons · Emoticons · Meanings · Intentions · Pragmatics · Communication · HCI

1 Introduction

In a communication act, humans naturally rely on various resources for better expressing their ideas, intentions and emotions. These resources include gestures and facial expressions, which indicate to an interlocutor how to interpret the communication acts.

A key aspect of communication refers to the shared understanding of intentions. Illocutions (acts performed by a speaker in producing an utterance) may result in different pragmatic effects depending on the interpretation of the speaker's intentions. For example, the phrase "please, leave the room" might be interpreted as an order/command or a gentle request. This might depend on the situation, intonation and corporal expressions. Although some words can characterize intentions, such as, "suggest", "ask",

© Springer International Publishing AG 2017
S. Hammoudi et al. (Eds.): ICEIS 2016, LNBIP 291, pp. 414–435, 2017.
DOI: 10.1007/978-3-319-62386-3_19

"expect" and "apologize", in many situations the speaker's intentions are formulated in an implicit way, without explicit use of words that indicate the real intentions.

In computational systems, in which communication remains predominantly based on text, intentions are not always clearly stated and shared. In some cases, the involved parts are unable to perform a successful communication. Frequently, inadequate interface design solutions result in various interaction barriers, leading to misunderstandings and disagreements between the participants of a conversation [5]. These problems can create difficulties for users to manage, retrieve and interpret the available content, as well as to interact effectively and satisfactorily with others. A possible solution would be to automatically capture and infer the intentions by using natural language processing techniques. However, this task is extremely complex, since the interpretation is highly dependent on social and cultural issues.

Although recent research literature has addressed some pragmatic aspects in interaction design [4], there is still a lack of interactive solutions and techniques to allow users to explicitly declare their intentions using computer systems. Our previous investigations preliminarily studied design alternatives to support users dealing with these issues [7]. Nevertheless, novel techniques and concrete design solutions are still required to enable users to express their intentions.

Whereas the use of so-called emoticons in interactive interfaces has been exploited to support the expression and transmission of emotions [6], we argue that icons can also bring benefits to the communication by supporting users in expressing their intentions.

This article proposes a method to design icons to express different classes of intentions. We call these expressive icons, created or selected with the proposal of representing and emphasizing users' intentions, "*intenticons*". This study thoroughly instantiates the method with 40 subjects, including undergraduate students in a Bachelor in Information Systems course. We consider as content for communication the software programming domain. Our investigation makes the following contributions:

- Define a method aiming at associating emotional icons with intention classes;
- Apply the proposed method to select and adapt groups of icons to express each class of intention based on experiments with users;
- Conduct an evaluation to examine the value of the specified *intenticons* to a set of real users distinct from those involved in the participatory activities.

This research adopts Semiotics [10] and Speech Act Theory [12] as frames of reference. The two theories provide means to structure and classify intentions according to different dimensions of the illocutions, as proposed by Liu and Li [8]. Based on this referential, the proposed method includes several steps to select icons with the users' participation. The designers and users also discuss and propose improvements in the icon selection and design in a participatory way. Obtained results point out the quality of the association between icons and classes of intentions and reveal the effectiveness of the proposal to achieve representative icons.

The article is organized as follows: Sect. 2 presents the state-of-the-art in emoticons applied to computer-mediated communication, and the used theoretical framework for intention classification. Section 3 defines the proposed method. Section 4 describes the results encompassing the participatory activities to obtain the *intenticons*. Section 5 reports on the evaluation conducted to investigate the adequacy of the *intenticons* to a distinct group of participants and discuss the findings. Section 6 draws conclusions and points out future investigations.

2 Background

According to Huang *et al.* [6], Computer Mediated Communication (CMC) poses additional difficulties to sharing emotions due to limited means of expressing them. One way to mitigate these difficulties is by introducing special icons named emoticons. These icons contribute to the creation of a new language to express emotions in CMC environments.

Studies of Huang *et al.* [6] also indicate positive results highlighting the value of emoticons for improving the CMC effectiveness and users' satisfaction. The authors pointed out that, when compared with text-based communications, integrating resources such as emotive expressions and gestures enhance the quality of information. This may refer to the possibility of emoticons to change the users' perceptions and interpretation of the received messages.

Users might feel more comfortable to express emotions in interfaces with informal style. In this sense, emoticons also contribute to increase the level of interpersonal interaction, as they improve the capacity of expressing emotions.

There are numerous studies about the representation of emotions in CMC. These researches indicate various advances in computer communication mechanisms. Derks *et al.* [2] present an extensive review of studies that reveal differences and potentials of CMC compared to face-to-face communication. Based on the analyzed studies, Derks *et al.* [2] emphasize the richness of emotions in CMC.

Emoticons are vastly disseminated in instant message interfaces and social networks. However, they can also be explored in professional settings, such as professional discussion forums. Luor *et al.* [9] investigated the effects of using emoticons on the communication of instant messages about professional tasks at the workplace. Their results point out the potential of emoticons to increase the expressiveness of text messages. The authors reported that workers recognize the utility of emoticons at the workplace. Other studies explored the use of emoticons in various working situations. For example, Thoresen and Andersen [13] studied the effects on the use of emoticons in the organizational communication from a socio-psychological perspective.

In this context, a relevant issue is how to choose an icon suitable to communicate a felling on a specific situation. Urabe *et al.* [14] present a system for recommending emoticons. Their results demonstrate the effectiveness of their system for 10 categories of emotions. The experiments also highlight users' difficulties in selecting an emoticon to represent the emotion that they want to express.

Carretero *et al.* [1] analyzed the use of expressive speech acts by students during online interactions. The study covers 13 types of expressive acts, *i.e.*, acts to express their feelings and emotions. The results reveal that the use of typography resources and emoticons can improve the expressiveness in various situations, *e.g.*, to thank or apologize.

The surveyed studies mostly stress the importance of emoticons for expressive CMC interactions. Although users' intentions are often associated with emotions, the communication and expression of intentions are scarcely addressed in literature. In contrast, our work focuses on the use of icons to inform intentions.

Studies of Dresner and Herring [3] adopted Speech Act Theory to analyze the linguistic role of emoticons in CMC. The authors emphasized that emoticons do not always work as "emotional icons"; they are also associated with other signs, which do not have the primary role of transmitting emotions, *i.e.,* they are indirectly related to emotions. In particular, Dresner and Herring [3] investigate the roles that the emoticons take as signs to express approaches and intentions. Their results indicate that emoticons assign the desired "illocutionary force" within the related text.

Our research aims to further explore the process of selection and design of emoticons when considering their role of illocutionary force. We contribute with techniques to the design and selection of suitable and expressive icons for the communication of intentions. In order to associate users' intentions with icons, we adopt the conceptual framework, which is based on Speech Act Theory and Semiotics [8].

Semiotics is a discipline that studies signs, their meanings and meaning-making processes. A sign is something that represents something to someone in some respect or capacity [10]. Among others, people use signs to share meanings and express intentions. While Semantics studies the relations between signs and objects, Pragmatics studies the relation between signs and the behaviour of sign-using agents [10].

The communication between a "speaker" and a "hearer" can be studied with Speech Act Theory [8]. Speech Acts [12] are utterances that have performative functions in language and communication. Searle proposes four types of Speech Act: locutionary acts, illocutionary acts, propositional acts and perlocutionary acts.

A locutionary act refers to the act of uttering an expression. An illocutionary act carries the speaker's intentions that are to be perceived by the hearer. The effects of an illocutionary act on the hearer are called perlocutionary effects. Perlocutionary effects comprise changes of sentiments or mental states, and perlocutionary acts are not necessarily linguistic. In this work, we focus on locutionary and illocutionary acts.

A speech act or message can be distinguished into two parts: the function and the content. The content manifests a message's meaning. Meaning and interpretation are dependent on the environment, in which the message is uttered, *i.e.,* they depend on the speaker and the hearer (in a certain situation). The function specifies the illocutions and reflects the speaker's intentions.

Inspired by Speech Act Theory and based on Semiotics, Liu and Li [8] proposed a framework for classifying illocutions using three dimensions. One dimension distinguishes between descriptive and prescriptive "inventions", another between affective and denotative "modes", and the last one between different "times", namely past/present and future.

If an illocution is related to the speaker's personal modal state mood, it is called affective, otherwise denotative. If an illocution has an inventive or instructive effect, it is prescriptive, otherwise descriptive. The classification of the "time" dimension is based on when the social effects of the message are produced, *i.e.,* in the future or the present/past.

The three dimensions result in eight different classes: 1. **Proposal** (future, prescription and denotative)—*e.g.*, request, command, promise and guarantee; 2. **Inducement** (future, prescription and affective)—*e.g.*, threaten, warn and temp; 3. **Forecast** (future, description and denotative)—imagin *e.g.*, predict and assume; 4. **Wish** (future, description and affective)—*e.g.*, wish, hope and desire; 5. **Palinode** (present/past, prescription and denotative)—*e.g.*, retract, annul and revoke; 6. **Contrition** (present/past, prescription and affective)—*e.g.*, regret and apologize; 7. **Assertion** (present/past, description and denotative)—*e.g.*, assert, report and notify; 8. **Valuation** (present/past, description and affective)—*e.g.*, judge, complain and accuse.

3 Specifying Intenticons with Participatory Practices

We propose a method to determine *intenticons*. The five-step method is inspired by the participatory method "Icon Design Game" [11] for supporting designers in the creation of icons and other graphical user interface elements. The general objective of this method is to identify the "best" graphical representation of a concept.

Figure 1 illustrates the five steps. First, participants and an icon set are selected. Second, participants explore the icons and freely associate concepts (short phrases). Third, participants associate icons with classes of illocutions. Fourth, participants choose the most representative icons from step three. Fifth, participants discuss and possibly adapt the icon selection.

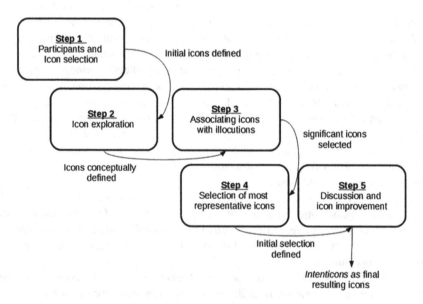

Fig. 1. Proposed five-step method.

In the following, we describe the five steps in more detail.

Step 1. Participants and Icon selection

1. Choose between 15 and 20 participants. According to the authors' experience, this number has shown to be adequate for this type of activity.
2. Designers propose the initial set of candidate icons.
3. Designers explain the objectives and the process of the activities to the other participants.

Step 2. Icon exploration

1. Participants describe concepts they associate with the icons on sticky-notes. At this point, the participants do not know yet the framework presented in Sect. 3, *i.e.*, concepts expressed by the participants are uninfluenced by the definition of illocution classes.
2. This process is iterative, one icon at a time. After each icon, facilitators collect the created sticky-notes.

Step 3. Associating icons with illocutions.

1. Designers create scenarios that illustrate the illocutions.
2. Designers present classes of illocutions, one at a time, using previously created illustrative scenarios to exemplify illocutions in the context of participants.
3. Participants individually write on sticky-notes the identifiers of the icons they think best denote the illocution, informing up to three icons in decreasing order of significance.

Step 4. Selection of most representative icons.

1. Designers distribute lists of illocutions and the respective icon set proposed during the previous step.
2. Participants individually choose a unique icon they think is most representative for each class of illocution.

Step 5. Discussion and icon improvement.

1. Designers present the results of the previous steps and conduct a debriefing with the participants. Discussion topics include, but are not limited to: possible changes in the association of illocution and icon; additional icons, in case no or few adequate icons where identified for an illocution; ambiguities/conflicts of icon-illocution association; removal of icons.
2. At the end of the discussion, the designers present the final set of *intenticons*.

4   Method Instantiation

The proposed method was applied in the Informatics lab at the IASP (São Paulo Adventist Institute – Hortolândia – SP, Brazil) in April 2015. The participants of the study included 2 HCI researchers with experience in interaction design, who were responsible for the conduction of the method, 1 graphic designer who designed the initial icon set, 2 local lecturers who acted as facilitators and 40 undergraduate students of an Information Systems course.

All 40 students—aged 20 to 61, 12 female—were in the seventh semester. The students and facilitators participated in the activities during two different days. On the first day, steps 1 to 4 were conducted. During the second day, step 5 was conducted using the focus group method in which the icons were presented in a shared screen by a beamer.

The research materials such as annotation forms were situated within the context of software programming. Sample phrases to represent illocution classes were taken from an online forum about Web development. For instance, a phrase to represent the illocution class "proposal" (request, command, promise, guarantee) was, "Please, take a look at HTML Media Capture". For all illocution classes, there was at least one representative phrase previously selected by the researchers. After presenting the initial set of icons to the participants, designers made available the annotation forms for each illocution.

The presentation and analysis of results explore the following topics:

1. Selection and initial design of icons;
2. Theory-free assignment of concepts to icons;
3. Analysis of quantitative distribution of icons for each illocution class and initial selection;
4. Analysis of detected ambiguities;
5. Proposal of improvements in icons and debriefing sessions;
6. Final selection of *intenticons*.

4.1   Selection and Initial Design of Icons

The initial icons were derived from preliminary studies [7] and from web searches associated with keywords related to the definition of the illocution classes. For instance, the class Proposal can be further described by terms request, command and promise. The goal was to obtain a limited initial set and the selection criteria included the relevance in making explicit intentions according to the classes of illocutions. To this end, designers selected images that had descriptions matching one of the eight classes, and that were judged as representing the respective class to some degree. A graphic arts professional redesigned the icons to maintain a uniform visual quality. Figure 2 shows the initial set of obtained icons numbered from 1 to 34.

Fig. 2. Initial icon set numbered from 1 to 34.

4.2   Theory-Free Assignment of Concepts to Icons

Table 1 shows the three most frequent concepts that participants assigned to each icon during the "icon exploration" (step 2 of the method proposed in this section). These results also consider an analysis performed by the involved researchers to detect the most representative concepts for each icon. The results indicate that various used concepts and terms depict people's ordinary language. Several verbs are used in the gerund form to portray the action represented by the icon, *e.g.,* crying.

4.3   Analysis of Quantitative Distribution of Icons for Each Illocution Class and Initial Selection

In order to determine the most relevant icons for each illocution class, we examined different frequencies of participants' assignments of icons to illocution classes. Three separate analyses were performed to understand the influence of icons defined as the most significant and most representative as the result of Step 3 and Step 4.

During analysis 1, we focused on how many times an icon appeared with the highest priority during Step 3. For analysis 2, we computed how many times an icon appeared in any of the three slots used during Step 3. In analysis 3, we counted how many times an icon was chosen as the most representative for an illocution class during Step 4.

Appendix A presents tables that summarize the three analyses for the eight illocution classes with all results obtained. To better examine the selection process of the icons, we chose to graphically present the distribution of occurrences for a few illocution classes that pose more difficulties (with highest concentration of occurrences in the top-five icons and those with the lowest concentration). Furthermore, to support and

Table 1. Most frequent concepts associated to the icons.

1	Hopeful anxious timidity	13	vanity seductive sensual	25	OK! sure agrément
2	Suspicious watching over keep an eye on	14	Passionate dreaming gentle	26	Yes sir! prepared Copy that
3	Thoughtful doubtful imagining	15	Fear apprehensive worried	27	greeting great Nice
4	Fear silent secret	16	Happiness wonder Beauty!	28	astonished frightened scared
5	Underdog sad agonized	17	aid help lonely	29	deluded in love wishing
6	Deception Disappointed Disapproved	18	cool small wink smartness	30	ashamed Sorry my love! Pardon
7	kidding playing mocking	19	oracle guessing Forecasting	31	Disappointed unmotivated upset
8	It was not me! doubt confusion	20	Optimistic idea light	32	sarcastic laughs guffaw
9	Apologies sorry Pardon	21	frightening angry raging	33	deep sadness crying depressed
10	happy Fake smile forced laugh	22	doubt thoughtful analytical	34	inattentive carefree tedium
11	suspicious thoughtful questioned	23	Regretful sheepish mistake		
12	Yes sir Copy that Determined	24	Attention Stopped! Stop!		

justify the selection of icons, Table 2 presents the occurrences in percentage of the top-five icons for each analysis and illocution class.

Figure 3 presents the distribution of occurrences for all icons in the analysis 1, 2 and 3 regarding the "Proposal" class. This indicates a concentration of occurrences on the top-five icons. As shown at Table 2, the top-five icons represent 50.50%, 50.93% and 56.22% for the three analyses, respectively. Similarly, Fig. 4 presents the distribution of occurrences for icons assignment in the analysis 1, 2 and 3 for the "Assertion" class. In this case, the top-five icons obtained 39.24%, 35.03% and 38.85% of the

Table 2. Percentage of occurrence for top-five icons.

	Top-5: analysis 1	Top-5: analysis 2	Top-5: analysis 3
Proposal	50.50%	50.93%	56.22%
Inducement	45.00%	42.26%	50.00%
Forecast	46.15%	36.32%	49.35%
Wish	66.67%	64.10%	69.23%
Palinode	51.28%	48.72%	55.13%
Contrition	66.67%	51.28%	69.23%
Assertion	39.24%	35.03%	38.85%
Valuation	51.57%	50.52%	55.35%
MEAN	52.14%	47.40%	55.42%

occurrences in the analysis 1, 2 and 3, respectively (*cf.* Table 2). Although less concentrated than in the Proposal class, the top-five icons still remains useful to the next steps in this investigation.

According to results at Table 2, although we had not a uniform distribution of the occurrence for the top-five icons, they represent around 50% in average. Thus, we selected five icons with highest frequency for each class based on the analyses (initially relying on analysis 2 and then refined afterwards).

The obtained results also allow discarding less frequent icons for some illocution classes, *e.g.*, 4, 5 and 6 for illocution class "Proposal" (details in in Appendix A). While some icons appear with high frequencies in different illocution classes, there are a few "distinctive icons". For example, the icon 22 refers to the most frequent in Forecast class, and only in Forecast, although it appears with a higher or similar absolute frequency in Assertion, Proposal and Valuation. The distribution of Palinode is very similar to Contrition, as can be seen in Fig. 5, which shows the normalized frequency counts of the two illocution classes, *i.e.*, the frequency count of and icon divided by the respective highest frequency count. This indicates potential ambiguities between icons, which are mitigate in the next step.

Table 3 presents the initial set of *intenticons* for each illocution class. This list was defined using only frequency counts and no statistical analysis. As a result, there are icons with a relatively high frequency difference compared to other icons (*e.g.*, icons 25 and 27 for Proposal class). We also observe icons with only a small difference compared to icons that did not enter the selection, *e.g.*, icon 3 for Inducement with a frequency count of 13 compared to a count of 12 for icons 11, 16, 22 and 24.

4.4   Analysis of Detected Ambiguities

Table 3 indicates a repetition of several icons for different classes of illocution, which potentially reveal ambiguities among icons. In particular, we observe that the participants deemed icons 27, 25, 20 and 18 as appropriate for the illocution classes *Proposal, Inducement, Desire* and *Valuation*. This result suggests the need of reworking these icons because they present difficulties in their interpretation.

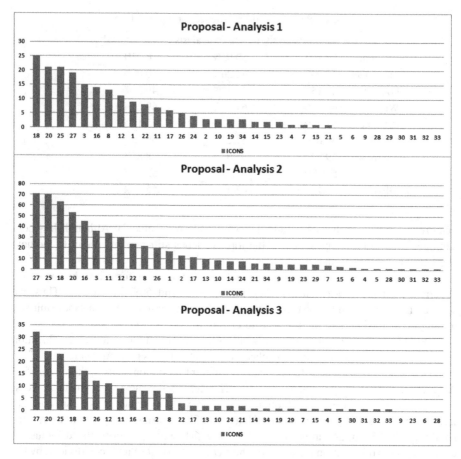

Fig. 3. Occurrence of icons for proposal class.

Similarly, the icons 11 and 20 appear as representative of both *Forecast* and *Assertion*. Considering the dimensions in the illocution classification framework, even though these two classes of illocution are organized into different periods in the time dimension, they are in the same invention and mode dimension, *i.e.,* both are denotative and descriptive. This scenario justifies the qualitative debriefing that can further clarify possible misunderstandings identified and mitigate these issues.

4.5   Proposal of Improvements in Icons and Debriefing Sessions

During Step 5, designers also introduced a new icon set to encourage discussion (Fig. 6). The new icons are identified with letters from A to T. The aim was to expand the diversity of choices for the representation of classes of illocution. The results of quantitative analyses informed the design of the new icons, where alternatives were defined to minimize ambiguities.

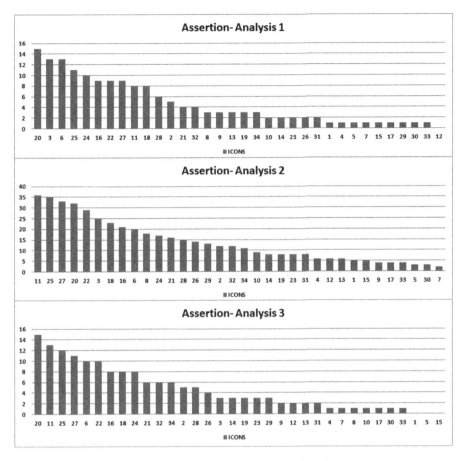

Fig. 4. Occurrence of icons for assertion class.

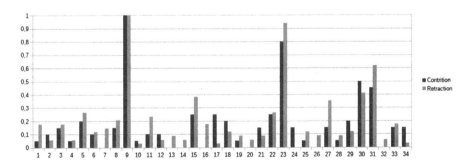

Fig. 5. Normalized frequency counts of contrition and retraction.

This step involves a debriefing session based on the results obtained from the previous steps. Firstly, designers chose the five *intenticons* to represent each class of illocution (Table 3). They presented to the participants the *intenticons* to make an

Table 3. Initially selected *Intenticons*.

Illocution	Intenticons				
	1ˢᵗ	2ⁿᵈ	3ʳᵈ	4ᵗʰ	5ᵗʰ
Proposal	27	25	18	20	03
Inducement	27	20	25	24	18
Forecast	22	11	20	03	02
Wish	27	25	18	16	01
Palinode	09	23	30	15	27
Contrition	09	23	30	15	22
Assertion	11	27	25	20	22
Valuation	27	25	18	16	20

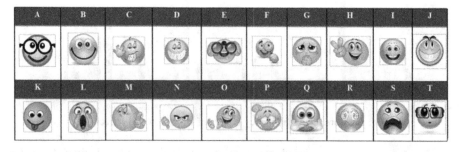

Fig. 6. Additional intenticons explored.

overview of the illocution classes. Prompted about the detected ambiguities among illocution classes, the participants reported that they had realized that many icons were out of context for some classes of illocutions.

The designers discussed the ambiguous *intenticons* with the participants. Subsequently, based on the initial selection of intenticons (Table 3), and considering the ambiguities as well as the additional icons (Fig. 6), the participants selected at least three ambiguity-free *intenticons* in a group session.

More specifically, in the debriefing session, designers went over each *intenticon* asking the participants to which extent each icon represented the class of illocution. They then took into account the participants' opinion to make additions and removals of icons in each class. Successively, they carried out discussions concerning all available *intenticons*. When an inaccurate case was detected, the choices were jointly revised and decided which category the icon best fit.

4.6   Final Selection of *Intenticons*

Table 4 shows the *intenticons* selected by the debriefing session developed with the participants. We found that while for some illocution classes the initial selection of icons remained in the final set (*e.g., Proposal*), for some other classes, the selected icons were fully reviewed. This may be due to the organization of the debriefing session, where designers did not impose any restrictions to maintain icons in one class or another. This result revealed the choice of new icons that did not appear in the first selection.

5   Evaluation and Discussion

To assess the representativeness and generalizability of the determined *intenticons* achieved by the proposed participatory method, we conducted a preliminary evaluation with a different group of participants. In the following, we present the experimental procedure and involved participants, as well as the obtained results. Afterwards, we discuss the main findings.

5.1   Procedure and Subjects

This evaluation was conducted with 22 students (6 females) aged 19 to 51 years. The students were graduate students in Computer Science of the Faculty of Campo Limpo Paulista and undergraduate students of an Information Systems course of the IASP Faculty.

The evaluation occurred on July of 2015 using a Web-based form. The invited participants were contextualized regarding the experiment and accessed the online form. For each illocution class, the *intenticons* resulted as the most representative according to the final selection were presented. The participants assigned a score to each *intenticon* to denote its representativeness to each illocution class according to their understanding using a Likert scale, ranging from 1 ("none") to 5 ("very high"), to represent the representativeness of the *intenticon*.

Table 4. *Intenticons* set after the debriefing outcome.

Illocution	Intenticons				
Proposal	27	25	18	C	H
Inducement	16	J		G	
Forecast	22	11	20	03	19	F
Wish	29	14	01		
Palinode	09	23	30	31	
Contrition	P	R	N	33	
Assertion	26	12	O	A	D
Valuation	I	K	06	10	

5.2   Results

Table 5 presents the mode of the representativeness item for each *intenticon*. This result reveals that most of the *intenticons* has acceptable representativeness for the illocutions classes, even when we consider a different group of users as compared with those involved in the initial selection and design phases. Only few icons like H, N, A and D present a mode value equal to 1, which indicates that the participants judged that such choices were inadequate to the illocutions.

5.3 Discussion

This research explored an alternative way of facilitating human communication through computer systems. While literature has studied icons to represent emotions, few empirical studies exist for elaborating explicit visual means to express intentions. Both Web and mobile applications could exploit the selection of resulting icons from our study.

Results of this study indicate the potential of the method to identify and evaluate icons to represent intentions. The initial steps of the method allow participants to preliminarily experience the icons, and enable designers to understand how users make sense of the originally proposed icons. Furthermore, the method enables a refinement of icons followed by a final selection, reached via debriefing sessions.

The initial selection is based on a quantitative analysis, which might result in ambiguous icons. The debriefing step is thus required to improve icon selection. Potential ambiguities may be related to several factors: (i) participants may have interpreted the icons superficially; (ii) the proposed icons may not be specific enough; and (iii) participants may have had difficulties in understanding the illocution classes. Regarding the latter factor, participants may not have been able to make the necessary distinctions between the existing classes (*e.g.*, between *Palinode* and *Contrition*), which may have influenced the assigned icons during the execution of the case study.

The preliminary validation process involved a second user population distinct from the participants of the initial study. We examined the extent to which the obtained *intenticons* are relevant to this second group of users. The conducted evaluation used a *Likert* scale and explored the mode value to analyze the adequacy of the *intenticons* to the illocution classes. Although the findings are satisfactory, a thorough evaluation is still required to deeply assess the quality of the associated *intenticons*.

The conducted quantitative analyses are likely to affect the initial selection of *intenticons*. Future research might investigate to what extent they can influence the results of obtained *intenticons*. Further studies could conduct alternative evaluation methods considering other criteria and exploring additional statistical techniques. We aim to understand the influence of the *intenticons* in distinct communities, and situations of communication addressing the impact of the *intenticons* in specific application contexts. The influence of user's profiles in the obtained results also requires additional investigation, since this work focused on computer science students as subjects in the case study. Experiments towards these issues can strengthen the quality of the *intenticons*, enhancing our understanding of its use in communicating intentions.

Table 5. Evaluation of the *Intenticons*.

Illocution	*Intenticon*	Mode of the Likert scale
Proposal	27	3
	25	4
	18	3
	C	3
	H	1
Inducement	16	4
	J	4
	G	5
Forecast	22	4
	11	5
	20	4
	03	4
	19	5
	F	4
Wish	29	5

Illocution	*Intenticon*	Mode of the Likert scale
Wish	29	5
	14	5
	01	5
Palinode	SORRY 09	5
	OOPS! 23	5
	SORRY 30	5
	31	5
Contrition	P	5
	R	5
Contrition	N	1
	33	5
Assertion	26	5
	12	3
	O	4

Illocution	Intenticon	Mode of the Likert scale
Assertion	A	1
	D	1
Valuation	I	4
	K	3
	06	5
	10	3

6 Conclusion

The perception of intentions plays a key role in human communication. Users require effective ways of expressing their intentions more explicitly through computer systems mediated communication. In this article, we argued that icons expressing emotions could help users communicate their intentions. We proposed a method to associate icons with intention classes, through several steps, representing a systematic approach to find the most adequate *intenticons*. The method was instantiated with participatory activities yielding encouraging empirical results. The proposed technique was effective in selecting icons and enabled resolving ambiguities. The foreseen debriefing sessions were relevant for improving the selection and mitigating inaccurate cases. The conducted evaluation revealed to which extent the resulting icons are representative for the two different set of users who participated in the study. Future investigations involve further quantitative and qualitative analyses that can contribute with refinements in the method and to the resulted *intenticons*.

Acknowledgment. We thank the São Paulo Research Foundation (FAPESP) (Grant #2014/14890-0) and National Counsel of Technological and Scientific Development (CNPq) (Grant #308618/2014-9). We also thank colleagues from the InterHAD research group for the insightful discussions. The opinions expressed in this work do not necessarily reflect those of the funding agencies.

Appendix A – Analysis Result of Icon Frequency

See Tables A.1 and A.2.

Table A.1. Quantitative analysis of Proposal, Inducement, Forecast and Wish.

Icons	Proposal			Inducement			Forecast			Wish		
	A_1	A_2	A_3	A_1	A_2	A_3	A_1	A_2	A_3	A_1	A_2	A_3
1	9	17	8	0	2	0	3	7	1	8	14	4
2	3	13	8	7	9	3	4	12	6	0	1	0
3	15	36	16	6	13	5	8	12	5	1	3	0
4	1	1	1	0	2	1	1	1	1	0	0	0
5	0	1	1	0	1	0	1	2	1	0	1	0
6	0	2	0	1	3	3	2	4	0	0	0	0
7	1	4	1	3	6	1	1	2	0	0	0	0
8	13	22	7	1	5	2	6	13	0	0	2	1
9	0	5	0	0	1	0	1	3	0	0	0	1
10	3	9	2	0	5	0	1	4	1	1	6	1
11	7	34	9	6	12	5	6	18	6	0	0	0
12	11	30	11	3	8	3	1	3	1	2	5	4
13	1	10	2	0	0	0	1	3	0	2	2	2
14	2	8	1	1	5	2	0	3	0	2	13	4
15	2	3	1	0	1	0	0	4	1	0	0	0
16	14	**45**	8	6	12	2	0	4	2	12	25	8
17	6	12	2	0	1	0	3	7	2	1	2	1
18	25	**63**	18	6	**18**	7	2	10	2	11	28	9
19	3	5	1	2	2	0	3	6	4	3	4	2
20	21	**53**	24	11	**22**	9	9	18	11	4	12	2
21	1	6	2	1	4	1	1	4	1	1	3	1
22	8	24	3	4	12	5	7	23	10	0	3	1
23	2	5	0	1	3	0	0	3	0	0	1	0
24	4	8	2	5	12	8	3	7	1	0	0	0
25	21	**70**	23	5	**23**	9	4	9	4	9	34	13
26	5	20	12	1	11	2	1	5	2	1	2	0
27	19	**71**	32	5	**25**	7	4	13	1	12	48	20
28	0	1	0	0	2	0	0	4	3	0	0	0
29	0	5	1	1	5	3	2	4	0	7	15	2
30	0	1	1	0	1	0	0	1	0	1	2	0
31	0	1	1	1	4	0	0	8	4	0	2	0
32	0	1	1	0	1	0	1	7	3	0	4	1
33	0	1	1	0	0	0	1	3	2	0	1	0
34	3	6	1	3	8	2	1	7	2	0	1	1

Table A.2. Quantitative analysis of Palinode, Contrition, Assertion and Valuation.

Icons	Palinode			Contrition			Assertion			Valuation		
	A_1	A_2	A_3	A_1	A_2	A_3	A_1	A_2	A_3	A_1	A_2	A_3
1	3	6	2	0	1	1	1	5	0	5	10	2
2	1	2	1	1	2	1	5	12	5	8	13	7
3	4	6	2	1	3	0	13	25	3	7	16	6
4	1	2	0	0	1	0	1	6	1	0	2	0
5	7	9	3	1	4	0	1	3	0	2	5	1
6	3	4	1	2	2	1	13	20	10	3	7	3
7	0	5	1	0	0	0	1	2	1	2	6	0
8	2	7	2	1	3	1	3	18	1	1	7	2
9	12	34	15	10	20	11	3	4	2	0	1	0
10	0	1	0	0	1	0	2	9	1	3	9	4
11	0	8	4	1	2	0	8	36	13	6	23	6
12	1	2	1	0	2	0	0	6	2	3	10	3
13	2	3	2	0	0	0	3	6	2	3	4	2
14	0	2	0	0	0	0	2	8	3	2	12	3
15	5	13	8	0	5	3	1	5	0	3	10	3
16	3	6	3	0	0	0	9	21	8	17	36	15
17	1	1	1	2	5	1	1	4	1	2	3	0
18	2	4	2	1	4	1	8	23	8	8	46	11
19	0	3	0	0	1	0	3	8	3	3	5	2
20	1	2	0	0	0	1	15	32	15	18	35	14
21	1	3	1	1	3	1	4	16	6	5	6	2
22	3	9	1	1	5	0	9	29	10	4	20	6
23	12	32	8	6	16	4	2	8	3	1	6	1
24	0	0	0	1	3	1	10	17	8	2	4	1
25	1	4	1	0	1	0	11	35	12	16	61	18
26	0	3	1	0	0	0	2	14	4	3	11	2
27	1	12	5	1	3	2	9	33	11	23	63	30
28	1	3	0	1	1	0	6	15	5	2	6	3
29	1	4	0	0	4	0	1	13	3	1	13	4
30	4	14	7	6	10	6	1	3	1	1	2	2
31	2	21	3	2	9	3	2	8	2	0	5	0
32	1	2	1	0	0	0	4	12	6	1	5	2
33	2	6	2	0	3	0	1	4	1	0	4	0
34	1	1	0	0	3	1	3	11	6	4	11	4

References

1. Carretero, M., Maíz-Arévaloa C., Martíneza M.A.: An analysis of expressive speech acts in online task-oriented interaction by university students. In: 32nd International Conference of the Spanish Association of Applied Linguistics (AESLA), pp. 186–190 (2015)

2. Derks, D., Fischer, A.H., Bos, A.E.R.: The role of emotion in computer-mediated communication: a review. Comput. Hum. Behav. **24**, 766–785 (2008)
3. Dresner, E., Herring, S.C.: Functions of the nonverbal in CMC: emoticons and illocutionary force. Commun. Theor. **20**, 249–268 (2010)
4. Hornung, H., Baranauskas, M.C.C.: Towards a conceptual framework for interaction design for the pragmatic web. In: Jacko, J.A. (ed.) HCI 2011. LNCS, vol. 6761, pp. 72–81. Springer, Heidelberg (2011). doi:10.1007/978-3-642-21602-2_8
5. Hornung, H., Pereira, R., Baranauskas, M.C.C., Bonacin, R., Dos Reis, J.C.: Identifying pragmatic patterns of collaborative problem solving. In: IADIS International Conference WWW/Internet, Madrid, Spain, pp. 379–387 (2012)
6. Huang, A.H., Yen, D.C., Zhang, X.: Exploring the potential effects of emoticons. Inf. Manag. **45**(7), 466–473 (2008)
7. Jensen, C.J., Dos Reis, J.C., Bonacin, R.: An interaction design method to support the expression of user intentions in collaborative systems. In: Kurosu, M. (ed.) HCI 2015. LNCS, vol. 9169, pp. 214–226. Springer, Cham (2015). doi:10.1007/978-3-319-20901-2_20
8. Liu, K., Li, W.: Organisational Semiotics for Business Informatics. Routledge, Abingdon (2014)
9. Luor, T., Wu, L., Lu, H., Tao, Y.T.: The effect of emoticons in simplex and complex task-oriented communication: an empirical study of instant messaging. Comput. Hum. Behav. **26**, 889–895 (2010)
10. Peirce, C.S. Collected Papers. Cambridge. Harvard University Press, Harvard University Press (1931–1958)
11. Rocha, H.V., Baranauskas, M.C.C.: Design e Avaliação de Interfaces Humano-Computador. NIED/UNICAMP, Campinas (2003)
12. Searle, J.R.: Speech Acts: An Essay in the Philosophy of Language. Cambridge University Press, Cambridge (1969)
13. Thoresen, T.H., Andersen, H.M.: The Effects of Emoticons on Perceived Competence and Intention to Act. BI Norwegian Business School (2013)
14. Urabe, Y., Rzepka, R., Araki, K.: Emoticon recommendation for Japanese computer-mediated communication. In: IEEE Seventh International Conference on Semantic Computing, pp. 25–31 (2013)

Towards Advanced Security Engineering for Enterprise Information Systems: Solving Security, Resilience and Usability Issues Together Within Improvement of User Experience

Wilson Goudalo[1,2(✉)], Christophe Kolski[1],
and Frédéric Vanderhaegen[1]

[1] LAMIH-UMR CNRS 8201, University of Valenciennes,
59313 Valenciennes, France
wilson.goudalo@abe-engineering.net,
{christophe.kolski,
frederic.vanderhaegen}@univ-valenciennes.fr
[2] Research and Innovation Department, ABE - Advanced Business Engineering,
77400 Lagny, France

Abstract. In our era of the service industry, information systems play a major place, even a vital position for businesses, organizations and individuals. Information systems are facing new ongoing security threats, more sophisticated and of different natures. In this context, it is important to prevent attackers from achieving their outcomes, manage the inevitable breaches, and minimize their impacts. Security practices must be conducted in an engineering framework; engineering of security has to be improved. For this, it is proposed to develop innovative and broad systemic approaches that operate together on several axes, by improving user experience. We track and solve Resilience, Security and Usability issues jointly in enterprise information systems. In this paper, we position socio-technical systems according to well-known information systems of enterprises and organizations. We treat the paradigms of socio-technical systems and we focus on the interplay between resilience, security and usability. A case study illustrates the proposed approach; it details the elaboration of design patterns for improving user experience.

Keywords: Enterprise information system · System resilience · Information security · Privacy · Human-Computer Interaction · Usability · User experience · Socio-technical systems · Design patterns

1 Introduction

Information systems, and more precisely the services they deliver, have completely invaded our lives and play an increasingly prominent role. This is verified for individuals, as well as for organizations and for enterprises [1]. Information systems are composed of business applications, application components and technical components,

© Springer International Publishing AG 2017
S. Hammoudi et al. (Eds.): ICEIS 2016, LNBIP 291, pp. 436–459, 2017.
DOI: 10.1007/978-3-319-62386-3_20

other IT resources and not IT resources, to which are added infrastructures of security and security guidelines, according to a security policy (if it is in place). The overall vision of security is often dotted with ruptures and the harmonized control is not easy at all levels.

Security and privacy concerns are crucial in many services [2–5]. As a quality attribute, the meanings of security have evolved, and the technologies in the industry and in the standards have adapted to this evolution. In the field of IT systems, the initiatives were mostly based on "securing the perimeter". In the case of Information system and the extended enterprise, initiatives have evolved into guaranteeing security strategy in depth. To improve the security strategy in depth, Goudalo and Seret [6] proposed a methodological approach that operates on building a membership canvas of all stakeholders of the company.

Therefore, there is an urgent need for new approaches focusing on human aspects including usability to ensure the security of systems. Indeed systems are used by humans, although they are increasingly automated. Ferrary showed that human resources are now at the heart of the business model of organizations and indicated "the human factor as a main source of operational risk in banking" [7]. Cranor and Garfinkel's book indicates the research trends in security and usability [8]. Clarke and Furnell's book presents the state of the art on "the human aspect in success of the security" [9]. Most initiatives are carried on specific security solutions. We notice a lack of research on the overall engineering of security from the point of view of HCI (Human-Computer Interaction).

Our propositions have taken inspiration from the following three motivations.

1. The Breakthroughs and developments of engineering of software and information systems (IS) are inspirational opportunities for building security engineering approaches. The perpetual emergence of new areas of researches in information systems shores up the interest in engineering methods. The CAME (Computer-Aided Method Engineering) is an ancient discipline which remains relevant, both for researchers and for professionals in industries. An analysis of existing CAME is summarized in [51]. The discipline of engineering of methods is concerned with the definition of new engineering methods for information systems. It is a discipline of conceptualization, construction and adaptation of methods, techniques and tools for IS development. The engineering of methods also addresses the development of new methods from existing methods.

2. Many achievements of the systems engineering are being applied to information security, with success. These achievements relate to the concepts, paradigms, techniques and tools. Security engineering has to include the understanding of the operational environment of the enterprises and organizations; it operates specifically on the security related objectives of enterprises and organizations. Security engineering treats the vulnerabilities, threats, and risks against assets of organizations and enterprises. Corporate assets include not only what the organization possesses, but also what it has right to, and represent value for it and for its operations. A summary of security engineering approaches is presented in [52]. Security policy development and security management imitate the formalism of processes of

information system, actually business process formalism [31, 48]. New international standards are increasingly developed in this direction [53].

3. The study of Ponemon Institute shows the causes of the data breach in 2015 [54]. In this study, malicious or criminal attacks are around 46%, system glitches (both IT and business process failures) are around 29% and human factors (negligent employee or contractor) around 25%. In similar studies, the total costs from cyber events are estimated about $10 billion annually [55]. Whatever companies and organizations do for information security, incidents occur and disrupt the providing of services worthy of provable confidence. Advanced engineering of enterprise information system security becomes crucial.

We suggest a socio-technical systems resilience approach, through design patterns based on user experience. Socio-technical approaches can help the design of organizational structures and business processes as well as the design of technical systems. Socio-technical system approaches aim to model all together human, social and technological capabilities in using and dealing with value added services.

In this extended paper [39], we introduce first the concept of socio-technical systems as an engineering approach. We also explain how resilience, usability and security can be addressed by using a socio-technical systems approach. We introduce then our socio-technical systems resilience approach, through design patterns based on improvement of user experience. A case study on medical analysis laboratory is used to illustrate the application of our suggested approach. The paper ends with a discussion, a conclusion, and suggestions for future researches.

2   Paradigms of Socio-Technical Systems

This section presents the positioning of the socio-technical systems in relation to information systems of companies and organizations. It appears that the socio-technical systems include classical concepts of information systems and also the entire social environments, which include both the cyber and the physical worlds. Then we recall the concepts of security, privacy and usability in socio-technical systems.

2.1   Socio-Technical Systems and Information Systems

The concept of *socio-technical system* was created in the context of labor studies by the Tavistock Institute in London by the end of the 50's [10, 11]. Sperber and Wilson treat the relevance of communication (and cognition) in social context [12]. Socio-technical systems aim to model all together human, social and technological capabilities in using and dealing with value added services. Singh defines socio-technical systems (STS) as multi-stakeholder cyber physical systems [13]. They contend with complexity and change in both the cyber and the physical (social) worlds.

Socio-technical approaches can help the design of organizational structures and business processes as well as technical systems. It is largely acknowledged that systems which are developed using a socio-technical approach are more likely to be acceptable to end-users and to deliver real value to stakeholders. There are notable differences between IT systems and socio-technical systems modeling and engineering approaches in terms of interactions (Fig. 1):

(1) IT systems modeling focuses on the technical description of the components of the systems and the interactions between them in order to deliver a certain service.
(2) Social systems include all human interactions and cooperation, on social and cultural values.
(3) Information systems include all users' interactions with the IT systems, integrating their organization, implementation and management.
(4) Social-technical systems provide a way of understanding all human interactions with the various IT systems, their components, as well as cooperation with other systems. Socio-technical systems approach also the interactions between the systems, all the stakeholders and their organization and the entire social environment, both the cyber and the physical worlds.

These dimensions define the information in terms of interactions among actors, which can be: social reliance (actors rely on others to achieve their goals), and information exchange (actors exchange relevant information). As it will be detailed

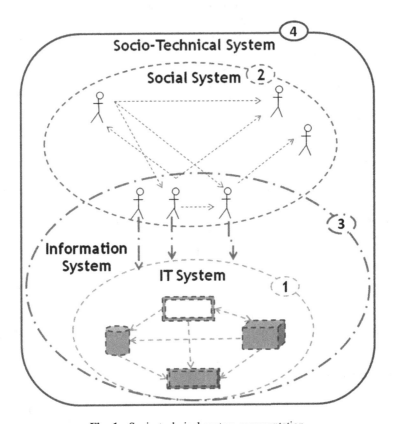

Fig. 1. Socio-technical system representation.

later on, many security issues arise from the interaction between actors, and on how the exchanged information is accessed. Therefore, user experience is a main concern when analyzing security.

2.2 Security and Privacy in Socio-Technical Systems

In socio-technical systems, a set of human and automated agents (organized or not) interact to complete tasks, according to a certain objective. These have converging and/or diverging characters or conflicting objectives. Feelings and conflict situations are quickly transposed into the socio-technical systems.

In other words, users of the systems can be animated by malicious intents. This is the case of hackers who find their playground in the socio-technical systems. At the same time, the systems process personal data, sensitive data and very private character data. The tasks and data are sensitive and highly valuable.

In socio-technical systems, privacy is an important matter as well and must be protected. Actually, in the case of medical health data, the privacy requires special attention in terms of confidentiality. This is one of the objectives of security. Another objective of security is to guarantee the safety, the integrity and the reliability in processing all tasks. Difficulties of security in socio-technical systems arise in ensuring these objectives, due to two reasons.

First, solutions of security (a too constraining usage) may constitute security vulnerability or may prevent the completion of tasks. Secondly, users' behavior (errors, unintentional actions) may constitute security vulnerability. Human factors are a main source of operational risk in companies [7], and the trust of users in the socio-technical system is necessary [3]. Clarke and Furnell's work reports success of security from the human point of view [9].

2.3 Usability Difficulties in Socio-Technical Systems

Socio-technical systems expose users to social and to technological issues. Users resort to technology to deal with social issues and vice versa. Usability is a property that depends on interactions among users, systems, tasks, and environments where processes are operated in both the cyber and the physical words. Human factors are the main source of operational risk in companies [7]. Usability concerns human factors. Usability is not a specific property of persons or of things, which we may measure by a "usability thermometer", or evaluate by applying widely accepted scientific formulas [14].

Usability difficulties are focused on: Personal human factors experiments; Measuring behaviors and attitudes captured when users complete the key tasks; Measuring capabilities of the systems to provide adequate conditions for carrying out tasks [15].

3   Foundations

This section defines the concepts of resilience applied to socio-technical systems, usability and security. It also concerns the interplay between them.

3.1   Resilience Applied to Socio-Technical Systems

Resilience is a major concern nowadays, in order to prevent an incident and more to restore a safer state after an accident or intentional fault [16, 17]. Resilience, actually in relation to the concern of accident [18], is applied in many domains such as socio-technical systems engineering.

Luzeaux [19] wrote that "resilience is obtained via the capacity to monitor conditions at the edges of the performance envelope, and the ability to adapt the operational behavior of the system to potential developments in this envelope".

Luzeaux [19] defined the four functions of the resilience, which are "avoidance (capacity for anticipation), resistance (the capacity for absorption), adaptation (the capacity for reconfiguration) and recovery (the capacity of restoration)". Resilience is considered as an active virtue integrated in all nowadays operations and systems, especially in the field of defense [20]. Today, geopolitical and economic strategies integrate simultaneously the five axes of influence (Cyber, Space, Air, Maritime, and Land), for achieving the activities and operations of Prevention, Protection, Mitigation, Response, Recovery, Correction, and Rescue. Infrastructure protection and functional continuity are aligned to make an active virtue integrated, the Resilience. Virtue is defined as "the capacity to take appropriate and correct action that benefits both the actor and others", by Roman philosopher Lucius Annaeus Seneca [57].

Resilience is also applied in the field of information technology and security. In this case, resilience is defined as "the capacity to perform during an incident (unintentional accident or intentional fault) and then to come back to a normal state" [21].

In this context, we define resilience as the capacity to prepare and adapt facing perpetuating evolutionary conditions and to restore full capability after an incident (an accident or an attack). In the face of ongoing security threats, it is crucial to prevent attackers from achieving their outcomes, manage the inevitable breaches, and minimize their impacts. It becomes necessary to develop innovative and broad systemic approaches that operate together on several axes; we propose to take especially into consideration the improvement of user experience.

3.2   Usability Models

HCI researchers have suggested different approaches in usability studies. Hertzum and his colleagues included cultural aspects in usability studies [22]. Bevan suggested including flexibility and safety to create a more comprehensive quality-of-use model [23]. Seffah and his colleagues suggested quality-of-use schemes that included 10 factors, 26 sub-factors, and 127 specific metrics [24]; see also [25]. Winter and his colleagues proposed a two-dimensional model of usability that associated a large number of system properties with user activities [26].

In socio-technical systems, usability rhymes with both the absence of usability problems and the measurements of effectiveness, efficiency, and satisfaction. Usability implies the ergonomic quality of the Human-Computer Interaction, regardless of the type of access media.

In terms of ergonomic requirements, the ISO has published a number of standards. The ISO 9241-12 published in 1998 [27] proposes seven principles for the presentation of information: *Clarity* (the content is displayed quickly and accurately), *Discriminability* (the information can be distinguished with precision), *Brevity* (only the information required for the task are displayed), *Consistency* (the same information is presented identically on the entire application), *Detectability* (information is properly encoded in the right place), *Readability* (the information is easy to read), *Comprehensiveness* (the meaning of terms is clearly understandable). The ISO 9241-110, published in 2006 [28], describes seven high-level principles for the design of dialogues: suitability for the task, self-descriptiveness, controllability, conformity with user expectations, error tolerance, suitability for individualization, and suitability for learning.

Shackel proposed three criteria to measure usability: performance of the task, user satisfaction and costs of use [29]. For the performance of the task, two sub-criteria are considered: the effectiveness and efficiency of interaction. An interaction is effective if users can perform the task successfully. An interaction is efficient if users can perform the task successfully for an acceptable period, with a consumption of acceptable resources. Satisfaction of users during the interaction considers the performance of the task and subjective feelings. The cost of the use considers, beyond the consumption of acceptable resources, the impact of the interaction on the health and safety of users, and on the reputation integrity of users in the socio-technical systems. The system must adapt to any user, within the predefined population, without distinction of age, size, ethnicity, educational or linguistic level, as well as those who have difficulty with some physical or cognitive operations. This adaptation must also comply with security requirements.

3.3 Security and Privacy Models

The family of standards ISO 2700x [30] is entirely dedicated to information security including the organizational dimension (private or public companies). The standards present how to establish, implement, maintain and continually improve a management system for information security. These standards model security in terms of confidentiality, integrity and availability of information by applying a risk management process. They give to all interested parties (users, operators and owners of socio-technical systems) the insurance that security risks are managed appropriately.

On one hand, we noticed how security risks are managed using a harmonized process, and secondly we noticed the three fundamental criteria of security that are confidentiality, integrity and availability of information. Briefly, we develop each of these four points:

1. The process incorporates the interested parties and their respective requirements. It takes into account the interfaces and dependencies between the activities of the organization and its stakeholders within the extended enterprise.
2. Confidentiality (Information should neither be made available or disclosed to a user, entity or unauthorized process).

3. Integrity (The information must not be modified, altered or destroyed in an unauthorized manner).
4. Availability (Access by an entity, an authorized user or process to the services offered by the socio-technical system must always be possible; Operations to illegally occupy the processing time must be detected). Other properties of the security of Information Systems, such as Proof, Traceability and Authenticity derived from these three basic criteria.

The security criteria characterize constraints or properties on system assets, describing their security needs. The harmonious process brings the answer, dealing with company issues that are human, financial, branding, regulatory and legal. Goudalo and Seret [31] define the process for the engineering of security of enterprise information systems in seven major activities designated by the term *Security Acts*. The first two of them (*Identifying business assets* and *Defining security goals to achieve*) assess security needs on corporate assets. Other international standards also address security and security risks of information system. This is the case of the ISO 15408 (Common Criteria, CC) focusing on three audiences that are producers, evaluators and users, the ISO 13335 and ISO 21827. We also identify local standards and norms as Cramm (in the United Kingdom), Mehari and Ebios (in France), Octave (USA and Canada). The basic criteria of security remain the same, and to them are added the various properties and attributes of security such as proof, trace, non-repudiation, identification, authentication, accountability, reliability, privacy, trust and others.

In socio-technical systems, the attributes of *Privacy* and *Trust* undeniably join to security. Westin, in his notable book "Privacy and freedom" opening the modern field of law and privacy, defined Privacy as "the request of individuals, groups and institutions to determine for themselves (on their own) when, how and to what extent information about them can be communicated to others" [32]. Alain Westin adds that "every individual is constantly engaged in personal adjustment process in which balance the desire for intimacy with the desire of disclosure and communication." Moreover, Privacy is a legal topic with a critical issue, since disruption of Privacy deals with penal/criminal law [33]. We use Privacy as both the confidentiality and the integrity of information dealing with the private aspects of individuals, groups and institutions in society. In her course materials [15, 34], Cranor defines different views on privacy: Privacy as limited access to oneself (the extent to which we are known to others and the extent to which the others have a physical access to us); Privacy as control of information (beyond limit of what others know about us, we must control, which implies individual autonomy, we can control the information in a meaningful way).

The presence of respect for the privacy policy (Privacy) builds consumer confidence. Rousseau et al. [35] define the trust as a psychological condition including the intention to accept vulnerability based on positive expectations of the intentions or behavior of another. Trustworthiness (reliability from the point of view of security) defines the property of a system which performs only what is required (except for an interruption of the environment, user errors and human operators, and attacks by hostile parts) and that does not make things [36].

3.4   User Experience in Socio-Technical Systems

The socio-technical system approach facilitates the identification and formulation of user experiences. A positive user experience is usually based on convenience (time savings or reduced physical or mental work), the confidence that the socio-technical system "works properly", and the perception of its usefulness. The concept of "works properly" implies (instills) the trust. According to Sasse [37], the user experience takes into account all the usability criteria, with additional factors [15]. Birge [38] emphasizes the lack of research on the design of technical solutions for communication and information technology in the field of "user experience and security" (Trust and User eXperience - TUX).

In summary, the security objective is to evaluate, eradicate and prevent errors, faults and attacks. If occurrences, the resilience objective is to tolerate and outdo the impacts, and to guarantee services in degraded mode according to the conditions of the service layer agreements. The objectives of security and resilience must be ensured, while maintaining a positive user experience. We specify that a good usability (HCI and positive user experience) should promote the success of the security and resilience, and *vice versa*.

It is proposed a joint conceptual model of security, of resilience and of usability in socio-technical systems, with the aim of improving user experience [39]. The resulting conceptual model operates

- on the three concepts of Assets, Incident Risks and Solutions;
- and on a homogeneous metric system to manage these three concepts, from the point of view of security, of resilience and of usability together.

4   User eXperience Improvement Built-in Approach of Socio-Technical Systems, Based upon Design Patterns

Today, most of the security built-in systems are not easily usable. Users who have to use these systems often bypass the security devices and this behavior generates security gaps.

The issue is to replace a security built-in system approach by user experience improving built-in socio-technical system approach; we propose this approach to be based on design patterns. This socio-technical approach takes into account interdependence between security, resilience and usability.

In such a way, this approach allows adapting facing perpetual evolutionary of usage conditions and facing usability problems. Figure 2 portrays the underlying process in the proposed approach. Three stages compose the approach: (1) Identify the boundaries, (2) Analyze risks, (3) Define solutions.

We use patterns to describe the problems and the solutions of security/usability problem. Patterns have been widely considered in many human endeavors that require a combination of skill and training. In the 70's architect Alexander pioneered the recognition, naming, and use of patterns, while working on urban planning [40]. In the late 80's computer scientists working in the field of object-oriented design discovered

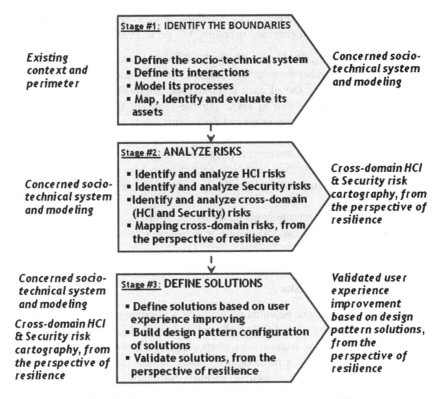

Fig. 2. User experience based design pattern approach.

Alexander's work and adapted design patterns to software [41]. Schumacher [42] argues that the security engineering can benefit from the use of patterns, but he fails to present specific patterns to accomplish this goal. The Open Group has edited a book on security design patterns [43], but has not addressed the alignment between usability and security.

The proposed approach is detailed in the three following sections.

4.1   Stage #1: Identify the Boundaries

This stage consists in defining the boundaries of the eco-systems including the entire social environment and the various actors. We integrate their interactions in both the cyber and the physical worlds, using BPMN (Business Process Modelling Notation) to model the processes, activities (sub-processes) and individual tasks performed by each actor involved in the process. The detailed description of the interactions between the technical components of the information system is described using UML diagrams including use cases. Links between the BPMN and UML diagrams (misuse cases) are also described during this stage [44].

We evaluate the assets and define the enterprise objectives on the assets, from the perspective of security, resilience and usability. We perform the tasks below.

- List the main assets (hardware, physical, software, human, documentary, and immaterial); asset is also data, service, business process and procedures.
- Specify the contexts of use of each asset and the responsible of each main asset. This responsible would have to know the use made of the asset, its utility, its intrinsic value and the consequences of the corruption of asset.
- Determine the intrinsic value of these assets, their sensitivity to the company, according to the business strategy, the legal and regulatory requirements.
- Classify assets and define their quotation, according to criteria of security, resilience and usability. The functional dependency between assets must be taken into account;
- Express the needs and requirements on the assets, from the perspectives of security, resilience, usability, and user experience improvement.

4.2   Stage #2: Analyze Risks

This stage produces the list of potential problems. It is possible to use different methods to analyze the description of the socio-technical system produced during the previous stage: for instance including cognitive walkthrough [45, 46]; marked Petri Nets; simple and cross-domain risk analysis methods [47]. Risks include on the one hand security threats (such as faults, frauds, blackmail, identity usurpation) and on the other hand usability issues and technical glitches. They lead to malfunction, denial of service or destruction of parts of the socio-technical system.

The study focuses on the problem, the origins and the reasons as well as the consequences of not improving some aspects. This study highlights the relations of proximity and interdependence between the HCI and the privacy security. Our proposal uses firstly a multi-domain approach to risk analysis, and secondly it focuses on human factors. Problems are documented using for instance a storytelling approach detailing user experience, its failures and its possible improvement points (other methods are available in the literature). Problem documentation is based on learning and operational feedback about any other kind of incidents dealing with these risks.

We summarize the stage #2 in five points:

- Identify and analyze usability risks;
- Identify and analyze security risks;
- Highlight the risks of incidents of technical glitches (failure, design errors, procedural inconsistency ...);
- Identify and analyze cross-domain risks (security, usability and resilience together), taking into account the propagation of risk;
- Perform the global mapping of risks, from the perspective of resilience and user experience improvement.

Risk analysis is not an *obvious* activity. Finally, we would like to recall the following elementary tasks that make the difference in risk analysis:

- Identify vulnerabilities inherent to each asset.
- Identify threats to which each asset is exposed.
- Estimate the intrinsic probability of occurrence of each threat.
- Study the impacts of occurrence of each threat, and the possible propagation (due to the bounce attacks and to the functional dependency between assets).
- Estimate the likelihood of occurrence of each threat (taking account of the real context, that is to say existing measures in their environment). In other words, the actual probability of occurrence is defined.
- Assess the overall level of risk faced each asset taking into account each of the elements obtained above.

4.3   Stage #3: Define Solutions

In the final stage, we resort to user experience in order to define the solutions that solve the points highlighted during the second stage. Actually, we look for the best improvement of user experience that underlies these identified points. The significant question addressed here is what makes the solution seen as a better – or worse – design concept, from a usable security perspective. Thus, how to detect a bad design in order to correct it?

We note four types of risk treatment: risk acceptance, risk avoidance, risk reduction and risk transfer. Following the decision on the type of risk treatment, we have to assess residual risks. The residual risks are appreciated against the organization's objectives. The controls applied in the security solutions are of four natures: corrective, detective, deterrent and preventive. A good security solution should ensure the adequacy between the three components of the triplet (nature of control, type of treatment, security goals).

We base the actions of this stage on various experiments both in industry and academic research. As mentioned in Sect. 3.3, Goudalo defined seven security acts constituting the engineering of information security. Although several researchers have discussed usable security design, Kai-Ping Yee has proposed a list of guidelines for addressing valid and nontrivial problems specific to usable security design [49]: path of least resistance, active authorization, revocability, visibility, self-awareness, trusted path, expressiveness, relevant boundaries, identifiability and foresight.

This stage consists also in documenting each pattern using the format:

- Name of the design pattern;
- Description of the problem (or class of problems);
- Description of the solution;
- Consequences of applying the design solution;
- Validity of the solution. Qualitatively, each pattern should improve the user experience, e.g. according to one of the guidelines given by Kai-Ping Yee. Quantitatively, patterns should enhance in a measurable way the compromise between usability and security.

The design patterns for resilient built-in socio-technical systems must integrate both usability and security concerns in order to design efficient and usable security systems. These design patterns have to complete other works dealing with security architecture of systems [50].

5 Case Study

The case study, called *FI MedLab*, is related to the information system in a medical laboratory, also called clinical laboratory. Credibility of medical laboratories is paramount to the health and safety of the patients relying on the testing services provided by these labs. The international standard in use today for the accreditation of medical laboratories is ISO 15189 – Medical laboratories – particular requirements for quality and competence. A laboratory conducts tests on clinical specimens in order to get information about the health of a patient as pertaining to the diagnosis, treatment, and prevention of disease. Such information is highly security-sensitive, any error may have a direct impact on patient safety, privacy and the reputation of the laboratory.

An information system is in use in most medical laboratories today. It allows collecting data about patients, test records and interpretation of test results. Information security and privacy risks have grown with the rapid growth in the number and types of people who have a legitimate role to provide access, use and transform the information and medical records. Tension often exists between security, privacy controls and usability needs. For example, access to the information system can be delayed by the need to first authenticate to ensure the user is legitimate, and is provided with the right level of system access he or she is requested. Some information has to be quickly available to a physician in the case of an emergency situation, but has not to be communicated broadly, since it deals with health and privacy. On the other hand, disclosing such information is a punishable offence, in many countries, for instance the article 226-22 of the French Penal Code.

The same can be said about anyone who wants to enter medical or private data in the system. Data entry errors because of a usability issue have fatal impact on the integrity of data, which is a key measure of security and privacy.

5.1 Stage #1: Identifying the Boundaries

FI MedLab is a socio-technical system which involves patients, internal and external operators, laboratories or medical partners, medical equipment suppliers, regulatory agency as well as IT services and applications providers, sometimes datacenters. The socio-technical system comprises various operational business processes (BP) that are grouped into three categories: pre-analytical, analytical and post-analytical processes (see Table 1).

Some operators have to access to certain kinds of information, but not to other ones. This depends upon the level of authorization and the user authentication. So, within the organizations, groups of users with respective roles and responsibilities have to be

Table 1. Three business processes of *FI MEDLAB*.

1.	**Prepare the medical tests**
1.1	*Manage the patient file (Create, Update, or Archive) (see Table 2)*
1.2	Register a request for medical tests
1.3	Charge the demand for medical tests
1.4	Collect and sample the blood of a patient,
1.5	Receive the blood sample extracted elsewhere
1.6	Process and store the blood samples prior to analysis
2.	**Realize the medical tests**
2.1	*Switch on and calibrate the devices (see Table 2)*
2.2	Pass a series of tests (technical analysis)
2.3	Validate the technical tests
2.4	Maintain the equipments
3.	**Conclude the medical tests**
3.1	Interpret the biological validation tests
3.2	Archive the blood samples
3.3	*Communicate the results (see Table 2)*
3.4	Archive the results

defined. Figure 3 shows a simplified model of these business processes using BPMN (Business Process Modeling Notation).

The activities (sub-processes) consist of tasks. We will detail some activities, that illustrate Stage#2 "Analyzing risks" (see Fig. 2).

5.2   Stage #2: Analyzing Risks

Table 2 is a detailed description of three of the sub-processes detailed in the previous section. We will use this description to explain how we have been analyzing risks of usability, privacy and security in the socio-technical system of *FI MedLab*.

Such risks are due to the interdependence between usability and security. Users need to access to information, function of their role and their task. But the modality to access this information depends upon the context of the task (indoor/outdoor, time pressure…), the quality of the security device, its adequacy to the task and its context.

As a matter of example, we have investigated more deeply the following scenarios.

Scenario T1: The patient gives his business address. He does not notice that the results of his medical tests will be sent to this address and the administrative operator does not indicate this helpful clarification to the patient. When results reach the patient, he is absent and his assistant handles the mail, like any business mail. This is a serious problem in terms of privacy and confidentiality that we detect during this phase. This scenario deals with the confusion between professional and personal information, within the professional email box. The assistant can open the email box and read the emails in this box, since these emails are supposed to be professional.

Scenario T2: The manager of technical operations faces serious difficulties in being accepted by the biometric authentication system. The camera system is not well

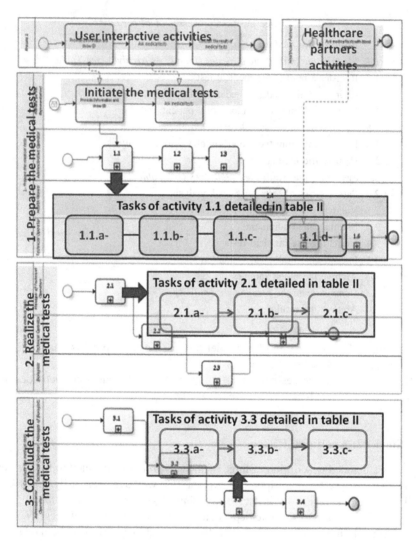

Fig. 3. Modelling business processes (with focus on tasks with potential problems)

positioned for this manager sportsman who measures 1.92 m (for information, the average height of his colleagues is 1.76 m). The manager is not comforTable 1n such a situation; he can no longer find his good inclination to be authenticated. In this context, he runs the backup procedure; he logs into the system and activates the devices. The devices are initialized, but do not load the signatures of the biologists' managers (who interpret the biological validation of tests). There is no alert. The manager does not notice the error. We are faced with a problem of usability and ergonomics (first on the internal procedures of the system and secondly, on the communication user interfaces). This problem creates security vulnerability on all the medical tests that will be

Table 2. Three detailed activities.

1.1	**Manage the patient file (Create, Update, or Archive)** *Input: identity document of patient or his representative* *Output: updated patient record* *Tasks:*
1.1. a	The patient or his representative indicates the required information to the administrative operator of FI MedLab, including address for sending medical analysis results
1.1. b	The administrative operator of FI MedLab enters information in the FI MedLab socio-technical system, for creation and/or update of the patient's record
1.1. c	A scheduled event triggers and alerts the administrative operator to archive records of some patients
1.1. d	The administrative operator carries out the administrative processing and archives the corresponding patients' records
2.1	**Switch on and calibrate the devices** *Input: identity document of the manager of technical operators* *Output: devices switched on and calibrated for operating medical tests* *Tasks:*
2.1. a	The manager performs biometric authentication (retinal scan and scan of the identity document)
2.1. b	The authenticated manager starts and calibrates the devices
2.1. c	The devices initialize and load the signatures of the biologists' managers (who interpret the biological validation of tests)
3.3	**Communicate the results** *Input: Results validated and interpreted* *Output: Results communicated by three ways (sent to the physician, sent to the patient by mail, made available on the secure website of FI MeddLab)* *Tasks:*
3.3. a	Administrative operator sends the results to the physician
3.3. b	Administrative operator sends the results to the patient address by mail
3.3. c	Administrative operator puts the results on the secure website of *FI MedLab*

performed during the day (no traceability and no respect for integrity on the interpretation and validation of medical test results).

The security device does not fit to the task and to the users. The user bypasses the security device, using a backup procedure. Moreover, there is no alarm alerting this barrier bypassing. This kind of behavior deals with barriers bypassing rules; it is a critical security issue.

Scenario T3: The patient is on vacation when medical analysis results are ready. From his vacation location (Cayman Islands), he decides to access the secure website of *FI MedLab*. He receives a message asking to enter the code that has just been sent to his phone via SMS. This may lead to three problems: a privacy problem (the vacation location could be a "non-public information", but is found out by the web site security system of *FI MedLab*, leading to potential rumor about the reputation of the patient); a trust and confidence problem (one category of patients could say: "*I have too much confidence in the FI MedLab system, as I feel that my data is protected*", another category of patients could say: "*I do not have any trust in the FI MedLab system, I feel spied*"); a problem of comfort and simplicity (due to the additional verification).

This scenario deals with the context of the task, namely, vacation. Moreover, it deals with the low level of the security device that can open to fraudulent access to information with bad consequences such as identity usurpation or blackmail ("I feel spied").

5.3   Stage #3: Developing Solutions

The previous three scenarios describe a user experience; each one of them highlights a usability, resilience, security or privacy problem.

Scenario T1, for example, details a typical problem of privacy and confidentiality, due to misunderstanding of the use made of the information requested to the user (the patient or responsible). Table 3 details possible solutions of this problem.

Table 3. Design pattern solution for trouble T1.

Design pattern solution for trouble T1	
Name	Awareness
Description of the problem	Misunderstanding and poor knowledge of the use made with the information requested from the user
Description of the design pattern solution	Provide users with the explanation, understanding and analysis of any of the information indicated in the socio-technical system. This will require an individualized support and pedagogy. Operationally, we can put flyers and (interactive) information terminals in the lobby of FI MedLab. An alternative solution should be to "send all mail of the results via letters"
Consequences	Another solution consists to add a tag "confidential personal information" in the object of the message, and a note presenting the law inside the text of the message, in order to alert the assistant and "to increase" its awareness

In Scenario T2, it is a more complex problem with several interrelated dimensions: T2.1 - Bad usability of the biometric authentication system; T2.2 - Non-effectiveness of the emergency procedure; T2.3 - Difficulties in understanding the emergency procedure by the manager; T2.4 - Detecting barrier bypassing by the manager. Tables 4, 5, 6 and 7 describe four possible solutions.

In Trouble T3, we are faced with three problems again: T3.1 - Feeling of privacy problem; T3.2 - Feeling of trust and confidence problem; T3.3 - Comfort and simplicity

Table 4. Design pattern solution for trouble T2.1.

Design pattern solution for trouble T2.1	
Name	Anticipation
Description of the problem	Bad usability of biometric authentication system
Description of the design pattern solution	Repositioning the camera and reconfiguring the biometric authentication system to account for all employees of the team. People need to use secure solution, in simple and efficient way
Consequences	Simple and efficient usage of secure solution is an important step, for ensuring the security in the context of a socio-technical system

Table 5. Design pattern solution for trouble T2.2.

Design pattern solution for trouble T2.2	
Name	Regular test of the procedures
Description of the problem	Non-effectiveness of the emergency procedure
Description of the design pattern solution	The repetition frequency of the tests and their results should be integrated into the systems of controlling and auditing
Consequences	This problem is well-known in safety issues of critical systems. The repetition of exercises develops more confidence of operators, and in case of failure they still trust the procedures. Regularly testing the emergency procedures is a way to improve the user operator experiences

Table 6. Design pattern solution for trouble T2.3.

Design pattern solution for trouble T2.3	
Name	Training of operators
Description of the problem	Lack of mastering the emergency procedure by the manager
Description of the design pattern solution	Training of operators in all the procedures they will face. These training activities should be embedded in the systems of controlling and auditing
Consequences	This problem is well known in critical systems. Operator training helps improve their user experience

problem. The search for improved user experience provides an effective response to all of these three points (Table 8).

These representative scenarios illustrate that usability problems impact security, and conversely. By identifying business processes, the roles and tasks of users, as well as their needs for private information or, on the opposite, the inability to access to this private information, context of use and other usability issues, we have elaborated design patterns. Such design patterns are the keystone of resilient built-in socio-technical systems, since they integrate security and usability issues together.

Table 7. Design pattern solution for trouble T2.4.

Design pattern solution for trouble T2.4	
Name	Detection and alert following barrier bypassing
Description of the problem	Due to usability problems, the security device is bypassed, using a backup procedure
Description of the design pattern solution	Usage of security device has to be monitored in order to detect barrier bypassing and to alert the system security administrator. Then, the security administrator can improve security device usability and adapt it to the current usage
Consequences	This problem is also well-known in critical systems in which such a pattern is suggested

Table 8. Design pattern solution for trouble T3.

Design pattern solution for trouble T3 (T3.1, T3.2, T3.3)	
Name	Sensitization and pedagogy
Description of the problem	Eventual stress of the user
Description of the design pattern solution	In the early stages, provide users with explanations allowing a better understanding of the functioning of the socio-technical systems
Consequences	In the era of service industry, personalized monitoring and pedagogy are a good way to improve user experience

6 Discussion

Nowadays, security must not be treated at the expense of usability. Several studies show how to take into account usability in the implementation of specific security features. Various tools have been proposed to provide more usable user interfaces for a specific security mechanism, or more easy-to-use security technologies; approaches have been proposed to design and to ensure trade-offs between security and usability [49]. However, there is still a need for global security approach, the security engineering that may take into account usability issue. The right balance between security and usability promotes user confidence and improves user experience. As part of the new threats that organizations face, resilience is a major concern in order to prevent an incident risk and more to restore a safer state after an accident or intentional fault [16, 17]. In case of occurrence of risk incident, the resilience objective is to tolerate and outdo the impacts, and to guarantee services in degraded mode according to the conditions of the service layer agreements (SLA). In this work, we proposed an attempt of advanced engineering that solves Security, Resilience and Usability issues together in enterprise information systems.

Our attempt of advanced engineering does not replace existing ISRAM (Information Security Risk Assessment Methods) [56]. It uses and extends them. Especially:

- Asset identification and asset quotation occur within business-driven perspective (stage #1 Identify the boundaries), like business processes, main business services. Its first benefit is the identification of the current key critical resources (through dependency graph). Its second benefit is to facilitate the join of business executives to security concerns.
- Risk analysis occurs through cross-domain analysis; and it uses qualitative and quantitative approaches valuation. Detailing activities to highlight the potential risks of incidents would be similar to the *method of scenarios*. One of its benefits is the ability to focus on the most important aspects, at each time, depending on the context. We did not consider in this paper the calculation of probabilities of occurrence of the risks or on the notions of exposure factor, annualized loss expectancy or annualized rate of occurrence.
- The solution search seems looking for the best improvement of the user experience behind all the points identified in stage #2. The formalism of design pattern inspires a combination of skill and training. The improvement of the user experience must be continuous, to lessen the risk (mitigating damages, inhibiting propagations, depleting occurrences, fixing vulnerabilities, user awareness, improving user interfaces).

The value of information to organizations is growing dramatically. However, for some kinds of information, like medical records, where a single corruption on data could be a matter of life or death, the value of secure data cannot be measured in terms of monetary value alone. An advanced engineering approach, solving Security, Resilience and Usability issues together, is in consequence necessary.

7 Conclusion and Future Work

From a perspective of enterprises and organizations, this research work addresses the actual information security needs. They take into account nowadays context of service industry, overlapping cyber and physical worlds, social environment and IS, professional and personal aspects, business objectives and privacy requirements. Security attacks have become crucial, they are professionalized increasingly, they are sophisticated and they use social engineering. Security is one of the most important issues for the achievements of service industry promises.

We propose to treat information security within an engineering method that brings together all stakeholders of company. This engineering method is advanced and operates on business processes, their decomposition and operational variants, in order to: discover the main assets in their context of use, identify the real value of assets and their dependencies, identify and assess risk incidents of security, resilience, usability and technical glitches. The proposed approach treats together security, resilience and usability issues; its solutions are based on design pattern approach for improving user experience continuously. The risks are not treated in isolation, but in their correlations. Indeed we have taken into account the functional dependency of asset, the cross-domain risk assessment and the interplay between security, resilience and usability. Human point of view and user experience are considered in this advanced security engineering for enterprise IS. Our advanced security engineering will overcome the lack of training and experience in security, the lack of security in terms of corporate strategy (operations, procedures) and the difficulties of communicating about security issues.

Despite the various tools proposed in the literature and in industry to provide more easy-to-use security technologies, despite the added values of our advanced security engineering approach, other challenges are still needed. How to raise awareness and effectively convey a good sense of usability as a security attribute? How to define the suitable framework that will facilitate a weighted consideration of security in the thoughts, decisions and activities? We plan to address such issues in the future, while elucidating a design pattern based engineering that will integrate explicitly measures of trust, privacy and other subjective criteria measuring user experience for all stakeholders.

Acknowledgments. The authors thank Prof. Ahmed Seffah (Lappeenranta University of Technology) for his numerous relevant remarks and suggestions on preliminary versions of this paper. They thank also warmly Dr. Jean-René Ruault for his strong contribution to the previous versions.

References

1. Larson, R.C.: Service science: at the intersection of management, social, and engineering sciences. IBM Syst. J. **47**, 41–51 (2008)
2. SBIC (Security for Business Innovation Council): The Time is Now: Making Information Security Strategic to Business Innovation. RSA Security, Bedford (2008)
3. IBM Corporation 2014: Understanding Big Data So You Can Act with Confidence. Doc. Ref. IMM14123USEN June 2014. http://www-01.ibm.com
4. KPMG International: Managing the Data Challenge in Banking. Why is It So Hard? Document published on June 2014. http://www.kpmg.com
5. Umhoefer, C., Rofé, J., Lemarchand, S.: Le big data face au défi de la confiance. Document published on June 2014. http://www.bcg.fr
6. Goudalo, W., Seret, D.: Towards the engineering of security of information systems (ESIS): UML and the IS confidentiality. In: Proceedings at 2nd International Conference on Emerging Security Information, Systems and Technologies, pp. 248–256. IEEE Computer Society Washington, DC (2008)
7. Ferrary, M.: Management des ressources humaines: Marché du travail et acteurs stratégiques. Ed. Dunod, Paris (2014)
8. Cranor, L.F., Garfinkel, S.: Security and Usability: Designing Secure Systems that People Can Use. Ed. O'Reilly, Newton (2005)
9. Clarke, N., Furnell, S.: 8th International Symposium on Human Aspects of Information Security and Assurance (HAISA 2014). Nathan Clarke, Plymouth (2014). (Ed. by S. Furnell)
10. Trist, E.L., Higgin, G.W., Murray, H., Pollock, A.B.: Organizational Choice: Capabilities of Groups at the Coal Face under Changing Technologies. The Loss, Rediscovery & Transformation of a Work Tradition. Tavistock Publications, London (1963)
11. Emery, E.: The next thirty years: concepts, methods and anticipation. Hum. Relat. **20**, 199–237 (1967)
12. Sperber, D., Wilson, D.: Relevance: Communication and Cognition, 2nd edn. Wiley, Hoboken (1995)

13. Singh, M.P.: Norms as a basis for governing sociotechnical systems. ACM Trans. Intell. Syst. Technol. (TIST) – Spec. Sect. Intell. Mob. Knowl. Discov. Manag. Syst. Spec. Issue Soc. Web Min. Arch. **5**(1), 21 (2013). (New York, NY, USA)

14. Lewis, J.R.: Usability: lessons learned… and yet to be learned. Int. J. Hum.-Comput. Interact. **30**(9), 663–684 (2014)

15. Cranor, L.F., Blase, U.: Usable Privacy and Security. Lecturer Materials, Courses, CyLab, Carnegie Mellon University, January 2015

16. Laprie, J.C.: From dependability to resilience. In: Proceedings of 38th Annual IEEE/IFIP International Conference on Dependable Systems and Networks (DSN 2008), Supplemental Volume, Anchorage, USA (2008)

17. ReSIST 2015: Resilience for Survivability in IST. A European Network of Excellence. http://www.resist-noe.org

18. Hollnagel, E., Woods, D.D., Leveson, N.: Resilience Engineering. Concepts and Precepts. Ashgate, Aldershot (2006)

19. Luzeaux, D.: Engineering large-scale complex systems. In: Luzeaux, D., Ruault, J.-R., Wippler, J.-L. (eds.) Complex Systems and Systems of Systems Engineering, pp. 3–84. ISTE-Wiley, London (2011)

20. Palin, P.J.: Resilience: Cultivating the Virtue. http://www.hlswatch.com/2013/08/29/resilience-cultivating-the-virtue/. Accessed 22 July 2016

21. ANSSI: Résilience de l'Internet français. http://www.ssi.gouv.fr/

22. Hertzum, M., Clemmensen, T., Hornbæk, K., Kumar, J., Shi, Q., Yammiyavar, P.: Usability constructs: a cross-cultural study of how users and developers experience their use of information systems. In: Aykin, N. (ed.) UI-HCII 2007. LNCS, vol. 4559, pp. 317–326. Springer, Heidelberg (2007). doi:10.1007/978-3-540-73287-7_39

23. Bevan, N.: Extending quality in use to provide a framework for usability measurement. In: Kurosu, M. (ed.) HCD 2009. LNCS, vol. 5619, pp. 13–22. Springer, Heidelberg (2009). doi:10.1007/978-3-642-02806-9_2

24. Seffah, A., Donyaee, M., Kline, R.B., Padda, H.K.: Usability measurement and metrics: a consolidated model. Softw. Qual. J. **14**, 159–178 (2006)

25. Braz, C., Seffah, A., M'Raihi, D.: Designing a trade-off between usability and security: a metrics based-model. In: Baranauskas, C., Palanque, P., Abascal, J., Barbosa, S.D.J. (eds.) INTERACT 2007. LNCS, vol. 4663, pp. 114–126. Springer, Heidelberg (2007). doi:10.1007/978-3-540-74800-7_9

26. Winter, S., Wagner, S., Deissenboeck, F.: A comprehensive model of usability. In: Gulliksen, J., Harning, M.B., Palanque, P., Veer, Gerrit C., Wesson, J. (eds.) DSV-IS/EHCI/HCSE -2007. LNCS, vol. 4940, pp. 106–122. Springer, Heidelberg (2008). doi:10.1007/978-3-540-92698-6_7

27. ISO 9241-12: Ergonomic requirements for office work with visual display terminals (VDTs). Part 12 Presentation of Information (1998)

28. ISO 9241-110: Ergonomics of human-system interaction. Part 110 Dialogue Principles (2006)

29. Shackel, B.: Usability - context, framework, definition, design, and evaluation. In: Shackel, B., Richardson, S. (eds.) Human Factors for Informatics Usability, pp. 21–37. Cambridge University Press, Cambridge (2009)

30. ISO/IEC 2700x: Information technology Security techniques (2010)

31. Goudalo, W., Seret, D.: The process of engineering of security of information systems (ESIS): the formalism of business processes. In: ECURWARE 2009, 3rd International Conference on Emerging Security Information, Systems and Technologies, pp. 105–113. IARIA (2009)

32. Westin, A.F.: Privacy and freedom. Wash. Lee L. Rev. **25**: 166 (1968) http://scholarlycommons.law.wlu.edu/wlulr/vol25/iss1/20
33. French Penal Code: De l'atteinte à la vie privée, article 226-1 (2015)
34. Cranor, L.: Usable Privacy and Security. Lorrie Cranor's Courses (2006). http://cups.cs.cmu.edu/courses/ups-sp06/
35. Rousseau, D.M., Sitkin, S.B., Burt, R.S., Camerer, C.: Not so different after all: a cross-discipline view of trust. Acad. Manag. Rev. **23**(3), 393–404 (1998)
36. Schneider, F.B.: Trust in Cyberspace. Committee on Information Systems Trustworthiness. National Research Council, Washington, D.C. (1998)
37. Sasse, M.A.: Red-eye blink, bendy shuffle, and the yuck factor: a user experience of biometric airport systems. IEEE Secur. Privacy **5**(3), 78–81 (2007)
38. Birge, C.: Enhancing research into usable privacy and security. In: SIGDOC 2009: Proceedings of 27th ACM International Conference on Design of Communication (2009)
39. Goudalo, W., Kolski, C.: Towards advanced enterprise information systems engineering - solving resilience, security and usability issues within the paradigms of socio-technical systems. In: Proceedings of 18th International Conference on Enterprise Information Systems (ICEIS 2016) – vol. 2, pp. 400–411 (2016)
40. Alexander, C., Ishikawa, S., Silverstein, M.: A Pattern Language: Towns, Buildings, Construction. Oxford University Press, New York (1977)
41. Salloway, A., Trott, J.R.: Design patterns par la pratique. Eyrolles, Paris (2002)
42. Schumacher, M.: Security Engineering with Patterns: Origins, Theoretical Models, and New Applications. LNCS, vol. 2754. Springer, Heidelberg (2003)
43. Blakley, B., Heath, C., and members of The Open Group Security Forum 2004: Security design patterns. Technical report G031, The Open Group, April 2004. http://www.opengroup.org/publications/catalog/g031.htm
44. Piètre-Cambacèdés, L.: Des relations entre sûreté et sécurité. Ph.D in Software and Network, Paris (2010)
45. Wharton, C., Rieman, J., Lewis, C., Polson, P.: The cognitive walkthrough method: a practitioner's guide. In: Nielsen, J., Mack, R.L. (eds.) Usability Inspection Methods, pp. 105–140. Wiley, New York (1994)
46. Mahatody, T., Sagar, M., Kolski, C.: State of the art on the cognitive walkthrough method, its variants and evolutions. Int. J. Hum.-Comput. Interact. **26**(8), 41–785 (2010)
47. DCSSI: 'Fiche d'expression rationnelle des objectifs de sécurité (2009). http://circulaire.legifrance.gouv.fr/pdf/2009/04/cir_1982.pdf
48. Goudalo, W.: Toward engineering of security of information systems: the security acts. In: Proceedings of 5th International Conference on Emerging Security Information, Systems and Technologies, pp. 44–50. IARIA (2011)
49. Yee, K.-P.: User interaction design for secure systems. In: Deng, R., Bao, F., Zhou, J., Qing, S. (eds.) ICICS 2002. LNCS, vol. 2513, pp. 278–290. Springer, Heidelberg (2002). doi:10.1007/3-540-36159-6_24
50. Ruault, J.R, Kolski, C., Vanderhaegen, F., Luzeaux, D.: Sûreté et sécurité: différences et complémentarités. In: Conférence C&ESAR, Résilience des systèmes numériques, Rennes, France (2015)
51. Niknafs, A., Ramsin, R.: Computer-aided method engineering: an analysis of existing environments. In: Bellahsène, Z., Léonard, M. (eds.) CAiSE 2008. LNCS, vol. 5074, pp. 525–540. Springer, Heidelberg (2008). doi:10.1007/978-3-540-69534-9_39
52. Jacobs, S.: Engineering Information Security: The Application of Systems Engineering Concepts to Achieve Information Assurance. Wiley, Hoboken (2011)
53. ISO/IEC 27032: Information Technology – Security Techniques – Guidelines for Security (2012)

54. Ponemon Institute LLC: 2015 Cost of Data Breach Study: Global Analysis. Benchmark Research Sponsored by IBM, Independently Conducted by Ponemon Institute LLC (2016)
55. Romanosky, S.: Examining the Costs and Causes of Cyber Incidents. Working document (2016).   https://www.ftc.gov/system/files/documents/public_comments/2015/10/00027-97671.pdf. Accessed 22 July 2016
56. Behnia, A., Rashid, R., Chaudhry, J.: A survey of information security risk analysis methods. Smart Comput. Rev. **2**(1), 79–94 (2012)
57. Stanford Encyclopedia of Philosophy: Seneca, chapter the Vertue. http://plato.stanford.edu/entries/seneca/#Vir. Accessed 22 July 2016

Enterprise Architecture

Business Model Loom: A Pattern-Based Approach Towards the Definition of Business Models

María Camila Romero$^{(\boxtimes)}$, Mario Sánchez, and Jorge Villalobos

Systems and Computing Engineering, Universidad de Los Andes, Bogotá, Colombia
{mc.romero578,mar-san1,jvillalo}@uniandes.edu.co

Abstract. To understand what an organization does one must comprehend the business model, which describes the way in which an organization acquires raw materials, transforms them into a product or service that is delivered to a client, and gains money in exchange. In consequence, it is possible to decompose the model into four core processes: supply, transformation, delivery, and monetization, which have both structural and behavioral dependencies among them. Unfortunately, identifying the business model demands an overall view of the business, and most representations focus only on the structural part leaving aside the interactions between core processes. The objective of this paper is twofold. Firstly, it presents a conceptualization and representation for business models that is capable of handling their components and interactions. Secondly, it uses the proposed representation to introduce a catalog of business patterns applicable in the design, portrayal, and analysis of business models. Each pattern includes the basic participants, resources, activities and interactions that must be accounted for in order to perform the core process. When different patterns are joined together, a complete business model can be portrayed.

Keywords: Business model · Structural view · Behavioral view · Business model pattern

1 Introduction

Business models describe what an organization does, also understood as the way in which it transforms, delivers and monetizes value. Though this definition is quite simple, it has led to different interpretations and consequently, a great variety of models that try to embrace the concept. However, this broad selection of models has also contributed to a lack of formality in the idea itself [1]. It is no longer clear how business models are supposed to be used, designed, or described. In addition to the scarcity of standards, there is a dearth of means to define and communicate business models, so that they can be understood, analyzed, and improved upon.

With a precise definition of a business model, small and medium enterprises (SME) could perceive various benefits. Since their main concern is staying afloat

© Springer International Publishing AG 2017
S. Hammoudi et al. (Eds.): ICEIS 2016, LNBIP 291, pp. 463–487, 2017.
DOI: 10.1007/978-3-319-62386-3_21

in the market, long term decisions are not part of their priorities, leading to two possible outcomes: either they grow and manage to position in the market, or they fail, cease to exist [2] and stop contributing to the economic growth, innovation and employment of their country [3]. With a well defined business model, SMEs would be able to recognize the different relationships present in their business and plan ahead, in order to execute a successful strategy.

The critical problem with current business model representations is the focus on a structural dimension (e.g., Osterwalder's Canvas [4], or Gordijns e3-value [5]. In particular, they leave (mostly) aside the specification of how business models components interact and behave in order to make the model work. Therefore, only a partial understanding of the business can be achieved with these business models. Additional artifacts are thus required, especially to achieve the goals behind Enterprise Modeling and Enterprise Engineering efforts.

This paper proposes two contributions. Firstly, it presents a conceptualization and representation of business models that includes all of their elements and allows further and more advanced analysis and understanding. Secondly, it introduces a catalog of business patterns which targets all the aspects of a business model. These patterns are intended to be the starting point for understanding and improving business models, especially in small and medium enterprises. By applying the patterns under our proposed conceptualization, it is possible to portray a complete business model and understand what the enterprise does and the maim components required.

The paper is organized as follows. Section 2 discusses the current understanding and representation of business models. Then, Sect. 3 presents our proposal for understanding business models by showing all its elements and the way in which they can be graphically represented. Next, the designed catalog of business patterns is introduced, and a few selected patterns are presented. Section 5 explains the way in which the patterns can be applied to portray a complete business model. Finally, related work is presented in Sect. 6, and in Sect. 7 the paper is concluded.

2   Understanding Business Models

A business is defined as a commercial activity in which one engages in, in exchange for money. Regardless of the product or service that is being exchanged, to produce the desired revenue every business transforms, delivers, and monetizes value. The way in which they do so, is known as a business model.

Several attempts to define what a business model is, have led to a diversity of interpretations. In turn, the concept has become blurry and there are no formal representations for it. This scenario explains the success of tools such as Alexander Osterwalder's Business Model Canvas [4]. The simple yet complete representation of the business model, has been adopted worldwide for describing businesses. By identifying 9 key elements, a canvas is able to communicate how a business works on a superficial level, and even propose alternative designs in order to adjust the model in a changing environment. Thus, these 9 elements allow the description of the business model, by defining its structural components.

2.1   Core Processes

Another perspective for understanding business models is the way in which an organization acquires supplies, transforms them into products and services, delivers these products and services, and obtains some money in exchange i.e., monetizes products and services. Accordingly, a business model can be decomposed into the four processes shown in Fig. 1: *Supply*, where the business performs all the activities necessary to acquire raw materials; *Transformation*, in which supplies are processed, typically adding value to them, in order to obtain the desired good or service; *Delivery*, that considers the distribution of the product or service to the client, and all the activities that lead to this delivery (e.g., marketing, customer acquisition); and *Monetization*, where the business performs the activities associated to the generation of revenues.

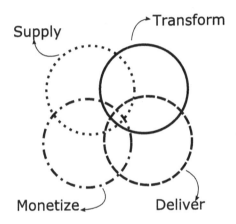

Fig. 1. Business model processes.

The order in which these processes are performed and the specific nature of their activities, varies depending on the type of product or service offered. Manufacturing businesses with a traditional model, first acquire their raw materials (Supply) to transform them (Transformation) and deliver the resulting products to the client (Delivery) which pays for them (Monetization) and generate revenue. Other businesses require a different sequence. For instance, transformation and delivery may be performed simultaneously, if the product or service is transformed as it is delivered. A business that exemplifies this sequence is private education: an educational service that is provided, is transformed (adding value) as it is being delivered and it is only at the end, when students graduate, that the complete service that was paid for is perceived.

2.2   Structural and Behavioral Viewpoints

Business models comprise two aspects which can be analyzed from two complementary points of view: structural elements, which include the business model components and their structural relations; and dependencies and interactions between said components.

When business models are analyzed from the structural viewpoint, the first elements to study are their four main processes (Supply, Transform, Deliver, and Monetize) and their relations. This includes analyzing the participants in each one of these processes and their responsibilities, as well as the activities that they have to perform. Special attention is also paid to the resources required to perform the activities, such as machines, communication and delivery channels, as well as financial resources. All these resources and activities generate costs, which are considered part of the structural viewpoint as they are attributes that shape the model. Well known representations, such as Osterwalder's Canvas, or Gordijin's e3-value [5], are well suited to describe a business model from the structural point of view.

On the other hand, in the behavioral viewpoint the foremost element is the order in which processes are performed. This depends on the interactions among participants and resources, and defines dependencies between activities: since the outputs of an activity are the inputs of the next one, flows are thus established both within and between the processes. These flows can be of *Cash*, *Information*, or *Value*: they represent the main, transversal linkage between components in the business model. The study of flows is thus necessary for the understanding of a business model. Unfortunately, current representations are not expressive enough for describing them and leave them to be figured out by the readers intuition. The following section presents a proposal that tackles precisely this problem.

3   Re-understanding Business Models

The conceptualization of a business model which we propose to fully describe a business model, including both the structural and behavioral aspects, is grounded in the following types of building blocks: Zones, Flows and Channels, Gateways, and Processors. These are described in the following pages and their role in a business model structure is discussed, along with the way in which they interact with each other. Together with the description of the concepts, we present a graphical representation for the business models.

3.1   Zones

A *Zone* represents a core process in a business model. A Zone contains participants, resources, flows, channels, and gateways (see Fig. 2): participants perform activities which generate flows and define sequences depending on the order of generation, and the origin and target of each flow. Each zone also has a frontier to determine the process' scope and the points where interactions with other zones are established. Processors act as mediators between zones and are depicted in the frontier of zones.

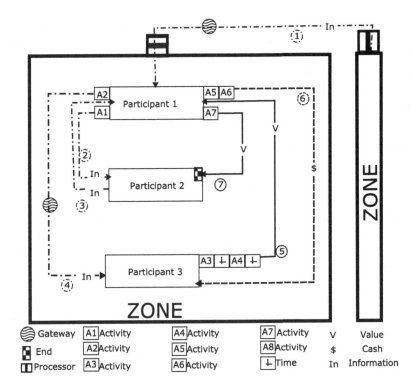

Fig. 2. A zone and its components.

Figure 3 presents three ways in which the four zones (S: Supply, T: Transformation, D: Delivery, M: Monetization) can be organized in order to describe different interactions in the model. Some models present more than four zones which means that they perform one or more of the four core processes in different ways. For instance, a business may gather raw materials from two different suppliers, involving different activities and participants interacting at different times.

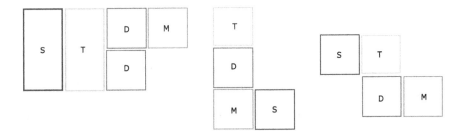

Fig. 3. Organization of zones in a business model.

Every zone includes participants, resources, activities, flows, gateways and processors. What varies among them are the actual components, which depend on the specific process represented. For example, the Supply zone might involve participants such as suppliers and clients, and activities such as placing orders, while the Delivery zone contemplates participants like distributors and activities like transporting the product.

3.2   Flows and Channels

A *flow* can be defined as a continuous relation between two participants, resources, or activities, established through a *channel*. The channel connects the output of its starting point to the input of the ending one. Flows can be characterized into three types. If the output is a document, a communication, or any other type of data, the flow is an *information flow*. If the output is a product or service, it is a *value flow*. And finally, money outputs mean that it is a *cash flow*.

Figure 2 presents the way in which flows are represented inside a zone. Since there is no structural difference between the flow and the channel, they are represented as one sole component. Value flows are presented with a black solid line. They appear as suppliers provide raw materials, as the business transforms them into the desired product, and as they are delivered and acquired by the client. It is thus possible to say that the business and the client establish a value flow as the latter acquires a product or service in exchange for money. This last element is associated to the cash flow, which is presented with a dashed line. As it was mentioned, there is a cash flow every time that a payment takes place, which leads to the appearance of these flows in scenarios such as the business paying to its suppliers and intermediaries. The information flow, presented with a chain like line, generates every time there is a communication and information is exchanged.

The three types of flows can be found inside zones and between them because there are also cause-effect relations between processes. Figure 4 shows an interaction between zones, established by the tree types of flows. These flows cross the different zones through processors, the fourth type of component that will be presented.

3.3   Gateways

As flows relate processes and the components within them, it is necessary to know when variations in volume take place. If the volume of a flow changes, it may be related to a change in the relation between the two connected agents. For instance, if business sales decrease, it may be due to an alteration in the relationship with the client. In order to know this, a *gateway* is used to control the flow.

A gateway is defined as a control mechanism that regulates flows among zones or agents, depending on the quality of the relationship among them. Acting as a push-pull mechanism, the gateway is able to tell whether a relationship has changed and if so, the way in which the volume varies. If a relationship worsens, the flow is pushed, and if it gets better, it will get pulled. In the business, the gateway may be represented by an area or actor in charge of looking after the relationships. Figure 4 presents the gateway as a waved circle crossed by a flow.

3.4 Processors

Processors are the most complex building block since they depend on the zones that are being connected, and the flows that cross them. A processor is defined as the entry and exit point of a zone, capable of allowing a certain type of flow cross the zone and interact with the elements inside another.

Figure 4 shows three types of processors that correspond to the three types of flows. The squares represent the information processor, the rectangle the value one, while the pentagon the cash one.

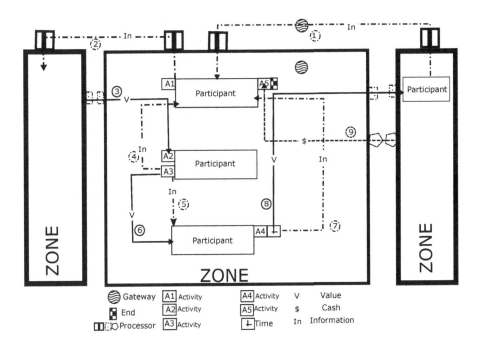

Fig. 4. Connected zones.

As processors allow the circulation of flow through zones, they permit the cause-effect relations that trigger the execution of an activity or process and at the end, they establish the connection between the processes. Figure 4 presents a view of several zones connected through flows crossing processors. This intertwining of processors and flows is like weaving a business model.

3.5   Meta-Model

To formalize the structure for the understanding of the business model that was just presented, a *meta-model* was built. A graphical representation using UML is shown in Fig. 5. In this figure, it is possible to see the business model and the decomposition into four processes with the correspondent structural and behavioral elements. By identifying the elements that compose the meta-model, it is possible to represent many business models regardless of the product or service being offered. This is possible since the representation process is not defined by the value proposition, but by the main building blocks that lead to the composition of the business model. When the zones are defined, so are the core processes, which in turn explains the way in which the business performs its different activities. Moreover, by recognizing participants and resources, the business model description is enriched and the different relationships in it are defined. As these relationships are characterized, flows begin to emerge and the business recognizes the points where money, information and value are exchanged.

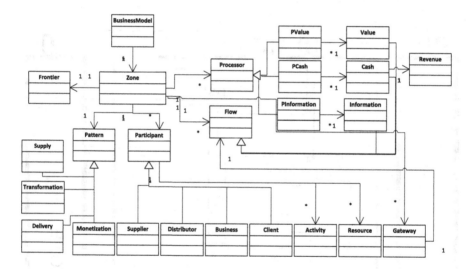

Fig. 5. Business model metamodel.

4   Business Patterns

The difference between business models is explained not only by differences in their component's structure, but also in the behavior and interaction among them: the unique combination of processes and the way in which they interact is what explains why each business operates the way it does.

It is fair to assume that the transformation process is unique for each business since it is the core point where value is added, where the actual strategy of the company is evidenced, and where competitive advantages are created. On the other hand, the supply, delivery and monetization processes do not differ enormously from one model to another. In fact, there is enough bibliography describing alternative designs and methods on each one of these topics to safely assume that each possible configuration for these processes has already been described somewhere (e.g., the ever expanding supply-chain corpus).

Considering this, we attempted to collect a significant number of the possible configurations for the Supply, Delivery, and Monetization processes in order to organize a catalog of Business Patterns. The goals behind this where two. Firstly, a pattern can be understood as a known solution to a well-known problem [6]. Therefore, by building the catalog we are making these solutions more accessible to those that are defining their business model, or re-defining their existing one. Secondly, we attempted to create a structured body of knowledge about business models which can be analyzed and used as the base for the definition of new businesses. In this sense, the catalog provides a set of *building blocks* to define a new business model under restrictions or expectations.

The sources for the catalog included standards such as the SCOR framework [7] and Osterwalders monetization patterns. For the moment patterns in the catalog only cover the business aspects of each process. However, it should be possible to expand the catalog in order to include aspects such as typical IT support for each situation described in the catalog (see Table 1).

The following pages present an extract of the patterns from the catalog, selected for illustration purposes. For each pattern a diagram is presented to illustrate the activities and flows within each zone. Furthermore, the interaction with the other zones are also presented.[1]

Table 1. Business patterns catalog.

CATEGORY	PATTERN
Supply	S1 - source stocked product
Supply	S2 - source make to order
Supply	S3 - source engineer to order
Deliver	D1 - deliver stocked product
Deliver	D2 - deliver make to order product
Deliver	D3 - deliver engineer to order product
Deliver	D4 - deliver retail
Monetization	M1 - asset sale
Monetization	M2 - advertising
Monetization	M3 - freemium
Monetization	M4 - licensing
Monetization	M5 - usage fee

---

[1] The complete catalog can be found in the following URL http://backus1.uniandes. edu.co/enar/dokuwiki/doku.php?id=wpatterns.

4.1 Supply Patterns

Supply patterns explain the way in which a business acquires raw materials from its providers. The following are three patterns extracted from the SCOR framework: source stocked products, source make to order and source engineer to order. Each pattern presents three main agents: the supplier, which typically is a different organization; business logistics, which are the coordinator of supply management activities; and the warehouse which stores and organizes supplies.

S1 - Source Stocked Product. The first pattern describes a supply process in which orders are made to maintain a stock of raw materials that allow the fulfillment of clients' orders in a defined period of time. This pattern is triggered by the client's demand (1) which tells the business the amount of product that may be needed and, consequently, the amount of supplies that must be ordered. Inventory is then checked (3), and necessary materials are ordered (4) based on actual inventory levels. Afterwards, the supplier prepares the order, which involves a certain time lead time, and then submits the raw materials (5). The business receives the order, for it (6), and stores the received materials in the warehouse (7) (Fig. 6).

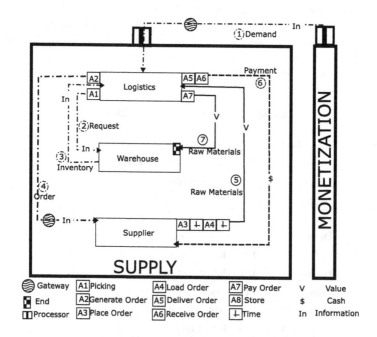

Fig. 6. Source stocked product.

S2 - Source Make to Order. This pattern describes a supply process in which raw materials are produced and delivered based on a client's order. In particular, once the order is placed (1), an information flow tells the supplier that the product must be made (2). Once the product is ready it is delivered to the business (3) which in turn pays for the supplies (4) and stores them in the warehouse (5).

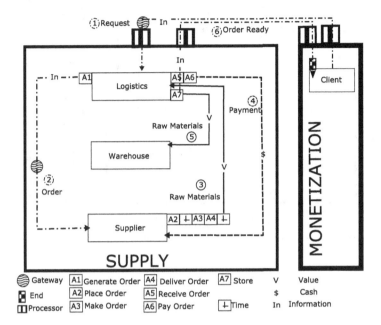

Fig. 7. Source make to order.

S3 - Source Engineer to Order. This supply pattern describes a supply process in which raw materials are designed, produced and delivered based on an order (1). In particular, there is a negotiation event where the final product design (2) is defined (3). Later, there is a placed order (4) that indicates the supplier that the product must be produced and delivered. Once the supplies arrive (5), the payment is done (6) and the materials are stored (7) (Fig. 8).

4.2   Delivery Patterns

The second core process in the business model, delivery, initiates after value is transformed. Delivery patterns include two types of participants: distributors and final clients. It is important to note that the distributor can represent the business itself, or a third party in charge of the activity. We now present four delivery patterns extracted from the SCOR framework.

D1 - Deliver Stocked Product. The first pattern describes a process in which the client maintains a stock of the product offered by the company. After the client's order(1) is placed (2), the product is picked from the warehouse (3,4)

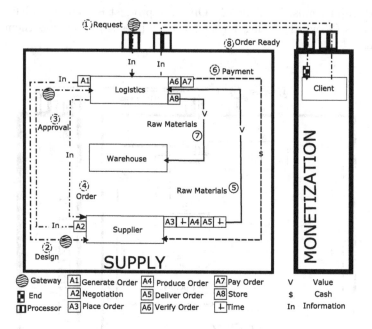

Fig. 8. Source engineer to order.

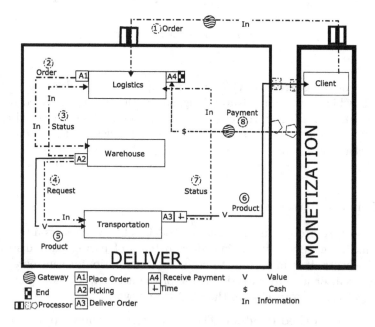

Fig. 9. Deliver stocked product.

and delivered (5). Once it reaches the client (6,7), the payment is received (8). Depending on the relationship quality between the client and the business, the product demand may vary. See Fig. 9.

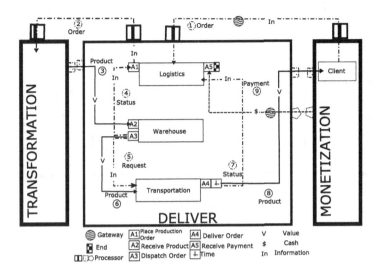

Fig. 10. Deliver make to order product.

D2 - Deliver Make to Order Product. The second pattern describes the distribution of products that are manufactured or provided given a client's order. In this case, an order is placed (1) along with the key information to initiate value transformation. These elements are recognized by the distributor and communicated into the value transformation zone (2). After the production and lead time are over, the product is placed in the warehouse (3,4) and dispatched (5,6). Once the order is delivered and received by the client (7,8), the payment is received (9). Like the previous pattern, the relationship with the client determines the amount of product ordered (Fig. 10).

D3 - Deliver Engineer to Order Product. The third pattern describes the distribution of a product whose design and production are defined and triggered by the client. Since the process involves an order and a negotiation, it begins with the client communicating the desired design and conditions of the distribution and payment (1). This information is delivered to the business, evaluated, and communicated to the client (2). When the negotiation is complete, the order is placed (3) and the distributor proceeds to communicate the clients final design, and adjust the distribution requirements. Once the product is ready (4), it is stored in the warehouse (5) where it is picked and dispatched (6,7). After the expected arrival time, the client receives the product (9–10) and pays for it (11) (Fig. 11).

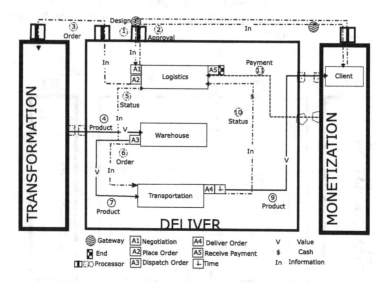

Fig. 11. Deliver engineer to order product.

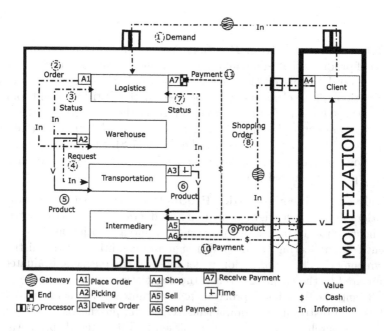

Fig. 12. Deliver retail.

D4 - Deliver Retail. The final delivery pattern describes a special type of business model: Retail. In this case, the distributor delivers the final product to a spot where clients acquire it. As in markets, and stores, this model considers clients acquiring the desired value in a physical location; therefore, the delivery reaches a middle point. In particular, depending on the demand (1), an order is placed (2), products are picked (3, 4, 5) and the orders are delivered to an intermediary (6, 7). The latter sells (8) the product to the client (9, 10) and sends the payment (11) (Fig. 12).

4.3 Monetization

The third group of patterns is proposed taking into account revenue stream models adopted in the market. Five different patterns are now presented, even though there are some similarities between them. Actors in these patterns are the business and the client that is acquiring or receiving the products and services produced (the ultimate recipients of value).

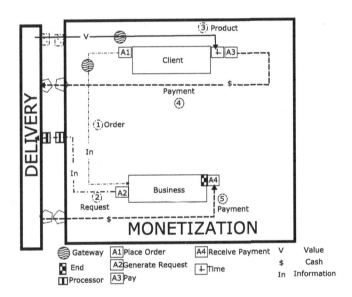

Fig. 13. Asset sale.

M1 - Asset Sale. The first pattern is perhaps the most common one when it comes to monetization. In this case, it describes value monetization based on a onetime payment that the client does to buy the desired product or service. It starts with an order placed to the business (1) which triggers an order to deliver (2) the product. Once the product reaches the client (3), the payment is received (4, 5) (Fig. 13).

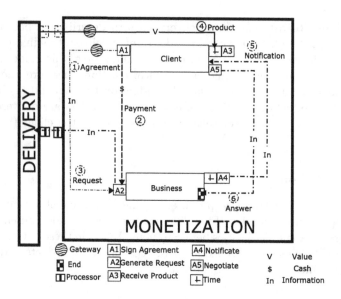

Fig. 14. Advertising.

M2 - Advertising. The second pattern describes monetization based on advertisement. In this case, a company generates revenue streams by giving clients a space to advertise their own businesses or products. The pattern starts with an agreement or contract (1) that defines how long is a company able to advertise, its value, and the granted space. This contract generates a payment (2) and an order (3) that grants the defined conditions (4). Once the contract time is over, so is the advertisement and the client is given the chance (5) to extend renegotiate the contract or end it (6) (Fig. 14).

M3 - Freemium. The third pattern describes a freemium model in which clients acquire the product for free during a period of time, or with less characteristics or functionalities. This pattern starts with a client order(1) to receive value for free accepting certain constraints (Such as the time in which value will be received, or the value that is accessible). Once the order is placed (2), the product is delivered (3) until the agreed time is over, or the client desires to request premium(4). If it does so (5), a payment is received (6) and the product is delivered or upgraded (7, 8) (Fig. 15).

M4 - Licensing. The licensing pattern describes a model based on the acquisition of a product or service through a license, which is bought by a client for a certain amount of time. The pattern starts with a client that buys a license (1, 2), this generates a request (3) that triggers the distribution of the product (4). Once the license time is over (5), the client is given the chance to renew it (6, 7) (Fig. 16).

M5 - Usage Fee. The final monetization pattern is usage fee, which describes a model in which the business charges for the usage of its product. In this case,

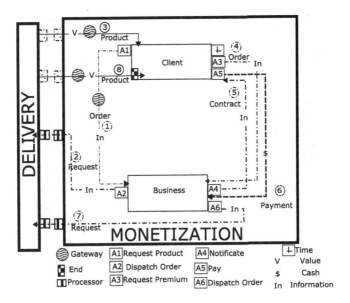

Fig. 15. Freemium.

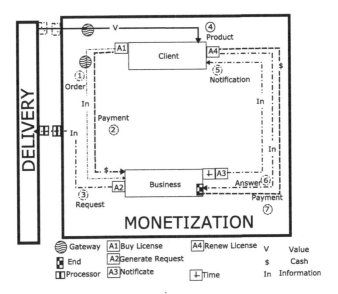

Fig. 16. Licensing.

a client places an order to use the product (1). After it is delivered (2,3) and the billing period is over, a bill is generated based on the usage (4) (That may be quantified depending on the business). The client pays (5) and may keep using the product as long as it pays the bill (Fig. 17).

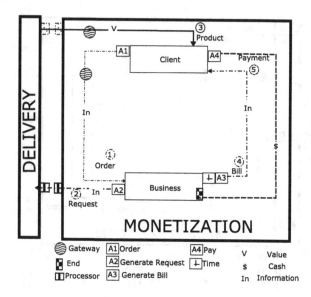

Fig. 17. Usage fee.

5 Weaving Business Model Patterns

When zones are joined among them, it is possible to represent the complete business model for an organization. For this purpose, it is necessary to understand flows in the business models, that is continuous relations between an origin and a target point. Flows can either be found inside a zone (in which case the origin and targets may correspond to participants, activities or resources) or between them (in which case the origin and targets will be found in different zones). This scenario allows to use them as the connector between two zones as every time that a flows leaves a zone and enters another one, it weaves them together.

An adequate representation of a business models depends on the correctness of the weaving. These implies that the appropriate patterns are used when describing each zone, and that the connection among them is accurate. To guarantee this correctness one must be sure that the flows do not present dead ends (lack of origins or targets) and that their type does not change when crossing the zones.

In this section we present a guide on how to connect zones in order to present a complete business model. We will first introduce the basic steps that must be followed, and then we will exemplify said steps with a case study.

5.1 Joining Zones

In order to join zones and represent the complete business model, it is important to follow 4 basic steps.

The first step is to identify the core processes that compose the business model and to arrange them. There should be four of them at least, one for each type of core process, but depending on the characteristics of the business and the difference between processes it is possible to have more.

After processes are identified, the second step is to arrange the zones. If a zone generates an input for another zone, they should be placed one next to the other. In case there is more than one zone of a given type, or if it is perceived as if two core processes are performed simultaneously, zones should be placed one on top of the other.

After a complete zone arrangement, the third step is to identify patterns. Since there are no particular patterns associated to the transformation process, it may be portrayed as a black box. If it is necessary to define a participant or activity in the zone, it is possible to place it in the box without many details. For the supply, delivery and monetization zones, it should be possible to identify the adequate patterns from the presented catalog.

The fourth step is the refinement of connections and correction of the weaving. Given a zone arrangement with patterns, it is first necessary to relate the participants in the pattern with the participants in the business model. Any actor or business area that is portrayed in the pattern, should be consistent to the business model. Moreover, if there is no explicit distinction between the participants that are mentioned in different zones, it is safe to assume that they refer to the same one. After participants are well defined, the flow connections must be verified.

When using the patterns, there are predefined connections between zones. For instance, the supply patterns consider orders generated from the client in the monetization zone. This is also the case with delivery zones which consider requests from the client in the monetization zone as well. All of these predefined connections must be verified: it must be guaranteed that they have an origin and a target correspondent to the business model, and that they cross the appropriate processors. Moreover, zones should be weaved at least by one flow. This does not necessarily imply that the flow must be explicit. In the case in which two zones refer to the same actor, there are "unseen" flows, as the information, value or money that the actor posses is constant among the zones. Therefore, every time that two zones present the same actor, it can be assumed that there is an unseen flow that connects them. Finally, if the business model describes a flow that is not described by the pattern, it should be portrayed in the zone.

These steps are now illustrated in a case study.

5.2   Case Study: An Editorial

To exemplify the way in which business patterns may be used to weave a complete business model, we will use a study case based on an editorial. To keep the example short enough to fit the paper, we will focus only on 5 core processes of the business model.

In this case, the editorial produces and sells school and college textbooks. To produce a book, the editorial must first get a manuscript from its author. To do so, the author is asked to deliver it. Once the manuscript arrives to the editorial, it is edited and formatted, a book cover is designed, and the final copies are printed. These copies are then gathered from the warehouse and delivered to two types of clients: libraries and people who directly contact the editorial. In the end, both types of clients buy a desired amount of book copies.

Describing the Business Model. The first step towards the representation of the business model, is identifying the core processes that compose it. First we identify a supply process associated to the manuscripts that arrive to the editorial. Secondly, we can spot several processes associated to a transformation process. In our case, formatting the manuscript, designing the book and printing the copies, are all part of the transformation process that the editorial must undergo in order to sell books. Once the copies are ready, we find two delivery processes: the one associated to intermediaries, and one associated to final clients. As they involve two different types of clients, it is appropriate to represent them with two different zones. Finally, we distinguish a monetization process that relates to the clients buying the copies, regardless of their type.

Portraying the Model. Once the core processes are identified and its execution order specified, we may use the zones and patterns to represent the business model. As there are five core processes we must use five zones. The first two zones will correspond to the supply and transformation processes, and they will be placed next to each other as they are performed successively (Fig. 18).

The delivery zones follow the transformation zone, and they both must be placed one on top of the other as the delivery processes are executed simultaneously (Fig. 19).

Finally, a monetization zone will follow these two zones, to portray they way in which the books are sold. Figure 20 shows the arrangement that must be used to portray the business model.

S   T

Fig. 18. Editorial supply and transformation zones.

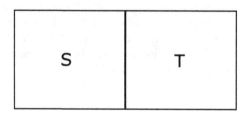

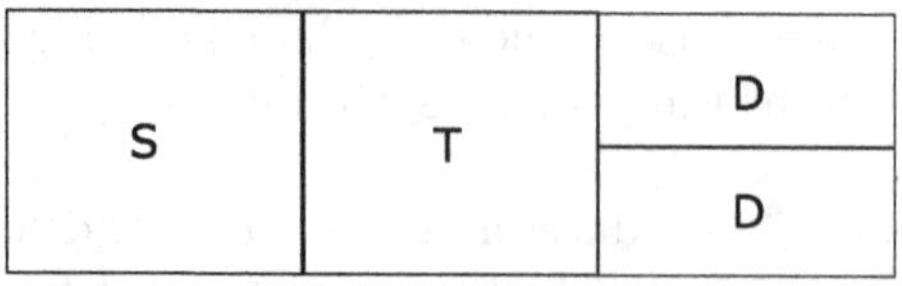

Fig. 19. Editorial supply, transformation and delivery zones.

Fig. 20. Editorial zone arrangement.

Using Patterns. Following the placement of the zones, we define the patterns that describe them. For the transformation zone we will use the black box. In the case of the supply process we find that the manuscripts arrive after they are ordered to the author, ant thus it is possible to describe it with a *Source Make to Order* pattern. Regarding the delivery processes, both can be portrayed using the *Delivery Stocked Product* pattern, as both clients order a certain amount of copies to be delivered. Finally, the monetization process is associated to clients paying for a product, therefore the *Asset Sale* pattern is appropriate to portray said process.

In order to weave the patterns and avoid any type of dead ends it is necessary to adequately define the participants in each pattern. To do so we start by portraying each zone shown in Fig. 20 with the correspondent pattern. In the supply zone, we will get a view similar as the one presented in Fig. 7. In this case we define that value flows as the manuscript is delivered by the author (the supplier); moreover, participants such as "Warehouse" may be replaced by the Editorial itself as there is no information on who is in charge of storing the manuscripts. It is important to note that in this case, the order that triggers the process is received from the Editorial and not by the final client in the monetization zone. With this in mind we can place inside our transformation zone and Editorial participant that not only transforms the manuscripts into book copies, but also places the order of new manuscripts. Finally, by portraying an Editorial in the Supply and Transformation zones we guarantee no dead ends because, although there is no explicit flow that connects the two zones, portraying the same participant defines said connection.

In the case of the delivery zone, we find a view as in Fig. 9. As in the supply scenario, we define participants like "Warehouse" as "Editorial" not only because of a lack of information but also to guarantee a connection among the transformation and delivery zone. This change must be present in both zones. Finally, the monetization zone establishes a view as the one in Fig. 13. In this case the "Business" participant is replaced with the "Editorial" and the order made to the delivery zone is connected to the flow associated to the "Place Order Activity". Although the order is initially made by the client, we show that an area in the Editorial is the one that orders directly to the logistics area. The remaining flows are connected according to the pattern.

Figure 21 shows the editorial's business model portrayed with the correspondent patterns and changes. As it is possible to see the flows that leave the delivery and monetization zones are duplicated in order to connect both delivery zones.

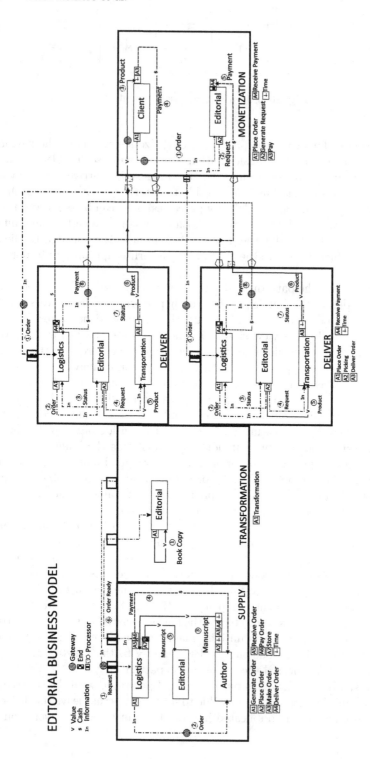

Fig. 21. Editorial business model.

6   Related Work

Business models and the different behaviors that emerge as they execute, have been matter of investigation for several authors. In particular, it is possible to find definitions and complete designs and representations of what a business model should look like. One of the most recognized efforts is Osterwalder's, who proposes both a structure for the model, and a method to use it [4]. Besides the well-known business model canvas, the author proposes several patterns to take into account when designing a business model. These patterns are based on five types of business models: unbundled, long tail, multi-sided, free and open business. Each pattern is appropriate for certain types of businesses [8].

Business patterns established around the RossettaNet standards are other example of designs considering business models. Though the standard considers the interaction between participants with a business purpose, it is possible to generate patterns that guide the execution of a business model. In particular, it is possible to generate patterns that describe order and shipment processes and use them to evaluate the business model execution [9].

Taking into account the scope of business models, patterns centered on specific elements are also possible to find. For example, value-exchange patterns have been designed after analyzing models of real businesses. In these designs, agents and interactions are specified taking into account what type of value is being delivered. The visual representation is also offered [10].

Moreover, efforts in generating guides for specific audiences are also in existence. For example, there is a business plan conception pattern language oriented to support entrepreneurs in the conception and design of their business models. Through a series of questions and descriptions, key aspects of the business model are addressed and depending on the concerns of the entrepreneur, several solutions for fulfilling them are offered [11].

The amount of examples, patterns and guides generated towards the comprehension and adoption of successful business models, is considerable. From languages, to visual representations, to definitions, there is a wide variety of options when it comes to designing a business model. As it has been shown, these patterns can derive from existing companies, frameworks, or tendencies in the market. Regardless of where they come from, their purpose remains similar: to guide and provide a standard in the design of a business model.

Still, the expressiveness needed in order to communicate the business model approach described in this paper, can not be achieved with the discussed visualizations. Since there are five building blocks that need to be considered (zones, flows and channels, processors and gateways), it is necessary to count with notations that allow their representation. In Osterwalder's case although there is a notion of zones and channels, the flow concept is implicit within the canvas and the definition of the relationships among agents turns out to be more complex. The e3-value notation, on the other hand, is quite useful for the visualization of flows and processors, however, the detail level is not enough for the purposes of the proposed business model approach. In particular, since e3 value groups the different types of flow in one type (value), there is a need to define explicitly the element that is flowing. Furthermore, there is not a clear representation of the activities that lead to the flow establishment, and without, it is not possible to define the resources or participants key in each relationship. Considering the lack of a complete representation for the building blocks and their components, defining a new notation was appropriate.

7 Conclusion

A business model describes the way in which a business receives and transforms inputs to create value and build products and services which are then delivered and monetized. Even though the concept is simple and interpretations abound, it is not formalized and there is a lack of comprehension of many business models. Furthermore, the semantics of a business model depend both on its structural features (components and their relations) and its behavior. The latter includes the interaction between these components and especially the flow of information, cash and value between them.

In order to understand both the structural and the behavioral aspects of a business model, we have proposed an interpretation based on the concepts of zone (or processes), processors that connect zones, flows that represent exchanges of value, information and cash, actors which perform activities, and gateways that regulate the exchanges. By using these elements it should be possible to have a more profound understanding of business models in order to better communicate and analyze them.

Using this conceptualization, pattens for supply, delivery and monetization were identified in the SCOR model and in the literature. Each pattern details a way in which a process can be performed, including the participating actors, their activities, and the exchanges of value, cash and information. Moreover, by joining these patterns it is possible to describe a complete business model and give an overall description of what the business does along with the main participants, activities and resources associated. Depending on the level of maturity of enterprises, these patterns should serve to understand their business models, or as a starting point for designing novel business models based on well known solutions.

References

1. Lindgren, P., Rasmussen, O.: The business model cube. J. Multi Bus. Model Innov. Technol. 1(3), 135–180 (2013)
2. Frick, J., Ali, M.M.: Business model canvas as tool for SME. In: Prabhu, V., Taisch, M., Kiritsis, D. (eds.) APMS 2013. IAICT, vol. 415, pp. 142–149. Springer, Heidelberg (2013). doi:10.1007/978-3-642-41263-9_18
3. Robu, M.: The dynamic and importance of SMEs in economy. USV Ann. Econ. Public Adm. 13(1(17)), 84–89 (2013)
4. Osterwalder, A., Pigneur, Y.: Business Model Generation: A Handbook for Visionaries, Game Changers, and Challengers. Wiley, Hoboken (2010)

5. Gordijn, J., Akkermans, H.: Designing and evaluating e-business models. IEEE Intell. Syst. **16**(4), 11–17 (2001)
6. Gamma, E., Helm, R., Johnson, R., Vlissides, J.: Design Patterns: Elements of Reusable Object-Oriented Software. Addison-Wesley Longman Publishing Co., Inc., Boston (1995)
7. Supply Chain Council: SCOR: Supply Chain Operations Reference Model Version 9. The Supply Chain Council, Inc. (2008)
8. Osterwalder, A., Pigneur, Y., Bernarda, G., Smith, A.: Value Proposition Design. Wiley, Hoboken (2014)
9. Telang, P.R., Singh, M.P.: Abstracting and applying business modeling patterns from RosettaNet. In: Maglio, P.P., Weske, M., Yang, J., Fantinato, M. (eds.) ICSOC 2010. LNCS, vol. 6470, pp. 426–440. Springer, Heidelberg (2010). doi:10.1007/978-3-642-17358-5_29
10. Zlatev, Z., van Eck, P., Wieringa, R.: Value-exchange patterns in business models of intermediaries that offer negotiation services (2004)
11. Laurier, W., Hruby, P., Poels, G.: Business plan conception pattern language. In: Kelly, A., Weiss, M. (eds.) CEUR Workshop Proceedings, vol. 566, pp. C4-1–C4-27. CEUR (2010)

Method and Practical Guidelines for Overcoming Enterprise Architecture Adoption Challenges

Nestori Syynimaa[1,2]([⊠])

[1] Department of Computer Science and Information Systems,
Faculty of Information Technology, University of Jyväskylä, Jyväskylä, Finland
`nestori.syynimaa@gmail.com`
[2] Founder and Principal Consultant Gerenios Ltd., Tampere, Finland

Abstract. During the last few years, interest towards Enterprise Architecture (EA) has increased, not least due to anticipated benefits resulting from adopting it. For instance, EA has been argued to provide cost reduction, technology standardisation, process improvement, and strategic differentiation. Despite these benefits, the EA adoption rate and maturity are still low. Consequently, EA benefits are not realised. A major reason hindering the adoption is that EA is not understood correctly. This paper aims for minimising the effect of the lack of understanding EA to adopting EA. Based on the research conducted in Finnish public sector, we propose an improved Enterprise Architecture Adoption Method (EAAM) to overcome the EA adoption challenges. EAAM is built using Design Science approach and evaluated using Delphi method. Some practical guidelines for applying EAAM are also provided to help organisations to overcome EA adoption challenges.

Keywords: Enterprise Architecture · Adoption Method · Design science · Delphi · Guidelines

1 Introduction

Enterprise Architecture (EA) has received a lot of attention during the last decades. In the last couple of years the interest has increased dramatically. Leading scientific conferences, such as ICEIS, even has a separate track dedicated to EA. One of the reasons for the increased interest is the number of anticipated benefits resulting from adopting EA. For instance, EA has been argued to provide cost reduction, technology standardisation, process improvement, and strategic differentiation [1]. Using a set of case-studies, Ross *et al.* [2] demonstrated how these benefits could create sustainable value to organisations. Despite these and other benefits to be gained, EA is not widely adopted in organisations [3, 4].

In this paper, we propose an improved EA adoption method and provide some practical guidelines to help organisations to adopt EA and, consequently, realise the EA benefits.

The structure of the paper is as follows. First, in this section, we introduce the key concepts of EA, the traditional EA adoption process, and some adoption challenges.

© Springer International Publishing AG 2017
S. Hammoudi et al. (Eds.): ICEIS 2016, LNBIP 291, pp. 488–514, 2017.
DOI: 10.1007/978-3-319-62386-3_22

Research methodology used in the paper is introduced in Sect. 2. Our proposal of improved Enterprise Architecture Adoption Method (EAAM) is introduced in Sect. 3, followed by some practical guidelines in Sect. 4. Section 5 concludes the paper, including some directions for the future research.

1.1 Enterprise Architecture

Enterprise Architecture has many definitions in the current literature. Vague definitions are confusing both practitioners and scholars [5–9]. EA is seen as a verb, something we do, and as a noun, something we produce [10]. From the various definitions in the literature [11–16] we adopt the following synthesis: "Enterprise Architecture can be defined as; (i) a formal description of the current and future state(s) of an organisation, and (ii) a managed change between these states to meet organisation's stakeholders' goals and to create value to the organisation" [17]. As such, we accept the double meaning of EA as a noun and a verb.

With this definition in mind, we can identify three processes related to *EA development cycle* as illustrated in Fig. 1 using ArchiMate notation. The first process (P2) is describing the current state of the organisation. The second process (P3) is describing the future state of the organisation. Difference between these two is that P2 is merely a description of the current state of the organisation, whereas P3 includes also elements of planning. The third process (P4) is the managed change where the (planned) future state of the organisation is implemented. There is also a fourth process related to EA, the adoption (P1), which precedes the other three processes. During the adoption the state of the organisation is changes from the state where EA is not adopted to the state where it is adopted.

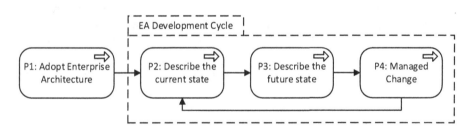

Fig. 1. Enterprise architecture processes.

1.2 Enterprise Architecture Adoption

We define Enterprise Architecture adoption as a process, where an organisation starts using EA methods and tools for the very first time. It is an instance of teleological organisational change aiming for the realisation of EA benefits, e.g., change for a purpose [18].

The traditional EA adoption process is illustrated in Fig. 2 using BPMN 2.0 notation. It is a high level process consisting of two activities. The mandate for the EA adoption is seen crucial by both scholars and practitioners [19–29]. Therefore the first activity is to *acquire a mandate* for EA adoption. If the mandate is not given the adoption process terminates. If the mandate is given the process continues to the another activity called *Conduct EA adoption*. This collapsed sub-process is expanded in Fig. 3.

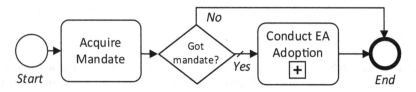

Fig. 2. Traditional EA adoption process.

The first task in the *Conduct EA Adoption* process is to *select EA framework*. EA frameworks, such as TOGAF, usually consists of a development method and a governance model which are distinctive to the framework. Therefore the remaining tasks of the process depends on the selected framework. As it can be noted, the remaining tasks are same than the processes P2, P3, and P4. This is because during the adoption these steps are executed once before entering the normal EA development cycle.

1.3   EA Adoption Challenges

As stated, EA adoption is an organisational change aiming for the realisation of EA benefits. About 70 per cent of organisational change initiatives fail [30–32]. This is also the case with EA adoption. Consequently, the anticipated benefits of the adoption are not realised.

For instance, in Finland, EA is made mandatory in public sector by legislation [33]. The Act of Information Management Governance in Public Administration requires public sector organisations to adopt EA by 2014. In 2014 the EA maturity in state administration was 2.6 or below in the 5 level TOGAF maturity-model [34]. Several studies has found that EA is not well understood in Finnish public sector [8, 35–37]. According to recent PhD studies [36, 37] the lack of EA knowledge is one of the main reasons hindering EA adoption

2   Research Methodology

In this paper we have adopted Design Science (DS) approach [38] to improve the traditional EA adoption method. DS is a research approach aiming to develop scientific knowledge by designing and building artefacts [39]. As such, DS is concerned about the utility value of the resulting artefacts [40]. There are three types of artefacts to research: (i) a technology artefact, (ii) an information artefact, and (iii) a social artefact [41]. In this paper we are building a method, which according can be categorised as a technology artefact [41].

This paper follows Design Science Research Model (DSRM) by Peffers *et al.* [42]. DSRM process consists of six phases: (i) problem identification and motivation, (ii) defining objectives for a solution, (iii) designing and developing an artefact,

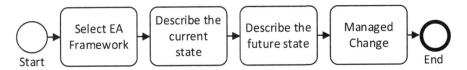

Fig. 3. Conduct EA adoption process.

(iv) demonstration of the usage of the artefact, (v) evaluation of artefact's utility, and (vi) communication.

Typical outcome of DS is a tested and grounded Technological Rule (TR), which can be defined as "a chunk of general knowledge, linking an intervention or artefact with a desired outcome or performance in a certain field of application" [39, p. 228]. The form of a TR is "if you want to achieve Y in situation Z, then perform action X" [39, p. 227]. Tested TR means a rule which has been tested in the context it is intended to be used [43]. Grounded TR (GTR) is a rule which reasons for its effectiveness are known [43, 44]. In this paper, we will seek for GTRs which would improve the traditional EA adoption method.

EA adoption is a process where the current state of the organisation is changed. This is comparable to the DS problem-solving situation illustrated in Fig. 4. The desired state of EA adoption is the organisation where EA is adopted and embedded to organisation's processes. However, it is possible to end up with a final state where the desired state is not achieved or it is achieved only partially.

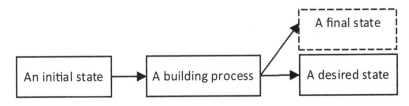

Fig. 4. DS problem-solving situation [45].

In order to evaluate whether the improved EA adoption method works as intended, we should perform the adoption using the method in a real-life setting. Given the time and resources required by EA adoption, real-life evaluation is practically not possible. Therefore, we will adopt a Delphi method to evaluate the utility of the method.

Delphi method is a research process where experts' judgements about the subject are iteratively and anonymously collected and refined by feedback [46]. It is typically used in forecasting but can be used also when developing and evaluating methods [47].

3   Enterprise Architecture Adoption Method

In this section we will introduce the Enterprise Architecture Adoption Method (EAAM) and describe its building process and evaluation. The section is organised following the phases of DSRM process.

3.1   Problem Definition and Objectives

As stated earlier, various studies have noticed the lack of EA knowledge in the Finnish public sector. For instance, it has been argued that current definitions of EA are inconsistent and thus confusing both researchers and practitioners [8]. This is a problem especially among practitioners; "EA was not thoroughly understood by the public sector authorities" [8, p. 170]. This is supported by other study [35]; EA is underutilised due to lack of understanding it properly. In general, poor communication have been found to be one of the factors contributing to EA adoption failures [27]. This problematic also because the perceived value of EA is directly influenced by how EA is understood [48]. Thus it can be argued that the lack of understanding of EA concepts is a major cause hindering EA adoption. As such, it is important to minimise or remove this cause. Therefore, our problem definition for EAAM is as follows: *How to minimise the effects of the lack of understanding EA concepts to EA adoption process?* This leads us to the objective of the EAAM, which is *to improve the traditional EA adoption method to minimise the effect of lack of understanding of EA concepts.*

3.2   Design and Development

In this sub-section the concepts and theories related to organisational change are introduced and discussed.

3.3   Readiness for Change

Besides organisation culture [49], also readiness for change has an impact on successful change [50].

According to Holt *et al.* [51] the most influential factors of change readiness are (i) *discrepancy* (the belief that a change was necessary), (ii) *efficacy* (the belief that the change could be implemented), (iii) *organisational valence* (the belief that the change would be organizationally beneficial), (iv) *management support* (the belief that the organizational leaders were committed to the change), and (v) *personal valence* (the belief that the change would be personally beneficial). [51]. This implies that the content, context, and process of EA adoption together with individual attributes affects the readiness for EA adoption. More specifically, individuals should believe that EA adoption is necessary, possible, beneficial to organisation, and supported by top-management. They should also feel that EA adoption would be beneficial to themselves. Similarly, managers who understand the change efforts are more less resistant to change [52].

Communication has an important role in organisational change. It has a positive effect to the readiness for change [53]. On the other hand, uncertainty has a negative effect to readiness for change, which can be influenced by communication. This implies that readiness for EA adoption can be increased by communication, either directly or by decreasing uncertainty.

General acceptance models [see for example 54] suggests that individual acceptance of information technology (IT) is influenced by beliefs and attitudes, which in turn is influenced by *Managerial interventions* and *Individual differences* Individual acceptance is conceptually similar to the readiness for change. Both are influenced by beliefs and attitudes. These beliefs can be influenced by managerial intervention, e.g., communication. Therefore, in order to increase the likelihood of EA adoption success, the readiness for change needs to be increased by a proper communication by managers.

3.4 Individual and Organisational Learning

Learning can be defined as a transformation where "the initial state in the learner's mind is transformed to the new state which is different from the initial state if learning has occurred." [55, p. 14, italics removed]. *State of mind* consists of following cognitive beliefs; *beliefs (knowledge), values,* and *know-how*. Skills are included in know-how. If learning occurs, the state of mind is transferred to a new state of mind with different cognitive beliefs. Learning can occur through acts in reality or by learner's own thinking. The former learning mode means learning by perceptions, by having new experiences, or by acquiring information. [55].

The current position of IS research is rooted in methodological individualism, which sees organisations as collection of individuals [56]. This theoretical point of view is problematic, as it suggests that if the new people are coming in to the organisation, a new organisation would emerge [57]. Therefore, according to Lee [57], the better conceptualisation would be that the organisation stays (somewhat) the same, and the people moving in would change towards the organisation's culture.

Organisational learning can be explained using *4I framework*, where learning occurs on individual, group, and organisational levels. These levels are linked by four processes; *intuiting, interpreting, integrating,* and *institutionalising.* "*Intuiting* is a subconscious process that occurs at the level of the individual. It is the start of learning and must happen in a single mind. *Interpreting* then picks up on the conscious elements of this individual learning and shares it at the group level. *Integrating* follows to change collective understanding at the group level and bridges to the level of the whole organization. Finally, *institutionalising* incorporates that learning across the organization by imbedding it in its systems, structures, routines, and practices" [58, p. 212].

Individual learning is in a crucial part on the organisational learning, as organisations are "after all, a collection of people and what the organisation does is done by people" [59]. Also, "change is not just about how people act, but it is also about how they think as well" [60, p. 49]. It can said that organisational learning has occurred, when EA concepts are understood on individual level, and EA processes and methods adopted and embedded to organisation's routines.

Individual and organisational learning has direct implications to EA adoption. Organisational level learning occurs only through individuals. Similarly, individuals learn from the organisation. However, organisation is not the only source of learning for individuals. Learning may occur whenever the individual is interacting with the reality (i.e., communicating, perceiving, observing) but also by barely thinking [55].

Therefore, in order to adopt EA in an organisation, individuals of the organisation needs to learn EA.

3.5   Effects of EA Training and Understanding EA Benefits

Hazen *et al.* [61] studied why EA is not used to a degree which realises its benefits. The study is based on the UTAUT by Venkatesh *et al.* [54]. The study is especially interested in which *performance expectancy* drives organisational acceptance of EA. Performance expectancy is defined as "the degree to which an individual believes that using the system will help him or her to attain gains in job performance" [54, p. 447]. According to findings, *partial mediation* model explains the EA use significantly more than *full* or *no mediation* models. The partial mediation model implies that in order to increase EA knowledge, individuals' performance expectancy of EA needs to be increased along with proper EA training.

Nassiff [48] studied why EA is not more widely adopted, by analysing how organisation's executives value EA. According to his findings, EA has four meanings among executives; *Business and IT alignment, a holistic representation of the enterprise, a planned vision of the enterprise,* and *a process, methodology, or framework enhancing enterprise decision making.* Also 16 unique benefits of EA were identified. Value of EA is directly influenced by how the EA is understood in the organisation. Regardless of the meaning of EA, three common benefits were expected; alignment between business and IT, better decisions making, and the simplification of system or architecture management. Findings implies that in order to increase the individual's performance expectancy of EA adoption, EA benefits needs to be communicated according to what EA means to the individual. This implication actually means also adopting *andragogy* instead of *pedagogy* as an assumption of learning; individual learning is depending on and occurring on top of the past experiences of the individual [62]. These past experiences and existing "knowledge" can have a negative effect to learning EA adoption, as individuals "have a strong tendency to reject ideas that fail to fit our preconceptions" [63, p. 5].

3.6   Role of Managerial Intervention and Leadership Style

Makiya [64] has studied factors influencing EA assimilation within the U.S. federal government. EA was adopted gradually, starting from adoption (as defined in this paper) ending to assimilating EA as an integral part of organisation. The research was divided in to three three-year phases. During the first phase (e.g., adoption) factors like parochialisms and cultural resistance, organisation complexity, and organisation scope had a significant influence. According to the findings, parochialisms and cultural resistance did not exist in phase two, likely due to coercive pressure by organisation. This can be interpreted so that by using a force mandated by organisational position, one can greatly influence EA adoption. This is conceptually similar to *managerial intervention*, but also to *situational* and *social influence*. It should be noted that this approach had no effect in the phase three, so it should be utilised only during the adoption phase. According to study, labelling EA as an administrative innovation instead of a strategic tool could help in value perception and adoption of EA.

Vera and Crossan [65] has expanded the model of organisational learning by Crossan *et al.* [66]. They added the concept of *learning stocks*. Learning stocks exists in each level of organisational learning, namely individual, group, and organisation levels. These learning stocks contains the inputs and outputs of learning processes, taking place between layers. They argue that different leadership styles (transactional or transformational) needs to be used based on which type of organisational learning (feed-forward of feedback) needs to be promoted.

There are some behavioural differences between transactional and transformational leadership styles. These styles are not exclusive but should be used accordingly based on the situation [65]. Transactional leadership is based on "transactions" between the manager and employees [67]. They are performing their managerial tasks by rewards and by either actively or passively handling any exceptions to agreed employee actions. Transformational leadership style aims to elevating the interests of employees by generating awareness and acceptance of the purpose of the group or initiative [67]. This is achieved by utilising charisma, through inspiring, intellectual stimulation, and by giving personal attention to employees. Thus it can be argued that transactional leadership style suits better in a situation where *status quo* should be maintained. Similarly, transformational leadership style works better in a situation where organisation faces changes.

The feed-forward learning allows organisation to innovate and renew, whereas the feedback process reinforces what has already learned. There can be two types learning; learning that reinforces institutionalised learning and learning that challenges institutionalised learning. Transformational leadership have a positive impact to learning when current institutionalised learning is challenged, and when organisation is in a turbulent situation. In turn, transactional leadership have positive impact to learning when the institutionalised learning is reinforced, and when organisation is in a steady phase [65].

The role of managerial or leadership style to organisational and individual learning is significant. The key is the current organisational learning stock or institutionalised learning regarding to EA adoption. If EA adoption conflicts with the current institutionalised learning, the transformational leadership should be used in order increase the feed-forward learning. Vice versa, if EA adoption does not conflict with the current institutionalised learning, the transactional leadership should be used to increase feedback learning.

Espinosa *et al.* [68] have studied the coordination of EA, focusing on increasing understanding how coordination and best practices lead to EA success. According to study, cognitive coordination plays a critical role in effectiveness of architecting. Their model consists of two models, static and dynamic models. Whereas the static model affects the effectiveness on "daily basis", a dynamic model strengthens group cognition over the time. There are three coordination processes in the model: *organic*, *mechanistic*, and *cognitive*. Mechanistic coordination refers to coordination of the routine aspects with minimal communication by using processes, routines, specification, etc.

Organic coordination refers to communication processes used in more uncertain and less routine tasks. Cognitive coordination is achieved implicitly when each collaborator have knowledge about each other's tasks, helping them to anticipate and thus coordinate with a reduced but more effective communication. As it can be noted, the term "cognitive" is not referring to term cognition, which is usually defined as a "mental action or process of acquiring knowledge and understanding through thought, experience, and the senses" [69]. Instead, they are referring to the *shared cognition* of a high performance group of individuals having similar or compatible knowledge, which can coordinate its actions without the need for communication [70].

According to the findings by Espinosa *et al.* [68], cognitive coordination plays a central role in strengthening the other two coordination mechanisms. Therefore, in order increase the effectiveness of EA adoption, the shared cognition of individuals within the organisation needs to be strengthened. This can be achieved by providing similar level of EA knowledge to all individuals.

3.7 Emerging EA Adoption Method

In this sub-section, we first sum up the concepts presented in previous sub-sections and form a list of propositions based on these concepts and their interrelations (Table 1). Based on these proposition, six Ground Technological Rules (GTRs) are presented (Table 2), and finally EAAM process descriptions are introduced.

By *EA Benefits* we refer to all those benefits that may result of adopting Enterprise Architecture. These benefits influences *Performance Expectancy (PE)*, which refers to individual's expectations towards EA adoption (P1). *Individual's Learning Stock* refers

Table 1. Propositions of EA adoption method.

ID	Explanation	Source
P1	Understanding EA benefits influences performance expectancy	Nassiff [48]
P2	Executive's understanding of EA meaning influences benefits	Nassiff [48]
P3	Performance expectancy influences EA training	Hazen *et al.* [61]
P4	Individual's and organisation's learning stocks influences each other	Crossan *et al.* [66]
P5	Performance expectancy influences EA adoption	Hazen *et al.* [61]
P6	Managerial intervention influences feed-forward and feedback learning	Crossan *et al.* [66]
P7	Individual's learning stock influences EA adoption	Agarwal [71] Elving [53] Espinosa *et al.* [68] Hazen *et al.* [61] Holt *et al.* [51]
P8	Executives individual Attributes influences leadership style	Bass [67] Crossan *et al.* [66]
P9	Managerial invention influences EA adoption	Agarwal [71] Makiya [64]

Table 2. Grounded technological rules.

ID	Explanation
R1	If you want to acquire a mandate for Enterprise Architecture adoption from top-management, explain *Common EA Benefits*
R2	If you want to acquire a mandate for Enterprise Architecture adoption from top-management in a situation where manager's view to EA is more business oriented, rating of the organisation's EA maturity is low, or EA experience is low, explain *Alignment Specific Benefits*
R3	If you want to acquire a mandate for Enterprise Architecture adoption from top-management in a situation where manager's EA experience is high, perception of EA complexity is low, or current EA authority is low, explain *Planned Vision Specific Benefits*
R4	If you want to acquire a mandate for Enterprise Architecture adoption from top-management in a situation where manager's current EA authority is high, explain Decision Making *Specific Benefits*
R5	If you want to improve organisational learning during EA adoption in a situation where EA challenges the *current organisational learning, use Transformational Leadership Style. Otherwise use Transactional Leadership Style*
R6	If you want to improve EA adoption, use *Coercive Organisational Pressure*

to all individual's current knowledge, know-how, values, and processes related on changing these (i.e. learning). *Performance Expectancy* influences *Individual's Learning Stock* (P3) by giving some meaning to EA's performance properties. *Performance Expectancy* also has a direct influence to *EA Adoption* (P5). *Individual's Learning Stock* influences *EA Adoption* (P7), as it contains all individual's knowledge, know-how, and values related to Enterprise Architecture. Managers' and executives' *Individual Learning Stock* influences *EA Benefits* (P2) in terms of his or hers capability to comprehend possible benefits related to EA adoption. Similarly, managers' and executives' *Individual Learning Stock* influences how they are capable in using *Managerial Intervention* to increase EA adoption success (P8). *Organisation's Learning Stock* refers to the current organisation's institutionalised knowledge (i.e., patents), know-how (i.e., processes, instructions, rules), and values (i.e., culture). Feed-forward and feedback learning occurs between *Organisation's Learning Stock* and *Individual's Learning Stock* (P4). As organisations are composed of its members, changes in *Organisation's Learning Stock* (i.e., organisational learning) may only occur through *Individual's Learning Stock*. *Organisation's Learning Stock* however is only one of many sources that influences *Individual's Learning Stock*. *Managerial Intervention* refers to those actions which organisation's managers and executives may use to increase the success of EA adoption. *Managerial Intervention* has a direct influence on *EA Adoption* (P9), as managers and executives may provide coercive pressure to "force" EA adoption. *Managerial Intervention* influences also organisational learning (P6) taking place between *Individual's* and *Organisation's Learning Stocks* where managers and executives may promote learning by choosing their leadership style accordingly.

Based on the propositions, six GTRs are provided in Table 2. As suggested by propositions P1, P2, P3, P4, P5, and P7, understanding EA benefits influences the EA adoption indirectly through performance expectancy and individual's learning stock. In order to acquire the mandate for EA adoption from the top-management, GTRs R1 to R4 are provided. As suggested by propositions P6 and P9, managerial intervention influences EA adoption indirectly by influencing organisational learning, and directly. Use GTRs R5 and R6 to influence indirect and direct learning, respectively.

Based on the propositions and the GTRs provided above, three process descriptions are formed using BPMN 2.0 notation. First description, *EA adoption* process, can be seen in Fig. 5. The process consists of four tasks; *Explain EA benefits*, *Acquire Mandate*, *Organise EA learning*, and *Conduct EA adoption*. When compared to the traditional EA adoption process seen in Fig. 2. Two tasks are added. The first new task, a collapsed sub-process of *Explaining EA Benefits* is expanded in Fig. 6. The second new task, a collapsed sub-process of *Organising EA Training* is explained in Fig. 7. The logic of the process is as follows. A mandate from top management of the organisation is a requirement for EA adoption. In order to increase the likelihood of getting the mandate, one needs to explain the benefits of EA to management. If mandate is given, the next task is to organise EA training to increase the understanding of EA concepts. After these tasks are completed, the actual EA adoption can be started.

The *process of explaining EA benefits* can be seen in Fig. 6. This process has two actors, the *EA responsible* and *Manager*. The manager refers to the manager or executive whose support to EA adoption is seen as important.

Fig. 5. Improved EA adoption process.

The first task of the process is to *explain common EA benefits*, such as alignment of business and IT. Next task is to *assess manager's views to EA* in terms of EA business orientation, organisation's EA maturity, EA experience, perception of EA's complexity, and current EA authority. Based on the assessments, one should explain the *more specific EA benefits* accordingly. For example if the manager's EA experience is low, one should explain the benefits specific to alignment, such as increased operational effectiveness and process improvements.

The *process of providing EA training* can be seen Fig. 7. This process has also two actors, *EA responsible* and *Employees*, which represents organisation's personnel. First task is to *assess organisation's current learning stock*, i.e. what is organisation's current knowledge, know-how, and values related to Enterprise Architecture. As we are in the adoption phase, the level of EA specific knowledge is ought to be low, but one

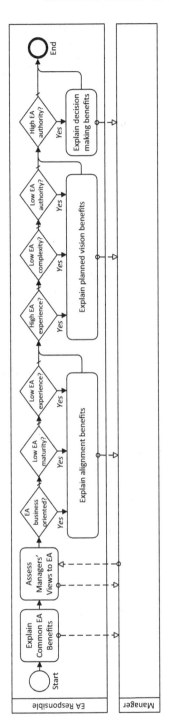

Fig. 6. Explain EA benefits process.

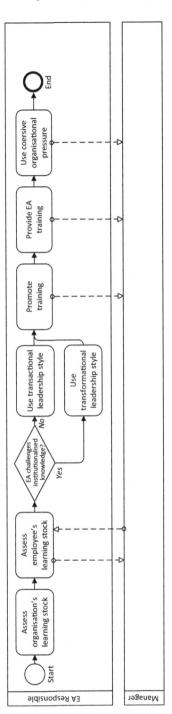

Fig. 7. Organise EA training process.

should assess capabilities and practices such as project management, change management, and internal communication. Second task is to *assess employee's learning stock*. Based on these two learning stock assessments, one should choose a proper leadership style. If *EA adoption challenges institutionalised learning*, i.e. it is different than *status quo*, one should choose to *use transformational leadership style*. If the learning does not challenge institutionalised learning, one should choose to *use transactional leadership style*. By using the chosen leadership style, next task is to *promote learning* accordingly. Next task is to *provide EA learning* based on assessments of current learning stocks. The last task is to *use coercive organisational pressure*.

3.8   Evaluation

Purpose of the evaluation of our Enterprise Architecture Adoption Method (EAAM) is to assess whether it has the intended affect. The evaluation design follows the guidelines by Venable *et al.* [72]. Target of the evaluation is the product, EAAM, and evaluation takes place *ex-post*. The audience of EAAM is mainly EA responsible, i.e., EA champions, project managers, EA architects, etc.

Delphi method was selected as an evaluation method. For the evaluation, a panel of top Finnish EA expert was carefully selected from both industry and academia. Panel consisted of 11 members of different roles; professors (2), CIOs (3), consultants (2), EA architects (2), and development managers/directors (2). Evaluation consists of three rounds.

For the first round, using open-ended questions, experts were asked to read the EAAM method description and compare it to the traditional adoption method. For the second round, first round answers were transformed to claims (n = 31) and were sent back to experts for rating (disagree-neutral-agree). The scale $(-3, -2, -1, 0, 1, 2, 3)$ was formed so that it could be treated as an interval scale as defined by Stevens [73] which allowed us to calculate mean and standard deviations. For the third round, claims were sent to experts for rating including the average opinion of the panel. This allowed experts to re-assess their opinions to each claim.

The purpose of the evaluation is to have an unanimous opinion of the experts about EAAM. Thus the interest lies in the claims having a high mean and low standard deviation. Claims were ordered by their z-scores calculated with the formula $z = (x - \mu)/\sigma$ where x is the mean value of the particular claim, μ is 0 (the centre of the scale), and σ is the standard deviation of the particular claim. The higher the z-score is, the more unanimous are the experts. To include only the most unanimous claims, a critical z-value for 0.95 significance was used as a threshold. The critical value for 0.95 is 1.65 as calculated by Excel 2007 NORMSINV function. Claims with the z-score less than 1.65 are thus rejected, which leaves us 16 statements of EAAM seen in Table 3.

Table 3. Evaluation statements.

z	Statement
5.33	Considered and appropriate leadership style helps in adoption because it is all about changing the way to perform development
4.64	Benefits of the adoption and the temporal nature of the resulting extra work is understood better, because the benefits are communicated using the target group's comprehension and point of view
3.77	The meaning of the top-management's own example for the organisation is becoming more aware, because by the commitment of the top-management also the rest of the organisation is obligated to the EA adoption
3.33	IM department's estimates of change targets are improved, because the anticipation of changes are improved and visualised
2.83	The average of organisation's individuals' willingness to change will change to more positive, because the communication of benefits increases the formation of positive image and the acquirement the mandate from top-management
2.67	The reasons for actions will be communicated
2.67	Top-managements support to EA as a continuous part of organisation's normal management and operational development increases, because the recognition of the purpose and justification of EA-work, and communication of benefits, builds the foundation to acquire the mandate of top-management
2.36	The total development of organisational knowledge would be improved in general, because also other actors beside the top-management are taken into account
2.36	The leadership point of view is correct because the communication of EA is shaped according to the target group
2.13	Setting the target and objectives of the adoption can be performed faster and in managed manner because the participants has a common picture of concepts, objectives, and methods before the actual execution phase
2.04	The commitment and motivation to the adoption increases, because the understanding of reasons and objectives of EA increases
1.85	Effects to the quality of results and to communicating them are positive, because the meaning of broad-enough knowledge is emphasised
1.76	Documentation of QA system is improved, because method has a positive effect in the creation of basic documentation
1.76	Improves commitments and possibilities to acquire the mandate, because the person responsible for adoption is helped to improve targeting and content of the communication, and to considering the appropriate influencing methods and approaches
1.76	Definitions of the roles and tasks are naturally forming according to the target, because the communication using the language of the target group affects the understanding of the benefits of each group
1.67	Securing of top-management's commitment to adoption of EA and similar concepts increases, because the adoption is strongly based on top-management's commitment and communication of the adoption

4   Some Practical Guidelines

In this section, some practical guidelines for applying Enterprise Architecture Adoption Method are provided. The section consists of four sub-sections following the EAAM process steps, i.e., *Explain Enterprise Architecture Benefits*, *Acquire Mandate*, *Organise Enterprise Architecture Training*, and *Conduct Enterprise Architecture Adoption*.

4.1   Explain Enterprise Architecture Benefits

The first phase of EAAM is to explain EA benefits to the organisation's management in order to "sell" the EA adoption. In this sub-section the steps of *Explain EA Benefits Process* (see Fig. 6) are explained. Purpose of this step is to increase the likelihood of securing the mandate for EA adoption from the top-management.

4.1.1   Explain Common Enterprise Architecture Benefits

The first task of the *Explain EA Benefits Process* is to explain the common EA benefits to organisation's management. Common EA benefits are those anticipated benefits that interests and can be understood by everyone regardless of their role.

The first common benefit is the *Alignment of business and IT*. This refers to "applying Information Technology (IT) in an appropriate and timely way, in harmony with business strategies, goals and needs" [74, p. 3]. Alignment allows organisations to generate business value from IT. For instance, organisation can achieve strategic goals and realise business benefits [75].

The second common benefit is *Make better decisions*. This benefit is premised on high-quality information which supports decision making.

Third common benefit is *Simplification of system or architecture management*. Reduced complexity of management reduces also risks associated to managing systems of architectures.

4.1.2   Assess Managers' Views to EA

The second phase of the *Explain EA Benefits Process* is to assess the managers' views to EA. There are five qualities or characteristics to be assessed.

The first quality to assess is whether managers see EA as a business or technology oriented. For instance, EA can be seen as the glue between business and IT, as the link between strategy and execution, or as the means for organisational innovation and sustainability [76]. The first view to EA refers to technical orientation and the two latter ones to business orientation.

The second quality to assess is how the managers see the organisation's current EA maturity. Maturity can be assessed using different methods and models. One framework to use is Architecture Capability Maturity Model (ACMM) developed by US Department of Commerce [77].

The third quality to assess is the managers previous EA experience. In other words, have managers previously involved in EA initiatives in their current or previous organisations.

The fourth quality to assess is how complex the managers see the EA. Sometimes EA deliverables, such as, architecture descriptions, are seen too complex [78].

The fifth quality to assess is the managers authority on EA related matters. This is tightly coupled for the first assessed quality, i.e., is EA seen as business or IT oriented. For instance, if EA is seen as the glue between business and IT, CIO typically has all required authority. However, if EA is seen as the means for organisational innovation, typically only CEO has the required authority to make EA related decisions.

4.1.3 Explain Specific EA Benefits

The third phase of the *Explain EA Benefits Process* is to explain specific EA benefits according to each manager's views to EA as assessed in the previous phase. There are ten benefits to be explained as listed in Table 4.

Table 4. EA views and benefits [adapted from 48].

EA view/benefit	Orientation		Maturity		Experience		Complexity		Authority	
	Bus	Tech.	Low	High	Low	High	Low	High	Low	High
Adaptability and agility	x		x		x					x
Increase operational effectiveness	x		x		x	x	x		x	
Increase revenues and cost reduction	x		x		x					x
Process improvement	x		x		x					
Standardisation and consistency	x		x		x					x
Win new business	x		x		x					
Planning						x	x		x	
Product selection						x	x		x	
Speak a common language						x	x		x	
Move the organisation forward										x

The first benefit is *Adaptability and agility*. This refers to organisation's capability to respond to external events. For instance, the ability to quickly change organisational processes is currently seen as a strategic necessity [2].

The second benefit is *Increase operational effectiveness*. EA enables organisations to digitalise their processes. If this digitalisation is focused on the processes that do not change on regular basis, organisations may increase their operational effectiveness [2].

The third benefit is *Increase revenues and cost reduction*. EA provides details about the organisation's current state, including its business, information, information systems, and technology. Such information can used as a basis for removing overlapping assets and improving re-use. This can result to cost reduction and increased revenues.

The fourth benefit is *Process improvement*. This benefit can partly be seen as a subset of the previous benefits. Information about the current business architecture, including processes, allows organisation to improve their processes. For instance, organisation may decide to adopt ITIL processes for their IT service management processes. However, the focus should be on those business processes where the most value can be realised.

The fifth benefit is *Standardisation and consistency*. Also this benefit is partly covered with previous benefits. Information about the current state of the organisation allows standardisation of, for instance, business processes, used vocabulary, desktop software, and server hardware. This, in turn, may lead to cost reduction and process improvement.

The sixth benefit is *Win new business*. This benefit can be seen as result of agility and standardisation. Agile organisation with standardised processes and operations may allow it to expand business to other markets and geographical areas [2].

The seventh benefit is *Planning*. This benefit refers to the organisational ability to change organisation in a planned way. This allows organisation to evolve proactively.

The eighth benefit is *Product selection*. This benefit refers to the ability to focus on those investments that provides the best value. The holistic information about the current state of the organisation allows assessing and selecting the investments which capture the most value.

The ninth benefit is *Speak a common language*. Describing the current and future states of the organisation in a formal way helps everyone to interpret and understand things in the same way. Using a formal and agreed notation helps to interpret descriptions even with low prior knowledge on the subject [79].

The tenth benefit is *Move the organisation forward*. This benefit refers to organisation's ability to achieve its goals. These goals can be described as the future state of the organisation and communicated using a common language. The managed change between the current and future states can be used to achieve the organisation's goals.

4.2   Acquire Mandate

The second phase of the EAAM is to acquire mandate from the top-management. This mandate can be, for instance, in a form of Request for Architecture Work (RAC) [13]. Typically the RAC is a high-level document including [13, p. 494]:

- Organisation sponsors
- Organisation's mission statement
- Business goals (and changes)
- Strategic plans of the business
- Time limits
- Changes in the business environment
- Organizational constraints
- Budget information, financial constraints
- External constraints, business constraints
- Current business system description
- Current architecture/IT system description
- Description of developing organization
- Description of resources available to developing organisation

The formal mandate emphasises the support from top-management, allowing smoother adoption process.

4.3 Organise Enterprise Architecture Training

The third phase of EAAM is to organise EA training see (Fig. 7). The purpose of the training is to increase organisation's EA knowledge to reduce organisational change resistance caused by the lack of EA knowledge.

4.3.1 Assess Organisation's Learning Stock

The first phase of the *Organise EA training* process is to assess organisation's learning stock. As discussed earlier, organisational learning stock refers to knowledge embedded to organisation. E.g., organisation's structures, strategy, procedures, and culture [65]. Also organisation's capabilities are part of this learning stock. Typical organisational capabilities which EA adoption will affect are listed in Table 5.

Table 5. Organisational capabilities affected by EA adoption [13, p. 17].

Financial management	Communications and stakeholder management
Performance management	Quality management
Service management	Supplier management
Risk management	Configuration management
Resource management	Environment management

Each of the mentioned capabilities are utilised during the EA adoption. Therefore the level of each capability should be assessed. Capabilities can be defined as tangible and intangible assets which organisations use to implement their strategies [80]. One example of these assets is the organisation's processes. For example, financial management capability consists of people and financial management processes. Thus the mature of the capability can be assessed by assessing the related processes.

There are many maturity models which could be utilised. Typically these models consists of 5 maturity levels. In TOGAF, process maturity is assessed using levels listed in Table 6. Another widely used framework is included in COBIT, which maturity levels are listed in Table 7.

Table 6. EA process maturity levels [13, pp. 685–689].

Level	Description
0: None	No enterprise architecture program. No enterprise architecture to speak of
1: Initial	Informal enterprise architecture process underway
2: Under development	Enterprise architecture process is under development
3: Defined	Defined enterprise architecture including detailed written procedures
4: Managed	Managed and measured enterprise architecture process
5: Optimising	Continuous improvement of enterprise architecture process

Table 7. COBIT process capability levels [75, p. 53].

Level	Description
0: Incomplete process	The process is not implemented or fails to achieve its process purpose. At this level, there is little or no evidence of any systematic achievement of the process purpose
1: Performed process	The implemented process achieves its process purpose
2: Managed process	The previously described performed process is now implemented in a managed fashion (planned, monitored and adjusted) and its work products are appropriately established, controlled and maintained
3: Established process	The previously described managed process is now implemented using a defined process that is capable of achieving its process outcomes
4: Predictable process	The previously described established process now operates within defined limits to achieve its process outcomes
5: Optimising	The previously described predictable process is continuously improved to meet relevant current and projected business goals

4.3.2 Assess Employee's Learning Stock

The second phase of the *Organise EA training* process is to assess organisation's employees' learning stock. Employee's learning stock refers to employee's individual competence, capability, and motivation [65]. First step is to identify skill categories required in EA adoption. Typical skill categories are listed in Table 8. The next step is to assess employees' proficiency in each category. Proficiency levels can be assessed using levels listed in Table 9.

Table 8. EA team skill categories [13, p. 695].

Category	Description
Generic skills	typically comprising leadership, team working, inter-personal skills, etc.
Business skills and methods	typically comprising business cases, business process, strategic planning, etc.
Enterprise architecture skills	typically comprising modelling, building block design, applications and role design, systems integration, etc.
Program or project management skills	typically comprising managing business change, project management methods and tools, etc.
IT general knowledge skills	typically comprising broker ing applications, asset management, migration planning, SLAs, etc.
Technical IT skills	typically comprising software engineering, security, data interchange, data management, etc.
Legal environment	typically comprising data protection laws, contract law, procurement law, fraud, etc.

Table 9. Skills proficiency levels [13, p. 696].

Level	Description
1: Background	Not a required skill, though should be able to define and manage skill if required
2: Awareness	Understands the background, issues, and implications sufficiently to be able to understand how to proceed further and advise client accordingly
3: Knowledge	Detailed knowledge of subject area and capable of providing professional advice and guidance. Ability to integrate capability into architecture design
4: Expert	Extensive and substantial practical experience and applied knowledge on the subject

4.3.3   Use a Proper Leadership Style

The third phase of the Organise EA training process is to select and use a proper leadership style. Leadership style refers to the style which managers use to lead their organisation, project, or like. This style can be either transformational or transactional [67], as discussed earlier in Sub-sect. 3.2. Characteristics of these styles are listed in Tables 10 and 11, respectively. For short, transformational leadership style works best when change is needed in organisation and transactional leadership style when the current state needs to be enforced.

Table 10. Characteristics of transformational leader [67, p. 22].

Characteristic	Description
Charisma	Provides vision and sense of mission, in stills pride, gains respect and trust
Inspiration	Communicates high expectations, uses symbols to focus efforts, expresses important purposes in simple ways
Intellectual stimulation	Promotes intelligence, rationality, and careful problem solving
Individualised consideration	Gives personal attention, treats each employee individually, coaches, advises

Table 11. Characteristics of transactional leader [67, p. 22].

Characteristic	Description
Contingent reward	Contracts exchange of rewards for effort, promises rewards for good performance, recognises accomplishments
Management by exception (active)	Watches and searches for deviations from rules and standards, takes corrective action
Management by exception (passive)	Intervenes only if standards are not met
Laissez-Faire	Adbicates responsibilities, avoids making decisions

Using a proper leadership style while organising EA training is crucial. When the knowledge and skills required by EA adoption is challenging organisation's current learning stock, the transformational leadership style needs to be used [65]. Similarly, if the required knowledge and skills does not challenge organisation's current learning stock, the transactional leadership style should be used [65]. It should be noted that some capabilities may be in better shape while others. For instance, Supplier Management might be very mature while Risk Management might be practically non existing. In such case, transactional leadership style should be used while organising Supplier Management training, and transformational leadership style while organising Risk Management training.

4.3.4   Promote EA Training

The fourth phase of the *Organise EA training* process is to promote EA training. Promoting refers to advertising the right training to right audience. The proper leadership style should be used during the promoting accordingly.

4.3.5   Provide EA Training

The fifth phase of the *Organise EA training* process is to provide EA training. This is the most crucial phase of the *Organising EA learning* process. In this phase, the required knowledge and skills are taught to individuals, and eventually, to organisation. Training can be provided as any other training, e.g., internal or external instructor-led training, e-learning, and self-study.

4.3.6   Use Coercive Organisational Pressure

The sixth phase of the *Organise EA training* process is to use the coercive organisational pressure. This means that as the new knowledge is trained and learned, applying this new knowledge needs to be enforced. Using coercive organisational pressure means adopting the transactional leadership style, focusing on searching deviations from using EA and taking corrective actions as required [67]. Coercive pressure has a crucial moderating role while assimilating EA to organisation's learning stock, but only when used as a temporary solution [64].

4.4   Conduct Enterprise Architecture Adoption

The fourth phase of EAAM is to conduct EA adoption (Fig. 3). In this phase the value and benefits of EA are realised as the organisation is adopting EA.

4.4.1   Select EA Framework

The first phase of the *Conduct EA Adoption Process* is to select the EA framework. Typically, EA framework consists of governance model and development method, including management and utilisation processes, roles, and description templates. Some examples of EAFs are The Open Group Architecture Framework (TOGAF), The Department of Defence Architecture Framework (DoDAF), Federal Enterprise Architecture Framework (FEAF), and Capgemini's Integrated Architecture Framework (IAF). TOGAF is currently the de-facto standard and mostly used EAF in both public and private sector [81]. Organisations should select the framework that best suits for its purposes.

4.4.2 Describe the Current State

The second phase of the *Conduct EA Adoption Process* is to describe the current state of the organisation. The descriptions to be produced depends on the selected EA framework and the purpose of adopting EA. Also the notation used to create the descriptions depends on the framework. However, some frameworks, such as TOGAF, does not contain any notation. In such case, it is recommended to use de-facto standard notations, such as, ArchiMate [82] and BPMN [83].

The descriptions of the current state should be value free, i.e., they should be objective representations of the reality without assessing the "goodness" of current solutions.

4.4.3 Describe the Future State

The third phase of the *Conduct EA Adoption Process* is to describe the future state of the organisation. The descriptions of the future state should be produced using the same notation used to describe the current state. Organisation's strategic goals and decisions are embodied to future state descriptions and should be perceived similar way by everyone.

4.4.4 Perform the Managed Change

The fourth phase of the *Conduct EA Adoption Process* is to perform the managed change from the current state to the future state of the organisation. In this phase the organisation is changed to match the desired future state. The breadth and depth of the change depends on many things, such as, the strategic level of EA.

Organisation may use any methodology or processes to perform the change, as long as it is managed. For instance, organisation may utilise best practices like PRINCE2 [84].

5 Conclusions

As stated in the problem definition, the purpose of the EAAM is to improve the traditional EA adoption process to minimise the effects of lack of understanding EA and related concepts. For this purpose, EAAM introduced two new sub-processes: *Explain EA benefits* and *Organise EA learning*.

Goal of the *Explain EA benefits* process is to increase the likelihood of getting a mandate from top-management for EA adoption. This is achieved by explaining EA benefits based on each manager's characteristics. Experts' statements supports achievement of this goal strongly, as most of the statements are related to this process. This also indicates the importance of securing top-management mandate.

Goal of the *Organise EA learning* process is to increase the understanding of EA concepts. This is achieved by assessing the current learning stock and by providing appropriate training with a help of appropriate leadership style. Experts' statements supports also achievement of this goal.

According to March and Smith [85, p. 261] "Evaluation of methods considers operationality (the ability to perform the intended task or the ability of humans to effectively use the method if it is not algorithmic), efficiency, generality, and ease of use". The first two criteria, operationality and efficiency is evaluated above; EAAM can be used to perform intended task (e.g., adopt EA in an organisation) and it is efficient. The last two criteria, generality and ease of use, can be evaluated only by applying EAAM in other settings. The practical guidelines applying EAAM helps in assessing the generality and ease of use.

It cannot be argued that EAAM would be the best alternative solution to the traditional EA adoption method. However, as demonstrated in previous section, it can be argued that EAAM is better than the traditional EA adoption method.

5.1   Limitations and Future Work

As with all research this research is not without limitations. EAAM was evaluated with a panel of EA experts. Therefore, the first direction for future work is to evaluate it in a real-life setting by instantiation. To increase its generalisability, EAAM should be instantiated outside the Finnish public sector. In this paper, the ease-of-use of EAAM was not assessed. As suggested for instance by Venkatesh *et al.* [54], ease-of-use is important. Thus our second direction for future research is to assess EAAM's ease-of-use in a real-life setting.

5.2   Conclusion

The EAAM method emphasises the importance of acquiring the mandate for EA adoption from the top-management and the importance of a proper EA training. EAAM helps in acquiring the mandate by formulating the argumentation of EA benefits according to the individual's interests. Moreover, EAAM helps in EA training by providing directions in choosing a proper leadership style to promote EA training. Thus by following EAAM, organisations can minimise the effects of the lack of EA knowledge.

To support the adoption of EAAM, some practical guidelines are provided. This should help practitioners in their EA adoption endeavours to realise EA benefits in their organisations.

References

1. Schulman, J.: Enterprise Architecture: Benefits and Justification. Gartner (2003)
2. Ross, J.W., Weill, P., Robertson, D.C.: Enterprise Architecture as Strategy: Creating a Foundation for Business Execution. Harvard Business School Press, Boston (2006)
3. Schekkerman, J.: Trends in Enterprise Architecture 2005: How are Organizations Progressing?. Institute for Enterprise Architecture Developments, Amersfoort (2005)
4. Computer Economics. http://www.computereconomics.com/article.cfm?id=1947

5. Hjort-Madsen, K.: Enterprise architecture implementation and management: a case study on interoperability. In: HICSS-39, Proceedings of 39th Annual Hawaii International Conference on System Sciences (2006)
6. Sembiring, J., Nuryatno, E.T., Gondokaryono, Y.S.: Analyzing the indicators and requirements in main components of enterprise architecture methodology development using grounded theory in qualitative methods. In: Society of Interdisciplinary Business Research Conference, Bangkok (2011)
7. Valtonen, K., Mäntynen, S., Leppänen, M., Pulkkinen, M.: Enterprise architecture descriptions for enhancing local government transformation and coherency management: case study. In: 2011 15th IEEE International Enterprise Distributed Object Computing Conference Workshops (EDOCW), pp. 360–369 (2011)
8. Lemmetti, J., Pekkola, S.: Understanding enterprise architecture: perceptions by the finnish public sector. In: Scholl, H., Janssen, M., Wimmer, M., Moe, C., Flak, L. (eds.) Electronic Government, vol. 7443, pp. 162–173. Springer, Berlin (2012)
9. Pehkonen, J.: Early phase challenges and solutions in enterprise architecture of public sector. Master's Degree Programme in Information and Knowledge Management, p. 107. Tampere University of Technology, Tampere (2013)
10. Fehskens, L.: Len's Lens: eight ways we frame our concepts of architecture. J. Enterp. Archit. **11**, 55–59 (2015)
11. Zachman, J.A.: Enterprise architecture: the issue of the century. Database Program. Des. **10**, 44–53 (1997)
12. CIO Council: A Practical Guide to Federal Enterprise Architecture (2001)
13. The Open Group: TOGAF Version 9. Van Haren Publishing, Zaltbommel (2009)
14. ISO/IEC/IEEE: Systems and software engineering – architecture description. ISO/IEC/ IEEE 42010:2011(E) (Revision of ISO/IEC 42010:2007 and IEEE Std 1471-2000), pp. 1–46 (2011)
15. http://www.gartner.com/it-glossary/enterprise-architecture-ea/
16. Dietz, J.L.G., Hoogervorst, J.A.P., Albani, A., Aveiro, D., Babkin, E., Barjis, J., Caetano, A., Huysmans, P., Iijima, J., van Kervel, S.J.H., Mulder, H., Op't Land, M., Proper, H.A., Sanz, J., Terlouw, L., Tribolet, J., Verelst, J., Winter, R.: The discipline of enterprise engineering. Int. J. Org. Des. Eng. **3**, 86–114 (2013)
17. Syynimaa, N.: Theoretical perspectives of enterprise architecture. In: 4th Nordic EA Summer School, EASS 2013, Helsinki, Finland (2013)
18. van de Ven, A.H., Poole, M.S.: Explaining development and change in organizations. Acad. Manag. Rev. **20**, 510–540 (1995)
19. North, E., North, J., Benade, S.: Information management and enterprise architecture planning – a juxtaposition. Probl. Perspect. Manag. **4**, 166–179 (2004)
20. Kaisler, H., Armour, F., Valivullah, M.: Enterprise architecting: critical problems. In: Proceedings of 38th Annual Hawaii International Conference on System Sciences, HICSS-38, pp. 224–234. IEEE, Washington, DC (2005)
21. Shupe, C., Behling, R.: Developing and implementing a strategy for technology deployment. Inf. Manag. J. **40**, 52–57 (2006)
22. Gregor, S., Jones, D.: The anatomy of a design theory. J. Assoc. Inf. Syst. **8**, 312–335 (2007)
23. Iyamu, T.: Enterprise architecture as information technology strategy. In: 2011 IEEE 13th Conference on Commerce and Enterprise Computing (CEC), pp. 82–88 (2011)
24. Iyamu, T.: The factors affecting institutionalisation of enterprise architecture in the organisation. In: Hofreiter, B., Werthner, H. (eds.) Proceedings of IEEE Conference on Commerce and Enterprise Computing, CEC 2009, pp. 221–225. IEEE, Los Alamitos (2009)

25. Liu, Y., Li, H.: Applying enterprise architecture in China e-Government: a case of implementing government-led credit information system of Yiwu. In: WHICEB 2009, 8th Wuhan International Conference on e-Business, pp. 538–545 (2009)
26. Carrillo, J., Cabrera, A., Román, C., Abad, M., Jaramillo, D.: Roadmap for the implementation of an enterprise architecture framework oriented to institutions of higher education in Ecuador. In: 2010 2nd International Conference on Software Technology and Engineering (ICSTE), pp. V2-7–V2-11. IEEE (2010)
27. Mezzanotte, D.M., Dehlinger, J., Chakraborty, S.: On applying the theory of structuration in enterprise architecture design. In: 2010 IEEE/ACIS 9th International Conference on Computer and Information Science (ICIS), pp. 859–863 (2010)
28. Vasilescu, C.: General enterprise architecture concepts and the benefits for an organization. In: 7th International Scientific Conference, Defence Resources Management in the 21st Century, pp. 1–9. Regional Department of Defence Resources Management Studies, Romanian National Defence University, Braşov (2012)
29. Struijs, P., Camstra, A., Renssen, R., Braaksma, B.: Redesign of statistics production within an architectural framework: the Dutch experience. J. Off. Stat. **29**, 49–71 (2013)
30. Hammer, M., Champy, J.: Reengineering the Corporation: A Manifesto for Business Revolution. Nicholas Brearly, London (1993)
31. Beer, M., Nohria, N.: Cracking the code of change. Harvard Bus. Rev. **78**, 133–141 (2000)
32. Kotter, J.P.: A sense of urgency. Harvard Business Press, Harvard (2008)
33. Finnish Ministry of Finance: Act on Information Management Governance in Public Administration (643/2011) (2011)
34. Finnish Ministry of Finance: Tietoja valtion tietohallinnosta 2014. Valtiovarainministeriön julkaisuja 27/2015. (Information on the state information management 2014. Publications of the Ministry of Finance 27/2015), p. 60. Ministry of Finance, Helsinki (2015)
35. Hiekkanen, K., Korhonen, J.J., Collin, J., Patricio, E., Helenius, M., Mykkanen, J.: Architects' perceptions on EA use – an empirical study. In: O'Conner, L. (ed.) Proceedings of 15th IEEE Conference on Business Informatics (CBI), pp. 292–297. IEEE, Los Alamitos (2013)
36. Seppänen, V.: From problems to critical success factors of enterprise architecture adoption. Jyväskylä Stud. Comput. **201**, 250 (2014). University of Jyväskylä, Jyväskylä
37. Syynimaa, N.: Enterprise architecture adoption method for higher education institutions. p. 262. Gerenios Ltd., Tampere, Finland (2015)
38. Hevner, A., March, S., Park, J., Ram, S.: Design science in information systems research. MIS Q. **28**, 75–106 (2004)
39. van Aken, J.E.: Management research based on the paradigm of the design sciences: the quest for field-tested and grounded technological rules. J. Manag. Stud. **41**, 219–246 (2004)
40. Vaishnavi, V., Kuechler, B.: Design science research in information systems (2013). desrist. org
41. Lee, A.S., Manoj, T.A., Baskerville, R.L.: Going back to basics in design: from the IT artifact to the IS artifact. In: Proceedings of 19th Americas Conference on Information Systems, pp. 1–7 (2013)
42. Peffers, K., Tuunanen, T., Rothenberger, M.A., Chatterjee, S.: A design science research methodology for information systems research. J. Manag. Inf. Syst. **24**, 45–77 (2007)
43. Houkes, W.N.: Rules, plans and the normativity of technological knowledge. In: de Vries, M.J., Hansson, S.O., Meijers, A.W.M. (eds.) Norms in Technology, vol. 9, pp. 35–54. Springer, Dordrecht (2013)
44. Bunge, M.: Technology as applied science. Technol. Cult. **7**, 329–347 (1966)

45. Järvinen, P.: On design research – some questions and answers. In: Matulevičius, R., Dumas, M. (eds.) BIR 2015. LNBIP, vol. 229, pp. 113–125. Springer, Cham (2015). doi:10.1007/978-3-319-21915-8_8
46. Skulmoski, G.J., Hartman, F.T., Krahn, J.: The Delphi method for graduate research. J. Inf. Technol. Educ. **6**, 1–21 (2007)
47. Päivärinta, T., Pekkola, S., Moe, C. E.: Grounding theory from delphi studies. In: 32nd International Conference on Information Systems, Shanghai, pp. 1–14 (2011)
48. Nassiff, E.: Understanding the Value of Enterprise Architecture for Organizations: A Grounded Theory Approach, vol. 3523496, p. 135. Nova Southeastern University, Ann Arbor (2012)
49. Burnes, B., James, H.: Culture, cognitive dissonance and the management of change. Int. J. Oper. Prod. Manag. **15**, 14–33 (1995)
50. Jones, R.A., Jimmieson, N.L., Griffiths, A.: The impact of organizational culture and reshaping capabilities on change implementation success: the mediating role of readiness for change. J. Manag. Stud. **42**, 361–386 (2005)
51. Holt, D.T., Armenakis, A.A., Feild, H.S., Harris, S.G.: Readiness for organizational change: the systematic development of a scale. J. Appl. Behav. Sci. **43**, 232–255 (2007)
52. Washington, M., Hacker, M.: Why change fails: knowledge counts. Leadersh. Org. Dev. J. **26**, 400–411 (2005)
53. Elving, W.J.L.: The role of communication in organisational change. Corp. Commun.: Int. J. **10**, 129–138 (2005)
54. Venkatesh, V., Morris, M.G., Davis, G.B., Davis, F.D.: User acceptance of information technology: toward a unified view. MIS Q. **27**, 425–478 (2003)
55. Koponen, E.: The development, implementation and use of e-learning: critical realism and design science perspectives. University of Tampere (2009)
56. Lee, A.S.: Retrospect and prospect: information systems research in the last and next 25 years. J. Inf. Technol. **25**, 336–348 (2010)
57. Lee, A.S.: Thinking about social theory and philosophy for information systems. In: Mingers, J., Willcocks, L. (eds.) Social Theory and Philosophy for Information Systems, pp. 1–26. Wiley, Chichester (2004)
58. Mintzberg, H., Ahlstrand, B., Lampel, J.: Strategy Safari: the Complete Guide Trough the Wilds of Strategic Management. Financial Times Prentice Hall, London (1998)
59. March, J.G., Simon, H.A.: Organizations. Wiley, Oxford (1958)
60. Kitchen, P.J., Daly, F.: Internal communication during change management. Corp. Commun.: Int. J. **7**, 46–53 (2002)
61. Hazen, B.T., Kung, L., Cegielski, C.G., Jones-Farmer, L.A.: Performance expectancy and use of enterprise architecture: training as an intervention. J. Enterp. Inf. Manag. **27**, 6 (2014)
62. Knowles, M.S.: The Modern Practice of Adult Education. New York Association Press, New York (1970)
63. Mezirow, J.: Transformative Learning: Theory to Practice. N. Dir. Adult Contin. Educ. **74**, 5–12 (1997)
64. Makiya, G.K.: A multi-level investigation into the antecedents of Enterprise Architecture (EA) assimilation in the U.S. Federal Government: a longitudinal mixed methods research study. vol. 3530104, p. 296. Case Western Reserve University, Ann Arbor (2012)
65. Vera, D., Crossan, M.: Strategic leadership and organizational learning. Acad. Manag. Rev. **29**, 222–240 (2004)
66. Crossan, M.M., Lane, H.W., White, R.E.: An organizational learning framework: from intuition to institution. Acad. Manag. Rev. **24**, 522–537 (1999)
67. Bass, B.M.: From transactional to transformational leadership: learning to share the vision. Org. Dyn. **18**, 19–31 (1990)

68. Espinosa, J.A., Armour, F., Boh, W.F.: The role of group cognition in enterprise architecting. In: 2011 44th Hawaii International Conference on System Sciences (HICSS), pp. 1–10 (2011)

69. Oxford University Press. http://oxforddictionaries.com/

70. Cannon-Bowers, J.A., Salas, E.: Reflections on shared cognition. J. Org. Behav. **22**, 195–202 (2001)

71. Agarwal, R.: Individual acceptance of information technologies. In: Zmud, R.W. (ed.) Framing the Domains of IT Management: Projecting the Future Through the Past, pp. 85–104. Pinnaflex Education Resources, Cincinnati (2000)

72. Venable, J., Pries-Heje, J., Baskerville, R.: A comprehensive framework for evaluation in design science research. In: Peffers, K., Rothenberger, M., Kuechler, B. (eds.) Design Science Research in Information Systems. Advances in Theory and Practice, vol. 7286, pp. 423–438. Springer, Berlin Heidelberg (2012)

73. Stevens, S.S.: On the theory of scales of measurement. Science **103**, 677–680 (1946). (New Series)

74. Luftman, J.: Assessing business-IT alignment maturity. Commun. Assoc. Inf. Syst. **4**, Article 14 (2000)

75. ISACA: COBIT® 5. A Business Framework for the Governance and Management of Enterprise IT. ISACA, Rolling Meadows (2012)

76. Lapalme, J.: Three schools of thought on enterprise architecture. IT Prof. **14**, 37–43 (2012)

77. http://ocio.os.doc.gov/ITPolicyandPrograms/Enterprise_Architecture/PROD01_004935

78. Raadt, B., Schouten, S., Vliet, H.: Stakeholder perception of enterprise architecture. In: Morrison, R., Balasubramaniam, D., Falkner, K. (eds.) ECSA 2008. LNCS, vol. 5292, pp. 19–34. Springer, Heidelberg (2008). doi:10.1007/978-3-540-88030-1_4

79. Mayer, R.E., Gallini, J.K.: When is an illustration worth ten thousand words? J. Educ. Psychol. **82**, 715–726 (1990)

80. Ray, G., Barney, J.B., Muhanna, W.A.: Capabilities, business processes, and competitive advantage: choosing the dependent variable in empirical tests of the resource-based view. Strateg. Manag. J. **25**, 23–37 (2004)

81. Cameron, B.H., McMillan, E.: Analyzing the current trends in enterprise architecture frameworks. J. Enterp. Architecture **9**, 60–71 (2013)

82. http://www.opengroup.org/subjectareas/enterprise/archimate

83. http://www.omg.org/spec/BPMN/2.0/

84. https://www.axelos.com/best-practice-solutions/prince2

85. March, S.T., Smith, G.F.: Design and natural science research on information technology. Decis. Support Syst. **15**, 251–266 (1995)

A Procedural Approach for Evaluating the Performance of Business Processes Based on a Model of Quantative and Qualitative Measurements

Thiago Mendes[(✉)] and Simone Santos

Centro de Informática, Federal University of Pernambuco,
Av. Jorn. Anibal Fernandes, Recife, Brazil
{trms,scs}@cin.ufpe.br

Abstract. Evaluating the performance of processes is of vital importance if organizations are to seek continuous improvements. It is by measuring processes that data on their performance is provided, thus showing the evolution of the organization in terms of its strategic objectives. These results will serve as the basis for making better decisions, thereby leading to continuous improvement. The approach set out in this paper is prompted by the relative lack of empirical investigations into performance measures contained in the literature and the difficulties that organizations face when trying to verify the results of their business processes. Based on analyzing studies selected in a Systematic Review of the Literature, there it was found the need to propose a new approach to evaluating business processes that brings together elements and recommendations selected from the analyzed approaches. In the evaluation of the proposed approach, a case study is discussed, to verify its applicability.

Keywords: Strategic alignment · Business process management · Performance measurement

1 Introduction

Organizations undertake their activities in a context that is characterized as being highly competitive, complex and subject to rapid mutations in addition to which customers demand more and more and all of which arises from greater access to information. Business processes help organizations to see to it that their activities become more flexible and that they enhance the quality of their products and services, thereby making themselves suit the demands of the market and thus leading to the natural development of the Organization. Against this background, organizations need to integrated management by running an interactive system of processes that carry out work with a view to delivering value to their customers. From this perspective, the concept of Business Process Management (BPM) has emerged as a management approach that shifts the focus from functional units to controlling the performance of business processes in achieving their objectives.

© Springer International Publishing AG 2017
S. Hammoudi et al. (Eds.): ICEIS 2016, LNBIP 291, pp. 515–534, 2017.
DOI: 10.1007/978-3-319-62386-3_23

The results of the processes are directly linked to the mission and objectives of the organization, since the processes represent the implementation of the strategy. The focus of process management is underpinned by key business strategies that establish the direction of the organization. In this context, [2] reinforces that the need for measurement in process management is a critical factor. It uses measurements that make it possible to monitor the performance of processes, thus contributing towards monitoring processes, thus contributing to checking how well these processes meet the strategic objectives set.

According to [3], issues related to performance measures and to defining what should be measured in relation to business processes should be directly linked to the strategic priorities of each organization.

BPM initiatives need to be evaluated to check the alignment between the strategic, tactical and operational aspects of processes, thus making it possible to verify the results achieved in accordance with the objectives outlined. Business processes should be designed by the administration, after having established measures of performance (Powell et al., 2001), which should reflect the desired direction given in the strategic objectives, and serve as a basis for the control of processes. By so doing, this will make it easier to see if the objectives of the organization are being attained.

However, according to both [5, 6], the effects of BPM programs are often not easily visible as to whether or not value is being generated for organizations. This is because organizations are unaware of or do not have good control over the operation of their processes. The result of this is to create performance indicators that reflect departments' prompt results, defined by a functional management focused on a vertical view [7]. Thus, measures and evaluation of performance end up targeting the functional performance of departments and individuals when they should focus on the outcomes of the process.

According to [8], organizations have difficulty in defining what should be measured, and end up measuring less complicated aspects such as productivity, cost, time; and often neglect indicators linked to strategy. Based on their analysis of empirical studies, [7] verified there is a gap between the analysis, implementation and conduct of processes as well as between strategic management and operational running; for which they give as a possible explanation that a methodological orientation of systems that measure the performance of Business Processes is lacking.

[2] takes the view that the sustainability of a BPM initiative is adversely affected in several ways when the value added to the organization cannot be measured due to the fact that several BPM initiatives are not supported by reports or measures that managers who contribute to the decision-making process understand. In the analysis of [7], various models for assessing the performance of Business Processes use numerical parameters and artificial and simplifying measures in an attempt to assess these processes. However, various processes of a qualitative and non-deterministic nature end up not being evaluated effectively.

Arising from the idea that various processes are not evaluated or that this evaluation is difficult when using these measures, possible problems or performance results may remain invisible to managers, and thus make hardly any contribution to the decision-making process and consolidate the gap between strategy and business processes [7].

When searching for studies related to initiatives on measuring business process performance, the paper by [9] was evaluated. Based on a systematic review of the literature, this study classified measurement initiatives in business process management into two distinct categories: measures for models and measures for running or assessing BPM activities; the former being related to the static properties of the processes represented based on the models, and the latter, corresponding to measures related to running processes, thus allowing results obtained and expected to be compared with the strategic objectives. The study shows that 77% of performance measures are related exclusively to the models of the processes, thus giving evidence of the lack of models that aim to evaluate the results of the Business Processes themselves.

The measurements for running a BPM program are related to customer satisfaction, and have been studied in less depth in the Computer Sciences than in other areas. These measures seek to quantify how the process is carried out over time, thus allowing the results measured to be compared with the expected results and thus providing information that contributes to improving business processes [9], which are the focus of this research study.

What prompted this research is related to the difficulty for organizations of finding comprehensible measurements to assess whether the results of the business processes are reflecting the strategic objectives noting the paucity of empirical research on using models and performance measurement systems in the literature. This leads us to following research question:

Which approach best meets the evaluation of business processes, with a view to bringing about a greater alignment between process indicators and strategic objectives?

Based on the model proposed by [10], which was adapted from the GQM (Goal Question Metric) method, the overall objectives of this research are: (1) to analyze metric models or approaches for assessing business processes proposed in the literature; (2) to put forward an approach to evaluating business processes that contributes towards better aligning indicators of processes and strategic objectives; (3) to check its applicability from the standpoint of leaders, analysts and owners of the process; (4) to do all these in the context of business processes of a public organization.

The rest of the article discusses the systematic review of the literature in Sect. 2. Then, the Approach put forward in this paper is described (Sect. 3). Section 4 presents the results obtained by applying the Approach and in Sect. 5 final remarks are made, the contributions of the paper listed and suggestions for future studies made.

2 Systematic Review of the Literature

The Systematic Review methodology adopted in this paper is a form of research that uses the literature on a given subject as a source of data [11]. This approach is a means for identifying, evaluating and interpreting various research studies which are available and especially relevant to a specific research question, subject area, or phenomenon of interest.

According to [12], there are specific reasons that contribute to conducting a systematic review, such as:

- Consolidating evidence and results obtained in previous studies on a given topic;
- Identifying gaps in current research or theory, thereby offering a theoretical basis to improve research studies;
- Having the ability to provide background and theoretical models so as to position new themes and research opportunities appropriately;
- Enabling new hypotheses on a given research theme to be refuted, validated or developed.

The systematic review approach indicated by [12] is divided into three stages/ordered phases: planning, execution and analysis of the results.

The objective of this review is to analyze, more specifically, what the performance measures or indicators are and how they are being used in the context of managing business processes to ensure that processes and strategic objectives are aligned. Based on this analysis, we set out to answer the following Research Questions:

RQ1- What are the metrics and indicators that are being used when evaluating business processes?

RQ2- Do the studies have rules, guidelines or sets of guidance notes on how to use the metrics presented?

RQ3- What is the context in which the metrics are being used?

2.1   Planning the Review

In the automatic search strategy, a few key words taken from the research question were selected. The list of keywords was defined in conjunction with the supervisor of the research study and are given in Table 1 below.

Table 1. Key-words and synonyms.

Key-words	Synonyms
Metrics	Measured
Assessment	Evaluation
Measure	Measurement
Application	Utilization
Performance indicators	–

When formulating the search string, the keywords listed in the Table above were used. These describe the terms related to evaluating business processes according to [13]. The second group of words used was: "business process", "BPM" and "business process management". This group focuses a set of words related to business processes, which are the elements that will be measured.

The search string was formed by combining the terms described above with Boolean operators (AND/OR). The formulated string was entered on the search engines of digital libraries to obtain the studies related to the terms used.

Automatic searches were conducted in the following digital libraries:

- Association for Computing Machinery – ACM (http://portal.acm.org/portal/);
- IEEE Computer Society (http://www.computer.org/web/search);
- Emerald Insight (http://www.emeraldinsight.com/search/advanced);
- Science Direct (http://www.sciencedirect.com/science/search);
- Springer Link (http://link.springer.com/advanced-search).

The libraries of the IEEE Computer Society and the Association for Computing Machinery (ACM) are specific to the Computer area. Initially only the titles of the articles were read and, if in doubt, the summary was also evaluated.

The strategy of manual search was also used in order to complement the automatic strategy, thus allowing an investigation to be made in pre-defined locations that, possibly, could include articles related to the topic of interest.

When conducting manual searches, some conferences, journals and the references of the articles found were used. Only articles published after 2004 were evaluated. The search sites and the articles selected are listed below:

AMCIS (Americas Conference on Information Systems). Article selected: Year 2011: Limitations of Performance Measurement Systems based on Key Performance Indicators.

CAISE (Conference on Advanced Information Systems Engineering): No article was selected.

ICSE (International Conferences on Software Engineering): No article was selected.

BPM Conference (International Conference on Business Process Management): The following articles were selected:

Year 2005: Using software Quality characteristics to measure Business Process Quality.

Year 2012: Defining Process Performance Indicator by Using Templates and Patterns.

The article entitled: An examination of the literature relating to issues affecting how companies manage through measures, from year 2005 (https://dspace.lib.cranfield.ac.uk/handle/1826/3035) was selected for analysis. The article was chosen for further analysis based on the analysis of the references of some articles.

After carrying out automatic and manual searches and searches on the references of articles, the process of selecting studies began, which will be described in the next sub-section.

2.2 Selection of the Primary Studies

The step of selecting primary studies is about assessing the relevance of the articles to the research questions. The inclusion criteria used to select articles are as follows:

IC1 – Studies published from 1 January 2004;

IC2 – Studies that describe metrics, measurements and performance indicators that make it possible to evaluate the results of business processes;

IC3 – Studies that present rules and guidelines or for constructing and/or using measurements for evaluating business processes.

The following criteria were used to exclude articles:

EC1 – Studies published before 1 January 2004;

EC2 – Tutorials or seminars or abstracts;

CE3 – Documents that have not been written in English will be deleted;

CE4 – Repeated studies (separate articles, but with the same or similar content) or of little relevance;

CE 5 - Documents that do not have the full text of the paper available on the internet and whose author(s) also cannot be contacted will be deleted;

CE6 – Documents that clearly deal with other matters not relevant to the purpose of this systematic review will be deleted;

CE7 – Articles that present measurements for evaluating models of business processes;

CE8 – Studies that are simply limited to the presentation of measurements, without describing how to calculate them or do not provide a guide on how to use them.

Table 2 shows, respectively, the Digital Library (Digital Library), the filters used (Filters), the number of returned items in each library (Results), the number of articles whose titles were analyzed (Checked) and the number of articles selected for review after a second reading (Selected).

Table 2. Results of the searches.

Digital library	Filters	Results	Checked	Selected
IEEE	From 1 January 2004	342	342	10
ACM	From 1 January 2004	827	827	1
SpringerLink	From 1 January 2004	976	976	4
Science Direct	From 1 January 2004	512	512	1
Emerald	From 1 January 2004	720	720	9
TOTAL	From 1 January 2004	3,377	3,377	25

Having made an initial selection of the articles, a second filter was used. This consisted of making a a more thorough and detailed search, which meant reading, in full, the text of the articles initially selected in the automatic and manaua searches. In this phase, the help of 2 (two) other researchers to read the articles was requested. The decision whether or not include articles in the final selection had to be discussed by the 3 researchers. Table 3 lists all the articles used for this review which contributed to achieving the results. The first column shows the the IDs of the articles selected and the second gives the titles of the articles.

Tables 2 and 3 present the approaches investigated related to the evaluation criteria described above.

Table 3. Final result of selecting the studies.

ID	Title of article
EP6	Optimizing process performance visibility through additional descriptive features in performance measurement
EP7	Organizational performance measures for business process management: a performance measurement guideline
EP9	Research on key performance indicator (kpi) of business process
EP11	The research of metrics repository for business process metrics
EP13	Two cases on how to improve the visibility of business process performance
EP15	Performance measurement in business process outsourcing decisions: Insights from four case studies
EP22	Quality evaluation framework (QEF): modelling and evaluating quality of business processes

2.3 Critical Analyses of the Approaches

The different approaches discussed above show variations in the methodology, specifications and even as to how business processes are evaluated. In order to assess these approaches, a set of criteria was defined which addresses both the theory, based on the selected references, and some aspects of usability. The criteria used were:

- Methodology: Ad-hoc (Ah) OR Systematic (Sy);
- Types of measures: Quantitative (Qt) AND/OR Qualitative (Ql);
- Context of Applications: Specific (S) OR Generic (G);
- Processes supported by systems: Yes OR No;
- Efficiency: Yes OR No;
- Effectiveness: Yes OR No;
- Empirical validation: Yes OR No.

The criterion of Methodology is related to the attention to the way in which an approach can be used to evaluate a business process. Approaches classified as systematic ones are those that describe a set of rules, guidelines, processes or activities needed to use the measures presented. On the other hand, ad-hoc approaches focus only on describing performance measures, without, at first being interested in the way that such approaches can be put into practice.

The criterion called types of measures concerns the nature of the measures presented in the selected approaches. Quantitative measurements are those based on numerical performance indicators, while qualitative measures consist of textual descriptions and narratives about factors of success of the process and which often require interpretation.

The criterion called application is related to the context in which a particular approach can be used. Certain approaches present measures that are sufficiently generic so that they that can be applied in different contexts and business processes of very different natures. Approaches classified as specific are those used in a specific business process or those of a similar nature.

Some approaches have performance measures that are established from information generated by business process automation systems. In other words, the use of the measures presented is associated with making information available by means of systems. The criterion of processes supported by systems is related to the concern for analyzing if the performance evaluation of the process depends, in principle, on some support by means of systems such as a BPMS (Business Process Management Suite), for example.

The aim of using criteria of efficiency and effectiveness is to describe whether the approaches analyzed present measures to evaluate the productivity and performance (efficiency) of processes, as well as their ability to do what is needed, which is correct in order to reach a certain goal or outcome (effectiveness). Efficiency involves the way in which an activity or process is performed; effectiveness refers to whether this results in meeting customer's needs in all their restrictions. In [14], efficiency is a measure of the extent to which an organization's resources are used economically, and effectiveness refers to the extent to which the objectives are achieved.

The criterion of empirical validation is concerned with assessing the practical utility of the measures proposed in the different approaches. Empirical validation occurs by conducting experiments, case studies or research in a real context, and helps to determine the effectiveness of these measures.

In the seven approaches investigated, only two describe a systematic and procedural way, guidelines using the performance measures presented. The other studies are much more concerned with describing the performance measures of business processes than with how they can be used. The EP13 study presents some general guidelines for using performance measures, but does not describe them in detail.

All approaches presented quantitative performance measures, based on numerical performance indicators. On the other hand, only two articles, qualitative measures for evaluating the performance of processes, but these are about similar measurements, since both studies are by the same authors.

Regarding the context of the application, two approaches are linked to a specific domain, such as, for example, Article EP15 which presents measurements derived from specific outsourcing contracts, while five approaches have greater applicability.

Two articles describe performance measures dependent on information obtained because business processes had been automated, while five others do not mention the need to use systems in order to use the measures presented.

The seven approaches investigated describe performance measures to evaluate the efficiency of business processes. As to measures to evaluate the results of processes (effectiveness), only two articles do not describe them. Finally, three approaches were empirically validated by using case studies or applying them in a real context.

Tables 4 and 5 present the approaches investigated related to the evaluation criteria illustrated above.

Based on the criteria presented and discussed earlier in this paper, we considered that a systematic approach (which enables the metrics presented to be used consistently), which brings together quantitative and qualitative performance measures, generically (measures not linked to a specific context or domain), not dependent on using systems that provide an evaluation of efficiency (resources) and effectiveness

Table 4. Evaluation criteria (Methodology, Measures and Application).

Articles	Evaluation criteria					
	Methodology		Measures		Application	
	Ah	Sy	Qt	Ql	S	G
EP6	X		X	X		X
EP7		X	X			X
EP9	X		X		X	
EP11	X		X			X
EP13	X		X	X		X
EP15	X		X		X	
EP22		X	X			X

Table 5. Evaluation criteria (System support, Efficiency, Effectiveness and Empirical validation).

Studies	Systems	Efficiency	Effectiveness	Validated
EP6	No	Yes	Yes	No
EP7	No	Yes	Yes	No
EP9	Yes	Yes	Yes	No
EP11	Yes	Yes	No	No
EP13	No	Yes	Yes	Yes
EP15	No	Yes	Yes	Yes
EP22	No	Yes	No	Yes

(results) and which had been validated empirically could be considered ideal, or the approach that best meets how to evaluate the performance of business processes.

From the analysis of the selected approaches, there was a need to propose a systematic approach that would combine relevant and complementary aspects of the studies that had been previously analyzed.

3   Approach Proposed for Evaluating the Performance of Business Processes

Of the approaches investigated, the one that comprises the largest number of requirements, set out in the previous section, is Article EP13. However, it does describe in great detail how this approach can be used. Moreover, the approaches presented in articles EP7 and EP22 do give a detailed description of the the process for using performance measures.

It was arising from these considerations that our approach was defined. It brings together the model of performance measures described in EP13, but using it as a guide to using the measures presented, and the procedural description defined in Article EP7.

3.1   Process for Evaluating the Performance of Processes

The evaluation process defined in EP7 is illustrated in Fig. 1 below:

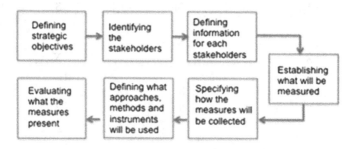

Fig. 1 Process for using performance measures.

The aim of the activities illustrated in the process flow is to lead to proposing a guideline for measuring the performance of business processes. In order to provide adequate guidance for assessing performance, on following this procedural description, a description will be given below of the steps and some artifacts or suggestions that may contribute to making such an assessment.

Defining the Strategic Objectives. According to Vuksicet et al. (2008), the performance measures of business processes should be aligned to the organizational goals and objectives. The first activity in the process of evaluating the performance of a process consists of defining the strategic objectives to be achieved by the results of the processes. These objectives are defined by the owners of the process in the organization, and can be obtained from the strategic planning documents.

Identifying the Stakeholders. After identifying the objectives of the process, the stakeholders in the conduct of the process must be identified, i.e., those responsible for the process, those taking part in the activities, clients, beneficiaries, sponsors and others. Process mapping artifacts or even the use of a RACI matrix can contribute to defining who the stakeholders in implementation are.

Defining the Information Required for Each Party. The information needs of each stakeholder can be very different, and require the performance measures to be adapted to their requirements.

The activity of mapping makes it possible to define the roles and responsibilities of each participant during the implementation of the process more clearly and objectively, thereby contributing to defining the information required for each party and assisting in defining the performance measures.

Establishing What will be Measured. In this stage what is sought is to identify what measures are useful for evaluating the performance of the process in relation to its goals, in achieving the strategic objectives. Performance reports or accounting documents can be used to identify performance measures of the process.

Specifying How the Measures will be Collected. When identifying the performance measures of a process, a process for collecting these measures needs to be identified. In the case of processes supported by systems, data collection is automated. In order to develop an action plan for identifying and collecting performance measures in non-automated processes, an adaptation of the5W2H management tool was proposed as an artifact for this step. The information is organized as follows:

- Description of the measure (What): Defines what this measure means.
- Rationale (Why): Defines the end, the purpose of using the measure.
- Instruments to obtain measures (From where): Specifies the instruments (media) from where the data of the measures can be collected.
- Frequency (When): Determines the frequency or time interval at which the information of the measures needs to be collected.
- Responsible (Who): Describes the sector or department responsible for providing information on a particular measure.
- Process for obtaining measures (How): Details what process will be undertaken to obtain the measures.
- Costs (How much): Describes the costs for obtaining the measure.

Defining What Approaches, Methods or Instruments will be Used. There are several approaches and frameworks that use different methods for measuring performance, described in the literature, as well as various tools that support these evaluation methods.

Based on the critical analysis of the approaches presented in Sect. 3, it was found that the model in EP13 has the largest number of criteria. Thus, it is recommended that this is used in step for evaluating the process. Subsection 3.2 presents how the measures in the EP13 model are systematized.

Assessing What the Measures Present. The performance measures of business processes should be related to (or the same as) measures existing in the organization that are used to monitor the success of the strategy.

3.2 Adapting the Evaluation Model

The performance measures defined in Article EP13 require a greater capacity of interpretation due to the way they are presented. The paper presents the measurements in the form of questions such as: Are the numerical parameters linked to quality, such as cycle time, probability of failure or average number of interruptions? This could hamper their use by individuals who evaluate their business processes.

Given this configuration, the measurement model was systematized in an attempt to make it orderly, coherent, clear and understandable by the parties that may use it. The model originally defined in EP13 was discussed together with two BPM experts until the model shown in Tables 6 and 7 was reached.

Also added to the model described above was an auxiliary table, which describes in detail each of the indicators presented. Such as, for example, *"Process Cycle time:*

Table 6. Model for systematizing the measurements (Efficiency).

	Efficiency	
NP (*)	**Indicators**	**Types of indicators**
	Key Performance Indicator (KPI)	- Time cycle of the process
		- Countable amounts of process outputs
		- Number of returned processes
		- Number of processes carried out
		- Downtime
		- Percentage of the budget used
DP (**)	Process Success Factors (PSF)	- Benefits, scope and steps of the process
		- Information systems, databases or interfaces used
		- Description of the success of the process
		- Documents and information produced and delivered

(*) Numeric Parameters; (**) Descriptive Parameters.

Table 7. Model for systematizing the measurements (Effectiveness).

	Effectiveness	
NP (*)	**Indicators**	**Types of indicators**
	Metrics of the Process (PMX)	- Probability of failure
		- Average number of interruptions
		- Time-cycle approval meetings
		- Number of approval meetings
		- Number of approvers/officers-in-charge
DP (**)	Description of the Components which comprise the Process (PO)	- Departments responsible, informed or affected
		- Role of approvers or officers-in-charge
		- Interfaces with other departments
		- Conditions and restrictions
		- Initiators, beneficiaries and customers of the process
		- Key people or information system for a step of the process or shared backup

(*) Numeric Parameters; (**) Descriptive Parameters.

corresponds to the time required for performing the process, i.e. the time between the start and end of the process".

The approach proposed for evaluating the performance of business processes dealt with in this study consists of the process for measuring performance, artifacts and the model of systematic measures described in this Section. In order to ensure the validation of the approach, it was applied in a real business process of an organization, and this is described in the next section.

4 Results and Discussion

The process that was selected to validate the proposed approach is called Pro-equipment, linked to the Pro-rectorate for Research and Postgraduate Subjects (PROPESQ) of a Brazilian Federal Institution of Higher Education (IFES, in Portuguese).

Pro-equipment procures equipment intended for shared use in the structure of scientific and technological research of post-graduate programs of the recommended IFESs and is funded by the Coordination Unit for Improving the Qualifications and Experience of Higher Education Personnel (CAPES). The selection of this process, to validate the proposed approach, occurred in a timely manner in view of the demand for having it mapped and optimized, requested through PROPESQ together with the IFES Office for Processes to which the author of this research is linked.

4.1 Defining the Objectives of the Process

The first interview was attended by two representatives of the Research Board (DPQ in Portuguese) and three process analysts of the Processes Unit of the institution were also present. The two participants are directly responsible for the performance of the process.

Initially a description of the following points was requested:

P1 – "What is the objective of mapping and optimizing the process?"

According to Respondent 2, the main problem of this process is the lack of transparency of the information on the results, when he states that:

E2 – "We have partial and not effective control, for example, we know the input volume of resources, we know how much CAPES makes available, and we even know how much of the resources were earmarked because the Accounts Department of PROPESQ send us this information on a spreadsheet, if we request it. From there on, we have no feedback, we do not know if the teacher received it."

P2 – "What is the Objective of the Pro-Equipment Process?"

E1 – "To stimulate scientific production by acquiring equipment intended for shared use in postgraduate laboratories of the university."

4.2 Identifying Stakeholders in the Process

P5 – "Who are the stakeholders in the process?" Specifically those in charge (the owners of the process), participants of the activities (sectors), clients, beneficiaries and sponsors.

CAPES acts as the sponsor, the clients of this process were defined as the teachers and/or research groups. Finally, the participants in the activities when the given process was being carried out were: the Director of Research (DPQ/PROPESQ), the

Accounting Board (DC/PROPESQ), the Agreements Sector (PROPLAN), the Legal Department (Office of the Rector), the Rector, The National Purchases Sector (PRO-GEST), the Importations Sector (PROGEST) and the Publishing Sector (PROGEST).

4.3   Defining the Information Necessary for Each Party

At this stage we were invited to the meetings, prior to which the stakeholders described above, excluding the sponsor of the process (CAPES). This was justified by the fact that CAPES is configured as an entity external to the University context in which one does not have dominion over the rules and procedures used.

Four meetings were held with the following representatives: 02 (DPQ/PROPESQ), 01 (DC/PROPESQ), 01 (Agreements Sector/PROPLAN) and 01 (PROGEST). At this stage the process was modelled collaboratively using the BizAgi Process Modeler.

The process starts when CAPES releases the official notice. Then, the Board of Research (DPQ) sets an internal schedule of activities before submitting a single proposal.

Generally, the amount of resources requested by the projects is greater than the amount initially made available by CAPES. Therefore, the DPQ convenes a committee to assess and recommend what projects should be submitted. The end result of the projects selected internally is announced and submitted to CAPES.

These projects will be further evaluated by CAPES, who may refuse some requests. Projects approved at this stage are announced by DPQ. After this step, the term of decentralization of credit is sent to PROPLAN, the process is reviewed, and the document is sent to the Legal Department, which will analyze items such as dates, terms, rubrics, data, etc. The Legal Department must give its assent in writing to ensure the process continues. If so, the process is sent for the signature of the Rector of the institution. The process for requesting ear-marking is then returned to PROPLAN which monitors that CAPES has released the funds and PROPLAN notifies the Accounting Sector of PROPESQ.

The Accounting Sector of PROPESQ then starts the activity of mounting the ear-marking process for each piece of equipment. At this moment, a request is made to the coordinators of the subprojects for a series of documents. Subsequently, the accounting entry for the committed funds is made via PROGEST, and there follows a new phase of analysis by the Legal Department. After being approved by the Legal Department, the process goes to the Publishing Sector in PROGEST, and the flow of the process proceeds to the National Purchases or Importations Sector so that the purchase can be made.

4.4   Defining What will be Evaluated in the Process

At this stage there were two interviews with those responsible (DPQ) for this process. Initially the interviewee was asked whether there is an accounting report on the performance of the process.

According to E1 - "CAPES demands an indication of how the previous buying process was conducted. We describe, when asked, only what was actually ear-marked".

For interviewee E2, this kind of report is based on measures that do not reflect, in a satisfactory manner, that achieving the objectives of the process was verified.

E2 - "Ear-marking is only the first stage of the expenditure budget, where the funds were granted, but there is no guarantee the equipment will be purchased."

When asked: "What are the important performance measures for making a satisfactory assessment of the results of this process?"

E1 - "In my opinion we should have information about whether or not the equipment was purchased, was actually installed in the laboratory and which research groups are using it".

Still on the measures that should be used to evaluate the process, interviewee E2 stated that:

E2 - "Besides the amount ear-marked and bits and pieces to be paid, which are data that we can get easily, we need to know the quantity and description of the pieces of equipment bought, how many and which ones are awaiting delivery and installation, and what the institutional outcomes are (number of dissertations, theses, descriptive reports on patents generated or information on the rendering of research services to other institutions) that have been achieved".

4.5   Specifying How the Measures will be Collected

At this stage a meeting was held with the same representatives who took part in the mapping of the process meetings. Initially, a projection of the mapping process was presented, followed by a set of measures that were extracted. The measures presented to the participants were:

- Total amount ear-marked;
- Amount spent the ear-marked resources;
- Amount in smaller bills to be paid;
- List of equipment purchased;
- List of delivered equipment;
- List of installed equipment and;
- Academic indicators.

For each of the measures proposed the artifact for specifying the collection process defined in the approach was discussed jointly by the participants and filled in. Table 8 shows an example.

4.6   Applying the Performance Assessment Model

At this stage, four meetings were held with the members already described: (02) representatives of DPQ/PROPESQ, (01) representative of the Accounting Sector/PROPESQ, (01) representative of the National Purchases Sector and the Importations Sector of PROGEST. Meetings were held separately. The procedure for conducting this step may be described in three phases:

Table 8. Collection process for academic indicators.

Academic Indicators	
Description of measure	Corresponds to descriptive reports on data from the scientific production supported by the equipment purchased. Reports may contain descriptive information about numbers of dissertations, theses, patents obtained as a result of using the equipment, as well as descriptions of services rendered to other institutions
Justification	One of the strategic objectives of PROPESQ is to encourage scientific production in the university. Products purchased by Pro-equipment are intended to contribute to achieve this goal. Academic indicators enable the results of this process to be made more visible in relation to achieving the strategic objectives
Instruments to obtain measures	Scientific production reports from research laboratories that have equipment coming from Pro-equipment funds
Periodicity	*Ad hoc*
Officer-in-charge	Coordinators of postgraduate laboratories
Process for obtaining measures	Meetings or requests via email
Costs	Time

- Presentation of the Model – in this stage the presentation was made, using a print document format, of the model of measures defined to the interviewee.
- Recording of the participants' responses – the interviewees' answers were recorded in the document.
- Summary of the responses – in this stage, the responses were combined in a single Table, thereby eliminating redundancies and inconsistencies in a single frame.

Table 9 presents some of the indicators obtained in this step:

Table 9. Model for sytematizing the measures (Efficiency).

	Efficiency	
NP (*)	*Indicators*	*Types of indicators*
	Key Performance Indicator (KPI)	- Amount raised from CAPES - Amount of funds spent; ear-marked (Percentage used of the budget)
DP (**)	Process Success Factors (PSF)	- Steps: Official notice published, term of decentralization of credit undertaken, Review and analysis of the process, Release of Credit Authorized, Constructing ear-marked funds, review and analysis of the funds ear-marked followed by legal approval, Publication in the Official Gazette of the Union, Purchase and control of acquisitions made
		- Information systems, databases or interfaces used: SICAPES (the CAPES Integrated System), net purchases (Purchases Portal of the Federal Government), SICAF (System for the Unified Registration of Suppliers)

(*) Numeric Parameters; (**) Descriptive Parameters.

4.7   What the Measures Present

The process for measuring performance provides a better understanding of their real needs, and thus make it possible that better decisions and actions can be made in the future. After analyzing the literature and the case study, it would be valid to suppose that seems to be important that the measurements of business processes should be related to the measurements the organization already has that are used to monitor the success of the strategy.

A set of measures for the process as a whole, and its "partitions" (steps, departments, phases, etc.) were set out in the previous section so as to reflect certain performance characteristics for each interested management level. These measures describe by means of generating information the real state of the configuration of the process, thus enabling aspects of performance to be evaluated such as complexity in operations, bottlenecks, redundant activities, excessive documentation and approvals. In addition, they make it possible to evaluate the results of the process as to achieving the objectives set, according to some of the clients of this process.

Regarding Pro-equipment, a check was made on the opportunity to insert some improvements into the process. The following optimization proposals were discussed, as a result:

1. Integrating the Superintendence of Works (SPO in Portuguese) into the early stages of the process, specifically into the (internal) evaluation step of the sub-projects to be submitted to CAPES. The function of the SPO is to carry out assessment in order to identify if the laboratory to which the equipment will go, has the infrastructure needed for its installation. In several situations it was reported that the purchase of equipment had been made but the research lab did not have an infrastructure appropriate for its installation. Currently, the process for guaranteeing resources for renovations, or purchase of equipment to ensure the effective installation of the equipment is only started from the moment that the equipment is delivered to the university.

2. The urgency to seek the guarantee of funds for the purchase of equipment by ear-marking funds encouraged the actors of the department responsible not to check the (full) requirements of documentation defined by legislation for the formation of these processes (ear-markings). The process very often did not follow its "normal" flow, where and if it was published in the Official Gazette of the Union without necessarily obtaining the approval of the Legal Department. This deviation in the flow led, in various situations, to delays in conducting the process due to non-observance of the applicable legislation.

3. Information on the results obtained for the research based on acquiring equipment was practically non-existent or difficult to monitor. As a proposed solution which was discussed between the actors of the process is the creation of the role of research lab coordinator. The proposal is awaiting the approval of the rector of the university. One of these responsibilities is to draw up laboratory performance reports on its coordination in terms of research supported by the equipment purchased.

Organizations, in general, need to constantly check whether the performance of their business processes are compatible with the objectives set. For this there are different approaches or models using different methods to evaluate the performance of business processes. It appears from the results obtained in the systematic review of the literature that there is no single or universal approach that is the most appropriate evaluation of these processes.

At first, the adoption of the model, which combined quantitative performance measures (that permit performance to be measured and managed) and qualitative measures (which allow grounding the critical analysis of the results), manages to gather important information about the performance of the process in relation to the strategic goals and objectives set. However, it is seen because of the evaluation of the performance measures surveyed that the process which includes defining performance measurements directly associated with the strategic objectives set by those taking part in the process seems to be much more effective than using a static model of performance measures of generic processes.

From the case study analysis, it was also concluded that it is important that managers or owners of the processes have the understanding that will obtain relevant information about what they actually decided to measure, according to their assessment needs. In the case study evaluation, a check was also made on the need, for the participants of the process, to define performance measurements that are simple to interpret, measure and obtain. In this context, it was found that using very complex performance measures or those that are difficult to measure would not be appropriate, since the cost of obtaining them could adversely affect how doing so is made operational.

The risk in evaluating the approach in the context of a specific case should be noted and, in this case, the owners of the process may have only a partial view of the organizational goals and strategies, and how this process can achieve such goals. Thus, this requires a broader analysis between interrelated processes around similar strategic objectives and should have the complementary view of other participants in these processes.

The selected measures have not yet been implemented in practice, before writing this article, mainly due to the difficulty of change in a very short time interval in the public service context. To some extent, this adversely affected evaluating the effectiveness of the approach. On the other hand, the subsequent collection of the results of the process using the measures selected, can be considered a future opportunity for expanding this research.

5 Conclusions

The aim of the BPM approach is to provide pertinent information on running business processes, thus contributing to being able to make improvements and so that processes can be managed, thereby making better decision making possible. In this context, it is essential to use metrics that enable the initiative to be monitored, thus helping to verify how well the processes meet the strategic objectives set.

However the performance measurement initiatives do not seem to be as effective as evaluating the results of the process as to achieving the strategic objectives. This, therefore, hinders the capacity to visualize what the effects of BPM initiatives in organizations are.

In this context, the main objective of this research was to identify which model for evaluating the performance of business processes best fits the evaluation of business processes, with a view to a greater alignment between the indicators of the process and the strategic objectives.

With regard to reaching the overall goal, a systematic review of the literature was conducted in order to identify the approaches that had performance measures to evaluate results of business processes (Obj. 1). After carrying out the review, we identified seven studies that present and describe the measures used to evaluate the results of business processes. Then, a comparative analysis of approaches was made using criteria that consider theory and usability, assembled from the papers assessed (Obj. 2). At this stage, what was recognized was the need to develop a procedural approach to evaluating business processes based on complementary aspects of the approaches analyzed.

After defining the approach, an empirical study was conducted in order to apply it (Obj. 3), and to obtain an evaluation based on the perception of the leaders of the process as to its usefulness (Obj. 4). The results indicate that, in general, the approach was positively evaluated as to its effectiveness in providing relevant information on the performance of business processes in relation to the objectives set. Nevertheless, complementary assessments need to be made after the defined performance measures have been effectively used.

Regarding the overall objective of the research, which consisted of verifying which approach best serves the evaluation of business processes, with a view to greater alignment between the process indicators and the strategic objectives, it may be noted that there is no single approach that adequately assesses the performance of business processes.

The approach to measurement used should consider the organizational context and several variables can be measured and evaluated with regard to business processes. However, it falls to managers to undertake the tasks of identifying, selecting and defining measures that are adequate for and aligned with the organization's objectives. The model used has a large number of indicators that can and should be adapted to different organizational contexts, from which the most important for use in practice should be selected. Finally, it is essential that an organization uses several indicators when evaluating its business processes, since the use of a single indicator can hardly represent the broad context needed to support effective decision making.

In order to complement the results found in this research, we propose the approach should be used in several different business processes, with a view to verifying its real results for the different characteristics of operations and dynamics of an organization such as: culture, size, area of activity, and so on.

534   T. Mendes and S. Santos

References

1. ABPMP: Guia para o Gerenciamento de Processos de Negócio - Corpo Comum de Conhecimento - (BPM CBOK®). Versão 2.0 (2009)
2. Smith, G., Furt, S.: How (not) to fail at BPM. In: BPM.COM (2009). http://bpm.com/how-not-to-fail-at-bpm.html
3. Trkman, P.: The critical success factors of business process management. Int. J. Inf. Manag. 30(2), 125–134 (2010)
4. Powell, S.G., Schwaninger, M., Trimble, C.: Measurement and control of business process. Syst. Dyn. 17, 63–91 (2011)
5. Kueng, P., Krahn, A.: Building a process performance measurement system: some early experiences. J. Sci. Ind. Res. 58(3–4), 149–159 (2001). National Institute of Science Communication and Information Resources, New Delhi
6. Škrinjar, R., Bosilj-vukšić, R., Indihar-štemberger, M.: The impact of business process orientation financial and non financial performance. Bus. Process Manag. J. 14(5), 738–754 (2008)
7. Pidun, T., Felden, C.: Two cases on how to improve the visibility of business process performance. In: 2012 45th Hawaii International Conference on System Science (HICSS), pp. 4396–4405, 4–7 January (2012)
8. Leclair, C., Cullen, A., Keenan, J.: Use a metric framework to drive BPM excellence. In: Forrester (2012)
9. González, L., Rubio, F., González, R., Velthuis, M.: Measurement in business processes: a systematic review. Bus. Process Manag. J. 16(1), 114–134 (2010)
10. Wohlin, C., et al.: Experimentation in Software Engineering – An Introduction, 1st edn. EUA: Kluwer Academic Publishers, Berlin (2000)
11. Sampaio, R.F., Mancini, M.: Systematic review studies: a guide for careful synthesis of the scientific evidence. Revista Brasileira de Fisioterapia 11(1), 77–82 (2007)
12. Kitchenham, B.: Procedures for performing systematic reviews. Joint Technical report, TR/SE-0401 and NICTA 0400011T.1, Keele University (2004). http://www.idi.ntnu.no/emner/empse/papers/kitchenham_2004.pdf
13. BPM CBOK – Guia para o Gerenciamento de Processos de Negócio. Corpo Comum do Conhecimento – ABPMP BPM CBOK V3.0, Association of Business Process Management Professionals (2013)
14. Corrêa, H.L., Corrêa, C.A.: Administração de Produção e Operações, 2nd edn. Atlas, São Paulo (2006)

Reliability of AAL Systems Modeled as BPMN Business Processes

Ana Respício[1(✉)], Ricardo Martinho[2], and Dulce Domingos[3]

[1] Departamento de Informática and CMAFCIO - Centro de Matemática,
Aplicações Fundamentais e Investigação Operacional, Faculdade de Ciências,
Universidade de Lisboa, Lisboa, Portugal
alrespicio@fc.ul.pt
[2] Polytechnic Institute of Leiria and CINTESIS - Center for Health Technology
and Services Research, Porto, Portugal
ricardo.martinho@ipleiria.pt
[3] LaSIGE, Faculdade de Ciências, Universidade de Lisboa, Lisbon, Portugal
mddomingos@fc.ul.pt

Abstract. The use of Ambient-Assisted Living (AAL) systems has been spreading across several countries, with the ultimate purpose of improving the quality of life of patients. These systems often reflect complex architectures including several components such as sensors, gateways, Information Systems or even actuators, as well as messaging and transmitting protocols. Failures in these systems can have severe impact on a monitored patient, and most components foresee some kind of compensation countermeasures to increase reliability. Nevertheless, these measures are often self-contained to a single component and do not address the overall AAL system reliability, disregarding precedent and successor activities and interactions that exist for each time a certain value is registered or a certain alert is triggered. In this paper, we propose a new approach to calculate the overall reliability of an AAL system. We take a Business Process Management (BPM) approach to model the activities and interactions between AAL components, using the Business Process Model and Notation (BPMN) standard. By extending the BPMN standard to include reliability information, we can derive the overall reliability of a certain AAL system. To prove this approach, we also present a reliability study considering scenarios with single and pairwise reliability variations of AAL system components. With this approach, healthcare managers can benefit from important overall reliability information of an AAL system, and better allocate the appropriate resources (including hardware or health care professionals) to improve responsiveness of care to patients.

Keywords: Ambient-Assisted Living · Reliability · Business processes · BPMN

1 Introduction

The major purpose of Ambient-Assisted Living (AAL) systems is to improve the quality of life and care responsiveness for patients at risk while staying at their homes and performing their normal daily routines [10]. AAL provides them with an overall

© Springer International Publishing AG 2017
S. Hammoudi et al. (Eds.): ICEIS 2016, LNBIP 291, pp. 535–550, 2017.
DOI: 10.1007/978-3-319-62386-3_24

surveilled environment, allowing the delivery of care where and when needed, and also supporting caregivers, families and care organizations.

Applications of AAL not only provide continuous health monitoring through, for instance, vital signs recording for medical history analyses, but also play a major role in detecting emergency situations. In turn, caregivers and/or other health professionals can better organize their care business processes by receiving alerts and actuating when needed, and with the appropriate resources. Some AAL applications can even replace (self) care activities, such as auto injecting insulin when blood sugar values increase at a certain rate.

Although many times associated with support in assisting elderly people (see for instance H2020 calls of European Commission), AAL systems can also be used in patients suffering from chronic diseases such as diabetes, asthma and heart attacks. Therefore, the impact of a less reliable system can range from a false alarm transmitted to a certain caregiver and/or emergency unit service, to serious patient injury due to wrong, delayed or even non-delivered care.

Current research works and industry products related with AAL and overall to Internet of Things (IoT) applied to healthcare already provide redundancy checks and alerts to prevent greater impacts to patients using them (see, for instance, [20, 24]). Nevertheless, these efforts to increase reliability are usually self-contained to some components of an AAL system, i.e., reliability is commonly evaluated for each component, regardless of its position in a certain sequence of activities to trigger some action (alert, register or even actuate).

In this work, we present our new and consolidated approach to calculate the overall reliability of an AAL system, by using a Business Process Management (BPM) approach and the Business Process Model and Notation (BPMN) [18] standard de facto for modelling AAL business processes. We consider each component of an AAL system as part of a business process containing essentially sensors, actuators and gateways, which interact through a sequence of activities, decision nodes and messages in order to produce alerts, to register values in a centralized (healthcare) Information System, or even to trigger actuators to provide immediate care. Since these interactions are usually subjected to several conditions, we model them as BPMN process models, in order to calculate their combined reliability. This way, we can derive the overall AAL system reliability, such as in the following example: a measure is taken by a heart rate sensor, transmitted through a network, evaluated through an Information System, and the appropriate alerts are triggered to prevent potentially fatal consequences for the patient.

We extend [14] and apply our approach to perform three analyses: (1) overall AAL system reliability calculus based on most common reliability values for its individual components; (2) overall AAL system reliability against single-component reliability variation, and (3) overall AAL system reliability against pairwise component reliability variation.

This paper is organized as follows: Sect. 2 presents background on AAL and a typical AAL system scenario modelled with BPMN. In Sect. 3 we refer to related work on reliability applied to most common components of an AAL system, and in Sect. 4 we explain how we include reliability information in an AAL BPMN process model, in order to calculate its overall reliability and how we apply the Stochastic Workflow

Reduction (SWR) algorithm to compute the reliability of combined BPMN process elements. Section 5 presents the three application scenarios for the calculus of the overall reliability for a typical AAL system. Finally, Sect. 6 concludes the paper and presents future work.

2 Background

This section presents a typical AAL process model (see for instance the proposals of [2, 6]).

The AAL BPMN process model, as illustrated in Fig. 1, uses a collaboration diagram with four pools, one for each participant or AAL component [10, 16, 21, 23].

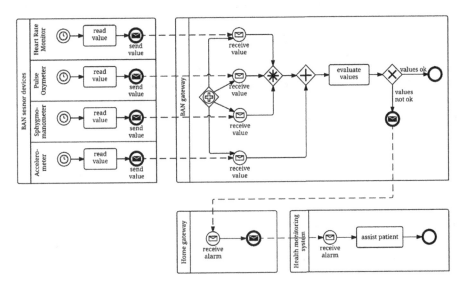

Fig. 1. AAL BPMN process model.

The Body Area Network (BAN) sensor devices are used for monitoring vital signs, i.e., heart and body activity in this example (based on [20]). The heart activity is assessed through the heart rate, the blood oxygen, and the blood pressure, by using a heart rate monitor, a pulse oxymeter and a sphygmomanometer, respectively. The system monitors the body activity by using an accelerometer. While this process only uses sensors, BANs can also include actuators. For instance BAN devices can, on a diabetic patient, auto inject insulin through a pump, while monitoring the insulin level [11].

As defined in this process, sensors read values from the patient from time to time by using a timer and send them to the BAN gateway. The interaction between sensors and the BAN gateway can also be implemented through the request-request paradigm, where the BAN gateway starts the interaction asking for the values. Depending on sensor computational capabilities, they can also filter the data they transmit, sending only values that are considered relevant. However, for this reliability study, these differences are not significant.

The BAN gateway, another participant of the process, is responsible for the communication inside that BAN and to the home gateway. Besides it receives the values from sensors, it also validates, aggregates and analyses these values. The reception of sensor values is modelled with a BPMN Event-Based Parallel Gateway. The information about heart rate should be provided by at least two out of three devices, and this behaviour is modelled with a BPMN Complex Gateway. After evaluating sensor values, the BAN gateway sends an alarm to the health monitoring system (HMS) to assist the patient, in case any emergent situation is detected. The communication between the BAN gateway and the HMS is performed through the home gateway. Smart phones or wireless routers can be used as home gateways. They communicate with the BAN gateway through wireless technologies (Bluetooth or WiFi, for instance) and provide the connectivity to the internet. From the point of view of the process model we could omit the Home gateway pool, as it does not define any business logic. However, this way, the participants of the process are coherent with the components of a generic AAL architecture and it simplifies the reliability study as the process includes all the components and connections.

Finally, with the health monitoring system, caregivers and physicians monitor patients remotely.

3   Related Work

The *reliability of a system at time t*, denoted by $R(t)$, can be defined as the probability of the system to be up continuously in time interval $[0; t]$ [13]. This metric is adequate for systems operating continuously, where a single momentary failure can have a high or even critical impact.

McNaull et al. discuss the quality issues of each component of an AAL system. BAN devices (sensors and actuators) reliability depends on their quality and manufacturer [15]. According to the same authors, the mean-time between failures (MTBF) metric can be used to assess it. In addition, sensors data quality (accuracy) also interferes with reliability as anomalous values can be discarded, for instance, in BAN gateways. Quality of data depends on sensor calibration as well as on the correct use and application of sensors. For instance, other heat sources can affect temperature sensors.

In [20] a use case where the health of patients is monitored considering heart and body activities is presented. The system uses a heart rate monitor, a pulse oxymeter, and a sphygmo-manometer to monitor the heart activity. The body activity of patients is monitored with an accelerometer on knees and a motion detector in the room. Taking into account the required reliability of the system, the authors determine the minimal combinations of sensors the system needs. However they only use the information about the reliability of each device.

BAN gateways can be used to increase the reliability of the system. They may evaluate sensor data and detect anomalous and inconsistent values, considering the expected ones, which may have been established during the testing period of the AAL system [15]. In case of anomaly, erroneous sensor values are discarded and BAN gateways can request for new sensor values. If the problem persists, the BAN gateway can alert the health monitoring system. Another way to increase system reliability is by defining a fault tolerant behaviour for the BAN gateway.

Body sensors and actuators communicate with each other and with the BAN gateway using mostly wireless technologies, such as IEEE802.15.4/ZigBee [8]. The latest international standard for wireless BAN (WBAN) is the IEEE802.15.6 [9]. Home and BAN gateways also communicate through wireless technologies (Bluetooth or WiFi, for instance).

Reliability of wireless networks depends on interferences of other devices; obstruction of the signal due to lifts or wall, and attenuation, i.e., the strength of the signal reduces during transmission.

Baig et al. [1] compare wireless transmitted data with manual recorded data and hospital collected data. They use a total of approximately 2500 transmissions of 30 hospitalized patients and they conclude that, in wireless transmitted data, losses vary from 20% (blood glucose) to 80% (blood pressure and heart rate). They also conclude that data losses were mainly due to distance and data transmission delays were due to poor signals, signal drops, connection loss and/or poor location.

Despite the evaluation of the reliability of each AAL component is crucial, it is not sufficient to study the overall system. This way, in the following, we present related work about computing reliability for composite tasks and/or even for the overall process.

Indeed, while reliability has been a major concern for networking, critical and real-time applications, as well as middleware [20, 24]; the increasing use of workflow, specifically, in more critical systems, justifies the works on workflow reliability.

In the context of workflow modelling, Cardoso [3] defines task reliability as the probability that the components operate on users demand, following a discrete-time model. In this context, the failure rate of a task can be described by the ratio number of unsuccessful executions/scheduled executions. The task reliability, denoted by $R(A)$, is the opposite of the failure rate, that is:

$$R(A) = 1 - failureRate(A).$$

In the same work, Cardoso proposes a predictive Quality of Service (QoS) model for workflows and web services that, based on atomic task QoS attributes, is able to estimate the QoS for workflows, considering the following dimensions: time, cost, reliability, and fidelity. To compute QoS for the overall workflow, the author developed the Stochastic Workflow Reduction algorithm, which applies a set of reduction rules to iteratively reduce construction workflow blocks until only one activity remains. The QoS metrics of the remaining activity corresponds to the QoS metrics of the process.

Cardoso defines reduction rules for the following construction blocks: sequential, parallel, conditional, loop, fault tolerant, and network systems [3]. He applies his proposal to the METEOR workflow management system [12]. To estimate the reliability of web services compositions, [5] generalizes the Cardoso proposal, covering all the generic workflow patterns of [25].

Within the WS-BPEL context, in [17], the authors compute the reliability of WS-BPEL processes taking into account most of the workflow patterns that WS-BPEL can express, while the method of [7] also incorporates advanced composition features such as fault, compensation, termination and event handling.

Using Unified Modeling Language (UML) models, Rodrigues et al. annotate system component interactions with their failure probabilities [23]. They convert them into a formal executable specification, based on a probabilistic process algebra description language, which are executed on PRISM. This way, they can, for instance, identify the components that have the highest impact on the reliability system.

By focusing their work on BPMN, Respício and Domingos [22] calculate the reliability of BPMN business processes by using the Stochastic Workflow Reduction method of Cardoso [3, 4]. To meet this goal, they extend BPMN with reliability information and identify the BPMN process blocks for which they can apply one of the reduction rules.

The work we describe in this paper applies and extends the proposals of [22] to evaluate the reliability of AAL processes.

4   Reliability Information in BPMN Processes

To include reliability information in BPMN business processes we use the extension, whose XML Schema we present in Listing 1. The definition of this extension is based on the work proposed in [22].

The extension has two elements. The first element, named `Reliabil-ityInformation`, has two attributes: the `requiredReliability` which defines the minimum accepted reliability value for the process or flow node, and the `calculatedReliability` which is the reliability of atomic activities and events (initialised with a pre-determined value) or the reliability for decomposable activities (sub-processes) and processes computed using the SWR method [3].

The second element is the `Probability`. The probability value is used with conditional `SequenceFlow` elements within conditional process or loop process blocks and defines the probability of the process execution path of taking them.

Listing 1. BPMN extension for reliability - XML Schema.

```
<?xml version="1.0" encoding="UTF-8"?>
<xsd:schema xmlns:xsd="http://www.w3.org/2001/XMLSchema"
xmlns="http://.../relybpmn"
xmlns:bpmn=http://www.omg.org/spec/BPMN/20100524/MODEL
targetNamespace="http://.../relybpmn">
  <xsd:import namespace="http://www.omg.org/spec/BPMN/20100524/MODEL"
    schemaLocation="BPMN20.xsd"/>
  <xsd:group name="relyBPMN">
    <xsd:sequence>
     <xsd:element name="ReliabilityInformation"
                  type="tReliabilityInformation"
                  minOccurs="0" maxOccurs="1"/>
     <xsd:element name="Probability"
                  type="tProbability"
                  minOccurs="0"
                  maxOccurs="1"/>
    </xsd:sequence>
  </xsd:group>
  <xsd:complexType name="tReliabilityInformation" abstract="false">
    <xsd:attribute name="requiredReliability" type="xsd:decimal"/>
    <xsd:attribute name="calculatedReliability" type="xsd:decimal"/>
  </xsd:complexType>
  <xsd:complexType name="tProbability" abstract="false">
    <xsd:attribute name="value" type="xsd:decimal"/>
  </xsd:complexType>
</xsd:schema>
```

The reliability of processes is calculated with the SWR method [3] (it is similar for decomposable activities). This method applies a set of reduction rules to the process, iteratively, until only one activity remains. The reliability of the remaining activity corresponds to the reliability of the process.

Table 1 presents the application of the six reduction rules of Cardoso to BPMN, identifying the BPMN process blocks for which the reduction rules can be used [22].

As the AAL BPMN process subject of our study also has events (see Fig. 1), we use the same reduction rules for process blocks composed by events or activities, in an undifferentiated way.

In addition, when using reduction rules with collaboration diagrams, they are applied to the overall diagram by omitting pools and lanes. However, to overcome the limitations of the block structured approach of Cardoso, where one starting point and one ending point are needed, we transform the collaboration diagram by adding two new gateways. To have a unique starting point, we add an Exclusive Event-Based Gateway without any incoming sequence flows and with one outgoing sequence flow to each start event of the collaboration diagram. Similarly, to have a unique end point, we add an Inclusive or Merge Gateway with an incoming sequence flow from each end event and without any outgoing sequence flows [19].

Table 1. Reliability of the reduced block [22].

Initial Block	Reduced Block	Reliability of the Reduced Block
Sequential	Activity AB	$R(AB) = R(A) * R(B)$
Parallel	Activity A → Activity B1n → Activity C	$R(B1n) = \prod_{1 \le i \le n} R(Bi)$
Conditional	Activity A → Activity B1n → Activity C	$R(B1n) = \sum_{1 \le i \le n} p_i R(Bi)$
Loop	Activity A'	$R(A') = \dfrac{(1-p)\,R(A)}{1 - pR(A)}$
Activity A / Activity A / Activity A	Activity A'	$R(A') = R(A)^k$
Fault Tolerant	Activity A → Activity B1n → Activity C	$R(B1n) =$ $\sum_{I_1=0,1} \cdots \sum_{I_2=0,1}(\phi(\sum_{i=1}^n I_i - k) * \prod_{i=1}^n 1 - I_i + (2I_i - 1)R(Bi))$
Network	Activity A'	$R(A') = R(P1)$

5 Reliability Study

This section presents a case study focusing on the reliability evaluation of the AAL process presented in Sect. 2.

Initially, process designers set up the minimum accepted values for the reliability of activities and sub-processes (requiredReliability). The BPMN process model is then enriched, through the relyBPMN extension, considering these values as well as pre-estimated values of the attributes calculatedReliability (initialized with pre-estimated values for atomic activities and events) and Probability. Then, the SWR algorithm iteratively computes the calculatedReliability for sub-processes, reaching the reliability value for the overall process (the collaboration diagram).

In the following, we describe the application of this method to assess the reliability of the collaboration diagram displayed in Fig. 1, considering different scenarios and variation of reliability of different AAL system components.

The experiment started by establishing a base case scenario and computing the corresponding reliability. After, a sensitivity analysis on the process reliability was made. The objective of this analysis was to evaluate the impact on the reliability of the overall process resulting from variations of the reliability of separate elements. This analysis was made in two phases. Firstly, we made vary the reliability of separate elements individually. Secondly, the reliability values of a pair of elements were varied in a discrete mode and for each pair of values the process reliability was computed.

5.1 Evaluation of the Overall AAL System Reliability in the Base Case Scenario

In [20], Parente et al. propose reliability values for the type of sensors used in our use case, namely the Heart Rate Monitor (HRM), the Pulse Oxymeter (POxy), the Shyg-momanometer (Shygm), and the Accelerometer (Acc), which are used to initialise the attribute calculatedReliability of the tasks "read value".

Based on the measures of [1], we establish the reliability value associated to the transmission from sensors to the BAN gateway, which is used to initialise the cal-culatedReliability of the "receive value" tasks. For setting the reliability value for the transmission from the BAN gateway to the HMS, through the home gateway, we consider both connections together to simplify the study. This reliability value is used to initialise the calculatedReliability of the task "receive alarm" of the HMS.

The base case scenario, as illustrated in Table 2, considers the values proposed in [20] for the reliability of sensors; the value 0.992 for the reliability of transmission from sensors to the BAN gateway; and the value 0.99 for the reliability of transmission from the BAN gateway to the HMS.

Table 2. Reliability values for activities and transmissions for the base case scenario.

BAN devices (sensors)	Raw reliability		
	Sensor	Sensors to gateway	BAN gateway to HMS
HRM	0.8	0.992	0.99
POxy	0.7	0.992	0.99
Shygm	0.6	0.992	0.99
Acc	0.9	0.992	0.99
Overall reliability	0.6901		

The `calculatedReliability` attribute was set to 1.0 for the remaining activities and events, such as the process start, the evaluation of the received values in the BAN gateway, and the "assist patient" activity. In addition, the `requiredReliability` value for all process activities and events was set to 0.6, as this was assumed to be the minimum acceptable reliability.

The reduction rule for the fault-tolerant gateway considers four feasible combinations of receiving two out of three signal devices: (HRM, POxy, Shygm), (HRM, POxy), (HRM, Shygm), and (POxy, Shygm).

For the base case scenario, the reliability of the process takes the value 0.6901. This value is above the required reliability value, meaning the base case is feasible for implementation in a real life system.

5.2   Impact of Individual Reliability Component Variation *versus* Overall AAL System Reliability

The study continued by making variations on different reliability values and assessing the resulting reliability of the global AAL system modelled as a BPMN process. We separately altered the reliability of the following elements: (1) each sensor, (2) the transmission from sensors to the BAN gateway, and (3) the transmission from the BAN gateway to the HMS through the home gateway.

Figure 2 displays the results of this study. Chart (a) displays the results of the variation of the Accelerometer reliability in three scenarios. The base case scenario corresponds to fix all the other values of the original base case (Table 2) and making the reliability of the accelerometer vary in the interval [0.6; 1], using steps of 0.01. The worst case scenario differs by setting the reliability values of the remaining sensors to 0.6 (the minimum allowed value), while for the best case the reliability of the other sensors was set to 0.99 (considering an optimistic value).

Chart (b) shows the effects on the process reliability due to variation of the HRM reliability considering the same scenarios. As receiving (or not) information from the other sensors in the fault tolerant gateway has the same impact, this chart would be the same for the sensors POxy and Shygm. Chart (c) displays the impact of varying the reliability of transmission from the sensors to the BAN gateway, for similar scenarios – worst case (all the sensors' reliability set to the minimum 0.6), base case (all values set to the base) and best case (all the sensors' reliability set to 0.99). Finally, chart (d) discloses the dependence of process reliability from the reliability of the transmission from the BAN gateway to the HMS, using the previous scenarios.

The results reveal that the reliability of the process is mostly sensitive to reliability variations of the transmission from the sensors to the BAN gateway (chart (c)), then to variations of the accelerometer reliability (chart (a)), to variations of transmission from the BAN gateway to the HMS (chart (d)), and, finally, to the reliability of a single sensor (HRM, Pulse Oxy, Shygm) (chart (b)). The analysis of scenarios for the different charts allows concluding that the process reliability is more sensitive to variations of the value under analysis in the best case scenario and less sensitive in the worst case scenario. Nevertheless, the process reliability is insensitive to reliability variations of the sensors HRM, POxy, and Shygm for the best case scenario.

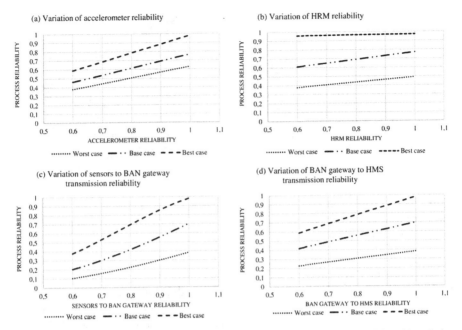

Fig. 2. Impact on the process overall reliability due to varying separate reliabilities: (a) variation of accelerometer reliability (upper left); (b) variation of HRM reliability (upper right); (c) variation of sensors to BAN gateway transmission reliability (lower left); (d) variation of BAN gateway to HMS transmission reliability (lower right).

The charts also allow identifying variation ranges for reliability values of the different elements that meet the required reliability for the overall process. In addition, few conditions allow to reach an overall reliability greater than 0.9 – if the transmission from the sensors to the BAN gateway has a reliability of at least 0.92.

5.3 Impact of Pairwise Component Reliability Variation versus Overall AAL System Reliability

The third phase of the study consisted of making pairwise variations on the reliability values of sensors and assessing the resulting reliability of the overall AAL system. We changed the reliability of the following pairs of sensors: (1) the shygmomanometer together with the accelerometer, and (2) the shygmomanometer together with the pulse oxymeter. The reliability value of the shygmomanometer sensor is associated with the fault-tolerant (parallel event-based) gateway in the AAL system BPMN process (Fig. 1), while the accelerometer is not, and both results are joint further in the parallel gateway before the "evaluate values" task. The charts in Fig. 3 show two perspectives of the variation of the overall reliability resulting from this pairwise variation. The reliability of both sensors was varied from 0 to 1 considering increments of 0.01, and for each pair of values the corresponding overall reliability was computed.

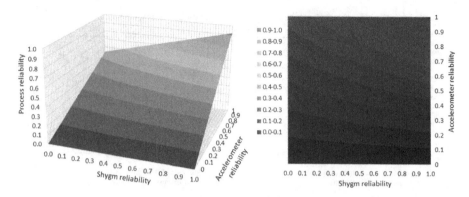

Fig. 3. Value of the process reliability resulting from the joint variation of the shygmo-manometer reliability and the accelometer reliability (a) 3D view; (b) lines of equal reliability and bands. (Color figure online)

The charts give evidence to the lines of equal reliability (isolines) and the resulting bands. Each isoline divides two contiguous areas of different colours (two bands). All points in the same isoline correspond to combinations of one value for Shygm reliability with a value for the Accelerometer reliability that lead to the same reliability of the overall system. By a band we understand the area between two consecutive isolines, which includes reliability values between those values represented by the two isolines. By an isoline interval we understand the variation of reliability between two consecutive isolines. The isoline interval is equal to 0.1 and is the same over all the displayed charts. The surface is plotted using a heat-color scale, where red represents the lowest reliability band [0.0–0.1] and dark green colours the band for the highest reliability [0.9,1].

Chart (a) of Fig. 3 displays a 3D perspective of the process reliability surface in function of reliabilities of the sensors Shygm and Acc. It can be observed that an increase in the accelerometer reliability has a higher impact for high values of the Shygm reliability – the slope of the surface projection, in the plane process reliability-accelerometer reliability, increases as the Shygm reliability increases. Similarly, the impact of varying the Shygm reliability is higher for high Acc reliability values – the slope of the surface projection in the plane Shygm reliability-accelerometer reliability increases as the accelerometer reliability increases.

The highest reliability band, representing values of process reliability between 0.9 and 1, is almost inexistent, and corresponds to values of Shygm and Acc reliability very close to 1. The second highest reliability band, representing a reliability between 0.8 and 0.9, corresponds to Acc reliability values greater than 0.9 together with Shygm reliability values greater than 0.75.

The charts reveal a tendency of a behaviour following a regular pattern. The lines are continuous and monotone.

Chart (b) exhibits a projection of the process reliability surface in the plane Shygm reliability-Acc reliability.

From this chart we can also perceive that the process reliability is stable in the Shygm reliability axis meaning that this component has a small impact in the overall process reliability when compared with the Accelerometer reliability. This is revealed by the shape of the bands which are almost parallel to the XX axis. On the opposite, an increase in the Acc reliability highly impacts on the increase of the process reliability, especially for higher values of the Shygm reliability where the bands are tinier.

Process reliability values greater than the required reliability value (0.6) are only obtained for combinations where the Shygm reliability is greater than 0.6 and the Acc reliability is greater than 0.7.

These conclusions are in line with the composition of the process, where the result of Accelerometer joints with the result of the fault-tolerant gateway block involving the Shygmomanometer (2 out of 3).

The same type of analysis could be reproduced for a pairwise variation of the reliability values of the Accelerometer and any other of the sensors in the fault-tolerant gateway: the Pulse Oxymeter or the Heart Rate Monitor, as their reliability contributes the same way for the process reliability.

The charts in Fig. 4 plot the process reliability surface in function of the reliability values of the sensors Shygm and pulse oxymeter (POxy). Again, a 3D perspective is given in chart (a) while chart (b) shows the projection of the process reliability surface in the plane Shygm reliability-POxy reliability. The same heat colour scale was used for plotting the process reliability values. Ten intervals for variation of the process reliability were considered. Each of these intervals corresponds to a reliability band in the chart. Contiguous bands are separated by a reliability isoline (where all points correspond to the same reliability value).

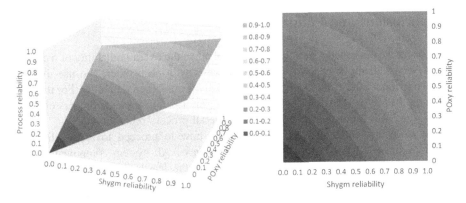

Fig. 4. Value of the process reliability resulting from the joint variation of the shygmo-manometer reliability and the pulse oxymeter reliability (a) 3D view; (b) equal reliability lines and bands. (Color figure online)

Chart (a) shows that the process reliability is more sensitive to variations of the POxy reliability for smaller values of the Shygm reliability – the slope of the surface projection, in the plane process reliability-POxy reliability, decreases as the Shygm reliability increases. The same way, the impact of varying the Shygm reliability decreases for higher values for the POxy reliability – the slope of the surface projection in the plane Shygm reliability – accelerometer reliability decreases as the POxy reliability increases.

There are no combinations of the Shygm reliability and the POxy reliability that lead to process reliability values greater than 0.9. The higher reliability band plotted corresponds to the interval [0.8, 0.9].

The projection of the process reliability surface in the plane Shygm reliability-POxy reliability is represented in chart (b) of Fig. 3. In this case the shape of the isolines is concave downward, opposite from the isolines shape in Fig. 3-chart (b), which is slightly concave upward. The analysis of these lines confirms that the process reliability depends equally from both sensors reliability. However, the isolines and bands provide additional information on the combination of Shygm and POxy reliability values that lead to process reliability values in a given interval.

It can be observed that the process reliability is more stable in zones of higher reliability for both sensors, where the bands are larger, corresponding to a smaller surface slope.

For our case study, only process reliability values greater than 0.6 are feasible. Thus, only points in the area above the isoline of value 0.6 correspond to feasible combinations of Shygm and POxy reliabilities. These points are in the three "upper" bands of the chart.

The sensors Shygm and POxy are joint within the fault-tolerant (parallel event-based) gateway. This means that the results of this type of analysis would be the same for any pair of sensors involved in this gateway – Shygm and HRM or POxy and HRM.

6   Conclusions and Future Work

In this paper we presented a new approach to calculate the overall reliability of a certain AAL system and the way its components interact with each other. We use a BPM approach to model these interactions and to derive the combined reliability. For this, we extend the BPMN language to include reliability information for each process element and use the SWR algorithm to calculate the overall process reliability.

The study presented in Sect. 5 exemplifies how to proceed to assess different conditions of an AAL BPMN process that involves AAL system components. This assessment can be made at design time to analyze the feasibility of the process, for instance, if a minimum level of reliability is assured. It allows to identify both individual and pairwise components which have the highest impact on process reliability and, therefore, to support the design the AAL system architecture and set the reliability requirements for its individual components.

Additionally, reliability can be computed at run time to monitor process executions hence providing an approach to identify low reliability services. In that case, for instance the sensor timers could be adjusted as well as the transmission rate increased at run time.

We are working on further developing this reliability concept within BPMN business processes, by considering not only its control-flow language elements (activities, gateways, loops, sequence and parallel flows), but also its resource and data language elements, such as resource definitions, assignments and data objects.

For this, we intend to extend a Business Process Management System (such as jBPM - www.jbpm.org), in order to include reliability information in BPMN processes, as well as runtime reliability monitoring features. These features can then help health care professionals to better allocate resources to provide the adequate care to certain monitored patients, taking into account the overall reliability of the AAL system in place.

Acknowledgments. This work is partially supported by National Funding from FCT - Fundação para a Ciência e a Tecnologia, under the projects PTDC/EEI-ESS/5863/2014, UID/MAT/04561/2013 and UID/CEC/00408/2013. The authors thank Carlos Albuquerque and Ana Paula Claúdio for the insightful conversations.

References

1. Baig, M.M., GholamHosseini, H., Connolly, M.J., Kashfi, G.: A wireless patient monitoring system for hospitalized older adults: acceptability, reliability and accuracy evaluation. In: IEEE-EMBS International Conference on Biomedical and Health Informatics (BHI), pp. 330–333. IEEE Press (2014). doi 10.1109/BHI.2014.6864370
2. Bui, N., Zorzi, M.: Health care applications: a solution based on the internet of things. In: Proceedings of the 4th International Symposium on Applied Sciences in Biomedical and Communication Technologies, p. 131 (2011). ACM. doi:10.1145/2093698.2093829
3. Cardoso, A.J.S.: Quality of service and semantic composition of workflows. Doctoral dissertation. University of Georgia (2002)
4. Cardoso, J., Sheth, A., Miller, J., Arnold, J., Kochut, K.: Quality of service for workflows and web service processes. Web Semant.: Sci. Serv. Agents World Wide Web 1(3), 281–308 (2004). doi:10.1016/j.websem.2004.03.001
5. Coppolino, L., Romano, L., Mazzocca, N., Salvi, S.: Web Services workflow reliability estimation through reliability patterns. In: International Conference on Security and Privacy in Communications Networks and the Workshops, pp. 107–115. IEEE (2007). doi:10.1109/SECCOM.2007.4550316
6. Dar, K., Taherkordi, A., Baraki, H., Eliassen, F., Geihs, K.: A resource oriented integration architecture for the Internet of Things: a business process perspective. Pervasive Mobile Comput. **20**, 145–159 (2014). doi:10.1016/j.pmcj.2014.11.005
7. Distefano, S., Ghezzi, C., Guinea, S., Mirandola, R.: Dependability assessment of web service orchestrations. IEEE Trans. Reliab. **63**(3), 689–705 (2014). doi:10.1109/TR.2014.2315939
8. IEEE: IEEE Standard for Local and metropolitan area networks - Part 15.4: Low-Rate Wireless Personal Area Networks (LR-WPANs) (2011)
9. IEEE: IEEE Standard for Local and metropolitan area networks - Part 15.6: Wireless Body Area Networks (2012)
10. Islam, S.M.R., Kwak, D., Kabir, M.H., Hossain, M., Kwak, K.: The Internet of Things for health care: a comprehensive survey. IEEE Access **3**, 678–708 (2015). doi:10.1109/ACCESS.2015.2437951

Respício et al.

11. Jara, A.J., Zamora, M.A., Skarmeta, A.F.: An Internet of Things-based personal device for diabetes therapy management in ambient assisted living (AAL). Pers. Ubiquit. Comput. **15** (4), 431–440 (2011). doi:10.1007/s00779-010-0353-1

12. Krishnakumar, N., Sheth, A.: Managing heterogeneous multi-system tasks to support enterprise-wide operations. Distrib. Parallel Databases **3**(2), 155–186 (1995). doi:10.1007/BF01277644

13. Koren, I., Krishna, C.M.: Fault Tolerant Systems. Morgan Kaufmann, San Francisco (2007)

14. Martinho, R., Domingos, D., Respício, A.: Evaluating the reliability of ambient-assisted living business processes. In: Proceedings of the 18th International Conference on Enterprise Information Systems. Scitepress, pp. 528–536 (2016). doi 10.5220/0005917005280536

15. McNaull, J., Augusto, J.C., Mulvenna, M., McCullagh, P.: Data and information quality issues in ambient assisted living systems. J. Data Inf. Qual. (JDIQ) **4**(1), 4 (2012). doi:10.1145/2378016.2378020

16. Memon, M., Wagner, S.R., Pedersen, C.F., Beevi, F.H.A., Hansen, F.O.: Ambient assisted living healthcare frameworks, platforms, standards, and quality attributes. Sensors **14**(3), 4312–4341 (2014). doi:10.3390/s140304312

17. Mukherjee, D., Jalote, P., Gowri Nanda, M.: Determining QoS of WS-BPEL compositions. In: Bouguettaya, A., Krueger, I., Margaria, T. (eds.) ICSOC 2008. LNCS, vol. 5364, pp. 378–393. Springer, Heidelberg (2008). doi:10.1007/978-3-540-89652-4_29

18. Object Management Group: Business Process Model and Notation (BPMN) Version 2.0. (2011)

19. Ouyang, C., Dumas, M., Ter Hofstede, A.H., van der Aalst, W.M.: Pattern-based translation of BPMN process models to BPEL web services. Int. J. Web Serv. Res. (JWSR) **5**(1), 42–62 (2007)

20. Parente, G., Nugent, C.D., Hong, X., Donnelly, M.P., Chen, L., Vicario, E.: Formal modeling techniques for ambient assisted living. Ageing Int. **36**(2), 192–216 (2011). doi:10.1007/s12126-010-9086-8

21. Rashidi, P., Mihailidis, A.: A survey on ambient-assisted living tools for older adults. IEEE J. Biomed. Health Inf. **17**(3), 579–590 (2013). doi:10.1109/JBHI.2012.2234129

22. Respício, A., Domingos, D.: Reliability of BPMN Business Processes. Procedia Comput. Sci. **64**, 643–650 (2015). doi:10.1016/j.procs.2015.08.578

23. Rodrigues, G.N., Alves, V., Silveira, R., Laranjeira, L.A.: Dependability analysis in the ambient assisted living domain: An exploratory case study. J. Syst. Softw. **85**(1), 112–131 (2012). doi:10.1016/j.jss.2011.07.037

24. Siewiorek, D., Swarz, R.: Reliable Computer Systems: Design and Evaluation. Digital Press (2014)

25. van Der Aalst, W.M., Ter Hofstede, A.H., Kiepuszewski, B., Barros, A.P.: Workflow patterns. Distrib. Parallel Databases **14**(1), 5–51 (2003). doi:10.1023/A:1022883727209

Author Index